PURCHASING
AND
MATERIALS
MANAGEMENT
TEXT AND CASES

McGraw-Hill Series in Management

Fred Luthans, *Consulting Editor*
Keith Davis, *Consulting Editor*

Porter and McKibbin: *Management Education and Development: Drift or Thrust into the 21st Century?*

Prasow and Peters: *Arbitration and Collective Bargaining: Conflict Resolution in Labor Relations*

Quick and Quick: *Organizational Stress and Preventive Management*

Rue and Holland: *Strategic Management: Concepts and Experiences*

Rugman, Lecraw, and Booth: *International Business: Firm and Environment*

Sayles: *Leadership: Managing in Real Organizations*

Schlesinger, Eccles, and Gabarro: *Managing Behavior in Organizations: Text, Cases, and Readings*

Schroeder: *Operations Management: Decision Making in the Operations Function*

Sharplin: *Strategic Management*

Steers and Porter: *Motivation and Work Behavior*

Steiner and Steiner: *Business, Government, and Society: A Managerial Perspective, Text and Cases*

Steinhoff and Burgess: *Small Business Management Fundamentals*

Sutermeister: *People and Productivity*

Walker: *Human Resource Planning*

Weihrich: *Management Excellence: Productivity through MBO*

Werther and Davis: *Human Resources and Personnel Management*

Wofford, Gerloff, and Cummins: *Organizational Communications: The Keystone to Managerial Effectiveness*

McGraw-Hill Series in Marketing

Allen, Spohn, and Wilson: *Selling Dynamics*
Anderson: *Professional Sales Management*
Baier: *Direct Marketing*
Bennett: *Marketing*
Berkman and Gilson: *Advertising*
Bowersox, Cooper, Lambert, and Taylor: *Management in Marketing Channels*
Britt, Boyd, Davis, and Larréché: *Marketing Management and Administrative Action*
Buell: *Marketing Management: A Stategic Planning Approach*
Corey, Lovelock, and Ward: *Problems in Marketing*
Dobler, Burt, and Lee: *Purchasing and Materials Management: Text and Cases*
Guiltinan and Paul: *Marketing Management: Strategies and Programs*
Guiltinan and Paul: *Readings in Marketing Strategies and Programs*
Johnson, Kurtz, and Scheuing: *Sales Management: Concepts, Practices, and Cases*
Kinnear and Taylor: *Marketing Research: An Applied Approach*
Loudon and Della Bitta: *Consumer Behavior: Concepts and Applications*
Lovelock and Weinberg: *Marketing Challenges: Cases and Exercises*
Monroe: *Pricing: Making Profitable Decisions*
Myers: *Marketing*
Rossiter and Percy: *Advertising and Promotion Management*
Russell, Beach, and Buskirk: *Selling: Principles and Practices*
Shapiro: *Sales Program Management: Formulation and Implementation*
Stanton: *Fundamentals of Marketing*
Wright, Winter, and Zeigler: *Advertising*

PURCHASING AND MATERIALS MANAGEMENT

TEXT AND CASES

FIFTH EDITION

Donald W. Dobler
Colorado State University
Emeritus

David N. Burt
University of San Diego

Lamar Lee, Jr.
Late Professor of Management
and Director of Purchasing
Stanford University

McGRAW-HILL PUBLISHING COMPANY

New York St. Louis San Francisco Auckland Bogotá Caracas
Hamburg Lisbon London Madrid Mexico Milan Montreal New Delhi
Oklahoma City Paris San Juan São Paulo Singapore Sydney Tokyo Toronto

This book was set in Palatino by the College Composition Unit
in cooperation with General Graphic Services, Inc.
The editors were Bonnie Binkert and Linda Richmond;
the production supervisor was Salvador Gonzales.
The cover was designed by Karen K. Quigley.
New drawings were done by J & R Services, Inc.
R. R. Donnelley & Sons company was printer and binder.

PURCHASING AND MATERIALS MANAGEMENT
Text and Cases

2 3 4 5 6 7 8 9 0 DOC DOC 9 4 3 2 1 0

ISBN 0-07-037047-8

Library of Congress Cataloging-in-Publication Data

Dobler, Donald W.
    Purchasing and materials management: text and cases / Donald W.
Dobler, David N. Burt, Lamar Lee, Jr.—5th ed.
        p.   cm.—(McGraw-Hill series in management) (McGraw-Hill
series in marketing)
    Bibliography: p.
    Includes index.
    ISBN 0-07-037047-8
    1. Industrial procurement.   2. Purchasing.   3. Materials
management.   I. Burt, David N.   II. Lee, Lamar.   III. Title.
IV. Series.   V. Series: McGraw-Hill series in marketing.
HD39.5.D62   1990
658.7—dc20   89-12575

To Lamar Lee, Jr.,
a good friend and colleague
who planted the seed.

CONTENTS

REQUIREMENTS PLANNING•CAPACITY REQUIREMENTS
PLANNING•CONTROL OF SHOP FLOOR ACTIVITIES•
MANAGEMENT CONSIDERATIONS•CLOSED LOOP MRP
SYSTEM•MRP II SYSTEM•BUYER-PLANNER CONCEPT•
VENDOR SCHEDULER CONCEPT•CONTRACT BUYING•
RELATIONSHIPS WITH SUPPLIERS•JUST-IN-TIME
SYSTEM•IMPACTS ON PURCHASING

PREFACE

A manager typically has three major resources with which to work—capital, personnel, and materials. This book focuses on materials—specifically, the management of materials and the control of material costs in business and institutional enterprises. It emphasizes purchasing as the primary materials activity; at the same time, it explicitly integrates the purchasing activity with all other materials activities. Further, the book views the purchasing and materials function in the context of a total business operation; it consistently relates this function to relevant activities in the engineering, operations, marketing, and finance functions, as well to the business as a whole.

The past decade has been marked by numerous important developments—technological, economic, and social. Many of these have impacted both the significance and the conduct of an organization's materials management activities. As a result, the purchasing and materials function has undergone a complete reevaluation by top management. Hence, a number of new strategies and techniques have emerged during this period.

In a growing number of firms, integrated strategic planning for long-term material requirements has become a normal way of life. The increasing emphasis on improved material quality and realiability has been little short of phenomenal. Widespread use of statistical process control and related techniques has been a logical consequence of this effort. At the same time, both domestic competition and international competition have produced major efforts to control and reduce *total* material costs, with an emphasis on the reduction of inventories and related unproductive activities and costs. In turn, these efforts have prompted many firms to experiment with the just-in-time (JIT) concept, to shrink their supplier bases, to utilize more single and dual sourcing arrangements, and to do so with the use of longer-term contracts and partnering arrangements with their suppliers. Concomitant with these

developments has been refinement for practical use of the electronic data interchange (EDI) concept, along with more extensive and sophisticated use of
MRP and MRP II planning and control systems.

The 5th edition of this book deals directly with these changes—and integrates them into the ongoing purchasing and materials function at both a
conceptual and an operations level. *New* 5th edition chapters address the development and management of the buying plan, purchasing's role in new
product development, production planning and its relationship to inventory
management, the purchasing of services, the intricacies of supplier management, managing for quality, and ethical and professional standards. In addition, this new edition gives substantially expanded treatment to the topics of
international sourcing, negotiation, computer-based systems, EDI developments, and JIT applications.

This book is written primarily for college students preparing for careers in
business. It is equally as useful for students with career interests in any business area as it is for those interested in the purchasing and materials management field. To achieve optimum performance in their own areas, all functional managers should understand the general concepts, approaches, and
problems in purchasing and managing materials.

This book is written also as a general reference for people already in business. Without any loss of academic soundness, it is designed to serve as a
useful working tool for the business practitioner. It is particularly useful as a
basic reference in preparing for the *Certified Purchasing Manager* examination.

Purchasing and Materials Management: Text and Cases is an adaptable text. It
provides a sound and complete introduction to the purchasing and materials
function. For the sophisticated reader, the book also offers advanced discussions and cases. Consequently, it is a useful text for a basic course in a community college or for a four-year undergraduate curriculum. It is also appropriate for a more advanced course in an M.B.A. curriculum, or in
professional training programs for government and industrial buyers. Undergraduate schools offering a course in purchasing may choose to cover
only part of the book. For this reason, the book is designed so that the specialized activities in Chapters 22, 23, 24, 27, 31, and 32 may be omitted if time
does not permit complete coverage. Also, Chapters 8, 16, 17, 26, 28, and 29
may be covered briefly to present only general concepts, rather than treating
these topics in depth. For schools that include the subject of purchasing and
materials management as part of a course in production or marketing or industrial engineering, the first fifteen chapters of the text plus Chapters 18
through 21 and 25 through 26 will provide the beginning student with the
basic concepts of purchasing and materials management. In graduate or industrial courses, it is suggested that the complete text be used and that all
topics and advanced cases be covered as thoroughly as time allows.

In developing this text, the authors have drawn freely on the research and
experience of scholars and business executives who have studied the subject.
A heavy debt is owed and acknowledged to these myriad contributors to

knowledge in the field of purchasing and materials management. In developing an original statement of concepts, the contributions of these individuals have been blended with the practical and academic experience of the authors. Some of the concepts have been modified in the revised editions of the book to accommodate the suggestions of hundreds of students and scores of teachers who have generously given the authors the benefit of their constructive criticism.

The cases for this book have been drawn from many sources. The authors are indebted to the National Association Of Purchasing Management, IBM, Westinghouse Electric Corporation, McGraw-Hill, Inc., Harbridge House, The Purchasing Management Association of Connecticut, and The University of San Diego for making selected cases available.

The authors are indebted to so many people that individual acknowledgement is impossible. However, they wish particularly to thank David E. Reeves and O. Richard Blanton who read much of the original manuscript and offered many helpful suggestions. For their contributions to the 5th edition, the authors also wish to thank Dean Emeritus Larry Smith, Jimmy Anklesaria, Charles Blue, James Caltrider, David Lamm, Richard Moss, Warren Norquist, Robert O'Neil, Richard Pinkerton, Roger Rourke, Wally Sanabria, Thomas Tasso, and Charles Tepliz. Thanks, too, to Judy Mersino for her administrative support.

The authors would also like to express their thanks for the many useful comments and suggestions provided by colleagues who reviewed this edition during the course of its development, especially to Kevin Beidelman, Coastline Community College; John M. Browning, University of North Florida; Walter Dember, State University of New York at Buffalo; Eugene L. Magad, William Rainey Harper College; Robert Reck, Western Michigan University; Steve Remington, Winona State University; and particularly to Martin E. Rosenfeldt, University of North Texas, for his extensive and perceptive contributions. In part, as a result of the suggestions of these reviewers, the 5th edition of this book has been reorganized, revised, and updated in its entirety.

A special debt of gratitude is owed to Elaine Dobler and Sharon Burt. Their understanding and assistance in the preparation of the manuscript made a difficult task distinctly easier. We sincerely thank them both.

Donald W. Dobler
David N. Burt
Lamar Lee, Jr.

ONE

THE FUNCTIONS OF PURCHASING AND MATERIALS MANAGEMENT

THE ROLE OF PURCHASING AND MATERIALS MANAGEMENT IN BUSINESS

KEY CONCEPTS

- Purchasing's roles
    - A function of business
    - Materials and productivity
    - Manager of outside manufacturing
- The purchasing function
    - Purchasing function versus purchasing department
    - Profit potential
    - Return on investment
- Relations with other departments
    - Purchasing and engineering
    - Purchasing and production
    - Purchasing and marketing
    - Purchasing and finance
- Consolidation of materials activities
    - Procurement management
    - Materials management
    - Physical distribution management
    - Logistics management
- The systems approach

This introductory chapter presents an overview of the book's two major subjects—purchasing and materials management. The purchasing function is discussed in the first portion, and the materials management concept is reviewed in the latter part of the chapter.

There are two basic types of purchasing in the business world: purchasing for resale and purchasing for consumption or conversion. Purchasing for resale is performed by merchants and speculators. From the beginning of time, purchasing for resale has been the prime responsibility of merchants. The quest for goods to sell was the motivating force that led to the discovery of the New World and the riches of the Indies. Ancient merchants spent some of their time dealing with sales problems, but they devoted by far the largest portion of it to the search for suitable purchases of new and desirable materials.

The basic problem of the merchant has not changed. Following the techniques of their predecessors, today's merchants determine what consumers want, buy it at a price to which they can add a profitable markup, and sell it to the customer at a satisfactory level of quality and service. For example, if a merchant decides his customers want washcloths when in fact they want sponges, his purchase will be a failure, regardless of any other consideration.

Today's merchants serve as the executive heads of trading firms. Additionally, they serve as the department heads in most merchandising houses, including department stores and mail-order houses. Every department within a merchandising house is normally a profit-centered unit. The buyers who head the units typically are completely responsible for the operation of their departments, including profits and losses. They must decide whether their customers want washcloths or sponges, and then buy what is wanted at a price which will permit resale at a profit.

Purchasing managers who buy materials for internal consumption or conversion are called *industrial buyers*. These buyers are faced with problems different from those of merchandise buyers. For industrial buyers, the decision of "washcloths or sponges" is still an important problem, but it is *not* the paramount problem. Industrial buyers have other, more important problems. They participate in determining what products their company should make, what components or parts of these products the company should manufacture, and what components or parts should be purchased from outside suppliers. They correlate their purchasing actions with sales forecasts and production or demand schedules. They select suppliers from whom purchases can be made on a continuing and mutually profitable basis. Most important, they integrate the efforts of their departments with those of the other departments of the firm.

This book is concerned primarily with industrial buyers and how they contribute to the managerial decisions and to the profit of their firms. However, many of their basic problems, such as inventory control, buying at the right price, and negotiation, are problems that also confront the merchandise buyer. It should be noted that institutional buyers (school, hospital, etc.) and government buyers (city, county, state, and federal) are included in the definition of industrial buyer.

PURCHASING'S PLACE IN BUSINESS

What is the role of purchasing in business management? Why is it important? To answer these questions, the purchasing function will be observed from three points of view: first, as a function of business; second, as one of the basic elements required to accomplish productive work; and third, as the department responsible for outside manufacturing.

Purchasing as a Function of Business

Purchasing is one of the basic functions common to all types of business enterprise. These functions are basic because no business can operate without them. All businesses are administered or managed by coordinating and integrating these six functions:[1]

1 *Creation,* the idea or design function
2 *Finance,* the capital acquisition and financial planning and control function
3 *Personnel,* the human resources and labor relations function
4 *Purchasing,* the acquisition of required materials, services, and equipment
5 *Conversion,* the transformation of materials into economic goods and services
6 *Distribution,* the marketing and selling of goods and services produced

The design engineering department, the finance or controller's department, the personnel or human resources department, the purchasing department, the production department, and the sales or marketing department are the common industrial titles of the organizational units responsible for performing these six functions. In nonindustrial enterprises, the same basic functions must be performed, but they may be identified by different names.

Depending on a company's size, these basic functions may be supervised by a single manager or by individual managers for each function. Regardless of how they are supervised, they are performed by someone in every business. Some small firms, for example, do not have a purchasing department; nevertheless, the purchasing function must still be performed. Sometimes it is performed by the president; at other times it is performed by an executive who administers several basic functions, including purchasing.

By its very nature, purchasing is a basic and integral part of business management. Why is this fact important? For a business to be successful, all its individual parts must be successful. It is impossible for any organization to

---

[1]Some authorities now include a seventh, *research.*

achieve its *full* potential without a successful purchasing activity. In the long run, the success of a business enterprise depends every bit as much on the purchasing executive as it does on the executives who administer the other functions of the business.

This is not to imply that all purchasing departments are of equal importance to the success of their companies. They are not; their importance varies widely. The importance of any individual business function within a specific organization is dependent on a number of factors. Among these factors are the type of business, its goals, its economic circumstances, and how the enterprise operates to achieve these goals. In some situations purchasing can function in a perfunctory manner without jeopardizing a company's profit. These situations, however, are exceptions. Similar exceptions can be found in marketing, finance, or any other function of business. For example, in a firm selling a highly advanced technical product, the marketing department usually does not have weighty responsibilities. Engineering excellence does more than efficient marketing techniques to sell the product. On the other hand, marketing a highly competitive standard product requires selling ability of the highest order. In such companies, the marketing department has a position of major importance.

It also is interesting to note that the basic functions of business vary in importance within a given firm, over time, as the firm passes through its life cycle. For example, in the early life of the Hewlett-Packard Company (HP), a highly successful producer of precision electronic instruments, design engineering was the dominant function of the company. The company's products were so far advanced technically, and demand for them was so great, that their cost was relatively unimportant. HP products were literally self-selling. Under such circumstances, neither purchasing nor marketing was a very important function within the company.

With the passage of time, however, conditions changed. Competent competitors entered the market. Consequently, HP products could no longer be sold at just any price, because the insatiable market for its products disappeared. As a result of these changes, the company had to reevaluate and reorganize its purchasing and marketing functions. As a consequence, purchasing and marketing are now functions of major importance.

Purchased Materials as Resources or Elements of Productive Work

The basic goal of any industrial activity is the development and manufacture of products that can be marketed at a profit. This goal is accomplished by the appropriate blending of what management authorities historically have called the *five M's:* machines, manpower, materials, money, and management. Materials today are the lifeblood of industry. No industrial organization can operate without them. Materials of the appropriate quality must be available at the right time, in the proper quantity, at the needed location, and at an acceptable price. Failure to fulfill any of these responsibilities concerning materials adds to company costs and decreases company profit just as surely as do outmoded production methods, inefficient personnel, and ineffective selling.

Materials have not always been so vital. During the nation's industrial development, the relative importance of the five M's has continually shifted. In the management sense, materials became important around 1900. Before then they were rightfully taken for granted, as they presented no significant problem in either availability or cost. The role of the purchasing function in business can be seen more clearly after exploring the reasons which caused the shift in the relative importance of the five M's.

During the first hundred years of the United States' industrial system, productivity increased very little. The availability of manpower and horsepower exceeded machine power almost one hundredfold. This relationship started to change around 1850. Between 1850 and 1950 an unbelievable increase in productivity took place. In 1850, productive power was divided as follows: 2 percent machine power and 98 percent horsepower and manpower. By 1900, this division of power became approximately equal. In 1950, the 1850 power relationship was reversed: 98 percent machine power and 2 percent horsepower and manpower. (See Figure 1-1.)

Because manpower was the first source of productive power, the initial industrial emphasis was on the human element. As machines became more

FIGURE 1-1
Power source relationships, 1850 to 1950. The light-shaded columns represent machine power, and the dark-shaded columns represent horsepower and human labor.

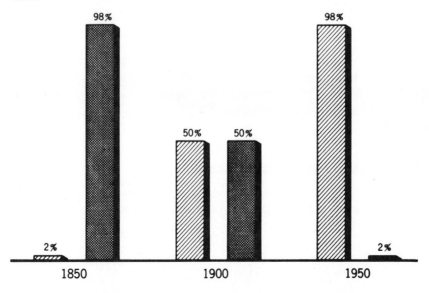

productive, the emphasis shifted toward them. As new products, specialized labor, and materials distribution became more complex, emphasis shifted toward scientific management. Still later, as both the complexity of materials and the volume of production skyrocketed, materials became an increasingly important element of cost. Consequently, emphasis naturally shifted toward this element of the five M's.

Before 1900, both industrial machines and the items they produced were relatively simple. The manufacturing process was uncomplicated and slow. Materials and components of production were simple, readily available, and cheap. Distribution was restricted to a limited area. In fact, a prerequisite to production for almost one hundred years was location of the plant close to plentiful and cheap materials. This prerequisite in turn limited the area of distribution, or the market. Within these constraints, labor costs represented the major portion of production expense.

The introduction of better machines, coupled with scientific management to develop and utilize more sophisticated man-machine systems, made possible the factory system, which in turn sparked many industrial changes. Inventions such as the steam turbine, the electric motor, and automatic controls changed the entire complex of manufacturing. Gradually, materials became more complex, labor became more specialized, and mechanization increased. These changes inevitably led to specialization in manufacturing and to longer production runs.

As the volume of production increased, labor costs per *unit* decreased. The reduction of unit labor costs increased the relative cost and importance of materials in the manufacturing process. *Percentagewise, labor costs went down while materials costs went up.* This change in the value of materials relative to total production costs continues to this day. For example, in 1945 materials represented approximately 40 percent of the manufacturer's total cost to produce an airplane. In 1955 the materials proportion of total cost increased to around 50 percent. Today it is over 60 percent.[2]

In addition to the frame of reference established by the five M's, other perspectives can also be utilized in describing how the goals of manufacturing are accomplished. Many management authorities see the overall manufacturing responsibility as one of managing resources. The three basic resources managed are the capital assets resource, the human resource, and the materials resource.

Purchasing as the Manager for Outside Manufacturing

The materials which go into a typical company's products can originate from either of two sources. The company's production department is the first

---

[2] "General Statistics for Industry Groups," *Annual Survey of Manufacturers, 1985*, U.S. Bureau of the Census, Government Printing Office, Washington, D.C., 1986, p. 8.

source; this department converts raw materials into processed parts. The company's purchasing department is the second source. This department not only purchases raw materials, which the production department converts into processed parts, but it also purchases finished parts and components. The parts made by the production department are combined in assembly with the items bought by the purchasing department to make the company's final products.[3]

The percentage of industrial components being purchased externally is constantly increasing compared with the percentage being manufactured internally. The trend toward specialization within our factory system inherently brings about such a situation. The increasing specialization of technology and labor, the increasing complexity of new materials, and the increasing cost of high-volume specialty machines all tend to cause most industrial firms to buy more and make less. Not even the largest manufacturing concerns have sufficiently high volume requirements to compete with specialty manufacturers in all fields. For example, RCA (a division of General Electric), one of the nation's largest manufacturers of electronic equipment, buys nearly all its capacitors and resistors. This purchasing action is taken not because RCA cannot make these components, but because it can buy them more cheaply from a specialty supplier.

The trend in manufacturing is toward the development of three distinct types of factories. The first type does not make finished end products; it is equipped with costly high-volume specialty machines and produces machined and fabricated parts in large quantities at low unit cost. These parts are sold to numerous factories of the second and third types. The second type of factory, like the first type, does not make finished end products; it makes subassemblies. The required parts for the subassemblies come from factories of the first type, or from the parts it makes, or from a combination of both. The third type of factory makes finished end products. As economic circumstances dictate, this type of factory assembles the finished product from a combination of the parts it makes (usually parts that are unique to its product) and the standard parts or subassemblies it buys from factories of the first and second types.

In the multiple-type factory system of today, any company generally uses two distinct sources of supply: *inside* manufacture and *outside* manufacture. The production department is responsible for inside manufacture, including the authority to schedule production in economical quantities, and to do so far enough in advance to have materials available when needed.

The purchasing department, on the other hand, has the responsibility and authority to schedule the delivery of outside production. Purchasing executives have the same managerial interests concerning their outside

---

[3] The Du Pont Company was among the first to recognize the importance of whether a company should make something itself or let its purchasing department buy it. See Ernest Dale, *The Great Organizers*, McGraw-Hill Book Company, New York, 1960, p. 53.

production as production executives have concerning their internal production. Both must schedule accurately. Production executives are interested in low unit costs and high quality. Purchasing executives are interested in keeping their suppliers' costs down. In addition, they are
interested in maintaining scheduled deliveries and good quality control to
assure that production schedules are met and to minimize the costs of inspection and unacceptable materials.

THE PURCHASING FUNCTION

Purchasing Function versus Purchasing Department

From the preceding overview, it is clear that the purchasing function is an
integral and essential part of business management. All the functions of business must mesh into a unified whole if management is to fulfill its basic responsibility of optimizing company profit. Each function of business must
share in this responsibility.

There is a fundamental distinction, however, between the purchasing
function and the purchasing department. They are not necessarily the same.
As a function, purchasing is common to all types of business enterprise. The
purchasing department, however, is an organizational unit of a firm whose
duties may include some part or all of the purchasing function. This distinction between *function* and *department* is not always appreciated or understood
by top management. Nevertheless, the purchasing function is usually performed most economically and effectively by a specialized, centralized purchasing department, directed by a skilled purchasing manager. However, the
purchasing function does not have to be performed in such a manner. In theory it can be performed, and in practice it sometimes is performed, by any
number of different company executives or departments.

The activities performed by modern purchasing departments are shown in
Table 1-1. A series of studies conducted by one of the authors involved 186
firms and produced these results.

"Buying," as used in Table 1-1, includes activities such as interviewing
salespeople, negotiating with potential suppliers, analyzing bids and making
awards, selecting suppliers, issuing purchase orders, handling problems
with suppliers, and maintaining appropriate records. A review of the data
makes it clear that the *primary* responsibilities of the typical purchasing department today focus on buying activities, value analysis, and purchasing research, including long-range materials planning. This focus is the product of
an evolutionary process spanning the last forty years.

Prior to the 1950s, more often than not, the purchasing department was a
clerically oriented order-placing unit. In the ensuing years, progressive firms
shaped their purchasing operations with a managerial emphasis, stressing
the specialization of individual purchasing activities, professionalism, and
contribution to the firm's profit. During the early to mid 1970s, the managerial orientation was augmented with an emphasis on longer-range strategic

TABLE 1-1
PURCHASING DEPARTMENT RESPONSIBILITIES

Activity	Number of purch. depts. responsible	Percentage of purch. depts. responsible
Buying	186	100
Value analysis	139	75
Purchasing research	131	70
Inventory control	96	52
Auditing invoices	82	44
Stores	79	42
Standardization	63	34
Receiving	51	27
Traffic	48	26
Subcontracting	28	15

planning for materials. In many firms, this activity was integrated into the organization's strategic planning process.

Unfortunately, in a relatively small number of firms, the purchasing department is still viewed as a clerically oriented operation. In such cases, the various management responsibilities associated with the purchasing function generally are performed by other functional and upper-level managers. In this book, however, to preclude the need for making numerous qualifying statements, it is assumed that the major portion of the purchasing function is assigned to the purchasing department. Hence, unless otherwise noted, reference to the purchasing department also means the purchasing function.

Profit Potential

How can purchasing increase company profit? For the typical firm, purchasing is responsible for spending over half of every dollar the firm receives as income from sales and other sources. More dollars are spent for purchases of materials and services than for all other expense items combined, including expenses for wages, taxes, dividends, and depreciation. Figure 1-2 illustrates the percentage distribution of the sales dollar for the *average* manufacturing firm.[4] In high-technology firms, such as instrument manufacturers, the cost of materials (34.4 percent) is well below the composite industry average of 56 percent. On the other hand, in the petroleum industry the cost of materials (90 percent) is far above the composite average. Table 1-2 details materials cost data for these and other major U.S. industries.

[4] "Statistics for Industries," *Annual Survey of Manufacturers: 1985,* U.S. Bureau of the Census, Government Printing Office, Washington, D.C., 1987, p. 1–4–8. Also, *Statistical Abstract of the U.S., 1986,* Government Printing Office, Washington, D.C., 1987, pp. 723–732.

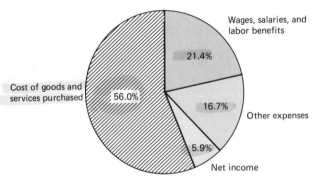

FIGURE 1-2
Percentage distribution of the sales dollar for the average U.S.
manufacturing concern in 1985.

TABLE 1-2
MATERIALS COSTS AS A PERCENTAGE OF SALES INCOME

Industry	Purchased materials (in millions)	Sales (in millions)	Materials to sales ratio
Food and kindred products	$ 197,274.5	$ 301,562.0	65.4%
Tobacco products	6,625.7	18,506.8	35.8
Textile mill products	32,258.3	53,276.5	60.5
Apparel and other textile products	29,130.2	56,993.1	51.1
Lumber and wood products	33,168.8	54,185.1	61.2
Furniture and fixtures	14,764.3	31,293.8	47.2
Paper and allied products	53,039.0	93,414.4	56.8
Printing and publishing	39,103.8	111,885.0	34.9
Chemicals and allied products	101,696.1	197,311.3	51.5
Petroleum and coal products	161,291.2	179,134.9	90.0
Rubber and miscellaneous plastics products	35,754.1	71,324.0	50.1
Leather and leather products	4,444.1	8,567.2	51.9
Stone, clay, and glass products	26,178.8	55,064.1	47.5
Primary metal industries	70,603.1	110,300.8	64.0
Fabricated metal products	70,490.3	139,579.7	50.5
Machinery, except electric equipment	102,831.3	215,080.2	47.8
Electric and electronic equipment	83,079.1	192,731.5	43.1
Transportation equipment	180,856.2	301,386.0	60.0
Instruments and related products	20,982.1	61,008.2	34.4
Miscellaneous manufacturing industries	12,442.4	26,527.1	46.9
All industries	1,276,013.4	2,279,131.7	56.0

Source: Annual Survey of Manufacturers: 1985, U.S. Bureau of the Census, Government Printing Office, Washington, D.C., 1987, p. 1-8.

   The fact that purchasing is responsible for spending over half of most companies' total dollars highlights the profit-making possibilities of the purchasing function. Every dollar saved in purchasing is equivalent to a new dollar of profit. Figure 1-3 illustrates this point. In simplified flowchart form, the figure shows, above the dashed line, key operating accounts that appear on a firm's operating statement. The interaction of these accounts produces a firm's profit margin, defined as:

$$\text{Profit margin} = \frac{\text{operating income}}{\text{sales}}$$

Below the dashed line are selected balance sheet asset accounts that, when related to sales, produce one measure of a firm's asset turnover rate, defined as:

$$\text{Asset turnover rate} = \frac{\text{sales}}{\text{total assets}}$$

   Top management's performance frequently is evaluated on the basis of the rate of return management is able to earn on the total capital invested in the business. Although return on investment (ROI) can be measured in various ways, one common measurement is:

FIGURE 1-3
A graphic view of the relationships of basic elements which influence return on investment. The figures in parentheses reflect a 5% reduction in the cost of materials.

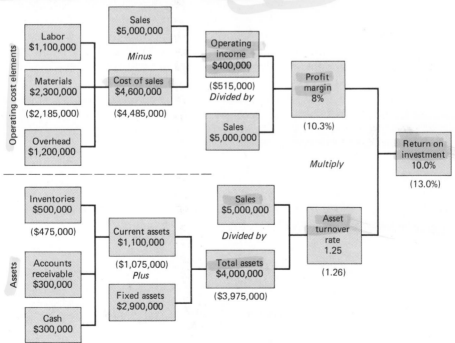

$$\text{ROI} = \frac{\text{operating income}}{\text{total assets}} = \frac{\text{operating income}}{\text{sales}} \times \frac{\text{sales}}{\text{total assets}}$$

Therefore,

$$\text{ROI} = \text{profit margin} \times \text{asset turnover rate}$$

A firm's profit margin reflects management's ability to control costs relative to revenue. The asset turnover rate reflects management's ability to effectively utilize the firm's productive assets. Hence, a firm's management can improve ROI (and managerial performance) in three ways: (1) by reducing costs relative to sales, (2) by getting more sales from available assets (or increasing sales proportionately faster than investment), or (3) by some combination of the two. As seen in Figure 1-3, purchasing can contribute to ROI *both* by increasing profit margins and by increasing the asset turnover rate.

The numbers within the boxes shown in Figure 1-3 represent the current operating figures for the Able Company. The parenthetical figures that appear below the boxes represent new operating data resulting from an assumed 5 percent ($115,000) reduction in materials costs. Such a cost reduction would increase profit margins from 8 percent to 10.3 percent, and ROI from 10 percent to 13 percent. This equals a 0.6 percentage point [(13 − 10)/5] improvement in return on investment for each 1 percent reduction in materials costs.

The 5 percent cost reduction used in the example is certainly a realistic expectation in a firm whose purchasing operation may not be particularly progressive or well run. In a well-managed operation, a more reasonable target might be in the 2 to 3 percent area. By inserting experimental figures into the ROI formula, the reader can determine the results and relative attractiveness of other approaches to profit or ROI improvement.

It was noted earlier that every dollar saved in purchasing is equivalent to a new dollar of profit. An additional dollar of income from sales, however, is not a new dollar of profit; applicable expenses must be deducted from the sales dollar to determine the remaining profit.

Returning to the Able Company illustration, a 5 percent reduction in materials costs ($115,000) produced a profit increase of $115,000. If the same profit increase were to be generated by increasing sales, what sales increase would be required? At the existing 8 percent profit margin, the following calculation provides the answer:

$$\text{Profit increase} = \text{New sales} \times 0.08$$

$$\$115,000 = \text{New sales} \times 0.08$$

$$\text{New sales} = \frac{115,000}{0.08} = \$1,437,500$$

This represents a sales increase of 28.8 percent:

$$\frac{1,437,500}{5,000,000} \times 100 = 28.8$$

So, for comparative purposes, in this case, the same absolute profit improvement can be achieved by reducing materials costs 5 percent or by increasing sales 28.8 percent—approximately a 6 to 1 ratio. If the profit margin were greater than 8 percent, the ratio would be somewhat less; if materials costs, as a percentage of sales, were higher, the ratio would be somewhat greater. Profit is the difference between income and outgo. And most progressive managers strive to improve the firm's profit position both by increasing sales revenues and by reducing the various elements of operating cost.

In practice, though, the cost of materials easily can vary as much as 10 percent, depending on the skill with which the purchasing function is organized and operated. This is why there are usually more opportunities available for reducing purchasing costs 5 percent than there are for increasing sales volume 25 to 30 percent. Also, additional profit from purchasing savings can normally be made without increases in expense. If an increase is required, it is usually for only one person to do analytical work. On the other hand, additional profit from increased sales volume normally entails both increases in expenses and increases in the risk of capital. Additional expenses are incurred for such things as an expanded sales force, a larger advertising budget, additional plant capacity, overtime production pay, or some combination of these factors. Additional profit from sales, therefore, entails increased capital risk and increased management effort. Additional profit from purchasing normally entails only increased management effort, plus an occasional modest increase in management expense.

RELATIONS WITH OTHER DEPARTMENTS

A purchasing department is the hub of a large part of a company's business activity. By its very nature, purchasing has continuing relationships with all other departments in the firm, as well as with the firm's suppliers. Purchasing operations cut across all departmental lines. Purchasing and other departments (production, engineering, marketing, and finance) often view common problems differently. This is a normal and healthy situation—provided the departmental opinions are held objectively. Figure 1-4 provides a graphic illustration of purchasing's many interfaces within the organization.

Purchasing and Engineering

Purchasing, engineering, and production have many mutual problems. Design engineering, like production, greatly influences the amount of time purchasing has to handle a procurement assignment. Engineering usually has

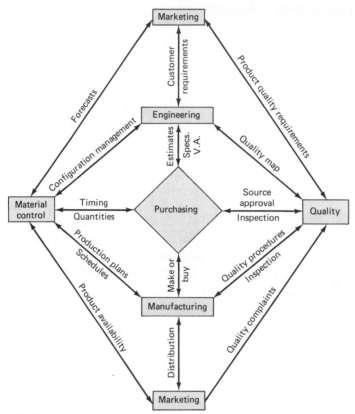

FIGURE 1-4
The many internal interfaces of the purchasing function.

the initial responsibility for preparing the technical specifications for a company's products and the materials that go into them. To exercise this responsibility effectively, engineering must have the constant help of purchasing and production. A number of firms have initiated early purchasing and early supplier involvement programs to assist in this effort. The prices paid for production materials and the costs to fabricate them are inextricably related to their specifications. Similarly, specifications can be written in a manner that reduces or enlarges the number of firms willing to supply specific items. If profit is to be maximized, the materials specified by engineering must be both economical to procure and economical to fabricate, and they should normally be available from more than one efficient, low-cost producer.

Purchasing and engineering occasionally differ in their concepts of materials problems. This is understandable. Engineers naturally tend to design conservatively; hence, their specifications provide amply for quality, safety, and performance. By training, the engineer may be inclined to seek the "ideal" design, material, or equipment without complete regard for cost or timing. The buyer, on the other hand, often believes it is appropriate to reduce the designer's performance goals and safety margins, and to work closer to actual performance requirements. Is an expensive design with a high safety factor necessary if a less costly design with a lower safety factor will do the job? Why use costly chrome plate if brushed aluminum is adequate? Clearly, such conflicting departmental interests cannot always be resolved easily. The answers to such problems are seldom clear cut. Mutual understanding and a willingness to give and take are required from both sides if mutually satisfactory solutions are to be reached.

Purchasing and Production

The purchasing-production relationship begins when the production department transmits its manufacturing schedule or materials requisitions to the purchasing department. Purchasing subsequently translates these documents into a procurement schedule. Purchase timing is often a cardinal difficulty in making this translation. When production does not allow purchasing sufficient time to purchase wisely, many needless expenses inevitably creep into the final costs of a company's products. When purchasing has inadequate time to develop competition or to negotiate properly, premium prices are certain to be paid for materials. Costly *special production runs* and *premium transportation* costs are two additional factors that frequently result from inadequate purchasing lead time.[5]

The most serious problem stemming from insufficient procurement lead time is a production shutdown. In most process types of operation (chemicals, cement, paint, flour, etc.), equipment either runs at nearly full capacity or it does not run at all. Consequently, material shortages in these industries can be catastrophic, resulting in complete production stoppage. Losses resulting from material shortages in nonprocess industries are not always so disastrous or apparent. A production shutdown in a metal fabricating shop, for example, can be piecemeal. The indirect costs of such shortages, consequently, are often hidden in production costs. One or two machines from a large battery of perhaps fifty can be shut down as a routine occurrence. Conventional accounting records fail to reveal the financial impact of this kind of slow profit-draining inefficiency.

Coordination between purchasing and production pays off in many ways. For example, a more expensive alternative material that will save the company money can on occasion be selected. This may sound like a paradox. "Pay more and save more"—how can this happen? Savings in manufacturing and assembling costs often can exceed the increased purchase costs. In

---

[5] It is purchasing's responsibility to keep production informed concerning what lead times are for all categories of production materials.

the normal manufacturing operations of casting, forging, machining, grinding, stamping, and so on, some materials are much more economical to work with than others. For example, the government has saved thousands of dollars by using bronze instead of steel extrusions in aircraft elevator and rudder counterweights. Bronze costs more than steel, but savings in machining time more than offset the increase in material cost. In this case, not only is the direct cost reduced, but as an added benefit skilled machinists and expensive machine tools are freed to do other high-priority work.

The potential consequences of a production stoppage cause many production managers to advocate an excessively large inventory of production materials. Again, this is understandable. For production managers to reach their main manufacturing objective of low unit costs, they must keep the production line operating. A large inventory is a logical safeguard to prevent possible production stoppages resulting from materials shortages.

Purchasing shares in the production manager's desire to keep the production line operating. In fact, to do so is purchasing's first objective. In addition to keeping the production line operating, however, purchasing has the related objective of accomplishing the task with the minimum reasonable capital investment in inventory, a major concern which production typically does not share with equal intensity. The cost of carrying inventory is high—usually between 25 and 35 percent of the average inventory value per year. Reconciling these two conflicting company objectives (one calling for a higher inventory than the other) requires capable, informed, and understanding department heads. Although chief executives themselves must occasionally resolve the issue, it should normally be resolved by the department heads.

The scenarios just described are but a few of the numerous operating situations that illustrate the continuing and coordinative nature of the purchasing and production relationship.

Purchasing and Marketing

All companies recognize the direct relationship between the marketing function and profit. In their enthusiasm to increase sales, however, many companies overlook the leaks in profit that can occur when the sales activity is not properly meshed with the purchasing and production activities.

The purchasing-production-sales cycle has its genesis in a sales forecast. Most sales forecasts include two important parts: (1) an estimate of sales based on what has happened in the past to a company's products, territories, and markets; and (2) an adjustment of this estimate to include changes the company expects in its future sales. The changes reflect alterations in the marketing program and shifts in economic and competitive conditions. The sales forecast is the basis for the production schedule, which in turn is the basis for the purchasing schedule. The sales forecast also influences a firm's capital equipment budget, as well as its advertising campaigns and other sales activities.

Prompt communication to production and purchasing of changes in the sales forecast permits these departments to modify their schedules as painlessly and economically as possible. Changes in the production schedules should be communicated immediately to sales. This action permits sales to alter its distribution schedule in a manner that will not alienate customers. Purchasing must immediately transmit to sales, as well as to other management groups, information concerning increases in materials prices. This permits sales to evaluate the effect of price rises in price estimates given for future sales quotations, on current selling prices, and on plans for future product lines.

Purchasing and sales must wisely blend their interests in the delicate area of *reciprocity* (buying from customers). If satisfactory *legal* reciprocal transactions are to be developed, they must be pursued with an understanding of the true costs of reciprocity. Buying from friends can be good business, but not when it is done at the expense of product quality or company profit. In a zest for increased sales, a company can lose sight of the fact that increased sales do not always result in increased profit. Sometimes increased sales result in *decreased* profit if they simultaneously require an increase in purchasing costs.

A purchasing department can be of major help to its sales department by serving as its practical sales laboratory. A firm's purchasing department is the target for many manufacturers' sales departments. Purchasing's files are replete with sales literature, policies, and promotional approaches of a broad range of manufacturers and distributors. Buyers are aware of the personal selling methods that sales representatives have used most effectively on them. They are equally aware of sales practices that fail or that irritate them. Therefore, a company's buyers can be an excellent source of information for developing and refining the company's own sales policies and procedures.

Purchasing and Finance

Purchasing's relationship with finance is different from its relationships with production, engineering, and sales. The difference stems from the fact that cost determinations cannot be hidden in the purchasing-finance relationship as they often can in the other relationships. The importance of good financial planning is highlighted by the fact that poor financial planning is the major cause of business failure. Among the basic data needed by an organization for proper planning of its working-capital and cash-flow positions are accurate sales forecasts and accurate purchasing schedules. It is just as important for purchasing to inform finance of changes in its schedule as it is to inform production and sales of these changes.

There are many economic factors that periodically bring about favorable and completely unexpected buying opportunities. For example, a supplier may momentarily have excess capacity because of the cancellation of a large order. During the period that this condition exists, the supplier may sell products at prices designed to recover only out-of-pocket costs.[6] This may be done because it is in the long-term interest of the firm not to reduce its labor force. The potential income from such unexpected buying opportunities must be weighed against the potential income from other alternative uses of the company's capital. Acquiring new equipment, adding to plant facilities, and increasing sales and promotional efforts are some of the alternative uses of capital that a company must consider. Usually, the alternative offering the greatest income in the long run should be selected, since no firm has enough capital to satisfy all requirements.

Regardless of the price advantage obtainable, the right time to buy from the standpoint of business conditions is not always the right time to buy from the standpoint of the company's treasury. If the purchasing department makes commitments to take advantage of unusually low prices without consulting the finance department, the company could find itself paying for these purchases with funds needed for other purposes. On the other hand, if the finance department does not strive diligently to make funds available for such favorable buying opportunities, the company may have to pay higher prices later for the same material.

Prompt payment of suppliers is a key contributor to good supplier relations. During the 1970s, Timex had a policy of paying its suppliers the day the supplier's invoice and the receiving report arrived in the accounts payable office. Thus, Timex became a preferred customer of many of its suppliers. During the two material shortage periods of the 1970s, Timex's preferred customer status allowed it to avoid the shortage problems experienced by most firms. Hence, a cooperative relationship between purchasing and finance clearly can impact the development of good supplier relations.

CONSOLIDATION OF MATERIALS ACTIVITIES

The preceding discussions make it clear that a number of functional interdependencies exist among many of a firm's materials activities, even though they may be located in several different departments. Figure 1-5 shows the flow of materials decisions and related activities through a typical firm—the firm's materials system. A decision or an action taken at any point in the materials chain usually impacts a number of other decision points in the chain. Clearly, these activities make up one or more subsystems, which are part of a firm's larger production or operations system. Consequently, most organizations find it necessary to coordinate the various materials activities very carefully.

The required coordination can occur in two ways. First, it may be achieved by developing a straightforward set of reporting, communication, and con-

---

[6]A manufacturing concern can be thought of as having two sets of costs: out-of-pocket costs and all other costs. Out-of-pocket costs include direct costs paid for making a specific product. They do not include rent of the factory, taxes, insurance, etc., all of which must be paid whether or not a specific product is made. See Chapter 11.

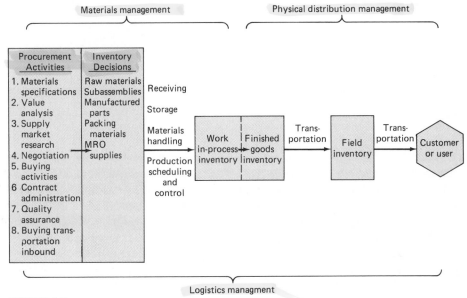

FIGURE 1-5
Systems management concepts imposed on the flow of materials and related activities in a firm's materials system.

trol procedures designed to enhance coordinated decision making among the involved groups or departments. The second approach involves an organizational rearrangement that consolidates some of the individual materials activities into larger groups for administrative purposes. In this case, coordination typically is easier to achieve because one manager has line responsibility and authority for those activities grouped in his or her operating unit, with the possibility of developing a more effective team-oriented operation.

The four consolidation or systems management concepts most commonly found in American business today are identified as: (1) procurement management, (2) materials management, (3) physical distribution management, and (4) logistics management. Although most practitioners and theorists currently do not agree on all the functional and operating details included in each approach, general agreement does exist with respect to the basic concepts themselves, as indicated in Figure 1-5.

Procurement Management

The procurement concept encompasses a wider range of supply activities than does the purchasing concept. And it typically includes a broadened view of the traditional buying role, with more buyer participation in related materials activities. Specific activities usually included are:

1 Participation in the development of requirements and their specifications

2 Managing value analysis activities
3 Conducting supply market research
4 Managing supplier negotiations
5 Conducting traditional buying activities
6 Administering purchase contracts
7 Managing supplier quality
8 Buying inbound transportation

Materials Management

Materials management, as practiced in business today, can be defined as a union of the major materials activities. Operationally, it utilizes an integrated management approach to planning, acquisition, conversion, flow, and distribution of *production materials* from the raw-material state to the finished-product state. Activities typically found in a materials management operation are:

1 Procurement activities
2 Inventory management
3 Receiving activities
4 Stores and warehousing
5 In-plant materials handling
6 Production planning, scheduling, and control
7 Traffic and transportation
8 Surplus and salvage

Physical Distribution Management

As the name implies, physical distribution management focuses on all the materials activities that come after the completion of a finished product—from finished goods inventory to customer delivery and service. Marketing people often refer to physical distribution as the "other (last) half of marketing." Specific activities include:

1 Sales order processing
2 Finished goods inventory management
3 Finished goods handling and movement
4 Finished goods traffic and transportation
5 Occasionally, customer service
6 Occasionally, production control

Logistics Management

As seen in Figure 1-5, logistics management is an encompassing combination of materials management and physical distribution management activities. On the basis of the preceding discussions of the latter two concepts, it is clear that a number of similarities exist between them. Not only are the activities involved in both concepts a part of the same overall materials system, many of the skills required to perform the respective operating activities are also similar. The same skills and knowledge required to control production inventories are also those used to control finished goods inventories. Similarly, the materials management and physical distribution skills used in traffic, materials planning, and materials handling are identical skills. Although physical distribution is the final stage of the marketing process, the training and orientation of physical distribution personnel is much more akin to that of materials management personnel. These factors have combined to produce the logistics management concept.

THE SYSTEMS APPROACH—A SYNTHESIS

It was during the late 1950s and the 1960s, when attention had focused on the *management* of the purchasing and materials activities, that serious attention was first given to the various systems management approaches in most companies.[7] On the supply side, the virtues of procurement management and materials management generated considerable appeal for firms genuinely interested in controlling materials costs. During this period, a number of Fortune 500 companies hired their first corporate vice president for procurement or materials management. The trend continued into the 1970s and accelerated dramatically after the oil embargo and subsequent materials shortages during 1973 and 1974. At the same time, the critical nature of some materials commanded the attention of top management, and materials generally became a significant element in the corporate strategic planning process.

Today the vast majority of U.S. firms embrace the procurement management concept and integrate it into their day-to-day operations. Although not quite to the same extent, the materials management approach to supply management has also been accepted widely throughout American business. Responsible estimates indicate that approximately 70 percent of the major U.S. manufacturing firms currently utilize some operating form of the materials management concept.[8] The physical distribution management concept is used to a lesser extent, typically by firms with a dominant marketing/distribution orientation, whereas only a limited number of firms employ the all-encompassing logistics management concept. Regardless of the systems approach used, however, experience has proven that integration of selected

---

[7] For an interesting discussion of the controversies and developments that occurred during the transition period, see Richard L. Pinkerton, "What the Experts Think about Purchasing/Materials Management Functions, Education, and Training," *Journal of Purchasing*, August 1970, pp. 54–67.

[8] "The Speedup in Automation," *Business Week*, Aug. 3, 1981, pp. 55–68; Jeffrey G. Miller and Peter Gilmour, "Materials Managers: Who Needs Them?" *Harvard Business Review*, July–August, 1979, pp. 143–153; Harold E. Fearon, *Purchasing Organizational Relationships*, N.A.P.M. Inc., Tempe, Ariz., 1988, p. 17.

materials activities for operating and management purposes typically reduces the *total costs* associated with acquiring and managing materials.

In day-to-day business operations, the primary contribution a materials management operation makes is improved communication, coordination, and control of the interrelated materials activities. Buck-passing possibilities are minimized—as are the possibilities for interdepartmental squabbles—and the organization's ability to plan proactively and to react to problems quickly is improved immensely.

The *specific form* of materials organization most appropriate for one firm may not be the best form for another. A brief discussion of two materials activities will illustrate why the unique nature of a specific firm's operating activities influences its form of materials organization so heavily. Assume that a plant *purchases* all the parts, components, and subassemblies for the product it manufactures. In this situation, if production were uniform, the production planning schedule and the purchasing schedule, allowing for lead time, would be similar or identical. Consequently, for this firm to achieve optimal control over materials and costs, production control should realistically be included in the materials management department. Assume now that a plant *manufactures* all the parts, components, and subassemblies that are used in producing its product. In this situation, there may be very little similarity between the production planning and purchasing schedules. Therefore, in this firm, a strong case could be made for locating production control within the production department.

In practice, the theoretical extremes discussed above seldom exist. For most firms, the production planning and purchasing schedules overlap significantly. Unfortunately, this frequently produces a continuing source of conflict. One of the paramount advantages of materials management is that it forces coordination between purchasing and production control. Purchasing and production control are both responsible for the on-time delivery of production materials. Division of this authority between two different operating units inevitably leads to conflict. When materials do not arrive on time, production control is seldom satisfied to work through the purchasing department. Frequently, production control personnel proceed to expedite the late materials directly with the supplier. Since the expediting of purchased materials and negotiation with suppliers are basic purchasing responsibilities, conflict ensues. Such conflict is much more readily resolved when production control and purchasing report to a single boss—the materials manager.

As with purchasing and production control, substantial benefits also accrue when inventory management, value analysis, receiving, stores, and surplus and salvage are placed in a materials management department. (Each of these activities and its role in the materials system is discussed in a separate chapter later in the book.)

Probably the single greatest benefit a firm receives from having a materials manager is that this manager thinks as the president and other top-level vice presidents do—that is, in terms of the firm as a whole. Managers of individual materials functions, such as purchasing, inventory, and traffic, usually are compelled to think more narrowly in terms of the unique responsibilities associated with their specific functions. Consider a typical situation. In practice, production and purchasing often develop a tacit agreement on carrying a higher level of inventories than a good materials manager would normally sanction. High inventories protect production from manufacturing delays and purchasing from production pressures. If top management complains of high inventories, production and purchasing blame each other for the condition. One large firm, with sales exceeding $1 billion, recently reduced inventories over 25 percent after creating a materials management organization and appointing an experienced top-management person as its new vice president for materials. Many other firms have experienced similar results.

CONCLUSION

As purchased materials become more complex and sophisticated, they usually become more expensive relative to the function they serve. The result is that they become a more important part of the buying firm's overall cost structure. And as the buying firm's productivity increases, the same labor effort produces more finished products. This phenomenon also increases the relative importance of purchased materials in the total cost structure.

In addition to technological and productivity changes, numerous national and international forces also impact the purchasing and materials management function. Several examples will clarify this point. Important materials periodically become scarce, both at home and abroad; similarly, the assurance of energy sources also becomes more critical with each passing year. Interest rate volatility is becoming a way of life; hence, material cost savings make proportionately larger contributions to profit. At the same time, profit margins of U.S. firms are declining relative to those of their foreign trading partners. Collectively, all these emerging phenomena make effective procurement and management of materials an increasingly important ingredient in achieving stable and profitable business operations.

Generally speaking, effective management and control of operations can be achieved only when a firm is analyzed and controlled as a total operating unit (a total system). In the cost area, uncoordinated cost reductions can be misleading, because cost reductions made in one area frequently pop up as increased costs in other areas. For example, purchasing costs can be reduced by buying in larger quantities—and passing increased carrying costs along to inventories. Or inventories can be reduced to an unreasonably low level, passing additional costs along to production in the form of operating delays and to purchasing in the form of higher ordering costs, additional receiving activities, payments, etc.

This trade-off situation has led to the widespread use of various systems management approaches in the materials area. In addition to the commonly accepted procurement management concept, some form of the materials management approach is now employed in a significant majority of U.S. industrial firms. Extensive use of computer-based information and control systems by business firms has served as an operational catalyst to facilitate this development. Management has been forced to rethink the design and the significance of the interrelationships existing among a firm's operating functions. Computer-based systems in the production and sales areas, in fact, *require* more closely coordinated operation of production planning, inventory control, purchasing, warehousing, receiving, and accounting. Thus, the trend is toward *system optimization* rather than suboptimization of the efforts of individual operating units in the firm.

Despite some disadvantages, a systems approach to coordinating and managing a firm's activities has proved to be extremely beneficial. In addition, a rewarding fringe benefit is the synergism produced among the departments when they coordinate and integrate their materials interests. The benefits typically achieved by a firm making the transition to materials management are reflected in greater profit, stemming from increased inventory turnover, greater productivity, fewer stockouts, improved supplier deliveries, increased equipment utilization, better materials planning, and reduced conflict among the firm's functional managers.

FOR DISCUSSION

1-1 Describe the two types of purchasing in the business world. Discuss the differences between the two. Have you had any experience with either? Explain how your experience relates to the discussion in this chapter.

1-2 "Purchasing is more important in an industrial firm today than it was one hundred years ago." Discuss.

1-3 What challenges does knowledge of the potential of good purchasing offer you? How can this purchasing course help you?

1-4 Do you think it would be easier for a company to increase its profit by increasing the efficiency of purchasing or by increasing sales? Explain.

1-5 How does efficient purchasing improve ROI? Discuss.

1-6 Economists frequently make the statement that labor costs make up the bulk of industrial expenditures today. Does this contradict the view taken in this chapter? Discuss.

1-7 Discuss the problems involved in purchasing-production relationships.

1-8 How can increased purchasing costs sometimes result in greater profit for a company? Is it possible to "pay more and save more"? Explain.

1-9 Discuss the problems involved in the daily operating relationships between purchasing and design engineering.

1-10 Explain how sales and purchasing can help each other by establishing a good relationship.

1-11 "The responsibilities of a firm's purchasing function and its purchasing department are not always the same." Explain.

1-12 Discuss how the economic changes both in the United States and abroad are influencing purchasing's role in business management.

1-13 Discuss the benefits that can result when materials activities are integrated.

1-14 "Generally speaking, a firm can attain effective control over the bulk of its costs only when it is analyzed and controlled as a total operating unit." Do you agree with this statement? Discuss.

1-15 Discuss the important differences between purchasing and procurement.

1-16 Define and discuss the significance of the materials management concept.

1-17 What are the important differences between materials management and physical distribution management? Could these two organizational units realistically be combined into one organizational unit?

1-18 What has accelerated industry's recent trend toward materials management? Explain fully.

1-19 Explain why materials management losses are not readily visible and sales and production losses are.

1-20 Discuss the benefits that a typical firm could expect from making the transition to materials management.

CASES FOR CHAPTER 1

The Centennial Company, page 727
The Privileged Fly, page 789
Metropolitan University (in the Instructor's Manual)

OBJECTIVES AND POLICIES

KEY CONCEPTS

- Objectives of purchasing and materials management
  - The managerial perspective
  - The functional level
  - Strategy for specific buying plans
- Basic operating policies
  - Policies defining purchasing responsibility
  - Policies affecting external relationships and image
  - Policies on pricing and supply sources
  - Policies concerning ethical practices
  - Policies concerning minority business enterprises
- The policy manual

OBJECTIVES

The objectives of purchasing and materials management can be viewed from three levels: (1) a very general managerial level, (2) a more specific functional or operational level, and (3) a detailed level at which precise strategic buying plans are formulated.

From a top managerial perspective, the general objectives have traditionally been expressed as the *five rights* which management expects the department to achieve—the acquisition of materials:

1 Of the *right quality*
2 In the *right quantity*
3 At the *right time*
4 From the *right supplier*
5 At the *right price*

A sixth factor implied in these items includes the desired *services* necessary for optimal supply and utilization of the materials.

Even the casual observer will detect just a bit of the "apple pie and motherhood" syndrome reflected in these five rights. Idealistically, they are all highly desirable. In practice, the department can rarely fulfill them all equally, because in a given procurement conflicts inherently exist between some of the objectives. Usually some trade-offs must be made. From a practical point of view, materials personnel seek a reasonable balance among them.

From an operating or functional perspective, then, it is necessary to probe more deeply to develop a set of statements that provide practical and useful targets for decision-making purposes. In this sense, the eight basic objectives of purchasing and materials management are identified and discussed briefly below. Each of the items is the topic of one or more chapters later in the book.

1 *To support company operations with an uninterrupted flow of materials and services.* This is the most fundamental of all purchasing and materials management objectives. In a logistical sense this is a key reason for the existence of the department. Responsibility for performance of the function is located in a single operating unit, thereby facilitating coordination and control of the supply activities.

2 *To buy competitively.* Buying competitively involves keeping abreast of the forces of supply and demand that regulate prices and availability of materials in the marketplace. At times, it also involves an understanding of a supplier's cost structure, coupled with an ability to minimize the supplier's costs within reason—then to negotiate price and service arrangements that are fair relative to the supplier's costs. A buyer who pays significantly more than his or her competitor does for a given material or service generally is not buying competitively.

3 *To buy wisely.* Buying wisely involves a continual search for better values that yield the best combination of price, quality, and service, relative to the buyer's needs. This frequently involves coordination with users in defining the need. It may also involve coordinating and reconciling users' needs with suppliers' capabilities to achieve optimal value considering both issues. A firm that purchases a silver-plated part when a copper-plated part could perform the function just as well usually is not buying wisely.

It is the combination of buying competitively and buying wisely that typically contributes most to the profitability of the firm.

4 *To keep inventory investment and inventory losses at a practical minimum.* Although maintaining a large inventory is one way to achieve objective number one, it is also costly. Generally speaking, most firms today pay in indirect costs between 25 and 35 percent of the average inventory value per year for the convenience of having the inventory available. Hence, the materials management job is to achieve a reasonable balance between the level of inventory required to support operations and the cost of carrying the inventory.

Through proper buying, packaging, and storing, it is also the department's objective to minimize losses that occur as a result of deterioration, obsolescence, theft, and so on.

5 *To develop reliable and effective sources of supply.* Cooperative suppliers that are willing to work with a buyer to help solve the buying firm's problems and to minimize its materials-related costs are an invaluable resource. Progressive buyers today tend increasingly to "buy suppliers," as opposed to simply "buying products." The identification, investigation, selection, and in some cases development of competent and responsive suppliers is a buyer's paramount responsibility. It is difficult indeed for a firm to perform optimally if it cannot depend on the planned performance of a reliable contingent of suppliers.

6 *To develop good relationships with the vendor community and good continuing relationships with suppliers.*[1]   Good relationships with suppliers are imperative, and good relationships with potential suppliers are invaluable. The achievement of the preceding objective on a continuing basis is virtually impossible if mutually satisfactory continuing relationships are not maintained. Potential suppliers are much more interested and eager to acquire a firm's business if the buying firm is likely to be a "good customer." And, when a contractual relationship has been formed with a supplier, the myriad operating problems that inevitably arise throughout the life of the contract are much more easily and effectively solved when the relationship is sound and mutually beneficial. Suppliers naturally direct their research, provide advance information on new products and prices, and in general give better service to such customers.

7 *To achieve maximum integration with the other departments of the firm.* It is essential for buyers to understand the major needs of their using departments, so that these needs can be translated into materials support actions. While these actions vary from firm to firm, they normally require

---

[1]In the purchasing literature, "supplier" and "vendor" are generally used interchangeably, and there is no objection to this practice. In this text, where a distinction seems desirable, *suppliers* are considered to be sellers with whom the buyer does business, and *vendors* (a generic term) are all other sellers.

the purchasing and materials operation to support a using department in one or more of its major responsibilities. The most common types of support involve actions such as developing materials standardization programs (in coordination with ongoing design programs), forecasting future prices and general business conditions, performing economic make-or-buy analyses, and serving as a repository of information and data from suppliers regarding new materials, processes, prices, and materials availability.

8 *To administer the purchasing and materials management function in a professional, cost-effective manner.* Management should expect the preceding seven objectives to be achieved in a professional manner at a cost that is commensurate with their value to the total organization. This involves the acquisition and development of highly competent personnel who are motivated to perform their responsibilities effectively, with the overall goal of helping the firm maintain a competitive position in its industry. Such personnel also serve as a reservoir of talent from which future executives of the firm can be drawn.

A part of this composite effort also involves the development of operating policies and procedures that facilitate accomplishment of departmental objectives at the lowest reasonable operating costs.

These objectives apply in principle to all categories of industrial buying activities: manufacturing concerns, governmental units, schools, hospitals, and all other types of buying units that buy for consumption or conversion. A nonprofit activity, of course, cannot seek to "maximize its profit." It can, however, seek to maximize the benefits the organization receives from its appropriated or endowed dollar. A principle common to all types of purchasing activities is to obtain the greatest *value* from each dollar the purchasing department spends.

Under the first objective (uninterrupted materials flow), for example, a manufacturing concern seeks to support its production schedule; the U.S. Navy seeks to support its ships, aircraft, and bases; and a hospital seeks to support its patients. The principles underlying the first objective apply with equal force to all types of organizations. It is the same with the other seven objectives; they apply to all types of industrial buying. The principles are also equally applicable to operations of all sizes, large and small. There are many situations where a slight change in the phraseology of a specific objective is required to make it fit a particular operating environment. The fact remains, though, that only the words change; the principles remain the same.

At the beginning of the chapter, it was noted that purchasing and materials management objectives can be viewed from three levels. The first two levels, managerial and functional, have now been reviewed.

The third level focuses on the detailed objectives that are developed when precise buying plans are made (usually annually) for each of the major categories of materials the firm uses in its operations. These objectives are spawned from the functional-level objectives just discussed, and are applied to fulfill the specific needs associated with each type of purchase. The precise set of objectives for each material typically varies because the usage requirements, the operating conditions, and the markets in which each material is purchased usually are different. Consequently, the specifics and the subtleties of these objectives are discussed later in the book in the technical chapters dealing with topics such as quality, sourcing, pricing, production and inventory planning, developing the buying plan, and so on. At this point, it is sufficient simply to say that all subsequent strategic buying objectives are based on the eight functional objectives just discussed.

BASIC OPERATING POLICIES

What is a policy? A *policy* is a statement that describes in very general terms an intended course of action. After the fundamental objectives of an activity are established, policies are developed to serve as general guidelines in making operating decisions that channel actions toward achievement of the objectives.

Before proceeding further, it should be emphasized that this entire book deals largely with matters of policy. Chapters 6, 7, and 19 focus on numerous policies influencing the quality of materials. Chapters 12 through 15 investigate pricing policies. Chapters 20 and 21 consider policies of production scheduling and inventory management, and so on. Every chapter deals with various matters of policy which relate to a specific phase of materials management. The remainder of this chapter is concerned with fundamental *operating* policies—broad policies of particular interest to top management. These policies deal with things such as purchasing authority, external relationships, and the firm's general conduct and image. These policies lie close to the heart of the purchasing and materials management function, yet their influence permeates the entire company operation.

Policies Defining Purchasing Responsibility

Centralization of Purchasing To decentralize the purchasing function needlessly is to deny a firm some of its potential profit. Centralization of the purchasing function is essential for attainment of both optimum operating efficiency and maximum profit.

Centralization of purchasing, as discussed in this book, is concerned solely with the placement of purchasing *authority*. It has nothing to do with the location of buying personnel. Centralization exists when the entire purchasing function is made the responsibility of a single person. This person is held accountable by top management for proper performance of purchasing activities. Decentralization of purchasing occurs when personnel from other functional areas—production, engineering, marketing, finance, and so on—decide on sources of supply, negotiate with vendors directly, or perform any of the other major functions of purchasing.

Most companies today view the centralization of purchasing as a logical and desirable evolution of Frederick Taylor's basic concept of the specialization of labor. The extent to which the efficiencies of functional specialization are realized when a firm creates a purchasing department, however, depends largely on the authority delegated to that department. When functioning properly, centralized purchasing produces the following benefits:

1 Duplication of effort and haphazard purchasing practices are minimized by the central coordination of all company purchases.
2 Volume discounts are made possible by consolidating all company orders for the same and similar materials. In addition, a firm is able to develop and implement a unified procurement policy, enabling it to speak with a single voice to its suppliers. In this way, the firm gains maximum competitive advantage from its total economic power.
3 Transportation savings can be realized by the consolidation of orders and delivery schedules.
4 Centralization develops purchasing specialists whose primary concern is purchasing. With training, purchasing specialists inevitably buy more efficiently than less skilled individuals who view purchasing as a secondary responsibility.
5 Suppliers are able to offer better prices and better service because their expenses are reduced. Their sales personnel have fewer people to call on, fewer orders to prepare, fewer shipments to make, fewer invoices to prepare, and fewer financial records to keep. Under these conditions, supplier goodwill and responsiveness naturally follow.
6 More effective inventory control is possible because of companywide knowledge of stock levels, material usage, lead times, and prices.
7 Line department managers do not have to spend time purchasing. They can devote full time and effort to their basic responsibilities. (When given purchasing responsibility, too often the overriding concern of line managers is to get what they want, when they want it, to the exclusion of all other purchasing considerations.)
8 Fewer orders are processed for the same quantity of goods purchased, thus reducing purchasing, receiving, inspection, accounts payable, and recordkeeping expenses.
9 Responsibility for the performance of the purchasing function is fixed with a single department head, thereby facilitating management control.

Despite the general advantages of centralization, *complete* centralized purchasing is neither always possible nor always desirable. Three types of situations justify some decentralization. The first of these is found in companies that process *single natural raw materials*. Many such firms separate the purchase of the key raw material from the purchase of other materials. Firms in the textile, leather, and tobacco industries are good examples.

In these industries, the raw materials are products of nature that are purchased in unstable markets whose prices fluctuate widely. Buying typically takes place at auctions conducted in small local warehouses. In such markets, a practical knowledge of grades is equally as important as a knowledge of prices. Buyers of these commodities usually guard their specialized know-how with secrecy, frequently handing it down from one generation to the next.

A second situation justifying some decentralization of purchasing authority exists in *technically oriented firms that are heavily involved in research.* In these firms some exceptions to complete centralization are always desirable. Many one-time purchases in the research, design engineering, and related departments can be handled more effectively by professional personnel in these departments. Moreover, the dollar volume of such purchases is usually relatively small.

In the research situation, scientists often do not know exactly what they want. Consequently, they must frequently discuss concepts with one or more vendors before it is possible to select specific pieces of hardware. The design engineer concerned with developing a prototype must frequently talk with the supplier at the completion of each developmental step. These circumstances dictate giving engineers and scientists flexibility and a small portion of the firm's purchasing authority. *After specifications become firm,* however, the purchasing department should assume full responsibility for procurement.

The third situation justifying a different type of decentralization is found in the *operation of multisite institutional and manufacturing organizations.* This interesting topic is discussed fully in Chapter 5.

The purchase of nontechnical odds and ends also often calls for a partial decentralization of purchasing. Petty cash fund purchases of less than $50 or so are a good example. Decentralizing through the use of a petty cash fund can be a money saver. Most firms estimate that it costs between $40 and $100 to process a formal purchase order. For many small purchases, the cost of the paperwork exceeds the cost of the item purchased. Even though the user may pay more for the item if it is bought through petty cash without purchasing assistance, the extra cost is more than offset by the saving in processing costs.

The danger of losing purchasing control (i.e., efficiency and profit) does not stem from a partial decentralization of the purchasing function per se. Some decentralization is necessary as a matter of common sense. The real danger of loss stems from *excessive* decentralization. What percentage is excessive? Generally speaking, if 95 percent or more of the dollar volume purchased is handled by the purchasing department, decentralization should not be considered a problem. However, the appropriate level of decentralization must be determined for each firm from an analysis of the individual factors involved in its operations. One thing is certain: Operating departments seldom try to assume the functions of a purchasing department if the purchasing department is doing a good job for them.

Implementing Centralization

The Manager of Purchasing and Materials is hereby granted the authority and the responsibility for procurement of all materials, equipment, supplies, and services necessary to maintain the Company as a vigorous, growing, and profitable business enterprise.

Within this authority, the Manager of Purchasing and Materials may delegate to other specific individuals the responsibility for the performance of some of the specific procurement duties.

Only those persons delegated specific written authority are authorized to commit Company funds for materials, equipment, supplies, or services. No other individuals are authorized to commit Company funds for these purposes.

The preceding statement is found in one firm's policy manual. When accompanied with the purchasing manager's subsequent list of individuals to whom specific purchasing authority is delegated, this statement communicates clearly to all company personnel the firm's policy on the procurement of materials and services.

Most well-managed firms include similar statements in their policy manuals. In addition, an external document is required to communicate the same message to those outside the business—suppliers and others who might do business with the firm. Some type of concise orientation or information booklet usually is prepared for this audience.

In summary, it is essential that appropriate internal and external personnel know and accept the fact that the purchasing department holds full authority for negotiating, concluding, and following up purchases. This does not mean that purchasing should not request technical assistance from appropriate operating departments when it is needed. Obviously, it should! As purchases become increasingly complex from a technical point of view, it is common to utilize a buying team comprised of individuals from several departments. The point is that the purchasing department bears the managerial responsibility for the planning and conduct of the procurement actions.

Liaison Responsibility for External Contacts   Stemming from this basic policy, most companies issue a series of additional policy statements which give more precise guidance in specific situations. For example, when an operating department head wishes to talk with a vendor's sales or technical representative, the request normally should be made to the purchasing department. The appropriate buyer then makes the initial contact, arranges the appointment, and keeps informed of significant aspects of the discussion that might influence future purchasing activity.

Channeling such external contacts through the purchasing department serves several useful functions. It permits buyers to maintain reasonable control of vendor relations—one of their major responsibilities. The operating department head, for example, may not know about other commitments the buyer has made on related matters with other suppliers. The buyer thus acts as a company coordinator. Moreover, the procedure keeps buyers aware of pending discussions and enables them to plan for and integrate these activities into related purchasing activities already under way. The same logic applies to correspondence between operating departments and vendors.

Selection of Suppliers and Contract Provisions   One of the most important responsibilities of a purchasing organization is to locate and/or develop suppliers that are competent and uniquely qualified to fulfill the buying firm's needs. Staying abreast of the large number of potential suppliers in the marketplace, and their respective capabilities and potential, can be a difficult and time-consuming task if it is done well. Consequently, most firms have a policy that requires buyers to spend a certain percentage of their time searching for, identifying, and investigating potential suppliers in the markets for their most important materials.

Similarly, most departments make it a policy to see all first-time callers from potential suppliers' organizations. Following the initial visit, buyers become much more selective in deciding which business callers to see, limiting their interviews to those sales representatives whose firms' products correspond closely with the buying firm's needs.

Clearly, except in predetermined situations, no one outside the purchasing department should be given the authority to commit the firm to a purchase from a particular supplier. The matters of supplier selection, price determination, and the development of specific contractual provisions lie at the heart of the purchasing department's fundamental responsibility.

Various unique or emergency conditions, however, may produce a situation where it is in the firm's best interest to delegate specific purchasing authority. In such cases, delegation of the authority should be accompanied with adequate plans and constraints to ensure that the purchasing department does not lose control of its purchasing responsibilities. A firm also must make certain that its purchasing department is placed in the best possible bargaining position. Toward this end, it should be clearly understood that no one outside of purchasing is to give potential suppliers any indication of product preference, current sources of supply, price or performance data for competing products, or any other information which would weaken the firm's purchasing position.

The Review of Material Specifications and Requests   The purchasing department's responsibility and authority to critically review material specifications and purchase requests is a policy of paramount importance. It must be stated clearly and unequivocally in the firm's policy manual. One company phrases its policy this way:

> The purchasing department and...subsidiary purchasing agents have the *duty* and the *authority* to request consideration of specifications or quantity of material requisitioned if, in the opinion of the buyer, the interest of the company or its subsidiaries may be better served. However, any change in the purchase request is prohibited unless it is approved by the person or department initiating the requisition, the bill of materials, or the production plan.

Without the establishment of this basic policy, the profit-making potential of centralized purchasing is severely curtailed. Its importance cannot be overemphasized.

Some companies go even further. They utilize a procedure that brings appropriate buying personnel into material specification considerations early in the development process. Using this approach, material specifications are, in fact, jointly developed by design (or using department) and purchasing personnel. Other firms simply require purchasing to review and approve all material specifications before a new product leaves the drawing boards.

In the interest of controlling expenditures, a firm typically delegates the authority to approve routine purchase requisitions only to specified individuals in each using department. This practice establishes the groundwork for a policy requiring that all requests for purchase be submitted in writing. Except in a rare emergency, oral requisitions should not be accepted. This policy obviously eliminates numerous costly communication errors. More important, however, is the fact that it requires operating departments to plan their material requirements more carefully. This in turn results in less ill-advised impulse buying, and it also reduces costly rush buying activities in the purchasing department.

Policies Affecting External Relationships and Image

Most companies spend a great deal of money to develop a favorable public image. Madison Avenue derives its livelihood from the efforts of business executives to convince the public that their companies are "the good guys in the white hats." Irrespective of public relations and advertising expenditures, however, a firm's purchasing and sales departments contribute heavily to the shaping of its public image. Most of a firm's contacts with the business community are managed by these two departments.

The development of sound vendor relations is a major responsibility of the purchasing department, for two reasons. First, good vendor relations contribute to the formation of a good public image. Second, the treatment and service that a supplier gives a customer depends to a great extent on the way the supplier feels about the customer. However the matter is viewed, it is in purchasing's best interest to establish policies that promote favorable relationships with the vendor community. Some of the more important issues are discussed briefly in the following pages.

Salespeople   Perhaps the simplest thing a purchasing department can do to promote favorable vendor relations is to treat all salespeople fairly and courteously. As noted earlier, most companies make it a policy to see all salespeople on the first call, as long as their products are remotely relevant to the firm's needs. To permit more efficient planning and utilization of a buyer's time, many companies establish regular calling hours for vendors' representatives (perhaps four hours a day, four or five days a week). As a rule, this conserves time for buyers and salespeople alike.

Orientation and Policy Booklets   Careful and complete communication with potential suppliers facilitates the development of good relations. Toward this end, many companies prepare an orientation booklet which is given to all vendors calling on the purchasing department. Such booklets typically contain a brief description of the company's operations and products or services, a directory of its buyers and the types of materials each buys, and a statement of major purchasing policies and practices that potential suppliers should know about.

The Kaiser Corporation distributes a small booklet which, in addition to explaining the purchasing department's calling hours, sets forth a number of ground rules which affect the company's relationships with vendors. Several key policies included are:[2]

- Our purchasing departments are the sole agents at the plant who have authority to commit the company to purchases, large or small.
- We prefer to limit the number of our suppliers to an extent that those suppliers will value our business and will endeavor to meet legitimate competition.
- We secure competitive prices whenever possible, giving due consideration to assurance of supply and prompt delivery.
- We buy from vendors nearest the point of use, other considerations being equal.
- Suppliers' representatives can deal with our plant Purchasing Managers secure in the knowledge that they are protected from any unfair advantage of competing suppliers through "second looks" or personal relationships.

To the extent that orientation booklets apprise a firm's potential suppliers of its basic policies and procedures, they can be very helpful and can prevent exasperating misunderstandings. A buyer must always bear in mind that statements which are *not* made in oral discussions with a vendor's representatives may tell the vendor more than statements that are made. Incomplete communication can give rise to incorrect rumors and speculations highly detrimental to the relationship. For these reasons, many firms follow the policy of communicating relevant purchasing policies to their potential suppliers by means of the written word, stated in a precise yet congenial manner.

Competitive Bids Nothing offers more potential danger to a firm's reputation for fair dealing than a poorly handled competitive-bidding situation. Consequently, most firms establish definite policies to guide all buying personnel in handling bidding activities, both *before* and *after* the issuance of requests for bid.

Despite the fact that no legal requirements compel a private firm to award a contract to the low bidder, the competitive-bidding process itself implies that the lowest qualified bidder will get the contract. It is this expectation that motivates a vendor to compute its costs and assess its competitive position carefully before submitting its bid. To consistently obtain vendors' best prices

[2]*Welcome to Kaiser Aluminum & Chemical Corporation Purchasing Department.* Kaiser Aluminum & Chemical Corporation.

on the first bid, a buyer should therefore, in most cases, award the contract to the low bidder. This situation gives rise to two important policies:

1 Sound competitive-bidding practice demands that a buyer be willing to do business with every vendor from whom he or she solicits a bid. The resulting policy states that all vendors requested to bid must be determined *in advance* to be *qualified* suppliers for the job in question.
2 Whenever the lowest bidder does not receive the contract, the buyer is required to explain the decision. A short memorandum to this effect should be filed with the order or with the quotation analysis.

As simple as the preceding policies sound, they can be quite difficult to follow in practice. The fact that very few vendors are *equally* qualified or motivated to handle a specific purchase makes it virtually impossible to evaluate bidders on the basis of price alone (except for highly standardized, off-the-shelf products). This situation, at times, justifies the selection of someone other than the low bidder. Even though justified, such a decision often is difficult to explain satisfactorily to the unsuccessful bidders who quoted lower prices than the successful bidder. And, though a buyer may try to prevent unsuccessful bidders from learning the successful bid price, this is usually impossible. In a competitive industry, "grapevines" are too numerous and too effective to permit the keeping of many price secrets. Thus, even when the decision to award the contract to a high bidder is fully justified by a combined evaluation of quality, service, and price, it can still produce unfavorable vendor relations. Hence, the need for the policies and their enlightened observance is clear.

Chapter 10 stresses the importance of allowing each vendor only one bid on a competitively bid contract. In the interest of fairness, all firms must be accorded the same treatment. The buyer should treat all bid data confidentially and should not divulge one bidder's data to another bidder, either before or after the contract has been awarded. All bidders should be advised of the bid closing date, and no bids should be accepted after that date. If, for extraordinary reasons, the bid date is extended to give an interested vendor more time, it is the buyer's responsibility to notify *all* bidders of the new bid closing date.

The rules of common courtesy require the buyer to notify all unsuccessful bidders that the contract has been awarded. This allows those firms to release production capacity that may have been reserved for this potential contract. It is important that bidders be told of their failure to get the contract in a courteous and objective manner. Although a vendor realizes that it cannot get every order, it is likely to be more competitive on future jobs if it is not dissatisfied with its treatment on the current job.

Presale Technical Service   The purchase of certain technical items requires a potential supplier to conduct a presale study of the buyer's specific application of the items to be purchased. Firms in some industries customarily make such studies as part of their regular sales efforts. Selling prices in these industries are set so that the revenue from successful efforts covers the cost of unsuccessful presale studies.

In other industries, however, vendors' prices provide for very little presale engineering work. Purchasing policy therefore must establish distinct limits with respect to the acceptance of presale technical services. While buyers want all the assistance legitimately available, they cannot afford to place their companies under obligation to a vendor by accepting an unreasonable amount of presale service.[3]

The incurrence of such an obligation usually leads to one of two undesirable results. First, the buyer can place the order with the vendor to whom he or she is obligated; however, some disadvantage may result if another vendor proves to be more desirable. Second, the buyer can place the order with the most favorable supplier, regardless of the obligation to the vendor providing the unusual service. Even though the latter may have no legal claim to the order or to compensation for its services, the vendor may frequently feel or say that the buyer has taken an unfair advantage. Whether or not this is true, of course, depends on the explicit agreement reached in prior negotiations. In reality, however, at this point the truth of the matter is of little significance to the buyer. What is important is the fact that as a result of the ensuing rumor, the buyer's firm may be viewed with suspicion by some members of the business community.

Purchasing policy must guard against such problems, however innocently they may arise. Before accepting a vendor's offer to make a presale study, the buyer must estimate the amount of money involved and determine whether the offer is consistent with standard practice in the industry. Any service exceeding normal industry practice should be *purchased* completely apart from the basic purchase of material or equipment.

Samples   One way to assess the quality of a product is to actually use or test a sample before ordering a significant quantity. In an effort to get a foot in the door, many salespeople request a buyer to accept a free sample of a product and "try it out."

The buyer may find it advantageous to accept such an invitation. It is an inexpensive and effortless way of learning about new, potentially useful products. If the cost of the sample is more than several dollars, however, the buyer should elect to pay for the sample. Such prudence removes any possible obligation that could result from accepting free material.

On the other hand, if the buyer sees no possible value in investigating a sales representative's product, he or she should explain the reason to the sales representative and decline the sample. Once a sample is accepted, the buyer is ob-

---

[3] Unfortunately, some salespeople deliberately employ this technique to gain a psychological advantage. If, for any reason, a buyer is under obligation to a seller, the buyer's conscience may well compel him or her to evaluate the relative positions of various vendors differently than would be the case if he or she were under obligation to none of the vendors.

ligated to see that it gets a prompt and fair test. Further, the vendor is entitled to a complete report of the test as well as an evaluation of the firm's probable use for the product. This procedure requires time and administrative effort. Under the constant pressures of daily business, buyers occasionally tend to handle samples in a haphazard and inconsistent fashion. Yet, nothing irritates a sales representative more than to learn two months later that his or her sample has not even been tested. Such irritation inevitably influences his or her attitude toward the buyer's firm. In the interest of good vendor relations, therefore, a definite policy (and related procedures) should be established to ensure fair and uniform treatment of all samples by all buyers.

Plant and Distribution Center Visits Every company should require its buyers to periodically visit the operations of major suppliers. Such visits yield three distinct benefits. First, they provide an opportunity for a buyer to learn more about the current technical or manufacturing aspects of the materials he or she buys. Second, these visits enable a buyer to discover a great deal of inside information about specific suppliers. In no other way can buyers become intimately acquainted with their suppliers' strengths and weaknesses or with the unique conditions under which each supplier operates. Third, site visits permit a buyer to develop valuable personal acquaintances and business friendships with suppliers' personnel.

Despite the impersonal nature of most major business decisions, daily business activities and negotiations are conducted by people who prefer to deal with someone they know and like. A buyer who is known personally in a supplier's operation sheds his or her inconspicuous role as a name on the customer mailing list and becomes a living personality. When a buyer has to expedite an order, ask a special favor, or ask a delicate question to which he or she wants a frank answer, there is no substitute for honest and friendly communication on a first-name basis with someone in the supplier's organization. Any purchasing department that fails to recognize this basic truth deprives itself of some of the fun of business, as well as some very tangible benefits.

Policies on Pricing and Supply Sources

Pricing and sourcing decisions represent major activities and outputs of a purchasing operation. They obviously produce a substantial impact both inside and outside the buyer's firm. Consequently, the manner in which these activities are handled and the nature of the decision-making processes are extremely important. For these reasons, it is essential that carefully conceived policies be included in the policy manual to facilitate sound and consistent actions.

Dozens of these policies are discussed in Chapters 9 through 12. Major topics include the use of competitive bidding and the use of negotiation, the number of sources to utilize (single or multiple), the size of sourcing firms, specialty firms, local firms, foreign firms, distributors and manufacturers, and the selection criteria to be utilized in considering the various options.

This brief discussion is included at this point in the text simply to make the reader aware of the importance of these types of policies in the development of effective relationships with suppliers and potential suppliers.

Policies Concerning Ethical Practices

Purchasing professionals in any organization have ethical obligations to three groups of people—*employers, suppliers,* and their *purchasing colleagues.* Because external perceptions of a firm's purchasing personnel are so important in building the firm's reputation, most organizations include in their policy manuals a series of statements much like these:

1 Purchasing personnel must not become involved in any situation that produces a conflict of interest or dilutes their performance for the firm.
2 Purchasing personnel must not become involved in any situation that results in the development of a sense of personal obligation to any supplier.
3 Buyers must treat all vendors fairly, without bias or prejudice.
4 Buyers are obligated to strive for an equitable settlement of business dealings for both firms—the buyer's firm and the supplier's firm.
5 Purchasing personnel are expected to protect any information that is proprietary to the buying firm or to individual vendors' firms.
6 Purchasing personnel are expected to conduct themselves generally in ways that bring credit to them personally, to their firms, and to the larger body of purchasing colleagues.

The topic of ethics is discussed extensively in Chapter 30.

Purchases for Employees A topic that increasingly is considered to border on the area of ethics is the use of a firm's buying power to purchase major consumer products at a significant discount for employees.

Thirty years ago, a majority of U.S. industrial firms routinely handled these types of purchases—major appliances, household furnishings, building materials, and so on—as a fringe benefit for their employees. Today the number of firms engaged in this practice has shrunk to a small minority. Four factors have combined to produce the decline.

1 The potential ethical problem, in a macro sense, has disturbed a number of firms, both buyers and suppliers. When a firm's purchasing department makes such a purchase from a distributor with whom it normally does company business, it usually buys at a price discount to which it is entitled by virtue of its annual volume of purchases. Industrial prices are frequently 30 to 50 percent below retail prices for comparable items. So, when a purchase is made for the personal use of an employee, *the employee is receiving the discount earned by the firm's purchasing power.*
2 A disadvantage of this practice to the buying firm obviously is the administrative cost involved in the action. Such special orders are time-

consuming and, in an operation of several thousand people, can add up to a substantial internal cost for the buying firm.

3 All employee reactions are not always favorable. Most purchases of this type do not carry the normal dealer return privileges, installation and maintenance service, and so on. If the employee has problems, often there is very little recourse available. Hence, some personal dissatisfaction sometimes results.

4 Finally, some state legislatures have viewed the practice as discriminatory and as a form of unfair competition to retail dealers. The result in a handful of states has been the passage of trade diversion laws which make it illegal for a firm to sell any products, except those it manufactures, to its employees.

In total, these factors have reduced the practice markedly in recent years. Although some firms still have a policy providing this type of purchasing service for their employees, most do not.

Policies Concerning Minority Business Enterprises

During the past decade and a half, this country has witnessed a growing sensitivity on the part of U.S. business firms to their potential roles in helping solve some of the country's major socioeconomic problems. This expanded role as responsible corporate citizens has included extensive participation in a wide variety of youth development programs, secondary and higher education support activities, and community charity efforts, as well as genuine support for affirmative action and equal employment opportunity programs. In addition to these highly visible activities, a less visible—but no less important—thrust has gradually emerged in the form of a variety of minority business procurement programs.

The late 1960s and the early 1970s saw ten years of social unrest in the United States that were unparalleled in recent times. In response to the needs revealed by this situation, the federal government took a number of legislative steps designed to bring more minorities into the mainstream of American economic life. One of these efforts focused on expanded development of qualified minority business enterprises (MBE).[4] Key legislative actions implemented to promote this effort are noted briefly below.

• *1969—Executive Order 11485:* Established the U.S. Office of Minority Business Enterprise within the Department of Commerce, for the purpose of mobilizing federal resources to aid minorities in business.

• *1971—Executive Order 11625:* Gives the secretary of commerce the authority to: (1) implement federal policy in support of MBE programs, (2) pro-

---

[4] A minority business enterprise is defined as any legal entity, organized to engage in commercial transactions, that is at least 51 percent owned, controlled, or operated by one or more minority persons.

vide technical and management assistance to disadvantaged businesses, and (3) coordinate activities between all federal departments to aid in increasing minority business development.

• *1978—Public Law 95-507:* Mandates that if a buyer's firm is awarded a federal contract that exceeds $10,000, the buyer is required to make "maximum efforts" in awarding subcontracts to small minority businesses.

If the federal contract exceeds $500,000 ($1,000,000 for construction projects), *prior to contract award* the buyer's firm must submit an acceptable buying plan that includes percentage goals for the utilization of minority businesses. The plan must also detail procedures for identifying and dealing with the minority businesses.

MBE policy requirements are clear for firms that do business with the federal government. The requirements of Public Law 95-507 do not apply to firms that deal only in the private sector. Nevertheless, a majority of the country's large firms have supported the concept underlying the minority business development thrust. In 1972 the National Minority Purchasing Council (now renamed the National Minority Supplier Development Council) was formed voluntarily to accelerate the acceptance of minority vendors through improved communications between majority and minority firms. Most metropolitan areas throughout the country have their own local or regional minority purchasing councils which, as a rule, are strongly supported by the local purchasing management association.

The bottom line of this activity is summarized in the following quotations of two industrial purchasing executives:[5]

> When we help all segments of the business community, we're helping ourselves. American commerce and industry will only be as strong as the segments that make it up. If MBEs are a segment of the total business pie, it's in our interest to assist them, because we are a part of the same pie.

> To find the lowest responsible bid that meets the needs of our company, we need to find vendors and distributors that allow us both to have effective, fair, and considerate competition—and that includes *all* possible sources.

In conclusion, it is fair to say that a majority of firms subscribe to a policy on minority buying that includes all or most of the following elements:

1 The firm intends to award some portion of its business to qualified minority business enterprises.
2 Within practical limits, the firm will supply technical and managerial assistance for a reasonable period of time to help the MBE become a "qualified" vendor.
3 In the long run, the MBE must compete favorably with other potential suppliers on all purchase decision criteria.

[5]R. T. Williams, *Doing Business with Minority Vendors,* The Publication Center Inc., Alexandria, Va., 1985, pp. 7 and 8.

THE POLICY MANUAL

It is appropriate at this point to state explicitly an underlying concept which has only been implied in the preceding discussions of policies: If policies are to function effectively, it is imperative that they be placed in written form. A policy is a communication—an important one. It is important that the message reach those who are to receive it as clearly and accurately as possible. The complexity of a modern firm necessitates the establishment of many diverse policies, all of which cannot possibly be remembered with accuracy. The normal turnover of employees and managers compounds the difficulty. Moreover, because policies are general statements, minor differences in interpretation are inevitable. It is essential, therefore, that care be taken to ensure the accuracy of policy communications.

Consequently, most firms disseminate policy statements to their employees via some type of written policy manual. A policy manual typically has at least two distinct sections, one containing *company* policies and one containing *departmental* policies. The section on company policies spells out in unmistakable terms the responsibility and authority of all departments. It is essential that these policies carry top-management approval and that they be communicated to every department head.

The second section on departmental policies is directed to the personnel of each respective operating department. In the case of purchasing, departmental policies inform personnel of the expected patterns of conduct for major buying activities and for relations with vendors and other external personnel. The use of a policy manual clearly facilitates consistent basic conduct among all departmental personnel. It is particularly important to foster consistent performance among buyers because their dealings with vendors can significantly influence the firm's public image. A policy manual also facilitates the training of personnel.

The specific style, format, and contents of purchasing manuals vary widely. Some firms include only policies, while others include policies and procedures. Still others add organization charts, job descriptions, sample departmental forms, and other detailed data which, in total, completely describe the purchasing department's operation. The particular format used is not important. One style may fit one company's need better than another. What is important is that all major policies and operating procedures be committed to writing. They must be stated simply and unambiguously in a manual that is easy to use and that is kept current.

CONCLUSION

What does management expect of a good purchasing operation? It should expect performance that provides an intelligent balance among its basic materials objectives—the *five rights*. Given that purchasing's first responsibility is to support operations with a satisfactory flow of materials, based on a given set of operating and market conditions, purchasing's charge is to provide optimal value to the organization. It does this by combining in the right proportions the various elements of material quality and cost, tempered with the needed touch of supplier know-how and service. Unfortunately, the difficult part of this balancing act is that the conditions and the requirements change—with time and with different materials. Hence, the optimal purchasing mix changes. This is the challenge for purchasing management in achieving what otherwise would be a reasonably simple set of basic objectives.

Policies are the general guidelines designed to assist these decision makers as they develop plans to "zero-in" on their moving target. The policies channel their actions, as well as those of their non-purchasing colleagues, toward attainment of the desired objectives.

Purchasing policies serve two general functions: (1) They establish the ground rules for purchasing's relationship with other departments, and (2) they inform purchasing personnel about the expected conduct of departmental activities.

Policies of the first type should establish clearly the centralized purchasing function. They should also specify the function's responsibilities with respect to the development of material specifications, supplier selection, price determination, and contract administration. Policies of the second type should provide guidance for departmental personnel in conducting activities that influence the firm's relationships with external individuals and with external organizations.

A vendor's perceptions about the buyer's firm are important. What vendors think about the firm's practices, as they reflect such things as competency, honesty, and fair play, definitely influences the type of relationship that develops between the firm and the business community. Some years ago, C. W. McVicar of Rockwell International summed up the idea very well:[6]

> Friendship can even be cultivated by the manner in which a salesman is told he has lost, or cannot have, an order. These may seem small things, but courtesy, square-dealing, honesty, and straightforwardness beget friendship. They are appreciated by vendors and the buyer benefits largely from them. The salesman who receives brusque treatment is not likely to make an extra effort to render special services, to offer new ideas readily, or to speak as favorably of either the buyer or the company as he would if he felt he had been given fair and courteous treatment.

This sage observation is still sound today—and it will be just as valid when we enter the twenty-first century.

---

[6] George W. Aljian (ed.), *Purchasing Handbook,* McGraw-Hill Book Company, New York, 1966, p. 3–24.

FOR DISCUSSION

2-1 Define and explain the "five rights."

2-2 What is the major difficulty in achieving the five rights in practice? Give an example.

2-3 What is the difference between "buying wisely" and "buying competitively," as described by the authors?

2-4 "Objectives of purchasing and materials management can be viewed from three levels." Identify and discuss the significance of these three levels from a practical point of view.

2-5 Define a policy. How do you think a policy differs from a procedure?

2-6 Some business executives believe that a company should operate with as few policies and procedures as possible, because they think such things inhibit the creative thinking of managers and employees. Comment on this idea in general. Comment on the idea as it relates specifically to purchasing policies.

2-7 Assume that you have just become the purchasing manager for an electric appliance manufacturer employing 4,000 people. You have been asked to rewrite the section of the company's policy manual that includes policies defining the purchasing department's responsibilities. Write these policies as you think they should appear in the company manual.

2-8 Assuming the same conditions as in question 2-7, write a policy for the complete handling of competitive bids in your firm.

2-9 What problems can arise in the handling of presale technical services? Discuss.

2-10 Prepare for your boss (the vice president for purchasing in a medium-size machinery manufacturing firm) a detailed report discussing the concept of centralized purchasing, including its strengths and weaknesses.

2-11 What ethical obligations does a buyer have? Discuss.

2-12 Assume you are the purchasing manager for a machinery manufacturing firm of 700 employees. Every year you use approximately $1,000,000 worth of lubricants, which you purchase from one supplier who is selected on the basis of competitive bids every January.

The sales representative for your current supplier makes his usual monthly call to your office on the first day of October. After discussing the normal business problems, he extends an invitation (through your office) to a group of your company executives and supervisors to attend a party.

Those invited are:

1 The purchasing manager, her assistant, and three buyers

2 The plant manager and his assistant

3 The chief design engineer and four engineering section heads
4 The maintenance superintendent and his three foremen
5 The production manager and his staff assistant
6 The controller and her assistant
7 The sales manager
8 The industrial relations manager

Supplier's personnel attending are:

1 Two corporate sales managers and the district manager
2 Several sales representatives
3 A representative from the corporate research department
4 Two representatives from the corporate technical applications department

The party is planned for Friday evening in the private dining room of a local hotel and includes the following program:

6:30–7:30	Cocktail hour
7:30–8:30	Dinner
8:30–9:00	Informal discussion and slides of the supplier's technical research activities and achievements
9:00–9:30	Film of the Olympic Games
9:30–10:00	Film—"New Dimensions in Musical Entertainment"
10:00–	Adjourn for continuation of the cocktail hour

Discuss in detail how (and why) you would handle this situation.

CASES FOR CHAPTER 2

World-Wide Industries, page 819
Sampson Products Corporation, page 800
Senator Foghorn, page 810
The Old Oak Furniture Company (in the Instructor's Manual)
The Hertz Boys (in the Instructor's Manual)

CHAPTER **3**

OPERATING PROCEDURES

KEY CONCEPTS

- Effective procedures
- General procurement procedures
    Definition, description, and transmission of need
    Supplier selection and order preparation
    Order follow-up
    Receipt and inspection
    Invoice audit and order completion
- Purchasing records
    Open orders; closed orders; purchase log
    Commodity record
    Supplier record
    Contract and tool records
- Handling rush orders
- Handling small orders
    Blanket orders; systems contracting
    Contracting/MRP systems
    Telephone orders; electronic systems
    Petty cash; C.O.D. systems
    Purchase order draft system
    Consignment and supplier delivery systems

A procedure outlines in detail the specific actions to be taken to accomplish a given task, within the guidelines of any applicable policies. In short, it establishes the way of doing things.

Procurement procedures, and the documents they utilize, serve two fundamental purposes within a firm:

1 They provide the framework and the direction for accomplishing the supply and materials management activities effectively and efficiently.
2 They provide the means for processing information inputs from outside the department to produce output communications needed by individuals in other departments to do their jobs in a coordinated and timely manner. (Figure 3-1 identifies the numerous departments that are affected by procurement procedures.)

Chapters 6 through 26 suggest procedures and policies for the specific materials activities discussed in those chapters. The purpose of this chapter is to identify and discuss the basic *operating* procedures, documents, and records that integrate the specialized activities of those chapters into a complete operational purchasing cycle.

In operation, these basic procedures can be implemented manually, by means of a computer-based system, or most commonly by a combination of the two. The next chapter, Chapter 4, discusses the implementation of procurement procedures in a computer-based environment.

GENERAL PROCUREMENT PROCEDURES

A purchasing department buys many different types of materials and services, and the procedures used in completing a total transaction normally vary among the different types of purchases. However, the general cycle of activities in purchasing most operating materials and supplies is fairly standardized. The following steps constitute the typical purchasing cycle:

- Recognize, define, and describe the need
- Transmit the need
- Investigate and select the supplier
- Prepare and issue the purchase order
- Follow up the order (including expediting and de-expediting)
- Receive and inspect the material
- Audit the invoice
- Close the order

Figure 3-1 outlines these steps in operational form. More important, it details the minimum flow of communication documents required for a system to function smoothly and efficiently. The precise form the documents take varies widely from one company to another. The important point to note, however, is that a properly controlled purchase requires extensive communication with numerous work groups. Procurement procedures constitute the framework within which this task is accomplished.

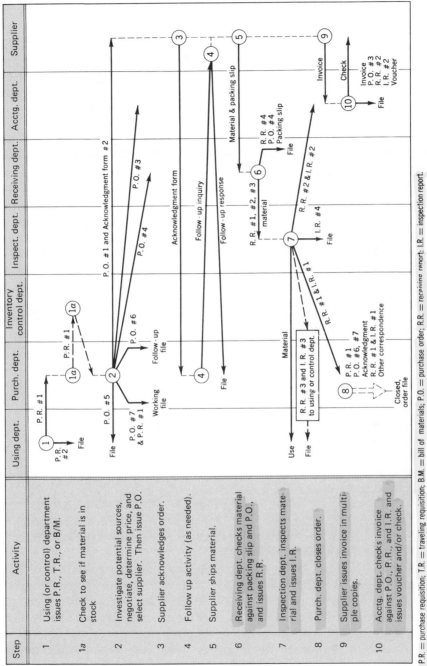

FIGURE 3-1
General procedure and document flow chart for a typical purchasing cycle.

51

Recognition, Definition, Description, and Transmission of the Need

The need for a purchase typically originates in one of a firm's operating departments or in its inventory control section. Transmission of the need to the purchasing department is usually accomplished by one of four forms: (1) a standard purchase requisition, (2) a traveling purchase requisition, (3) a bill of materials, or (4) a material requirements planning (MRP) schedule.

Standard Purchase Requisition The purchase requisition is an internal document, in contrast with the purchase order which is basically an external document. Most companies use a standard, serially numbered purchase requisition form for requests originating in the operating departments. The user generally makes a minimum of two copies. One copy is sent to purchasing; the other is retained in the using department's file. Some companies use as many as nine copies of the requisition for communication with other interested departments. Purchase requisition formats vary widely because each company designs its format to simplify its own particular communication problems. The essential information which every requisition should contain, however, includes a description of the material, quantity and date required, estimated unit cost, operating account to be charged, the date, and an authorized signature. A typical purchase requisition is shown in Figure 3-2.

Traveling Purchase Requisition Many companies use a "traveling requisition" to communicate to purchasing the material needs that originate in the inventory control section. In a manually operated system, a traveling requisition is a simple printed card that is usually filed with the inventory control record for each item carried in inventory. The following data typically appear on a traveling requisition: (1) a complete description of the item, including reference to applicable specifications; (2) a numbered list of approved suppliers and their addresses; (3) last prices paid to various suppliers; (4) reorder point and order quantity values; and (5) a record of usage. If desired, the card can also include supplier performance information and other historical data. Figure 3-3 illustrates a commonly used traveling requisition format.

When the stock level drops to the reorder point in a manual system, an inventory clerk takes the traveling requisition from the file, notes the current stock level and the desired delivery date on the card, and sends it to the purchasing department. To indicate that the requisition has been sent to purchasing, a colored signal clip is usually attached to the inventory record card. This procedure eliminates the typing of a purchase requisition. Since the traveling requisition contains information the buyer would otherwise have to locate in his or her own files, it also conserves time. After reviewing the requisition, the buyer pencils the small quantity of required order data in the provided columns. The purchase order is then prepared directly from the

FIGURE 3-2
A typical purchase requisition form. (*Courtesy of Storage Technology Corporation.*)

traveling requisition. After the buyer signs the purchase order, the traveling requisition is returned to the inventory control section and refiled with its respective inventory record card.

In companies using computerized inventory control systems, the work of the inventory control clerk is done automatically by a computer. In such cases, the computer typically produces a purchase requisition that contains essentially the same information as the traveling requisition.

Bill of Materials and MRP Schedule   When a design engineer completes the design of a part or an assembly, he or she makes a list of all the materials (and quantity of each) required to manufacture the item. This specially structured list is called a *bill of materials*. (In some cases it is possible to include the bill of materials directly on the engineering drawing.) The bill of materials, along with a production schedule, can be sent directly to purchasing as notification of the production department's need for materials. Total requirements are obtained by simply extending the bill of materials for the production quantity scheduled.

FIGURE 3-3
A typical traveling requisition.

In many firms using computerized production and inventory control systems, such as an MRP system, this entire procedure is accomplished by the computer. It produces a complete requirements schedule for a given time period, containing most of the information needed by the buyer.

These procedures obviously eliminate the necessity of preparing numerous purchase requisitions. They are efficient methods of transmitting the need for materials used in an intermittent manufacturing process or for materials required for a uniquely designed, one-time project.

Definition and Description of the Need Chapters 6 and 7 discuss in depth the formulation and utilization of material specifications and standards; Chapter 6 also deals extensively with the various methods of describing quality. Regardless of the form of transmission used, material requirements must be defined effectively, and the most appropriate methods of description should be selected for the situation at hand. The point to be understood here is that *clear, complete, appropriate* definition and description is a joint responsibility of the user and the buyer. One of the reasons why every purchase requisition should be approved by designated departmental supervisors is to ensure that requisitions are initially reviewed by qualified individuals and subsequently come to purchasing in correct form. The buyer's responsibility is then threefold. First, he or she checks the requisition for accuracy and completeness, including internal data such as the account to which the purchase will be charged. Second, the buyer determines that the need has been adequately defined. Finally, he or she must ensure that the appropriate method of description has been used to guarantee a satisfactory purchase for the user and, at the same time, provide all possible latitude in the selection of a supplier.

The Stock Check With the exception of traveling requisitions that originate in the inventory control section, when purchase requests arrive in the purchasing department, they are checked to see if the requested item is carried in stock. In many cases, a buyer can tell simply by looking at the requisition whether it involves a stock material. If adequate stock is on hand, no purchase is necessary.

Some companies route all requisitions for tools, supplies, and production-type materials to inventory control before they are sent to purchasing. If a sizable percentage of a firm's requisitions involve stores-type items, this procedure expedites the supply process and reduces clerical work in the purchasing department. It also apprises inventory control of the non-stock items that are being ordered repetitively and, therefore, might advantageously be carried in stock.

Supplier Selection and Preparation of the Purchase Order

As soon as a need has been established and precisely described, a buyer begins the investigation of vendors to select a source of supply. In the case of routine items for which supplier relationships have already been developed, little additional investigation may be required to select a good source.[1] The purchase of a new or a high-value item, on the other hand, may require a lengthy investigation of potential suppliers. After selecting a preliminary group of potential sources, the buyer may employ the techniques of competitive bidding or negotiation, or both. When competitive bidding is used, the buyer initiates the procedure by requesting quotations from a selected group of vendors with whom he or she is willing to do business. Although "request for quotation" forms vary widely among firms, typically they contain the same basic information that will subsequently be included on the purchase order. Figure 3-4 provides an illustration.

---

[1]In practical purchasing terminology, these types of purchases are termed "rebuys" or "modified rebuys."

REQUEST FOR QUOTATION

STORAGE TECHNOLOGY CORPORATION
303-673-5151
MATERIAL PROCUREMENT
P.O. BOX 98
2270 SO. 88th ST.
LOUISVILLE, COLORADO 80027

DATE:

REQUEST NUMBER:

INSTRUCTIONS: STORAGE TECHNOLOGY CORPORATION REQUESTS YOUR PROPOSAL (RFQ) ON THE GOODS OR SERVICES LISTED BELOW. PLEASE FURNISH ALL INFORMATION AS REQUESTED. UPON COMPLETION, RETURN RESPONSE AND ONE COPY OF THIS RFQ TO THE BUYER.

TO:

IT IS STORAGE TECHNOLOGY'S INTENTION:
☐ To Make a One-time Buy Only.
☐ To Issue One or More Purchase Orders Over a Period of _____
☐ To Enter Into a Corporate Agreement to Extend Over a Period of _____
☐ Other_____

PLEASE PROPOSE ON THE ABOVE IN THE FOLLOWING MANNER:
1. ☐ On Exact Quantity Only.
   ☐ From_____to Indicated Quantity, Indicating all Price Breaks.
   ☐ On 25%, 50%, and 100% of Quantity.
   ☐ Over_____
2. **MAXIMUM STC LIABILITY IN THE EVENT OF TERMINATION:**
   A)____Days Work-in-Process.
   B)____Days Material.
3. Other _____

COMPLETE THE FOLLOWING:
Minimum Quantities
Deliverable Per Week_____Month_____ Payment Terms:_____
Earliest Delivery:_____ F.O.B. Point:_____
Deliveries To Be Made From_____To_____
Set-Up Costs:_____ Tooling Costs:_____
Deliveries To Be Scheduled_____
Other Costs (please indicate):_____

Specify the Identity of the Individual(s) or Firm (in the event of a local representative) Authorized to Contractually Commit Your Firm in Negotiations and the Execution of Any Resultant Agreement:_____
Minority Owned & Operated Enterprise ☐ YES ☐ NO

THE FOLLOWING ENCLOSURES MUST BE COMPLETED AND RETURNED WITH YOUR PROPOSAL, IF INDICATED BY "X".
☐ Cost Breakdown Requirement ☐ Certificate of Non-Segregated Facilities
☐ Value Engineering Questionaire ☐ Certificate of Employment of Handicapped

DESCRIPTION OF ITEM(S)

ITEM	STC PART NUMBER	DESCRIPTION	EC LEVEL	ESTIMATED USAGE

ADDITIONAL INFORMATION AND REQUIREMENTS

1. ANY PURCHASE ORDERS ISSUED SHALL BE SUBJECT TO AND CITE THE TERMS AND CONDITIONS ON THE REVERSE SIDE OF THIS RFQ. ANY EXCEPTIONS TO THESE TERMS AND CONDITIONS MUST BE SUBMITTED IN WRITING AND RETURNED WITH YOUR RESPONSE. ANY PREPRINTED TERMS AND CONDITIONS ON ANY PROPOSAL FORM SHALL BE INVALID AND OF NO EFFECT. TOOLING REQUIRED FOR ANY ORDER SHALL BE SUBJECT TO ATTACHMENT T 100.
2. ALL GOODS OR SERVICES BOUGHT, RENTED, OR LEASED AS A RESULT OF THIS RFQ WILL BE SUBJECT TO THE FOLLOWING ENCLOSED SPECIFICATIONS (INDICATED BY "X"):
   ☐ SPEC #3092 ☐ SPEC #2925 ☐ SPEC #3043 ☐ SPEC #26000 ☐ SPEC #26001
   ☐ SPEC #33118 ☐ SPEC #2926 ☐ SPEC #21010 ☐ SPEC #21002 ☐ SPEC #3049 ☐ SPEC #QP5003
   ☐ SPEC #3011 ☐ SPEC #3012 ☐ SPEC #33200 ☐ SPEC #33120 ☐ SPEC #23200 ☐ SPEC #E52925
   ☐ SPEC #QP5007 ☐ OTHER_____
3. IT IS STC'S POLICY TO INSURE AN EQUAL OPPORTUNITY FOR ALL QUALIFIED PROSPECTIVE SUPPLIERS. THEREFORE, ALL CONTACTS WITH STC PERSONNEL RELEVANT TO THIS RFQ MUST BE THROUGH THE BUYER. UNAUTHORIZED CONTACTS AT ANY TIME MAY BE THE BASIS FOR DISQUALIFICATION.
4. ALL DRAWINGS, SPECIFICATIONS, PART LISTS, ETC. RECEIVED FROM STC SHALL REMAIN THE PROPERTY OF STC. ANY DISCLOSURE TO THIRD PARTIES WITHOUT AUTHORIZATION BY STC MAY BE THE BASIS FOR DISQUALIFICATION.
5. STC RESERVES THE RIGHT TO REJECT ANY AND ALL PROPOSALS AND TO WAIVE SPECIFIC REQUIREMENTS AT ITS DISCRETION.
6. ALL PRICES PROPOSED MUST BE FIRM FOR_____DAYS.
7. "ALL PROPOSALS TO BE PHONED IN WITH WRITTEN CONFIRMATION TO FOLLOW."
8. YOUR PROPOSAL, ONE COPY OF THIS RFQ AND ALL ENCLOSURES REQUIRING RESPONSES MUST BE IN OUR POSSESSION BY_____ A.M. _____ P.M. _____

IF NOT PROPOSING, PLEASE SO INDICATE AND RETURN ENTIRE PACKAGE TO THE BUYER.

REPLY TO THE ATTENTION OF _____
Material Procurement

FORM STC-0890B

PHONE

FIGURE 3-4
A typical request for quotation form. (*Courtesy of Storage Technology Corporation.*)

Once a supplier has been selected, the purchasing department prepares and issues a serially numbered purchase order. In most cases the purchase order becomes a legal contract document. For this reason, the buyer should take great care in preparing and wording the order. Quantity requirements, price, and delivery and shipping requirements must be specified accurately. Quality specifications must be described precisely. If engineering drawings or other related documents are to be considered an integral part of the order, they should be incorporated clearly by reference. In the event that sampling inspection is to be used, sampling plans and conditions of acceptance should be stated or referenced on the order. Similarly, any other important factor affecting the acceptability of the product should be stated precisely. In short, the order should include all data required to ensure a satisfactory contract, and it should be worded in a manner which leaves little room for misinterpretation by either party.

In addition to those provisions that are unique to each contract, most firms also include as a part of every contract a series of terms and conditions that are standard for all orders (typically called "boilerplate"). These terms and conditions are designed to give legal protection to the buyer on such matters as contract acceptance, delivery performance and contract termination, shipment rejections, assignment and subcontracting of the order, patent rights and infringements, warranties, compliance with legal regulations, and invoicing and payment procedures. Each company develops its terms and conditions of purchase in accordance with its own unique needs. Consequently, much variation exists among firms. The terms and conditions which are printed on the back of one firm's purchase order form are reproduced in Figure 3-5.

Most companies prepare their purchase orders on multipart snap-out forms similar to the one shown in Figure 3-6. These multipart forms provide enough copies of the order to satisfy both internal and external communication needs. Although one preparation completes all copies, the various copies of the form may be printed with slightly different formats as the use of each demands. Seven is the *minimum* number of copies most commonly required. The typical distribution procedure is as follows:

- Copy 1 and copy 2 (the acknowledgment copy) are sent to the supplier.
- Copy 3 informs the accounting department of the purchase. It is used by accounting in checking and issuing payment for the seller's invoice.
- Copy 4 advises the receiving department that it can expect to receive shipment of the order on a particular date. Receiving uses its copy to identify and check the incoming shipment.
- Copy 5 informs the user of the details of the order so he or she can plan the work and budget accordingly.
- Copy 6 remains in the purchasing department open-order file and is often used for purposes of order follow-up and expediting. (See pages 60–61.)

Terms and conditions

The following terms and conditions and any specifications, drawings, and additional terms and conditions which may be incorporated by reference or appended hereto are part of this purchase order. By accepting the order or any part thereof, the Seller agrees to and accepts all terms and conditions.

1 The cash discount period available to Buyer shall commence on the date of the receipt of the merchandise or on the date of receipt of the invoice, whichever may be the later.

2 In the event of Seller's failure to deliver as and when specified, Buyer reserves the right to cancel this order or any part thereof without prejudice to its other rights, and Seller agrees that Buyer may return part or all of any shipment so made and may charge Seller with any loss or expense sustained as a result of such failure to deliver.

3 In the event any article sold and delivered hereunder shall be covered by any patent, copyright, or application therefore, Seller will indemnify and save harmless Buyer from any and all loss, cost, or expense on account of any and all claims, suits, or judgments on account of the use or sale of such article in violation of rights under such patent, copyright, or application.

4 Seller guarantees that the design and performance of all items being purchased conform with the requirements of applicable insurance and government health and safety regulations, including regulations administered by OSHA and EPA.

5 Seller agrees not to use the name of Buyer or to quote the opinion of any of Buyer's employees in any advertising without obtaining the prior written consent of Buyer.

6 Buyer may at any time insist upon strict compliance with these terms and conditions notwithstanding any previous custom, practice, or course of dealing to the contrary.

7 Seller agrees to indemnify, defend, and hold harmless Buyer, its trustees, officers, agents, and employees, of, from, and against any and all claims and demands which may arise in any way out of the furnishing of goods or services hereunder, including, without limitation, claims and demands arising from injury to or death of personnel of Buyer or for damage to the property of Buyer, except those arising by reason of the negligent or willful act of Buyer, its officers, agents, or employees.

8 It is the policy of the Buyer to give favorable consideration to those suppliers who do not discriminate against any employee or applicant for employment because of race, creed, color, or national origin.

FIGURE 3-5
Terms and conditions of purchase appearing on the back of a typical purchase order.

- Copy 7 becomes the buyer's working document and is filed in purchasing's open-order file.

Some firms organize their personnel into a larger number of specialized work groups and therefore require more copies of the order to complete the communications system. In any event, all parties involved in the transaction should receive a copy of the order. This communication has two objectives: (1) to permit planning and efficient conduct of the individual activities and (2) to integrate the efforts of the individual groups into a smoothly functioning supply operation.

After an order has been issued, changes in company requirements frequently require a change in the contract. In such cases, the buyer issues a

FIGURE 3-6
A typical purchase order form. (*Courtesy of Storage Technology Corporation.*)

change order, following the same procedures as were followed for the original order. When accepted by the supplier, the change order either supplements or replaces the original order.

Acknowledgment and Follow-Up of the Order

In most cases, the original copy of the purchase order which is sent to the supplier constitutes a legal "offer" to buy. No purchase "contract" exists, however, until the seller "accepts" the buyer's offer. The seller's acceptance can take one of two forms: (1) performance of the contract or (2) formal notification that the offer is accepted.

The purpose of sending the supplier an acknowledgment form along with the purchase order is twofold. First, it is a form that can be completed conveniently and returned to the buyer, acknowledging acceptance of the order. At the same time, the supplier can indicate whether or not it is able to meet the desired delivery date. If a supplier ships the ordered item immediately from stock it frequently disregards the acknowledgment form.

If shipment is *not* made immediately, an acceptance should be sent to the buyer. Although the acknowledgment form usually serves this purpose, some sellers prefer to use their own forms, which state their terms and conditions of sale. In either event, the buyer should check the acceptance closely to see that the supplier has not taken exception to any provisions of the order. If the seller's acceptance terms are different from those on the buyer's order, the law holds that they will automatically be incorporated in the contract unless they materially alter the intent of the offer, or unless the buyer files a written objection to their inclusion. In cases where the seller's and the buyer's terms are in direct conflict, the law omits such terms from the contract, leaving settlement of the differences to private negotiation or legal adjudication.[2] In view of the posture adopted by the courts on this matter, it is amply clear that a buyer must review suppliers' order acceptances with great care.

The purchasing department's responsibility for an order does not terminate with the making of a satisfactory contract. Purchasing bears full responsibility for an order until the material is received, inspected, and accepted.

Even though a supplier intends to meet a required delivery date, many problems can arise to prevent it from doing so. When there is a reasonable chance that the supplier may not stay on schedule, important orders with critical delivery dates should receive active follow-up attention. At the time such orders are placed, the buyer should determine specific dates on which follow-up checks are to be made.

Numerous follow-up systems can be used. In one manual system, the follow-up copy of the order is simply filed in a calendar file under the date the order is to be checked. Each day a clerk withdraws the orders to be checked that day. In a second system, the orders are filed alphabetically by supplier. The upper edge of each order has numbers from one to thirty-one printed on it; a colored flag is subsequently attached to each order at the number corresponding with the next follow-up date. A clerk reviews these files daily or semiweekly to withdraw the orders requiring follow-up. In an automated purchasing system, the computer checks the programmed follow-up dates and notifies the buyer when follow-up is required.

In all systems, follow-up communication with the supplier usually takes one of two forms. A letter, a wire, or a telephone call is typically used for most critical orders. Routine follow-up for the less critical orders is usually accomplished by mailing a preprinted inquiry to the supplier.

In some firms, follow-up procedures are conducted by the buyer handling the order. In others, follow-up activities are conducted by a separate expediting group. This subject is discussed in Chapter 5.

Although relatively few in number, some firms maintain a force of follow-up personnel in the field. Such firms typically purchase a great

---

[2] This subject is discussed in depth in Chapter 29.

deal of critical material or major equipment on very tight delivery schedules. To ensure that all material is available when needed, these firms track critical purchases by having traveling follow-up representatives personally visit suppliers' plants. In some situations these field personnel have the additional responsibility of attempting to speed up (expedite) or even delay (de-expedite) delivery as the buyer's timing requirements undergo unexpected changes.[3]

Receipt and Inspection

The next step in the purchasing cycle is receipt and inspection of the order. When a supplier ships material, it includes in the shipping container a packing slip which itemizes and describes the contents of the shipment. The receiving clerk uses this packing slip in conjunction with his or her copy of the purchase order to verify that the correct material has been received.[4]

After a shipment has been inspected for quantity and for general condition of the material, the receiving clerk prepares a receiving report. In some cases, the report is prepared on separate receiving department forms. However, the trend in most companies today is to reduce the clerical work by preparing the receiving report forms during the same typing or printing operation that prepares the purchase order. In these situations, the receiving report forms are included in the snap-out purchase order form. A typical form is shown in Figure 3-7. To complete the report, the receiving clerk merely records the identification and receiving figures in the appropriate spaces included on the form.

Copies of the receiving report are typically distributed as follows:

- Copy 1 is used by the purchasing department in closing out its working file of the order.
- Copy 2 is used by the accounting department in reviewing the order for payment.
- Copy 3 is sent to the user as notification that the material has arrived, or as a delivery copy if immediate delivery is made. (If another notification system is used, this copy can be omitted.)
- Copy 4 is retained in the receiving department's operating record file.

Before some shipments can be accepted, technical inspection is necessary. (A discussion of these procedures is found in Chapter 19.) In some companies, distribution of the receiving report is withheld until the technical in-

---

[3] The term "expedite" is used rather loosely in industry. In a more precise sense, "follow-up" involves activities to ensure delivery as scheduled. To "expedite" involves actions to achieve an earlier delivery than that originally planned. To "de-expedite" is to attempt to delay delivery beyond the original schedule.

[4] A complete discussion of the procedures to be followed when short or damaged shipments are received is found in Chapters 23 and 29.

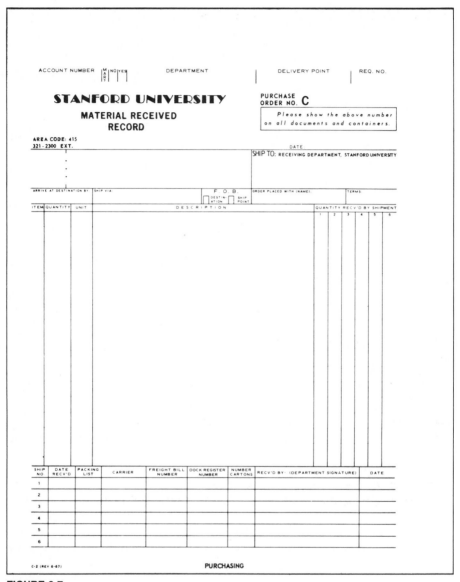

FIGURE 3-7
A receiving report form, reflecting a purchase order format different from that shown in Figure 3-6. (*Courtesy of Stanford University.*)

spection report has been prepared. In other companies, distribution of the receiving report precedes distribution of the inspection report. Some firms send an inspection report to every department that gets a receiving report, so their records of *actual* receipts will be complete. Other companies provide copies only to purchasing, accounting, and inspection.

The Invoice Audit and Completion of the Order

Occasionally, a supplier's billing department makes an error in preparing an invoice, or its shipping department makes an incorrect or incomplete shipment. To ensure that the purchaser makes proper payment for the materials actually received, sound accounting practice dictates that some type of review procedure precede payment to the supplier.

A typical procedure involves a simultaneous review of the purchase order, the receiving report, and the invoice. By checking the receiving report against the purchase order, the purchaser determines whether the quantity and type of material ordered was in fact received. Then by comparing the invoice with the purchase order and receiving report, the firm verifies that the supplier's bill is priced correctly and that it covers the proper quantity of acceptable material. Finally, by verifying the arithmetic accuracy of the invoice, the correctness of the total invoice figure is determined. Auditing invoices is a repetitive, time-consuming task that should be handled as efficiently as possible. It should also be conducted soon after receipt of the invoice to permit the accounting department to make prompt payment and obtain any applicable cash discounts. As mentioned in Chapter 1, prompt payment also aids the firm's efforts to establish and maintain good supplier relations. Because of the high cost of auditing invoices, many companies do not verify the accuracy of low-dollar-value invoices.

Invoice auditing is technically an accounting function. Theoretically, the purchasing department's job is completed when an order has been received in the plant and is ready for use. In practice, however, some firms assign the invoice auditing responsibility to accounting, while others assign it to purchasing. This difference of opinion focuses on questions concerning the efficiency and accuracy with which invoices can be checked when the task is assigned to the accounting department.

In the purchase of complex or technical materials, a strong case can be made for assigning the auditing task to the buyer who handled the order. This individual is familiar with the materials and their technical nomenclature, with prices and contract provisions, and with all ensuing negotiations. Invoices for such orders often are difficult to interpret and evaluate without a detailed knowledge of these things. Hence, such an audit done by an accounting clerk may be open to question. Auditing invoices for the purchase of most standard materials, on the other hand, is a routine clerical task. And a majority of most firms' orders fall in this category. Hence, there is no reason to burden a buyer with this job, which can be done satisfactorily by clerical personnel.

Figure 3-1 indicates that the purchasing department closes its purchase order file before the invoice is audited. This is usually the case if accounting audits the invoice. When purchasing audits the invoice, its records are closed after the audit. Closing the order simply entails a consolidation of all documents and correspondence relevant to the order; the completed order is then filed in the closed-order file. In most firms, a completed order consists of the purchase requisition, the open-order file copy of the purchase order, the acknowledgment, the receiving report, the inspection report, and any notes or correspondence pertaining to the order. The completed order file thus constitutes a historical record of all activities encompassing the total purchasing cycle.

PURCHASING DEPARTMENT RECORDS

The files of a purchasing department contain an endless flow of operating data. Despite its huge volume, much of this information can be useless in daily operations unless it is organized in a manner which makes it readily accessible. Although the unique needs of each purchasing department dictate the specific structure of its records system, the following basic records are essential for the effective operation of most purchasing departments:

- File of open orders
- File of closed orders
- Purchase log
- Commodity record
- Supplier record
- Contract record
- Special tool record

File of Open Orders

All buyers need immediate access to information concerning the status of their outstanding orders. Because reference to these orders most frequently requires identification by the supplier's name, the filing system customarily is indexed alphabetically by suppliers' names. Within each supplier's subfile, orders are arranged in ascending numerical sequence.

Although practice varies widely, each order folder commonly contains the purchase requisition, the working copy of the order, the returned acknowledgment form, follow-up data, and all notes and correspondence that pertain to the order. Some companies also file competitive bids with the order. Others prefer to file bids in a separate price file or with the commodity record. When the bid is not filed with the order, the order folder must contain a cross-indexing reference.

Some firms also maintain a separate numerical file or log of purchase requisitions. The file makes it easy to locate a purchase order needed to answer questions from a requisitioner who can identify the order only by requisition number. In such situations, it is essential to note the purchase order number on the requisition. When follow-up activities are conducted by a separate expediter, all information pertaining to the purchase is contained in his or her working file. To reduce paperwork, duplicate information is frequently omitted from the open-order file.

File of Closed Orders

The closed-order file provides a historical record of all completed purchases. It frequently serves as a useful reference when questions arise concerning past orders and when certain historical data are needed to guide future decisions. Specific inclusions of the file were discussed above.

It is difficult to generalize about the length of time such records should be kept. Nearly all firms retain their closed orders at least three years. Normally, any order files kept beyond three years should be retained only on a highly selective basis. In a large firm, records retention is costly. Therefore, if commodity and supplier records are properly maintained, only unique and high-value orders are generally worth keeping longer than three years.

Purchase Log

Every purchasing department should maintain a numerical record of all purchase orders issued. The record need not be elaborate, but it should contain the purchase order number, the status of the order, the supplier's name, a brief description of the material purchased, and the total value of the order. Such a record summarizes the commitments for which the purchasing executive is responsible. In the event that the working copy of an order is misplaced, basic data concerning the purchase can be found in the log. The log further serves as a convenient record from which summary administrative data can be extracted concerning such matters as the number of small orders, rush orders, and total orders issued; the volume of purchases from various suppliers; the value of outstanding commitments; and so forth.

The purchase logs of some firms consist of a sequential list of purchase orders recorded in a journal or in the computer data base. Other firms accomplish the same objective simply by filing, in numerical sequence, the follow-up copy or an additional copy of the order.

Commodity Record

The file of commodity records constitutes a vast reservoir of materials data that makes efficient "mass production purchasing" possible. A commodity record card or computer file should be maintained for each major material and service that is purchased repetitively. Typically included in the record is a complete description of the material or service, with full reference to necessary engineering drawings and specifications which might be filed elsewhere. Also included should be a list of approved suppliers and their price schedules. Competitive quotations may be included in the file, although it is more common to summarize bid data in the record, note a cross reference to the original quotation, and place all quotations in a separate file.

The preceding data provide a buyer with the basic information initially required in a repetitive purchase investigation. In making the purchase decision, the buyer supplements this information with numerous qualitative considerations concerning individual suppliers, such as their current work loads, internal problems, quality performance, and so on. Some companies, however, also include in the record a complete purchase history for the item. For every purchase, the purchase order number, purchase quantity, price, delivery performance, and quality performance are recorded. In deciding how much detailed information to keep in its commodity record, each firm must weigh the value of the information against the cost of transcribing it.

When a firm uses a traveling requisition system for repetitively purchased inventory items, the traveling requisition and inventory record duplicate the commodity record. In such cases, there is no need to maintain a separate commodity record.

Supplier Record

To provide quick access to information about suppliers, most companies centralize such information in a single record file. A separate card or computer record is maintained for each major supplier. In this record is recorded the address, telephone number, and the names of personnel to contact on specific matters of inquiry. Selling terms and routing instructions for shipping purposes also usually are included. Although the practice varies, many firms additionally summarize in this record the supplier's delivery and quality performance, as well as the annual volume of materials purchased from the supplier.

In a matter of seconds, these records enable a buyer to obtain a wealth of summary information about any important supplier.

Contract Record

Today most firms are purchasing an increasing number of items on a long-term contractual basis. In such cases, it is usually convenient to consolidate all contracts in a separate file. In addition to providing immediate access to all contract documents, this file also apprises all buying personnel of the materials that are purchased in this manner. If the number of contracts is large, it is desirable also to list them in summary form to provide a bird's-eye view of all contract purchases and their expiration dates.

Special Tool Record

Many companies have no need for this record. However, such a record is essential to those firms that purchase many items requiring special tooling for their manufacture. On some orders the purchaser buys the required dies, jigs, fixtures, and patterns; on others the supplier owns them. By maintaining a record of special tools, the buyer can summarize for quick reference the special tools owned, the age and location of each, and the essential mounting and operating characteristics of each.

RUSH ORDERS

Every department executive tries to develop an orderly and systematic pattern of operation that efficiently utilizes the resources of that department. In a well-run purchasing department, systematic analysis and processing of most orders is completed in two to four days after the requisition is received.

How should purchasing handle the emergency needs that inevitably arise in any business operation? Clearly, a special procedure for processing *rush* requisitions is needed. The key elements of such a procedure are discussed in the following paragraphs.

Even in the case of emergencies, it is unwise to accept oral requisitions—in person or over the telephone. Too much chance for erroneous interpretation of the requirement exists. The requisitioner should state the need in writing and, preferably, deliver it to the buyer in person. For purposes of identification, emergency requisitions can be printed on paper of a different color, or they can be identified with a visible emergency sticker. Typically, the buyer should process these requisitions immediately and telephone emergency orders to the supplier. In no case, however, should an order be placed without assigning it a purchase order number. For most purchases, a confirming purchase order subsequently should be mailed to the supplier. In cases where the emergency is less urgent, the buyer may process such requisitions at appointed times twice daily (say, at 10:30 A.M. and 2:30 P.M.).

Purchasing's basic responsibility is to the departments it serves. Yet, purchasing should not permit users to take unfair advantage of its emergency service. Only justifiable requests should receive this service. Rush orders always cost more than if they were handled through the normal purchasing system. Higher prices frequently are paid because rush purchases are not investigated as thoroughly as those handled in the normal routine, and premium-cost transportation typically is used. Furthermore, the interruption of a buyer's scheduled work by the emergency request invariably produces inefficiency in normal purchasing department activity.

Consequently, steps should be taken to discourage all rush orders that arise because of poor planning in the using departments. In practice, three approaches have proved successful. The first involves a concerted effort to coordinate the activities of the using group or production scheduling and purchasing. Some companies require that realistic order points for inventory materials be established jointly by production scheduling and purchasing. In other firms operating on a job-order basis, purchasing is required to issue periodic lead time reports to users for all major classes of materials. A second approach, designed to reduce unjustifiable requests, requires the requisitioner to obtain approval from a general management executive for all emergency requisitions. A modification of this approach requires an after-the-fact review of all rush orders by top management. Still another approach assesses the requisitioning department a predetermined service charge for each emergency requisition processed.

THE SMALL-ORDER PROBLEM

Small orders are a perennial problem in *every* business—and a serious problem in some. Examination of a typical company's purchase order file reveals that a sizable percentage (sometimes up to 80 percent) of its purchases involve an expenditure of less than $250. In total, however, these purchases constitute a small percentage (seldom more than 10 percent) of the firm's annual dollar expenditures. Clearly, no manager wants to devote more buying and clerical effort to the expenditure of 10 percent of his or her funds than to the expenditure of the other 90 percent. Yet this frequently is what happens. The very nature of business requires the purchase of many low-value items. Nevertheless, small orders are costly to buyer and seller alike. It costs a seller only a few cents more to process a $1,000 order than it does to process a $10 order. The following sections discuss various methods a purchasing manager can use to minimize the small-order problem.

Centralized Stores System

A stores system is the first approach typically used to reduce the volume of small-order purchasing activity. When experience shows that the same supply items are ordered in small quantities time after time, the logical solution is to order these items in larger quantities and place them in a centralized inventory for withdrawal as needed. An analysis of repetitively used production materials leads to the same action for the multitude of low-value items. If usage of an item is reasonably stable, an optimum order quantity can be computed using a basic economic order quantity approach. There is, of course, a limit to the number of items and the financial investment a firm can place in inventory.

Blanket or Open-End Order System

A stores system solves the small-order problem only for items that are used repetitively. A *blanket*, or *open-end*, order system helps solve the problem for the thousands of items a firm cannot carry in inventory, as well as some that it does carry.

Briefly, the general procedure used for this type of purchase is as follows. On the basis of an analysis of past purchases, the buyer determines which materials should be handled in this manner. After bidding or negotiation, the buyer selects a supplier for each item, or family of items, and issues a blanket order to each supplier. The order includes a description of each item, a unit price for each item when possible, and the other customary contract provisions. However, no specific order quantities are noted. The blanket order typically indicates only an estimated usage during the period of coverage. It also states that all requirements are to be delivered upon receipt of an authorized release from the buyer. On receiving a requisition for one of the materials, the buyer merely sends a brief release form to the supplier. On the release form are noted the blanket order number, the item number, and the quantity to be delivered. Receiving reports are filed with the original order, and at the end of the month are checked against the supplier's monthly invoice. At the end of the period, the order may be renewed or placed with another vendor, depending on the supplier's performance record.

Most companies develop their own unique modifications of the basic procedure. For example, instead of advising suppliers of order releases by means of a written form, some companies simply issue releases to local suppliers by telephone. By noting such releases on the order, the buyer still retains adequate control.

In the event that material is needed immediately (and the supplier is nearby), some firms allow the using department to pick up the material without notifying the purchasing department. The employee obtaining the material simply endorses and enters the proper accounting charge on the sales receipt, a copy of which is sent to the buyer. This document then serves as the receiving report. This procedure is particularly applicable to the frequent purchase of various repair parts, when specific needs are not known and the equipment is dismantled. It also works well for purchasing special processing services, such as heat-treating and plating, when the service is required quickly but cannot be planned in advance. This variation of the basic blanket order procedure can easily be abused and possibly can lead to petty fraud. It is therefore important to entrust its use only to responsible operating personnel and periodically to review the endorsed sales receipts.

The blanket order system offers five important benefits:

1 It requires fewer purchase orders and reduces clerical work in purchasing, accounting, and receiving.
2 It releases buyers from routine work, giving them more time to concentrate on major problems.
3 It permits volume pricing by consolidating and grouping requirements.
4 It can improve the flow of feedback information, because of the grouping of materials and suppliers.
5 Because some suppliers will stock material for prompt delivery, this system may reduce the buyer's lead times and inventory levels.

To function effectively in the long run, however, any blanket order system must provide adequate internal control. Absence of the control element encourages petty fraud and poor supplier performance. The elements essential to effective control are:

1 A numbered purchase order, including proper internal accounting charge notations

2 A record of authorized delivery releases

3 Bona fide evidence of receipt of the material

Systems Contracting

At this point a few words need to be said about systems contracting. Though frequently used as a basic purchasing strategy, as well as an approach for minimizing the small-order problem, systems contracting, in reality, is simply an extensive and more sophisticated development of the blanket order purchasing concept. Some firms call it "stockless" purchasing.

As its name implies, systems contracting involves the development of a corporatewide agreement, often a one- or two-year requirements contract, with a supplier to purchase a large group or "family" of related materials. The items to be purchased are usually described in detail in a "catalog" that becomes part of the contract. Estimated usage usually is included, along with a fixed price for each item and an agreement by the supplier to carry a stock of each item adequate to meet the buyer's needs. Various types of supplies and commonly used operating items, typically purchased from distributors, are the materials most often covered by these types of agreements.[5]

In addition to the benefits of blanket order purchasing, a major objective of systems contracting is to minimize both the buyer's and the supplier's administrative costs associated with the purchases. The operating procedures of the two firms are integrated to the extent practical. For example, users in the buyer's various operating locations usually send their purchase requisitions directly to the supplier holding the contract for the item. The requisition thus serves as the purchase order. The supplier then simply maintains a list of such shipments on a "tally sheet," identifying each by the requisition number (or a supplier-assigned number), and periodically (monthly or semimonthly) submits the tally sheet to the buyer for payment in lieu of an invoice.

These types of integrated procedures and shortcuts typically develop a closer relationship between the two firms and reduce paperwork and associated costs markedly. The buyer's inventories and carrying costs obviously decline as well.

Term Contracting System Coupled with MRP

On page 53 the engineering bill of materials was discussed as a device for communicating production material needs to the purchasing department.

---

[5] For a good discussion of systems contracting in MRO buying, see J. A. Lorincz, "Systems Contracts Put Control in MRO Buying," *Purchasing World*, May 1986, pp. 51–54.

Some firms that use an MRP computer-based scheduling system have carried this concept one step further, moving closer to achievement of a "paperless" purchasing operation.

The logic of an MRP system converts bills of materials into aggregate requirements schedules for each individual part used in the products being manufactured. Using these precise MRP schedule requirements, some firms utilize a two-step approach to eliminate both the purchase requisition and the purchase order. First, the buyer establishes a long-term contract (one year or longer) with a supplier for each part. Second, material needs are transmitted directly to suppliers simply by sending them updated copies of the weekly (or monthly) material requirements schedule. The MRP schedule thus serves as *both* the purchase requisition and the purchase order (or release). Suppliers simply deliver to the schedule. At the Boston Gear Works, for example, this approach works smoothly, involving purchasing personnel only on a management-by-exception basis after the initial purchase contracts are developed.[6]

Telephone Order System

Most companies now use a telephone ordering system to reduce the paperwork associated with small-order purchasing. Under this system, when the purchasing department receives a requisition, it does not prepare a formal purchase order. Instead, the order is placed by telephone, and the requisition is used in the receiving procedure.

Although many variations of this system are in use, it is important that the requisition form be designed to provide all data necessary for internal communications and control. One company uses a six-part form which includes all data normally included on a conventional purchase order. When the order is placed, one copy of the requisition is sent to the requisitioner, one goes to accounting, one remains in purchasing, and three copies are sent to receiving. When the material arrives, all receiving data are noted on the latter copies. One of these copies is sent to accounting, one is sent to purchasing, and the final copy either goes to the requisitioner or remains in a permanent receiving file.

One large firm in the electrical industry reportedly places most of its *small* orders by telephone—this translates to approximately 60 percent of *all* orders placed during the year. The system goes one step further in the elimination of paperwork; the firm's suppliers send no invoices for telephone purchases. A firm price is determined during the initial telephone conversation and is recorded on the requisition. When the material is received as ordered, the accounting department issues payment on the basis of the purchase requisition.

[6] John Fitts, "On the Road to Paperless Purchasing," *Purchasing World*, May 1982, pp. 48–50.

Electronic Ordering Systems

A number of electronic communication systems currently are available to transmit material purchase requests without writing orders or talking on the telephone. One of the first was the Data-Phone Communication System, which has since been superseded by more advanced systems. The hardware of these systems consists of a magnetic or punched card reader connected to a telephone in the purchaser's office and an interpreting unit connected to a telephone in the supplier's office. With this system, the buyer simply places a purchase requisition (in magnetic or punched card form) in the card reader and dials the supplier's telephone number. The requisition data are then transmitted over telephone lines to the supplier's interpreting unit.

Another approach in this evolving process utilizes a computer terminal as the input device at the buyer's site. The terminal is tied to a telephone line through a modem. The data signal is then communicated via the telephone line to a printer or other receiving device at the supplier's site.

Such electronic systems will have limited use for *general* purchasing activity until a buyer's major suppliers acquire the necessary equipment and operating systems. Rapid growth in usage, however, *is* occurring among industrial supply firms. In situations where buyers find their use feasible, such systems can expedite the purchasing process, reduce paperwork, and simplify internal accounting and control. They are particularly applicable to the purchase of repetitively used items whose recurring orders can be placed using the same card or input source. Clearly, the use of an electronic ordering system requires a master agreement, or similar contractual arrangement, with the supplier.

The next step in the evolutionary development of this concept—computers talking to computers—is now a reality in a growing number of firms across the country. The topic of electronic data interchange is discussed in the next chapter.

Petty Cash System

Most firms today use a petty cash fund for making small one-time purchases. For this purpose, many firms define "small" as $30 to $50. It is often less expensive for an individual user (or a purchasing delivery employee) to buy minor items personally and pay for them from a petty cash fund than it is to buy them through the conventional purchasing system. Any inefficiencies that may arise because of a lack of buying skill are more than compensated for by the savings resulting from not placing a purchase order.

C.O.D. System

Some firms find it economical to make small one-time purchases on a C.O.D. basis. Material can be ordered by telephone and paid for on arrival. Payment can be made using petty cash or a departmental check written on an account set up for such purchases.

Purchase Order Draft System

Some years ago the Kaiser Aluminum and Chemical Corporation instituted a blank check type of ordering system to reduce the paperwork required by its numerous small purchases.[7] The system has since been adopted by a number of companies. Unlike the preceding systems, the draft system requires preparation of a formal purchase order for every purchase. However, the bottom quarter of the purchase order is a bank draft—a blank check to be filled in by the supplier. When it receives the order, the supplier detaches the draft and fills it in for the exact amount of the invoice, less any cash discount. The draft is actually constructed in the form of an envelope. The supplier then places one copy of the invoice in the envelope and deposits it in the bank as an immediate cash payment. The draft can only be deposited, not cashed. The buyer's bank pays the draft when it is received and debits the buyer's account daily for the total number of drafts paid.

Each draft usually is limited to a sum of $1,000 (or some other predetermined figure printed on the face of the draft). To provide adequate control, the amount of each returned draft can be checked against its accompanying invoice or receiving report. Kaiser performs this audit by computer. Like the telephone system, the draft system does not permit back ordering. Each order is considered complete as it is shipped. This system does not significantly reduce the purchasing work associated with small orders, but it virtually eliminates the work of the accounts payable section.

Supplier Stores/Consignment System

If a purchaser buys a large enough volume of certain materials from a single supplier, the supplier sometimes can afford to staff a small "store" at the purchaser's plant and operate it on a consignment basis. Some suppliers find that annual purchases of approximately $100,000 justify such a branch operation. Users then simply go to the store and sign for their purchases. At the end of the month the company is billed for its purchases just as if the user had "gone downtown" to buy the material.

This system clearly is not a short-term arrangement. The purchaser, therefore, must take great care in selecting the supplier and in negotiating the terms of the agreement.

---

[7] For an interesting discussion of the historical development of this system, see "Blank Check Solves Small Order Problem," *Purchasing*, Nov. 5, 1962, pp. 78–82.

Supplier Delivery System

The supplier delivery system is somewhat similar to a supplier stores system, but it is more feasible for firms with a smaller volume of purchases. Many suppliers who are not willing to set up a store at the buyer's plant are willing to stock numerous miscellaneous materials and make daily or semiweekly deliveries. The buyer typically reviews and accumulates purchase requisitions for such materials. The supplier's delivery person then picks them up on the specified day, and at the same time delivers the material ordered on the preceding batch of requisitions. This continuous shuttle service provides reasonably fast delivery and also reduces the purchaser's paperwork and inventory problems. Properly designed, the system can provide for adequate accounting control.

CONCLUSION

Every business unit develops a series of procedures to assist operating personnel in carrying out the policies and plans of the unit. In total, these procedures establish the ground rules for the daily activities of the department.

The *specific* procedures employed by each firm should be designed to meet the unique needs of that firm. *Generally* speaking, properly designed procedures should accomplish four objectives:

1 Accomplish each task satisfactorily with a minimum of time, effort, and paperwork.
2 Effectively communicate and coordinate the efforts of one work group with another.
3 Minimize overlapping efforts and group conflicts by clearly designating responsibility for each step of the procedure.
4 Permit effective management by exception.

While accomplishing tasks efficiently within the materials functions is important, perhaps the *most* important feature of procurement procedures is the communication and coordinative impact they have on other operating units throughout the organization. Purchasing and its related materials functions cannot flourish alone. They need the understanding, cooperation, and respect of the operating units they work with and serve. Enlightened policies coupled with sound operating procedures establish the foundation on which this relationship is built.

FOR DISCUSSION

3-1 One executive has said that the development of many of her company's procedures was a waste of time. Could there be any merit to this statement? Why do executives develop procedures and record them in procedure manuals? Explain.
3-2 What basic objectives should a good procedure fulfill?

3-3 List and discuss the steps in the purchasing cycle.

3-4 What improvements can you make to the procedures illustrated in Figure 3-1? Explain.

3-5 Write a series of procedures for the tasks constituting the complete purchasing cycle when a bill of materials is used to transmit the need to the purchasing department.

3-6 How does a traveling purchase requisition differ from a standard purchase requisition?

3-7 Write a procedure for auditing invoices.

3-8 Design a commodity record card (include related requirements). Design a contract record summary sheet.

3-9 Design a supplier record card (include related requirements). Design a special tool record.

3-10 Assume that you are a maintenance supplies buyer. A maintenance foreman calls you to inquire about a purchase order you placed two weeks ago. The foreman has lost his copy of the order, but he does have his copy of the requisition. How would you locate your copy of the purchase order to get the information he requests? Explain.

3-11 What is the value of maintaining a purchase log?

3-12 Write a procedure to be used in handling rush orders.

3-13 What does a purchasing executive mean by the "small-order problem"? Explain.

3-14 Explain briefly the various techniques that might be used to help solve the small-order problem.

3-15 How does a blanket purchase order system work? What are its advantages? What are its disadvantages?

3-16 How does systems contracting differ from blanket order purchasing?

3-17 What impact do you think the computer will have on the small-order problem of most businesses?

3-18 Explain how the purchase order draft system works. What are its pros and cons?

CASES FOR CHAPTER 3

Blozis Company, page 715
WVC Industrial Chemicals Company, page 821
Futronics, Inc., page 740
The Oakland School District, page 778
Metropolitan University (in the Instructor's Manual)

4

COMPUTER-BASED SYSTEMS

KEY CONCEPTS

- A computerized materials management system
    Inventory control and purchase requisitions
    Purchase orders and change orders
    Follow-up and expediting
    Receiving, inspection, and stores requisitions
    Invoices and payment
    Management reports
- Impact on daily operations
- The use of microcomputers
- Electronic data interchange
    Standards requirements

"A computer is in effect a huge file, a superfast calculating machine, and a printer rolled into one. It stores basic data in its memory and translates the data for procurement action."[1]

The preceding chapter discussed the basic procedures, documents, and records typically found in most firms' procurement operations. Although computerized systems were mentioned occasionally, the discussion was set primarily in the context of a manual operation using traditional office equip-

---

[1] S. F. Heinritz, Paul V. Farrell, and Clifton L. Smith, *Purchasing: Principles and Applications,* 7th ed., Prentice Hall, Englewood Cliffs, N.J., 1986, p. 57.

ment and clerical methods. This chapter discusses the characteristics of a computer-based procurement system, along with the changes it brings to the department in performing key activities.

Effective use of a computer offers a purchasing or materials manager a number of important advantages. Because of its ability to process huge volumes of data rapidly, a computer can do much of the routine clerical work, thus freeing departmental personnel from many dull repetitive tasks. This means that a department can operate with fewer clerical people, or that existing personnel can spend their time on more creative purchasing work.

Most managers agree that the *primary advantage* a computer offers a buyer or a materials planner is the immediate availability of much more complete data for use in making cost-effective materials-related decisions. Because of its speed, a computer can supply virtually instantaneous reports which otherwise might take a small army of clerks weeks to prepare and update. The timeliness of such reports enables a materials executive to manage by exception and to do a more effective and more profitable job of purchasing and managing the flow of materials throughout the operation.

A COMPUTERIZED MATERIALS MANAGEMENT SYSTEM

When a system is computerized, the basic activities of the procurement process remain essentially the same as when the system was operated manually. What changes is the way in which the activities are performed.

In a computer-based system, for the most part, the same records that are maintained in a manual system are stored in disc or tape files that are readily accessible to the computer's central processing unit (CPU). Although the specific format and data contents vary among systems, the records readily available to the computer for display or processing typically are:

- Open-order file
- Order/parts behind schedule file
- Supplier record file
- Material (commodity) record file
- Inventory record file

These computer files usually contain the same detailed data (and perhaps more) that was discussed in the design of manual operating procedures in the preceding chapter.

Every company that automates its materials activities utilizes the computer in a slightly different manner. The data inputs vary from firm to firm, as do the desired data outputs. The form and timing of various reports depend to a great extent on the operating needs of each particular firm. Generally speaking, however, the *basic* materials activities which can be performed well by a computer-based system are the same in all cases. They are:

1 Maintenance of inventory records
2 Computation of order quantities

3 Preparation of purchase requisitions for inventory items
4 Preparation of requests for quotation
5 Preparation of purchase orders
6 Maintenance of order status records
7 Distribution of accounting charges
8 Automatic preparation of follow-up memos
9 Posting of delivery and quality records, by part and by supplier
10 Preparation of numerous operating reports for management
11 Auditing of invoices and preparation of checks for payment
12 Electronic data interchange communications

Three types (and sizes) of hardware are used today in computer-based purchasing operations. The first is a large mainframe system that purchasing shares with most other operating units in the organization. In most cases, the cathode ray tube (CRT) input terminals are located at the appropriate purchasing work stations and linked to the processing hardware, which is usually located elsewhere in a centralized computer center. The second type of system frequently found in purchasing departments today is built around the use of a minicomputer. As its name implies, the mini is simply a miniature version of larger mainframe units. This type of system frequently (but not always) is dedicated for use in the purchasing and materials management activities of the firm. Operationally, this system functions much like a mainframe system, usually with better accessibility but with reduced memory and capacity. Finally, materials management operating systems in smaller companies are sometimes handled adequately by a network of microcomputers (PCs) that constitute purchasing's own freestanding system. Some of these units may have the capability to access larger corporatewide data bases that are part of the firm's mainframe system.

In all of these systems, authorized personnel communicate directly with the computer data base through the terminal for purposes of entering and recalling data, as well as performing calculations and other machine processing activities. Through the use of computer security codes, each individual's data access is usually restricted to that portion of the data base he or she needs to use in performing his or her job.

Figures 4-1 and 4-2 show in schematic form the general operation of an on-line computerized materials management system.

Inventory Control and Purchase Requisitions

In an automated materials system, all inventory and part records (including engineering drawings and bills of material) are filed in memory accessible to the CPU. For each part either one record or several different records can be maintained. In either case, certain standard information is included, such as the part number, its name, required descriptive data, historical usage data, and the current inventory balance. Additionally, price data from recent purchases as well as price quotation information are also on file. Just as in a man-

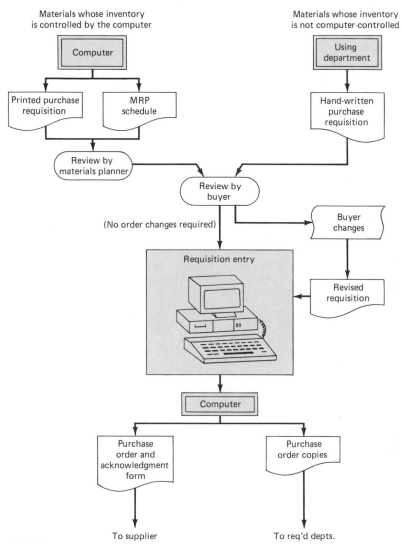

FIGURE 4-1
Schematic diagram of the materials ordering activity in a computerized materials
management system.

ual system, the file memory contains such information as supplier names and
addresses, shipping terms, quality and delivery performance data, purchase
history, and open orders.

Each time the machine posts a stores withdrawal requisition for a particular part, it updates the balance on hand and compares this figure with a
specified reorder point figure. When the balance falls below this level, the
computer prints out a purchase requisition. The quantity that the machine

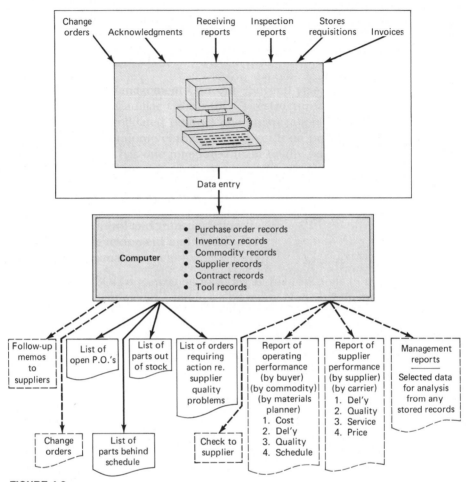

FIGURE 4-2
Schematic diagram of the activities subsequent to placement of the purchase order in a computerized materials management system.

orders may be a predetermined order quantity or the quantity required by a planned period production schedule.

In the case of items controlled by an "order point" inventory control system, software is available to compute the most economical quantity, just as a buyer might do manually. Quantity calculations are based on predetermined figures for inventory carrying costs and acquisition costs, and on current figures for part usage and price; these data are filed in memory.[2] Thus, the com-

---

[2]This discussion focuses on the use of an order point inventory control system. The operation can be automated just as easily for items that are controlled under a cyclical review or MRP system of inventory control. The cyclical review system frequently is used extensively in companies

puter automatically produces printed purchase requisitions which contain most of the information (including the appropriate accounting charge) that normally would appear on a manually prepared requisition. For the buyer's use, the requisition also can contain monthly usage data for the past year, a listing of past purchase orders and prices, and a summary of the most recent price quotations from different vendors.

The computer, however, cannot determine the urgency of a firm's need for a part. Consequently, for other than normal delivery requirements, exact shipping dates, order follow-up dates, and carrier designations must be specified by the buyer. For this reason and for purposes of control, an automated system usually provides for a review of all purchase requisitions by the material planner and by the buyer. In the event that production needs fluctuate, the planner changes the requisition accordingly before sending it to the buyer. The buyer analyzes the requisition in terms of potential suppliers' performances under current conditions. He or she also considers future quantity and quality requirements, as well as other intangible factors, and makes any changes deemed appropriate. At this point, a purchase order number is also assigned.

Note that all purchase requisitions for parts whose inventory is *not* controlled by the computer must be finalized manually by the buyer. From this point on, however, a purchase order (PO) can be created and handled in the automated materials system without difficulty.

Purchase Orders and Change Orders

For computer-generated requisitions, if the buyer makes no changes, the purchase order can be prepared simply by adding the name of the desired supplier and a purchase order number—and instructing the computer to print out the requisition in the form of a purchase order. When data are added and changes are made to the requisition, or in the case of manually generated requisitions, all new data is keyed directly into the computer through a terminal with the instruction to print out the corresponding purchase order.

At the same time the computer prepares the purchase order to be mailed to the supplier, it can produce an acknowledgment form for the supplier, copies of the purchase order for internal distribution, and forms to be used as the receiving and inspection reports. While producing purchase orders, the computer also produces and files in memory a cumulative list of all outstanding purchase orders. This becomes the major "working" order file.

In the event an order is changed after it has been issued, a change order form is prepared by the buyer and processed by the computer. This and sub-

---

that cannot accurately forecast production demands more than a month or two in advance. In fact, computerization of inventory control in such cases reduces clerical costs of operating the inventory control system immensely.

sequent documents are processed by the machine in the same way as the original purchase order. With accompanying documents, they simply replace the original order.

Follow-Up and Expediting

The file of open purchase orders can be processed as frequently as desired to produce current information for purchasing personnel. Today most firms update open orders once a day to provide purchasing with up-to-the-minute status reports.

One of the most important outputs of the open-order processing operation is the follow-up communication. At the time a purchase requisition is converted into an order, the buyer instructs the computer to print out a follow-up memo at specified dates prior to the scheduled delivery date. Such a system assures periodic review of every purchase order, regardless of departmental work load or employee absenteeism. The computer, as instructed, faithfully reproduces follow-up memos, according to a predetermined format; hence, mailing these communications is the only clerical effort required of purchasing personnel. Upon receipt of a supplier's response, the buyer or expediter gives attention only to those orders requiring further follow-up work.

Orders whose delivery is behind schedule are brought to the attention of the buyer by a "behind schedule" report.

Receiving, Inspection, and Stores Requisitions

When an order is received, the receiving clerk (or a terminal operator) utilizes a remote CRT terminal to enter the conventional receiving information directly into the computer's order record. Simultaneously, the machine produces the printed reports required for the use of other company personnel. Receiving reports thus can be generated in multiple copies for the buyer, the materials planner, and other using departments. For those orders requiring technical inspection, inspection reports are produced in conventional form and are processed periodically by the computer to update the open-order file and the inventory record file.

As previously indicated, stores requisitions that are prepared in conventional form are entered through a terminal and processed periodically to update inventory records.

Daily updating of the open-order records and the parts inventory records, coupled with the computer's speed, permits the preparation of numerous daily operating reports to facilitate the buyer's job. Four commonly used reports are:

- List of open purchase orders
- List of orders or parts that are behind schedule
- List of parts that are out of stock

- List of orders or parts that require action because of supplier quality or related problems

Such reports are of tremendous value to individual buyers. They provide a buyer with a summary of critical, up-to-the-minute information about his or her orders that is virtually impossible to obtain manually. These summary reports also permit the buyer to manage by exception—that is, to concentrate efforts on those orders requiring attention in time to prevent the development of serious purchasing problems.

Invoices and Payment

When an invoice for an order is received, it is keyed directly into the computer through a terminal. The computer then audits the invoice by comparing the item, the quantity, and the price with corresponding information recorded in the updated purchase order (and receiving) files. The computer also verifies the price extension. Any discrepancies are noted on an output error list. If no discrepancies are found, the unit signals a printer to write a check to the supplier for the amount of the invoice less any applicable discount.

Accounting charges for the order can be distributed in the conventional manner from a printed copy of the purchase order, or they can be distributed by the computer. If the accounting system is computerized, distributions can be made by the machine during the processing of the accounting records.

Management Reports

In its initial design, an automated materials management system can be developed to accumulate various data useful to managerial personnel for control purposes. The computer's speed permits monthly or weekly analysis and summary of much information that is outside the realm of feasibility in a manually operated system. While managers in different firms may desire different types of reports, most materials executives want to evaluate the performance of suppliers, carriers, and commodities, as well as their own individual personnel and departments.

It is entirely possible to purchase or develop computer software to provide periodic reports of each supplier's and carrier's performance with respect to such things as volume of business, late deliveries, rejected shipments (because of poor quality), transit damage, or price trends. Such reports can even be broken down by product lines, in the case of multiproduct suppliers. Likewise, the computer can prepare reports on the performance of individual buyers, materials planners, and departments. Such reports can include figures on number of orders, blanket orders and materials handled, dollar volume of orders by commodity, percentage of open orders, prices paid versus target prices, percentage of late deliveries, percentage of rejected shipments, percentage of schedules missed, etc. Some companies even develop formulas for determining performance indexes for suppliers and buyers and have the computer automatically compute the indexes monthly. The computer offers materials executives an endless number of possibilities for developing data to improve management decisions and control.

THE IMPACT OF A COMPUTER-BASED SYSTEM ON DAILY OPERATIONS

Although a computerized materials management system produces major benefits for all types of organizations, in a relative sense it is most beneficial to firms that (1) carry a large number of diversified materials in inventory, (2) process a large number of purchase orders, (3) buy a large number of different items, or (4) deal with a large number of different suppliers.

The first observable change a computer-based system makes in the traditional purchasing office routine is in the generation and processing of purchase requisitions. As a rule, a majority of the firm's purchase requisitions are prepared by the computer, including virtually all the requisitions for materials carried in inventory. Items whose inventory cannot be controlled effectively by a computer on a continuing basis are primarily those with extremely unstable usage patterns. Requisitions for these items as well as for "new buys," normal "one-time" purchases, and certain emergency and critical items are usually generated manually.

A second, and related, change produced by an automated system focuses on the utilization of people. A computer-based system frees buyers and other professional personnel from a vast amount of routine work associated with the initiating and processing of requisitions. One company found that prior to the installation of an automated system, the average buyer spent nearly 50 percent of his or her time processing purchase requisitions. After installation of the system, requisition processing required only a fraction of this time. Automation thus permitted the typical buyer to devote a majority of the time to creative buying activities such as vendor investigation, negotiation, value analysis, and various types of purchasing research.[3]

Another difference, with significant managerial implications, is that the system regularly provides buyers and managers with a large variety of new and valuable detailed control data. One aircraft manufacturer found that report data enabled it to reduce delays in manufacturing because of fewer late shipments, reduce its inventory investment, reduce average material costs, do a better job of planning cash flows, improve its cost accounting control,

---

[3] For an interesting variety of case study experiences, see: (1) Steve Springer, "The Role of the PC in the Purchasing Environment," *The Hoosier Purchaser*, March/April 1988, pp. 12–13; (2) T. F. Dillon, "Caterpillar Connects with EDI," *Purchasing World*, August 1986, pp. 62–64; (3) R. L. Janson, "How Computers Give Purchasing People a Break," *Purchasing World*, September 1981, pp. 64–68.

and increase the speed and effectiveness of the total procurement operation.[4]

Still another change is seen in the relationships developed between purchasing and other materials activities. These relationships, particularly with production control, are somewhat closer under an automated system. The computer is the common bond which draws all materials activities into an integrated system. This situation simulates the development of a materials management type of organization. Even where the traditional forms of organization persist, buyers find themselves working more closely with their counterparts in the production control department. The design of the system and the speed with which it functions minimize buck-passing between the two and tend to make specific materials problems company problems, rather than departmental problems.

Finally, compared with a traditional purchasing operation, the general tenor of activities in an automated department is upgraded and focuses more sharply on the managerial and creative responsibilities of the purchasing function. Fewer clerks and expediters are required. The buyer's role, if developed as a logical extension of the old one, involves more analytical work and more purchasing research.

THE USE OF MICROCOMPUTERS

Microcomputers, or personal computers (PCs), are commonly found in most business offices today, including purchasing and materials management offices. In the latter case, micros are used primarily to increase the productivity and effectiveness of procurement personnel. The increase is accomplished in two ways:

1 By making it possible for individuals to do more thorough *analytical* work that leads to more effective materials decisions.
2 By making it possible simply to increase the volume of work that can be handled—hence, increasing the individual's productivity.

Three types of micro applications are found most frequently in the materials environment—analytical, data base, and communications.

Analytical Applications

The most common technique used in the various analytical applications is "spreadsheet" analysis. A *spreadsheet* (developed either on paper or on a PC) is simply a matrix of rows and columns into which relevant data elements are inserted for different operational alternatives (e.g., suppliers, operating plans, and so on). Many of the data elements for each alternative are related

---

[4] For a detailed discussion of this case see Dean S. Ammer, *Materials Management and Purchasing*, Richard D. Irwin, Inc., Homewood, Ill., 1980, pp. 589–594.

mathematically, and it is the PC's ability to make such calculations quickly that makes it so useful for this type of analysis.

Spreadsheet analysis is used most commonly in purchasing offices for activities such as: (1) the evaluation of competitive bids, (2) the analysis of various quantity discount purchase alternatives, (3) cost-price analysis for different potential suppliers, (4) make-or-buy analysis, and (5) the quantifiable aspects of value analysis. In all of these various analyses many of the data elements are variable as they relate to each other (different quantities, different service, different costs and prices, and so on), and they typically vary among alternative suppliers, plans, and so on. So the job of the analyst is to make the calculations, develop comparable data among the alternatives (compare apples to apples), and then analyze the findings to determine the best course of action. The value of a PC-based spreadsheet analysis in this work is obvious.

"What if" analysis is a similar type of spreadsheet application that can give management extremely useful data for planning purposes. This approach, in effect, simulates the operation of a total system under different operating conditions. For example, a materials manager might conduct an inventory system simulation. Suppose he or she wants to know the effects on costs and service of reducing the inventory levels of certain commodity classifications, or of developing various supplier stocking arrangements for certain materials, or of developing a JIT purchasing plan with selected suppliers—"what if" we did such and such? Once the system is modeled on the spreadsheet, the manager can change a given variable, and within seconds the computer will show the impact of the modification on the entire system.

Data Base Applications

When the data records maintained in the computerized operating system are originally designed, practical considerations typically limit the amount of information to be contained in each record. In the course of their work, however, certain buyers or buying groups may have unique needs for more detailed or refined information about certain suppliers, operations, data needed for forecasting, and so on. A microcomputer or a networked micro system in the department can be used to expand selected operating data files for such purposes.

Records that frequently are enhanced in this way include those dealing with materials and market variables, suppliers, services, quotations, and contracts. When such records are expanded by using a PC, it is important to integrate the system carefully with the purchasing operating system and to provide adequate data security so that unauthorized individuals cannot modify the basic record.

Communications Applications

PC software is commonly available to provide "electronic mailbox" and "electronic bulletin board" capabilities, as well as word processing capability.

Many purchasing departments use electronic mail communications among personnel within the department, as well as with users in operating departments. The bulletin board feature can be used to communicate material lead-time changes, price changes, information about supplier problems, and similar types of information that purchasing and other individuals throughout the organization need to know.

As in all departments, word processing capability can be a real time saver in purchasing. The repetitive preparation of various reports, requests for quotation, and so on, in which some data remain constant from one preparation to the next while other data change, represents an excellent opportunity to increase productivity by using this PC capability.[5]

ELECTRONIC DATA INTERCHANGE

Once a firm has an effective computer-based purchasing system in operation, a logical extension of that system is to link it, in one way or another, with the order-handling computer system of selected suppliers. The term generally given to this type of buyer-supplier communications operation is *electronic data interchange—EDI*. In an evolutionary sense, EDI simply is an advanced step in the continuing drive toward the development of a "paperless" purchasing operation that began with techniques such as the blanket order, systems contracting, consignment purchasing, and various data-phone techniques discussed in the preceding chapter.

In its purest sense,

> EDI is the direct electronic transmission, computer to computer, of standard business forms, such as purchase orders, shipping notices, invoices, and the like, between two organizations. In a purchasing environment, documents are transmitted 'over the wire,' eliminating the need to generate hard copies and to distribute them manually. By utilizing EDI, a buyer and a supplier are operating in a near real-time environment, which can reduce material delays by shortening procurement lead times.[6]

Types of Operations

In practice, applications based on the EDI concept take several forms. The first step in many firms is the transmission of data from a dedicated terminal in the buyer's operation to a terminal (and perhaps printer) in the supplier's operation. Technically, this is not a pure EDI operation because a terminal operator is required to input data generated by the buyer's automated purchasing system,

---

[5] Detailed discussions of PC applications in purchasing are found in: (1) Jeff Pinkerton, "Using Spreadsheets as a Purchasing Tool," *Purchasing World*, October 1986, pp. 34–36; (2) Steve Springer, "The Role of the PC in the Purchasing Environment," *The Hoosier Purchaser*, March/April 1988, pp. 12–13; (3) E. B. Lohaus, "Purchasing Decisions and the Computer," *Guide to Purchasing*, NAPM, New York, 1985, pp. 3.17.1–3.17.16.

[6] Robert M. Monczka and Joseph R. Carter, "Implementing Electronic Data Interchange," *Journal of Purchasing and Materials Management*, Summer 1988, p. 2.

and an operator frequently is required to receive the data at the supplier's location. Nevertheless, in this type of proprietary system transmission is instantaneous and most of the key benefits accrue to both organizations.

Another similar application, terminal to computer, involves transmission from the buyer's terminal to the supplier's electronic mailbox at its computer site. In this case, operation is about the same as in the preceding example, except no operator is required at the receiving site. However, it is necessary to ensure that the supplier's system is ready to receive the communications before transmission is begun.

The last stage, in what is sometimes an evolutionary process, is computer-to-computer communication. Both the buyer and the supplier have electronic mailboxes into which the other party can deposit purchase orders, acknowledgments, invoices, and related communications. Because neither party has access to the internal files of the other, the integrity of proprietary data is maintained. This system represents operational development of the concept to its fullest extent; the two firms' computers literally talk with each other in a standardized language. Figure 4-3 shows in simplified schematic form the flow of communications in this system, as compared with a traditional hard copy system.

Standards Requirements

For the two firms' computers to communicate with each other effectively, they must "talk the same language." To accomplish this requirement operationally, it is necessary for both firms to use certain standard procedures. These technically based requirements involve two types of procedures—communication standards and message standards.

Communication Standards   Communication standards provide guidelines for the *transmission* of electronic data. These standards help to ensure that the message is received and can be processed by the receiver. Issues covered include:[7]

- The speed at which the data can be transmitted
- The timing of the placement or retrieval of information to or from the mailbox
- The requirement for passwords and the coding of data
- The matching of equipment to be used

Message Standards   Message standards provide guidelines for the *content* of the data to be transmitted. These standards help to ensure that the meaning of the data is clear to both parties. The standards cover:[8]

---

[7] Margaret A. Emmelhainz, "Electronic Data Interchange in Purchasing," *Guide to Purchasing,* NAPM Inc., New York, 1986, p. 6.
[8] *Ibid.*

TRADITIONAL TRANSMISSION OF DOCUMENTS

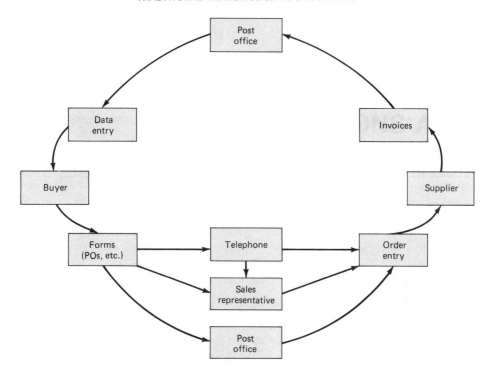

ELECTRONIC TRANSMISSION OF PURCHASING DOCUMENTATION

Direct Transmission

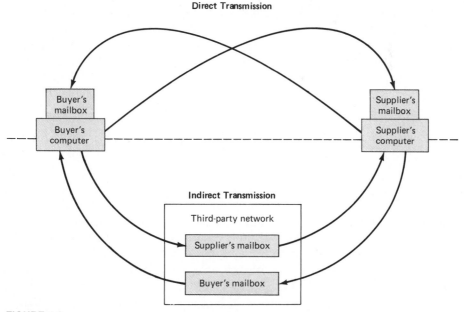

FIGURE 4-3
Simplified schematic of communication flows in traditional and electronic transmission systems.
(Source: *Based on Margaret A. Emmelhainz, "Electronic Data Interchange in Purchasing,"*
Guide to Purchasing, *NAPM Inc., New York, 1986, pp. 10–11.*)

- Definition of words and codes
- Meanings for specific terms of trade
- Methods of identifying specific products and terms
- Essential elements to be included in the transmission

To permit the development of EDI relationships among large numbers of different buying and supplying firms, it is important that essentially the same message standards be used by all firms. Consequently, a variety of industry groups have developed standards for their industries. Most of these standards are based on a structure developed by the Transportation Data Coordinating Committee, which was subsequently expanded and refined by the American National Standards Institute (ANSI). The current set of standards most commonly used by industrial purchasers and sellers is identified as ANSI X12, which carries the strong support of the National Association of Purchasing Management. These standards accommodate virtually all forms of purchasing-related documents.

Each buying firm's computer system typically generates its purchasing data in an internal format that is unique to that firm. Hence, prior to electronic transmission the internal data format must be translated into the ANSI X12 format. The buying firm can do the translation with specially designed software, or it can employ a "third-party network" firm to do the job.

Third-Party Networks

A third-party network firm functions as a central communications clearinghouse, much as a central check clearinghouse functions in the banking industry. It accepts the buyer's purchase orders, separates them by supplier, and at the appropriate times transmits them to the computer in each supplier's organization. In addition, a third-party network firm can provide certain value-added functions. One such function is the format translation function just mentioned. Other functions performed are those associated with the communication standards requirements. They involve primarily a matching of the buyer's and the supplier's compatibility requirements with respect to the speed of data transmission, the timing of data delivery, passwords and coding of data, and equipment.

If a buyer is working in the EDI mode with only one or a small number of suppliers, the buying and the selling firms usually can manage the translation and communication standards requirements satisfactorily. As EDI purchasing agreements expand to include a number of suppliers, these logistical management problems increase correspondingly and soon become impractical to handle. In this situation, third-party network firms usually are employed to manage the conversion processes of the interfacing companies. The lower portion of Figure 4-3 diagrams the resulting information flows.

Benefits

Once an EDI system is in place and functioning properly, it produces a number of clear-cut operating benefits for the buying firm. An obvious reduction in paperwork and related administrative requirements contributes noticeably to increased productivity. Because data are transmitted directly between computers, accuracy of the data throughout the process typically is increased. For the same reason, more complete and faster feedback of order status information is possible. Finally, and perhaps most important, purchasing lead time is reduced. This produces additional time that can be utilized for planning, solving problems, and so on. The net result frequently is the reduction of troublesome materials and operations delays.

There is little doubt that the EDI approach will be utilized increasingly in the future for purchases that involve a number of standard inventory items obtained from a given supplier, or repetitive high-volume purchases of production materials (standard or special) that can be supplied by one or a small number of firms.

CONCLUSION

During the past two decades, we have witnessed the evolution of one of the most important trends in the history of organized society—the increasingly sophisticated use of computers. Although these amazing electronic devices have found applications in virtually every type of human endeavor, the business sector is a major beneficiary.

Within a business operation, no functional area is likely to benefit more from computerization than the materials activities. In addition to its capabilities for processing enormous quantities of data, producing timely management reports, and developing EDI operations, a computer provides another capability that is particularly important to management. Its speed in performing mathematical computations produces a quantitative analytical capability infinitely greater than that possible in a manual system. Consequently, numerous operations research techniques and "what if" models now can be used to analyze materials problems to generate data for planning purposes. Managers can investigate alternative plans with quantitative precision and, hence, make decisions based on more factual data and more informed assumptions and judgments than was previously possible.

Managers must not lose sight of the fact, however, that a computer is only as capable as the people who design the software and the systems in which it is used. Finally, it is essential to remember that the integrity of the output is no greater than the quality and integrity of the data the computer-based system is asked to process.

FOR DISCUSSION

4-1 How does a computer determine when the order point has been reached in an automated inventory control operation? Explain how this computer capability is used in developing other operating elements of an automated purchasing system.

4-2 Explain how an automated purchasing system such as that shown in Figures 4-2 and 4-3 works in practice.

4-3 "The uninformed person sometimes envisions an automated purchasing system as one in which most purchasing personnel are simply replaced by a computer." Comment. Discuss the impact computerization has on departmental staffing requirements.

4-4 In what ways does a buyer's job change when his or her company computerizes the purchasing operation?

4-5 Discuss in detail the benefits a purchasing department might expect to obtain from computerizing its operation. What problems or disadvantages might be expected?

4-6 It is frequently said that managers and buyers can truly "manage by exception" in a purchasing department that is automated. What is your reaction to this statement?

4-7 "The design and speed of an integrated computer-based purchasing operation minimize buck-passing between purchasing and production control personnel." Comment.

4-8 Discuss how you would proceed, as a purchasing manager, to determine whether you should computerize your purchasing system.

4-9 How can a microcomputer be used in a purchasing department?

4-10 Explain how purchasing productivity can be increased by the use of microcomputers.

4-11 Give a detailed illustration of how a buyer might use "what if" analysis in his or her work.

4-12 What is EDI? How does it work in practice?

4-13 Why do standards need to be developed for effective EDI use? Explain the two types of standards used.

4-14 Discuss the role of third-party network firms in EDI operation.

CASE FOR CHAPTER 4

Julberg, Inc., page 748

ORGANIZATION

In any group activity, three principal factors largely determine the level of performance attained by the group as a whole:

- The capabilities of the individuals
- The motivation of the individuals
- The organizational structure within which the individuals function

This chapter focuses on the last factor.

The first two factors are obvious to most business people. However, to many people the third is less clear. In the case of purchasing, the function's location in the management hierarchy of a firm is important, for this decision either facilitates or limits the influence purchasing policies and actions can have on the firm's total performance. Within the department itself, the form of organization selected influences the types and levels of expertise developed and also, to a great extent, the effectiveness with which the talents of individuals are utilized.

The starting point in thinking about various potential organization structures is a delineation and an analysis of the work to be done by the unit—the responsibilities and activities discussed on pages 97–98. In small firms, these duties may be handled by a purchasing manager and one or two assistants; everyone wears several hats. In large organizations, the department may consist of 100 to 150 purchasing professionals. The possibilities for various types of specialization in this type of organization are great indeed. Although there is no precise relationship between the size of a firm and the size of its purchasing department, several informal studies have indicated that purchasing departments frequently employ from 0.7 to 1.2 percent of the total number of employees in the firm.

LOCATION OF THE PURCHASING FUNCTION IN AN INDUSTRIAL ORGANIZATION[1]

A firm's organizational structure reflects management's basic attitudes toward the major activities involved in its operation. Where should the purchasing function fit in a firm's organizational structure? A recent study funded by the National Association of Purchasing Management (NAPM) among the *Fortune 1000* firms reveals the reporting relationships shown below:[2]

Percent of firms	Purchasing reports to
34%	President or executive vice president
25	Vice president of manufacturing
29	Other functional vice presidents
12	Other units

---

[1] The discussion in this chapter is set in a manufacturing environment because the various organizational approaches are most fully developed in that setting. The concepts discussed, however, are just as applicable in the nonmanufacturing environments of service-oriented institutions and government. The only thing that changes is the terminology.

[2] Harold E. Fearon, *Purchasing Organizational Relationships*, NAPM, Inc., Tempe, Ariz., 1988, p. 28.

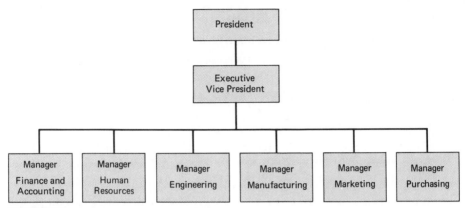

FIGURE 5-1
Skeleton organization for a medium-sized firm, with purchasing as a top-level function.

The two most commonly found alternatives are shown schematically in Figures 5-1 and 5-2.

In a given firm, how does one tell whether purchasing is a top-level function that should report to a general management executive, as do marketing and production, or a subfunction that should report to one of the top functional executives? Answers to these questions can be determined only by finding the answers to several more basic questions. How important is the purchasing activity to the total company operation? Will the company suffer significantly if purchasing does not perform as effectively as it might? How important is it that purchasing activities be coordinated closely with engi-

FIGURE 5-2
Skeleton organization for a medium-sized firm, with purchasing as a second-level function.

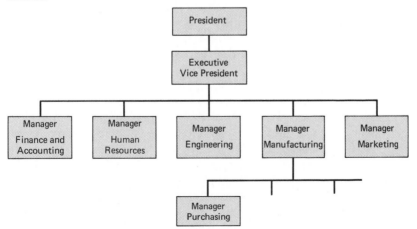

neering and finance activities? Is it essential that materials costs be tightly controlled?

Due to the varied nature of different firms' products and operations, answers to the preceding questions differ among firms. The importance of purchasing in any specific firm is determined largely by four factors:

1 *Availability of materials.* Are the major materials used by the firm readily available in a competitive market? Or are some key materials bought in volatile markets subject to periodic shortages and price instability? If the latter condition prevails, creative performance by analytical purchasing professionals is required; this typically is a top-level group.

2 *Absolute dollar volume of purchases.* If a company spends a large amount of money for materials, the sheer magnitude of the expenditure means that top-flight purchasing can usually produce significant profit. Small unit savings add up quickly when thousands of units are purchased.

3 *Percent of product cost represented by materials.* When a firm's materials costs are 40 percent or more of its product cost (or its total operating budget), small reductions in material costs increase profit significantly. Top-level purchasing usually pays off in such companies.

4 *Types of materials purchased.* Perhaps even more important than the preceding considerations is the amount of control purchasing personnel actually have over materials availability, costs, and services. Most large companies use a wide range of materials, many of whose price and service arrangements definitely can be influenced by creative purchasing performance. Some firms, on the other hand, use a fairly small number of standard production and supply materials, from which even a top-flight purchasing department can produce little profit as a result of creative management, pricing, and supplier selection activities.

Value analysis and purchasing-engineering coordination activities produce handsome profits for a company like General Electric. On the other hand, the types of materials required by some companies leave little room for savings to be produced by such creative effort. A manufacturer of conventional storage batteries, for example, would appear to have little need for sophisticated value analysis work after product designs have been refined several times.

Economic analysis and other profit-oriented activities conducted by purchasing research groups likewise are much more lucrative when dealing with some materials and markets than with others. Purchasing for a technical research and development organization, for example, is often primarily a service activity. In such a firm, materials costs and market trends are not the important concerns they are in a production-oriented firm.

When business operations are viewed in the light of the preceding criteria, it is evident that many firms can benefit from a high-caliber, creative purchasing department. In such companies purchasing should be a top-level, profit-making function that receives close attention from general management. In other firms, purchasing performs primarily a service activity for a major operating function. In such cases, purchasing properly should report to that functional executive. Similar types of considerations dictate the location of all departments in an organization. In most companies, for example, engineering and marketing are top-level functions; in some companies, however, they perform a secondary function and are organized accordingly.

ORGANIZATION FOR PURCHASING IN A SINGLE-PLANT COMPANY

A Basic Approach to Organization

The nature of purchasing activity permits effective use of the functionalization concept. Purchasing work divides naturally into five distinct classifications, each of which encompasses a fairly wide range of activities. In most cases the classifications can be further divided into more specialized tasks, each of which still involves working with different problems, different products, and different vendors. This happy circumstance permits the attainment of a high degree of specialization, without creating motivational problems for most purchasing personnel. Moreover, this type of functionalization permits reasonable flexibility in expanding the work force to meet operational demands.

The five classifications of work found in a purchasing operation are:

1 *Management.* Management of the purchasing function involves all the tasks associated with the management process, with emphasis on the development of policies, procedures, controls, and the mechanics for coordinating purchasing operations with those of other departments. On an exception basis, it also involves the management of unique supplier and commodity problems.

2 *Buying.* This includes a wide variety of activities, such as working with users to help develop requirements and specifications, reviewing requisitions, analyzing specifications, investigating vendors, analyzing vendor capabilities, interviewing salespeople, studying costs and prices, analyzing bids, negotiating, and selecting suppliers.

   Some firms have expanded the buying job and now see it as "supplier management." This additional responsibility involves continuing work with a supplier to improve supplier capability and performance, particularly in the quality area.

3 *Follow-up and expediting.* Order follow-up activity involves various types of supplier liaison work, such as reviewing the status of orders, writing letters, telephoning and telegraphing suppliers, and occasionally visiting suppliers' plants.

4 *Special research work.* A well-developed purchasing operation has an unending number of special projects or studies requiring specialized

knowledge and uninterrupted effort. These projects commonly are found in the areas of formal value analysis, economic and market studies, special cost studies, special vendor investigations, and systems studies.

5 *Clerical.* Every department must write orders and maintain working files, catalog and library materials, and records for commodities, suppliers, prices, and so on.

The precise manner in which purchasing work is subdivided and grouped depends on the size of the department, which in turn depends on the size of the company. The size of the purchasing department typically runs somewhat over 1 percent of the total company work force in small firms to substantially less than 1 percent in large firms.

In a small company, say 150 employees, purchasing frequently is a two-person department. The purchasing manager handles all work in the first four classifications, and a secretary performs the clerical work. As the size of the department increases, additional personnel are usually assigned joint buying and follow-up duties. At this point, buyers begin to specialize on the basis of broad classifications of the commodities which they buy, and each buyer typically does his or her own follow-up and expediting work. As the department grows, buyers continue to specialize in increasingly narrower commodity classifications. Eventually, the follow-up and expediting work may be withdrawn from the buyers and assigned to expediters, who may specialize in somewhat the same manner as buyers. Continued growth finally results in the addition of one or more staff personnel who specialize in various kinds of special projects.

The Typical Organization Structure

Figure 5-3 illustrates a typical structure for the internal organization of a purchasing department in a medium-sized firm.[3]

Manager of Purchasing The chief purchasing executive assumes various titles in different companies, such as manager of purchasing, director of purchases, or, occasionally, purchasing agent. In a small department, he or she usually performs major buying activities as well as the required management duties. As the department grows, most of the manager's time is devoted to management issues, except for the negotiation of a few major contracts.

Buyers Buyers and their assistants perform the actual buying activity and work directly with suppliers. Each buyer, and assistant if the job requires one, handles a specific group of materials.

---

[3] A common modification of this basic pattern entails the assignment of expediting personnel and clerical personnel to each buying group. This kind of structure is a "pure" commodity-type organization. It reduces the possibility of divided responsibility among buyers and expediters, and some firms feel that it tends to increase employee job satisfaction. On the other hand, this type of organization can be more costly and less flexible, especially in small companies.

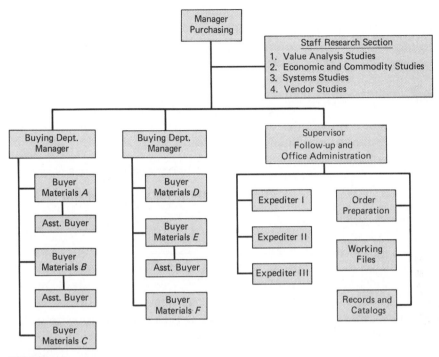

FIGURE 5-3
A typical basic structure for the internal organization of a single-plant purchasing department in a medium-sized firm.

For buying purposes, materials can be grouped in two ways: (1) materials whose purchase requires similar buying skills and technical knowledge can be grouped together, or (2) materials that are used in the same finished product (or by the same operating department) can be grouped together. The former practice is the more common. Grouping materials that have similar buying and technical characteristics permits a buyer to become a technical specialist. For example, he or she may specialize in buying electronic parts, metal castings, or abrasive materials. In most firms today this is highly desirable. As materials continue to become more complex, specialized knowledge of their characteristics, manufacturing processes, and markets is indeed required to purchase them intelligently. Table 5-1 illustrates a classification of materials used in a typical production operation. For assignment to buyers, these classifications are organized into larger groups on the basis of required buying skills. Exact groupings depend on the size of the department and the volume of material usage.

If a buyer's materials are grouped by similarity of end use, one buyer may buy some or all of the parts for finished product A, and another buyer may buy the parts for finished product B. Or one buyer may handle the materials used by the fabrication department and another may handle the components

TABLE 5-1
A CLASSIFICATION OF MATERIALS USED IN A TYPICAL MANUFACTURING OPERATION

1	Abrasives	18	Machine tools
2	Adhesives	19	Office furniture and equipment
3	Bearings	20	Office supplies
4	Castings	21	Packaging material
5	Chemicals	22	Paint
6	Coal	23	Plastic parts
7	Containers	24	Powdered metal parts
8	Electrical and electronic components	25	Printed materials
9	Electrical and electronic assemblies	26	Power sources
10	Electrical cable and wire	27	Pumps
11	Fasteners	28	Rubber goods and parts
12	Forgings	29	Safety clothing
13	Fuel oil	30	Sheet metal parts
14	Hardware	31	Shop supplies
15	Laboratory supplies	32	Stampings
16	Lubricants	33	Tooling
17	Machined parts		

for the assembly department. Generally speaking, when materials are grouped by end use, the buyer buys a wider range of items and becomes less of a specialist than would be the case under the preceding method. This arrangement also produces some duplication of effort because several different buyers invariably buy some of the same types of materials.

A major advantage of grouping materials by end use, however, is the fact that buyers do not become immersed in their own technical specialities. They have a tendency to identify to a greater extent with the product or the department for which they are buying. In these circumstances, the buyer frequently feels that he or she is an integral part of a *specific* production effort. Companies favoring this form of organization believe that the loss of technical buying specialization is more than compensated for by the added effectiveness of the purchasing-production team effort that results. The extent to which this is actually true in a specific situation depends on the range and complexity of materials purchased by each buyer and the effectiveness achieved by the team effort.

Buying Supervisors   The size of the buying staff and the complexity of the purchases handled determine the need for buying supervision. In some departments eight or ten buyers can report directly to the purchasing manager or to a line assistant. In other cases, each commodity buying group is headed by a senior buyer who reports to the chief purchasing executive. Possibly the most common arrangement is depicted in Figure 5-3. In this case, buyers are organized into larger groups on the basis of similar commodity characteristics. An intermediate manager, who reports to the chief executive, is assigned to each group (sometimes called a buying department). These managers are variously titled senior buyers, assistant purchasing agents, purchasing agents, or buying department managers, consistent with the title of the top purchasing executive. The duties of these individuals typically encompass both managerial and actual buying activities.

Expediters The most common form of organization for the follow-up and expediting activity is shown in Figure 5-3. Formation of a separate expediting department permits a high degree of specialization; additionally, it facilitates an even distribution of the work load and efficient utilization of expediting personnel.

However, there is a wide difference of opinion concerning the most effective arrangement for handling the expediting activity. Some firms require each buyer to do his or her own expediting. Because of the buyer's status and intimate knowledge of the order, these firms believe that a buyer can obtain more effective results from suppliers than can someone of lesser status in the organization. More important, companies using this approach want the buyer to assume *total* responsibility for each of his or her orders. They feel the buyer can do this best by personally participating in all phases of the purchase. Additionally, if a buyer is responsible for all phases of an order and for all vendor contacts, it is easier to measure and control his or her performance.

Since much follow-up and expediting is routine work, however, it often represents an inefficient use of a buyer's time. Some companies therefore develop a hybrid organization. To achieve the benefits of specialization, they assign the follow-up and expediting function to a separate expediter. So that the buyer can retain full control of his or her orders, though, each expediter is assigned directly to one buyer (for a buying group). Thus, the expediter does his or her work as directed by the buyer, and the buyer is held fully accountable for his or her orders. In practice, the expediter usually handles all routine follow-up inquiries and calls on the buyer for assistance with the difficult or delicate expediting problems. This form of organization, when fully developed, produces a commodity-type organization structure that minimizes the division of responsibility between buyers and expediters and tends to produce a beneficial esprit de corps among buyers, expediters, and clerical personnel assigned to a particular commodity group. In addition, this approach helps develop an internal source of new buyers—its experienced expediters. This form of organization clearly may also be less flexible and more costly, especially in small firms.

Staff Research Personnel The number of staff specialists employed depends on the size of the department, the complexity of its operation, and the types of material it purchases. Theoretically, in making prepurchase investigations good buyers should perform nearly all the activities such staff specialists are hired to do. However, most companies now realize that under the pressure of daily operations, most buyers simply do not have time to conduct all desired investigations in adequate depth. This is particularly true for complicated purchases that influence future procurement efficiency. This fact, coupled with an awareness of the benefits specialization can produce in planning and research, has led many firms to organize such activities functionally within a special staff group. The specific activities of this group are discussed in the chapters dealing with value analysis and purchasing research. For these activities to yield optimum benefits, it is essential that their organization and implementation be carefully planned from a *companywide* point of view.

Organization by Product or Project

Few single-plant companies are large enough to support a separate purchasing department for each major product line the firm manufactures. A few large firms making a limited number of major products, however, do organize the total purchasing activity on the basis of product or project. General Motors is one of these companies.[4] In such firms each product division is largely autonomous and to a great extent operates its own manufacturing facility, complete with all supporting functions. The basic objective of this type of organization is to develop a group of employees whose interests and identification with a specific *production effort* transcend their identification with a functional department. This attempt to motivate individuals and to develop a smoothly coordinated team effort is based on the same reasoning as that involved in grouping buyers' materials by end use. Viewing the total operation from the standpoint of each *product manager*, this form of organization permits more effective coordination and control of all operating functions contributing to his or her production responsibility.

As top management views the purchasing activity, however, this decentralized form of organization can in some cases possess two disadvantages. First, when the autonomous divisions use many of the same materials, savings can be lost through the failure to consolidate requirements and exploit the company's full buying potential. Second, some duplication of buying effort always exists. Given a fixed number of buying personnel, this means that the firm is not taking full advantage of the potential benefits afforded by increased buyer specialization that would be possible under a consolidated purchasing effort. The seriousness of these two disadvantages largely depends on the size of the individual product divisions.

ORGANIZATION FOR PURCHASING IN A MULTIPLANT FIRM

A multiplant firm faces one additional organizational question that does not concern most single-plant companies: To what extent should purchasing activity be centralized at the corporate level? In practice, virtually every firm

---

[4] For an interesting discussion of General Motors' product line organization, see T. E. Drozdowski, "At BOC They Start with the Product," *Purchasing*, Mar. 13, 1986, pp. 62B5–62B11.

answers this question differently. Some firms centralize the activity almost completely, doing the buying for all plants at a central headquarters office. Others decentralize the function entirely, giving each plant full authority to conduct all of its purchasing activities. Still other firms—the majority of them—develop an organization somewhere between these two extremes. Each extreme approach offers significant benefits that are discussed in the following sections.

Advantages of Multiplant Centralization

Greater Buying Specialization   Perhaps the greatest benefit of centralization stems from the fact that it permits greater technical specialization among buyers. This leads to the development of more knowledgeable and more highly skilled buying personnel.

Assume that a firm has three plants, each employing a decentralized purchasing department of six buyers. Assume further that each plant uses eighteen different classes of materials and that each buyer is responsible for materials in three classes. It is not unusual to find that half of the material classes used by each plant are also used by the other plants. If the eighteen buyers were combined in a central department, they would have only thirty-six classes of material to purchase [9 common + (3 × 9) unique]. Thus, each buyer would have only two material classes to handle (36/18); each buyer's degree of specialization would be increased by one-third. Because materials purchased in the different classes normally vary in complexity and volume, the transformation does not occur this simply in practice. However, the example illustrates an important point. Centralization enables a firm to do a better technical job of buying, or it permits a job of buying comparable with that under decentralization to be accomplished with fewer buyers. It also provides for the capable buying of major capital equipment and construction services which are required only intermittently by any single plant, but which on a companywide basis represent a continuing purchasing activity.

In most companies, the importance of specialized buying cannot be overvalued. The complexity of industrial materials increases constantly. A buyer who does not fully comprehend the significance of a material's major technical and manufacturing characteristics cannot perform effectively. If buyers fail to perform with technical competence, the important buying decisions will ultimately be made in the using departments, and buyers will be relegated to a glorified clerical status.

Consolidation of Requirements   Just as single-plant centralization facilitates the consolidation of plant requirements, multiplant centralization facilitates the consolidation of material requirements at the corporate level. In most situations, such consolidation results in larger purchases from a smaller number of suppliers, yielding more favorable prices and increased supplier service. Increased purchase volumes also permit the negotiation of highly profitable *long-term* contracts for many production materials.

Easier Purchasing Coordination and Control   When all company purchasing activities are consolidated in one office, procedures for coordinating and controlling individual segments of activity can be effected more quickly and with less paperwork. Consolidation permits more direct administration and control of such important policies as those affecting supplier selection procedures, supplier relations, purchasing ethics, budget compliance, and the consistency of general purchasing practices among the various buying groups. In general, under this type of organization, the chief purchasing executive finds it easier to control the total efficiency of the corporate purchasing activity.

Effective Planning and Research Work   The existence of a centralized group to handle corporatewide purchasing requirements provides the concentrated staff know-how to improve purchasing research work. Virtually all purchasing planning needs—from internal systems design to strategic materials planning—can be conducted in more depth with greater efficiency for all purchasing operations throughout the corporation.

Advantages of Multiplant Decentralization

Easier Coordination with Operating Departments   From an operating standpoint, the greatest advantage of decentralization is that it facilitates the coordination of purchasing activities with the activities of using departments within each plant. When a complete purchasing unit is located at each operating site, purchasing personnel are close to the users' operating problems and develop a much better feel for unique plant needs and their implications in the purchasing area. Buyers can personally discuss purchasing matters with using supervisors any time they wish. Value analysts and technical coordinators can work daily with engineering personnel whenever necessary. Also, a plant purchasing department can develop a much closer working relationship between suppliers' technical representatives, buyers, and plant engineers than is possible under a centralized organization.

In brief, under a decentralized arrangement, purchasing personnel can participate more fully as members of a specific purchasing-production team.[5]

Speed of Operation   A purchasing department located at the plant clearly can respond more quickly to users' needs. The transmittal of information from plant to headquarters by means of a conventional paperwork system typically lengthens the purchasing procedure by one or two days. Of course, telephone, teletype, fax equipment, and computer links can be used in many cases, but often these are not practical as a regular method of communication. If most operating needs could be adequately planned, and plans always functioned according to schedule, the time delay factor would be a minor

---

[5] To prevent each plant from losing its identification in a *centralized* purchasing office, some companies using centralization locate a "plant coordinator" for each plant in the purchasing office. The coordinator's job is to act as a liaison between plant users and centralized purchasing; he or she looks after the particular procurement interests of his or her plant.

problem. In a dynamic business situation, however, unforeseen events cause enough deviations from schedule so that this is rarely the case.

Effective Use of Local Sources   If a firm's plants are geographically dispersed, it can be difficult for a centralized purchasing department to locate and develop potentially good suppliers in the locale of each plant. At times this difficulty deprives a plant of various technical and purchasing benefits resulting from close working relationships between plant personnel and suppliers. If plants are separated by great distances, decentralized purchasing departments in many cases may also be able to reduce material transportation costs by the wise use of local suppliers.

Plant Autonomy   A fundamental principle of management holds that the delegation of responsibility must be accompanied by the delegation of adequate authority to carry out that responsibility. A plant manager who is given full responsibility for the operation and profit performance of a plant can properly contend that he or she should have full authority over the expenditures for materials. Decentralization of purchasing gives a plant manager this authority.

Although entirely valid, the preceding idea implies that a plant manager has no control over materials expenditures if purchasing is centralized. This need not be true. While a plant manager has no line control over a centralized purchasing department, many firms develop coordinating committees to correct purchasing situations that are unsatisfactory to plant management. If these are established within the proper framework, a plant manager, through such a mechanism, can exercise satisfactory indirect control over the performance of a centralized purchasing department.

Factors Affecting Feasibility and Desirability of Centralization

Three factors determine how feasible or desirable centralization of the purchasing function may be in a given situation: (1) similarity of the classes of materials used in each of the plants, (2) size of each individual plant purchasing department, and (3) distance separating the individual plants.

Similarity of Materials Usage   If a firm's plants use entirely different materials, centralization of purchasing offers only minimal benefits; the major benefits of increased specialization and requirement consolidation cannot be achieved. In such cases, potential disadvantages of centralization usually outweigh the advantages gained from better coordination and control.

Most firms, however, generally have a greater similarity of materials usage among plants than is at first apparent. To make specialization profitable, the various plants do not have to use exactly the same *items*. The important thing is the similarity of *types* of materials (or markets). Specialization of buyers is accomplished on the basis of material (or market) *classifications*. Most firms find that their plants *do* use a number of the same *classifications* of materials.

The J. I. Case Company provides a classic illustration of this. Some years ago, when Case was considering a reorganization of its purchasing operations, it found that only about 5 percent of the 16,000 items it purchased were used by more than one of its five plants (each plant makes a different line of products—agricultural machinery, industrial tractors, materials-handling equipment, and construction equipment). However, analysis of these items by material classification revealed that of the total 191 classifications of material, over 75 percent were used by at least several plants. Further study of the situation led the Case Company to centralize its purchasing operation, whereas the initial decision had been to decentralize because of the dissimilarity of the items purchased.[6]

Plant Department Size   As a general rule, centralization is more advantageous when a firm's individual plant purchasing departments are not large. If plant purchasing operations are large, a high degree of buyer specialization may already have been achieved. Similarly, the benefits to be gained from consolidating requirements of large departments are less significant than those gained from consolidating the requirements of small plants. This is not to say that consolidation of large departments does not yield benefits. It usually does. The benefits, however, are not as significant as in the case of small departments, and they are frequently outweighed by the offsetting disadvantages.

Geographic Dispersion of Plants   The closer a firm's plants are situated geographically, the easier centralization becomes. Conversely, if much centralized buying is done, the more widely the plants are dispersed, the more serious the disadvantages of centralization become. Even if a centralized purchasing office has direct telephone and fax service to the production scheduling offices at each plant, when a plant is 1,000 miles distant, the problems of communication and coordination with that plant are difficult indeed.

The Trend in Industry

While the purchasing organizations of some multiplant firms are found at both ends of the centralization continuum, most are located somewhere between these two extremes. The NAPM study cited earlier found that 60 percent of the *Fortune 1000* firms employ a combined centralized/decentralized form of organization, 26 percent a centralized form, and 14 percent a straight decentralized form.[7] The trend clearly appears to be toward the general type of organization shown in Figure 5-4. This organization includes elements ofboth centralization and decentralization. Its objective is to reap the major benefits offered by both approaches.

---

[6] For a complete account of the Case Company's reorganization, see "J. I. Case Switches to Centralized Purchasing," *Purchasing Week,* May 6, 1963, pp. 18–19.

[7] Fearon, 1988, p. 26.

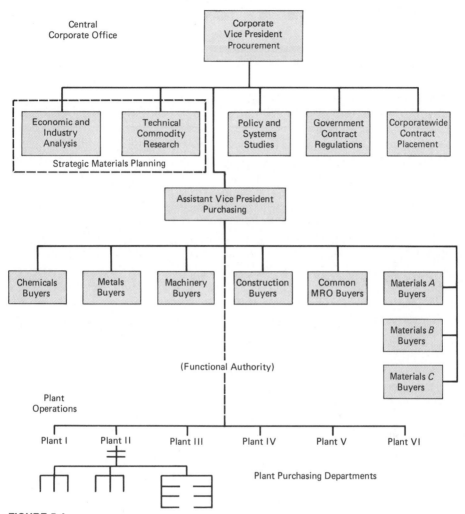

FIGURE 5-4
A multiplant purchasing organization with some activities centralized and some decentralized.

A centralized purchasing office is established at the corporate level, with the chief purchasing executive usually reporting to the president or executive vice president. Duties of the centralized office typically include planning, research, and specialized buying. Economic and industry analyses, technical commodity research, strategic materials planning, systems planning, and government contract regulation work are the most common types of planning and research activities. Buying activities conducted centrally vary widely from firm to firm; however, they focus on the material classifications for which highly specialized buying and requirements consolidation produce the greatest profit. In addition, many of the important long-term contracts are negotiated centrally on a companywide basis. Plant purchasing departments then issue orders against these contracts in accordance with their needs.

In most cases, the relationship between the central purchasing office and the plant purchasing departments is a "functional" relationship. This means that each plant has its own purchasing department, whose manager usually reports directly to the plant manager. By explicit agreement, however, the plant purchasing department relinquishes to the central purchasing department certain planning and buying responsibilities. The central department generally has no line authority over the plant manager of purchasing, but typically it does have the authority to determine specifically which materials will be purchased locally and which centrally. The central department also serves in a coordinating capacity by formulating and enforcing basic purchasing policy and by designing purchasing systems and procedures for all plants.

The increasing need in recent years for thorough long-range materials planning has increased the attention given to the strategic materials planning activity. A growing number of firms have consolidated existing activities or have established a new planning group at the corporate level to conduct these economic and technical investigations on a continuing basis. This phenomenon, coupled with a general increase in the volume of long-term contract buying, has produced a noticeable expansion of centralized purchasing efforts in some industries.

An Illustration[8]   The Hewlett Packard Company (HP) provides an interesting and somewhat unique illustration of several of the trends emerging in industry today. For years HP has thrived and grown while employing a strict policy of autonomy and accountability for each of its manufacturing divisions. In recent years, however, the firm created a corporate procurement and materials management group. The function of this central group is to provide support and guidance for the decentralized procurement groups at each of the individual divisions. HP currently has more than 1,000 buyers companywide, with approximately 180 purchasing people employed in the central procurement operation. The major responsibilities of the central group are:

1 To develop companywide forecasts for all divisions' component usage.
2 To qualify suppliers for critically important materials. This is done with a number of "commodity teams" staffed by central office specialists.
3 To help develop and manage corporate contracts for materials used by multiple divisions in excess of $200,000 per year.
4 To provide support to individual divisions for international procurement.

---

[8] R. M. Faltra, "How HP Buys Electronics," *Electronics Purchasing*, a special report, March 1987.

5 To monitor the companywide procurement system, including supplier performance, on a continuing basis.
6 To manage the data bases of component specifications and part control numbers.
7 To provide leadership for the development of corporate procurement strategy.

Note that the central group does not buy anything, per se. It serves uniquely in both leadership and staff supporting roles, in an operating system that is still decentralized to a great extent.

Procurement Strategy Teams The seventh item in Hewlett Packard's list of central procurement responsibilities—that of developing corporate procurement strategy—is clearly one of the group's most important functions. In HP this is accomplished by means of a group of "commodity procurement strategy teams." Each team is made up of members from various operating divisions from the areas of research and development, manufacturing, quality assurance and control, and purchasing. Each team is headed by a commodity manager from the central procurement group and focuses on a strategic group of materials purchased through a corporate contract. The team evaluates suppliers on the basis of technology, quality, cost, responsiveness, and delivery—and then decides which suppliers will get what portion of the business.

The team approach to strategy development is evolving as a trend in a number of major U.S. firms. Different firms use somewhat different techniques, but the concept is fundamentally the same. The General Motors Corporation utilizes a similar approach with its "purchasing steering committees" and its "commodity buying teams."[9]

THE MATERIALS MANAGEMENT CONCEPT

To this point, the discussion has dealt mostly with the organization of the purchasing function. In designing an organization structure for a total plant, management must decide how to group and coordinate the other activities whose major interest also focuses on the company's acquisition and utilization of materials. In addition to purchasing, the departments that are primarily concerned with materials are inventory (materials) control, receiving, stores, production scheduling, and traffic. To which functional executives should these departments report?

Chapter 1 discussed the materials management concept and its growing application in American industry. Historically, firms have divided responsibility for the various materials activities among two or three functional de-

[9] T. E. Drozdowski, "Purchasing At GM Restyles for the '90s," *Purchasing*, Oct. 24, 1985, pp. 56–60.

partments (i.e., purchasing, production, and marketing). This division of responsibility makes it difficult to coordinate the interrelated activities of the materials-oriented departments. More important, it makes effective identification and control of *total* materials costs extremely difficult, if not impossible. The materials management concept, and its related form of organization, has evolved in response to these needs.

Materials management provides an *integrated systems approach* to the *coordination* of materials activities and the *control* of total materials costs. It advocates assigning to a single operating department all major activities which contribute to the cost of materials. The objective is to optimize performance of the materials *system*, as opposed to suboptimizing the performance of individual operating units that are parts of the materials system. The organization of materials activities that stems from the materials management concept takes the general form shown in Figure 5-5.

Although the theory is simple and straightforward, its implementation provides some basis for differences of opinion. Top executives and management consultants do not agree completely on the exact form the materials management organization should take. In many cases, these differences in application of the concept are quite legitimate, simply because each firm is somewhat unique in terms of its specific orientation, its operating environment, and its specific problems. Consequently, some companies do not include all the materials activities in the materials management department. In

FIGURE 5-5
The general structure of an organization employing the materials management concept.

fact, the title of the department varies considerably from firm to firm. Some firms adopt the *philosophy* underlying the concept, but for various reasons assign some or all of the materials activities to a strong existing department (often the purchasing department), without creating a department bearing the materials management name.

Materials Management In Practice

Over the past twenty years, the organization structure shown in Figure 5-5 has become the "classical" materials management model. Various studies during this period, however, have identified not only a number of variations from the basic model, but have determined that the variations tend to cluster into a small number of specific patterns.[10] These patterns reflect two basic differences from the classical materials management model: (1) the level to which and the executive to whom the materials manager reports and (2) the specific functions included in the materials department.

One of the authoritative studies was conducted by Jeffrey Miller and Peter Gilmour of the Harvard Business School.[11] This study covered 206 firms of various sizes in a cross section of manufacturing industries. With respect to the reporting level, the study found that in 53 percent of the firms the materials manager reports to a general management executive—i.e., the president (or general manager), the executive vice president, or the vice president for administration. In other words, with respect to reporting level, these firms follow the classical model. On the other hand, in 43 percent of the firms the materials manager reports to the manager of manufacturing. In these firms the materials function is a second-level activity. (Four percent of the materials managers in the study report in a second-level position to the controller or the manager of finance.)

Results of the study were less clear concerning the specific functions included in the materials management department. However, three organizational clusters seem to emerge:

1 Approximately 50 percent of the firms include in the materials management department the functions shown in the classical model. A few also include the physical distribution function.
2 Slightly more than 25 percent of the firms utilize the classical model, but exclude production and inventory control from the materials management department.

[10] For details, review the following three studies: (1) Harold E. Fearon, *Purchasing Organizational Relationships,* NAPM, Inc., Tempe, Ariz., 1988, pp. 17, 36; (2) Ronald Baer and John Centimore, "Materials Management: Where It Stands—What It Means," *Purchasing,* special reprint, no date; and (3) Gary J. Zenz, "Materials Management and Purchasing: Projections for the 1980s," *Journal of Purchasing and Materials Management,* Spring 1981, pp. 15–20.
[11] Jeffrey Miller and Peter Gilmour, "Materials Managers: Who Needs Them?" *Harvard Business Review,* July–August 1979, pp. 143–153.

3 Slightly less than 25 percent of the firms include in the department all of the classical model functions except purchasing. In these cases, purchasing usually reports individually to a general management executive.

The Supplier Management Concept   Several years ago, General Motors' Buick-Oldsmobile-Cadillac Group (BOC) restructured its total operation on the basis of a consolidated product line organization—luxury vehicles, specialty vehicles, premium vehicles, and power train products.[12] Each of these four product lines has one integrated team totally responsible for the product, "bumper to bumper...cradle to grave." Included in each team is a materials management group responsible for the following functions:

- Production control
- Material control and transportation
- Supplier development and certification
- Supplier management

Clearly, the BOC organization includes all the functions in the classical materials management model—and just a bit more. Note that the purchasing function has been divided into two parts: (1) supplier development and certification and (2) supplier management. After a supplier has been selected, the first group works with the firm helping it develop manufacturing and quality capabilities until it passes the BOC test for supplier "certification." After the supplier becomes certified, the "supplier manager" (the former buyer) assumes responsibility for continued work with and management of the supplier.

The purpose of this expanded purchasing role is twofold. The first objective is to bring suppliers up to a certified level of performance by making a significant front-end investment in this activity before a supplier is really accepted as part of the BOC team. The second objective is to provide a closer, more intensive working relationship between the buyer and appropriate individuals in the supplier's organization. In this setting, the buyer truly functions as a supplier manager, responsible for continued supplier improvement in capability and performance, particularly in the area of quality.

Use of the supplier management concept is not confined to multisite organizations, or to those utilizing a materials management structure. However, the concept intrinsically fits well with the materials management philosophy, and it does require additional time and functional capability, which usually can be accommodated by a materials management type operation. In any case, an increasing number of firms are expanding the buying activity somewhat along these lines.

The Buyer-Planner Concept   Within the structure of a materials management organization, some firms have taken a different approach. These orga-

---

[12] T. E. Drozdowski, "At BOC They Start with the Product."

nizations have expanded the buyer's job, but in the opposite direction. In effect, they have merged the jobs of the buyer and the production control materials scheduler. The new job, aptly described by its title, is that of "buyer-planner."

The *buyer-planner* is responsible for determination of materials requirements, developing materials schedules, making order quantity determinations, and handling all the activities associated with the buying function. The concept is a logical extension of the basic materials management idea, simply applied at a micro level in the department. It is particularly applicable in a manufacturing operation utilizing an MRP-type system.

The concept has been adopted at an increasing rate the past few years, particularly in intermittent manufacturing operations. Firms that use it report three major benefits: (1) a smoother materials flow, (2) improved coordination with key suppliers, and (3) increased productivity.[13]

The fact that the approach eliminates one major interface (buyer/production planner), and its attendant problems, tends to smooth the materials flow. Additionally, a buyer-planner develops a better understanding of the total materials cycle. These two factors in combination usually increase the efficiency of the planning-buying activity. At the same time, because the buyer-planner sees the total materials requirements picture over an extended period of time, he or she frequently is able to match requirements more closely with a supplier's manufacturing capabilities and constraints. Lot sizing can be considered also from the supplier's point of view in developing order release schedules.

Practical Benefits   How do practicing managers view materials management? On the whole, very positively; approximately 70 percent of the nation's major manufacturing firms utilize it in one form or another. Mr. John Davin, former vice president for materials and facilities at GTE, summarizes his observations in the following statement: "While some may disagree with inclusion of certain specific jobs under the control of a materials manager, there is a general consensus as to the...benefits derived from the practice of materials management."[14] He cites his summary of the practical benefits as follows:

- *Profit contribution.* Integrated under a single manager, individual functions previously considered to be business expenses can focus on positive profit contributions through a coordinated profit center effort.
- *Lower total materials costs.* The total cost of buying, storing, and moving materials can be reduced by individual managers working in unison to achieve a single goal, thereby eliminating counterproductive efforts. A cost problem anywhere in the chain of materials activities can easily be pinpointed and resolved.

[13] Somerby Dowst, "Purchasing Knows What Management Wants," *Purchasing,* Jan. 26, 1984, pp. 87–89.
[14] P. V. Farrell and G. W. Aljian (eds.). *Aljian's Purchasing Handbook,* McGraw-Hill Book Company, New York, 1982, p. 19–13.

- *Optimum inventory levels.* Proper inventory levels, balancing costs with availability, are now a primary objective of a materials manager.
- *Maximized materials movement.* The horizontal management of materials places one manager in charge of materials from beginning to end. This unity of coordination and control reduces time lost through interdepartmental conflict.
- *Functional efficiency.* There is a general synergistic effect and upgrading of the materials functions because of their collective interactive management.
- *Job enrichment.* Members of a multifunctional department have an enlarged opportunity for promotion and personal development. In addition, the elimination of overlapping work reduces conflicts, improves morale, and increases job satisfaction.

A strong, integrated materials department, whose manager has equal status with the engineering and operations managers, offers one intangible yet important benefit which is not apparent on an organization chart. Such a department possesses the potential to exert a strong influence on indirect materials activities such as the standards program, the material specifications program, and the value analysis program. An organization structure containing a top-level executive whose primary responsibility is the *total* cost of materials without doubt establishes the foundation for developing profitable interdepartmental participation in these activities.

Effect on Purchasing Organization

What effect does the adoption of a materials management organization have on purchasing? It has no effect on the purchasing function per se. With respect to the purchasing function's status in the organization, if any change occurs, its status is usually enhanced because of the greater attention management gives to materials costs.

Internal organization of the purchasing department, in many cases, changes very little.[15] However, in cases where the supplier manager concept is used, as was noted in the GM illustration, a greater degree of functional specialization typically is employed in front-end supplier certification and in materials scheduling to provide sufficient time for the buyer to genuinely perform as a supplier manager. In cases where the buyer-planner concept is utilized, just the opposite occurs; the buyer's job is expanded to include materials scheduling. Hence, each buyer handles a smaller number of materials, over a broader range of functional activities.

The position of the chief purchasing executive changes significantly, however, if he or she previously reported to a general management executive.

---

[15] To facilitate coordination of buyers and production control schedulers, materials groupings may be modified so that a given buyer and a given scheduler tend to handle the same materials.

This position automatically moves down the executive hierarchy one level. Under the new organization, the purchasing manager reports to a materials manager, who now occupies his or her previous location on the organization chart. Although the materials manager has responsibilities that are considerably broader than purchasing, purchasing is the focal point of activity in the new department. For this reason, a competent purchasing executive, as well as an equally competent production control manager, is a logical candidate to fill the materials manager's position when the transition is made. In firms that have made the transition, approximately the same number of materials managers have moved up from purchasing as from production control.

In a multiplant company, the central purchasing office experiences approximately the same type of transition as the plant purchasing departments. However, the additional centralized activities for inventory control, production control, and stores tend to focus on the development of policies and systems; most operating activities usually remain decentralized.

CONCLUSION

The fundamental purpose of organization is to provide a structure that facilitates the motivation of people and the coordination of their efforts toward the common goals of the firm. A poorly designed structure can inhibit such accomplishments, just as a well-designed structure can facilitate them.

Location of the purchasing or materials department within a firm's organizational hierarchy is determined very simply by one factor—management's perception of the importance of the function. In a majority of manufacturing firms the purchasing/materials function reports to a top-management executive, but in a sizable minority it is seen as a second-level function.

In addition to the complexity of the markets and the value and complexity of the materials purchased, the type and amount of specialized expertise in purchasing also influence its profit potential—and its importance. Hence, over the long term, purchasing's position in the hierarchy can be influenced heavily by the department's internal pattern of organization. How purchasing chooses to specialize is important. It can specialize buying activities by material categories, and it can specialize by operating function (e.g., buying, expediting, purchasing research, value analysis, and so on). In practice, all but the smallest departments do some of both. But, with limited staff, each staffing decision represents a trade-off. The manager must decide which type of expertise (material or functional) is most useful to the firm at a given time and develop the organization accordingly. These needs, however, change from time to time.

This is why very few firms have organizational structures that are exactly alike. Each design represents a compromise solution to the different problems in each firm. It is for this reason, for example, that many multiplant firms decentralized purchasing in the 1960s, and, with the changing conditions of the late 1970s and 1980s, have moved back toward more centralized purchasing planning and, in some cases, buying activity. The increased use of materials management, but with a variety of different organizational patterns, is another illustration of this phenomenon.

Hence, managers constantly seek to maximize utilization of the capabilities of their human resources, following the sage observation of Dr. Harry Hopf:[16]

> That a business cannot permanently occupy levels of effectiveness higher than those clearly determined by the capacity of its executives is self-evident; but it is not generally understood that the influence of a superior organization upon the accomplishments of mediocre executives can raise the enterprise to heights not otherwise attainable.

FOR DISCUSSION

5-1 How do you distinguish between a good organization and a poor organization?

5-2 Some business executives say that overorganization is just as bad as underorganization. What is your reaction to this idea? Explain.

5-3 Where in a single-plant manufacturing company's organizational structure should the purchasing department be located? Explain.

5-4 Assume that you have been asked to study a plant's purchasing department and to recommend an ideal organization to the manager. Describe exactly what you would do and how you would conduct the study.

5-5 On what bases are materials grouped for buying purposes? Explain the strengths and weaknesses of each approach.

5-6 How and by whom should the expediting function be conducted in a purchasing department? Explain.

5-7 Discuss the advantages and disadvantages of centralized purchasing in a multiplant company.

5-8 When is it neither feasible nor desirable to centralize the purchasing activity in a multiplant company? Explain.

5-9 Is centralized multiplant purchasing likely to expand or decline in the decade ahead? Explain.

5-10 Commodity buying teams and procurement strategy teams are used with increasing frequency today. Explain how they are used. What advantages and disadvantages do they produce?

5-11 Discuss the supplier management concept.

5-12 Discuss the buyer-planner concept.

5-13 How does the materials management concept affect a firm's organization structure?

---

[16] Harry A. Hopf, as quoted by Ernest Dale, *Planning and Developing the Company Organization Structure*, American Management Association Research Report 20, New York, 1952, p. 17.

5-14 From an operating point of view, discuss the pros and cons of the materials management concept.

5-15 Why do some purchasing managers resist the adoption of a materials management form of operation? What reasonable arguments might be used to persuade them to change their minds? Explain.

CASES FOR CHAPTER 5

Northeastern Equipment Company, page 774
Smith-Jones Electronics Corporation, page 814
Blozis Company, page 715
G.A.R Manufacturing Company (in the Instructor's Manual)

TWO

THE GENERATION OF REQUIREMENTS

CHAPTER **6**

PURCHASE DESCRIPTIONS AND SPECIFICATIONS

KEY CONCEPTS

- Quality defined
- Specifications
    - Basic importance of specifications
    - How balanced specifications are developed
    - Writing specifications
    - Procurement importance of the specification
    - Commercial standards
    - Design specifications/Engineering drawings
    - Material and method-of-manufacture specifications
- Other purchase descriptions
    - Performance specifications
    - Function and fit specifications
    - Brand or trade names
    - Samples
    - Market grades
    - Qualified products
    - Combination of methods
- How to select the right approach to describing requirements

The purchase description forms the heart of the procurement. Whether or not a purchase order or contract will be performed to the satisfaction of the buying organization frequently is determined at the time the purchase description is selected or written, specifying the quality requirements. In no other form of communication is there a need for greater clarity and precision of expression.

QUALITY DEFINED

Quality frequently is defined as "fitness; merit; excellence." This is the definition most people have in mind when they think of quality. The Rolls Royce is taken for granted to be a quality automobile. The diamond is accepted without question to be a quality gem. People generally believe that "high quality" is something desirable in itself.

In industrial and institutional purchasing, quality has an entirely different meaning. Here quality is related to suitability and cost (not price),[1] rather than to intrinsic excellence. The best quality is that which can be purchased at the lowest cost to fulfill the need or satisfy the intended function for which the material is being purchased.

Quality has no meaning in purchasing except as it is related to function and ultimate cost. A few examples will clarify this point. It would be unnecessarily costly to print the pages of this book on the high-quality parchment used for college diplomas. Because of its high price, in most cases it would be needlessly wasteful to use silver as an electrical conductor, even though its conductivity is approximately 9 percent greater than that of copper. The high cost of labor for painting would make it foolish to attempt to save money on the price of the paint without considering its lasting qualities.

This chapter discusses the important aspects of written descriptions of quality and their impact on good purchasing. Such purchase descriptions serve a number of purposes, among them to:

- Communicate to the buyer in the purchasing department what to buy
- Communicate to prospective suppliers what is required
- Serve as the heart of the resulting purchase order
- Establish the standard against which inspections, tests, and quality checks are made

Purchase descriptions directly affect the quality and performance of the item purchased and the price paid. For example, unnecessarily tight tolerances result in needlessly high production costs and prices for purchased materials. Performance specifications that describe the function to be performed without specifying the materials and procedures to be used allow potential suppliers to propose alternative approaches to satisfying the requirement.

---

[1] Price is only one element of cost, as is discussed later in this chapter.

When purchasing with performance specifications, the buyer benefits through a "competition of concepts," frequently with significant savings. Many firms pay a "fair and reasonable" price for materials; however, they do not always pay the "right" price. The right price is paid only when the "right" material is specified and after all reasonable efforts to improve the purchase descriptions have been exhausted.

Purchase descriptions fall into two broad categories: detailed specifications and other purchase descriptions.

SPECIFICATIONS

Specifications are the most detailed method of describing requirements. Various types of design specifications are the detailed descriptions of the materials, parts, and components to be used in making a product. Hence, they are the descriptions that tell the seller exactly what the buyer wants to purchase. Because they impinge extensively on the activities of engineering, operations, purchasing, and quality, optimum specifications vitally influence the contribution made by all these departments to the firm's success.

In a manufacturing firm, when specifications are fixed, the final design of the product is also fixed. When the final design is fixed, the product's competitive stance and its profit potential are also fixed. Hence, developing proper specifications is an important management task. The task is difficult because it involves many variables, including the problem of conflicting human sensitivities and orientations. Many departments are capable of contributing to design; however, they frequently are thwarted from fully doing so because of conflicting views. Before the optimum in design can be achieved, these major conflicting views must be reconciled. For example, to gain a competitive advantage, the marketing department normally desires unique and nonstandard features in a product. Engineering sometimes desires features of design excellence which contribute little to sales potential and which may complicate the manufacturing process. Operations, to achieve its goals of low unit costs and long production runs, favors materials that are easy to work and designs which result in the smallest possible number of items in the product line. Such natural departmental differences regarding design problems can be resolved only by perceptive and skillful management.

Reduced costs usually result in increased profit. Direct attempts to reduce labor costs normally result in strong counter pressures. Labor unions and individual workers are innately suspicious of attempts to save money by reducing labor costs. Hence, when an attempt is made to reduce these costs, regardless of its justification, labor troubles often follow. Cost reduction in the design area sometimes also generates opposition. But through imaginative and creative thinking, costs in this area typically can be reduced more easily than in any other area. This is why the design area is an extremely fruitful field for management cooperation and coordination between engineering, operations, and purchasing.

Basic Importance of Specifications

The cost of materials alone clearly dictates that their selection is an important consideration during product design. The costs of many materials are firmly engineered into a product's specifications during the design stage, usually before purchase requests are submitted to the purchasing department. The design stage is the first (and sometimes the only) point at which numerous costs can be reduced and controlled. If costs can be, but are not, reduced at this point, it is possible that they will be built into the product permanently and will be hidden forever in the firm's cost accounting records. They will not show up on the firm's profit and loss statement as a loss; rather, they will continue indefinitely as an unnecessary and undetected profit drain.

As will be discussed in Chapter 26, "Value Analysis/Engineering," all is not lost if all unnecessary costs are not eliminated at the design stage. Markets, materials, and methods are constantly changing; hence, a second look to modify, simplify, or improve specifications will always be necessary, justified, and profitable. However, it is at the time of original design that the greatest dollar savings from both specifications and standardization are possible.

Preparing specifications for a product involves four major considerations:

1 Design considerations of function
2 Marketing considerations of consumer acceptance
3 Manufacturing considerations of economical production
4 Procurement considerations of markets, materials availability, supplier capabilities, and cost

As previously pointed out, it is not uncommon for these considerations to conflict with one another. Consequently, top management must provide the encouragement and direction that will motivate all departments to cooperate and seek a company solution, rather than departmental solutions. A design capable of solving the functional problem perfectly might very well present difficult production problems of machining or fabricating. A design could function well and be easy to produce, but present insoluble problems of materials procurement and pricing. All too frequently a product design is functionally sound, production is economical, and procurement is effective—but the consumer does not want to buy the product! Some years ago a major automobile manufacturer built a car that was superbly engineered and very economical to operate. These were the two qualities the manufacturer thought the consumer wanted most. This turned out to be an erroneous assumption. Because the car lacked some of the style features of its competitors, it did not sell well, and the manufacturer lost almost half its previous share of the total automobile market.

Interdepartmental conflicts of interest are seldom as grave as the extremes just cited. Although department managers do disagree occasionally, compromises usually can be worked out when the various aspects of the problem are understood and the organizational mechanism for resolving such conflicts has been established. Unfortunately, it appears that either industry in general does not understand this problem fully, or such conflicts are not adequately resolved because of limited direction from top management.

How Balanced Specifications Are Developed

Too often design engineers and production engineers resolve between themselves all four of the major considerations of specifications preparation, without consulting purchasing or the other concerned departments. This is regrettable because professional engineers seldom have the commercial experience and the market information required to resolve the procurement considerations of specifications. In their attempts to do so, they frequently develop stringent specifications that do not provide sufficient latitude to allow effective competition. In an article entitled "Three Essentials of Product Quality," management consultants Jack Reddy and Abe Berger write: "In most plants, management assumes that specs are correct and that stated tolerances are necessary. In our experience, this assumption is false; a significant fraction of valuable processing time in plants is inefficiently employed in refining products to unnecessarily tight specifications."[2]

When specifications conflicts arise, final authority for the decision should rest with the department having responsibility for the product's performance. This is usually the design engineering department. However, this is not a justifiable reason for engineering unnecessarily to subordinate the design considerations of manufacturing, procurement, quality, and marketing. From a company viewpoint, the right specifications are those that blend the requirements of all departments. Only such specifications can satisfy the goals of top management—i.e., increased sales, decreased costs, and the added corporate security which comes with an increasingly strong competitive position.

To develop specifications that properly balance product quality characteristics and product cost, management must coordinate the firm's technical and business skills. Four approaches can be used: (1) early purchasing involvement, (2) the formal committee approach, (3) the informal approach, and (4) the purchasing coordinator approach.

Early Purchasing Involvement More and more, progressive firms involve purchasing and potential suppliers during the early stages of new product development. Such early involvement optimizes the development of specifications since the technical and commercial issues are addressed at a point where there is maximum objectivity and flexibility. Prospective suppliers are provided rough function-fit specifications. As the item's configuration

---

[2] *Harvard Business Review,* July–August 1983, pp. 153–159.

takes form, more definitive specifications evolve. Progressive firms find that this approach is an element in their quest for quality at realistic costs.

The Formal Committee Approach   This approach recognizes that a good specification is a compromise of basic objectives. A specifications review committee is established, with representatives (as appropriate) from design engineering, production engineering, purchasing, marketing, operations (including production control), quality, and standards. When a new product design is proposed, all members of the committee receive copies of all drawings, bills of materials, and specifications. No design becomes final until it is approved by the committee. One electronics firm estimates that it saves over $1 million annually by using such a team to evaluate new specifications in this way.

The Informal Approach   This method emphasizes the concept of a buyer's responsibility to "challenge" materials requests. At the same time, top management urges designers to request advice from buyers and work with them on all items that may involve commercial considerations. Emphasis at all times is placed on person-to-person communication and cooperation between individual buyers and designers. Using this approach, a company-oriented, cost-conscious attitude is developed at the grass-roots level throughout the organization.

The Purchasing Coordinator Approach   One or more positions are created in the purchasing department for individuals, frequently called *materials engineers*, to serve in a liaison capacity with the design department. Typically, the materials engineer spends most of his or her time in the engineering department reviewing design work as it comes off the drawing boards. The materials engineer searches for potential purchasing problems in an attempt to forestall them before they become serious. This approach is highly structured, as well as expensive. It also is very effective. Therefore, it should be used whenever coordination problems stemming from the technical nature of a firm's product or from the magnitude of its cost justify such an investment.

The reader should not infer from this discussion any intent to derogate the work of the design engineer. None is intended. Often, for reasons of policy, tradition, or expediency, the design engineer is required to make decisions alone that could be made more effectively in collaboration with others. Nevertheless, billions of dollars are lost annually through the adoption of unnecessarily stringent specifications at the design stage.[3]

---

[3] *Purchasing* magazine annually devotes an entire issue to value analysis/engineering savings, most of which are derived from design modifications. See also James L. Lundy, *Effective Industrial Management*, Macmillan, New York, 1957, pp. 141–142.

Writing Specifications

After the design of a product is determined, the next step is to translate the individual part and materials specifications into written form. The need for clarity and precision of expression is important in all business communications. Nowhere is it more important than in the communications emanating from purchase contracts.

Optimal performance in all departments is contingent on good specifications. To meet the needs of all departments, a specification must satisfy the following requirements:

1 Design and marketing requirements for functional characteristics, chemical properties, dimensions, appearance, etc.
2 Manufacturing requirements for workability of materials
3 Inspection's requirements to test materials for compliance with the specifications
4 Stores' needs to receive, store, and issue the material economically
5 Production control's requirement to schedule the material economically
6 Purchasing's ability to procure material without difficulty and with adequate competition from reliable sources of supply
7 Production control's and purchasing's ability to substitute materials when such action becomes necessary
8 The total firm's requirements of suitable quality at the lowest overall cost
9 The total firm's requirement to use commercial and industrial standard material whenever possible and to establish company standards in all other cases where nonstandard material is used repetitively

Procurement Importance of the Specification

One of the basic requirements of a good specification is to satisfy the procurement consideration of markets, materials availability, and price. The specification must also be clear enough for both buyer and seller to be absolutely certain they are considering the same thing. Clarity in written expression is not always easy to achieve. One company recently lost $65,000 on a closed-circuit television installation because its written specifications misled the supplier into believing that a more expensive installation than the buyer really wanted was specified.

In addition to achieving clarity, care must be exercised to ensure that specifications are not written around a specific product, so as to limit competition. Several years ago, a fire chief wrote into the specifications for a new fire truck the requirement that the truck's 12-cylinder engine be produced by the manufacturer of the truck. This completely restricted the competition, since only one manufacturer of fire engines manufactured 12-cylinder engines in its own plant. Had the fire chief specified what was wanted in terms of performance characteristics, such as speed and acceleration, competition would have been plentiful. This example typifies one of industry's most common forms of specifications abuse, i.e., slanting specifications to one manufacturer's product, thus reducing or precluding competition. In this particular case, fortunately, the situation had a happy ending; the purchasing department challenged the specifications, and the fire chief agreed to rewrite them in a form permitting maximum competition. A significant savings resulted from this change.

As previously discussed, specifying unreasonable tolerances is another common specification difficulty. Unnecessary precision pyramids costs! It costs more to make materials to close tolerances, it costs more to inspect them, and more rejects typically result. The best method of avoiding such unnecessary costs is to adhere to the most economical method of manufacture while using standard specifications wherever possible. For example, in procuring 1,000 drive pulleys for use in vacuum-sweeper motors, the first decision would be to determine whether the pulleys could be manufactured satisfactorily by a casting process. Although this method dictates the use of looser tolerances, in large volumes its unit cost is considerably lower than that of a second alternative, machining the pulley from bar stock. The second decision would be to select an industrial standard for the part, regardless of the method of manufacture used. This decision leads directly to a consideration of standardization, an issue which is addressed in the next chapter.

There are three principal types of detailed specifications: commercial standards, design specifications (generally accompanied by engineering drawings), and material and method-of-manufacture specifications.

Commercial Standards

Recurring needs for the same materials have led industry and government to develop commercial standards for these materials. A commercial standard is nothing more than a complete description of the item standardized. The description includes the quality of materials and workmanship that should be used in manufacturing the item, along with dimensions, chemical composition, and so on. It also includes a method for testing both materials and workmanship. Commercial standards are a cornerstone of the mass production system; therefore, they are important to efficient purchasing and to the standard of living in the United States.

All nuts, bolts, pipes, and electrical items that are made to standard specifications can be expected to fit all standard applications, regardless of who manufactured the item. Materials ordered by standardized specifications leave no doubt on the part of either the buyer or the seller as to what is required. Standard specifications have been prepared for many goods in commercial trade. National trade associations, standards associations, national engineering societies, the federal government, and national testing societies all contribute to the development of standard specifications and standard methods of testing. Commercial standards are applicable to raw materials, fabricated materials, individual parts and components, and subassemblies.

Purchasing by commercial standards is somewhat similar to purchasing by brand name. In both methods, the description of what is wanted can be set forth accurately and easily. With the exception of proprietary products, most widely used items are standard in nature; hence, they are highly competitive and readily available at reasonable prices. There are many users of standard products; therefore, manufacturers who make them can safely schedule long, low-cost production runs for inventory. They do not need specific sales commitments before production. They know that materials will be ordered under these standard specifications when they are needed.

Inspection is only moderately expensive for materials purchased by commercial standards. Commercial standard products require periodic checking in addition to sight identification to assure buyers that they are getting the quality specified.

Commercial standard items should be used whenever possible. They contribute greatly to the simplification of design, purchasing procedures, inventory management, and cost reduction. Copies of standard specifications can be obtained from a number of government, trade association, and testing association sources. In fact, the easiest way to get a particular specification is to ask a manufacturer to provide a copy of the standard specification of the material or product that it recommends for the buyer's intended need.

Design Specifications

Not all items and materials used in industry are covered by standard specifications or brands. For many items, therefore, a large number of buying firms prepare their own specifications. By so doing, these buyers broaden their field of competition. All manufacturers capable of making the item described in the buyer's specifications are potential suppliers.

By preparing its own specifications, a company can often avoid the premium prices of brand name items and the sole-source problems of patented, copyrighted, and proprietary products. When preparing its own specifications, a company should attempt to make them as close as possible to industry standards. If any special dimensions, tolerances, or features are required, every effort should be made to attain these "specials" by designing them as additions or alterations to standard parts. This action will save time and money.

Describing requirements with chemical or electronic specifications, or with physical specifications and accompanying engineering drawings, entails some risk. For example, if a buyer details for a paint manufacturer the exact chemical specifications of the paint desired, the buyer assumes complete responsibility for the paint's performance. Should the paint fade in the first month, it is the buyer's responsibility. If a buyer specifies for a metal fabricator the exact dimensions wanted in a part, the buyer assumes all responsibility for the part's fitting and functioning. Should it develop that a part, to fit and function properly, must be 26.045 inches long, rather than 26.015 inches as specified in the purchase order, the responsibility for failure rests solely with the buyer.

The cost of inspection to assure compliance with company-prepared specifications can be high. The very nature of the materials purchased under this method of description tends to require special inspection.

Engineering Drawings

Engineering drawings and prints occasionally are used alone, but more typically in conjunction with other physical purchase descriptions. Where precise shapes, dimensions, and spatial relationships are required, drawings are the most accurate method of describing what is wanted. Despite their potential for accuracy, exceptional care must be exercised in using them. Ambiguity, sometimes present in this method of description, can produce costly repercussions. All dimensions, therefore, must be completely covered, and the descriptive instruction should be explicit.

Engineering drawings are used extensively in describing quality for construction projects, for foundry and machine shop work, and for myriads of special mechanical parts and components. There are four principal advantages in using drawings for description: (1) They are accurate and precise, (2) they are the most practical way of describing mechanical items requiring extremely close tolerances, (3) they permit wide competition (what is wanted can easily be communicated to a wide range of potential suppliers), and (4) they clearly establish the standards for inspection.

Material and Method-of-Manufacture Specifications

When this method is used, prospective suppliers are instructed precisely as to the specific materials to be used and how they are to be processed. The buyer assumes full responsibility for product performance. Further, the buyer assumes that his or her own organization has the latest knowledge concerning materials, techniques, and manufacturing methods for the item being purchased. In this case, purchasers see no reason to pay another company for this knowledge.

Material and method-of-manufacture specifications are used extensively by the armed services and the Department of Energy. A modified version of these specifications is used by industry. Large buyers of paint, for example, frequently request manufacturers of a standard paint to add or delete certain chemicals when producing paint for them. Large steel buyers make the same type of request when purchasing special steels. Chemical and drug buyers, for reasons of health and safety, sometimes approach full use of the material and method-of-manufacture technique in describing quality. Also, these specifications are used most appropriately in those situations where technically sophisticated buyers in large companies deal with small suppliers having limited research and development staffs. Normally, however, this technique is little used in industry because it puts such great responsibility on the buyer. It can deny a company the latest advancements in both technical development and manufacturing processes. Specifications of this type are expensive to prepare. Inspection generally is very expensive.

There are two important features of this method of description. First, the widest competition is possible, and thus good pricing is assured. Second, since the product is nonstandard, the antidiscriminatory provisions of the Robinson-Patman Act pose no barrier to obtaining outstanding pricing and service.

OTHER PURCHASE DESCRIPTIONS

Performance Specifications

A performance specification, in theory, is the perfect method of describing a requirement. Instead of describing an item in terms of its design characteristics, performance specifications describe in words, and quantitatively where possible, what the item is required to do. This type of description is used extensively in buying highly technical military and space products. For example, the product wanted could be a missile capable of being launched from a submarine with a designated speed, range, and accuracy. Or it could be a telemetering system capable of tracking and reporting missiles or satellites during their flight. Potential suppliers are told only the performance that is required. Though performance is specified in precise detail, suppliers are not told how the product should be manufactured or what material should be used in its manufacture.

Performance specifications are not limited to such complex items as spacecraft. Electronics, aircraft, and automobile companies, for example, frequently use this method to buy such common materials as electrical wire, batteries, and radios. A performance specification for wire may require it to withstand a given temperature, have a designated resistance to abrasion, and have a given conductivity capability. No mention is made in the specifications of materials to be used or how the wire is to be manufactured or insulated to give it the required characteristics. Manufacturers are free to make these choices as they see fit.

Industry uses performance specifications extensively to buy expensive, complicated machines and machine tools. Today, more production machines are replaced because of technological obsolescence than because of wear. Therefore, in buying such a machine, a firm should make every effort to obtain the ultimate in technological advancement. Often this can be done best by using performance specifications. To reduce and control the expense associated with this approach to describing requirements, descriptions should be written as explicitly as possible. Also, the product being purchased should be sectionalized into the greatest practical number of distinct components, with potential sellers required to quote on each component. This practice helps solve the difficult problem of comparing sellers' prices by allowing comparison of individual components.

There are two primary advantages of describing quality by performance specifications: (1) ease of preparing the specifications and (2) assurance of obtaining the precise performance desired. For complex products, it is by far the easiest type of specification to write. It assures performance and, if the supplier is competent, it assures inclusion of all applicable new developments.

Potential problems with performance specifications include inappropriate use, poor supplier selection, and pricing. Because performance specifications can be easy to prepare, indifferent buyers sometimes apply them inappropriately. Such buyers use performance specifications to avoid preparing more suitable descriptions that may lead to less costly purchases. Proper supplier selection is essential when performance specifications are used. In fact, the ability to select capable and honest suppliers is prerequisite to the proper use of performance specifications. Because the supplier assumes the entire responsibility for designing and making the product, quality is entirely in its hands. If the supplier is not capable, it cannot apply the most advanced technical and manufacturing knowledge. If it is not honest, materials and workmanship may be inferior. When using performance specifications, buyers must solicit competition among a number of capable sellers. Capable suppliers ensure quality; competition ensures reasonable prices.

Function and Fit Specifications

Such purchase descriptions are a variation of performance specifications and are used in *early supplier involvement (ESI)* programs. With this approach, the design team describes the function(s) to be performed, how the item is to fit into the larger system (e.g., automobile, computer, etc.), together with several design objectives (cost, weight, reliability). As ESI becomes more common, this approach to describing requirements undoubtedly will increase in popularity. With careful prequalification of suppliers, there are no significant disadvantages with this approach.

Brand or Trade Names

When manufacturers develop and market a new product, they must decide whether or not to brand it. Branding or differentiating a product is generally done to develop a recognized reputation and thus gain repeat sales, protect the product against substitutes, maintain price stability, and simplify sales promotion.[4] The primary reason most manufacturers brand their products is to obtain repeat sales. Consumers develop a preference for brands. There-

---

[4] Manufacturers also produce merchandise for wholesalers and retailers who market it under their own private brands. In such arrangements the manufacturer is relieved of marketing and promotional responsibilities.

fore, branded products can generally be sold at higher prices than unbranded products of similar quality. A brand represents the manufacturer's pledge that the quality of the product will be consistent from one purchase to the next. A buyer can be certain that a reputable manufacturer will strive to keep this pledge. Violation of the pledge carries the severest penalty possible— consumer rejection of the manufacturer's product.

Brand name products are among the simplest to describe on a purchase order. Thus, they save purchasing time and reduce purchasing expense. Inspection expense is also low for branded products. The only inspection required is sight verification of the brand labels. The brand is the quality ordered. The higher prices usually paid for name brands thus are offset to some extent by reduced description preparation and inspection costs.

A supplier's success in maintaining a consistent quality level is greatest in those situations where production and quality control are under its own supervision. If a supplier buys an item from several manufacturers (each exercising its quality control), the quality variation in all probability will be larger than if the supplier made the item or bought it from a single source. For this reason, it is important for buyers to know who is responsible for the production and quality control of all branded products they buy. In situations where tight quality control is essential, multiple sources of production should be avoided if possible.

It is often said that when a buyer purchases by brand name he or she eliminates competition by limiting the purchase to a single source of supply. If a buyer had to limit purchases to a single brand from a single source, this would represent a major disadvantage of purchasing by brand name. In fact, however, there are very few situations in which only one brand is acceptable for a given purpose. A profitable market for any item in a competitive enterprise economy attracts other manufacturers to make the item. Competition, therefore, is available by brands just as it is by other types of quality descriptions. In addition, the same branded product may be available from different wholesalers or jobbers who are willing to compete on price and service to get a buyer's order.

Competition among brands is usually attained by specifying "brand A or equal" on the bid forms. What does "or equal" mean? This question generates many arguments. Realistically, it means materials that are of equal quality and are capable of performing the function intended. Equal quality means similar quality of materials and similar quality of workmanship. Comparing the quality of materials is relatively easy, but comparing the quality of workmanship is particularly difficult. Here such nebulous considerations as precision of production, fit and matching of adjacent parts, types of finish, and shades of color must be resolved. The key to the "or equal" consideration is "Can the 'equal' perform the function for which the specified brand is desired?" If it cannot, it certainly is not equal; if it can, it is equal.

One practical way of resolving the "or equal" problem is to let the user department decide what is equal before prices are solicited. Only companies whose products are accepted by using departments as equal are requested to submit prices. This technique helps avoid wounded feelings among potential suppliers. It also permits requisitioning departments to make more objective decisions.

In some situations, purchasing by brand name can be made more effective by including in the purchasing description additional references or limitations. For example, if the buyer suspects that other materials can perform the desired function, reference in the description should give prospective suppliers the opportunity to offer such other materials for consideration. When limitations concerning physical, functional, and other characteristics of the materials to be purchased are essential to the buyer's needs, they should be clearly set forth in the brand name description. For example, in many purchases of equipment, interchangeability of repair parts is essential. When this is the case, this limitation should be spelled out in the brand name description.

For small quantities, brand buying is excellent.[5] The primary disadvantage of purchasing by brands frequently is higher price. Many categories of branded items sell at notoriously high prices. Antiseptics and cleaning compounds are common examples of such items. For these, another type of purchase description is preferable. When purchased by detailed or performance specifications, savings often exceed 50 percent. In recent years, buying drugs by generic name rather than by brand has resulted in spectacular savings for many hospitals; savings up to 70 percent are not uncommon.

Samples

Samples have been called the lazy person's method of describing requirements. When samples are used, the buyer does not have to look for an equal brand, pick a standard specification, or describe the performance wanted. Samples are neither the cheapest nor the most satisfactory method of purchase. Usually the money saved in description costs is substantially exceeded by the money spent on inspection costs. It usually is difficult to determine by inspection that the product delivered is, in fact, the same as the sample. Quality of materials and quality of workmanship are generally exceedingly difficult to determine from routine inspection. Therefore, in many cases, acceptance or rejection becomes a matter of subjective judgment.

Samples generally should be used only if other methods of description are not feasible. Color and texture, printing, and grading are three broad areas in which other methods of description are not feasible. A precise shade of green, for example, is difficult to describe without a sample. Proposed lithographic work is best judged by the vendor's proofs. Establishing grades for commodities such as wheat, corn, and cotton by samples has proved to be the best method of describing these products.

---

[5] Brand buying is mandatory in some situations. Common examples are when a supplier's production process is secret, when its workmanship exceeds all competitors', or when testing competitive items is too costly.

Market Grades

Grading is a method of determining the quality of commodities. A grade is determined by comparing a specific commodity with standards previously agreed on. Grading is generally limited to natural products such as lumber, wheat, hides, cotton, tobacco, food products, and so on. The value of grades as a description of quality depends on the accuracy with which the grades can be established and the ease with which they can be recognized during inspection. There are, for example, thirteen grades of cotton, each of which must be determined from an examination of individual samples. Trade associations, commodity exchanges, and government agencies all expend great effort in establishing and policing usable grades.

In buying graded commodities, industrial buyers often use personal inspection as a part of their buying technique. Just as individuals select by inspecting the shoes, dresses, and shirts they buy, so industrial buyers select by inspecting some of the commodities they buy in primary markets. There can be a significant difference between the upper and lower grade limits of many commodities. The difference is so great in some that materials near the lower limit of the grade may be unacceptable. Hence, inspection is critically important in buying many materials by market grade. Brewers and millers, for example, usually inspect all the grains they buy. Inspection is necessary if they are to obtain raw materials of the quality needed to produce a finished product of consistent quality.

Beef is an excellent illustration of the wide quality spread that can exist within a grade. Normally, 700-pound steers dressed and graded as "U.S. Prime" have a spread of roughly 40 pounds in fat content between the beef at the top of the grade and beef at the bottom of the grade. Such a wide spread may be a minor consideration to the purchaser of a 1-pound steak. However, to the industrial food service manager buying millions of pounds of beef, the difference can be thousands or hundreds of thousands of dollars.

Qualified Products

In some situations, it is necessary to determine in advance of purchase whether a product can meet specifications. These situations normally exist when: (1) it takes too long[6] to conduct the normal post-purchase inspections and tests that are required to ensure quality compliance, (2) inspection to ensure compliance with the quality aspects of the specifications requires special testing equipment that is not commonly or immediately available, and (3) the purchase involves materials concerned with safety equipment, life survival equipment, research equipment, or materials described by performance specifications.

When advance qualification is indicated, suppliers are prequalified by a thorough review and test of the entire process by which they ensure compli-

---

[6] The federal government and some large industrial firms have defined "too long" as a period exceeding 30 days.

ance with their specifications. After qualification, the products of the approved suppliers are placed on what is called a *qualified products list (QPL)*. Approved products are described by trade name, model number, part number, place of manufacture, and similar identifying data on the QPL.

Combination of Methods

Many products cannot adequately be described by a single method of description. In such cases, a combination of two or more methods should be used. For example, in describing the quality desired for a space vehicle, performance specifications could be used to describe numerous overall characteristics of the vehicle, such as its ability to withstand certain temperatures, to perform certain predetermined maneuvers in space at precise time sequences, and to stay in space for a specific period of time. Physical specifications could be used to describe the vehicle's configuration as well as the television cameras and other instruments it will carry. Commercial standards or brand names might be used to describe selected pieces of electrical or mechanical hardware used in the vehicle's support systems. A chemical specification could be used to describe the vehicle's paint. Finally, a sample could be used to show the color of this paint.

Few products are as complex as space vehicles; nevertheless, an increasing number of industrial products require two or more methods of quality descriptions. For instance, something as commonplace as office drapes could require chemical specifications to describe the cloth and fireproofing desired, physical specifications to describe the dimensions desired, and samples to describe the colors and texture desired.

Methods Used in Practice

A survey[7] of 168 manufacturing companies indicates that purchase requirements in these companies are described as follows:

Method	Percent of total items purchased
Brand name*	25
Commercial standards	26
Specifications	31
Combination	8
All other methods	10
	100

*Ninety-one percent of the purchasing executives buying brands stated they were able to get competition when purchasing by this method. Competition came from competitive brands accepted as equal and from competitive sources selling the same brand.

[7]An unpublished survey made by one of the authors at the Graduate School of Business, Stanford University, August 1973, revised July 1980.

Regardless of the method(s) used to describe purchase requirements, only the minimum quality needed for the product to perform the function intended should be specified. Overspecifying and including restrictive features in purchase descriptions cause delays and increase costs. The section of the purchase order including purchase descriptions should also include all applicable warranties.

HOW TO SELECT THE RIGHT APPROACH TO DESCRIBING REQUIREMENTS

While the decision on what type of purchase description to use may appear to be simple, there are many factors that complicate the issue. For small, noncritical procurements, brand names frequently best describe requirements. The use of a brand name as a purchase description is appropriate (1) to obtain the desired level of quality or skill when these are not described easily, (2) to gain the benefits of wide advertising of the brand name item that would aid in promotion of the purchaser's end product, or (3) to accommodate users who have a bias or prejudice (whether founded or unfounded) in favor of the brand. Such prejudices can be virtually impossible to overcome.

When brand names or samples are inappropriate methods of describing requirements, some type of specification will be employed. When selecting or developing the specification, consideration must be given to the importance of competition and the desirability of avoiding unnecessarily restrictive criteria.

Once a need has been identified and functionally described, and when the size of the contemplated purchase warrants, procurement research and analysis should be conducted to investigate the availability of commercial products able to meet the buyer's need. This research and analysis also should provide information to aid in selecting a procurement strategy appropriate to the situation. Procurement research and analysis involves obtaining the following information, as appropriate:

- The availability of standard products suitable to meet the need (with or without modification)
- The terms, conditions, and prices under which such products are sold
- Any applicable trade provisions or restrictions or controlling laws
- The performance characteristics and quality of available products, including quality control and test procedures followed by the manufacturers
- Information on the satisfaction of other users having similar needs
- Any costs or problems associated with integration of the item with those currently used
- Industry production practices, such as continuous, periodic, or batch production
- The distribution and support capabilities of potential suppliers

If a suitable commercial product is unavailable at a reasonable price, a determination should be made whether to use another type of detailed specification or a performance specification.

CONCLUSION

Specifications play an important role in the search for the right quality and the right value. They also assist in resolving the design conflicts which exist between engineering, manufacturing, marketing, and procurement. Specifications serve as the heart of the resulting purchase order or contract.

FOR DISCUSSION

6-1 Many firms pay a "fair and reasonable" price for materials; however, they do not always pay the "right" price. Explain.

6-2 Discuss the importance of specifications.

6-3 Discuss the role which the design department should play in a company's cost-saving program.

6-4 Why should several departments participate in the product development design? What are the impacts on profit, control, and quality?

6-5 What are the four major considerations involved in the development of specifications?

6-6 Why should a specification not be written around a specific product?

6-7 Discuss the benefits and weaknesses of commercial standards.

6-8 When using commercial standards, what is the relation between quality and inspection cost?

6-9 When would you recommend the use of a company-prepared specification? What are the major disadvantages?

6-10 Why does a performance specification not describe chemical or physical properties? What should it include? What are the potential problems with performance specifications?

6-11 Market grades are typically associated with commodities. Could other products also be graded?

6-12 What is a qualified product list? When are QPLs necessary?

6-13 Which factors must you consider when selecting the right approach to describing requirements?

CASES FOR CHAPTER 6

Dynamic Aircraft, page 733
The Big "O" Company, page 714
The Peach Computer Company, page 780
OCR, Inc. (in the Instructor's Manual)
Gotham City Buys Fire Engines (in the Instructor's Manual)
The Case of the Unruly Spider (in the Instructor's Manual)

STANDARDIZATION

STANDARDIZATION

Standardization Defined

In business practice, the concept of standardization is applied in two different areas. The first is concerned with the standardization of things—their size, shape, color, physical properties, chemical properties, performance characteristics, and so on. The present chapter investigates this usage of the standardization concept, which frequently is called "industrial standardization." The second application deals with the managerial aspects of business activity—standardizing such things as operating practices, procedures, and systems. This type of standardization, frequently termed "managerial standardization," is discussed in the chapters that deal with managing purchasing and materials activities.

Although minor differences are found in practice, *industrial standardization* can be defined as "the process of establishing agreement on uniform identifications for definite characteristics of quality, design, performance, quantity, service, and so on." A uniform identification that is agreed on is called a *standard*.

Two historical incidents illustrate the importance of standardization. Eli Whitney is best known to most Americans for his invention of the cotton gin, but his contribution to the development of standardization was a much greater accomplishment. The cotton gin is an important machine, but standardization is the prerequisite to mass production and mass prosperity.

Whitney's work on standardization started in 1801, when he accepted a contract to furnish 10,000 muskets to the United States government. It appeared that Whitney had fallen behind on his contract. He was summoned to Washington by Thomas Jefferson to explain his delay. The explanation is a little-known but extremely important landmark in American history. Whitney took with him a box containing the parts of ten muskets. On a table before his congressional interrogators, he separated these parts into piles of stocks, barrels, triggers, firing hammers, and so on. He asked a congressman to pick a part from each pile. Whitney then assembled these parts into a finished musket, repeating the process until all ten muskets had been assembled.

After his demonstration, it was easy for Whitney to explain his apparent delay. Rather than furnishing a proportional number of guns each month, as an artisan gunsmith would have done after individually making the parts for each gun and then assembling each gun in turn, Whitney had been working to design machine tools and dies with which he could mass-produce parts which were interchangeable with each other. He had standardized the parts. When his machine tools were completed, he was able to produce the 10,000 muskets in a period of time during which an artisan gunsmith could have produced only a few muskets. This effort gave birth to the techniques of mass production.

In short, Whitney discovered that by standardizing parts, the skills of artisans could be transferred to machines that could be operated by less-skilled labor. This, in turn, reduced the need for highly skilled labor, which, at the time, was in extremely short supply. Even more important, this practice introduced mass production and sizable industrial growth to the United States.

The burning to the ground of Baltimore's business district in 1904 clearly illustrates the need for standards in urban living. Like the battle that was lost for the lack of a horseshoe nail, Baltimore was lost for the lack of standard firehose couplings. Washington, New York, and Philadelphia all responded to Baltimore's cry for help. When their equipment arrived in Baltimore, however, the rescuers just stood by helplessly. There was no way to connect the different-sized hose couplings.

The Broad Implications of Standardization

There are three basic systems of production: job-shop or intermittent production, line or continuous production, and process production. The systems themselves can represent degrees of industrial progress. This is not to imply that in all cases progress lies in advancing from the job-shop to the process system of production. Each of these systems has its own applications and benefits. However, whenever feasible, production should progress from a less technologically sophisticated to a more technologically sophisticated system. Such a move will produce greater economic gains.

This concept of advancement is well understood in industry, although it is not always equally well applied. Less well understood is the fact that production systems are heavily influenced by standardization. If Eli Whitney introduced mass production in the United States, Henry Ford made it universal. Ford, however, misinterpreted one important relationship of standardization to mass production: he visualized mass production to mean a standard product produced on an assembly line. Ford thought he spoke correctly when he said, "The customer can have any color car he wants as long as it is black." Actually, he missed the full implication of mass production. Mass production is the production of many diverse products, assembled from standardized parts which themselves have been mass-produced.

A West Coast manufacturer who produces only a few hundred machines yearly for picking apples, harvesting beans, and picking tomatoes comes closer to the concept of true mass production than did Henry Ford. This firm produces only a few machines of a given type. It designs specialized machines from standardized parts which are mass-produced. The design engineers of this company are fully aware that their job entails more than designing specific machines which can perform functions that will make farming more efficient. To sell this company's unique machines at prices customers can pay, the machines must be designed from standard parts and assemblies that are themselves mass-produced.

Billions of dollars are saved by companies through standardization. A survey of the American National Standards Institute (ANSI) lists the following examples:

- A maker of business machines spends about $90,000 a year on standards work. It estimates annual savings at $500,000.
- A manufacturer of electronic equipment spends $24,000 annually on standards to save $125,000.
- A division of a major lubricating-equipment maker believes it saves $3.50 for every $1.00 spent on standards work.

- Two major standards projects of a certain manufacturing concern are tank design and minimum piping. Total savings equal $500,000.
- An engineering firm saves $25,000 per year, mostly on engineering and drafting time, through standards. The cost is $2,000.

How Standardization Reduces Costs

The use of standards permits a firm to purchase fewer items, in larger quantities, and at lower prices. Thus, fewer items are processed and stocked. This lowers purchasing, receiving, inspection, and payment costs. Stocking fewer items makes controlling inventories easier and less costly. The use of standardized approved items drastically reduces the number of defects in incoming materials. Consequently, the purchase of standardized materials saves money four ways: lower prices, lower processing costs, lower inventory carrying costs, and fewer quality problems.

Conversely, the use of nonstandard items, commonly referred to as "specials," almost always assures a firm of higher total acquisition and carrying costs. Additionally, because for specials there frequently is no history of manufacturing experience, using them can result in problems such as unknown quality, uncertain delivery schedules, and lack of uniformity.

AWAKENING INTEREST IN STANDARDIZATION

American industry is expanding its use of standardization noticeably. The American National Standards Institute reports that its number of American National Standards increased 75 percent during the 1970s.[1] The increasing speed of scientific and technological advancement now mandates the establishment of standards at the time new products are developed. Standardization after the fact is so expensive and difficult to administer that predesign or current design standardization is essential. New computer-aided design (CAD) systems provide considerable assistance in this regard.

As might be expected, the government imposes standardization requirements for major purchases. Joint Military Specification No. 81398 requires prime military contractors to develop standardization programs for systems and major items of hardware purchased. Under this specification, prime contractors also must stipulate to the government their procedures for imposing adequate standardization requirements on their subcontractors. Incentive awards are given to those contractors who use the smallest feasible number of different components in a system's design and who select the maximum feasible number of standardized items that are already in the military supply system.

---

[1] *1980 Annual Report,* The American National Standards Institute, Aug. 1, 1981, p. 9.

Kinds and Sources of Industrial Standards

In industry, there are two basic kinds of materials standards: (1) industry or national standards and (2) company standards. With the increasing use of international standards, there will soon be three. If a designer or user cannot adapt a national standard for his or her purpose, the second choice is to use a company standard. If the required part is truly a nonrepetitive "special," then use of a standard is impossible.

Where can one get standard specifications? Specifications for items that have been standardized can be obtained from the organizations that have developed them, such as those listed below:

- National Bureau of Standards
- American National Standards Institute
- American Society for Testing and Materials
- Underwriters' Laboratories
- Society of Automotive Engineers
- Society of Mechanical Engineers
- American Institute of Electrical Engineers
- Federal Bureau of Specifications
- National Lumber Manufacturers' Association

A catalog of United States standards, international recommendations, and other related information is published annually and distributed without charge by the American National Standards Institute.[2] The Institute is a federation of more than 100 nationally recognized organizations, trade associations, and technical societies, or groups of such organizations. Its members can gain ANSI assistance in developing any standard desired. Recommendations for establishing a standard can be made at any time. If, after appropriate research and debate, ANSI approves the recommended standard, it will be adopted as a United States standard.

Both the civilian and military departments of the United States government participate in standardization work that greatly assists industry. For example, the National Bureau of Standards (NBS), among other things, was established to serve "any firm, corporation, or individual in the United States engaged in manufacturing or other pursuits regarding the use of standards."

Among current NBS standardization accomplishments is the development of a specification for data transfers between CAD systems of different manufacturers and for transfers between CAD and computer-aided manufacturing (CAM) systems. This specification, called *Initial Graphics Exchange Specification (IGES)*, also provides a first step toward allowing data transfer from CAD to CAM systems, robots, and other manufacturing components. Until IGES was developed, it was necessary to convert design data from one CAD system to some transportable form, such as a blueprint, and then reenter the

---

[2] ANSI, 1430 Broadway, New York, N.Y., 10018.

data in the second CAD system. This was a slow and costly process. All the military services, NASA, NBS, and ANSI are now jointly working in the development of IGES.

At the request of the NBS, ANSI is currently considering IGES for adoption as a voluntary national standard. If IGES becomes an ANSI standard, data could readily be moved between any two systems that adhere to IGES. This, in turn, would increase the flexibility of computer manufacturing, make CAD/CAM sales more competitive, and make industry as a whole more productive.

Simplification

Simplification, a corollary of standardization, is another term for which recognized authorities have varying definitions. Most frequently, simplification means reducing the number of standard items a firm uses in its product design and carries in its inventory. For example, one company formerly used twenty-seven different kinds of standard lubricating greases in the maintenance of its machinery. Analysis showed that in some cases the same grease could be used for several different applications and that a total of only six kinds of grease were needed. Hence, through simplification the number of standard greases used was reduced from twenty-seven to six. Similar analysis showed that the number of standard bearings and fasteners used in production could be reduced by half. Reductions of this scope are commonplace. Here are some other typical examples:

- A large electrical manufacturer reduced its number of standard washers from 1,350 to 150 varieties.
- Another large company saves $250,000 yearly from simplifying its standard typewriter desks, formerly purchased at prices ranging from $60 to $500.
- Still another company saves $217,000 yearly from standardizing the paper towels used throughout its multiplant operations.
- The United States Navy saves several million dollars yearly from simplifying its stock of ball bearings.

The preceding examples illustrate that simplification can indeed produce big savings. Simplification savings result primarily from reduced inventory investment, more competitive prices, greater quantity discounts (because of larger volume purchases and the use of blanket orders), and reduced clerical and handling costs (because fewer different items have to be handled and controlled).

Some authorities consider simplification an integral part of standardization, rather than a corollary of it. They visualize the simplification process as taking place primarily at the design level, rather than at the stocking level. They think in terms of simplifying (or reducing) the number of related items that are approved as standards in the first place.

Results of No Simplification Program   Recently, a procurement system review was performed by one of the authors for a California instrument manufacturer. The firm was suffering from low sales volume brought on, in large part, by quality problems. In addition, the high cost of goods sold resulted in anemic profits. Purchasing was not involved in the design and development of new products. It soon became apparent that many of the firm's problems could be attributed to the absence of a simplification program, and that both of the cited problems were directly affected by this absence.

Engineers responsible for developing new products had no systematic way of drawing on the firm's previous experience with purchased materials. A connector, capacitor, or gate array designed into a product last year may have had either of two shortcomings: a low level of quality (i.e., a high level of defects) or a low level of reliability.[3] The designer of a new product frequently specified the same problem materials. This led to more waste in production and more avoidable field failures.

The absence of a simplification program affected the cost of goods sold in another way. In many instances, design engineers were specifying new materials that were similar, but not identical, to materials already in use for other products. This proliferation of materials resulted in small-quantity buys, usually at higher unit prices than would have resulted from higher-volume consolidated purchases. Further, unnecessarily high inventory carrying costs resulted.

Materials Catalog   A current, easily accessible materials catalog of approved standard items is the logical output of a standardization program. The catalog greatly aids the firm's design efforts. The availability of such a catalog virtually eliminates the possibility that designers will utilize materials which previously caused problems.

A Success Story   Several years ago, the corporate materials management department of a computer manufacturer began developing a catalog of approved parts. This catalog has been developed by the joint efforts of design engineering, reliability engineering, purchasing, and manufacturing engineering. It is a result of team effort which considers both the technical and commercial implications of the items included. The internal catalog is in contrast to a given supplier's catalog which, while simplifying the engineers' efforts to describe an item, places the firm in a single-source posture.

All items in the catalog have undergone and passed extensive quality analyses. All suppliers have been carefully qualified to ensure that they have the

---

[3] "Quality" has many definitions. As used in this book, *quality* is conformance to specifications that result in a product which meets customers' expectations, not the number of features or degree of sophistication of the product. *Reliability* is the degree of confidence or probability that an item will perform a specified number of times under prescribed conditions. This topic is discussed in detail in Chapter 19, "Managing for Quality."

ability to continuously supply high-quality materials. This catalog is made available to the design engineers who are responsible for the development of new products. These engineers are able to incorporate parts from this catalog without further approval. If they want to use a part which is not approved in the catalog, or which has a marginal technical or supplier rating, engineering management and materials management must agree on the use of the item. The development of the catalog has been expensive, but the rewards have been far greater. A dramatic reduction in quality problems with purchased materials and significant price and inventory cost reductions have been enjoyed. At present, this catalog is in a manual format and is updated semiannually. The catalog is being upgraded to make it available on a real-time electronic basis.

International Standards

The need for international standards is fundamental; by eliminating technical trade barriers, international standards facilitate increased international trade and prosperity.

In 1979, Congress passed the United States Trade Act to implement the Multilateral Trade Agreements, which, among other provisions, include an international standards code. Thirty signatory nations, including the United States, the European Economic Community, the Nordic countries, Canada, New Zealand, and Japan, currently use the code.

Establishing the Multilateral Trade Agreements, the mechanism used to create international standards, was relatively easy. However, actually getting international standards adopted will be a long and difficult task. Consider just a few of the existing difficulties. The United States is only in the early stages of implementing metric standards. Although metric standards are used in both Europe and Japan, product dimensions have not been standardized, so parts from these countries are not yet interchangeable. Standardizing electric power characteristics is a very difficult problem; for example, voltage requirements for electrical equipment vary significantly between the United States and Europe. In short, countries around the world currently have widely different standards for virtually everything, from safety to ecology.

Nevertheless, simply because there is no quick or easy way to get international standards adopted does not mean that progress will not be made. The economic stakes associated with the development of international standards are so high—in terms of increased international trade and prosperity—that progress, albeit slow, is inevitable. Because private organizations, national and regional governments, and other international organizations are all involved in the adoption process, political infighting is inescapable. This, of itself, precludes fast action.

The following facts are presented to give a feeling for some of the current progress being made in the development of international standards. The

American National Standards Institute represents the interests of the United States' voluntary standards system in programs carried out by non-treaty organizations,[4] such as the International Organization for Standardization (IOS), the International Electrotechnical Commission (IEC), and the Pan American Standards Commission (COPANT). IOS and IEC are the most important of over fifteen active international voluntary standards organizations. ANSI is a participating member in more than 800 international technical committees, subcommittees, and working groups. ANSI also holds the secretariat for a number of critically important committees. For example, it holds the post of secretariat for the IOS committee on plastics standardization. This group developed a standard glossary of technical terms and characteristics in French, English, German, and Russian. Producers and buyers of plastics in the world market now have a common reference point for doing business. This kind of progress eases the problems faced by American purchasing managers who buy abroad. Further progress in developing international standards will produce similar benefits for purchasing managers in all industrialized countries.

In summary, the concept and the advantages of international standards are widely recognized and accepted. Progress toward their implementation is being made. As in most international efforts, however, progress is slow.

Metric Conversion

Metric system measurements are among the important international standards. At one time, ANSI believed that adoption of the metric system, formally called the International System of Units (SI),[5] by U.S. industry was just about a dead issue. However, this is no longer the case; ANSI now considers adoption of a major portion of the metric system possible. There is no doubt that the United States places itself at a competitive disadvantage by remaining the world's only major industrialized, nonmetric country. It is generally agreed that conversion to the metric system will increase United States exports by a minimum of $2 billion annually.[6]

There are three primary obstacles thwarting speedy metric conversion: (1) cost, (2) the apathy of some industries, and (3) the fact that many U.S. firms are indifferent to the issue because they do not engage in foreign trade. Actually, the conversion cost is unknown, but it has been estimated to be as high as $20 billion.

Regardless of obstacles, there is evidence that the country is slowly adopting the metric system. In many fields, America has already gone metric. The

---

[4] The United States Trade Act of 1979 provides for ANSI to represent U.S. interests in nongovernmental international standards organizations.

[5] The International System of Units (SI) was defined and given official status by the Eleventh General Conference of Weights and Measures in 1960.

[6] National Bureau of Standards, *Special Bulletin 330.*

shutters of thousands of 8-, 16-, and 35-millimeter cameras daily click across America. Work is done daily in hundreds of repair shops on thousands of foreign automobiles manufactured to metric standards in foreign countries. General Motors' conversion to metric is over 90 percent complete.[7] U.S. pharmaceutical companies went metric over fifteen years ago, and the electronics industry has used the metric system since 1954.

In December 1975, Congress passed the Metric Conversion Act. Although the act provided only for voluntary action, monitored by the United States Metric Board, interested persons and associations had a focal point around which they could rally and exchange implementation plans and ideas. Additionally, the Department of Defense, under DOD Directive 4210.18, has established definite policies to implement the metric system within the DOD. The United States is NATO's largest member. It is the only member not using the metric system, making the establishment of NATO standards exceedingly difficult. The failure to establish such standards is dangerous from a defense point of view, as well as expensive.

How is the United States Metric Board progressing with its voluntary program? "Slowly," according to a survey of typical U.S. industrial firms. Products made to metric measurements now account for only 6 percent of U.S. sales. Far more common are soft conversion products—that is, products made to U.S. measurements but labeled with metric equivalents. Will everything eventually be metric? "Not likely," the Metric Board says. The change is strictly voluntary, and conversion is likely to occur only after the development of economic incentives such as those that now exist for firms engaged in foreign trade. With increasing world shortages of materials and with expanding world technology, more and more U.S. firms probably will be slowly forced to establish international markets for both the sale of their products and the purchase of their materials.

In short, total metric conversion would be possible only under two conditions: (1) if it were mandated by the federal government (which seems unlikely), and (2) when a firm or an industry clearly recognizes it is to its monetary advantage to change—a process that seems destined to be slow.

Organizing a Standardization Program

At this point, a standardization program is defined to include simplification. A standardization program can be organized in many ways. Because so many departments are affected by standards decisions, however, a committee effort is the most commonly used approach. A standards committee normally consists of representatives from engineering, purchasing, operations, marketing, and transportation. This committee typically is charged with the responsibility for obtaining input from all user departments, reconciling dif-

[7] "Coming: Fewer Types, Greater Economy for Purchasers," *Purchasing World*, February 1981, p. 44.

ferences between them, and making the final standards decisions. Theoretically, a member from any department could serve as head of the committee.
Purchasing is particularly well qualified to head the committee in companies
where materials complying with national standards and maintenance, repair,
and operating (MRO) items form a large portion of the company's total purchases. In companies that manufacture highly differentiated technical products assembled from parts made to company standards, engineering is well
qualified to head the committee.

The form of organization used, or who heads it, is not of major importance. It is important, however, that a firm has an effective standards program and that it attains the substantial benefits standardization affords. Regardless of the organization employed, the purchasing department occupies
a focal point in the process. It is only in purchasing that duplicate requests
for identical (or nearly identical) materials, overlapping requests, and
"special buy" requests from all departments become visible. Hence, no program for standardization can be optimally successful unless purchasing is assigned a major role in the program.

CONCLUSION

Many firms still do not fully appreciate the concepts embraced in standardization and its corollary, simplification. Nevertheless, the philosophies underlying these concepts played an important role in bringing the United
States to a position of industrial might. It seems highly probable that these
same philosophies will continue to be important in the future. Aided by increased automation, coupled with computer-aided design and computer-
aided manufacturing systems, standardization seems to be part of the answer to meeting the lower costs of some foreign competitors.[8] By further
standardizing its component parts, its processes, and its operations, U.S. industry can refine and streamline the system that made it a dominant industrial power. Such refinement should permit the production of additional lines
of low-cost, high-quality, differentiated products that will be competitive in
the world marketplace.

FOR DISCUSSION

7-1 What are the two areas of application for standardization?

7-2 Discuss the significance of Eli Whitney's invention of interchangeable
parts to modern manufacturing.

7-3 What are the three basic systems of production?

7-4 Explain why Henry Ford's early system of production fell short of a true
implementation of mass production.

---

[8] Recall the discussion and illustrations in Chapter 1 which depicted the direct relationship
between reductions in material costs and increases in profit margins and return on investment.

7-5 How might the use of standardization permit a firm to experience a reduction in costs?

7-6 What is ANSI and how might this organization be able to assist a developing firm?

7-7 What are the two basic types of materials standards currently in use in industry?

7-8 In what way is simplification a corollary to standardization?

7-9 Describe how the absence of a simplification program in a firm can affect the cost of goods sold.

7-10 How might a materials catalog aid in the use of standardization in engineering design efforts?

7-11 Discuss some of the difficulties encountered in attempting to establish international standards.

7-12 What are the three primary obstacles the United States faces in adopting metric conversion?

7-13 Which departments of a firm are normally involved in a standardization program?

7-14 How can management involve purchasing in the standardization program of a firm?

CASES FOR CHAPTER 7

MAKE OR BUY

KEY CONCEPTS

- Origination and types of make-or-buy investigations
- Factors influencing make-or-buy decisions
    - The time factor ⎱
    - The capacity factor ⎰ Cost considerations
    - Control of production or quality
    - Design secrecy
    - Unreliable suppliers
    - Suppliers' specialized knowledge and research
    - Small-volume requirements
    - Limited facilities
    - Work force stability
    - Multiple-sourcing policy
    - Managerial and procurement considerations
- The volatile nature of the make-or-buy situation
- Administration: personnel and procedures

A purchasing department is responsible for investigating all potential suppliers and for placing the order with the supplier which will, in the long run, provide a satisfactory product at the lowest *overall cost* to the company. Among the potential suppliers that should be considered is the buyer's own firm. In some cases, a company may be able to make a required component or provide a service more effectively or economically than it can buy it. On the other hand, historical policy decisions may at times prompt a company to provide certain parts or services internally that it could buy more advantageously from outside suppliers. Deciding whether a part or service should be purchased or produced in-house is known in industry as the *make-or-buy* issue.

A firm's objective is to arrive at make-or-buy decisions whose composite effect optimizes the utilization of its productive, managerial, and financial capabilities. Unfortunately, studies indicate that a surprisingly small number of firms (large or small) have developed a comprehensive make-or-buy policy that provides for consistent analysis of specific make-or-buy questions.[1]

HOW MAKE-OR-BUY INVESTIGATIONS ORIGINATE

In a going concern, past managerial decisions and the firm's long-range plans establish the current pattern of operations. This pattern dictates that some parts and components of the company's products will be made internally and that others will be purchased from outside suppliers. Within this framework, make-or-buy investigations can originate in one of several ways.

New Products

The development of a new product and the major modification of an old one are typical situations requiring make-or-buy investigations. Every major part of the new product should be studied well in advance to determine the most advantageous production and sourcing decisions. Careful analysis of a complete set of part requirements *prior* to pressing production demands is more effective than subsequent piecemeal analysis in obtaining optimum use of the firm's resources. For this reason, progressive firms, as part of the strategic planning process, include make-or-buy analysis as an integral part of their new product development procedures.

Unsatisfactory Supplier Performance

Unsatisfactory supplier performance for certain purchased parts and components may also trigger make-or-buy investigations. Less than desirable performance may occur for several reasons. It may stem from the supplier's inability to perform certain complex production operations satisfactorily, or from unstable quality performance. Often it results from poor service or from

---

[1]A recent study of English manufacturing firms confirms that this same situation exists in British industry. The researchers conclude "that make-or-buy decisions are often taken without a strategic perspective or an overall policy." David Ford and David Farmer, "Make or Buy—A Key Strategic Issue," *Long Range Planning,* vol. 19, no. 5, 1986, pp. 54–62.

unreasonable price increases. Sometimes a firm's value analysis program un-covers a purchased part whose cost is disproportionate to its value. The pos-sibility of making such parts should be investigated, as well as the possibil-ities of improving the present supplier's performance or finding a more efficient supplier.

Changing Sales Demand

Periods of significant sales growth or sales decline also generate situations that initiate make-or-buy analyses. Reduced sales result in reduced pro-duction activity, leaving plant facilities and workers idle. When this hap-pens, management naturally attempts to bring into its own shops work previously performed by outside suppliers. During periods of rising sales, management seeks external assistance in satisfying the production de-mands made on its limited facilities. During such periods, make-or-buy analysis of individual parts identifies the parts which are most profitable to make internally and those which can be purchased more economically from outside suppliers.

TYPES OF MAKE-OR-BUY INVESTIGATIONS

Specific make-or-buy issues can be grouped in two general categories. The first includes items for which the user currently possesses most of the nec-essary production potential. With only a *small* capital outlay for tooling or mi-nor equipment, the firm can produce each of the items in this category. The second category includes materials or services which the using firm cannot produce without making a sizable additional investment in tooling, facilities, or know-how.

Investigation of possibilities in the second category extends far beyond the traditional make-or-buy analysis. Most "make" alternatives requiring a sig-nificant capital investment become a matter of basic product determination, eliciting such fundamental questions as: What business do we really want to be in? These issues are directly related to a firm's fundamental business pol-icies—to long-range company objectives and financial plans. Matters of this type therefore call for top-management consideration, including extensive economic analysis of the type discussed in Chapter 16. Specifically, the in-vestment required for facilities and personnel to produce the item, and the revenue generated by the decision, must be expressed in the form of a net return to the business. This net return must be evaluated in terms of risk and in the light of possible returns and nonquantifiable benefits obtainable from alternative investments.

A third type of make-or-buy investigation, from a policy point of view, fre-quently lies somewhere between the two extreme types of issues. The dis-cussion to this point has implied that the buying organization has only two choices—make *or* buy. In reality, the firm may have three choices: (1) *make* the item completely, (2) *buy* the item completely, or (3) *buy* some portion of the item *and make* some portion of it. In processing operations, for example, for a given end product a specialty steel producer might elect to buy raw slab steel from another specialty mill—and then roll the steel into finished shapes itself, thus concentrating on the finishing operations. In fabrication and assembly types of operations, a buying firm might decide to buy the parts required for a given component—and then do the assembly work itself. The other alternatives would have been to make everything *or* to buy the finished component. Hence, more combination-type alternatives may be available than at first are apparent. And, again, the need for interdepartmental analysis and the establishment of managerial priorities is clear.[2]

In any case, the make-or-buy possibility requiring only a modest expenditure of funds in the event of a "make" decision is the type most commonly encountered by materials managers. A decision of this type usually does affect a firm's resource allocation plans; however, its effect on the firm's future is much less significant than is a decision requiring a major capital investment. Although the decision requiring a nominal expenditure of funds does not require *direct* top-management participation, *it does require coordinated study by several operating departments.* Top management's responsibility is to develop an operating procedure which provides for the pooling and analysis of information from all departments affected by the decision. In other words, *management should ensure that the decision is made only after all relevant inputs have been evaluated.*

FACTORS INFLUENCING MAKE-OR-BUY DECISIONS

Two factors stand out above all others when considering the make-or-buy question: *cost* and *availability of production capacity.* A good make-or-buy decision, nevertheless, requires the evaluation of many less tangible factors, in addition to the two basic factors. The following considerations influence firms to make or to buy the items used in their finished products or their operations.

Considerations Which Favor Making

1 Cost considerations (less expensive to make the part)
2 Desire to integrate plant operations
3 Productive use of excess plant capacity to help absorb fixed overhead
4 Need to exert direct control over production and/or quality
5 Design secrecy required
6 Unreliable suppliers
7 Desire to maintain a stable work force (in periods of declining sales)

---

[2]For a good discussion of this topic, see Michiel Leenders and Jean Nollet, "The Grey Zone in Make or Buy," *Journal of Purchasing and Materials Management*, Fall 1984, pp. 10–15.

Considerations Which Favor Buying

1 Suppliers' research and specialized know-how
2 Cost considerations (less expensive to buy the part)
3 Small volume requirements
4 Limited production facilities
5 Desire to maintain a stable work force (in periods of rising sales)
6 Desire to maintain a multiple-source policy
7 Indirect managerial control considerations
8 Procurement and inventory considerations

Cost Considerations

In some cases cost considerations indicate that a part should be made in-house; in others, they dictate that it should be purchased externally. Cost is obviously important, yet no other factor is subject to more varied interpretation and to greater misunderstanding.

A make-or-buy cost analysis involves a determination of the cost to make an item—and a comparison of this cost with the cost to buy it. The following checklist provides a summary of the major elements which should be included in a make-or-buy cost estimate.

To Make

1 Delivered purchased materials costs
2 Direct labor costs[3]
3 Incremental factory overhead costs
4 Incremental managerial costs
5 Incremental purchasing costs
6 Incremental inventory carrying costs
7 Incremental costs of capital

To Buy

1 Purchase price of the part
2 Transportation costs
3 Receiving and inspection costs[3]
4 Incremental purchasing costs

To see the comparative cost picture clearly, the analyst must carefully evaluate these costs, considering the effects of time and capacity utilization in the user's plant.

The Time Factor   Costs can be computed on either a short-term or a long-term basis. Short-term calculations tend to focus on direct measurable costs.

---

[3] It is assumed that all inspection costs associated with the "make" operation are included in the direct labor costs.

As such, they frequently understate tooling costs and overlook such indirect materials costs as those incurred in storage, purchasing, inspection, and similar activities. Moreover, a short-term cost analysis fails to consider the probable future changes in the relative costs of labor, materials, transportation, and so on. It thus becomes clear that in comparing the costs to make and to buy, the *long-term view* is the correct one. Cost figures must include all relevant costs, direct and indirect, and they must reflect the effect of anticipated cost changes.

Since it is difficult to predict future cost levels, *estimated average* cost figures for the total time period in question are generally used. Even though an estimate of future costs cannot be completely accurate, the following example illustrates its value.

Suppose the user of a particular stamped part develops permanent excess capacity in its general-purpose press department. The firm subsequently decides to make the stamped part which had previously been purchased from a specialized metalworking firm. Because this enables the firm to reactivate several unused presses, the additional cost to make the item is less than the cost to buy it. However, the user finds that the labor segment of its total cost is much higher than the labor segment of the automated supplier's cost. Should labor costs continue to rise more rapidly than the other costs of production, the user's cost advantage in making the part may soon disappear. Thus, an estimate of future cost behavior can prevent a "make" decision that might well prove unprofitable in the future.

The Capacity Factor When the cost to make a part is computed, the determination of relevant overhead costs poses a difficult problem. The root of the problem lies in the user's *capacity utilization factor*. As is true in most managerial cost analyses, the costs relevant to a make-or-buy decision are the *incremental costs*. In this case, *incremental costs are those costs which would not be incurred if the part were purchased outside*. The overhead problem centers on the fact that the *incremental overhead* costs vary from time to time, depending on the extent to which production facilities are utilized by existing products.

For example, assume that an automobile engine manufacturer currently buys its piston pins from a distant machine shop. For various reasons, the engine producer now decides that it wants to make the piston pins in its own shop. Investigation reveals that the machine shop is loaded to capacity with existing work and will remain in that condition throughout the foreseeable future. If the firm decides to make its own piston pins, it will have to either purchase additional machining equipment or free existing equipment by subcontracting to an outside supplier a part currently made in-house. In this situation, the incremental factory overhead cost figure should include the variable overhead caused by the production of piston

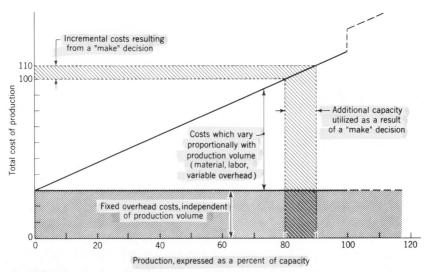

FIGURE 8-1
A representative case illustrating the incremental costs resulting from a "make" decision when operating at 80 percent of production capacity.

pins, *plus* the full portion of fixed overhead allocable to the piston pin operation.[4]

Now assume that the same engine manufacturer wants to make its own piston pins and that it has enough excess capacity to make the pins in its machine shop with existing equipment. Investigation shows that the excess capacity will exist for at least the next two or three years. What are its incremental overhead costs to make the pins in this situation? *Only* the variable overhead caused by production of the piston pins! In this case, fixed overhead represents sunk costs which continue to accumulate whether piston pins are produced or not. The total machine shop building continues to generate depreciation charges. Heat, light, and janitorial service are still furnished to the total machine shop area. Also, property taxes for the machine shop remain the same regardless of the number of machines productively employed. The firm incurs these same fixed costs regardless of the make-or-buy action it decides on. Such costs, under conditions of idle capacity, are *not* incremental costs and, for purposes of the make-or-buy decision, must be omitted from computation of the cost to make a new part.

The concept can also be observed from a slightly different point of view in the graphic representation of Figure 8-1. Note that a 12½ percent increase in

---

[4] In the event that piston pin production replaces production of another part, the piston pin operation should carry the same absolute amount of fixed overhead that was carried by the part replaced. In the case where new equipment is purchased to produce piston pins, the piston pin operation should be charged with the additional fixed overhead arising from acquisition of the new equipment.

production volume (an increase from 80 to 90 percent of capacity) can be achieved by a total cost increase of only 10 percent. This favorable situation results simply because the 12½ percent increase in production is accomplished by activating unused capacity. Fixed overhead costs are incurred irrespective of the decision to make piston pins by utilizing unused capacity.

Finally, consider a third common situation in which the same engine manufacturer wants to make its own piston pins. Investigation in this case reveals that enough excess capacity currently exists in the machine shop to permit production of the piston pins. However, management expects a gradual increase in business during the next several years, which will eliminate all excess capacity by the end of the second year. How should the make-or-buy decision be approached in this particular case?

As always, the starting point of the analysis is an estimate of the costs to make versus the costs to buy. For the first 1½ to 2 years, the cost to make piston pins will not include fixed overhead because excess capacity exists. Beyond two years, however, the cost to make must include fixed overhead; if piston pins are not made, increased production of some other part will, in the normal course of business, carry its full share of fixed overhead. One alternative is to consider the make-or-buy decision separately for each of the two time periods. While the analysis may indicate that it is profitable to make the pins in both cases, it will probably reveal that it is profitable to make the pins only for the first two years and to buy them beyond that date. In this case, several qualitative factors must be investigated to determine the practical feasibility of a split course of action. If the split course of action does not appear feasible, a second alternative is to compute a weighted average cost to make the pins during both time periods. The cost data can then be used in considering the total make-or-buy question.

In practice, an infinite number of situations exist between the two extremes of excess capacity and full capacity. Any attempt to categorize these situations and apply rules of thumb in analyzing them is arbitrary (and sometimes dangerous). There is no simple, absolutely accurate solution to any of these problems. Each situation must be analyzed in its own dynamic context.

In summary, an analyst should be guided by several basic ideas. First, *incremental costs* are virtually always the costs germane to the managerial decision-making process. Second, the determination of a realistic cost to make an item requires a realistic estimate of the future conditions of capacity. When capacity can be utilized by existing business or by alternative new projects, incremental overhead costs to make a new item must reflect total overhead costs. During any period when this condition does not exist, the incremental overhead to make consists only of variable overhead. When conditions of capacity normally oscillate frequently between partial load and full load, it is likely that the make-or-buy decision for a new project of substantial duration will turn largely on considerations other than comparative cost.

Precautions in Developing Costs If a firm decides to buy a part that it has made in the past, it must exercise particular care in interpreting the quotations it receives from potential suppliers. Some suppliers may prepare the quotation carelessly, with the mistaken idea that the user does not really intend to buy the part. Other suppliers may bid unrealistically low in an attempt to induce the user to discontinue making the part in favor of buying it. Once the user has discontinued its "make" operation, resumption of the operation in the future may be costly. Thus, the user may be at the mercy of the supplier in case the supplier later chooses to increase the price.[5] It is essential that the buyer carefully evaluate the reliability of all quotations in his or her attempt to determine a realistic estimate of the total cost to buy the part.

In estimating the cost to make a part, an analyst must ensure that the firm possesses adequate equipment and technical know-how to do the job. Moreover, in an industry where technological change occurs rapidly, a firm can find its equipment and know-how competitively outmoded in a few short years. Thus, the factor of obsolescence should also be given adequate consideration in determining the ultimate costs of equipment and personnel training.

The proper equipment to make an item may sometimes be easier to acquire than the properly skilled manpower. Large volume requirements, complex skill requirements, or unique geographic locations can precipitate shortages of adequately skilled manpower. In preparing cost-to-make estimates, the local manpower situation must be evaluated. Should it be necessary to import adequately skilled personnel, total labor costs can substantially exceed initial estimates.

In the case of a "make" decision, it is equally important to investigate the availability and price stability of required raw materials. Large users of particular materials generally find the availability and price structure of these materials much more favorable than do small unspecialized users. Wise analysts ensure that their estimates for raw material are realistic.

In estimating the cost to make a part for the first time, the analyst must also investigate several practical production matters. The first deals with the cost of unacceptable production work. What is the expected rate of rejected and spoiled parts? Equally important, what learning curve can the production department reasonably expect to apply? Answers to these questions may vary substantially, depending upon the complexity of the job and the type of workers and equipment available. The resulting influence on the make-buy cost comparison can be considerable, however, and realistic answers should be sought.

Finally, when a company decides to make a part, it assumes responsibility for all production problems stemming from the variability of the part's de-

---

[5]A long-term requirements contract may be used as a device to help forestall such price increases.

mand. Final cost estimates must therefore include any increased costs of production resulting from consequent production inefficiencies.

Control of Production or Quality

Consider now some of the factors other than costs that influence make-or-buy decisions. Two conditions weigh heavily in some firms' decisions to make a particular part—control of production and control of quality.

Production Requirements The need for close control of production operations is particularly acute in some firms. A company whose sales demand is subject to extreme short-run fluctuations finds that its production department must operate on unusually tight time schedules. This kind of company typically produces for stock those parts used in several different products. However, it produces to individual customer order the parts unique to a particular product or customer specification. Sales fluctuations for products using unique parts therefore influence the planning and scheduling of numerous assembly and subassembly operations, as well as single-part production operations. Efficient conduct of assembly operations thus depends on the firm's ability to obtain the unique unstocked parts on short notice.

Most suppliers serving a number of customers cannot normally tool up and fit an order for a unique part into existing schedules on a moment's notice. If a user cannot tolerate suppliers' lead time requirements, its only other major alternative is to control the part production operations itself. Thus, by making the item, the user acquires the needed control. It is possible to quickly revise job priorities, reassign operators and machines to specific jobs, and require overtime work as conditions demand.

Some firms also choose to make certain critical parts to assure continuity of supply of these parts to succeeding production operations. This type of vertical integration guards against production shutdowns caused by supplier labor problems, local transportation strikes, and miscellaneous supplier service problems. These are particularly important considerations when dealing with parts that feed an automated production operation whose downtime is tremendously expensive. If such action reduces the risk of a production stoppage, it may well justify the incurrence of extra materials costs.

Quality Requirements Unique quality requirements frequently represent a second condition requiring control of part production operations. Certain parts in technical products are occasionally quite difficult to manufacture. Compounding this difficulty, at times, is an unusually exacting quality specification the part must meet. In certain technological fields or in particular geographical areas, a user may find that the uniqueness of the task results in unsatisfactory performance by an outside supplier. Some companies find that their own firm is in a better position to do an acceptable production job than are external suppliers.

A user normally understands more completely than an outside supplier the operational intricacies connected with usage of the part. Therefore, if the using firm makes the part itself, there can be greater coordination between the assembly operation and the part production operation. Conducting both operations under one roof likewise eliminates many communications problems which can arise between a buyer and supplier whose operations are geographically separated. Finally, large users often possess technological resources superior to those of smaller suppliers. Such resources may be needed in solving *new* technical problems in production.

For example, one producer of hydraulic systems makes a practice of subcontracting production of some of the valves used in its systems. The production of one particular subcontracted valve involved difficult interior machining operations as well as tight quality requirements. Of the supplier's first four shipments, the systems manufacturer rejected 80 percent of the valves for failure to meet quality specifications. During the ensuing months, the systems manufacturer worked closely with the subcontractor in an attempt to solve the quality problem. With the passage of time, however, it became clear that the systems manufacturer was contributing considerably more to solution of the problem than was the supplier. Eventually, the systems firm decided to make the valve. Although production of the valve still remained a difficult task, the systems manufacturer was able to develop the techniques necessary to produce a valve of acceptable quality, with a greatly reduced reject percentage.

Design Secrecy Required

Although their number is small, a few firms make particular parts primarily because they want to keep secret certain aspects of the part's design or manufacture. The secrecy justification for making an item can be found in highly competitive industries where style and cost play unusually important roles. Also, a firm is more likely to make a key part for which patent protection does not provide effective protection against commercial emulation.

If design secrecy is really important, however, a firm may have nearly as much difficulty maintaining secrecy when it makes a part as it would when a supplier makes it. In either case, a large number of individuals must be taken into the firm's confidence, and once information leaks to a competitor, very little can be done about it. A firm can usually control security measures more easily and directly in its own plant, but it can never prevent an individual from becoming an informer if the person so chooses.

Unreliable Suppliers

A few firms decide to make specific parts because their experience has shown that the reliability record of available suppliers falls below the required level. The likelihood of encountering such a situation thirty years ago was infinitely greater than it is today. Competition in most industries today is so keen that grossly unreliable performers do not survive the competitive struggle. With one major exception, unreliable delivery or unpredictable service is confined largely to isolated cases in new, highly specialized lines of business where competition has not yet become established. Such businesses are usually characterized by low sales volumes, the requirement of highly specialized production equipment, or the unique possession of new technological capabilities.

The one major exception mentioned above is the case of the buyer who provides only an insignificant fraction of a specific supplier's total volume of business. Even the most reputable suppliers are forced at times to short-change very small accounts in order to give proper attention to their major accounts. Regardless of the reasonableness of the cause, however, consistently unreliable performance by a supplier is sufficient grounds for shifting suppliers or possibly reconsidering the original make-buy decision.

Suppliers' Specialized Knowledge and Research

A primary reason underlying most decisions to buy a part rather than make it is the user's desire to take advantage of the specialized abilities and research efforts of various vendors.

Lest the preceding discussion of "make" decisions distort the total procurement picture, bear in mind that the typical American manufacturing firm spends more than 50 percent of its sales dollar for purchases from external suppliers. Modern industry is highly specialized. No ordinary firm, regardless of size, can hope to possess adequate facilities and technical know-how to make a majority of its production part requirements efficiently. Large corporations spend millions of dollars on product and process research each year. The fruits of this research and the ensuing technical know-how are available to customers in the form of highly developed and refined parts and component products. The firm that considers forgoing these benefits in favor of making an item should, before making its final decision, assess carefully the long-range values that accrue from industrial specialization.

Small-Volume Requirements

When a firm uses only a small quantity of a particular item, it usually decides to buy the item. The typical firm strives to concentrate its production efforts in areas where it is most efficient and in areas it finds most profitable. The work of designing, tooling, planning, and setting up for the production of a new part is time-consuming and costly. These fixed costs are recovered more easily from long production runs than from short ones. More often than not, the small-volume user consequently searches for a potential supplier who specializes in production of the given part and can economically produce it in large quantities. Such specialty suppliers can sell to a large number of users in almost any desired quantity at relatively low prices.

Small-volume production of *unique, nonstandard* parts may likewise be unattractive to external suppliers. Every supplier is obligated to concentrate first on its high-volume, high-profit accounts. Thus, cases may develop in which a user is virtually *forced* to make a highly nonstandard part it uses in small quantities. Generally speaking, however, as the part tends toward a more common and finally a standard configuration, the tendency to buy increases proportionally.

Limited Facilities

Another reason for buying rather than making certain parts is the physical limitation imposed by the user's production facilities. A firm with limited facilities typically attempts to utilize them as fully as possible on its most profitable production work. It then depends on external suppliers for the balance of its requirements. Thus, during peak periods a firm may purchase a substantial portion of its total requirements because of loaded production facilities, and during slack periods, as internal production capacity opens up, its purchases may decrease markedly.

Work Force Stability

Closely related to the matter of facilities is the factor of work force stability. A fluctuating production level compels a firm to face the continual problem of contracting and expanding its work force to keep in step with production demands. Significant continuing fluctuation, moreover, adversely affects the type of workers such a firm is able to employ. The less stable an operation, the more difficult it becomes to retain an efficient work force.

At the time when a firm sizes the various segments of its production operation, many make-buy decisions are made. One factor which often bears heavily on the decision is the firm's desire to develop an interested, responsible group of workers with a high degree of company loyalty. Awareness that stable employment facilitates the attainment of this objective frequently prompts a firm to undersize its production facility by a slight margin. Its plan is to maintain as stable an internal production operation as possible and to buy requirements in excess of its capacity from external suppliers. This policy is most effective in firms whose products require a considerable amount of general-purpose equipment in the manufacturing operation. Equipment, as well as personnel, that can perform a variety of different jobs provides the internal flexibility required to consolidate or split work among various production areas as business fluctuates. This capability is necessary for the successful implementation of such a policy, because, as business increases, it is not feasible to place small orders for a large number of different parts with outside suppliers. It is much more profitable to farm out large orders for a small number of parts.

Firms that successfully solve their work force problems in this way frequently create problems in the purchasing area. External suppliers are, in effect, used as buffers to absorb the shocks of production fluctuations. This action transfers many of the problems associated with production fluctuations from the user to the supplier. The supplier's ability to absorb these production shocks is therefore an important consideration. In some instances it may be able to absorb them reasonably well; in others, it may not.[6] In all cases, however, the supplier prefers, as does the user, to maintain a stable production operation. Consequently, many suppliers are not interested in the user who buys only its peak requirements. The question naturally arises: Will a supplier ever be motivated to perform well for a buyer who uses the supplier only for surplus work? This question should be considered carefully before a "buy" decision of this type is made.

Multiple-Source Policy

Some firms occasionally make *and* buy the same nonstandard part. This policy is followed for the explicit purpose of having available a reliable and experienced second source of supply. Firms adopting a make-and-buy policy recognize that they may not always be able to meet their internal production schedules for certain parts. In case of an emergency, an experienced outside source is usually willing to increase its delivery of the part in question on a temporary basis until the situation is under control.

Managerial Control Considerations

Companies occasionally buy and make the same part for the purpose of developing managerial control data. Some firms use outside suppliers' cost and quality performance as a check on their own internal production efficiency. If internal costs for a particular part rise above a supplier's cost, the user knows that somewhere in its own production system some element of cost is probably out of line. An investigation frequently uncovers one or more problems, some of which often extend to other production areas. Consequent improvements may therefore exhibit a compounding effect as they reach into other operations where inefficiencies might otherwise have gone undetected.

---

[6] Two factors largely determine a supplier's ability to absorb fluctuating order requirements from a user. They are:

1 The similarity of the work involved in producing a particular user's requirement and in producing other customers' orders. The more similar the requirements are, the less is the expense of special planning and setup work for a particular user.

2 The extent to which other customers' orders offset the peaks and valleys in the supplier's production operation. The more stable the supplier's total production operation is, the less disturbing is the effect of an occasional fluctuating account.

Procurement and Inventory Considerations

A "buy" decision produces several significant benefits in the management of purchasing and inventory activities. For purchasing, such a decision typically means that it has fewer items to buy and fewer suppliers to deal with. Usually, though not always, when a component is made in-house a number of different materials or parts must be purchased outside to support the "make" operation. A corresponding buy decision usually involves only one or two suppliers and a relative reduction in the associated buying, paperwork, and follow-up activities. The same relative reduction in workload is passed on to the receiving, inspection, stores, and inventory management groups. Typically, inventory investment is also reduced.

One of the goals of most purchasing departments today is to achieve a reduction in the supplier base, simply to facilitate more effective purchasing and supplier management.

THE VOLATILE NATURE OF THE MAKE-OR-BUY SITUATION

Although make-or-buy investigations begin with a cost analysis, various qualitative factors frequently portend more far-reaching consequences than does the cost analysis. Therefore, a make-or-buy decision correctly approached considers the probable *composite effect* of all factors on the firm's total operation.

A thorough investigation is complicated considerably by the dynamics and uncertainties of business activity. Certain factors can hold quite different implications for a make-or-buy decision at different points in time and under different operating conditions. As pointed out, changing costs can turn a good decision into a bad one in a very short period of time. And future costs, complicated by numerous demand and capacity interrelationships, are influenced substantially by such variable factors as technological innovation and customer demand. The availability of expansion capital also influences make-or-buy decisions. An "easy money" policy, a liberal depreciation policy, or liberal government taxing policies tend to encourage "make" decisions. Contrary policies promote "buy" decisions. These federal policies fluctuate with economic and political conditions.

The tendency toward "make" decisions in order to stabilize production and work force fluctuation is usually greater in small firms than in large ones. In some small shops the loss of just a few orders results in the temporary layoff of a sizable percentage of the work force until additional orders can be obtained. Generally speaking, larger organizations do not have such severe problems because their fluctuations in production volume relative to total capacity are smaller. As large firms adopt compensation plans that move toward a guaranteed wage structure, however, they too will feel a similar pressure to favor "make" decisions.

Finally, the labor-relations climate within a firm can influence its make-or-buy decisions. A hostile union may seize the opportunity to irritate management as a result of the decision to buy an item previously made in-house. An amicable labor-management climate may evoke a very different union re-action.

To summarize, the point very briefly stated is this: Beware of rigid formu-las and rules of thumb that claim to produce easy make-or-buy decisions. The make-or-buy question is influenced by a multitude of diverse factors that are in a constant state of change. Under such conditions, few easy decisions turn out well in both the short and the long run. Moreover, the relevant fac-tors vary immensely from one firm to another. For these reasons, every com-pany should periodically evaluate the effectiveness of its past decisions to generate information helpful in guiding future courses of make-buy action.

ADMINISTRATION OF MAKE-OR-BUY ACTIVITIES

It is not difficult to find otherwise well-managed firms in which most make-or-buy decisions are inadvertently delegated to a clerk in inventory control or production control. It should now be apparent that this is a poor practice. In the first place, such a person normally does not have adequate information with which to make an intelligent decision from a companywide point of view. Second, even if adequate information were available, a typical clerical employee lacks the breadth of experience to evaluate fully the significance of the information and the resultant decision.

In most cases, make-or-buy decisions should be made, or at least reviewed, at a managerial level. The decision maker must be able to view such problems with a broad companywide perspective. Many progressive firms use the com-mittee approach to analyze make-or-buy alternatives. The committee is usually composed of department managers or high-level staff assistants. The impor-tant point to keep in mind is that all departments that can contribute to the de-cision, or that are affected by it, should have some voice in making it. The com-mittee approach accomplishes this directly by committee activity. In other cases, a formal mechanism must be established which facilitates, and indeed requires, the submission by all interested departments of relevant data and suggestions to the decision maker. Moreover, to ensure thoroughness and con-sistency, the system must detail the cost computation procedures to be used and assign cost investigations to specific operating groups.

In addition to providing an operational framework within which make-or-buy alternatives are investigated, a complete review system is necessary. The system should provide definite procedures for three important additional ac-tivities: (1) the entry of projects into the investigatory system, (2) mainte-nance of essential records, and (3) a periodic audit of important decisions.

Procedures should be established as part of a firm's product development program, compelling high-value parts in new products to enter the make-or-buy investigation process. In some cases, this investigation can be effectively integrated with preproduction value analysis/engineering investigations. Similarly, existing production parts should be subjected to a systematic review which searches for borderline make-or-buy items warranting full investigation.

Regardless of the source of entry, all make-or-buy investigations should be classified as "major" or "minor," based on the value of the part. In one firm all items involving expenditures under $25,000 are classed as minor. Subsequent investigations of minor items involve personnel from production, purchasing, quality control, and occasionally design engineering. Major items entail expenditures over $25,000, and additionally involve personnel from finance, marketing, and other production areas.

Certain summary records are essential to full utilization of the data developed in make-or-buy investigations. The investigation record should be designed to serve as a useful future reference. A brief discussion of all factors pertinent to the decision that was made should be included, as well as the primary reasons for the decision. Assumptions about future conditions should be stated. And an accurate summary of cost data should always be included. Records of this type provide the information required when a firm is forced to make quick decisions about subcontracting work under peak operating conditions, or about bringing work back into the shop when business slumps. Accurate records can mean the difference between a profitable decision based on *facts* and a hopeful decision based on intuition and hunches.

Finally, investigation records provide the basic data for postdecision audits.

CONCLUSION

If one takes a broad view of the American industrial scene over the past three decades, two characteristics stand out clearly: (1) As technology has advanced, most manufacturing firms have become much more specialized—in the words of researchers Peters and Waterman, they "stick to their knitting";[7] and (2) the cost of materials, expressed as a percent of total product cost, has continued to increase in most industries. These two factors lead to the inevitable conclusion that in the aggregate, American firms are buying more and making less. Planned or unplanned, the trend continues to develop. In a recent nationwide *Purchasing* magazine survey, 41 percent of the responding purchasing executives said that their firms have moved significantly to the buy side of the make-buy equation, as compared with just a few years ago.[8] The Ford Motor Company is a prime example.[9]

Yet, at the managerial level, many successful firms have not handled the make-or-buy issue in a well-organized, systematic manner. Instead, many have elected to deal with specific cases on an ad hoc basis as they arose. This

---

[7] T. J. Peters and R. H. Waterman, *In Search of Excellence*, Harper & Row, Publishers, New York, 1982, pp. 292–305.

[8] Somerby Dowst, "The Winning Edge," *Purchasing*, Mar. 12, 1987, pp. 52–60.

[9] D. D. Buss, "Ford Is Riding High with Smart Execution and Slashed Capacity," *Wall Street Journal*, Oct. 7, 1986, p. 1.

situation is understandable, yet ironic. In earlier years when the cost-price squeeze was less severe for many firms, poor decisions in this area did not affect earnings noticeably. Yet, in the aggregate, make-or-buy decisions do significantly affect a firm's ability to utilize its productive resources in an optimal manner.

Past practices are now changing. Three forces will continue to stimulate this change:

- *Pressures on profit margins* are severe, and will continue to increase—productive resources must be utilized more efficiently.
- *Firms continue to become more highly specialized* in products and production technology, producing greater cost differentials between making and buying for many users.
- *Computer modeling capability* is becoming commonplace; make-or-buy evaluation and control systems can be developed and handled quasi-automatically with this capability.

Refined management practice in this area is needed and clearly is within the grasp of most firms. Just as materials management organizations, MRP systems, and JIT systems have developed over the past several decades, so will implementation systems for make-or-buy analysis. Interaction of the three factors noted above will produce refined make-or-buy operating systems in many firms in future years.[10]

FOR DISCUSSION

8-1 Discuss briefly the basic objective of make-or-buy decisions.

8-2 Do all make-or-buy investigations require the same type of analysis? Explain.

8-3 How many types of make-or-buy alternatives can a firm have? Explain.

8-4 Develop in detail a procedure to be followed in conducting a make-or-buy cost analysis. (Include explanations necessary for the reader's full understanding of the procedure.)

8-5 List and briefly discuss the major difficulties that may be encountered in making a valid make-or-buy cost analysis.

8-6 Why may fixed overhead expenses in a specific plant be an incremental cost in the case of one make-or-buy investigation and not in the case of a similar investigation made at a later date in the same plant? Explain.

---

[10] Readers interested in a detailed examination of the make-or-buy issue should review two studies: (1) The classical study conducted some years ago by J. W. Culliton, *Make or Buy?* Research Study 27, Graduate School of Business Administration, Harvard University, Boston, 1942, 4th reprint, 1956. (2) The futuristic applications study, utilizing integer programming and dealing with the multiple product make-or-buy decision in a capacity constrained environment by F. C. Weston, Jr., "The Multiple Product Make-or-Buy Decision," *Journal of Purchasing and Materials Management*, Winter 1981, pp. 17–22.

8-7 Refer to Figure 8-1. How do you explain the fact that a 12½ percent increase in production produces only a 10 percent increase in production cost?

8-8 Are make-or-buy decisions influenced by the learning curve concept? Explain.

8-9 It has been said that make-or-buy decisions are much more critical in companies whose production operations are highly automated than in others. What is your reaction to this statement? Explain.

8-10 Some business executives strongly advocate vertical integration of production operations because they can eliminate payment of a profit to various middlemen. What is your reaction to this argument?

8-11 List and briefly discuss the major factors which tend to influence make-or-buy decisions in the direction of buying.

8-12 List and briefly discuss the major factors which tend to influence make-or-buy decisions in the direction of making.

8-13 Some companies claim that they can transfer much of the shock of sales fluctuations normally felt in the production operations to their suppliers. How can this be done? What problems frequently result when a firm attempts to do this?

8-14 The text states that most make-or-buy decisions are volatile in nature. What is meant by this statement? Explain.

8-15 To whom should a company assign the responsibility for make-or-buy decisions? Explain.

8-16 Discuss the acceptance and application of make-or-buy analysis in U.S. industry.

8-17 Discuss the make-or-buy trend that has developed in U.S. industry during the past several decades.

CASES FOR CHAPTER 8

Maine-Barnes, Ltd., page 755
Donley Brothers, page 730
The Muenster Pump Company, page 765
Three Vendors and a Tub (in the Instructor's Manual)

THREE

FUNDAMENTALS OF PURCHASING

SOURCES OF SUPPLY: PART I

To produce the best products worldwide you need more than ideas, designs and specifications. You need to choose the very best suppliers.... [1]

KEY CONCEPTS

- Development and maintenance of the supplier base
    - Sources of supplier information
    - Developing suppliers
    - Supplier goodwill
    - Partnerships/Collaborative purchasing
    - Supplier management
- Strategic and tactical issues in supplier selection
    - Early supplier involvement
    - Number of suppliers; Share of supplier's business
    - Improving purchasing efficiency
    - Buying locally/Nationally/Internationally
    - Manufacturer or distributor
    - Ethical considerations
    - Dishonest suppliers
    - Reciprocity

---

[1] *Xerox Commodity Teams*, October 1986, p. 3.

Selection and management of the right supplier is the key to obtaining the desired level of quality, on time, and at the right price; the necessary level of technical support; and the desired level of service. Buyers must take six important supplier-oriented actions in order to satisfy this responsibility. They must:

- Develop and maintain a viable supplier base
- Address the appropriate strategic and tactical issues
- Ensure that potential suppliers are carefully evaluated and that they have the potential to be satisfactory supply partners
- Decide whether to use competitive bidding or negotiation as the basis of source selection
- Select the appropriate source—or be the team leader responsible for this task
- Manage the selected supplier to ensure timely delivery of the required quality at the right price

The first two of these responsibilities are the subject of this chapter. The third, fourth, and fifth responsibilities are the subject of Chapter 10. Supplier management is addressed in Chapter 18.

DEVELOPMENT AND MAINTENANCE OF THE SUPPLIER BASE

Although some buyers rely on memory and experience for knowledge of sources of supply, competent buyers more correctly rely on the department's own records, published material, and personal contacts. Sources of information concerning suppliers are plentiful. The following information sources should prove helpful to a buyer in establishing a list of potential suppliers.

Sources of Supplier Information

Supplier Purchasing Information File Purchasing departments should keep supplier information files on past and present suppliers which include the name of each supplier, a list of materials available from each supplier, the supplier's delivery history, the supplier's quality record, the supplier's overall desirability, and general information concerning the supplier's plant and management. In addition to a departmental file, buyers usually maintain a personal supplier file for their own use. Supplier information files are important because many purchasing operations are repetitive; hence, it would be poor management indeed if buyers spent time repeatedly recapturing information which was once available to them but had been needlessly lost.

Supplier Catalogs Because catalogs are a commonly used source of supplier information, many purchasing departments maintain a catalog library. Here users examine the catalogs to locate the materials they need. The firm's buyers also use catalogs to determine potential sources of supply and, on occasion, to estimate prices.

Large firms frequently employ a full-time librarian for indexing and keeping their catalogs up-to-date. Without an indexing system, using manufacturers' and jobbers' catalogs can be excessively time-consuming. In addition to catalogs, purchasing libraries traditionally include a commodity file, a supplier name file, appropriate trade publications, and purchasing textbooks. A few libraries now have fully indexed microfilm catalogs containing information on many suppliers—primarily those in the electronics and aerospace industries.

Trade Registers and Directories   *Thomas' Register of American Manufacturers* is typical of several widely known trade registers and directories. These registers contain information on the addresses, number of branches, and affiliations of all leading manufacturers. Financial standings of firms are also frequently given. The registers are indexed by commodity, manufacturer, and trade name or trademark description of the item. Kompass Publications in Europe provides similar information for European firms.[2]

Trade Journals   Trade journals are another excellent source for obtaining information about possible suppliers. Advertisements in trade journals are often a buyer's first contact with potential suppliers and their products. Among the magazines in the purchasing field, *Purchasing* and *Purchasing World* are perhaps the best known and most widely read trade journals. Both contain purchasing, general management, and economic information that is valuable to all buyers and all purchasing managers. Specialized trade journals are available for more specific information about specific industries. For example, a buyer in the aircraft industry would routinely read *Aviation Week;* a buyer in the steel industry would routinely read *Iron Age.*

The Yellow Pages   Another commonly known directory is the classified yellow pages section of telephone directories. This source of information is frequently of limited value to industrial buyers because local telephone books list only local companies. However, buyers can readily obtain telephone books for all major cities from the telephone company. The size and capability of companies are also difficult to determine, as management and financial data are normally not included in the advertisements. The yellow pages do, however, have the virtue of being well indexed. Also, they can serve as a useful starting point if other sources have proved fruitless or if local sources are desired.

Filing of Mailing Pieces   Many mail advertisements are worth saving. These should be given a file number, dated, and indexed by the name and number of each publication. When buyers seek a new source, they can then refer to the index and review the appropriate brochures and booklets.

---

[2] Kompass Publications, Ltd., Windson Court, East Grimstead House, East Grimstead, Sussex, RH19-IXD, England.

Some purchasing departments ask prospective suppliers to complete a simple form giving basic information about themselves and their products. This information, which includes company name, address, officers, local representatives, and principal products, is kept in a set of loose-leaf notebooks or in a computer file. By referring to this standardized data, a buyer can obtain immediate, current information about potential new sources.

Sales Personnel   Sales personnel are excellent sources for information about suppliers and materials. Not only are they usually well informed about the capabilities and features of their own products, but they are also familiar with similar and competitive products as well. By the very nature of their specialized knowledge, sales people can often suggest new applications for their products which will eliminate the search for new suppliers. From their contacts with many companies, salesmen and saleswomen learn much about many products and services, and all this information is available to the alert, receptive buyer. This is a key reason why sales personnel should always be treated courteously and given ample time to make their sales presentations. To deny them this opportunity is to risk the loss of valuable information, including information concerning new and reliable sources of supply.

Trade Exhibits   Regional and national trade shows are still another way by which buyers learn about possible sources of supply. The use of exhibits as a means of sales presentations is increasing. Exhibits provide an excellent opportunity for buyers to see various new products and modifications of old products. They also offer buyers an opportunity to compare concurrently similar products of different manufacturers. Regional trade exhibits are sponsored periodically by many manufacturers, distributors, and trade organizations. For example, a large distributor of scientific apparatus and glassware holds annual trade exhibits in major cities throughout the country; electronics distributors hold similar exhibits. Invitations to these exhibits are sent to all interested purchasing and technical personnel in the area. Although buyers must often find time to visit trade exhibits after working hours, doing so is usually worthwhile. Exhibits offer a buyer an excellent opportunity to expand his or her knowledge of new products, new potential suppliers, and new ideas.

Company Personnel   Personnel from other departments in a buyer's firm can often provide purchasing with helpful information about prospective suppliers. Through their associations in professional organizations, civic associations, and social groups, these employees often learn about outstanding suppliers. Scientific, technical, and research personnel who use sophisticated materials or services always have many valuable suggestions to make regarding possible sources of supply. From their attendance at conventions and trade exhibits, and from their discussions with associates, these personnel are particularly well informed regarding new products, new methods, and new manufacturers.

Other Purchasing Departments Purchasing departments in other firms can be helpful sources of information regarding suppliers. Information exchanged among purchasing departments can be mutually beneficial for all participating companies; therefore, this source of information should be actively developed.

Local purchasing management associations, such as the local affiliates of the National Association of Purchasing Management, the Purchasing Management Association of Canada, the National Institute of Government Purchasing, and the National Association of Educational Buyers, publish a list of their members. The lists are indexed in two ways: alphabetically by name of each member and alphabetically by name of the member's company. One of the basic objectives of a purchasing association is that its members help each other in every possible way. Accordingly, members usually will do everything possible to help fellow members locate and evaluate new sources of supply. However, they will not, and they should not, exchange pricing information. That would be both unethical and illegal.

International Sources Because a high percentage of buyers now utilize international suppliers, information concerning foreign markets and companies is available from an increasing number of sources. Some of them are:

- The United States Department of Commerce, 1615 H Street, N.W., Washington, D.C., 20233 (has many publications of foreign agents, distributors, and buyers).
- Foreign commercial attachés, who are located in foreign embassies and consulates throughout the United States.
- American commercial attachés, who are located in U.S. embassies and consulates abroad.
- *Trade Directories of the World,* Croner Publications, Inc., 21105 Jamaica Ave., Queens Village, N.Y., 11428.
- The New York Chamber of Commerce and Industry, 99 Church Street, New York, N.Y., 10007.
- *Handbook of International Purchasing,* by Paul H. Combs, Cahners Books, 88 Franklin Street, Boston, Mass., 02110.
- The International Federation of Purchasing and Materials Management, York House, Westminister Bridge Road, London SE1 7UT, England.
- The United States Counsel of the International Chamber of Commerce, 1212 Avenue of Americas, New York, N.Y., 10036 (publishes many pamphlets of interest to buyers).
- The international departments of all large banks have considerable material on foreign buying.

Developing Suppliers

An adequate supplier base is essential to the economic well-being of a firm. Such a base is as much a resource as are research scientists or skilled production personnel. The supplier base is especially critical in high-technology industries and in industries where scarcity of materials is a potential occurrence.

Buyers are the first point of contact and are responsible for dealing with potential new suppliers. Obviously, the buyer should obtain information on the supplier's capability, resources, and product lines.

If the supplier has a new product or technology of possible interest, the buyer should arrange for conferences between the supplier and the firm's appropriate technical personnel. A buyer's responsibility is to provide advice and even coaching to ensure the success of such technical presentations. If possible, advance data and a sample of the product should be obtained from the supplier and distributed to interested company personnel. This allows the preparation of questions and helps to overcome the native tendency to resist change and new ideas.

After the presentation, the buyer becomes a communications conduit between the supplier and company personnel. Any complaints from suppliers who feel that they have been treated unfairly should be investigated—a buyer should do everything possible to generate supplier goodwill.

It is essential that all purchasing personnel recognize the importance of being available to suppliers. If buyers are not available, suppliers frequently will circumvent purchasing and go directly to the user. Some may have received advance information and subsequently may be successful in having the user specify their products as a sole-source requirement for the job. The results frequently are higher prices and a failure to consider competing technology.

The Importance of Supplier Goodwill

Business has long recognized that customer goodwill is a valuable asset. In fact, customer goodwill has legal recognition, and it is carried as an asset on many company balance sheets. Business is just beginning to realize that supplier goodwill is also an important company asset. A company develops customer goodwill by selling acceptable products at a fair price, supported by good service with the customers' interests in mind. The buying firm develops supplier goodwill by being open, impartial, and scrupulously fair in all its dealings with suppliers.

A company's purchasing department should motivate its suppliers to participate in a mutually profitable buyer-seller relationship. To create such motivation fully, it is essential that both buyer and seller completely understand the mutual advantage of a continuing relationship. Such a relationship permits the seller to learn the intricacies of the buyer's operations, and vice versa. The seller learns about the buyer's business problems—manufacturing, inventory, receiving, and overall operational problems. As the relationship develops, the supplier typically can reduce its direct selling effort; consequently, it can afford to direct additional effort to the study of mutual problems that may reduce prices. The end result of good supplier relations is a meshing of the operations of both companies. The seller's production and distribution facilities in reality become an extension of the buyer's production line.

Regardless of the managerial skills of a buyer, periodically difficulties will be encountered from which only a friendly supplier can extricate the buyer. Even the best sales and usage forecasts are vulnerable to error. Emergencies of many types continually arise in business. For example, unexpected increases in sales cause materials shortages. Unforeseeable declines in sales and plant breakdowns cause materials excesses. As a result of unexpected shortages and excesses, some orders have to be canceled, others spread out, and still others increased or accelerated. Purchasing departments must have suppliers motivated by goodwill to cooperate with them in such emergencies; otherwise, additional costs will be incurred needlessly.

Supplier relations impinge directly on a company's public relations objectives. Many individuals and organizations form their image of a company almost entirely from their contact with its purchasing department. It is important that a company's image be a favorable one because the nature of its image can influence both its profit and its future. A purchasing department, therefore, should strive to maintain good relations with all who call at its offices either in person or by telephone. Sales people are usually realistic. They realize that not every sales representative can get every order. Nonetheless, when a salesperson fails to get an order, particularly one on which he or she has worked unusually hard, disappointment is the natural result. The salesperson will, however, bear no ill will toward a purchasing department that has developed a reputation for fairness to all suppliers. Such a reputation is a valuable asset. Although a reputation for fairness does not appear on the balance sheet, it has real capital value—a value which is particularly enhanced during periods of short supply.

A salesperson's time is money; to waste it is to reduce his or her income. Therefore, when a salesperson arrives for an appointment, he or she should not be kept waiting longer than a few minutes. If it is apparent that a buyer cannot quickly see a caller who arrives without an appointment, the buyer should notify the visitor of this fact immediately. If possible, as a matter of common courtesy, the buyer should notify the salesperson in person.

Partnerships

A good supplier is an invaluable resource to the organization requiring its product or service. Such suppliers make a direct contribution to a firm's success. They can assist their customers with product development, value analysis, and timely delivery of the desired level of quality. Good buyer-seller relations facilitate the buyer's efforts to gain superior performance, extra service, cooperation on cost reduction programs, and a willingness to share in new processes and procedures. Two authorities present several arguments for what they call "voluntary collaboration,"[3] or partnerships:

- Every time a new set of partners comes together, a learning process is required. The potential for communication difficulties is much greater during early transactions than during later ones.
- Changing market conditions and changing technology that affect the buying process require adaptation on the part of buyers and sellers. Such adaptation can be much less painful under conditions of an ongoing and mutually beneficial relationship where the parties have teamed to adapt together.
- The likelihood of quality problems and late deliveries is greatly reduced in a continuing relationship.
- Open relationships can help to cushion bad times. Customers and suppliers who value each other, based on long-term relations and respect, are more likely to come to each other's aid during times of adversity.
- Suppliers learn from the behavior of an aggressive, price-optimizing purchaser. Such buyers will find it more difficult to obtain delivery of the required goods on time than will buyers who have developed continuing relations with their suppliers.
- Opportunistic buyers are more subject to shocks resulting from capacity or supply problems encountered by the supplier than are buyers who maintain continuing relations with their suppliers.
- Opportunistic buyers should expect less effective performance from suppliers who believe that they have little to lose in the way of follow-on business.

Long-term agreements encourage suppliers to invest research and development (R&D) dollars in order to propose technologically current, cost-effective, and high-quality solutions to the buying firm's needs. Properly priced life-of-product agreements encourage suppliers to invest in the equipment, training, and appropriate management systems required to be an efficient, low-cost producer. The buyer benefits from such an agreement in many ways: low "all-in-cost" (total cost), a dependable source of supply, and a partner familiar with his or her needs.

Such partnerships are a major departure from the more traditional quasi-adversarial relationships with suppliers. The buying firm must be open about its true needs (e.g., technology, quantities, and schedules). The buyer must agree to protect the supplier partner from sudden changes which might leave the supplier with unusable raw materials or finished goods. Trust must be developed and possible reform action enhanced. And, as will be seen in Chapter 18, a different set of supplier management skills must be developed and applied.

[3] David H. Farmer and Keith MacMillan, "Voluntary Collaboration vs. 'Disloyalty' to Suppliers," *Journal of Purchasing and Materials Management*, Winter 1976, pp. 3–8.

Another group of researchers recently has advanced three significant cost-based arguments against the traditional short-term competitive-based approach to source selection:[4]

- Significant cost reductions in manufacturing operations typically are achieved through the development and implementation of methods improvements and technological innovations. Such accomplishments generally require significant research and development expenditures and/or capital investment. Clearly, an uncertain business environment and the potential loss of business are negative factors in the management analysis of these types of opportunities. Suppliers tend to view such a situation as too risky, and perhaps too costly, and will be reluctant to make these types of long-term commitments without some assurance of obtaining an adequate return on investment. Consequently, major opportunities for cost reduction through R&D and capital investment typically are severely limited.
- The use of multiple-sourcing and competitive-bidding strategies requires that a buyer provide potential suppliers with fully developed and precisely described product specifications. In order to ensure uniformity of product quality, the buyer must insist that suppliers conform strictly to the specifications. Consequently, suppliers are not likely to take the initiative in considering modifications that may improve product quality or reduce production costs, since their commitment is tied only to the current contract. In essence, possible productivity improvement through value analysis/engineering is severely limited.
- Furthermore, by frequently changing suppliers, a buyer deprives his or her current supplier of the chance to reduce its production cost through the extended learning curve effect that accompanies many production activities. With accumulated experiences from continuing production, a supplier obviously would be in a better position to achieve certain improvements that could well result in reduced costs.

The Ford Motor Company is a leading advocate of supplier partnerships. Ford has found that its supplier partners invest in better tools and equipment, better methods, and far more training than under previous short-term adversarial relationships. As a result, quality, cost reductions, and flexibility (responsiveness) have all increased drastically.

Supplier partnerships do not just happen. Planning and the expenditure of effort on the part of both parties are required. Intel Corporation likens a supplier partnership to a marriage. The buying company must avoid marriage (partnership) without courtship. Intel stresses "formal supplier partner-

---

[4] Chan K. Hahn, Kyoo H. Kim, and Jong S. Kim, "Cost of Competition: Implications for Purchasing Strategy," *Journal of Purchasing and Materials Management*, Fall 1986, p. 6.

ships which feature written co-objectives and regular meetings between senior executives of Intel and its suppliers."[5]

Supplier Management

The challenging issue of managing suppliers is dealt with in detail in Chapter 18. At this point, however, it is essential to recognize that the buyer has many responsibilities associated with management of his or her suppliers. Satisfying these responsibilities should ensure that suppliers perform as required or that appropriate corrective action is taken to upgrade or eliminate them from the firm's supplier base.

In addition, purchasing must, on a periodic basis, analyze its suppliers' abilities to meet the firm's long-term needs. Areas that deserve particular attention include the supplier's general growth plans, future design capability in relevant areas, the role of purchasing or materials management in the supplier's strategic planning, potential for future production capacity, and financial ability to support such growth.

If present suppliers appear to be unlikely to be able to meet future requirements, the firm has three options: (1) it may assist the appropriate supplier(s) with financing and technological assistance, (2) it may develop new sources having the desired growth potential, or (3) it may have to develop the required capability internally.

STRATEGIC AND TACTICAL ISSUES IN SUPPLIER SELECTION

A buyer must consider many factors in selecting sources of supply. This section of the chapter investigates two broad areas of concern: characteristics of the supplying markets and acceptable ethical practices in these markets. These are the areas most buyers consider before getting down to the more specific factors of supplier selection.

Early Supplier Involvement (ESI)

A 1984 study indicated that when suppliers are involved early in the buyer's design process, they can apply their expertise in the following nine areas:[6]

- Material specifications
- Tolerances
- Standardization
- Order sizes
- Process changes in supplier's manufacturing

---

[5] Somerby Dowst, "The Right Suppliers Have the Right Stuff," *Purchasing*, Jan. 30, 1986, p. 95.

[6] Somerby Dowst, "Better-forged Links Bring in Better Designs," *Purchasing*, Sept. 6, 1984, pp. 67–75.

- Packaging
- Inventory
- Transportation
- Assembly changes in buyer's plants

Early supplier involvement is an accepted way of life at many progressive firms. "Not only is ESI desirable, it's absolutely necessary for establishing the high level of trust demanded by long-range projects."[7]

The *Purchasing* article advances four reasons cited by purchasing executives for utilizing ESI:

- Get supplier inputs before the design is frozen.
- Capitalize on the latest technology.
- Design cycles are getting shorter.
- Let the supplier know that it is part of the team.

ESI normally, but not always, results in the selection of a single source of supply. At most progressive companies, this selection process is the result of intensive competition between two or three carefully prequalified potential suppliers. The company selected becomes the single source of supply for the life of the item using its material.

Number of Suppliers

Should one, two, or more suppliers be used? In addition to the reasons discussed in the prior sections on partnering and ESI, the major argument for placing all of a firm's business with one supplier is that in times of shortage, this supplier will give priority to the needs of a special customer. Additionally, single sources may be justified when:

1 Better pricing results from a much higher volume
2 Quality considerations dictate[8]
3 The buyer obtains more influence—clout—with the supplier
4 Lower costs are incurred to source, process, expedite, and inspect
5 The quality, control, and coordination required with just-in-time manufacturing require a single source
6 The quantities to be purchased are small
7 The supplier holds critical patents
8 Significantly lower freight costs result

---

[7] James Dairs, Manager of Transportation Programs at G.E.'s Plastics Group, Pittsfield, Mass., quoted in "The Winning Edge" by Somerby Dowst, *Purchasing,* Mar. 12, 1987, p. 57.

[8] Dr. Edwards Deming, dean of America's quality gurus, has long advocated that buyers should strive to have one good source of supply in an effort to upgrade the quality of their products. Deming recommends that we "end the practice of awarding business on the basis of the price tag. Instead, depend on meaningful measures of quality, along with price. Move toward a single supplier for any one item, on a long-term relationship of loyalty and trust." *The Deming Guide to Quality and Competitive Position* by Howard S. Gitlow and Shelly J. Gitlow, Prentice-Hall, Inc., Englewood Cliffs, N.J., 1987, p. 51.

9 Special tooling is required, and the use of more than one supplier is impractical

10 A supplier agrees to carry the buyer's inventory (stockless purchasing)

On the other hand, if buyers use two or three suppliers, the purchasing firm may have a better chance of being protected in times of shortages, strikes, and so on, by having alternate sources of supply. Large companies buy in such volume that they usually can receive excellent pricing and service from two or more suppliers. For example, Sears, Roebuck and Company has, with full satisfaction, sometimes used as many as three manufacturers for its Kenmore refrigerator.

Certainly, if a single supplier's plant is closed because of a strike, a fire, or any other reason, its customers will be caught without material. When a General Motors transmission plant burned to the ground, for example, production was halted on three of its five lines of cars that utilized this transmission. Months passed before another division of General Motors was able to supply the needed transmissions.

Similarly, during a glass strike, all automobile companies that were using glass from a single source were forced to discontinue the use of tinted glass in their automobiles. One major corporation was forced to close its entire assembly line for lack of glass, tinted or clear. An independent automobile manufacturer, however, had been consistently buying some of its glass from a Canadian source as well as from its traditional U.S. source. When the strike occurred at its traditional source, the independent manufacturer merely ordered larger quantities of glass from its Canadian supplier. Although the Canadian source could not supply tinted glass, it could supply enough clear glass to keep production lines operating. Thus, at no time was this company forced to close down its assembly line. The airframe industry, on the other hand, has found that when high tooling costs are necessary, it simply is not feasible to make use of more than one supplier. However, if high tooling costs are not involved, many buyers prefer at least two suppliers for high-volume items.

When a buyer becomes dependent on a single-source supplier, there is a real danger that this source may take advantage of the buyer in future pricing decisions as volume requirements change. A single source may also become complacent. Such complacency can result in a less than satisfactory level of service, quality problems, and a failure to maintain its technological accuracy. The buyer's response to these dangers should be to proactively manage the supplier relationship, as discussed in Chapter 18.

Determining the number of suppliers to use for standard commercial items is always difficult. One practical solution used by many buyers is to utilize two suppliers for a material category that has an annual dollar volume of, for example, $250,000 or more. Two contracts could be placed, using a 70 percent/30 percent split. Such a distribution gives the supplier with the larger part of the business the required profit and incentive to perform any extra services the buyer may need, such as warehousing, special deliveries, and inventory and usage analysis. At the same time, the small supplier is stimulated to want more business; hence, it is competitively motivated to keep nipping at the heels of the larger supplier. Active competition thus stimulates both suppliers to vigorous performance. If the supplier with the larger portion of the business does not perform to the buyer's expectations, the distribution can be adjusted to give more business to the company with the smaller share.

Share of Supplier's Business

Many highly regarded firms try not to be more than 15 to 25 percent of any one supplier's business. They reason that if their purchases represent too large a share of the supplier's business and they discontinue a product or purchase an item from another supplier, they could put the initial supplier in a very difficult financial situation.

Improving Purchasing Efficiency

An innovative buyer may deliberately *develop a new supply source*, not because he or she needs it, but because doing so will improve the firm's purchasing efficiency. If necessary, the buyer may even provide the prospective new supplier with the financial, technical, and managerial help that is needed to enable the new source to achieve efficient production. Three unremitting forces spur this type of purchasing action: (1) rapidly changing technology, which continuously creates a need for new specialty suppliers; (2) expanding international trade, which brings large multinational companies to the doorstep of virtually every country in the world; and (3) an ever-increasing scarcity of raw materials.

Technology is changing so fast that 40 percent of the products which are sold in the United States today did not exist ten years ago. This rapid change, as far as a buyer's specific requirements are concerned, inevitably results in sources of supply getting out of balance. One alternative for correcting this imbalance is for buyers to develop new sources of supply.

International competition places great pressure on the quality and the price of industrial and retail goods produced by domestic firms. This pressure, in turn, makes it essential that professional buyers constantly be on the lookout for producers of high-value materials.

For years, to assure continuity of supply, manufacturers have integrated vertically, sometimes by acquiring their suppliers.[9] Many other companies similarly control some of their suppliers. Hence, supplier development is not a new concept. What is new is the increasing importance and urgency of obtaining reliable sources of supply. The world's population explosion, its

---

[9] For further insight into the issue of vertical integration, see "Reopening the Vertical Integration Case," by D. N. Burt and M. F. Doyle, *Harvard Business Review*, March-April 1989, pp. 190-191.

shrinking resources, and the formation of cartels (such as the OPEC bloc) have all combined to intensify the necessity of new source development.

Buying Locally

Sometimes community relations require greater use of local sources than could be justified solely by economic factors. One large hospital in a city of approximately 700,000 people, for example, has found that it must purchase at least half its materials requirements within the community; otherwise, local business people will not support the fund-raising campaigns needed by the hospital to obtain part of its required operating budget.

Local buying sometimes can be justified solely on an economic basis. A local supplier often can furnish smaller quantities of materials at lower prices than could be obtained from distant sources. Local suppliers also can maintain and finance a well-balanced inventory of materials for continuing local users. Working with local sources of supply and encouraging them to be capable suppliers is a part of progressive purchasing.

Two basic considerations are involved when deciding to buy locally or nationally. First, large dollar purchases should be placed at sources as close to the manufacturer as possible to obtain optimum prices and discounts. Second, small and medium dollar purchases should be placed with local sources when price differentials are small or when such action is necessary to keep materials physically available in the immediate area.

Most buyers prefer to patronize local sources whenever such action is prudent. A Stanford University research study found that approximately three-fourths of 152 buyers surveyed indicated a preference to buy from local sources whenever possible. Many of them were willing to pay slightly higher prices to gain the advantage of better service and immediate availability of materials offered by some local suppliers.

Local suppliers often can be made more effective if buyers from several firms coordinate their requirements. For example, a large number of oil companies actively drill for oil and gas in the area around Bakersfield, California. Because it is costly to shut down a producing well, historically each drilling company carried its own inventory of expensive valves, pumps, and similarly critical production components. A few years ago, buyers from each oil company involved met to discuss the possibilities of eliminating this costly, duplicate expense. They concluded that if the local suppliers would carry reasonable levels of the expensive items of inventory now carried by each oil company, and if the suppliers would guarantee around-the-clock delivery of these items in case of emergency, everyone would benefit economically. The suppliers were willing to render this kind of service for a reasonable profit. Now, instead of each oil company carrying, for example, a $25,000 valve which it may never use, the selected supplier carries one of these valves which is available to all companies. The price for the valve is slightly higher than when it was carried in the storeroom of each company. However, savings from lower valve inventories and from less valve obsolescence have reduced total costs for all companies substantially from their former level. Thus, this arrangement results in worthwhile gains for both the oil companies and the local suppliers.

Just-in-time manufacturing requires dependable sources of defect-free materials which arrive within a very tight time frame. Suppliers to JIT customers are meeting their requirements in three ways: (1) They are locating close to their customers[10]; (2) the suppliers are maintaining inventories of the material at nearby warehouses, or even on the customer's site under consignment; and (3) they are taking aggressive action to control the transportation of their materials to their customers.

In summary, local buying has the following advantages:

1 Closer cooperation between buyer and seller is possible because of close geographical proximity.
2 Delivery dates are more certain since transportation is only a minor factor in delivery. (Certainty of delivery is a prerequisite for just-in-time manufacturing.)
3 Lower prices can result from consolidated transportation and insurance charges. A local supplier, in effect, brings in many local buyers' orders in the same shipment.
4 Shorter lead times frequently can permit reductions or the elimination of inventory. In effect, the seller produces just-in-time or carries the buyer's inventory.
5 Rush orders are likely to be filled faster.
6 Disputes usually are more easily resolved.
7 Implied social responsibilities to the community are fulfilled.

Buying Nationally

National buying has the following advantages:

1 National sources, as a result of the economies of scale, can in some situations be more efficient than local suppliers and offer higher quality or better service at a lower price.
2 National companies often can provide superior technical assistance.
3 Large national companies have greater production capacity and therefore greater production flexibility to handle fluctuating demands.
4 Shortages are less likely with national companies because of their broader markets.

Buyers should give careful consideration to both the advantages and disadvantages of buying locally and buying nationally. In those situations

---

[10] For example, Chrysler builds additional buildings on-site and leases them to its suppliers. Robert M. Faletra, "How Chrysler Buyers Make Quality a Standard Feature," *Electronics Purchasing*, vol. 101, July 10, 1986, p. 62A15.

where economic and technical considerations justify the selection of local sources, it is the policy of most companies to buy locally. If this is not the case, national suppliers should be used.

Buying Internationally

This important buying consideration is discussed in detail in Chapter 11. It is mentioned here only to note that it is an important factor in supplier selection.

Manufacturer or Distributor?

In deciding whether to buy from a manufacturer or distributor, a buyer's considerations should focus largely on the distributor's capabilities and services, not on its location. In the steel industry, for example, distributors pay the same prices for steel as other buyers. Distributors, however, buy in carload lots and sell in smaller quantities to users whose operations do not justify carload lot purchases. The distributors realize a profit because large lots sell at lower unit prices than small lots. If buyers wish to purchase steel directly from the mill and bypass the distributor, they are perfectly free to do so; however, when they do, they usually forgo certain special services that a competent distributor is equipped to offer. Distributors, for example, have cutting and shaping tools, and skilled personnel to operate them. They maintain large, diverse inventories. They also are able to perform numerous customer services.

When the materials ordered from a distributor are shipped directly to the user by the manufacturer (a *drop shipment*), an additional buying decision becomes necessary. In this situation, the distributor does not handle the materials physically; it acts only as a broker.[11] Under such circumstances, a buyer is strongly motivated to buy directly from the manufacturer—if the manufacturer will sell to him or her.

Buyers should be aware that distributors stock many manufacturers' products. Hence, ordering from a distributor can significantly reduce the total number of orders a buyer must place to fill some of his or her materials requirements. If there were no distributors, orders for production as well as maintenance, repair, and operating (MRO) requirements would all have to be placed directly with many different manufacturers. This obviously would increase direct purchasing costs. Furthermore, for every additional purchase order placed, an additional receiving, inspection, and accounts payable operation is created.

In the final analysis, the manufacturer-distributor decision centers around one critical fact: the functions of distribution cannot be eliminated. The buyer

---

[11] Manufacturers' representatives, who usually deal only in technical items, also effect deliveries by drop shipments, and they act as brokers. Manufacturers' reps also aid a buyer by being able to furnish numerous product lines from a single source.

needs most of these functions; therefore, the buyer should pay for them once—but he or she should not pay for them twice. Either the distributor or the manufacturer must perform the essential distribution functions of carrying the inventory, giving technical advice, rendering service, extending credit, and so on. The buyer must decide for each individual buying situation how to best purchase the functions needed. The buyer must answer the question: Is it my company, the distributor, or the manufacturer that can perform the required distribution services satisfactorily at the lowest cost?

Miscellaneous Considerations

By the very nature of business, managers move up the executive ladder from functional to general management positions. Thus, it should not be surprising that all firms have a specific functional orientation or bias depending on the functional backgrounds of their top executives. Some firms have a marketing orientation; others have a production, financial, or engineering orientation. Competent buyers seek out suppliers having management orientations that best blend with the requirements of their own firms.

In searching for a new supplier, it is possible that a routine supplier evaluation might result in the selection of an efficient supplier who is also the major supplier of the buyer's major competitor. This could create an extremely dangerous situation. During periods of shortages, economic pressures assuredly would cause a seller to favor its older, large customers at the expense of its newer, less important customers. Obviously, a buyer should avoid such a situation.

In selecting suppliers, buyers also should consider the seller's general product mix and the types of markets served. These factors should fit well with the needs of the buyer's own company. How do the supply curves of the seller match the demand curves of the buyer? Would a long-term relationship be economically beneficial to both? Clearly, a buyer seeks positive answers to such questions.

Ethical Considerations

Buyers must be aware of potential conflicts of interest when selecting suppliers. A conflict of interest exists when buyers must divide their loyalty between the firm which employs them and another firm. In purchasing, this situation usually occurs when a buyer is a substantial stockholder in a supplier's firm or when he or she makes purchases from close friends and relatives. Conflicts of interest are discussed more fully in Chapter 30. The subject is introduced here solely to remind the reader that such conflicts always should be avoided in all source selection decisions.

Buyers should keep themselves as free as possible from unethical influences in their choice of suppliers. It is very difficult to maintain complete objectivity in this matter, for it is only human to want to favor one's friends. On occasion, friends can make unusually good suppliers. They will normally re-spond to emergency needs more readily than suppliers without a strong tie of personal friendship. On the other hand, buyers tend not to discipline or reprimand friends who perform poorly to the same degree as they do other suppliers.

Gifts which are intended to influence buying decisions have no place in a professional purchasing department. In most states commercial bribery is a criminal offense. Lunches with salespeople customarily are not considered gifts for the purpose of influencing decisions. Traditionally, they are judged to be a means of providing more time for the buyer and seller to discuss busi-ness problems. Beyond this point, the issue of undue influence may be raised. It is for this reason that many companies prohibit their buyers from accepting any gift beyond a simple meal. Regarding meals, firms should pro-vide expense accounts for members of their purchasing departments. This permits buyers to reciprocate with salespeople in paying for lunches, thus eliminating any suspicion of undue influence. Chapter 30 addresses ethical issues in greater detail.

Dishonest Suppliers

Dishonest sellers exist in the industrial world just as they do in the consumer world. This may surprise some readers, for it is logical to assume that dis-honest suppliers would not tackle experienced industrial buyers, but they do. Dishonest suppliers, therefore, can be a problem in source selection. A recurring technique used by dishonest suppliers is to contact a buyer by tele-phone, usually stating that the buyer has been referred to them by a top cor-porate executive—commonly one who cannot be contacted quickly or one who is located in another city. A typical story centers upon an unfortunate person who must liquidate the family stationery business immediately. The entire inventory of office supplies is offered at very low prices. If the buyer takes the offer, and many do, the result is always the same: poor quality, high prices, and late delivery. How many buyers take such offers? Several studies indicate that from 12 to 15 percent of buyers, at one time or another, have been swindled by dishonest suppliers.[12] It's caveat emptor, without a doubt—even in the industrial world.

A buyer's best protection against dishonest suppliers is the practice of thorough and prudent investigation before becoming seriously involved with a supplier. This type of professional purchasing performance, blended with a liberal dose of common sense, should keep buyers on safe ground in most cases.

What can buyers do if they are swindled by a dishonest seller? From a practical standpoint, in most cases, they have little legal recourse, but they

---

[12] *Wall Street Journal,* June 6, 1978, p. 29.

should attempt to expose such sellers. They should contact the nearest Better Business Bureau and the postal inspector if mail solicitation is involved. They should also inform the district attorney and the local purchasing association. Dishonest sellers cannot operate in the light of publicity. The reluctance of victims to admit that they have been swindled is one of a dishonest seller's greatest protections.

Reciprocity

When buyers give preference to suppliers who are also customers, they are engaging in a practice known as *reciprocity*.[13] The practice can be illegal, and the line between legal and illegal reciprocal practices frequently is very thin. A key criterion used by the courts in determining illegality is the degree to which reciprocal activity tends to restrict competition and trade. Hence, those who engage in reciprocal practices must do so with care and legal consultation.

The following cases clearly illustrate illegal practices. One of the nation's largest shippers was convicted of illegal reciprocity as a result of threatening to withdraw business from a large railroad if the railroad did not use a braking system manufactured by a subsidiary of the large shipper. Another large company was convicted of unlawful reciprocal dealing under its announced policy of "I will buy from you if you buy from me." Under this policy, by means of its economic power the company forced other companies to purchase its products at higher than market prices under the threat of losing the firm's high dollar business. *In contrast, it is entirely legal to buy from one's customers at fair market prices, without economic threat, and without the intent of restricting competition.*

Most buyers disapprove of the practice of reciprocity, even when legal, because it restricts their ability to achieve competition among potential suppliers. Thus it usually constrains purchasing's opportunity to increase profit by reducing the cost of materials. Those opposed to reciprocity cite the following dangers:

1 Reciprocity does not follow sound principles of buying and selling on the fundamental criteria of quality, price, and service.
2 Companies may relax their competitive efforts in technical and production areas as a result of reduced competition. Consequently, purchasing costs may be higher.
3 Sales departments may develop a false sense of security, resulting in deterioration of a firm's selling effort.

---

[13] Reciprocity becomes more insidious when it involves more than one tier of suppliers. For example, A is asked to buy from B, not because B is A's customer, but because B is C's customer, and C is A's customer, and B wants to sell to A. Obviously, it is possible for reciprocal relationships to extend to four or more tiers.

4 New customers may be hard to find because of preestablished relationships with competitors.

5 Company reputations may be impaired because of bad publicity resulting from reciprocity. Consequently, sellers of new, advanced products and processes will not waste their time with companies known to be tied up with reciprocal agreements.

6 Conspiracy and restraint-of-trade situations can develop, with their attendant legal dangers. The Antitrust Division of the Justice Department is taking the position that purchasing and materials managers are responsible for their own illegal actions regarding reciprocity; they can no longer transfer these responsibilities to top management.

Consequently, most U.S. firms proclaim a reciprocity policy similar to this one: "When important factors such as quality, service, and price are equal, we prefer to buy from our customers."[14]

Buyers find, however, that combinations of quality, service, and price are seldom exactly equal. If quality and price are equal, then the supplier would be selected solely on the basis of service. Service is seldom equal except for standard off-the-shelf items because, as was discussed earlier, in the majority of cases it is a supplier's capabilities that are being purchased, not commodities. To test the validity of this conclusion, readers should ask themselves questions such as the following and also should consider how many times they believe the answers would be the same for different suppliers:

- Does the supplier have an effective value-analysis program for its products?
- To what extent will the supplier provide engineering and design assistance?
- To what extent does the supplier have a service-shop organization that is available to me?
- Are repair parts available locally? On short notice? Will the supplier make available reserve production facilities to meet my emergency demands?
- To what extent will the supplier plan shipments to minimize my inventory?
- To what extent will the supplier help me cut acquisition costs such as qualifying visits, telephone calls, spoilage and waste?

The proponents of reciprocity contend that it is simply good business. They believe that if a buyer buys from a friend, both the buyer and the friend will profit in the long run. They maintain that service is better from suppliers who are also customers. They argue that reciprocity is a legitimate way to expand a company's markets. For example, a battery manufacturer states

---

[14] Some firms use vague phrases such as "Buy from customers when doing so will contribute to the greatest economic good of the firm."

that it only makes good sense to buy the brand of automobile that uses its company's batteries.

Companies manufacturing high-volume, highly competitive, standardized products are more susceptible to reciprocal pressure than companies manufacturing highly differentiated products. Industries most susceptible to reciprocal pressures typically include transportation, petroleum, steel, and cement.[15] Industries less susceptible to such pressures include those involved with electronic data processing equipment, electronics, and defense systems.

In the final analysis, reciprocity is neither a marketing problem nor a purchasing problem; rather, it is a management problem. If management believes that it can expand its markets permanently and add to the firm's profit legally by reciprocity, then this is the decision management should make. Conversely, if management believes profit will be increased by buying without the constraints of reciprocity, then that is the policy management should adopt. Although reciprocity can benefit a firm, no economist would argue that it benefits a nation's total economy.

CONCLUSION

The buyer's first responsibility in source selection is to develop and manage a viable source base. Once such a base is available, the buyer can focus on selecting the *right* source of supply, the subject of the next chapter.

FOR DISCUSSION

9-1 What should a buyer do in order to select reliable suppliers?

9-2 Why should a company develop and maintain a dependable supplier base? How often should the base be updated?

9-3 How can a purchasing department motivate its suppliers to participate in a mutually profitable relationship? Should the seller know about the buyer's business problems?

9-4 Explain the statement "The end result of good relations is the meshing of operations."

9-5 Describe and discuss supplier goodwill.

9-6 Elaborate on the concept of "voluntary collaboration" or "partnership." Are partnerships feasible in the high-tech industries? Low-tech?

9-7 Explain why Chan K. Hahn and his colleagues at Bowling Green State University are opposed to the traditional short-term competitive approach to source selection.

---

[15] As might be suspected, the firms in these industries tend to have the greatest interest in reciprocity. In many cases, however, large firms have altogether disbanded their reciprocity organizations under threat of antitrust violations. See Martin T. Farris, "Purchasing Reciprocity and Antitrust Revisited," *Journal of Purchasing and Materials Management*, Summer 1981, pp. 2–7.

9-8 How much aid should firms extend to regular suppliers? To new suppliers? What do you think are the long-term effects of vertical integration on productivity and competition?

9-9 Describe four benefits of voluntary collaboration.

9-10 Discuss three disadvantages of "opportunistic" buying.

9-11 What are four reasons cited by purchasing executives favoring early supplier involvement?

9-12 Does early supplier involvement exclude competition? Discuss.

9-13 Is there any relation between the number of suppliers and purchasing efficiency? Discuss the factors to be considered in making a choice between buying from single or multiple sources.

9-14 Evaluate the advantages and disadvantages of buying from a local source of supply.

9-15 Distinguish the factors to be considered when choosing between a distributor and a manufacturer.

9-16 What is reciprocity? Discuss the legality of this practice. What are the potential dangers of reciprocity? How can reciprocity benefit a person? How about a firm? A nation?

CASES FOR CHAPTER 9

SOURCES OF SUPPLY: PART II

EVALUATING A POTENTIAL SUPPLIER

After developing a comprehensive list of potential suppliers, the buyer's next step is to evaluate each prospective supplier individually. By a process of elimination, a selected list of potential suppliers is developed with whom the buying company may be willing to do business. The supplier list should be complete enough to bring to bear every type of competition desired, including:

1 Price competition resulting from identifying the lowest-cost producers or distributors.
2 Technological and quality competition, resulting from identifying potential suppliers who excel in good ideas, engineering planning, design, material quality, and production techniques.
3 Service competition, resulting from identifying those suppliers who are especially anxious to get contracts and who are willing to add "plus" values over and above functional value (quality) and price.

What kind of company makes the best supplier? It would be difficult to improve on the definition given by Professor Wilbur England of Harvard University:[1]

> A good supplier is one who is at all times honest and fair in his dealing with the customers, his own employees, and himself; who has adequate plant facilities, and know-how so as to be able to provide materials which meet the purchaser's specifications, in the quantities required, and at the time promised; whose financial position is sound; whose prices are reasonable both to the buyer and to himself; whose management policies are progressive; who is alert to the need for continued improvement in both his products and his manufacturing processes; and who realizes that, in the last analysis, his own interests are best served when he best serves his customers.

Type of Evaluation Needed

The type of evaluation required to determine supplier capability varies with the nature, criticality, complexity, and dollar value of the purchase to be made. It also varies with the buyer's knowledge of the firms being considered for the order. For many uncomplicated, low-dollar-value purchases, an examination of the information already available in the purchasing department (such as the supplier information file, catalogs, and brochures) is sufficient.

For complex, high-dollar-value, and perhaps critical purchases, additional evaluation steps are necessary. These steps can include surveys conducted by mail, telephone, or both—and then visits to the facilities of two or three carefully selected potential suppliers. As necessary, visits are followed by even more detailed analyses of the most promising suppliers' managerial and service capabilities. For an extremely difficult purchase, a supplier evaluation conference frequently is held at the buyer's plant to discuss the difficult purchase. From such a discussion, it is usually easy to differentiate among those suppliers who understand the complexities of the purchase and those who do not. By eliminating those who do not, the search for the right supplier is further narrowed.

---

[1] Wilbur B. England, *Procurement Principles and Cases*, 5th ed., Richard D. Irwin, Homewood, Ill., 1967, p. 405.

Preliminary Surveys

If an examination of existing data indicates that a supplier appears to be attractive, a telephone or mail survey should be conducted to obtain additional information. Such a survey should provide sufficient knowledge of the supplier to make a decision to include or exclude the firm from further consideration; clearly, this should precede any plant visits. The survey is based on a series of questions which cover the following areas: principal officers and titles, bank references, credit references, the annual history of sales and profit for the past five years, a referral list of customers, number of employees, space currently occupied, expansion plans (including sources of funds), current production defect rate for similar products, the number of inspectors used, the date when statistical process control was adopted, and a list of all equipment and tools which would be used to manufacture, test, and inspect the purchase in question.

Financial Condition

Preliminary investigation of a potential supplier's financial condition often can avoid the expense of further study. A review of financial statements and credit ratings can reveal whether a supplier is clearly *incapable* of performing satisfactorily. Financial stability is essential for suppliers to assure continuity of supply and reliability of product quality. Imagine the difficulty of getting: (1) a financially weak supplier to maintain quality, (2) a supplier who does not have sufficient working capital to settle an expensive claim, or (3) a financially unsound supplier to work overtime to meet a promised delivery date.

In addition to informing a buyer about a supplier's capability to perform a contract, financial information can be useful in other ways as well. Financially strong firms are usually managerially strong; hence, they generally make good suppliers. An analysis of a firm's balance sheet and operating statement is helpful to a buyer in numerous ways. For example, on discovering that a firm's financial condition has started to deteriorate, a buyer should tighten quality monitoring and consider either searching for a new supplier or reducing the size of the orders given to the distressed firm. Increasing profit margins alert a professional buyer to the fact that it may be possible to obtain price reductions—if the buyer has the purchasing skills and economic leverage to get such reductions. Falling profit margins may indicate that price rises are probable. In this case, the supplier either is becoming less efficient or is losing sales and working at lower percentages of capacity. In either case, price rises are likely, and they are certain if demand for the product is relatively inelastic.

Integrated firms with ample supplies of raw materials and adequate production equipment and capability make highly desirable suppliers. Even during depressed economic conditions, these firms have to make only minimum cash payments to outsiders; thus, they usually have ample resources available to serve their customers. On the other hand, firms that have to purchase their supplies on a hand-to-mouth basis or lease their buildings and equipment can, even in mild recessions, suffer cash squeezes that can affect quality, service, and prices.

Firms with sound working capital positions—that is, those that have enough cash to purchase required materials, pay employees, and extend credit as necessary to customers—can be particularly desirable suppliers. On the other hand, firms with weak working capital positions may be satisfactory suppliers only when business is good.

Buyers are not expected to be trained financial analysts. However, competent buyers should be able to interpret financial reports and to make intelligent comparisons from them. The financial information buyers routinely need is found in corporate annual reports, 10-K reports, Moody's Industrials, Dun and Bradstreet (D & B) Reports, D & B *Key Business Ratios*, and occasional consultations with a supplier's banker.

Dun and Bradstreet[2] publishes a booklet entitled *Key Business Ratios;* this annual publication is free. For each industry, this booklet cites the fourteen financial ratios that D & B considers most important in determining a firm's credit status. By comparing these ratios with those of the potential suppliers, purchasing can determine which firms are most likely to be reliable or unreliable suppliers, from a financial point of view. For example, a firm that ranks high in its industry on all fourteen ratios should be an outstanding supplier candidate. Conversely, firms ranking low in most of the ratio categories should be avoided.

Plant Visits

By visiting a supplier's plant or distribution facility, the sourcing team can obtain firsthand information concerning the adequacy of the firm's manufacturing or distribution capabilities and its management's technical know-how. Depending on the importance of the visit, the company may send representatives from only purchasing and engineering; or it may also include some combination of representation from finance, operations, quality assurance, marketing, and industrial relations. Occasionally, top management may also participate in the visit and the evaluation.

In planning plant visits, only a few outstanding potential suppliers' plants should be chosen for observation. In addition to observing production equipment and operations, there are other compelling reasons for plant visits. It is vital, for example, to determine a supplier's managerial capabilities and motivation to meet contractual obligations. To make such a determination properly requires an overall appraisal. Among the factors to be appraised are R&D ca-

---

[2] D & B's address is 99 Church Street, New York, N.Y. 10017.

pability; the appropriateness of equipment; the effectiveness of the production control, quality control, and cost control systems; the competence of the technical and managerial staffs; the morale of personnel in general; the quantity of back orders; the willingness of the supplier to work cooperatively with the company; and the quality of the key materials management activities.

The plant visit should be carefully planned to provide the required level of knowledge and insight into the potential supplier's operations, capacity, and orientation. The efficiency with which the plant visit is planned and conducted reflects on the buying organization. To provide the reader with a sense of the detail in which some plant visits are conducted, one firm's evaluation form is reproduced in the appendix on pages 210–217. This evaluative instrument is used by a high-tech firm that utilizes a number of single-source partnering arrangements.

Although it varies with the firm's size and organizational structure, the *initial orientation meeting* typically is attended by the buying team members and their management counterparts from the potential supplier's organization. In smaller firms, the president often leads the supplier group. In this session, the buying team provides general information and explains the interests of its company: its kind of business, a brief history, kinds of products, the importance of the item(s) to be purchased, and volume, quality, and delivery requirements.

The prospective supplier usually is requested to provide additional information on the company's history, current customers, sales volume, and financial stability. If classified or confidential data might be involved during design and production operations, the buying team must review the supplier's security control system. In the quality area, the buyer should attempt to understand the *supplier's attitude* toward quality by asking questions such as: How do you feel about Zero Defects? Do you employ statistical process control? Have you adopted a total quality commitment plan? Do you have a quality manual? Copies of the manual and the policy should be reviewed by the buying team's quality representative. The potential supplier also should be asked to describe *its own* supplier quality control program.

If the buying team is satisfied with the results of the introductory meeting, a tour of the facilities typically is made. Prior to the tour, the buying team should get permission to talk freely with various individuals working in the operation, not just hand-picked managers.

Supplier management often assumes that satisfactory operating controls are in place. In reality, however, experience frequently shows that some of these controls may not have been implemented, or that they may have been discontinued. When management describes these things, the buying team should respond, "That sounds excellent, we'd like to see them." The team should also check controls by asking such questions as, "How do you ensure that the most current drawing is in use?" "How do you segregate rejected materials?"[3]

As a cross-check on specific information obtained in the initial meeting, perceptive team members often ask shop and staff personnel similar types of questions. When supplier managers are not present, operating personnel should be asked about *their* understanding of the firm's quality systems, schedules, cost control efforts, and related requirements. Workers can also be asked about working conditions and turnover, about the firm's commitment to quality, about quality tools, and about training.

When observing plant equipment, buyers should determine whether the equipment is modern, whether it is in good operating condition, whether tolerances can be held consistently, and what the output rates are. Buyers also should look for special modifications or adaptations of equipment; these things often provide clues to the ingenuity of operating management personnel.

The first impression of a supplier's operation is generally obtained through observing the housekeeping of the plant itself. Is it clean and well organized? Are the machines clean? Are the tools, equipment, and benches kept orderly and accessible? Good housekeeping tends to be an indication of efficiency. Many buyers believe it is reasonable to expect that a firm displaying pride in its facilities and equipment will also take pride in the workmanship that goes into its products.

During the visit, buyers should investigate production methods and efficiencies. Is the just-in-time system utilized to a significant extent? Is material moving freely from storage to production areas? Are there any production bottlenecks? Is the production scheduling and control function organized and functioning well? Is reserve production capacity available? Is it available on a regular or an overtime basis? Does the supplier have a competent maintenance crew? And, finally, the buyer should determine whether inventory levels for both production materials and finished goods are adequate for his or her company's needs.

Employee attitudes are extremely important. In the long run, production results often depend more on people than on the physical plant. Do the employees seem to work harmoniously with one another and with their supervisors? Are they interested in quality and in improving the products they make? Is enthusiasm at a reasonable level? In short, do the people take pride in their jobs and in the firm—or do they view it as an eight-to-five clock-punching operation?

Management Normally, a buyer's first contact with a potential supplier is with a sales representative. A properly trained representative knows his or her product thoroughly, understands the buyer's requirements, gives useful suggestions to the buyer, commits the company to specific delivery prom-

---

[3]Warren E. Norquist, Director of Worldwide Purchasing and Materials Management, Polaroid Corporation, personal interview, October 1987.

ises, and follows through on all orders placed. This type of sales representative indicates that the supplier's firm is directed and managed by responsible and enterprising executives. A well-managed firm seldom experiences the instability that results from continual labor problems and always strives to reduce its cost. Such a company can be a good supplier.

When a buyer purchases an off-the-shelf item which a supplier has manufactured using its own design and tools, the buyer is primarily buying a *product*. However, when a buyer purchases a high-dollar-value item made to his or her firm's own unique specifications, for which the firm may or may not furnish special, high-cost tooling, *then the buyer is buying far more than just a supplier's production capability*. Technical competence in itself does not assure that a firm will be a good supplier. Rather, technical competence must be blended with good business management to ensure that a firm has the ability to be a "good source of supply" in the fullest sense of the term.

In the final analysis, it is a firm's *technical ingenuity* and *managerial ability*, coupled with its *financial strength*, that determines how effectively its physical and cash resources will be employed.

Service   "Service" is a term that varies in meaning, depending on the nature of the product being purchased. Specifically, good service always means delivering on time, treating special orders specially, filling back orders promptly, settling disputes quickly and fairly, and informing buyers in advance of impending price changes or developing shortages. In some situations, it means exceptional post-sale service. Service also can include actions such as stocking spare parts for immediate delivery, extending suitable credit arrangements, or warranting the purchased item's quality and performance to a degree beyond that normally required. In the aggregate, good service means that a supplier will take every reasonable action to ensure the smooth flow of purchased materials between the seller and the buyer.

What kinds of companies can give buyers the best service? Service is usually measured by a supplier's ability to comply with promised delivery dates, specifications, and technical assistance. How do forward-looking companies feel about the service they expect from their suppliers? A leading valve manufacturer has said, "We want a supplier to do more than simply quote prices from an engineering drawing. We want the supplying firm to know the parts thoroughly, so that it can use specialized knowledge of processing alternative designs and alternative materials to help us cut costs. We make it quite clear that cost-saving ideas can win a contract."

Another firm states its position this way: "We feel our approach in recognizing our specialty suppliers' expert knowledge and letting them work with responsible people in our organization has paid off handsomely. We have effectively expanded our purchasing knowledge and gained experience that might have taken years with another approach."

An electrical company holds the following view concerning specialty suppliers: "Common sense should tell us that they know more about the design and building of their products than we do. So it's only natural for us to draw on their skill and experience in coming up with a better end product of our own."

Just-in-Time Capabilities

When properly implemented, a just-in-time (JIT) system results in increased productivity and reduced costs through the elimination of waste. The benefits of JIT protect and enhance the success of firms that embrace it. Unfortunately, too frequently a key prerequisite to successful implementation of such a system is ignored: JIT requires virtually defect-free incoming purchased materials.

The vast majority of American manufacturers still operate under a materials/manufacturing system which tolerates a 1 to 3 percent defective rate in incoming purchased materials. This level of quality translates to 10,000 to 30,000 defects per million incoming parts. Using JIT, often there is no inventory of purchased goods awaiting inspection. There is, at most, a small inventory of purchased goods in the storeroom awaiting manufacture. Typically, there is no more than an hour's supply of items which have been processed through station C waiting to move through work station D. Inventory is squeezed out of the *total* system to detect waste, errors, and inefficiencies.[4]

Defects in purchased materials obviously disrupt such a system and result in lost production. Typically, JIT systems can tolerate incoming defect levels of only 100 or fewer parts per million (PPM). This level of quality has been found to be essential if the using firm is to enjoy the major benefits of JIT.

In addition to requiring virtually defect-free incoming materials, JIT requires a high degree of integration of the customer's and supplier's operations. The inevitable changes in a customer's production plans and schedules affect the supplier's schedules. Experience has demonstrated that dependable, single-source partnerships are virtually essential if the required level of integration is to result.

A firm that is considering the adoption of JIT manufacturing must focus on its suppliers' abilities and willingness to meet the stringent quality and schedule demands imposed by the system. A buyer must investigate carefully a potential supplier's capability as a JIT manufacturer. Michael McGrath has identified four stages of a supplier's typical progress into a JIT program. These stages are depicted in Figure 10-1.[5]

The Criticality of Qualifying Sources

By now, the cynical reader probably is thinking, "Come on. Qualifying suppliers can't be this critical or this complex!" A 1983 *Harvard Business Review*

---

[4] JIT systems are discussed extensively in Chapters 20 and 21.
[5] Michael McGrath, "Guidelines for Assessing Supplier JIT Capability," *Electronics Purchasing*, June 1988, p. 37.

CHART YOUR SUPPLIER'S JIT PROGRESS

SUPPLIER CHARACTERISTICS	STAGE 1 "Exploration"	STAGE 2 "Acceptance"	STAGE 3 "Pilot project"	STAGE 4 "Full implementation"
Overall Measurements:				
Knowledge of concepts	Hazy or no awareness	Understood	Applied	Teachers
Management commitment	Uncommitted	Superficial	Evaluating	Drivers
JIT customers	None	Talks with one or two	Contracts with several	Majority of output
Manufacturing Process:				
Quality programs	Not formalized	Quality circles	PPM targets	Low PPM achieved
Capacity flexibility	Very inflexible	Discussing options	Flexible work force	Flexible automation
Pull mechanisms	Shortage lists	Sales orders	Some Kanbans	All Kanbans
Batch sizes	Monthly to quarterly	2 weeks	Weekly	Daily
JIT purchasing	None	Talking with suppliers	Some JIT	Majority JIT
Supply Process:				
Delivery frequency	Monthly	2 weeks	Weekly to daily	As required
Delivery quality variance	Uncontrolled	5%	1%	Low PPM
Delivery quantity variance	± 10%	± 5%	± 1%	None
Delivery time variance	± Weeks	± Days	± Hours	None

FIGURE 10-1
Chart your supplier's JIT progress.

article cites the following example which demonstrates that, yes, qualifying sources carefully is essential:

> A leading copier manufacturer developed a new machine requiring 1,500 purchased parts, and buyers were given three months to find qualified bidders to supply these parts. In an attempt to obtain the lowest costs and still meet delivery schedules, the buyers selected 500 different vendors. After the buyers had placed the orders, a survey team determined the qualifications of the vendors making the 30 most critical parts, and [subsequently] reported that only six vendors could deliver parts consistently manufactured to specification, at the cost quoted. As it turned out, the company required a costly two-year program to correct the problems created during the three-month rush of placing orders without benefit of adequate information about vendor qualifications.

> Buyers and purchasing managers are often given unrealistically tight schedules.

In addition, they are usually isolated from engineering and quality control staff whose services they frequently need to fulfill their mission of buying at the lowest cost from qualified vendors. Major problems often arise when buyers try to assess a vendor's qualifications. Some of the information needed requires detailed sampling and analysis of the vendor's manufacturing process, and this has to be done by quality control engineers in close cooperation with the vendor's technical personnel at the vendor's plant. Inspecting a few selected pieces at the buyer's receiving dock does not fully describe the consistency of the product or the reliability of the vendor's tooling. Nor does it generate understanding of the vendor's interpretation of the manufacturer's specifications.[6]

COMPETITIVE BIDDING

Once a buyer has identified the potential suppliers he or she wishes to invite to submit bids (or proposals), a decision must be made whether to use competitive bidding or negotiation (or a combination of the two) as the basis for source selection. When competitive bidding is used by private industry, requests for bids are traditionally sent to three to eight potential suppliers depending on the dollar size and complexity of the purchase. Requests for bids ask suppliers to quote the price at which they will perform in accordance with the terms and conditions of the contract, should they be the successful bidder. Government buyers generally are not able to restrict the number of bidders to only eight. Rather, all suppliers desiring to bid are permitted to do so (for large purchases, the numbers are literally in the hundreds). Under competitive bidding, industrial buyers generally, *but not always*, award the order to the lowest bidder. By law, government buyers are routinely required to award the order to the lowest bidder, provided the lowest bidder is deemed qualified to perform the contract.

Five Prerequisites

The proper use of competitive bidding is dictated by five criteria. When all five criteria prevail, competitive bidding is an efficient method of source selection and pricing. The criteria are:

1 The dollar value of the specific purchase must be large enough to justify the expense, to both buyer and seller, that accompanies this method of source selection and pricing.
2 The specifications of the item or service to be purchased must be explicitly clear to both buyer and seller. In addition, the seller must know from actual previous experience, or be able to estimate accurately from similar past experience, the cost of producing the item or rendering the service.

---

[6] Jack Reddy and Abe Berger, "Three Essentials of Product Quality," *Harvard Business Review*, July–Aug. 1983, pp. 157–158.

3 The market must consist of an adequate number of sellers.
4 The sellers comprising the market must be technically qualified and *actively want* the contract—and, therefore, be willing to price competitively to get it. Frequently criteria 1, 2, and 3 prevail, yet there is no real competition because the sellers are not anxious to bid. Backlogs of work in some sellers' plants may prevent competition. Under such circumstances, additional orders would entail overtime operation and its attendant problems of scheduling difficulties and premium wage payment. Under such circumstances, if bids are made at all, they are at prices that include numerous contingencies.
5 The time available must be sufficient for using this method of pricing— suppliers competing for large contracts must be allowed time to obtain and evaluate bids from their subcontractors before they can calculate their best price. Bidders must also have time to perform the necessary cost analysis required within their own organization and to assure themselves of reliable sources of materials. The time required for preparing, mailing, opening, and evaluating bids is usually considerably longer than those unfamiliar with this system would expect. Thirty days is not an uncommon time.

Four Conditions When Competitive Bidding Should Not Be Used

In addition to satisfying the preceding five prerequisites, four other conditions should *not* be present when employing competitive bidding as the means of source selection:

1 Situations in which it is impossible to estimate costs with a high degree of certainty. Such situations frequently are present with high-technology requirements, with items requiring a long time to develop and produce, and under conditions of economic uncertainty.
2 Situations in which price is not the only important variable. For example, quality, schedule, and service may well be negotiable variables of equal importance.
3 Situations in which the purchasing firm anticipates a need to make changes in the specification or some other aspect of the purchase contract. When unscrupulous suppliers anticipate changes, they may "buy-in" with the expectation of "getting well" (and even wealthy) on the resulting changes.
4 Situations in which special tooling or setup costs are major factors. The allocation of such costs and title to the special tooling are issues best resolved through negotiation.

If these nine conditions are satisfied, then competitive bidding usually will result in the lowest price and is the recommended method of source selection. To ensure that the lowest prices are obtained, the competing firms must be assured that the firm submitting the low bid will receive the award. If the purchasing firm gains a reputation for negotiating with the lowest bidders *after* bids are opened, then future bidders will tend *not* to offer their best prices initially, believing that they may do better in any subsequent negotiations. They will adopt a strategy of submitting a bid low enough to allow them to be included in any negotiations. But their initial bid will not be as low as when they are confident that the award will be made to the low bidder without further negotiation.

When all these prerequisites to the use of competitive bidding are not satisfied, the *negotiation process* should be employed to select sources and to arrive at a price.

Several progressive purchasing professionals offer two additional arguments which favor the use of negotiation over competitive bidding for critical procurements:

1 The negotiation process is far more likely to lead to a complete understanding of all issues of the procurement. This improved understanding greatly reduces subsequent quality and schedule problems.
2 Competitive bidding tends to put great pressure on suppliers to reduce their costs in order to be able to bid a low (but profitable) price. This cost pressure may result in sacrifices in product quality, development efforts, and other vital services.

Normally the competitive bidding system itself, when all the prerequisite criteria prevail, evaluates quite accurately the many pricing factors bearing on the purchase being made. These factors include determinants such as supplier production efficiency, willingness of the seller to price this particular contract at a low profit level, the financial effect on the seller of shortages of capital or excesses of inventories, errors in the seller's sales forecast, and competitive conditions in general.

Because the proper uses of competitive bidding appear to be widely misunderstood, this system of pricing is frequently abused by both industry and government. Government officials, because of political pressures from Congress, tend to overuse competitive bidding. The reason for such behavior is easily understood. By stressing the applicability of competitive bidding as the best method of pricing, and by allowing all constituents the opportunity to compete, regardless of their qualifications, politicians can avoid disputes with their constituents. When competitive bidding is used in industry, too often buyers hold steadfastly to the unsound premise that purchasing judgment is not required. In reality, however, planning the preliminaries correctly for competitive bidding takes purchasing judgment of the highest order.

If the preliminary planning of tight specifications, proper selection of competing suppliers, correct quantities, precise delivery schedules, adequate time for placing bids, and general economic analysis is done correctly, selecting the successful bidder after the bids are evaluated is generally a routine matter. Except in unusual circumstances, the low bidder should receive the order. Purchasing judgment and analytical planning should normally be exercised *before* competitive bids are requested, not after the bids are in.

The general belief that adequate competition is a sound method of obtaining the right source and price is correct. However, the belief that competitive bidding assures adequate competition is wrong. Competitive bidding assures adequate competition and the right price only when the mandatory five criteria for this method of pricing prevail and the four cited situations are not present. Too often industry and government alike err in using competitive bidding to buy highly technical products with vague specifications. This practice inevitably leads to faulty cost estimates and contingency pricing. The contingency pricing on the part of suppliers is the result of the poor purchasing judgment of the buyer, who is guilty of incorrectly using a good and effective purchasing tool under inappropriate circumstances. It is also an error to use competitive bidding for purchases involving high engineering, setup, and testing costs.

Buyers must remember that sellers usually will bid on any product or service they are asked to bid on. It is not the seller's responsibility to tell a buyer that the wrong method of source selection and pricing is being used. However, if sellers do not have adequate cost information, do not fully understand the specifications, or already have large backlogs, they will factor into their bid prices contingencies for labor costs, materials costs, and all other possible costs they can think of. For example, if a supplier is not sure how many hours it will take to complete a job, its bid will be based on the estimated maximum number of hours. Sellers are not at fault for making high competitive bids to protect themselves just because buyers are naive enough to use an incorrect method of source selection and price determination. Caveat emptor! To buy wisely is the buyer's responsibility. Competitive bidding improperly used is not buying wisely. Competitive bidding properly used is an excellent method of selecting the right source and obtaining a fair price. Generally speaking, this method of sourcing and pricing is most applicable to highly standardized products that are widely used and produced abundantly for stock by many manufacturers and for standard services.

Two-Step Bidding/Negotiation

On occasion, large, technically oriented firms and the federal government use a modified type of competitive bidding called "two-step bidding." This method of source selection and pricing is used in situations where *inadequate specifications* preclude the initial use of traditional competitive bidding. In the first step, bids are requested only for technical proposals, without any prices. Bidders are requested to set forth in their proposals the technical details describing how they would produce the required materials, products, or services. After these technical bids are evaluated and it is determined which proposals are technically satisfactory, the second step follows.

In the second step, requests for bids are sent only to those sellers who submitted acceptable technical proposals in the first step. These sellers now compete for the business on a price basis, as they would in any routine, competitive-bidding situation. The price is determined in either of two ways: (1) award may be based solely on the lowest price received from those competing, or (2) the price proposals for the accepted technical approaches may be used as the beginning point for *negotiations*. It is important that the buyer specify *at the outset* which of the two procedures will be used.

THE SOLICITATION

Once a decision has been made whether to use competitive bidding or negotiation as the means of selecting the source, an *invitation for bids (IFB)* or a *request for proposal (RFP)* is prepared. The IFB or RFP normally consists of a purchase description of the item or service required, information on quantities, required delivery schedules, special terms and conditions, and standard terms and conditions. The legal implications of these documents and processes are discussed in Chapter 29.

When an RFP is used in anticipation of cost negotiations with one or more suppliers, the buyer should request appropriate cost data in support of the price proposal. The buyer must also obtain the right of access to the supplier's cost records that are required to support the reasonableness of the proposal. The cost data and the right of access must be established during the RFP phase of the procurement, at a time potential suppliers believe that there is active competition for the job. Details of the negotiation process are explored in Chapter 15.

SELECTING THE SOURCE

In many instances, one prospective supplier is obviously superior to its competition—and selection is a very simple matter. Unfortunately, though, the choice is not always so clear. In these cases, a numerical weighted-factor rating system can greatly facilitate the decision process.

A weighted-factor system calls for two activities: (1) the development of factors (selection criteria) and weights and (2) the assignment of ratings. The first step, identification of the key factors to be considered in the selection decision, along with their respective weights, typically is accomplished by a committee of individuals involved in the purchase (individuals from operations, design, and purchasing). An illustration of the approach is shown in Table 10-1.

Step two requires the assignment of numerical ratings for each of the competing firms. These assessments are based on the collective judgments of the evaluators after studying all the data and information provided by the potential suppliers, as well as that obtained in field investigations.

In effect, a weighted-factor rating system breaks a complex problem down

TABLE 10-1
AN ILLUSTRATION OF THE WEIGHTED FACTOR RATING APPROACH

Factors	Maximum rating (weights)	Supplier		
		A	B	C
Technical:				
Understanding of the problem	10	9	9	7
Technical approach	20	19	16	16
Production facilities	5	4	5	3
Operator requirements	3	2	3	2
Maintenance requirements	2	2	2	2
Totals	40	36	35	30
Ability to meet schedule	20	20	16	15
Price	20	16	20	15
Managerial, financial, & technical capability	10	10	8	8
Quality control processes	10	9	8	9
Rating Total	100	91	87	77

into its key components and permits analysis of each component individually. The approach is widely used in practice and generally leads to a fair and reasonably objective result.

CONCLUSION

Purchasing has many vital responsibilities. None is more crucial than selection of the right source. The right source provides the right quality, on time, at the right price, and with the right level of service.

Selection of the right source is more important today than ever before, since more buyers are entering into long-term partnerships with a single source of supply. The benefits of such partnerships are many, but the risks are great. Careful selection of suppliers and the professional management of the relationships are essential.

FOR DISCUSSION

10-1 What types of competition may be desired during source selection?

10-2 What factors affect the type of evaluation to be employed?

10-3 What is the objective of a preliminary survey?

10-4 In what ways is an analysis of the potential supplier's financial condition useful?

10-5 Where can the required financial data be located?

10-6 When should a plant visit be made? Who should make the visit?

10-7 What information should be obtained during the introductory meeting phase of a plant visit?

10-8 What are the reasons for conducting a tour of the supplier's facilities? What areas typically receive attention?

10-9 How does buying a standard product differ from buying a high-dollar-value item made to the firm's own unique specifications?

10-10 Define and discuss your concept of "service."

10-11 How does just-in-time manufacturing affect source selection?

10-12 What are the five prerequisites to using competitive bidding? Under what four conditions should competitive bidding *not* be employed?

10-13 Purchasing professionals offer two arguments in favor of the use of negotiation over competitive bidding for critical procurements. Describe and discuss these two arguments.

10-14 Why do government officials overuse competitive bidding?

10-15 Does competitive bidding assure adequate competition? Why?

10-16 Describe two-step bidding.

10-17 What extra requirement should a buyer impose when an RFP is used in anticipation of cost negotiations? Discuss.

10-18 Describe the weighted-factor rating system approach to source selection.

CASES FOR CHAPTER 10

APPENDIX:
Illustrative Plant Survey

After conducting preliminary surveys of potential suppliers of critical materials, equipment, or services, it frequently is desirable to conduct a plant visit to the one or two most attractive candidates. The purpose of such visits is to gain firsthand knowledge of the supplier's facilities, personnel, and operations. Such a visit normally is conducted by a team from the purchasing firm. Each member will study his or her area of expertise at the potential supplier's operation.

The plant survey shown in Figure 10-2 is used by one high-tech manufacturer. The evaluation form calls for yes or no answers to specific questions and evaluation ratings for all questions, asking the team member to evaluate how well the supplier is doing in a given area. The evaluation ratings are described below.

Rating	Description
10	The provisions or conditions are extensive and function is excellent.
9	The provisions or conditions are moderately extensive and function is excellent.
8	The provisions or conditions are extensive and are functioning well.
6/7	The provisions or conditions are moderately extensive and are functioning well.
4/5	The provisions or conditions are limited in extent but are functioning well.
2/3	The provisions or conditions are moderately extensive but are functioning poorly.
1	The provisions or conditions are limited in extent and are functioning poorly.
0	The provisions or conditions are missing but needed.

Assume that the purchasing firm's quality assurance (Q.A.) manager is rating a potential supplier on the sections entitled Quality Management (pages 215–216) and Quality Information (page 216). When these phases of the study are complete, the Q.A. manager is in a position to assign an average or overall rating for Quality Management on the first sheet of the survey (page 212).

Such an evaluation is used in at least two ways: (1) It now is possible to compare competitors' operations, with major emphasis on quality, and (2) actual or potential problem areas for an otherwise attractive supplier may be identified. The purchasing firm then may require that the area of concern be corrected or upgraded before award, or as a condition of award.

FIGURE 10-2
Plant survey

Company Name _____

Address _____

Phone _____

Management Officials:

Name   Position

_____   _____

_____   _____

_____   _____

_____   _____

_____   _____

Type of Manufacturing Service or Products:

_____

_____

FACILITIES

Employee breakdown:

Total plant area, sq. ft. _____   Design engineering _____

Number of buildings _____   Manufacturing engineering _____

Type of buildings _____   Research and development _____

Total number of employees _____   Purchasing _____

Sales volume $_____

OVERALL RATINGS

Design Information   ( )   Quality Information   ( )

Procurement   ( )   Calibration   ( )

Material Control   ( )   Inspection of Completed Material ( )

Manufacturing Control   ( )   Final Acceptance   ( )

Quality Management   ( )

Work Schedule

Hours_____ Shifts_____ Days Work_____

Percent of present production to full capacity _____%

Condition of production equipment _____

_____

Report prepared by _____ Title _____ Date _____

DESIGN INFORMATION

Control of design and manufacturing information is essential for the control of product. It consists of making sure that operating personnel are furnished with complete technical instructions for the manufacture and inspection of the product. This information includes drawings, specifications, special purchase order requirements, engineering change information, inspection instructions, processing instructions, and other special information. A positive recall system is usually considered necessary to ensure against use of superseded or obsolete information.

How well do procedures cover the release, change, and recall of design and manufacturing information, including correlation of customer specifications, and how well are procedures followed? (   )
How well do records reflect the incorporation of changes? (   )
How well does quality control verify that changes are incorporated at the effective points? (   )
How well is the control of design and manufacturing information applied to the procurement activity? (   )
Is there a formal deviation procedure, and how well is it followed? (   )
Does your company have a written system for incorporating customer changes into shop drawings? (Y/N)
Does your company have a reliability department? (Y/N)
Is reliability data used in developing new designs? (Y/N)
Is quality history fed back to engineering for improvements in current or future designs? (Y/N)
Does Q.A. review new designs? (Y/N)
Does your company have a sample or prototype department? (Y/N)
Does Q.A. review sample prototypes? (Y/N)
Is this information used in developing shop inspection instructions? (Y/N)
Are customer specifications interpreted into shop specifications? (Y/N)
Do drawings and specifications accompany purchase orders to suppliers? (Y/N)
Are these reviewed by Q.A.? (Y/N)
Are characteristics classified on the engineering documents as to importance? (Y/N)
Does Q.A. review new drawings with the intent of designing gauging fixtures? (Y/N)

PROCUREMENT—CONTROL OF PURCHASED MATERIAL

It is essential for the assurance of quality that outside suppliers meet the standards for quality imposed on the firm's own operations department. Sources should be under continuous control or surveillance. Incoming material should be inspected to the extent necessary to assure that the requirements have been met.

How well are potential suppliers evaluated and monitored? (   )
How well are quality requirements specified? (   )
How well are inspection procedures specified, and how well are they followed? (   )
How adequate are inspection facilities and equipment? (   )
How adequate are "certifications" which are used in lieu of inspection? (   )
How well are certifications evaluated by independent checking? (   )
How well are inspection results used for corrective action? (   )
Do you have an incoming inspection department? (Y/N)
   (If yes, list personnel) Inspectors _____ Supervisory _____ Quality Engineers _____
Are purchase orders made available to incoming inspection? (Y/N)
Is there a system for keeping shop drawings up-to-date? (Y/N)
Are written inspection instructions available? (Y/N)
Is sample inspection used? (Y/N)
Is gauging equipment calibrated periodically? (Y/N)
Is gauging equipment correlated with suppliers' equipment? (Y/N)
Are suppliers' test records used for acceptance? (Y/N)
Are commercial test records used for acceptance? (Y/N)

Is material identified to physical and chemical test reports? (Y/N)
Are records kept to show acceptance and rejection of incoming material? (Y/N)
Does your company have a supplier rating system? (Y/N)
Is it made available to the purchasing department? (Y/N)
Is the supplier notified of nonconforming material? (Y/N)
Does your company have an approved supplier list? (Y/N)
Does your company survey supplier facilities? (Y/N)
Does the incoming inspection department have adequate storage space to hold material until
   it is inspected? (Y/N)
Is nonconforming material identified as such? (Y/N)
Is nonconforming material held in a specific area until disposition can be made? (Y/N)
Who is responsible for making disposition of nonconforming material? _____

MATERIAL CONTROL

Control of the identity and quality status of material in-stores and in-process is essential. It is not enough that the right materials be procured and verified; they must be identified and controlled in a manner that will assure they are also properly used. The entire quality program may be compromised if adequate controls are not maintained throughout procurement, storage, manufacturing, and inspection.

How adequate are procedures for storage, release, and movement of material, and how well are
   they followed? ( )
How well are incoming materials quarantined while under test? ( )
How well are materials in-stores identified and controlled? ( )
How well are in-process materials identified and controlled? ( )
How well are materials in inspection identified and controlled? ( )
How adequate are storage areas and facilities? ( )
How well is access to material controlled? ( )
How well do procedures cover the prevention of corrosion, deterioration, or damage
   of material and finished goods? How well are they followed? ( )
How well are nonconforming items identified, isolated, and controlled? ( )

MANUFACTURING CONTROL

In-process inspection, utilizing the techniques of quality control, is one of the most satisfactory methods yet devised for attaining quality of product during manufacture. Because many quality characteristics cannot be evaluated in the end product, it is imperative that they be achieved and verified during the production process.

How well are process capabilities established and maintained? ( )
How well is in-process inspection specified? How effectively is it performed? ( )
How adequate are inspection facilities and equipment? ( )
How well are the results of in-process inspection used in the promotion of effective corrective action? ( )
How adequate are equipment and facilities maintained? How adequate are housekeeping procedures,
   and how well are they followed? ( )
Does your company have a process inspection function? (Y/N)
   (If yes, list on a separate sheet inspectors, supervisory and quality engineering personnel.)
To whom does process inspection report? _____
Are inspection stations located in the production area? (Y/N)
Are shop drawings and specifications available to inspection? (Y/N)
Is there a system for keeping the documents up-to-date? (Y/N)
Are written inspection instructions available? (Y/N)

214

Is there a system for reviewing and updating inspection instructions? (Y/N)
Is sample inspection used? (Y/N)
Do production workers inspect their own work? (Y/N)
Are inspection records kept on file? (Y/N)
Is inspection equipment calibrated periodically? (Y/N)
Is all material identified (route tags, etc.)? (Y/N)
Is defective material identified as such? (Y/N)
Is defective material segregated from good material until disposition is made? (Y/N)
Are first production parts inspected before a job can be run? (Y/N)
Is corrective action taken to prevent the recurrence of defective material? (Y/N)
Who is responsible for making disposition of nonconforming material? _____

Does your company use:
  X-bar and R charts? (Y/N)
  Process capability studies? (Y/N)
Are standards calibrated by an outside source that certifies traceability to NBS? (Y/N)
Are standards calibrated directly by NBS? (Y/N)
Are packaged goods checked for proper packaging? (Y/N)

QUALITY MANAGEMENT

The key to the management of quality lies in philosophy, objectives, and organization structure. The philosophy forms the primary policy and should include the broad principles common to good-quality programs. The objectives should be clearly stated in specific terms and should provide operating policies which guide the activity of the quality program. The organizational structure should clearly define lines of authority and responsibility for quality from top management down to the operating levels.

How adequate is the quality philosophy, and how well is it explained in operating policies and procedures? ( )
How adequate is the technical competence in the quality discipline of those responsible for assuring quality? ( )
How well does the organizational structure define quality responsibility and authority? ( )
How well does the organizational structure provide access to top management? ( )
How adequate is the documentation and dissemination of quality control procedures? ( )
How adequate is the training program, including employee records? ( )
The quality department reports to:
Name _____ Position _____
Other functions reporting at the same level are _____
Does the quality department have:
  Written quality policy and procedures manual? (Y/N)
  Written inspection instructions? (Y/N)
  A quality engineering department? (Y/N)
  Person or persons who perform vendor surveys? (Y/N)
  Incoming inspection department? (Y/N)
  In-process inspection department? (Y/N)
  Final inspection department? (Y/N)
  A quality audit function? (Y/N)
  A gauge control program? (Y/N)
  A gauge control laboratory? (Y/N)
  Other quality laboratories? (Y/N)
    (If yes, specify type) _____
  A quality cost program? (Y/N)
  A reliability department? (Y/N)
To whom does the inspection department report? _____

Who is responsible for analyzing customer complaints and goods returned for defective quality?
_____

Does the quality department use statistical tools (control charts, sampling plans, etc.)?   (Y/N)
Explain _____

Is government source inspection available to your plant?
Resident _____ Itinerant _____ No _____

QUALITY INFORMATION

Records should be maintained of all inspections performed, and the data recorded should be periodically analyzed and used as a basis for action. Quality data should always be used, whether it be to improve the quality control operation by increasing or decreasing the amount of inspection, to improve the quality of product by the initiation of corrective action on processes or suppliers, to document certifications of product quality furnished to customers, or to report quality results and trends to management. Unused or unusual data are evidence of poor management.

How well are records of inspections maintained?   ( )
How adequate is the record and sample retention program?   ( )
How well are quality data used as a basis for action?   ( )
How well are quality data used in supporting certification of quality furnished to customers? ( )
How well is customer and field information used for corrective action?   ( )
How well is it reported to management?   ( )

CALIBRATION—INSPECTION AND TESTING

Periodic inspection and calibration of certain tools, gauges, tests, and some items of process control equipment are necessary for the control and verification of product quality. Controlled standards, periodically checked or referenced against national standards, will assure the compatibility of vendor and vendee measurements. Inaccurate gauges and testers can compromise the entire quality control program and may result in either rejection of good material or acceptance of defective material.

How well do internal standards conform to national standards or customer standards?   ( )
How well are periodic inspections and calibrations specified?   ( )
How adequate are calibration facilities and equipment?   ( )
If necessary, is traceability to NBS adequate?   (Y/N)
If external calibration sources are utilized, how adequate is the program and how well is it executed? ( )
Does your company have a gauge control function?   (Y/N)
   (If yes, list personnel.)
Does your company have written instructions for operating inspection and test instruments? (Y/N)
Are all inspection instruments calibrated at periodic intervals?   (Y/N)
Are records of calibration kept on file?   (Y/N)
Is there a system to recall inspection instruments when they are due for calibration?   (Y/N)
Are the inspection instruments used by production calibrated?   (Y/N)
If so, are these instruments removed from use until they can be repaired or recalibrated? (Y/N)
Are shop masters calibrated at periodic intervals to secondary standards traceable to NBS? (Y/N)

INSPECTION OF COMPLETED MATERIAL

Does your company have a final inspection function?   (Y/N)
   (If yes, list inspection, supervisory and quality engineers on a separate sheet.)
To whom does the final inspection department report?_____
Are shop drawings and specifications available to inspection?   (Y/N)
Is there a system for keeping the documents up-to-date?   (Y/N)

216

Are written inspection instructions available?   (Y/N)
Is there a system for reviewing and updating inspection instructions?   (Y/N)
Is sample inspection used?   (Y/N)
Are inspection records kept on file?   (Y/N)
Are records of inspection results used for corrective-action purposes?   (Y/N)
Is inspection equipment calibrated periodically?   (Y/N)
Is all material identified (route tags, etc.)?   (Y/N)
Is defective material identified as such?   (Y/N)
Is defective material segregated from good material until disposition is made?   (Y/N)
Is reworked material submitted for reinspection?   (Y/N)
Who is responsible for making disposition of nonconforming material? _____

FINAL ACCEPTANCE

Final inspection, testing, and packing are critical operations necessary to assure the acceptability of material. The specifications must form the basis for these activities. And to the extent that certifications or in-process inspections are used, in lieu of final inspection, records of those activities should be reviewed to verify conformance.

How well are specifications used in determining the acceptability of material?   (   )
How well are certifications and in-process inspection records used in the final acceptance decisions?   (   )
How adequate are inspection procedures? How well are they followed?   (   )
How adequate are inspection facilities and equipment?   (   )
How well are inspection results used for corrective action?   (   )
How adequate are packing and order-checking procedures? How well are they followed?   (   )

CHAPTER 11

INTERNATIONAL SOURCING

KEY CONCEPTS

- The benefits and risks of foreign sourcing
  Why purchase foreign goods and services?
  Problems associated with foreign procurement
  Common definitions
- Getting started
- Identifying sources
  Foreign trade intermediaries
  Direct purchasing
  International procurement offices
- Preparing for discussions
- The nuances of negotiating overseas
  Preparation
  General considerations in Europe
  Japan
  Suggestions for negotiating with non-Americans
- Countertrade
  Definitions
  Purchasing's role in countertrade
  Creative countertrade

Purchasing products and services of foreign origin can be extraordinarily challenging. On the one hand, virtually all of the practices and procedures described in this book are applicable. At the same time, many new issues must be addressed if the buyer is to ensure that his or her organization receives the right quality, in the right quantity, on time, with the right services, at the right price.

THE BENEFITS AND RISKS OF FOREIGN SOURCING

Why Purchase Foreign Goods and Services?

International sourcing requires additional efforts when compared with domestic sourcing, but it can yield large rewards. One of the complexities of buying goods and services of foreign origin is the wide variability among the producing countries in characteristics such as quality, service, and dependability. Quality, for example, may be very high in products from one country but inconsistent or unacceptably low in products from a neighboring land. With this caveat in mind, let us look at six common reasons for purchasing foreign goods and services:

Quality   Discussions with purchasing managers lead to a surprising conclusion: the number-one reason for foreign sourcing is to obtain the required level of quality. In coming years, this factor is bound to decline in significance, as American suppliers continue to address their quality problems and adopt the total quality commitment concept. At the moment, however, buyers in a variety of industries still look offshore to fulfill their most critical quality requirements.

Timeliness   A second major reason for purchasing foreign goods and services is, in general, the dependability of the supplier in meeting schedule requirements. Once initial difficulties of the new business relationship have been overcome, many foreign sources have proven to be remarkably dependable. In this area, too, the performance of American suppliers has improved markedly during the last several years and, in all likelihood, will continue to become more reliable and more service-oriented. The growing use of flexible manufacturing systems and the increasing use of tightly controlled production planning systems, as discussed in Chapter 20, should enable American firms to equal or exceed the performance of their foreign competitors in the near future.

Cost   International sourcing generates expenses beyond those normally encountered when sourcing domestically. For example, additional communications and transportation expenses, import duties, greater costs when investigating the potential supplier's capabilities (see Chapter 10), and so forth, all add to the buyer's total costs. To illustrate the point, one major computer manufacturer uses a rule of thumb that a foreign material's price must be at least 20 percent lower than the comparable domestic price to compensate for these additional costs. *Nonetheless,* after all of the additional costs of "buying foreign" are considered, in the case of many materials it frequently is possible to reduce the firm's *total cost* of the material through international sourcing.

New Technologies   No country holds a monopoly on new technology. Foreign sources in some industries tend to be more advanced technologically than their American counterparts. Not to take advantage of such advanced technology can result in a manufacturer's losing its competitive position vis-à-vis manufacturers that incorporate the new technology.

Broadening the Supply Base   Professional buyers want to develop and maintain an adequate supply base for required materials. It may be necessary to develop foreign suppliers in order to have a competitive supply base.

Countertrade   Many countries require their nondomestic suppliers to purchase materials in their country as part of the sales transaction. These arrangements commonly are called barter, offsets, or countertrade. The tying of *sales into a country* with *the purchase of goods from that country* makes both marketing and procurement far more challenging than when pure monetary transactions are involved. For a buyer's firm to compete and make sales in many countries, increasingly it is necessary to enter into agreements to purchase items made in those countries. This topic is discussed in greater detail on pages 237 to 239.

Problems Associated with Foreign Procurement

The American Standard of Living   In a broad sense, the biggest risk in buying goods and services of foreign origin is the long-term impact on the U.S. standard of living. Stephen Cohen and John Zysman in their provocative book, *Manufacturing Matters*, argue that the ability of the American economy to maintain high and rising wages under conditions of openness to international competition is *not* enhanced by abandoning production to others.[1] Akio Morita, the chairman of Sony, warns America: "Unless U.S. industry shores up its manufacturing base, it could lose everything. American companies have either shifted output to low-wage countries or come to buy parts and assembled products from countries like Japan that can make quality products at low prices. The result is a hollowing of American industry. The United States is abandoning its status as an industrial power."[2]

In contrast to the situation described by these gentlemen, progressive purchasing managers at leading firms such as Xerox, Tennant, General Electric, Texas Instruments, and the Ford Motor Company work with their *domestic* suppliers to develop them into world-class manufacturers that compete successfully with nondomestic manufacturers. Thus, the buying firm, the supplier, and the American economy all benefit.

Culture and Communications   Perhaps the largest obstacles to developing mutually profitable business relations with foreign sources are the cul-

---

[1] Stephen Cohen and John Zysman, *Manufacturing Matters,* Basic Books, Inc., New York, 1987.
[2] Ibid., p. 60.

tural differences between the buyer and the seller. The nature, customs, and ethics of individuals and business organizations from two different cultures can raise a surprising number of obstacles to successful business relations. What is considered ethical in one culture may not be ethical in another. The intention of filling commitments, the implications of gift giving, and even the legal systems differ widely.

Language frequently poses a significant barrier to successful international business relations. Differences in culture, language, dialects, or terminology may result in miscommunication and cause problems. Both parties may think they know what the other party has said, but true agreement and understanding often may be missing. Think, for instance, of the confusion the simple word "ton" can create. Is it a short ton (2,000 lb), a long ton (2,240 lb), or a metric ton (2,204.62 lb)? The use of textbook English in practice raises innumerable interesting problems. For example, in the Far East, the word "plant" is interpreted to mean only a living organism.

Payment Terms and Conditions   From the buyer's point of view, the preferred method of payment is after receipt and inspection of the goods. However, it is customary in many countries for advance payments to be made prior to commencing work. Such a provision ties up the purchaser's capital. Letters of credit also are common in international commerce. Again, the purchaser's funds may be committed for a longer period of time than if a domestic source were involved, and a cost is incurred in obtaining the letter of credit.

The absence of fixed exchange rates can be a problem; it creates at least four potential situations, as described below.

Case 1   A contract calls for *payment in a foreign currency*. The exchange rate moves against the U.S. dollar during performance of the contract. For example, assume that a contract was awarded to a supplier in the Federal Republic of Germany for 1 million deutsche marks (DM 1 million). Assume further that the rate of exchange was U.S. $1.00 = DM 1.5; that is, one U.S. dollar purchased 1.5 deutsche marks at the time the contract was awarded. Ignoring all other costs, the dollar cost to the U.S. buyer would be

$$\frac{\text{DM } 1,000,000}{\text{DM } 1.5/\$} = \$666,666.66$$

Assume that the U.S. dollar weakens to the point that $1.00 buys only DM 1. The cost in dollars then becomes

$$\frac{\text{DM } 1,000,000}{\text{DM } 1.0/\$} = \$1,000,000$$

This is an increase of $333,333.33, or a 50 percent increase in the cost of the item in U.S. dollars. Note that the German supplier is no better off, since it receives only DM 1 million, while the U.S. purchaser has suffered the 50 percent increase in the cost of the item in *U.S. dollars.*

Case 2 A contract calls for *payment in a foreign currency* (DM), and the exchange rate improves for the U.S. dollar so that $1 now buys DM 2. The cost of the item in U.S. dollars now is

$$\frac{\text{DM } 1,000,000}{\text{DM } 2/\$} = \$500,000$$

The American buyer has reduced its costs from the initial likely amount of $666,666.66 to $500,000.00, a 20 percent saving.

Case 3 The contract is with a foreign supplier, *with payment in U.S. dollars*, and the dollar weakens. Assume that when the contract was awarded, the rate of exchange was U.S. $1 = DM 1.5; the cost of the item was DM 1 million, or $666,666.66. Were there no change in the rate of exchange, the supplier would convert the $666,666.66 received into DM 1 million. Unfortunately for the supplier, the dollar has weakened so that $1 will buy only DM 1. Now, when the supplier receives its $666,666.66 and has this converted to deutsche marks, it receives only DM 666,666.66, a 33⅓ percent reduction from what it expected under the former exchange rate. Quite obviously, the supplier will be very unhappy and may translate this either to nonperformance or to a demand for a price increase.

Case 4 The contract is with a foreign supplier *with payment in U.S. dollars.* The dollar strengthens. As with Case 3, the contract called for a payment of $666,666.66. Assume that the rate of exchange changed so that $1 U.S. purchases DM 2. When the supplier receives its $666,666.66 and has it converted to marks at the current rate, it will receive 666,666.66 × 2 = DM 1,333,333.32, a windfall gain of DM 333,333.33. While the German supplier may be delighted, the American buyer will tend to be less enthusiastic.[3]

Long Lead Times Variable shipping schedules, unpredictable time requirements for customs activities, the need for greater coordination in foreign purchasing, strikes by stevedores and maritime unions, and storms at sea (which can cause both delays and damage) usually result in longer lead times. Air freight may be used to offset some of the problems of variable shipping schedules, but at a significant increase in cost.

Additional Inventories The quantity of additional inventory needed when purchasing from foreign sources can be difficult to determine. Quite often, however, the additional inventories are not as large as one might expect. Nevertheless, inventory carrying costs must be added to the purchase, the freight, and the administrative costs to determine the true total cost of

---

[3]The reader interested in strategies for handling fluctuating exchange rates should read J. R. Carter and S. K. Vickery, "Managing Volatile Exchange Rates in International Purchasing," *Journal of Purchasing and Materials Management*, Winter 1988–89, pp. 13–20.

buying from foreign sources. Occasionally, when a U.S. industry is producing at full capacity, it is possible to get both faster delivery and lower prices
from foreign sources. Routinely, however, additional lead times, which traditionally exceed thirty days, must be considered in planning foreign purchases when surface transportation is involved. It should be noted that some
buyers do *not* add buffer stocks, relying on air freight in case of emergencies.

Quality As previously mentioned, foreign suppliers frequently are utilized because many of them can provide a consistently high level of quality.
But problems do exist. The United States is the only major nonmetric country
in a metric world. This frequently leads to manufacturing *tolerance problems.*
Additionally, nondomestic suppliers tend to be less responsive to necessary
design changes than do their domestic counterparts. In many cases, there is
the risk that production outside of the U.S. firm's control can result in "off-
spec" incoming materials. Potential rework or scrap costs could add substantially to the total cost of doing business.

Higher Costs of Doing Business The need for translators, communications problems, the distances involved in making site visits, and so on, all
add to the cost of doing business overseas. Port-order services are more complicated because of currency fluctuations, methods of payment, customs issues, and the utilization of import brokers and international carriers. Inadequate local (foreign) logistical support functions such as communication
systems (telephones, telexes, and FAX machines), transportation systems, financial institutions, and so forth, can complicate communications and product distribution.

Common Definitions

International purchasing involves a number of unique documents, activities,
and taxes. This section provides the normally accepted definitions for the
most important of these items. These definitions are abstracted from a National Association of Purchasing Management publication authored by N. A.
DiOrio.[4]

Import Duties When goods are dutiable, three types of rate may be assessed: ad valorem, specific, or compound rates. An *ad valorem rate*, which is
the type of rate most often applied, is a percentage of the appraised value of
the merchandise, such as 5 percent ad valorem. A *specific rate* is a specified
amount per unit of weight or other quantity, such as 5.9 cents per dozen. A
compound rate is a combination of both an ad valorem rate and a specific rate,
such as 0.7 cents per pound plus 10 percent ad valorem.

---

[4]N. A. DiOrio, "International Procurement," *Guide to Purchasing,* National Association of
Purchasing Management, 1987, pp. 11–12.

Dutiable or Free of Duty   Rates of duty for imported merchandise may also vary depending on the country of origin. Certain rate concessions are reflected in the tariff schedules for merchandise from least-developed countries. Most merchandise is dutiable under the most favored nation (MFN) rates of the tariff schedules. Merchandise from countries to which the MFN rates have not been extended is dutiable at the full or "statutory" rates of the tariff schedules.

Free rates are provided for many items in the tariff schedules. Duty-free status is also available under various condition exemptions. One of the more frequently applied exemptions from duty occurs under the Generalized System of Preferences. GSP-eligible merchandise qualifies for duty-free entry when it is from a beneficiary developing country and meets other requirements.

Assists   U.S. Customs requires that any "assist" supplied by the buyer for use in connection with the production of goods imported into the United States is dutiable and must be declared. Assists include: (a) components or similar items incorporated in the imported goods; (b) tools, dies, molds, and so on, used in their production; (c) engineering, development plans, and sketches performed or provided outside the buying country by other than the buyer's employees.

Rulings on Imports   The U.S. Customs Service makes its decision as to the dutiable status of merchandise when the entry is liquidated after the entry documents have been filed. When advance information is needed, the buyer should not depend on a small "trial" or "test" shipment since there is no guarantee that the next shipment will receive the same tariff treatment. An importer, or importer's broker, may get advance information on any matter affecting the dutiable status of merchandise by contacting the director of the port or district where the merchandise will be entered.

Customs Penalties   In most instances, the clearance of shipments through U.S. Customs is handled by *customs brokers* who serve as buyer's agents. Customs brokers generally conduct freight forwarding services in addition to their customs activities. Although brokerage fees vary according to the pricing policy of the customs brokers, arrangements can be negotiated based on a fixed fee for each shipment handled. Normal buying practice is to instruct the foreign supplier (1) to consign the shipment and (2) to airmail the original and required import documents to the selected customs broker.

Customs Invoice   A customs invoice is a special document or invoice, prepared by the seller, on a form supplied by the U.S. Treasury which may be obtained from any U.S. Consulate. It is used to clear merchandise through U.S. Customs. It must be distinguished from the commercial invoice.

Pro Forma Invoice   This document is used largely for banking purposes. It is an abbreviated invoice sent in advance of a shipment, usually to enable the buyer to obtain an import permit or an exchange permit, or both. The pro forma invoice gives a close approximation of the weights and values of a shipment that is to be made.

In the absence of a commercial or customs invoice at the time of entry to U.S. Customs, a pro forma invoice may be filed and a bond given for the presentation of the required invoice within a prescribed period.

Packing List   The purchase contract should require a specified number of packing lists to facilitate the identification and movement of the order and checking of containers and contents. The lists should detail the contents with descriptions, weights and measures, and markings.

Bill of Lading   As in the case of domestic shipments, a bill of lading is a receipt issued by a carrier for merchandise to be delivered to a party at some named destination. It is (1) a contract for shipment of merchandise; (2) a receipt for merchandise; (3) a document of title to the merchandise; (4) a document of freight charges (where indicated); and (5) a guide to the carrier's staff in handling the shipment.

An *ocean bill of lading* covers the movement of goods by water and may be issued in either a "straight" form or an "order" form. When a straight form is used, the consignee *must* be named in the bill. When an order form is used, either the consignee or a designee can be named. Steamship lines insist on surrender of an original bill of lading on both straight and order consignments. *Air waybills* are generally issued by air carriers in nonnegotiable form, and the carrier will effect delivery to a straight consignee only.

Inspection Certificate (when required)   An inspection certificate is a document normally prepared by an independent entity other than the exporter to attest to the condition, quality, or quantity of goods being shipped. It is requested by the importer as a means of assuring that the goods contracted for are those that the exporter has shipped.

Certificate of Origin (when required)   Certain commodities require a document certifying the country from which the goods originated as distinct from the country from which they were immediately exported. U.S. Customs regulations prescribe the conditions under which this certificate is required for entry.

GETTING STARTED

Raul Casillas, of the Alps Manufacturing organization, suggests:[5]

To help determine if a part, product, or process is a candidate for foreign sourcing, ask the following questions:

- Does it qualify as "high-volume" in your industry?
- Does it have a long life (two to three years)?
- Does it lend itself to repetitive manufacturing or assembly?
- Is demand for the product fairly stable?
- Are specifications and drawings clear and well defined?
- Is technology not available domestically at a competitive price and quality?

If the answer to all six questions is yes, then the buyer may want to evaluate the support network within his or her firm, asking the following questions:

- Is there engineering support to efficiently facilitate engineering change orders when they do occur?
- Will the buyer be able to allow sufficient time to phase out existing and "pipeline" inventory?
- Will the buyer's firm take the responsibility for providing the necessary education and training for those that will have to interact with and support foreign suppliers?
- Is the firm prepared to make a financial commitment for expensive trips to the supplier?
- Is management willing to change the approach, in some cases even the policy, of how business and related transactions are conducted?
- Is the buyer aware of the environment—i.e., current and forecasted exchange rates, general impact of tariff schedules, available technologies, and products from other countries, as well as their political climates, and leading economic indicators both in the U.S. and abroad?

If the answers to both sets of questions are all positive, foreign sourcing may be a realistic possibility for the buyer. A significant number of negative responses indicates the potential for real problems if an overseas sourcing arrangement is developed. Before a positive decision is made, however, the buyer needs to explore several issues with top management. First, do the required procedural and policy changes mesh satisfactorily with the firm's existing mode of operation? More important, is the overseas sourcing concept, and its underlying rationale, compatible with the firm's long-term plans? It is important that the program contribute positively to achievement of the firm's long-range goals—and that the commitment be made as something more than a short-term-strategy decision.

---

[5] Raul Casillas, "Foreign Sourcing: Is It for You?", *Pacific Purchasor*, November–December 1988, p. 9.

IDENTIFYING SOURCES

Foreign Trade Intermediaries

Once a decision has been made to consider goods of foreign origins, the simplest way to get started is through the use of an intermediary. Selection of the appropriate intermediary is a function of availability and of the services required. The use of such intermediaries typically adds an estimated cost of 15 to 20 percent[6] to the overall cost of the transaction, but in most cases, their use avoids many unforeseen problems. The buyer who is venturing into international sourcing is well advised to solicit the advice of colleagues from the local purchasing management association. Some typical intermediaries are described below.[7]

- *Import merchants* buy goods for their own account and sell through their own outlets. Since they assume all the risks of clearing goods through customs and performing all the intermediate activity, their customers are relieved of import problems and, in effect, can treat such transactions as domestic purchases.
- *Commission houses* usually act for exporters abroad, selling in the United States and receiving a commission from the foreign exporter. Such houses generally do not have goods billed to themselves, although they handle many of the shipping and customs details.
- *Agents* are firms or individuals representing foreign sellers. Since their commission is paid by the seller, their primary interests are those of the foreign exporter. They generally handle all shipping and customs clearance details, although they assume no financial responsibility of the principals.
- *Import brokers* act as "marriage brokers" between buyers and sellers from different nations. Their commissions are paid by sellers for locating buyers and by buyers for finding sources of supply, but they are *not* involved in shipment or clearance of an order through customs. They also may act as special purchasing agents for designated commodities on a commission basis. Like agents, import brokers do not assume any of the seller's fiscal responsibility.
- *Trading companies* are large companies which generally perform all the functions performed individually by the types of agencies previously listed. The worldwide operations and know-how of such firms offer significant advantages and convenience. The use of Japanese trading companies is particularly advantageous to U.S. importers since the Japanese government exercises a high degree of control over their operations. Standard directories and trade publications list such firms, their capabilities, and areas of service.

[6]N. A. DiOrio, *op. cit.*, p. 3.
[7]N. A. DiOrio, *op. cit.*, p. 7.

Direct Purchasing

After the buying firm has gained confidence in the quality of the foreign goods, and volume increases, it typically discontinues the use of foreign trade intermediaries for major procurements. Its major motivation is to avoid the intermediary's markup. The buyer should inform its suppliers of this new policy—and then visit each of the manufacturers, *without the intermediaries*, to negotiate new contracts. The buyer should anticipate resistance by both the intermediaries and their manufacturers. But this resistance normally can be overcome. In some cases, new suppliers may have to be developed due to the tight ties the foreign trade intermediaries may have with the existing supplier. Before taking such action, the buyer must ensure that his or her company is set up to handle items such as traffic, customs clearance, and international payments.[8]

Direct purchasing requires the involvement of the company in all aspects of the transaction; when properly conducted, it eliminates the added profit of the middleman. Outside agencies may be engaged to perform specialized services. For example, *customs brokers* can be used to handle entry requirements, *export brokers* to handle foreign clearances, and *freight forwarders* to arrange for transport. Such agents do not take title to the goods. They are used by most direct purchasers whose scale of activities does not warrant such in-house capability.

Identifying Potential Suppliers Potential foreign suppliers can be located through a wide variety of sources: current business publications, catalogs, associations, newspapers, the commercial attachés of foreign embassies and consulates, the U.S. Department of Commerce, local chambers of commerce, the International Chamber of Commerce,[9] official trade commissioners and government agencies represented in many major cities in the United States, international banks, the International Federation of Purchasing and Materials Management, and colleagues in the buyer's industry.

International Procurement Offices

When an organization's purchases in a foreign country or region warrant (e.g., $15 to $20 million per year), consideration should be given to establishing an international procurement office (IPO). Such an organization quickly becomes familiar with qualified sources, thereby expanding the buying firm's potential supplier base. IPO personnel can evaluate suppliers personally, negotiate for price and other terms, and monitor quality and job progress through direct site visits. IPO personnel are in a position to develop and maintain better

---

[8] Richard G. Novotny, "Global Search," *Electronic Buyers' News*, Dec. 19, 1988, p. 34.
[9] The International Chamber of Commerce is located at 1615 H Street N.W., Washington, D.C. 20062.

information on local conditions such as materials shortages, labor issues, and governmental actions than are U.S.–based buyers. The IPO also facilitates payments to the suppliers. IPOs normally are staffed by expatriates who have worked for the U.S. manufacturer—usually in a technical role.

Preparing for Discussions

Considerably more preparation is required for foreign sourcing of a crucial item than for purchasing from a domestic source.

Before dealing with identified candidate suppliers, the buying team should:

- Review the specifications and drawings.
- Determine in great detail what the quality requirements are.
- Identify specific production scheduling requirements.
- Determine (as a group) what percentage of the annual requirements for the item can be placed offshore.
- Determine requirements for special packaging.
- Identify likely lead times.
- Develop a clear idea of the price objective.
- Prepare a briefing on the buyer's firm. Frequently, much effort will be expended selling the potential suppliers on doing business with the buying firm. The briefing should include:
  Information on the relevant product line and related lines
  Actual and forecasted sales volume
  Customers
  Market share
  Unclassified corporate strategy information
  Annual reports
  An indication of why the buyer is soliciting the potential foreign supplier's interest (quality? price?)

Each supplier's country's trade council should be visited before the team departs. The buyer should take along samples (or photos) of required materials.

The Initial Meeting   It is essential that potential suppliers be visited and their facilities reviewed. Experience has shown that the controller of the target supplier usually occupies a very influential position. To gain his or her support, the buyer should describe how the supplier firm will get paid! The buying firm's technical people clearly must be part of the visiting team. The potential supplier will be judging the buying firm just as much as the buyer is judging the potential supplying firm.

THE NUANCES OF NEGOTIATING OVERSEAS[10]

Virtually all purchases from foreign suppliers are the result of negotiations. The success of each of these negotiations is influenced, in part, by the American negotiator's ability to understand the needs, and ways of thinking and acting, of representatives of the foreign firms.

Negotiating is a process that is greatly enhanced when negotiators understand their counterparts—the wants, needs, and frame of reference of those at the other side of the table. This type of understanding helps all negotiators reach a satisfactory agreement. U.S. negotiators perform more effectively in these negotiations if they understand the cultural and business heritage of their opposites—and the effect of this heritage on the opposites' negotiation strategies and tactics.

Intercultural communication can be difficult. Even when one overcomes the natural barriers of language difference, it is still possible to fail to understand and be understood. When one is unaware of the significant role culture plays in communication, there is a tendency to place the blame for communication failure on the other person. It may be obvious that there are language differences between cultural groups. Unfortunately, many busy American executives believe that a competent interpreter is all that is necessary to overcome these differences. The use of interpreters, while allowing communication to take place, does not obviate the need for an understanding of the non-American's culture.

The ability to understand a non-American's cultural background is of great practical advantage. It puts the non-American off his or her guard. He or she expects most Americans to be clumsy and able to do business only in the American way. The American heritage of team sports appears to result in what can best be described as good team players. This is not the case in Europe. The teamwork and team play commonly present on the American side is usually absent on the European side. The Japanese, on the other hand, are excellent team players.

Preparation

In addition to the conventional preparation for any negotiation, it is essential to conduct an extensive study of the culture(s). This should include reading about the history and customs of the country in question and discussions with others who have had experience dealing with its citizens. The focus of these preparations should be on the culture, not the language. Pan American's *World Guide* and Dow Jones Irwin's *Big Business Blunders* are good investments and good reading. Talk with others who have experienced living or working in the culture. Learn what the holidays are, what the units of measure are, what the currency exchange is, what topics are taboo, and so on.

[10] Much of the material contained in this section was developed by one of the authors under contract F33 615-80-C-5188, sponsored by the Air Force Business Research Management Center.

A second aspect of the cultural preparation process becomes important in cases where there is a strong likelihood of continuing relations (i.e., one or more transactions that would require a year or more for completion). Under such circumstances, the non-Americans (accompanied by their spouses) frequently visit the U.S. firm. The American hosts should go to considerable lengths to become acquainted with their counterparts (and their spouses) on a social basis. Americans should host the visitors in their homes (a rarity in Europe and the Far East). This will give the Americans and their spouses an opportunity to develop good relations with their counterparts. This bank of goodwill, while not a means of co-opting the foreign supplier, projects a desire and willingness to understand, which frequently proves to be invaluable during subsequent transactions.

One other aspect of the preparatory process needs to be emphasized: it takes much longer to negotiate with non-Americans. This is especially true if the foreign firm has not had extensive exposure to U.S. business practices and specifications. The longer time required is due to the different organization and mode of operation of most non-American businesses. In the case of European firms, it usually takes at least twice as much time, and up to six times as long is often required for Far East firms. The American negotiator must be aware of the requirement for additional time—and plan accordingly. He or she must be patient and thick-skinned when progress is slow.

General Considerations in Europe

Pricing The European concept of a fair and reasonable price is tied directly to the marketplace. "Whatever the market will bear" is often the sole basis for a European firm's pricing policy. Europeans tend to be unprepared to support their price proposals. Understanding this tendency should cause the American negotiator to conduct detailed and realistic cost analysis before entering negotiations, and to be prepared to deal with an opposite who may not know the firm's true costs.

Productivity Europeans tend to be sensitive to discussions that might show that their productivity is lower than that of their competitors. As a result, it has been found to be more effective to focus on rates rather than man-hours. Experienced buyers don't push for details on productivity.

Profit Objectives Many European firms are closely held by financial institutions, and return on investment and dividend payments tend to be lower than in the United States. Therefore, it frequently is possible to negotiate a lower target profit figure in Europe than in the United States.

Progress Payments Many European firms, like some American firms, tend to have cash flow problems. Frequently, it may be possible to gain a significant price concession if advance or progress payments are incorporated in the resulting agreement. However, this approach must not be treated in isolation. European financing rates may be considerably below American rates. Thus, it may be less costly to have the European supplier assign the contract payments to a local financial institution in order to obtain low-cost, temporary financing.

Tax Laws   It is desirable to be familiar with the tax laws in the European supplier's country. This may make it possible to negotiate significant price reductions.

Currency Issues   It is essential that the negotiator be given guidance from his or her firm's controller about the likely costs or advantages of using a particular currency. Then the negotiator should be free to negotiate the exchange rate as he or she would any other term or condition.

Tactics   The buyer should keep in mind the following tactical points:

- Frequent caucuses are helpful during negotiations with non-Americans, since the caucuses help relieve the tensions introduced by different cultural and business practices.
- The winner of a negotiation in some countries is the one who gains the *most* concessions, regardless of the value of the concessions. When a negotiator treats all concessions with equal importance, his or her counterpart should ensure that many issues are introduced and should take care in properly sequencing them.
- Usually the "package approach" is more productive than the sequential one. In using the package approach, each issue is addressed in turn. If agreement is possible, it is so noted. If agreement is not possible, the issue is deferred and finally included as part of a final package proposal. One negotiator was quite successful with what he called the "bucket approach." He would refer to his package proposal as a bucket, pointing out that if something were to be added, something else would flow out, and vice versa.
- Cancellation procedures are especially difficult to negotiate with European suppliers due to their inability to manipulate the size of their labor force. In some instances, rather than prolong negotiations on this issue, it may be better not to include cancellation procedures in the resulting contract. The issue is addressed only if cancellation later becomes necessary. In Europe, disputes over such issues as cancellation costs are resolved through arbitration or jurisprudence. In such cases, the decision goes beyond the terms of the contract in an effort to arrive at what is considered an equitable decision.
- Several approaches are possible in deciding what language to use at the negotiating table. In the 1950s and 1960s, it was common to employ negotiators who were native to the foreign country. Negotiations were conducted in the appropriate foreign language. A representative of the American firm would be present. The foreign employee would function

as an "intelligent interpreter"—one who conveyed the meaning, nuances, and intent, not merely a literal translation. Several American firms still utilize this approach.

- Even when the foreign supplier has excellent translators, many experienced buyers insist on bringing their own competent translator to all business discussions. An alternative approach, which seems to be equally successful, requires all discussions to be in English. Most European business officials have an excellent command of English. American negotiators who require all discussions to be in English contend that this produces a freer discussion and a better, quicker understanding.
- The recorder is in a powerful position—especially in dealings with foreigners. The experienced buyer attempts to appoint a member of his or her team as the official recorder.
- Many European firms like to start negotiations at a low level with emissaries who obtain information and then scurry back to their superiors. This approach can be a frustrating waste of time. It can be avoided by insisting that the key decision-maker be present.
- It is quite common in the U.S. culture to be open and frank in negotiations. This is especially true if one negotiator tends to be in a superior position to the other. For example, such a negotiator may indicate the target cost for a project to an unsophisticated supplier in order to convey the scope of the work. Many Europeans, however, do not react well to this degree of openness. In fact, such an approach often appears to be very dysfunctional.
- Most Europeans have a sense of humor, but their humor often tends to be localized. The typical American approach to joviality does not come off well in Europe. In fact, such joking can be dangerous.
- Care should be taken in the selection of American negotiators to avoid the *"ugly American" syndrome.* The American negotiator should not be loud and should not be a carouser.
- Europeans tend to be very title-conscious. Some American firms have found it desirable to "promote" their personnel while they are conducting business overseas.
- For some years after the end of World War II, many European firms derived a unique satisfaction from dealing with American customers. Those days, however, are long gone—the romance is over. It is now business as usual.

Japan

The Japanese are a source of wonderment and confusion. Their culture is vastly different from those of the United States and the European countries. Breakdowns in communication based on this cultural difference are common. But the effort to develop sound, mutually satisfying relations is an investment that usually yields an excellent return. Japanese firms typically are dependable and loyal suppliers.

Personal Characteristics   The Japanese are diligent, loyal employees of their firms. They are an especially polite people. They are much more concerned about the well-being of their firm and their country than of themselves as individuals. While Americans are usually better team players than their European counterparts, the Japanese out team-play the Americans. They are more concerned with saving face and achieving harmony than with achieving higher sales and profits. They are extremely cautious. If a proposed transaction requires recruitment of many new employees, the Japanese may refuse the deal if there is not a reasonable assurance of steady employment for the new personnel.

A Japanese negotiator should never be placed in a position in which he must admit failure or impotency. The Japanese resist pressure for deadlines and delivery dates; yet, once an agreement is reached, they treat their customers as valued members of their "family." While a great deal of time is required to reach a decision, the time required to implement the decision is far less than in America.

The Japanese possess great emotional sensitivity. Yet, they go to considerable lengths to conceal their emotions. They are uncomfortable when others lose control and show anger or impatience. Most are ill at ease in the presence of an egotistical, abrasive, or harsh individual, and they may break off negotiations to avoid dealing with such a person.

The Japanese, like most Orientals, appear to have *great difficulty with saying no*. Many American business representatives who have presented their ideas and requirements, and then assumed that an agreement had been reached, have learned later that the apparent agreement was based on the Japanese counterpart's desire to be polite, and not on reality! The Oriental custom of telling people what they want to hear, rather than the hard facts, can be extremely frustrating. When a Japanese says yes, but then draws his breath through his teeth—or when he says, "It is very difficult," he is probably saying no.

As in Europe, good personal relations are a great asset. An effort to speak a little Japanese is appreciated. Entertainment is an important part of the process of developing the personal relations and goodwill that are prerequisites to a good agreement. Gift giving is a common and accepted factor in Japanese business transactions. Usually, the gift is not of great monetary value. The most enhancing gifts are those that are selected with a knowledge of the recipient's preferences and a desire to bring happiness and pleasure.

Negotiations   Negotiating in Japan is a wondrous experience. When negotiating, it is necessary to convince the whole group whose activities will be influenced by the proposed transaction. It is desirable to begin discussions at as high a level as possible, since the first person contacted will be involved through the conclusion of the discussions. The Japanese negotiator typically asks what seems to be an endless list of questions—frequently far afield of issues bearing on the proposed transaction. He has learned that his colleagues will want such information and he must be prepared. The Japanese place great emphasis on decision by consensus. This consensus frequently is achieved through the "ringi" process. With ringi, a proposal is developed between buyer and seller. The pertinent facts and a recommendation then are circulated to all concerned members of the Japanese firm. Each recipient is expected to review the proposal and affix his seal to the accompanying routing slip. Questions and disagreements are then resolved at conferences until a consensus evolves.

Americans who are about to negotiate with a member of a Japanese firm are well advised to develop personal relations away from the negotiating room. The usual intense and rather dry American approach to doing business must be supplemented with a social relationship. The Japanese are accustomed to the use of entertainment as a means of becoming better acquainted and of developing goodwill. The feeling a Japanese has about his counterpart may have as much impact on the outcome of a transaction as do the cold facts. *Honesty* and *sincerity* are essential traits for the American negotiator.

Once the right degree of rapport has been established, it is possible to get on with the details of the negotiation. In these discussions, it is important for the American negotiator to realize that growth, steady employment, and superiority over competitors are far more important to the Japanese than are profits.

Americans tend to be uncomfortable with extended silences. The Japanese are not. They feel no compulsion to break a silence. American impatience or desire to hammer out an agreement often results in a breaking of the silences, which in turn may mean yielding or compromising on the point being discussed. Again, such silences are culturally inspired and are not ploys. A good negotiator will recognize that a silence indicates doubt or uncertainty and will be content to allow the silence to run its course.

During complex and protracted negotiations, a crisis may develop. This is not a ploy. Rather, one or more members of the Japanese firm have voiced disagreement or concern over the proposal. The crisis may continue for several days or weeks. It is important for the American buyer to keep communication channels open during this period, even if there are no formal meetings. When a crisis is protracted, the American should maintain discreet contact with those who favor the transaction and seek advice on how to get the negotiations back on track.

When final agreement appears to have been reached, it is essential to prepare a written contract. Many apparently minor points may have been put aside in the interest of reaching a general agreement. Compromise may be necessary to reach a final agreement on all points. While the Japanese are excellent conciliators, one must remember how important face is. They do not like the appearance of having made forced concessions. The American approach of "splitting the difference" results in an obvious compromise. A mutually acceptable agreement based on the facts—even if somewhat bent—should be the goal.

Suggestions for Negotiating with Non-Americans

When negotiating with non-Americans, the following summary of key points may be helpful.

- Speak slowly. Ask questions to check for understanding.
- Print business cards in both English and the language of the host country (this impresses the non-Americans and tells them that the buyer is sincerely interested in doing business with them).
- Constantly test understanding.
- Be sensitive to the culture of the supplier's negotiator(s). Read about his or her culture during the preparation phase. Ask questions of others who have had experience negotiating with individuals from that culture. Obtain information on local circumstances in the country.
- Be well prepared on all issues, especially technical ones.
- If continuing relations are likely, attempt to develop a personal rapport, a base of understanding, and a bank of goodwill.
- Find out who the supplier's negotiator is, who his or her family is, what the level of education is, the approximate income level, and what makes him or her tick.
- In Europe, be prepared for negotiations to take two or three times as long as in the United States. In Japan, negotiations may take six times as long as in America.
- Conduct extensive cost and price analyses before the formal negotiation meeting. Do not expect the supplier's negotiator to have a well-developed cost breakdown.
- Do nothing that might put the opposing negotiator in a face-saving position over the issue of productivity. Focus on rates, not man-hours.
- Attempt to establish a lower profit objective than would normally be acceptable in the United States.
- Become familiar with local tax laws.
- Obtain guidance from experienced international finance people on the issue of exchange rates and the likely costs or advantages of using a particular currency. Then negotiate the exchange rate just as any other issue.
- Arrange issues in such a manner that the opposing negotiator can win his or her share of the issues.
- Use the package approach of discussing each issue in turn, reaching agreement when possible, and finally developing an acceptable package addressing all issues.
- The recorder occupies an important position; he or she should be selected from the American team when possible.
- If possible, ensure that the head of the non-American team has the authority to reach agreement on behalf of his or her firm. In Japan, however, such an approach cannot be used; therefore, time must be allowed for the consensus process to function.
- Be extremely cautious about being frank and open during discussions.

Non-Americans are not accustomed to such an approach. It can be misunderstood and may be disruptive.

COUNTERTRADE

Countertrade refers to any transaction in which payment is made partially or fully with goods instead of money. Countertrade links two normally unrelated transactions: the sale of a product into a foreign country and the sale of goods out of that country. Countertrade normally is imposed by foreign governments in an effort to gain foreign exchange or foreign technology.[11]

Asim Erdilek, an economics professor at Case Western Reserve University, writes: "Countertrade, including barter and more complex forms of exchanging goods directly or indirectly, is less efficient than monetized multilateral trade. It raises transaction costs and hence discourages trade by limiting competition, choice, and flexibility. Countertrade is promoted by governments that restrict private foreign exchange transactions, prefer state-to-state trading, and keep their currencies inconvertible."[12] Robert Paul, Vice President of Materiel Management, Lockheed Corporation, recently cited the following advantages and disadvantages (from the selling firm's point of view) of countertrade:[13]

Advantages	Disadvantages
Facilitates sales	Complicates procurement
Expands competition	Requires development
Improves profit potential	Decreases "make" items
Opens responsive markets	Adds administrative costs
Improves ally's technology	Extends transportation time/cost
Locates superior artisans	Incurs duties and taxes
Develops new capabilities	Drains home technology
Retards inflation	Imposes unfamiliar specifications

An example of the persuasiveness of countertrade is reflected in Figure 11-1, which depicts the suppliers involved in McDonnell Douglas's MD-11 program.

Elderkin and Norquist indicate that total world countertrade was approximately $150 billion per year, or about 8 percent of the total volume of world trade in 1983. They also write that there is consensus on the following five points:[14]

1 Some 200 U.S. companies are now thought to be attempting countertrade transactions.

[11] The interested reader is encouraged to read *Creative Countertrade: A Guide to Doing Business Worldwide* by Kenton W. Elderkin and Warren E. Norquist, Ballinger Publishing Co., Cambridge, Mass., 1987.
[12] *Wall Street Journal*, Sept. 16, 1988.
[13] Third Annual Procurement Forum, University of San Diego, Oct. 28, 1988.
[14] Elderkin and Norquist, op. cit., p. 38.

Global engineering
Main MD-11 subcontractors

☐ Douglas Aircraft, Long Beach
☐ Other McDonnell Douglas locations

Vertical stabiliser & rudders (Aeritalia) Italy
Aft tail pylon (Rohr Industries) USA
Tail engine: (General Electric) USA; (Pratt & Whitney) USA or (Rolls-Royce) Britain
Extended tail cone (Mitsubishi) Japan
Horizontal stabiliser & elevators (CASA) Spain
Auxiliary power unit (Garrett) USA
Wing/fuselage fillets (Korean Air) South Korea
Vanes (Westland) Britain
Outboard flap (Embraer) Brazil
Spoilers (Fleet) Canada
Trailing edge panels (Heath Tecna) USA
Flap-hinge fairings (Fischer) Austria
Winglet (Aeritalia) Italy
Main gear (Cleveland Pneumatic) USA
Wheels & brakes (Bendix) USA. Automatic braking (Hydro Aire) USA. Brake monitoring systems (Labinal) France. Antiskid system (Loral) USA
Main gear strut door (Fleet) Canada
Main gear door (CASA) Spain
Pylon (Rohr Industries) USA
Engine: (General Electric) USA; (Pratt & Whitney) USA or (Rolls-Royce) Britain

Tail-engine inlet (Heath Tecna) USA

Aft fuselage & doors (Convair, USA a division of General Dynamics)

Center fuselage (Convair) USA
Overwing fuel tank (CASA) Spain
FWD fuselage (Convair) USA
Intermediate fuselage & doors (Convair) USA
Flight-deck avionics (Honeywell) USA
Air-conditioning units (Garrett) USA
Nose gear (AP Precision) Britain
Wheels & tires (Goodyear) USA
Doors (Convair) USA
Wing/fuselage fillets (Korean Air) South Korea

Centerline gear (AP Precision) Britain
Underwing fuel tank bladder (Goodyear) USA

FIGURE 11-1
An example of countertrade. (*Source: The Economist,* Sept. 3, 1988.)

2 About 45 companies are beginning their own counter trading companies.
3 It is generally believed that of the 155 nations in the United Nations only 20 to 30 do *not* counter trade.
4 Around 30 countries require countertrade in certain instances.
5 Everyone agrees that countertrade is growing and that much of the growth is taking place among the less developed countries.

Definitions

Barter This form of transaction preceded the use of money. Goods are exchanged for other goods with no money involved. This is the simplest form of countertrade.

Offset Under this form of transaction, some, all, or even more than 100 percent of the value of the sale is *offset* by the purchase (or facilitation of purchases by others) of items produced in the buying country. Offsets are categorized as direct and indirect. A *direct offset* involves close technological ties between the items sold and purchased. For example, when the government of Australia purchased helicopters made by Boeing, Boeing agreed to buy ailerons for the 727 from an Australian supplier. An *indirect offset* involves the purchase or facilitation of sales of commodities unrelated to the purchasing country. When the Swiss purchased F-5 aircraft, the manufacturer (Northrop) facilitated sales of Swiss elevators and other non-aircraft products in North America.

Counter Purchase   With this type of transaction, unrelated goods are exchanged. The U.S. manufacturer purchases goods in the foreign country from a supplier who is paid in local currency by the buyer of the manufacturer's goods.

Purchasing's Role in Countertrade

Historically, purchasing has been dragged screaming to the offset transaction by the firm's marketing people who are intent on making a sale. One of the authors was involved in such transactions during the 1970s. Little thought was given to the American seller's countertrade obligations until the purchasing government brought economic and political pressure to bear. At this point, the U.S. firm's buyers frantically began to see what could be purchased in the foreign country. A very uncomfortable relationship developed between the customer and the seller.

Both marketing and procurement people must recognize that they need to work as a team if countertrade is to operate to the firm's benefit. When countertrade is used to facilitate sales, purchasing should be involved *up-front*. Buyers should review the items their company requires. Similar requirements must be levied on the firm's suppliers so that they are in a position to assist the manufacturer in meeting its present or potential obligations.

Creative Countertrade

Elderkin and Norquist define traditional countertrade as focusing "on existing goods to be brought out of the host country and sold in existing world markets. Traditional countertrade must deal with the limitations of fitting what already exists into unresponsive markets."

"Creative countertrade," on the other hand, with its focus on creating future goods for *new market niches*, has greater flexibility and wider possibilities. Creative countertrade is broader than traditional countertrade. It includes not only traditional countertrade, but also foreign investment and international joint venture activities. It carefully analyzes the needs of all the major parties, including the potential development of new foreign suppliers, and creatively applies existing business tools to answer these needs.

Traditional countertrade provides quick-fix solutions to ongoing trade problems. But it lacks the depth and longer time horizons of creative countertrade." It seems likely that progressive firms will embrace creative countertrade as a means of both increasing sales and developing new dependable sources of supply.[15]

---

[15] Elderkin and Norquist, op. cit., pp. 122–123.

CONCLUSION

Foreign procurement is one of the most challenging aspects of purchasing. Many new problems are involved for the buying firms. Perhaps the most perplexing issue is that of balancing the purchasing firm's short-term interest with America's long-term need to be competitive.

FOR DISCUSSION

11-1 What is the number-one reason for purchasing foreign-made industrial products? What are five other reasons?

11-2 Describe the biggest risk in buying foreign-made goods.

11-3 What is the largest obstacle to developing mutually profitable business relations with foreign sources? Discuss.

11-4 How do payment terms and conditions differ with a purchase from a U.S. manufacturer?

11-5 Describe four possible outcomes of variable exchange rates on an international purchase.

11-6 What are the key contributors to longer lead times when purchasing internationally?

11-7 Define import duties, assists, and customs invoices.

11-8 Identify the sources of higher costs of doing business internationally.

11-9 What is the *simplest* way to start purchasing goods of foreign origin?

11-10 List and describe four foreign trade intermediaries.

11-11 Why would a purchaser prefer to buy directly from a foreign producer? How would such a purchaser proceed?

11-12 Describe the steps involved in preparing to meet with candidate suppliers.

11-13 Describe the initial meeting with a new foreign supplier.

11-14 Why is it important to understand a non-American's cultural background?

11-15 Describe the role of teamwork when dealing with non-Americans.

11-16 Describe six major nuances of negotiating overseas.

11-17 Describe the key cultural differences you would expect when preparing to deal with the Japanese.

11-18 Describe countertrade. What are its major advantages to a U.S. manufacturer? Disadvantages?

CASES FOR CHAPTER 11

The Dutzel Diesel Case, page 732
National Machine and Electronics, page 770
SDC Corporation, page 803
The Wide, Wide World of Purchasing (in the Instructor's Manual)

PRICING PRINCIPLES

KEY CONCEPTS

- General economic considerations
    - Conditions of competition
    - Variable-margin pricing
    - Differences between products
    - Six categories of cost
    - Regulation by competition
    - Break-even analysis
- Price analysis
    - Competitive price proposals
    - Regulated, catalog, and market prices
    - Historic prices
    - Independent cost estimates
- Purchasing design work
- "All-in-cost"
- Documenting a price analysis
- Discounts
    - Trade discounts
    - Quantity discounts
    - Cash discounts

Obtaining materials at the right price is important; it literally can mean the difference between a firm's success or failure. Professional buyers interpret the right price to mean a price that is fair and reasonable to both the buyer and the seller. Unfortunately, there is no magic formula for calculating precisely what constitutes a "fair and reasonable price." The right price for one supplier is not necessarily the right price for any other supplier, either at the same time or at different points in time. To determine the right price for any specific purchase, a number of constantly changing variables and relationships must be evaluated. This chapter discusses the most important of these variables and their relationships.

GENERAL ECONOMIC CONSIDERATIONS

Conditions of Competition

Economists of the classical school speak of a competitive scale that includes three fundamental types of competition: pure, imperfect, and monopoly. At the one end of the scale is *pure (or perfect) competition.* Under conditions of pure competition, the forces of supply and demand alone, not the individual actions of either buyers or sellers, determine prices.[1]

At the other end of the competitive scale is *monopoly.* Under conditions of monopoly, one seller controls the entire supply of a particular commodity, and thus is free to maximize its profit by regulating output and forcing a supply-demand relationship that is most favorable to the seller.

The competitive area between the extremes of pure competition and monopoly is called *imperfect competition.* Imperfect competition takes two forms: (1) markets characterized by few sellers and (2) those in which many sellers operate. When there are just a few sellers, an *oligopoly* is said to exist. The automobile, steel, and cigarette industries are examples of oligopolies. Generally, oligopolistic firms produce relatively few different products.

In contrast to oligopolies, the second form of imperfect competition exists where many sellers produce many products. This form of competition does not have a distinctive name. Most of the products sold in this market are *differentiated* (distinguished by a specific difference), although some are not. Sellers, however, spend much money and effort to persuade buyers that their products are different. This is the market in which the majority of the products made in the United States are traded.

In practice, the three categories of competition are not mutually exclusive; actually, they overlap considerably. When one considers both the buying and the selling sides of the total market, it is apparent that the number of market arrangements between individual buyers and sellers is very large indeed.

---

[1] Pure competition exists only under the following circumstances: The market contains a large number of buyers and sellers of approximately equal importance. The products traded are homogeneous (a buyer would not desire one particular seller's product over any other's). The buyers and sellers always have full knowledge of the market. The buyers always act rationally, and sellers are free to enter and to leave the market at will.

It is frequently suggested that oligopolists conspire and act together as monopolists to thwart price competition. The facts, however, indicate that price conspiracies among oligopolists are not the normal order of business. Although the U.S. Department of Justice does uncover a few conspiracies every year, any buyer who has purchased in oligopolistic markets knows that price competition can be intense. Chevrolet strives intensely to outsell Ford, and vice versa. This is not to say that oligopolistic industries do not periodically exercise monopolistic tendencies to their own advantage. They do. For example, in times of recession, it requires only a basic knowledge of economics, not a conspiracy, for oligopolies to lower production rates and thus direct a balance of the forces of supply and demand in their favor.

It should be noted that oligopolistic industries frequently hold firmly to their prices for long periods and appear noncompetitive. This appearance may be deceptive, however. Frequently, in order to gain a competitive advantage without notice, oligopolists shift their competitive efforts to other areas, such as service. Sellers may agree to perform such additional services as carrying customers' inventories, extending the payment time of their bills, or absorbing their freight charges. Such indirect price reductions are not advertised.

Consequently, the amount of service a firm is able to obtain usually correlates directly with the perception and skills of its purchasing personnel. Foreign competitors also greatly influence the freedom of U.S. oligopolies to raise their prices above fair market prices. For example, the freedom of U.S. automobile, steel, and electronic companies to raise prices is noticeably restrained because of foreign imports. For a number of items, specialty suppliers also compete effectively with oligopolies. Consequently, the competent buyer who learns to operate successfully within the practices of oligopolistic industries can definitely influence the firm's total cost of materials.

It is important to understand that oligopoly is not characteristic of industry as a whole. Most firms and industries operate somewhere in the area of imperfect competition. Millions of people, working in thousands of factories, produce hundreds of thousands of products substantially without governmental or any other outside direction. The firms that make up this market exercise almost complete control over their prices, and price conspiracies in this market are extremely rare. In fact, aside from utilities, transportation, and some manufacturing industries, the concentration of oligopolistic power is rare.

Most Prices Are Subject to Adjustment   It is because most firms are free, within broad limits, to adjust their prices at will that competent buyers can obtain better prices in direct proportion to their ability to analyze price. Prices can be negotiated very little with firms in the markets of pure competition or monopoly. They can be negotiated a great deal with firms operating in the markets of imperfect competition. The question then is: What proportion of the nation's total market falls within the area of imperfect competition? What percentage of a buyer's total purchases are subject to price flexibility?

Studies made by Theordore Kreps, of the Graduate School of Business of Stanford University, show the nation's economy to be approximately 70 percent free.[2] The results of similar studies by other authorities support Dr. Kreps's conclusion.[3] Buyers in most purchasing situations, therefore, have considerable latitude for negotiating prices with their suppliers. At the same time, however, every buyer should guard against the inducement of illegal price concessions. Buying personnel must understand the operation of federal and state restraint of trade laws. (See Chapter 29.)

Variable-Margin Pricing

Most industrial firms sell a line of products rather than just a single product. Very few firms attempt to earn the same profit margin on each product in the line. Most firms price their products to generate a satisfactory return on their whole line, not on each product in the line. Such a variable-margin pricing policy permits maximum competition on individual products. The profits from the most efficiently produced and "successfully priced" items are used to offset the losses or the lower profit margins of the inefficiently produced items.

An understanding of the theory of variable-margin pricing is essential if buyers are to obtain the right price. Because it is usually advantageous to them, whenever possible sellers use average profit margins for pricing orders. In some cases, this practice results in prices that sophisticated buyers realize are too high—particularly when low-cost, efficiently produced items are being purchased. Invariably when average margins are used, prices considerably above fair prices result for large, long-term purchases. When dealing with large, multiproduct firms which utilize this pricing approach, a buyer must also know which of the items purchased are high-margin and which are low-margin items. This fact is learned by noting the differences in volumes, manufacturing skills, and costs of the various producers.

The following case illustrates the practical concepts of the preceding discussion. A large, high-technology research firm successfully negotiated a $2.8 million annual contract for medical and scientific supplies. At the outset, the seller proposed that the contract be priced at cost plus the firm's annual gross profit margin of 19 percent. After several hours of negotiation, the contract was priced at cost plus a 6 percent profit margin. Had the buyer not understood the concept of variable-margin pricing, and not known which

[2]T. J. Kreps, "An Evaluation of Antitrust Policy," Joint Committee Print, 86th Cong., Study Paper no. 22, Government Printing Office, 1960, p. 42, Reconfirmed 1973.
[3]Studies by such outstanding economists as Paul Samuelson of M.I.T., George Stigler of Chicago, Warren Nutter of Virginia, and Clair Wilcox of Swarthmore have reached conclusions similar to those of Dr. Kreps.

items the seller produced efficiently, this contract would have cost his company an additional $320,000.

In their search for optimum prices, competent buyers are aided by analyzing the pricing methods of both full-line and specialty suppliers. Regrettably, only buyers from a few progressive firms actually make such in-depth analyses of the entire product line of the industries in which they do business. Rather, most buyers focus their analyses on just one product at a time (the product presently being purchased). Buyers are rewarded by directing their efforts toward the development of savings produced by recurring long-term cost reductions, rather than focusing on savings from short-term cost reductions. In short, optimal pricing comes to buyers who understand the pricing processes for complete product lines, in all firms, in all industries from whom they buy.

In the long run, a firm must recover its costs or go out of business. In the long run, for any given item, the price is roughly equal to the cost of the least efficient producer who is able to remain in business. *In the short run*, however, prices in the free, competitive segment of the economy (roughly 70 percent of the whole) are determined primarily by competition, that is, by supply and demand, and not by costs.

Differences between Products

There are many basic differences between the kinds of products marketed in the various segments of the economy. Some products in the competitive segment are *undifferentiated* products (not distinguished by specific differences), and others are *differentiated*. In some cases, the products are intrinsically different (differentiated); in others, manufacturers are successful in making their similar products appear different from those of their competitors. Even in those cases where a product cannot be made different in substance, producers can still get premium prices if they can persuade buyers *to believe* that their products are superior. Some producers spend huge sums of money on sales personnel and advertising to accomplish such a purpose. In the jargon of the economists, "They attempt to make the demand curve for the products of their firm somewhat inelastic." If their efforts are successful, they can charge higher prices for their products. On the other hand, if their efforts are defeated by the counter efforts of competitors, as is frequently the case, price competition comparable to that in pure competition can result. Grocers, for example, are well acquainted with this economic fact.

For both differentiated and undifferentiated products, producers compete on quality and service as well as price. The consumer market is more susceptible to producers' advertising claims than the industrial market; therefore, the major portion of advertising effort is directed toward the consumer market. Nonetheless, industrial buyers must be aware of advertising and sales tactics and be very careful that they determine quality from an analysis of facts, not from unsupported claims.

Six Categories of Cost

A buyer must understand variable, fixed, semivariable, total, direct, and indirect costs, and how these costs influence prices.

Variable Costs   These are items of cost that *vary directly and proportionally with the production quantity* of a particular product. Variable costs include direct labor wages, the cost of materials, and a small number of overhead costs which the supplier incurs in filling an order. For example, if a specific cutting tool costs $10 and lasts for 100 cuttings, each cut represents a variable cost of 10 cents. If three cuts were required in machining a specific item, the variable cost for cutting would be 30 cents. Thus, variable costs represent money sellers can keep if they do not perform a specific contract, and money they must pay if they do perform it.

Fixed Costs   Fixed costs *do NOT vary with volume*, but rather change over time. Fixed costs are costs sellers must pay simply because they are in business. They are a function of time and are not influenced by the volume of production. For example, if the lathe that held the cutting tool in the preceding example depreciates at the rate of $25 a month, this is a fixed cost. The seller has this $25 expense every month, whether or not any turnings are made during that period. Fixed costs generally represent either money the seller has already spent for buildings and equipment or money the seller will have to spend in the future for unavoidable expenses such as taxes and rent, regardless of the plant's volume of production. Other fixed costs include advertising and research and development, which may be increased or decreased from one time period to another, regardless of production volume.

Semivariable Costs   Generally, it is not possible to classify all production costs as being either completely fixed or completely variable. Many others, called semivariable costs, fall somewhere between these extremes. Costs such as maintenance, utilities, and postage are partly variable and partly fixed. Each is like a fixed cost, because its total cannot be tied directly to a particular unit of production. Yet, it is possible to sort out specific elements in each of these costs that are fixed as soon as the plant begins to operate. When the fixed portion is removed, the remaining elements frequently do vary rather closely in proportion to the production volume. For example, if a plant is producing an average of 5,000 items a month, it might have an average light bill of $700 a month. Should the number of units produced be increased to 8,000, the light bill might increase by $100 to $800. The $100 increase is not proportional to the production increase, because a certain segment of the light bill is fixed whether any production occurs or not. Above this fixed segment, however, light costs do vary in a fairly consistent relationship with production volume.

Total Costs The sum of the variable, fixed, and semivariable costs comprises the total costs. As the volume of production increases, total costs increase. However, the cost to produce *each unit* of product decreases. This is because the fixed costs do not increase; rather, they are simply spread over a larger number of units of product. Suppose, for example, that a single-product firm has the following cost structure:

Variable costs, per unit	$ 2.25
Fixed costs, per month	1,200.00
Semivariable costs:	
Fixed portion, per month	450.00
Variable portion, per unit	0.30

Under these circumstances, Table 12-1 shows how unit costs change as volume changes. To understand fully the intricacies of the volume-cost-profit relationship it is essential to understand variable, fixed, and semivariable costs.

Because it is difficult to allocate costs specifically as fixed, variable, and semivariable, accountants generally classify costs in two categories—direct costs and indirect costs. These are discussed briefly below.

Direct Costs These are costs that are specifically traceable to or caused by a specific project or production operation. Two major direct costs are direct labor and direct materials. Although most direct costs are variable, conceptually, direct costs should *not* be confused with variable costs; the two terms are rooted in different concepts. The former relates to *traceability* of costs to specific operations, while the latter relates to the *behavior* of costs as volume fluctuates. The salary of a production supervisor, for example, can be directly traceable to a product even though he or she is paid a fixed salary regardless of the volume produced. Returning to the illustration of the cutting tool, if a firm pays a worker 15 cents for making the three cuts required for each item, direct labor costs are 15 cents. If the value of the piece of metal being cut is 85 cents, direct costs for the item are $1.00.

TABLE 12-1
VOLUME–UNIT COST RELATIONSHIPS

Monthly production units	Variable costs	Fixed costs	Semivariable costs Fixed	Semivariable costs Variable	Total cost	Unit cost
500	$1,125	$1,200	$450	$150	$2,925	$5.85
1,000	2,250	1,200	450	300	4,200	4.20
1,500	3,375	1,200	450	450	5,475	3.65
2,000	4,500	1,200	450	600	6,750	3.375
2,500	5,625	1,200	450	750	8,025	3.21

Indirect Costs (Overhead)   These are costs that are associated with or caused by two or more operating activities "jointly," but are not traceable to each of them individually. The nature of an indirect cost is such that it is not possible (or practical) to measure directly how much of the cost is attributable to a single operating activity. Indirect costs can be fixed or variable, depending on their behavior (e.g., the portion of energy consumption that varies with the level of production is a variable overhead). So, it is important that the reader not confuse indirect costs with fixed costs.

Regulation by Competition

From a buyer's point of view, competition is the mainspring of good pricing. As previously discussed, most producers do not have the same real costs of production. Even when their costs are the same, their competitive positions can be quite different. Hence, their prices can also be quite different. Consider the following example. Assume that a buyer is ready to purchase 10,000 specially designed cutting tools. The buyer sends the specifications to five companies for quotations. All five respond. For the sake of simplicity, assume that direct costs in these five companies are identical. Assume further that each company uses the same price-estimating formula; overhead is figured as 150 percent of direct labor, and profit is calculated as 12 percent of total cost. Each company could then lay out its figures as follows:

Cost of materials	$12,000	
Cost of direct labor	3,000	
Cost of overhead*	4,500	(150 percent of direct labor)
Total cost	$19,500	
Profit	2,340	(12 percent of total cost)
Price	$21,840	

*To simplify the example, assume all overhead is classified as fixed; that is, it remains constant over a given range of production.

Even with all the controlling figures fixed, the companies more than likely would not quote the same price, because *the cost of production and profit are only two of the factors a seller considers in determining price.* In the final analysis, it is the factors stemming from competition that determine the exact price each firm will quote. That is, when faced with the realities of competition, the price any specific firm will quote will be governed largely by its need for business and by what it thinks its competitors will quote, not by costs or profits.

Who is responsible for final determination of the price to be quoted? Generally, it is the chief marketing executive; in some cases, it is the president of the company. Pricing is one of the most important management decisions a firm must make. As an objective, a firm tends to seek the highest price that is compatible with its long-range goals. What is the possible price range for the order in the preceding example? The out-of-pocket (variable) costs for this order are $12,000 for materials and $3,000 for direct labor, a total of $15,000. This is the lowest price any company should accept under any circumstances. The highest price is $21,840, based on the assumption that a profit in excess of 12 percent is not in the long-range interest of the firm. (Such a profit may attract additional competition to enter this market, which in turn would erode the profitability of the market.)

What could cause one of the firms to consider a price of $17,000? Keen competition among suppliers could. On the other hand, keen competition among buyers could drive the price higher. This is why competition, as a leveler, is such a dominant factor in pricing. If the firm had been unable to obtain a satisfactory volume of other business, it would gladly take this order for a price of $17,000. As a result of the order, the $15,000 out-of-pocket costs would be covered, the experienced work force could be kept working, and a $2,000 contribution could be made to overhead. Remember that the fixed overhead would continue whether or not the firm received this order.

In the long run, a firm must recover all costs or go out of business, for in the long run, plant and machinery must be maintained, modernized, and replaced. *In the short run,* however, it is generally better for a firm to recover variable costs and some portion of overhead rather than undergo a significant decline in business. This would not be true, of course, if such additional business would affect the pricing of other orders the firm has already filled or is going to fill.

Business in good times is not ordinarily done at out-of-pocket prices. A more traditional situation would be for each of the five firms to bid prices above the total cost figure of $19,500. How much above this figure each would bid would depend on the specific economic circumstances and expectations applicable to each firm. Those firms hungry for business would bid just slightly above the total cost figure of $19,500. Those with large backlogs and growing lists of steady customers (and therefore not in need of new business in the short run) would bid a larger profit margin (perhaps 14 percent). Sellers can be expected to evaluate competitive situations differently, depending on how much they want or need the business. Therefore, even with the simplifying assumption of identical costs, it is reasonable to expect bids in this situation to range from approximately $19,700 (1 percent profit) to $21,840 (12 percent profit). Prices close to out-of-pocket costs could be offered if the seller were attempting to obtain a desirable, prestigious account, or if the supplier desired to gain experience in a situation wherein additional large orders are expected to follow.

Varying Profit Margins   A seller must recover *all* costs from his or her total sales to make a profit. However, *each* product in the line does not have to make a profit, and all accounts do not have to yield the same profit margin. Bearing these thoughts in mind, the principal cost/competition implications of pricing can be summarized as follows: *Sound pricing policy dictates that sellers, in accordance with their interpretation of the prevailing competitive forces,* *quote prices that are high enough to include all variable costs and make the maximum possible contribution toward fixed costs and profit.*

Similarly, sound pricing policy dictates that, for any given purchase, buyers should use their knowledge of products, markets, costs, and competitive conditions to estimate the price range at which sellers can reasonably be expected to do business. Finally, with this information, a knowledge of the value of the buyer's ongoing business to a seller, and an appreciation of the value of this specific order, the buyer applies all relevant purchasing principles and techniques to purchase at prices as close as possible to the bottom of the estimated price range.

Break-Even Analysis

Break-even analysis is primarily a top-management planning tool. When conducted with precise cost data, break-even analysis helps management make intelligent decisions concerning proposed changes in the firm's product mix, the pricing of individual products, and the purchase of new production equipment.

Break-even analysis also can be used effectively by buyers. Buyers, however, use it differently than does top management or marketing. A buyer's break-even analysis focuses not on his or her own firm's products and costs, but on suppliers' products, costs, and production volume. By constructing and analyzing a supplier's break-even chart, a buyer can uncover clues concerning future price changes, and the reasons a supplier prices the way it does. Break-even analysis also is helpful when pricing changes in volume for specialty items.

What is a firm's break-even point? It is exactly what the term implies—the dividing point between profit and loss. It is the yearly volume of sales which produces enough revenue to cover total yearly expenses. Fixed costs prevent most firms from operating profitably at a low percentage of capacity. Consider a firm which incurs $2.5 million of fixed overhead. If it produces and sells only 1 unit, that unit of product costs $2.5 million in fixed costs alone. The more units that are produced, the lower the fixed cost per unit, and the more closely unit cost approaches unit selling price (up to the break-even point). At the break-even point, the *average* unit cost of all units produced exactly equals the average unit selling price. Beyond this point, the sales revenue generated by 1 unit of product is greater than its *total* cost of production; hence each sale produces a profit.

How can a buyer construct a supplier's break-even chart? The following six steps illustrate the procedure; the results are shown graphically in Figure 12-1.

1 Scale on graph paper the range of operating capacity from 0 to 100 percent on the horizontal scale. On the vertical scale, place the firm's actual and potential sales.

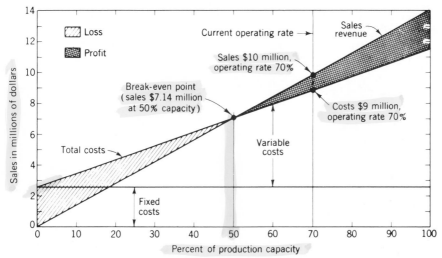

FIGURE 12-1
How to figure a firm's break-even point. (*Note:* For ease in illustrating the break-even concept,
the example shown has purposely been oversimplified. The sales and cost lines have been
shown as straight lines when in reality they are normally curved. See any current basic
economics text for a more complete explanation of marginal cost analysis.)

2 Take the total sales ($10 million, Figure 12-1) from the firm's latest finan-
cial statement (Table 12-2), and plot the value at the firm's normal operating rate for the period covered by the statement (70 percent in this
example).

3 Draw a line from 0 in the lower left-hand corner to the sales figure just
plotted, and extend it to the limit of the chart (see Figure 12-1). This line
gives a rough sales volume measured for every operating rate up to full
production capacity.

4 Take the fixed costs—rent, depreciation, interest charges, taxes, etc.—
which remain the same no matter what the operating rate is, locate the

TABLE 12-2
SELECTED FIGURES FROM COMPANY FINANCIAL REPORTS
(in Millions of Dollars)

	Fixed	Variable	
Total sales			$10.0
Total costs:			9.0
Direct labor		$2.0	
Direct material		3.0	
Factory overhead	$1.5	0.5	
Selling expenses	0.6	0.9	
General and administrative	0.4	0.1	
	$2.5	$6.5	
Net profit (before taxes)			$ 1.0

dollar sum of fixed costs on the vertical axis, and draw a line horizontally across the chart.

5 Take the total cost figure ($9 million) from the firm's financial statement
(Table 12-2), and position it above the same operating rate (70 percent)
as used for the total sales figure.

6 Connect that point with the beginning of the fixed-cost line (at 0 capacity, since fixed costs are total costs at that point), and extend the line to
the limit of the chart (see Figure 12-1). This line gives a rough indication
of costs for every operating rate.

*The break-even point is the point at which the total cost line intersects the total
revenue line.* To the right of that point, the vertical distance between the two
lines represents profit (sales revenue in excess of costs). To the left of the
point, losses are represented in a similar manner (costs in excess of sales revenue). The percentage of capacity at which the firm must operate to avoid
loss (50 percent in this example) can be read directly below the break-even
point.

Not all costs fall into the fixed and variable categories. Some are semivariable
(such as overtime costs resulting from increased use of maintenance personnel). For simplicity, in this example semivariable costs have been allocated between the fixed and variable groupings in Table 12-2.

If the analyst is interested only in the sales value, and not the operating
rate at the break-even point, this can be computed quickly without constructing the chart. The statement shows that variable costs are $6.5 million for
sales of $10 million. Therefore 65 percent of every sales dollar goes for vari-
able expenses. This means that 35 percent of sales contributes to fixed costs
and net profit. If there is no net profit—as is the case at the break-even
point—then the full 35 percent of sales just covers fixed costs. If fixed costs
equal 35 percent of break-even sales value, then

$$\$2.5 \text{ million fixed costs} = 0.35 \times \text{Sales at break-even point}$$

$$\text{Sales at break-even point} = \$2.5 \text{ million}/0.35 = \$7.14 \text{ million}$$

A check of the break-even chart verifies that $7.14 million in sales must be
made for the firm to break even.

If a buyer can approximate a supplier's break-even chart, he or she can
determine the approximate production rate (in percentage of capacity) that
the supplier must average during the year to attain a particular profit goal.
Then, by periodically observing the supplier's actual production levels, the
buyer can evaluate the success of the supplier's efforts and attempt to ascer-
tain what influence they may have on future pricing actions. *Thus, a buyer
knows that when a supplier's operating rate is close to the break-even rate and is declining, there is considerable pressure to increase sales revenue.* If demand for the
supplier's product is elastic, the buyer should well expect a future price reduction (as the supplier attempts to increase revenue on low-volume sales by

decreasing selling price). Such information clearly aids the buyer in developing the negotiating or buying strategy. *When he or she observes a supplier operating well above the break-even rate of production with volume steadily increasing, a buyer may well be able to negotiate more advantageous prices.* The success of negotiations, however, is conditioned significantly by the total demand situation in the industry.

Break-even analysis finds its most effective use when a buyer deals with companies in a process industry or with companies making one product or a small number of products. The reason for this is clear: an enterprising buyer usually can obtain adequate cost and sales data from published sources to approximate a supplier's break-even chart *in the aggregate* (on a companywide basis). Seldom, however, can the buyer obtain such information broken down accurately by major product lines for a multiproduct company. Hence, break-even analysis is considerably more effective in dealing with single-product companies than with multiproduct or multiplant giants.

In recent years, a significant economic phenomenon has affected the need for break-even analysis. Many firms have made substantial investments in capital equipment at relatively high interest rates. The result is that high machinery costs have effectively raised operating break-even points. For purchasing managers, this presents a fruitful opportunity for exploiting long-term, high-volume contracts. Under these circumstances, most suppliers need such contracts to keep their new machinery busy producing products for buyers at high, sustained production rates.

One final note of caution: the results of break-even analysis are no more reliable than the accuracy of the data used in the analysis. Since the cost information available to most people outside the supplier's firm does not include meaningful details of its origin, the break-even chart constructed by a buyer is at best a rough approximation. Consequently, it should not be considered a precise tool, but rather a general guide in determining buying and negotiating strategy.

PRICE ANALYSIS

Some form of price analysis is required for every purchase. The method and scope of analysis required are dictated by the dollar amount and circumstances attending each specific purchase. *Price analysis is defined as the examination of a seller's price proposal (bid) by comparison with reasonable price benchmarks, without examination and evaluation of the separate elements of the cost and profit making up the price.*

The buyer has four tools which may be used to conduct price analysis: (1) analysis of competitive price proposals, (2) comparison with regulated, catalog, or market prices; (3) comparison with historical prices; and (4) use of independent cost estimates.

Competitive Price Proposals

Chapter 10 described the conditions which should be satisfied before using competitive bidding as a means of selecting the source of supply. When this approach is employed, and the following additional conditions are satisfied, then the resulting low bid normally provides a fair and reasonable price:

- At least two qualified sources have responded to the solicitation.
- The proposals are responsive to the buying firm's requirements.
- The supplier competed independently for the award.
- The supplier submitting the lowest offer does not have an unfair advantage over its competitors.
- The lowest evaluated price is reasonable.

The buyer cannot apply this approach to pricing in a mechanical manner. He or she clearly must use common sense and ensure that the price is reasonable when compared with past prices, with independent estimates, or with realistic rules of thumb.

Regulated, Catalog, and Market Prices

Prices Set by Law or Regulation When the price is set by law or regulation, the supplier must identify the regulating authority and specify what the regulated prices are. With regulated prices, some governmental body (federal, state, or local) has determined that prices of certain goods and services should be controlled directly. Normally, approval of price changes requires formal review, hearings, and an affirmative vote of the regulatory authority. No supplier may charge more or less than the approved price.

Catalog Price An established catalog price is a price that is included in a catalog, a price list, or some other form that is regularly maintained by the supplier. The price sources must be dated and readily available for inspection by potential customers. The buyer should request a recent sales summary demonstrating that significant quantities are sold to a significant number of customers at the indicated price before accepting a catalog price.

Market Price A market price results from the interaction of many buyers and sellers who are willing to trade at a given (market) price. The forces of supply and demand establish the price. A market price is generally for an item or a service that is generic in nature and not particularly unique to the seller. Normally the daily market price is published in local newspapers or trade publications which are independent of the supplier.

Historic Prices

Price analysis may be performed by comparing a proposed price with historic quotes or prices for the same or similar item. It is essential that the base price was fair and reasonable (as determined through price analysis) and is a valid standard against which to measure the offered price. The fact that a historic price exists does not automatically make it a valid basis for comparison. Several issues must be considered:

- How have conditions changed?
- Were there one-time engineering, setup, or tooling charges?
- What should be the effect of inflation or deflation on the price?
- Will the new procurement create a situation where the supplier should enjoy the benefits of learning? (The concept of learning curve analysis is discussed in the next chapter.)

Independent Cost Estimates

When other techniques of price analysis cannot be utilized, the buyer may use an independent cost estimate as the basis for comparison. The buyer must determine that the estimate is fair and reasonable.[4] If price analysis is impractical or if it does not allow the buyer to reach a conclusion that the price is fair and reasonable, then cost analysis, the subject of the next chapter, should be employed.

PURCHASING DESIGN WORK

When a buyer contracts for the design as well as the manufacture of a special component, he or she must be careful not to create a future supplier relations problem. One facet of the potential problem centers about the matter of ownership of the special design. Another facet concerns the supplier's recovery of sunk costs in design work and tooling.

When a supplier agrees to design and manufacture a special component, who owns the resulting design—the supplier or the buyer? Who has the right to apply for a patent on the item? Further, who owns the special tooling the supplier must obtain to produce the item? The answers to these basic questions should be specified unequivocally in the purchase contract. By taking this precaution, the buyer can avoid the uncertainties and distasteful misunderstandings which at times accompany such purchases.

The purchase price stated in the contract should reflect the decision regarding ownership of the design and tooling. From a buyer's standpoint, the most desirable method of pricing is one which separates the supplier's charges into three categories: (1) price for design and development work, (2) price for special tooling and equipment, and (3) price for manufacturing. Under these circumstances, both parties know precisely what the buyer is paying for and what should be obtained in return.

---

[4]The development and use of independent cost estimates is described in detail in Chapter 4 of *Zero Base Pricing™: Achieving World Class Competitiveness Through Reduced All-in-Cost*, by D. N. Burt, W. Norquist, and J. Anklesaria, Probus Publishing, Chicago, Ill., 1990.

If a buyer can purchase design work and tooling completely apart from the manufactured components, the contract is usually clear-cut and no problems ensue. The buyer can do whatever he or she wishes with the design or tooling without infringing on the prerogatives of the supplier. Other things being equal, this is by far the most desirable type of contract. It makes the buyer less dependent on a single supplier who chooses to operate in a short-term-profit-maximizing mode in lieu of a partnership mode; it gives the buyer more leverage which can be used in stimulating competition among additional potential suppliers.

As anyone with good business sense would suspect, some suppliers are unwilling to accept contracts for continuing business on the basis just described. A shrewd supplier may well prefer to develop a proprietary product and, for a limited period of time, establish itself in a monopolistic position. It is this type of contract that generates supplier relations problems. Clearly, the buyer does not want to remain a captive customer of one supplier indefinitely. On the other hand, in the interest of fairness, the buyer is obligated to see that the supplier is adequately compensated for its original design and development work. Therefore, if the supplier will not divulge design and tooling costs, the buyer should write the purchase contract in a manner which compels the supplier to price the job so as to recover these costs within a reasonable period of time (usually within a year). For example, the contract might guarantee the purchase of a specified number of units, or it might state that the job will be opened for bid on an annual basis.

Although the original supplier has an inherent advantage over future bidders, it is nevertheless essential that the buyer state at the outset the intention to open the job to competition as soon as the original contractor has recovered the sunk costs and earned a reasonable profit. This approach is in keeping with the buyer's responsibility to treat all suppliers fairly, and at the same time to seek out the efficient, low-cost producer.

ALL-IN-COST

The modern professional buyer is concerned with obtaining the lowest "all-in-cost"—that is, the total acquisition and usage cost of the procurement to the buying firm. Price is only one of the components of all-in-cost. Other components are costs associated with transportation, storage, and administration, as well as the costs resulting from defective materials entering the conversion process. Defective materials costs include rework, lost productivity, and total costs incurred to the point the item is scrapped. In addition, postmanufacturing costs in the areas of warranty, service, and field failure costs resulting from defective materials should be included in all-in-cost.

> THE PROFESSIONAL BUYER RECOGNIZES THAT PRICE
> IS ONLY A COMPONENT OF ALL-IN-COST!

DOCUMENTING A PRICE ANALYSIS

A price analysis report is a written summary of the analysis for a given procurement. The report is prepared for each procurement to summarize the basis for the buyer's conclusion that a price is fair and reasonable. It is included in the purchase order or contract file.

The report may be a separate document, particularly if there is to be no negotiation conference. If competitive bidding was used to select the source and the price, an abstract of the bids received will suffice. The findings of the price analysis may be incorporated in the price negotiation memorandum as part of the explanation of the prenegotiation objective and as part of the justification for the resulting price. There are strong arguments, however, for requiring a written report of price analysis before the negotiation. The discipline of writing the report requires the buyer to sift through the data, reconstruct the process and its events, restate key issues and decisions, and state conclusions based on these findings.

The price analysis report should indicate:

- Information that was considered
- Weight given to each piece of information and why
- Logic supporting the determination that an offeror's price is or is not reasonable
- Soundness of that logic

The length and detail in a price analysis report depends on the nature of the procurement. Similarly, the specific elements included depend on what it takes to establish reasonableness and what is available.

DISCOUNTS

Discounts frequently are considered to be a routine, prosaic part of pricing. Perceptive buyers, however, recognize that this is not always the case. As will be illustrated in the discussion to follow, discounts can sometimes succeed as a technique for reducing prices after all other techniques have failed. The four most commonly used kinds of discounts are *trade discounts, quantity discounts, seasonal discounts,* and *cash discounts.*

Trade Discounts

These discounts are reductions from list price allowed various classes of buyers and distributors to compensate them for performing certain marketing functions for the original seller (the manufacturer) of the product. Trade discounts are frequently structured as a sequence of individual discounts (e.g., 25, 10, and 5 percent), and in such cases they are called *series discounts.* Those who perform only a part of the distribution functions get only one or two of the discounts in the series. If the retail price of an item with such discounts is $100, the full discounted price is calculated as follows: 25 percent of $100 = $25;

10 percent of ($100 − $25) = $7.50; 5 percent of ($100 − $25 − $7.50) = $3.38. The manufacturer's selling price, then, is $100 − $25 − $7.50 − $3.38 = $64.12.

An industrial buyer who purchases through distributors must, as a result of the very nature of series trade discounts, be certain that the buy is from the right distributor (i.e., the distributor obtaining the most discounts). The general guideline for a buyer is to get as close to the manufacturer as is practical. For example, a large buyer normally should not purchase paper requirements from a janitorial supply house which usually does not obtain all discounts in the series for paper. If an account is sufficiently large, the buyer should purchase from a paper distributor who normally does obtain all discounts in the series. Such a supplier can, at the same profit margin as the janitorial supply house, offer buyers lower prices. Buyers with very large accounts should purchase directly from paper manufacturers.

Quantity Discounts

These price reductions are given to a buyer for purchasing increasingly larger quantities of materials. They normally are offered under one of three purchasing arrangements:

1 For purchasing a specific quantity of items at one time
2 For purchasing a specified dollar total of any number of different items at one time
3 For purchasing a specified dollar total of any number of items over an agreed-upon time period

The third type of quantity discount noted above is called a *cumulative discount*. The period of accumulation can be a month, a quarter, or, more commonly, a year. For large-dollar-value, repetitive purchases, buyers should always seek this type of discount. Also, because unplanned increases in business occur with regular frequency, buyers should include in all quantity discount contracts a provision that if the total purchases made under the contract exceed the estimated quantities, then an additional discount shall be allowed for all such excesses.

Seasonal Discounts

Based on the seasonal nature of some products (primarily consumer products), their producers commonly offer discounts for purchases made in the off season.

Cash Discounts

In many industries, sellers traditionally offer price reductions for the prompt payment of bills. When such discounts are given, they are offered as a percentage of the net invoice price. When suppliers extend credit, they cannot avoid certain attendant costs, including the cost of tied-up capital, the cost of operating a credit department, and the cost of some bad-debt losses. Most sellers can reduce these costs by dealing on a short-term payment basis. Therefore, they are willing to pass on part of the savings to the buyers in the form of a cash discount.

Buyers should be aware of the importance of negotiating the highest possible cash discount. The most commonly used discount in practice is 2 percent 10 days, net 30 days. In industries where prompt payment is particularly important, cash discounts as high as 8 percent have been allowed. A cash discount of 2/10, net 30 means that a discount of 2 percent can be taken if the invoice is paid within 10 days, while the full amount should be remitted if payment is made between 10 and 30 days after receipt of the invoice.

A 2 percent discount, viewed casually, does not appear to represent much money. In one sense, however, it is the equivalent of a 36.5 percent annual interest rate. Because the bill must be paid in 30 days and the discount can be taken up to the tenth day, a buyer not taking the discount is paying 2 percent of the dollar amount of the invoice to use the cash involved for 20 days. In a 365-day year, there are 18.25 twenty-day periods (365/20 = 18.25). A 2/10 discount translates into an *annual* discount rate of 36.5 percent (2 percent times 18.25). If a firm does not have sufficient cash on hand to take cash discounts, the possibility of borrowing the needed money should be investigated. Under normal conditions, paying 10 to 15 percent for capital that returns 36.5 percent is good business. Capable buyers understand the time value of money. In some situations, generous cash discounts can be obtained either for prepayment or for 48-hour payment.

Various other types of cash discounts are in use. One common type is the *end-of-month (EOM)* dating system. This system of cash discounting permits the buyer to take a designated percentage discount if payment is made within a specified number of days after the end of the month in which the order is shipped. If materials are shipped on October 16 under 2/10 EOM terms, a 2 percent discount can be taken at any time until November 10.

Lower prices, in the form of higher cash discounts, are an ever-present source of price reduction which buyers should always explore. Frequently, sellers who will not consider reducing the prices of their products will consider allowing higher cash discounts. Such action accomplishes the identical result for the buyer. For example, a major petroleum company recently was able to gain a 6 percent price reduction on the purchase of a complex testing machine—a machine the manufacturer had never before sold below its listed $92,000 selling price. The $5,520 price reduction was achieved by the buyer's offering to pay one-half of the purchase price one week in advance of the machine's delivery to his company's testing laboratory.

LEGAL IMPLICATIONS OF PRICING

Pricing cannot always be decided solely on the basis of economic considerations. Legislation and court decisions, both federal and state, sometimes influence pricing. The major pricing laws are discussed in Chapter 29, "Legal Considerations."

CONCLUSION

Obtaining the *right* price is one of the buyer's most important responsibilities. When focusing on price, the buyer is concerned with the total cost, or all-in-cost, of the item or service being purchased.

Price analysis is a comparison process. Comparisons are made with other bids, prices commonly paid, historic prices, or independent cost estimates.

FOR DISCUSSION

12-1 Describe the three fundamental types of competition identified by the classical school of economics.

12-2 Discuss the pricing strategy of oligopolistic industries and the efforts they employ to maintain competitiveness.

12-3 Which classical market structure provides the best environment for price negotiations?

12-4 What is variable-margin pricing?

12-5 List and briefly describe the six categories of cost.

12-6 As the volume of production increases, the cost to produce each unit of product decreases but total cost increases. Why?

12-7 How might it be against the long-range interest of a supplier to establish a large profit margin?

12-8 Discuss the utility to a buyer of generating a supplier's break-even chart.

12-9 Why is break-even analysis more effective in dealing with single-product companies than with multiproduct ones?

12-10 What are the four tools which a buyer can use to conduct price analysis?

12-11 What are some of the issues involved in historical price considerations?

12-12 Discuss the problems involved in purchasing design work.

12-13 Describe the concept of all-in-cost.

12-14 Why should a buyer prepare a written report documenting his or her price analysis?

12-15 List and describe the four most commonly used discounting practices.

CASES FOR CHAPTER 12

Hardy Company, page 743
Collier Company I, page 728
Templeton Engine Company, page 817
Nationwide Telephone, page 772
A Problem of Price, page 791
World-Wide Industries, page 819
Campbell Typewriter Corporation (in the Instructor's Manual)

13

COST ANALYSIS

KEY CONCEPTS

- Cost analysis
    - Cost analysis defined
    - The capabilities of management
    - The efficiency of labor
    - The amount and quality of subcontracting
    - Plant capacity
- Direct costs
    - Direct labor
    - Direct materials
- Learning curves
    - The cumulative average curve and the unit curve concepts
    - Application of learning curves
    - Pitfalls in using learning curves
- Tooling costs
- Indirect costs
    - Engineering overhead
    - Materials overhead
    - Manufacturing overhead
    - General and administrative expenses
    - Selling expense
    - Recovering indirect costs
- Profit

COST ANALYSIS

Cost analysis should be employed when price analysis is impractical or does not allow a buyer to reach the conclusion that a price is fair and reasonable.

Cost analysis generally is most useful when purchasing nonstandard items and services.

Cost Analysis Defined

Cost analysis is defined as "a review and an evaluation of actual or anticipated cost data." This analysis involves the application of experience, knowledge, and judgment to data in an attempt to project reasonable estimated contract costs. Estimated costs serve as the basis for buyer-seller negotiation to arrive at mutually agreeable contract prices.

When a buyer anticipates that cost analysis will be required, he or she should include a request for a cost breakdown with each request for quotation. This is the proper time to make such a request, *not after* negotiations have started. Suppliers cannot complain that making this breakdown is an extra burden at this time, since they must perform such an analysis to prepare their bids. A simple procedure used by a number of progressive firms for obtaining cost breakdowns is to include the following statement with their request for quotations: "The buyer will not consider any quotation not accompanied by a cost breakdown." Not all suppliers readily provide cost-of-production information; however, the number refusing to do so for nonstandard items is becoming relatively small. An example of a typical cost breakdown request form is shown in Figure 13-1.

The purpose of cost analysis is to arrive at a price that is fair and reasonable to both the buyer and the seller. Estimates can be made with the help of one's engineering department or by analyzing the estimates submitted by the seller. To analyze a seller's costs, a buyer must understand the nature of each of the various costs a manufacturer incurs. The buyer must compare the labor hours, materials costs, and overhead costs of all competing suppliers as listed on their cost-breakdown sheets. Most important, he or she must determine the reasons for any differences, focusing on three principal elements of cost: direct, indirect (overhead), and profit. These cost elements were defined and discussed in the preceding chapter.

The buyer should always be conscious of the fact that costs vary widely among manufacturing firms. Some firms are high-cost producers, others are low-cost producers. Many factors affect the costs of specific firms, as well as the cost of individual products within any given firm. Some of the most important elements affecting costs are:

- The capabilities of management
- The efficiency of labor
- The amount and quality of subcontracting
- The plant capacity and the continuity of output

Each of these factors can change with respect to either product or time. For this reason, a specific firm can be a high-cost producer for one item and a low-cost producer for another. Similarly, the firm can be a low-cost producer

COST ANALYSIS	CHECK APPROPRIATE BOX: ESTIMATED COST ☐ HISTORICAL COST ☐ PERIOD COVERED:			
NAME OF SUPPLIER	INQUIRY OR PURCHASE REQUISITION NO.			
ADDRESS (Street, City, State)	QUANTITY	AT $ EACH	AMOUNT $	
ARTICLE				
TERMS AND DISCOUNT NET TOTAL OF QUOTATION $				

INDICATE WHETHER:
ANALYSIS OF COST AS OF _____ , 19____   COST PER ITEM ☐   OR TOTAL COST ☐

ITEM	AMOUNT	PERCENT OF COST
1. DIRECT MATERIAL		
2. LESS SCRAP OR SALVAGE		
3. NET DIRECT MATERIAL		
4. PURCHASED PARTS ·FROM SUBCONTRACTORS		
5. DIRECT PRODUCTIVE LABOR HOURS AT $		
6. DIRECT FACTORY CHARGES:		
(a) TOOLS AND DIES		
1. DIRECT WAGES HOURS AT $		
2. TOOLING BURDEN		
3. MATERIALS		
(b) SPECIAL MACHINERY		
(c) MISCELLANEOUS		
7. INDIRECT FACTORY EXPENSES (Burden), ON BASIS OF See Note[a]		
8. ENGINEERING AND DEVELOPMENT EXPENSES·DIRECT:		
(a) SALARIES AND WAGES HOURS AT $		
(b) BURDEN		
(c) OTHER		
TOTAL MANUFACTURING COST		
9. GENERAL AND ADMINISTRATIVE EXPENSE: PERCENT OF See Note[b]		
10. SELLING EXPENSE See Note[c]		
11. CONTINGENCIES See Note[d]		
12. OTHER EXPENSES See Note[e]		
13.		
14.		
15.		
16.		
17. TOTAL COST		
18. SELLING PRICE		

19. (a) Are the wage rates used in estimating the direct labor of the unit cost
         break-down the same as those now prevailing?
    (b) If "No," explain difference and indicate approximate amount thereof.

20. (a) What operating rate has been used in calculating the above estimate?
         Hours of operation per week?
    (b) At what rate is your plant now operating?
         Hours of operation per week?

_____   _____
(Supplier)   (Signature and title)

_____
(Date)

a State basis of allocation.
b State nature of expenses included and basis of allocation.
c State nature of expenses included and amount of advertising, if any,
   separately, and basis of allocation.
d Explain in detail.
e State nature of expenses, basis of allocation, and why related to the
   cost of this item.

FIGURE 13-1
Example of a typical request for a cost breakdown.

one year and a high-cost producer another year. These circumstances make it extremely important for a buyer to obtain competition among potential suppliers. Competition can be a buyer's key to locating the desired low-cost producer.

The Capabilities of Management

The skill with which management plans, organizes, staffs, coordinates, and controls all the personnel, capital, and equipment at its disposal determines the efficiency of the firm. Managements utilize the resources available to them with substantially different degrees of efficiency. This is one basic reason why finding the correct supplier (and price) is so profitable for astute buyers.

The Efficiency of Labor

Anyone who has visited a number of different firms surely has noticed the differences in attitudes and skills that exist between various labor forces. Some are cooperative, take great pride in their work, have high morale, and produce efficiently, while others do not. The skill with which management exercises its responsibilities contributes greatly to these differences between efficient and inefficient labor forces. Buyers are well rewarded for pinpointing suppliers with efficient labor forces.

The Amount and Quality of Subcontracting

When a contract has been awarded to a supplier (the *prime contractor*), the supplier frequently subcontracts some of the production work required to complete the job. The supplier's subcontracting decisions are important to a buyer because they may involve a large percentage of prime contract money. The first decision a prime contractor must make regarding subcontracts is which items should be made and which specific items should be bought. Should the prime contractor decide to buy some of those items which can be made more efficiently, and vice versa, the buyer suffers financially. Even if the prime contractor makes the correct "make" decision, it still is responsible for selecting those subcontractors which are needed for the "buy" items.

Subcontractor prices and performance directly influence the prices the buyer pays the prime contractor. Hence, the prime's skills in both making and administering its subcontracts are of great importance to the buyer. For this reason, buyers must be assured that their major suppliers have effective purchasing and subcontracting capabilities of their own.

Plant Capacity

A plant's overhead costs are directly influenced by its size. A plant can get too large for efficient production and, as a result, lose its competitive ability.

On the other hand, plants with large capital investments, or those manufacturing products on a mass-production basis, can be too small to attain the most efficient production levels. A buyer must be alert to detect firms whose operations are adversely affected by size.

Plant output is clearly one of the controlling elements in the cost/profit picture. Table 13-1 illustrates this concept numerically. Note how volume affects profit when variable costs change because of inefficient use of facilities beyond optimum plant capacity. Note also that while total profit continues to increase as production output increases, beyond a certain output profit increases at a decreasing rate. This relationship is an important one for buyers to keep in mind.

DIRECT COSTS

Except in industries with heavy fixed capital investments, direct costs are normally the major portion of total costs. As such, they generally serve as the basis on which sellers allocate their overhead costs. The astute buyer, therefore, must carefully investigate a seller's direct costs. A tiny reduction here (because they are relatively large) is worth more (price-wise) to the buyer than a major reduction in the percentage of profit (which is relatively small). Referring to Table 13-2, a 25 percent reduction in the $8 direct labor cost of situation 1 to the $6 direct labor cost of situation 2 results in a $6.05 ($33.88 − $27.83) reduction in price. A 25 percent reduction in profit would result in only a 77 cent reduction in price (0.25 × $3.08 = $0.77).

TABLE 13-1
HOW PRODUCTION VOLUME AFFECTS FIXED COSTS, VARIABLE COSTS, AND PROFIT

Production quantity	Selling price	Sales revenue	Fixed costs	Variable costs	Total cost	Total profit	Profit per unit of added production
0	$20	$ 0	$4,000	$ 0	$4,000	−$4,000	$15
100	20	2,000	4,000	500	4,500	− 2,500	15
200	20	4,000	4,000	1,000	5,000	− 1,000	15
300	20	6,000	4,000	1,500	5,500	+ 500	15
400	20	8,000	4,000	2,000	6,000	+ 2,000	15
500	20	10,000	4,000	2,500	6,500	+ 3,500	15
600	20	12,000	4,000	3,000	7,000	+ 5,000	14
700*	20	14,000	4,000	3,600	7,600	+ 6,400	12
800*	20	16,000	4,000	4,400	8,400	+ 7,600	10
900*	20	18,000	4,000	5,400	9,400	+ 8,600	

*Plant begins to strain capacity and administrative capabilities. The result is less efficient operation, i.e., overtime is required, less experienced workers are utilized, scheduling and handling of materials becomes less efficient, and variable costs per unit rise. Consequently, although profit continues to increase beyond a production quantity of 600, it increases at a decreasing rate.

TABLE 13-2
DIRECT COSTS AND PRICES

Cost elements	Situation 1	Situation 2
Material	$ 8.00	$ 8.00
Direct labor	8.00	6.00
Fixed overhead at 150 percent of direct labor	12.00	9.00
Prime cost	$28.00	$23.00
General and administrative overhead at 10 percent of prime cost	2.80	2.30
Total cost	30.80	25.30
Profit at 10 percent of total cost	3.08	2.53
Price	$33.88	$27.83

Direct Labor

During the development and production phase of a new item, a supplier typically experiences a heavy design and production engineering effort. These efforts will peak and then decrease. As they do, tooling and setup efforts increase, peak, and decline. Machining, assembly, and test effort then become the predominant users of labor. A buyer should be cognizant of these factors and should analyze a bidder's estimate to ensure that it is based on proper planning, applying reasonable expectations of efficiency in this regard.

When analyzing direct manufacturing labor estimates, the buyer should pay particular attention to the following:

- Allowances for rework
- Geographic variations
- Variation in skills

Allowances for Rework A buyer should carefully review a bidder's estimate of rework costs. Modern production techniques now make it possible to drastically reduce scrap rates. Effective purchasing by a supplier's organization can reduce the defect rates on incoming materials as much as 95 percent. The combined effect of reduced incoming quality problems and improved production and quality systems should reduce a supplier's requirement for rework markedly.

Geographic Variations Wage rates vary significantly from one part of the country to another. A buyer must ensure that the wage rates proposed are, in fact, the wage rates applicable in the areas where the work is to be performed. The Bureau of Labor Statistics provides current wage rates for different trades in different locations.

Variations in Skills The buyer, with assistance from the firm's industrial engineering or production departments, should review the types of labor skills proposed, to ensure that they are relevant and necessary for accomplishment of the required tasks.

Direct Materials

Direct materials are consumed or converted during the production process. Sheet metal, fasteners, electrical relays, and radios for automobiles are all examples of direct materials. In most cases, such materials normally are purchased from a wide variety of suppliers. And in some cases, the materials may have been produced or partially processed in other plants or divisions of the supplier's operation. The resulting costs should be scrutinized carefully for internal transfer charges and markups.

Further analysis of proposed materials costs frequently reveals a difference between the buyer's cost estimate for a given bill of materials and the bidder's estimate for the same bill. In such cases, the buyer should request supporting data from the supplier. In some cases, the labor component of the proposed materials costs should reflect a learning effect as more units are produced (this topic is discussed shortly). In any case, careful analysis and discussion should help identify the source of the variance.

LEARNING CURVES

In many circumstances, labor and supervision become more efficient as more units are produced. The *learning curve* (sometimes called the *improvement curve*) is defined as an empirical relationship between the number of units produced and the number of labor hours required to produce them. Production managers can use this relationship in scheduling production and in determining manpower requirements for a particular product over a given period of time. Buyers can use the relationship to analyze the effects of production and management "learning" on a supplier's unit cost of production.

Traditionally, the learning curve has been used primarily for purchases of complex equipment in the aircraft, electronics, and other highly technical industries. Recently, its use has spread to other industries. The learning curve is useful in both price and cost analysis. It is probably most useful in negotiations, as a starting point for pricing a new item. In addition to providing "buyer's insurance" against overcharging, the learning curve is also used effectively by government and commercial buyers in developing (1) target costs for new products, (2) make-or-buy information, (3) delivery schedules, and (4) progress payment schedules for suppliers.

The Cumulative Curve and the Unit Curve

In practice, two basic forms of the learning curve exist. The first curve, "the cumulative average cost curve," is commonly used in price and cost analysis. This curve plots cumulative units produced against the average direct labor cost or *average labor hours required per unit for all units produced*. The second, "the unit or marginal cost curve," is also used in labor and cost-estimating work. The unit curve plots cumulative units produced against the *actual labor hours required to produce each unit*. Figure 13-2 illustrates and compares the two types of curves.

Selection of the learning curve technique to use tends to be based on an organization's past experience. Ideally, whether one should use a cumulative or a unit curve is a function of the production process itself. Some operations conform to a cumulative curve, others conform to the unit curve. The only way to know which to use is to record the actual production data and then determine which type of curve fits the data the best. The relationship is strictly an *empirical* one.

Target Cost Estimation

If a new product is custom made to unique specifications, what should be paid for the 50th item? The 500th item? Obviously, costs should decline—but

FIGURE 13-2
Comparison of a cumulative average learning curve *A* and a unit learning curve *B*, plotted on an arithmetic grid.

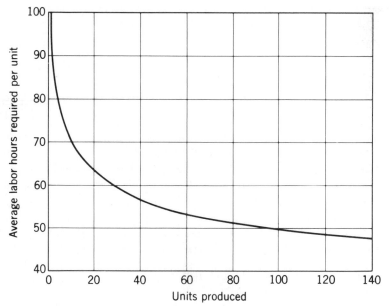

FIGURE 13-3
A 90 percent cumulative average learning curve, plotted on an arithmetic grid.

by how much? Analysis of the learning curve provides an answer. Cost reductions and estimated prices can be obtained merely by reading figures from a graph.

The learning curve is a quantitative model of the commonsense observation that the unit cost of a new product decreases as more units of the product are made because of the learning process. The manufacturer, through the repetitive production process, learns how to make the product at a lower cost. For example, the more times an individual repeats a complicated operation, the more efficient he or she becomes, both in speed and skill. This, in turn, means progressively lower unit labor costs. Familiarity with an operation also results in fewer rejects and reworks, better scheduling, possible improvements in tooling, fewer engineering changes, and more efficient management systems.

Suppose a buyer knows that it took a supplier 100 hours of labor to turn out the first unit of a new product, as indicated on Figures 13-3 and 13-4. The supplier reports that the second unit took 80 hours to make, so the average labor requirement for the two items is 180 ÷ 2 = 90 hours per unit. The production report for the first four units is summarized in Table 13-3.

Observe that the labor requirement dropped to 74 hours for the third unit and to 70 hours for the fourth unit. Column 4 shows that the average number of labor hours required for the first four units was 81 hours per unit. Investigation of the learning rate shows the following relationships:

FIGURE 13-4
The 90 percent cumulative average learning curve of Figure 13-3, plotted on a log-log grid.

- As production doubled from one to two units, *the average labor hours required per unit* dropped from 100 to 90, a reduction of 10 percent.
- As production doubled from two to four units, *the average labor hours required per unit* dropped from 90 to 81, a reduction of 10 percent.

Figure 13-3 indicates that the same learning rate continues as production of the new item increases. Each time production doubles, the average labor requirement for all units declines by 10 percent. Thus, the product is said to have a 90 percent learning rate, or a 90 percent learning curve. Note that this is based on the *cumulative average* learning curve phenomenon. The basic point revealed by the learning curve is that *a specific and constant percentage reduction in the average direct labor hours required per unit results each time the*

TABLE 13-3
NINETY PERCENT CUMULATIVE LEARNING CURVE DATA

Unit produced	Labor hours required	Cumulative labor hours required	Average labor hours required per unit
1st	100	100	100.0
2d	80	180	90.0
3d	74	254	84.7
4th	70	324	81.0

number of units produced is doubled. It is an established fact that specific learning rates occur with reasonable regularity for similar groups of products in many different industries.

Studies made in the aircraft, electronics, and small electromechanical subassembly fields indicate that learning rates of 75 to 95 percent are typical. However, learning curves can vary anywhere within the practical limits of 50 to 100 percent. As more units are produced, the effect of a constant learning rate on unit costs gradually diminishes. After several thousand units, the absolute reduction in cost from learning becomes negligible. Note in Figure 13-3 how the curve flattens out as the number of units produced increases. This is why learning curve analysis is of greatest value for new products.[1]

Most analysts prefer to plot the data for learning curves on log-log graph paper, as in Figure 13-4. The logarithmic scales on both the horizontal and vertical axes convert the curve of Figure 13-3 into a straight line (because a log-log grid plots a constant rate of change as a straight line). The straight line is easier to read, and it also simplifies forecasting since a constant learning rate always appears as a straight line on log-log coordinates. To verify the fact that both graphs represent the same thing, look at the number of hours needed to produce 100 units in Figures 13-3 and 13-4; both figures indicate about 50 hours per unit.

In addition to determining the direct labor component of price, the labor hour data also have the following purchasing applications.

Estimating Delivery Times   Since the learning curve can be used to forecast labor time required, it is possible to estimate how many units a supplier can produce over a specified time with a given labor force. This information can be extremely helpful to a buyer in scheduling deliveries, in planning his or her firm's production, and in identifying suppliers who obviously cannot meet desired delivery schedules.

Supplier Progress Payments   Since the learning curve reflects changing labor costs, it provides a basis for figuring a supplier's financial commitment on any given number of units. This information is important because suppliers often operate in the red during the initial part of a production run, until learning can reduce costs below the average price. Buyers can minimize supplier hardship by using the learning curve to break down an order into two or more production lots—each with successively lower average prices—and then set up progress payments based on the supplier's costs.

---

[1]Different types of labor generate different percentages of learning. Assembly-type labor generates the most rapid improvement and fabrication-type labor the least. Fabrication labor has a lower learning rate because the speed of jobs dependent on this type of labor is governed more by the capability of the equipment than the skill of the operator. The operator's learning in this case is confined to setup and maintenance times. In some situations, therefore, when a precise analysis is desired, a learning curve should be developed for each category of labor. Also, it should be noted that different firms within the same industry experience different rates of learning.

Application of Learning Curves

Before applying a learning curve to a particular item, a buyer must be certain that learning does in fact occur at a reasonably constant rate. Many production operations do not possess such properties. Gross errors can be made if a learning curve is misapplied; therefore, buyers must be alert to the following problems.

Nonuniform Learning Rates   Learning curve analysis is predicated on the assumption that the process in question exhibits learning at a reasonably constant rate. Direct labor data from such a process should plot in a straight line on a log-log grid. If a straight line cannot be fitted to the data reasonably well, the learning rate is not uniform and the technique should not be used.

Low-Labor-Content Items   Continued learning occurs principally in the production of products entailing a high percentage of labor. The learning opportunity is particularly high in complex assembly work. On the other hand, if most work on a new item involves machine time, where output tends to be determined by machine capacity, there is little opportunity for continued learning.

Small Payoffs   Obtaining historical cost data to construct a learning curve entails much time and effort, particularly when a supplier uses a standard cost accounting system. Therefore, learning curve analysis is worthwhile only if the amount of money which can be saved is substantial.

Incorrect Learning Rates   Learning varies from industry to industry, plant to plant, product to product, and part to part. Applying one rate just because someone in the industry has used it can be misleading. Intelligent use of learning curves demands that learning rates be determined as accurately as possible from comparable past experience.

Established Items   If a supplier has previously made the item for someone else, a buyer should not use the learning curve even if the product is nonstandard and new to the buyer. Since most of the learning has already been done on previous work, any additional cost reduction may well be negligible.

Misleading Data   Not all cost savings stem from learning. The economies of large-scale production spread fixed costs over a larger number of output units, thus reducing the unit cost of the item. However, this phenomenon has nothing to do with the learning curve.

An Example of Learning Curve Application: The Cumulative Average Curve   The following simplified example shows a basic application of the cumulative average learning curve concept in labor cost analysis and contract pricing.

The ABC Corporation has purchased 50 pieces of a specially designed electronic component at $2,000 per unit. Of the the $2,000 selling price, $1,000 represents direct labor. An audit of product costs for the first 50 units established that the operation is subject to an 80 percent cumulative average learning curve. What should ABC pay for the purchase of 350 more units?

Solution

1 Using log-log paper, plot 50 units (on the horizontal axis) against $1,000 direct labor cost on the vertical axis (see Figure 13-5).
2 Double the number of units to 100 on the horizontal axis and plot against a labor cost of $800 (80 percent as high as the original $1,000 cost).
3 Draw a straight line through the two cost points. The line represents an 80 percent learning curve, constructed on the basis of labor costs data for the first 50 units of production.
4 Locate 400 units on the horizontal axis (the total expected production of 50 original units plus 350 new ones). Read from the curve the labor cost of $510. This is the *average* expected labor cost per unit for the total production of 400 units.
5 To find the labor cost for 400 units, multiply 400 × $510, the direct labor cost per unit. The total is $204,000.
6 Subtract the labor paid in the original order to determine the labor cost of the new order of 350 units. Hence, subtract $50,000 (50 × $1,000)

FIGURE 13-5
Estimating labor cost for the new contract.

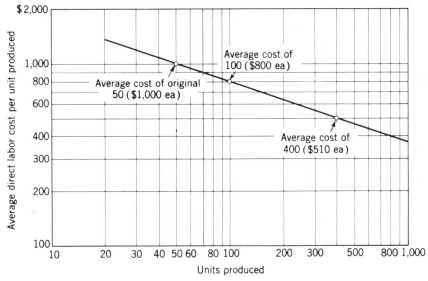

from $204,000. The answer is $154,000, the labor cost which should be paid for the new order of 350 units: $154,000 ÷ 350 units = $440 per unit labor cost, as compared with the original $1,000 per unit.

7 Now determine the cost for materials, overhead, and profit on the 350 units. Add this figure to the labor cost determined in step 6 to obtain the total price ABC should pay for the additional 350 units.

An Example of Learning Curve Application: The Unit Curve   The preceding application dealt with the use of a *cumulative average* learning curve. To illustrate the application of a *unit* learning curve, consider the following hypothetical situation.

Assume that a manufacturer receives an order to produce 515 units of a new product. After the necessary production and tooling design work is completed, the manufacturer begins production. Prior experience with moderately similar products leads the manufacturing manager to believe that a *unit* learning curve phenomenon probably will be experienced as production operations proceed.

To investigate this possibility, for the first 32 units produced, he records the production data shown in Table 13-4, columns 1 and 2. Then he makes the calculations shown in column 3. As production doubled (1 to 2, 2 to 4, 4 to 8, etc.), in each case it is clear that a significant learning effect was experienced. (The 2nd unit took 85 percent of the time required by the 1st unit, the 4th unit required 84.3 percent of the time required by the 2nd unit, and so on, as indicated in column 3). Although the rate varies slightly, the manager concludes that a unit learning curve of approximately 85 percent is a good indicator of the manner in which the process will behave during the production of the remainder of the order. (That is, that the 64th unit will require 85 percent of the time required by the 32nd unit, that the 128th unit will require 85 percent of the time required by the 64th unit, and so on.)

Consequently, he constructs the curve on a log-log grid—and reads directly from the graph that the 512th unit will require approximately 13.6

TABLE 13-4
THE MANUFACTURER'S PRODUCTION DATA

Column 1 Unit produced	Column 2 Labor hours required to produce the corresponding unit in col. 1	Column 3 Labor hours required as a percent of those required for the preceding unit
1	60	—
2	51	85.0%
4	43	84.3
8	37	86.0
16	31	83.8
32	26	83.9

direct labor hours for its production. Similar determinations for all units produced permit him to calculate the total number of labor hours for the complete job. Using this information, he can schedule production efficiently, as well as estimate the total labor cost the job will incur.

TOOLING COSTS

Most procurement authorities advocate that the buyer pay for and take title to special tooling. Such an approach allows the buyer maximum control. Analysis of production costs is easier and the tooling can be moved if circumstances dictate.

There should be an inverse relationship between the investment in tooling and the number of hours required to produce a unit of output. The buyer should ensure that the supplier plans to use sufficient tooling to minimize labor hours, but at the same time avoids investments which are not recovered through labor savings.

INDIRECT COSTS

Indirect costs represent 30 to 40 percent of many suppliers' total costs of production. Five of the most common indirect cost pools are engineering overhead, materials overhead, manufacturing overhead, general and administrative expense, and selling expense.

Engineering Overhead

This is the cost of directing and supporting the engineering department and its direct labor staff. Costs include supervisory and support labor, fringe benefits, indirect supplies, and fixed charges such as depreciation.

Materials Overhead

This category of overhead usually includes the indirect costs of purchasing, transporting incoming materials, receiving, inspection, handling, and the storage of materials.

Manufacturing Overhead

This category includes all production costs except direct materials, direct labor, and similar costs that can be assigned directly to the production of an item. Manufacturing overhead includes:

- The cost of supervision, inspection (some firms charge quality assurance or inspection as a direct cost), maintenance, custodial, and related personnel costs
- Fringe benefits such as social security and unemployment taxes, allowances for vacation pay, and group insurance

- Indirect supplies such as lubricating oils, grinding wheels, and janitorial supplies
- Fixed charges, including depreciation, rent, insurance, and property taxes
- Utilities

General and Administrative

General and administrative (G&A) expenses include the company's general and executive offices, staff services, and miscellaneous activities.

Selling

Selling expenses include sales salaries, bonuses and commissions, and the normal costs of running the department.

Recovering Indirect Costs

The supplier allocates overhead costs to specific operations. This allocation results in the use of an overhead rate for each indirect cost pool. The rate is determined by management personnel who select an appropriate base (or allocation vehicle) and then develop the ratio of the indirect cost pool dollars to that base. For example, the following allocation formula might be used for manufacturing overhead:

$$\frac{\text{Manufacturing overhead pool dollars}}{\text{Manufacturing direct labor hours}} = \frac{\$5,000,000}{1,000,000} = \begin{array}{c}\$5 \text{ per direct}\\ \text{manufacturing}\\ \text{labor hour}\end{array}$$

Overhead rates are generally established annually, typically before the start of the accounting period.

When determining the reasonableness of overhead rates, a buyer should not look only at the rate. He or she must consider the reasonableness of the indirect costs in the overhead pool and the appropriateness of the overhead allocation base. Since rates typically are established annually, the buyer should also ensure that the allocation rate used by a supplier is applied consistently.

PROFIT

There are no precise formulas which can be used to help form a positive judgment concerning the right price, of which profit is one component (price = cost + profit). There are, however, certain basic concepts of pricing on which scholars and practitioners do agree. One objective of sound purchasing is to achieve good supplier relations. This objective implies that the price must be high enough to keep the supplier in business. The price must also include a profit sufficiently high to encourage the supplier to accept the business in the first place, and, second, to motivate the firm to deliver the materials or services on time. What profit does it take to get these two desired results? On what basis should it be calculated?

If profit were calculated on a percentage-of-cost basis, the high-cost, inefficient producer would receive the higher profit (in absolute terms). To make matters even worse, under the cost concept of pricing, producers who succeeded in lowering their costs by attaining greater efficiency would be "rewarded" by a reduction in total profit. For example, if an efficient producer has costs of $1,000 and a fair profit is agreed to be 10 percent of cost, its profit would be $100. If an inefficient producer has costs of $1,500, its profit on the same basis would be $150. If by better techniques the efficient producer should lower its costs to $800, the reward would be a $20 loss in profit—from $100 to $80. Obviously, the concept of determining a fair profit as a fixed percentage of cost is unrealistic.

Another concept on which profit might be determined is the relationship of capital investment required to produce the profit. Profit might be calculated as a percentage of capital investment. However, under this system, it would still be possible for the inefficient producer to receive the greater reward. For example, suppose firm A makes a capital investment of $2 million to produce product X. Firm B, on the other hand, invests only $1 million in its plant to produce product X successfully. From the buyer's point of view, there is no reason why firm A, simply because of its greater investment, should receive a higher profit on product X than firm B. Firm B, in fact, is utilizing its investment more efficiently. Thus, profit calculated as a fixed percentage of a firm's capital investment is not a satisfactory method for a buyer to use in determining a fair profit.

In a competitive economy, the major incentive for more efficient production is greater profit and repeat orders. A fair profit in our society cannot be determined as a fixed percentage figure. Rather, it is a flexible figure that should be higher for the more efficient producer than it is for the less efficient one. Low-cost producers can price lower than their competitors, while simultaneously enjoying a higher profit. Consequently, one of a buyer's greatest challenges is constantly to seek out the efficient, low-cost producer.

Considerations other than production efficiency can also rightly influence the relative size of a firm's profit. Six of the most common considerations are discussed briefly below.

1 Profit is the basic reward for risk taking as well as the reward for efficiency; therefore, higher profits justifiably accompany extraordinary risks, whatever form they take. For example, great financial risk usually accompanies the production of new products. For this reason, a higher profit for new products is often necessary to induce a seller to take the risk of producing them.

2 A higher dollar profit per unit of product purchased on small special orders is generally justified over that allowed on larger orders. The justification stems from the fact that the producer incurs a fixed amount of setup and administrative expense, regardless of the size of the order. Consequently, the cost of production for each unit is greater on small orders than on large orders. Since producers incur this cost at the request of the buyer, they usually demand a proportionately higher absolute profit before accepting an order which forces them to use their facilities in a less efficient manner than they might otherwise do.

3 Rapid technological advancement creates a continuing nationwide shortage of technical talent. The cost in dollars and time of training highly technical personnel frequently makes it necessary to pay a higher profit on jobs requiring highly skilled people.

4 In the space age, technical reliability can be a factor of overriding importance. A higher profit is generally conceded as justified for a firm that repeatedly turns out superbly reliable technical products than for one producing less reliable products. Good quality control, efficiency in controlling costs, on-time delivery, and technical assistance that has resulted in better production or design simplification all merit profit consideration.

5 On occasion, because of various temporary unfavorable supply-demand factors (e.g., excessive inventories, a shortage of capital, a cancellation of large orders), a firm may be forced to sell its products at a loss in order to recover a portion of its invested capital quickly or to keep its production facilities in operation.

6 A firm that manufactures a product according to the design and specifications of another firm is not entitled to the same percentage of profit as a firm that incurs the risk of manufacturing to its own design. In the first instance, the manufacturing firm is assured of a sale without marketing expense or risk of any kind, provided only that it fulfills the terms of the contract. In the second instance, the manufacturing firm is without assurance that its product can be sold profitably, if at all, in a competitive market.

In summary, there is no single answer to the question: What is a fair profit? In a capitalistic society, profit generally is implied to mean the reward over costs that a firm receives for *the measure of efficiency it attains* and the *degree of risk it assumes.* From a purchasing viewpoint, profit provides two basic incentives. First, it induces the seller to take the order. Second, it induces the seller to perform as efficiently as possible, to deliver on time, and to provide all reasonable services associated with the order. Except in those temporary cases where a firm is willing to sell at a loss, the profit is too low if it does not create these two incentives for the seller.

CONCLUSION

Armed with an understanding of cost principles, the buyer now is in a position to conduct an analysis of a potential supplier's proposal. This analysis is a major step in preparing for negotiations, as described in Chapter 15.

FOR DISCUSSION

13-1 What are the principal elements of cost?

13-2 How might the application of experience, knowledge, and judgment to data assist in an attempt to project contract costs?

13-3 How can a reduction in direct cost generate more of a price savings for the buyer than a similar percentage reduction in the seller's profit?

13-4 Describe the factors that buyers must review when they select a seller that engages in subcontracting.

13-5 What must the buyer consider when he or she analyzes direct manufacturing labor estimates?

13-6 Discuss the two basic types of learning curves and their applications.

13-7 If each time the production rate doubles, the average labor requirement for all units declines by 20 percent, what would the learning rate be?

13-8 Why might a person working on a punch press exhibit a lower rate of learning than one working in a complex assembly operation?

13-9 How might the purchasing department apply learning curves?

13-10 What are some examples of misapplied learning curve use?

13-11 If a supplier has previously made an item, how is the learning curve affected?

13-12 List some factors that contribute to a supplier's "learning."

13-13 Why might it be discouraging for an efficient producer to have its profit for a job based solely on its costs?

13-14 Discuss some of the considerations, other than production efficiency, that can influence the relative size of profits.

13-15 Why shouldn't a firm that manufactures a product according to the designs and specifications of another firm be entitled to the same percentage of profit as if it had developed its own design?

CASES FOR CHAPTER 13

Frich Turbo Engine Company, page 738
A Problem of Price, page 791
Hartinco, Inc. (in the Instructor's Manual)
Black Motor Company (in the Instructor's Manual)
Collier Company II (in the Instructor's Manual)
Naval Operating Base, Arkladelphia (in the Instructor's Manual)

CHAPTER **14**

TYPES OF CONTRACTS AND ORDERING AGREEMENTS

KEY CONCEPTS

- Types of contracts
  - Fixed price contracts
  - Incentive contracts
  - Cost-type contracts
  - Considerations when selecting contract types
- Ordering arrangements
  - Effects of delivery times and dollar values on prices
  - Purchasing agreements
  - Systems contracts

TYPES OF CONTRACTS

One of the major pricing aids available to a buyer is a wide variety of contract types. The term *contract type* refers to the contract's pricing mechanism. To determine the best type of contract to use, a buyer must consider those available and the factors influencing the use of each. The most important factors are:

- The intensity of competition among potential suppliers
- Each supplier's cost and production experience in manufacturing identical or similar items
- The availability, accuracy, and reliability of pricing data
- The extent of the business risk involved

If it were always possible to purchase on a fixed price basis, selection of contract type would be no problem. In a rapidly changing economic and technological world, however, purchasing many items on a fixed price basis would be costly and wasteful. Generally speaking, as the complexity of the item being purchased increases, so does the complexity of the pricing mechanism. Industry and government use three basic types of contracts, as follows.

1 Fixed price
- Firm fixed price
- Fixed price with escalation/de-escalation
- Fixed price with redetermination
    Maximum price
    Flexible price
- Firm fixed price level of effort

2 Incentive
- Fixed price incentive
- Cost plus incentive fee

3 Cost-type
- Cost plus a percentage of cost
- Cost plus fixed fee
- Cost plus award fee
- Cost without fee
- Cost sharing
- Time and materials
- Letter contracts

The types of contracts noted above are arranged according to risk, with firm fixed price contracts (minimum risk to a buyer) at one end and cost contracts (maximum risk to the buyer) at the other end.

Fixed Price Contracts

Firm Fixed Price (FFP)   This is the most desirable type of contract. It is simply an agreement for the buyer to pay a specified price to the seller when the latter delivers what was purchased. If a fair and reasonable price can be determined, either by competition or by adequate price or cost analysis, a firm fixed price contract should always be used. Such a contract has many advantages. It requires minimum administration (no auditing of costs), it gives the seller the maximum incentive to produce efficiently, and *all financial risks are borne entirely by the seller.*

Fixed Price with Escalation (FPE)   For a contract involving a long period of production and a large amount of money, sellers usually prefer not to quote a firm fixed price because of the risk of inflation. If forced to do so, sellers often include in their price excessive contingencies for expected increases in costs. These expectations may or may not actually materialize. Hence, to avoid paying for something not received, the buyer should use an escalator clause. Such a clause should provide for both *upward* and *downward* changes in price as a result of changes in either materials prices or labor rates.[1] The escalation clause should be as simple as possible, and adjustments normally should be made in accordance with the prescribed movements of well-known, regularly published indexes. The two indexes most commonly used are the Bureau of Labor Statistics' Producer Price Index (for materials) and the Wage Increase Series by Standard Industrial Classification (for labor). Many other government and commercial indexes, however, are also used for escalation purposes. It should be noted that price adjustments of this type apply only to changes in labor rates and materials costs, not to overhead and profit and not to increases in the amounts of labor or materials.

Fixed Price with Redetermination (FPR) Redetermination as a means of pricing is different in concept from escalation. In contracts with escalation, the amounts of labor and materials required to complete the contract are known, but the labor rates or the prices of material are unknown. In cases involving price redetermination, the amounts of labor and materials (and in some cases their prices also) initially are unknown, but they become known with limited production experience.

Because of labor and materials unknowns, a firm fixed price contract initially would be impractical; however, enough is known so that a temporary estimated fixed price can be established. The buyer generally believes the agreed-upon price is too high, and he or she expects it ultimately to be lowered during a subsequent review. In the meantime, the buyer is protected from unknown raises. After an agreed-upon percentage of work has been performed under the contract, the unknowns are translated to knowns. At this time, the costs incurred to date are analyzed, future costs are estimated, and a fixed price is determined for the remainder of the contract. This new price may or may not be the same as the original temporary price. It may or may not apply to the items already produced, depending on the terms established. Learning experiences, expected future volume, expected increases in efficiency, and similar factors relating to future production all are considered in arriving at the firm price.

The earlier in the life of a contract that price redetermination can be made, the more effective this type of contract is. Thirty percent completion is typically a satisfactory redetermination point.

Maximum price redetermination provides that prices can be adjusted downward only at the time of redetermination. *Flexible price redetermination* means that

---

[1] Upward adjustments are normally limited to 10 percent or are tied directly to reliable and timely price indexes. Suppliers generally agree that only part of wage increases should be escalated because suppliers' productivity should improve with time. Guidance on the construction of escalation clauses may be found in *Zero Base Pricing ™: Achieving World Class Competitiveness Through Reduced All-in-Cost*, by David N. Burt, Warren E. Norquist, and Jimmy Anklesaria, Probus Publishing, Chicago, Ill., 1990.

price adjustments can be made upward or downward; however, an upward limit of 10 percent usually is imposed.

Firm Fixed Price Level of Effort   This type of contract is used primarily for research and development work. It is used when the work cannot be precisely described in advance, but the level of effort required to accomplish it can be described and also agreed on by the buyer and seller. Under this type of contract, the seller is obligated to a specified level of effort, for an agreed-upon time, and for an agreed-upon fixed price.

Incentive Contracts

Incentive contracts are appropriate when the following three conditions all exist:

1 A significant amount of uncertainty exists regarding the level of effort required to accomplish the task properly.
2 The supplier's management can, through its efforts, have an impact on the level of effort and costs required.
3 The size of the procurement justifies the efforts involved in establishing and managing the resulting contract.

Incentive and cost-type contracts are expensive to administer. All costs that are allowable under the contract must be agreed on in advance, and *subsequently they must be audited*. For this to be possible, the seller must have an accounting system that can separate the costs applicable to a specific cost contract. Despite advance agreement on what costs are allowable, intense arguments routinely develop between the buyer and the seller over the validity of certain cost inclusions.

What often seems to be a justifiable item of cost to the seller may not seem to be justifiable to the buyer. For example, a reasonable percentage of research expense for scientists' and engineers' salaries may be considered an entirely proper expense by the seller, even though these people did not work directly on the project. The buyer may have different feelings about including this type of cost as an expense against the contract.

There are two principal types of incentive contracts: (1) fixed price incentive ("fixed price" because a fixed price ceiling is established, above which the supplier assumes all cost liability) and (2) a cost plus incentive fee contract.

Fixed Price Incentive   This type of contract provides for *a target price, a ceiling price,* and *a variable profit formula*. This contract is generally used when a reasonable target price can be established but exact pricing is impossible without payment of a contingency.

The contract works like this. Suppose both buyer and seller agree that $990 is a reasonable *price objective* for item A. This price was calculated roughly as follows: target cost $900,[2] target profit $90, total price $990. The buyer intends to purchase large numbers of item A; consequently, he or she wants to be sure the seller has the maximum incentive to produce efficiently. Both parties agree that every dollar by which the seller reduces costs below $900 will be shared equally. For example, if costs are reduced to $800, the price will be:

$800	supplier's cost
50	supplier's share of savings below target cost of $900
90	target profit
$940	price to be paid

Both the buyer and the seller "saved" $50 because of increased efficiency and the cost reduction of $100 below target cost. At the upper limit, it was agreed that if costs equaled or exceeded the ceiling figure of $1,100, the seller would receive no profit and the maximum price to the buyer would be $1,100, regardless of the seller's costs. All costs between $900 and $1,000 reduce the seller's profit by 50 percent of these costs, just as they increase it by 50 percent of the cost "saving" below $900 (see Table 14-1). All costs between $1,000 and $1,100 reduce the seller's profit from $40 to $0 proportionally.

This type of contract has its greatest application in the purchase of high-cost, long-run production items. Initially it was used almost exclusively by the Department of Defense in the purchase of complex, expensive weapon systems which required lengthy development times. Now, however, it is used by sophisticated buyers in industry, particularly in the purchase of high-cost office and factory buildings, ships, and complex machines.[3] Occasionally it is also used for the purchase of low-value technical and construction products.

Cost plus Incentive Fee   This is a variation of the fixed price incentive contract. The buyer and seller agree beforehand on a tentative fee based on the estimated target cost. If the seller can reduce costs below target costs, both parties share in the reduction. Under this type of contract, a seller can lose all or part of its fee, but all costs must be paid by the buyer. (Occasionally, an administrative ceiling is used.) This type of contract is used in development work where successful results are reasonably certain. Target costs

---

[2]The target cost is the point at which there is equal likelihood that costs will go below or above.

[3]A modification of this basic contract type is now emerging with the incentive fee based on some combination of dollar cost and system performance. In the modified contract type, the supplier also agrees to meet certain quantified performance standards (such as specified range and accuracy in a missile system) as well as meeting cost goals. If performance is above standard, the supplier's fee is increased; if the performance is below standard, the fee is reduced. This combination of performance and incentive also can be used in cost plus incentive fee contracts. The new contract type is not a departure from the basic incentive concept; it is a refinement of it.

TABLE 14-1
PROFIT AND SAVINGS FROM A FIXED PRICE INCENTIVE CONTRACT

Seller's cost per unit	Profit per unit	Price per unit
$1,200	– $100	$1,100 (ceiling price)
1,100	0	1,100 (ceiling price)
1,000	40	1,040
900	90	990 (target price)
800	140	940
700	190	890

are not exact, but they are considered close enough to provide a basis on which management efficiencies can be rewarded with incentive fees.

Cost-Type Contracts

Cost-type contracts are used only when it is not possible to use any type of fixed price or incentive contract without including a large contingency fee. The distinctive difference between a fixed price and a cost-type contract is that *under cost pricing, the buyer assumes almost all the financial risks.* Generally, sellers do not have to achieve any performance results to be paid. They are guaranteed reimbursement for all their allowable costs, up to a predetermined figure. Beyond this point, they will do no additional work unless the buyer agrees to provide more money. Also, sellers are usually guaranteed a fee in addition to their costs. Therefore, *under a cost-type contract a seller has no effective incentive to keep costs, and thus prices, down.* This is a clear disadvantage to a buyer.

Cost plus Percentage of Cost Although used by the federal government extensively during World War I, *this is the most undesirable of all types of contracts.* Today it is outlawed for use by the federal government. Despite the obvious fallacy of the concept, "The higher the cost the greater the profit," this type of contract is still used to some extent in private industry, especially for the purchase of construction.

Cost plus Fixed Fee This contract type provides that the seller shall be paid for all allowable costs up to a stated amount, plus a fixed fee. The fixed fee is usually a percentage of the estimated target cost. For example, if the estimated target cost to perform the contract is $2,000 and a 5 percent profit fee is agreed on, the fee is $100; the fee remains fixed at $100 even if the cost rises to $3,000 or more, or if it is held to $1,000. This contract type is used primarily in research projects and exploratory studies where the level of effort required to achieve success, if it can be achieved at all, is unknown. Unlike the cost plus a percentage–type contract, this contract does not reward a supplier for inefficiency. On the other hand, neither does it penalize the supplier for inefficiency (the fee remains fixed irrespective of cost). Hence, like its preceding cousin, this type of contract also should be used only as a last resort.

Cost plus Award Fee (CPAF) This type of contract was pioneered by NASA when the agency was purchasing highly complex hardware and professional services in support of the space program. The award fee is a pool of money established by the buyer to reward the supplier on a periodic basis for the *application of effort in meeting the buyer's stated needs.* The key difference between the award fee and other fees is that the supplier's receipt of the fee is based on the buyer's *subjective evaluation* of how well the supplier applies its efforts in meeting the buyer's needs. The subjective aspect provides a flexibility to contracting situations in an uncertain environment. When properly used, the award fee benefits both the buyer and the supplier. Superior performance receives superior rewards in the form of a superior fee. The award fee also introduces an element of flexibility since the buyer can change the areas receiving supplier attention by providing advance guidance for any performance period. The award fee gives the buyer's management a flexible tool with which to influence performance.

Under a CPAF contract, a minimum fee is established (e.g., 2 percent) to ensure that the supplier will receive some revenue for its efforts. In addition, an award fee pool is established. Prior to each performance period (frequently a three-month period), the buyer informs the supplier which areas of performance should be emphasized during the period. For example, during the first four performance periods of a contract to develop software for a new computer, the buyer might tell the supplier: "Your award fee will be based 70 percent on how well you meet schedule and 30 percent on how well you control cost." At the end of each three-month evaluation period, the buyer's performance evaluation team would review the supplier's efforts in meeting these two objectives. Assume that during one of these periods the schedule slipped and costs exceeded the target as a result of a defect in a buyer-furnished computer for which the software was being developed. If, in the opinion of the evaluation team, the supplier applied outstanding effort in overcoming the problem, the team might recommend that a high percent of the fee available for that period be awarded—even though schedule and cost objectives were not met!

The buyer's award decisions are not subject to the disputes provision present in most contracts nor to arbitration. However, the supplier has certain protection. Performance evaluations are subject to review at higher management levels within the buying organization and the supplier is given an opportunity to present its case. The supplier's greatest protection from unreasonableness is the buyer's self-interest. Arbitrary action on the buyer's part would destroy both the desired harmonious working relationship and the effectiveness of the award fee.

Use of the award fee can be combined with other types of contracts. For example, a firm fixed price contract with an award fee provision could be used to purchase janitorial services. The presence of the award fee simplifies the contract administrator's job because excellent performance produces a bonus for the supplier.

Cost without Fee Nonprofit institutions, such as universities, usually do research work for both government and industry, without the objective of making a profit. Such research is done under cost-type contracts without a fee. Because universities do much of the nation's pure research, as distinguished from applied research done by industry, a growing number of contracts of this type are being used. Naturally, the universities recover all overhead costs, which generally include facilities costs and remuneration for personnel who work on the contracts. In recent years, high-technology firms have increased their use of this contract type.

Cost Sharing In some situations, a firm doing research under a cost type of contract stands to benefit if the product developed can be used in its own product line. Under such circumstances, the buyer and the seller agree on what they consider to be a fair basis to share the costs (most often it is 50:50). The electronics industry has found this type of contract especially useful.

Time and Materials In certain types of contracts, such as those calling for repairs to machinery, the precise work to be done cannot be predicted in advance. For instance, it cannot be known exactly what must be done to a large malfunctioning pump aboard a ship until it is opened and examined. Perhaps only a new gasket is required to put it in good working order. On the other hand, its impeller could require a major job of balancing and realignment. The time and materials contract is one method of pricing this type of work. Under this type of contract, the parties agree on a fixed rate per labor hour that includes overhead and profit, with materials supplied at cost.

Suppose a mechanic working on the ship's pump is paid $30 per hour. Assume also that overhead is calculated as 100 percent of the labor cost and profit is set at 10 percent of total cost. A billing rate for this mechanic for one hour would be calculated as follows:

Direct labor cost, per hour	$30
Overhead at 100 percent of labor	30
Total cost	$60
Profit at 10 percent of total cost	6
Billing rate, per hour	$66

If it took the mechanic two days (16 hours) to repair the pump, using $320 worth of material, the job price would be $1,376 (16 × $66 + $320).[4] Profit should be paid only on labor and overhead costs. Some sellers have been known to compute profit on materials, sales taxes, and so on.

A variation of the time and materials type of contract is called a labor-hour contract. In this type of contract, materials are not supplied by the seller; however, other costs are agreed to as in time and materials contracts.

Letter Contracts Letter contracts are used in those rare situations in which it is imperative that work start on a complex project immediately. Letter contracts are *preliminary contractual authorizations* under which the seller can commence work immediately. The seller can prepare drawings, obtain required materials, and start actual production. Under letter contracts, the seller is guaranteed reimbursement for costs up to a specified amount. Letter contracts should be converted to definite contracts at the earliest possible date.

Considerations When Selecting Contract Types

With such a wide variety of contract types available, a buyer must exercise considerable care in selecting the best one for a particular use. If a bid or a quoted price is reasonable, this will help the buyer decide to use a firm fixed price contract. On the other hand, if the fairness of the price is in doubt, a fixed price contract could entail excessive expense to the buyer and would be a poor choice. If price uncertainty stems from unstable labor or market conditions, escalation may be a solution. If the uncertainty is due to a potential improvement in production effort, an incentive contract may be the best answer. Plainly, the many factors that affect procurement costs can themselves guide the buyer in his or her selection of the best type of contract for a given purchasing situation.

The specific nature of the materials, equipment, or services to be purchased also can frequently point up advantages of one contract type over another. The more complex or developmental the purchased item, the greater the risks and difficulties in using a fixed price contract. Any uncertainty in design affects a seller's ability to estimate costs, as does a lack of cost experience with a new item. The details of any given purchase will themselves indicate the magnitude of the price uncertainties involved. A full understanding of these uncertainties permits buyers to allocate the risks more equitably between their firm and the supplier's firm through the proper choice of contract type.

---

[4]The alert reader will observe that this is really a cost plus percentage of cost contract. If the mechanic is a good worker, he might complete the job in 10 hours ($60 profit to his employer). If he is a poor worker, he could take 20 hours, and his employer would receive $120 in profit. Obviously, buyers must exercise close control over this type of contract to be sure that inefficient or wasteful methods are not used.

Timing of the procurement quite frequently is a controlling factor in selection of contract type. Allowing sellers only a short time to prepare their bids can reduce the reliability of the cost estimates and increase prices. A short delivery period usually rules out the effective use of incentive contracts. On the other hand, a long contract period allows time to generate and apply cost-reducing efficiencies, an ideal situation for an incentive contract. The facts of each procurement must be considered individually in determining which contract type the buyer should use.

Business practices in specific industries frequently can provide additional clues as to the best choice of contract type. The construction industry, for example, traditionally accepts a wider range of competitive fixed price jobs than the aerospace industry. The lumber industry accepts prices established by open auctions. Architects and engineers frequently will not enter into price competition with one another for architectural or engineering services; neither will some management consulting firms compete with one another on price. Business factors such as these help determine the best contract type in a great many purchasing situations.

The scope and intensity of competition definitely can influence the type of contract to use. If competition is intense and the prices bid are close, then the buyer can justifiably feel that the prices are fair and reasonable and use a fixed price contract. On the other hand, if competition is not adequate and the buyer has doubts concerning the reasonableness of prices, an incentive or cost contract may be appropriate.

In short, *the buyer's basic preference for a firm fixed price contract is just the starting point for an analysis of alternative contract choices.* As the buyer considers all available contract types, he or she must weigh the preference for fixed prices against the risks involved, the time available, the degree of competition involved, experience with the industry involved, the apparent soundness of the offered price, the technical and developmental state of the item being purchased, and all the other technical and economic information that affects the purchase transaction. Determination of the best contract type for a given situation requires a careful analysis of all the factors relevant to that situation.

ORDERING ARRANGEMENTS

Effects of Delivery Times and Dollar Values on Prices

Regardless of the type of contract used, the dollar value of the materials or services being purchased and their delivery schedules greatly influence contract prices.

Long-Term Contracts (Annual and Multiyear) Because of the economies of scale, large-quantity buyers generally purchase their high-dollar-value materials under long-term contracts. Historically, contracts made for longer than one year were normally limited to situations involving large start-up costs, substantial investments in capital equipment, or major expenses in connection with assembling and training specialized personnel. Today, however, contracts extending up to three years, sometimes five, are commonly used for the purchase of regular production materials. Such contracts eliminate duplicate yearly supplier investigations and purchasing administrative efforts. Lower prices and total purchase costs are the natural result.

In addition to the direct price benefits which accrue from the economies of scale, long-term contracts provide the buyer other benefits. For example, under such contracts, the seller is assured a large volume of business. It may adopt just-in-time manufacturing techniques or agree to carry inventories of the buyer's goods. Consequently, the buying firm can reduce its inventory. When the seller knows the buyer's delivery schedule well in advance, distribution costs and production costs can be reduced. Some of this saving should be passed along to the buyer. In times of scarcity, the buyer is assured of a reliable source of supply, as well as the best possible protection against unjustified price increases. Because long-term contracts are negotiated only once every few years, buying personnel are freed for other productive work such as supplier management, purchasing research, value analysis, and administration. The sophisticated buyer schedules major contracts to expire at equal intervals throughout the year in order to balance his or her workload.

The use of multiyear contracts is increasing. As markets for certain materials become more volatile and availability becomes more uncertain, long-term contracts can offer significant advantages for both the buyer and the seller. Larger volumes, over longer time periods, justify additional supplier investment in research training and tooling, thus assuring lower unit costs and prices.

Despite their benefits, however, long-term contracts do have inherent disadvantages. Buyers must consider the fact that competition is reduced during the term of the contract and that some new sources with exceptional capability may be excluded from participation during this period. In summary, tying up a portion of a buyer's business for too long may deprive that buyer of some of the advantages of a dynamic marketplace.

Most production materials are purchased with firm fixed price– or fixed price with escalation–type contracts. However, cost contracts with a predetermined profit rate are not uncommon, and fixed price with redetermination contracts are used occasionally.

Some of the contractual arrangements that buyers commonly use to cope with variable demand and varying delivery schedules are discussed below.

Definite Delivery–Type Contracts   When production schedules for the entire period of a contract are known, definite quantities for delivery on definite dates can be established. A contract with these provisions is called a "definite delivery–type contract." This is the ideal type of contract when such a degree of certainty is present.

Indefinite Delivery–Type Contracts In some cases, production schedules cannot be planned; hence, the quantities of materials required and their times of use, or both, are unknown. Materials and services for the support of such operations must be contracted for on an indefinite delivery schedule. There are three basic types of indefinite delivery contracts. In order of preference for the best pricing, they are (1) *definite quantity contracts*, (2) *requirements contracts*, and (3) *indefinite quantity contracts*.

Definite Quantity Contracts These provide for the purchase of definite quantities of materials or services—whose time of use is unknown. The contract therefore specifies that instructions regarding delivery schedules will be provided later. Because the quantities are known, very favorable prices are possible for this type of contract.

Requirements Contracts These contracts provide for the purchase from one supplier of *all* of a buyer's requirements, for a stipulated time period, for specified materials or services for a designated operation or activity. Requirements contracts typically are used in applications such as the support of a firm's automotive repair shop, with parts being purchased from a specific parts dealer during the life of the contract. To be certain that this type of contract is both legal and mutually satisfactory, the contract should provide for a *minimum quantity* the buyer is committed to take, and it should stipulate that neither party can terminate the contract during its life, as long as performance is satisfactory and as long as the buyer's requirements continue to exist. Without such provisions, requirements contracts have been found to be unenforceable.

Indefinite Quantity Contracts During an agreed-upon period of time, these contracts provide for the delivery of a specific category of materials or services. Quantities and delivery dates are indefinite, but the buyer is committed to purchase between designated high- and low-quantity limits.

The indefinite quantities associated with both indefinite quantity contracts and requirements contracts preclude optimum pricing. However, the contracts represent a total volume of business that, although indefinite, is large enough for suppliers to want and to price competitively to get.

Purchasing Agreements

To reduce costs, purchasing and materials managers have developed a number of methods for consolidating groups of similar items into purchasing "bid-bundles." Contracts resulting from such groupings collectively are known as *purchasing agreements*. Individually, they are referred to as *annual contracts, national contracts, corporate contracts, pricing agreements, blanket orders, open-end orders*, and so forth. All of these agreements originate from purchasing's initial efforts to *reduce the paperwork associated with relatively small orders* and to *increase a supplier's total volume of business,* thus reducing its unit costs and permitting it to sell at lower prices.[5]

From this initial effort to reduce prices by increasing volume, purchasing managers have gradually added other benefits to purchasing agreements. As a result, such agreements now range from the simple to the complex. The purpose of the simplest agreement is solely to reduce prices and increase operating efficiency. The purpose of the most complex agreement (called a systems contract) is to reduce costs in every possible buyer and supplier operation bearing on the agreement. The simpler forms of purchasing agreements are discussed at length in Chapter 3, "Operating Procedures." Systems contracts are discussed below.

Systems Contracts

The words "systems" and "contracts" have a variety of definitions in business today. In purchasing parlance the term "systems contracts" has a very specific meaning. A systems contract is a contract that authorizes designated employees of the buying firm, using a predetermined release system, to place orders directly with the supplier for specified materials during a given contract period. The contract is finalized only after an attempt has been made to integrate as many buyer-seller materials management functions as possible. For example, careful analysis usually makes it possible to reduce the combined inventories of the buyer and the seller. Frequently, the same release form used by the buyer to order materials can also be used by the seller for stock-picking and delivery of materials, and so on. While systems contracts have certain features in common with other purchasing agreements, it is this integration of buyer-seller operations that clearly distinguishes systems contracts from other types of contracts.

Systems contracts are referred to by some writers as *stockless purchasing.* This definition stems from the fact that if this method of contracting were used to the ultimate, a buyer's company would not have to maintain any inventories at all. Not everyone agrees that systems contracting should be stockless purchasing. Most authorities do agree, however, that one principal objective of systems contracting is to reduce the buyer's inventories to a level as low as is consistent with assured continuity of supply. There is general agreement, too, that order releases under systems contracts should usually be made by personnel from the using department. Most authorities similarly agree that maintenance, repair, and operating (MRO) materials are the cate-

---

[5]Whenever a supplier's volume of business increases, buyers should request lower prices. The request may not always be successful—especially if the supplier suspects that no other firm will sell at lower prices. Nonetheless, buyers should not hesitate to request lower prices, because sellers can offer any price reduction that is less than their reduction in unit costs and still make higher profits.

gories of materials best suited for purchase using systems contracts. However, some of the most profitable arrangements under systems contracts apply also to critical raw materials. Finally, there is general agreement that systems contracts are an excellent way of "simultaneously cutting costs while building efficiencies through simplification."[6]

The following example illustrates a typical application of this method of contracting. A large U.S. firm that has production operations in five Latin American countries uses and maintains field inventories of thousands of individual repair parts and components. These materials are used to support a wide variety of activities which use many types of heavy equipment. For example, to operate several railroad systems, there are locomotives, many types of cars, stations, roundhouses, and shops. To operate numerous large agribusinesses, there are various types of tractors, heavy-duty trucks, many large pumps, power plant equipment, and every imaginable kind of production equipment. All of this equipment requires supply support. Before systems contracts were used, stores inventories were the principal supply support used to keep all equipment operational. Most purchases of needed parts and components were made in the New Orleans market. Emergency items were purchased for direct delivery to users; all other purchases were made for delivery to various inventory sites.

In total, the company had twenty-eight categories of support materials. To develop systems contracts, each category was jointly reviewed in a special meeting by the firm's executives and their counterparts in those supplier organizations that were capable of supplying the company's requirements. During these review conferences, both groups explored each other's major operating problems and found that through a planned, cooperative effort mutual benefits could be achieved. Subsequently, systems contracts proposals were solicited and received. Five systems contracts were negotiated from the initial proposals, and additional contracts were negotiated from later proposals.

Competition for these contracts was excellent. This was not the case, however, until the decision to use systems contracts was made, after the joint conferences were held, and the estimated yearly usage for each material category was disclosed to the potential suppliers. The sellers were surprised at the total dollar amounts. Because each seller had been getting only a part of the total quantity, no one seller could know what the total dollar value was. In return for being awarded the company's total annual business for one category of materials, sellers agreed to keep on hand for immediate shipment those items in the company's inventory that showed active usage in the past year. Without giving a supplier all of the company's yearly business for a category of material, getting such an agreement would not have been possible.

---

[6] For a thorough discussion of systems contracting, see William J. Hannaford, "How Effective Is Systems Purchasing?" *Journal of Purchasing and Materials Management*, Summer 1979, pp. 13–19.

In the final analysis, the company saved well over 20 percent in materials costs on all contracts. Additionally, the large inventory stocks whose yearly carrying costs were approximately 35 percent of the average inventory value were no longer necessary.

Under these systems contracts, order releases were made almost entirely by individual production and warehouse units. Many were made by telephone and teletype. Paperwork was reduced, billing was simplified, and equipment downtime for lack of repair parts was greatly reduced. Additionally, to the present day, suppliers continue to make profit-improving suggestions—they have been assured that such action will favorably influence the selection of the next year's suppliers. In addition to these benefits, total savings for the first year exceeded $2 million. The largest savings came from inventory reductions.

CONCLUSION

The vast majority of purchases are made with the use of firm fixed price (FFP) contracts. But when there is much uncertainty about important aspects of the agreement, use of an FFP contract will result in the buyer's paying a significant contingency fee. The buyer has an array of contract types at his or her disposal. Selection of the right type of contract can result in significant savings.

The buyer also has a variety of ordering agreements from which to choose. Selection of the right type of ordering agreement can reduce the supplier's costs, resulting in lower prices. Administrative costs and inventory carrying costs also may be reduced through selection of the right ordering arrangement.

FOR DISCUSSION

14-1 What are the three basic types of contracts used by industry and government today? Briefly describe each.

14-2 Why is a cost-type contract considered risky to the buyer?

14-3 Describe an escalation clause. Discuss the circumstances when it may be appropriate. What benefits flow to each party?

14-4 How does redetermination as a means of pricing differ from escalation?

14-5 Explain the mechanics of a firm fixed price type of contract. What are the benefits for each party? What are the dangers?

14-6 Name the conditions which might exist that would call for the use of an incentive contract.

14-7 What are the two principal types of incentive contracts?

14-8 What are the main differences between a fixed price and a cost-type contract? When would one elect to use a cost-type contract?

14-9 Why is the cost plus percentage of cost type of contract the most undesirable of all contracts?

14-10 Under what situation might both buyer and seller agree to engage in cost sharing?

14-11 Discuss some of the considerations that must be employed when selecting a particular contract type.

14-12 What are some of the buyer's benefits from long-term contracting with the seller? How does the seller benefit?

14-13 List and briefly describe the contracts buyers commonly use when faced with variable quantities and delivery schedules.

14-14 How might "bid-bundles" aid purchasing and materials managers in cost reduction?

14-15 Discuss the means by which a systems contract can effect a reduction of the buying company's inventory level.

CASES FOR CHAPTER 14

CHAPTER **15**

NEGOTIATION

KEY CONCEPTS

- Objectives of negotiation
- When to negotiate
- The buyer's role in negotiation
    - The buyer acting alone
    - The buyer as team leader
- The negotiation process
    - Preparation
    - Establishing objectives
    - The dynamics of negotiation
    - The four phases of face-to-face negotiation
    - Techniques
- Negotiating for price
    - Price analysis negotiation
    - Cost analysis negotiation
- Documentation
- Characteristics of a successful negotiator

Negotiation is one of the most important as well as one of the most interesting parts of professional purchasing. In industry, and at most levels of government, the term "negotiation" frequently causes misunderstandings. In industry, negotiation is sometimes confused with "hassling" and "price chiseling." In government, negotiation is frequently visualized as a nefarious means of avoiding competitive bidding and of awarding large contracts surreptitiously to favored suppliers.

Webster's dictionary defines *negotiation* broadly as "conferring, discussing, or bargaining to reach agreement in business transactions." To be fully effective in purchasing, negotiation must be utilized in its broadest context—as a decision-making process. In this context, negotiation is a process of planning, reviewing, and analyzing used by a buyer and a seller to reach acceptable agreements or compromises. These agreements and compromises include all aspects of the business transaction, not just price.

Negotiations differ from a ball game or a war. In those activities, only one side can win; the other side must lose. In successful negotiations, both sides win something. The "winnings," however, are seldom equally divided; invariably, one side wins more than the other. This is as it should be in business—superior business skills merit superior rewards.

OBJECTIVES OF NEGOTIATION

Five major objectives are common to all negotiations:

1 To obtain a fair and reasonable price for the quality specified
2 To get the supplier to perform the contract on time
3 To exert some control over the manner in which the contract is performed
4 To persuade the supplier to give maximum cooperation to the buyer's company
5 To develop a sound and continuing relationship with competent suppliers

Fair and Reasonable Price

In the majority of cases, the establishment of a fair and reasonable price for the desired level of quality becomes the principal focus of the negotiation process. This aspect of negotiation ranges in complexity from the use of price analysis to the more complex analysis of the potential supplier's cost elements.

On-Time Performance

Inability to meet delivery schedules for the quality and quantity specified is the single greatest supplier failure encountered in purchasing operations.

This results primarily from (1) failure of requisitioners to submit their purchase requests early enough to allow for necessary purchasing and manufacturing lead times and (2) failure of buyers to plan the delivery phase of negotiations properly. Because unrealistic delivery schedules reduce competition, increase prices, and jeopardize quality, it is important that buyers negotiate delivery schedules which suppliers can realistically meet, without endangering the other requirements of the purchase.

Control

Deficiencies in supplier performance can seriously affect, and in some cases completely disrupt, the operations of the buyer's firm. For this reason, on important contracts buyers should negotiate for controls which will assure compliance with the quality, quantity, delivery, and service terms of the contract. Traditionally, controls have been found to be useful in areas such as man-hours of effort, levels of scientific talent, special test equipment requirements, the amounts and types of work to be subcontracted, and progress reports.

Cooperation

Cooperation is best obtained by rewarding those suppliers who perform well with future orders. In addition to subsequent orders, however, good suppliers also expect courtesy, pleasant working relations, timely payment, and cooperation from their customers—*cooperation begets cooperation*.

Continuing Relations

When negotiating with suppliers, a buyer should recognize that current actions usually constitute only a part of a continuing relationship. Negotiating conditions which permit buyers to take unfair advantage of sellers invariably, with time, change to conditions which allow sellers to "hold up" buyers. For this reason, the buyer must realize that any advantage not honestly won will, in all likelihood, be recovered by the supplier at a later date—probably with interest. Thus, as a matter of self-interest, buyers must maintain a proper balance between their concern for a supplier's immediate performance, on the one hand, and their interest in the supplier's long-run performance on the other.

In summary, the objectives of negotiation require investigation, with the supplier, of every area of negotiable concern—considering both short-term and long-term performance. The buyer's major analytical tools for negotiating prices were discussed in the preceding chapters—such things as price, cost, break-even, learning curve, and cost-volume-profit analyses. Additional negotiating tools, as well as the development of strategy and tactics for negotiation, are discussed throughout this chapter.

WHEN TO NEGOTIATE

Negotiation is the appropriate method of purchasing when competitive bidding is impractical. Some of the most common circumstances dictating the use of negotiation are noted below.

- When *any of the five prerequisite criteria for competitive bidding are missing.*
- When many *variable factors bear* not only on price but also *on quality* and *service.* Many high-dollar-value industrial and governmental contracts fall into this category.
- When *early supplier involvement* (as described in Chapter 27) is employed.
- When the business *risks and costs* involved *cannot be accurately predetermined.* When buyers seek competitive bids under these circumstances, excessively high prices inevitably result. For self-protection, suppliers factor every conceivable contingency into their bids. In practice, not all these contingencies occur. Hence, the buyer unnecessarily pays for something not received.
- When a buyer is *contracting for a portion of the seller's production capacity,* rather than for a product the seller has designed and manufactured. In such cases, the buyer has designed the product to be manufactured and, as an entrepreneur, assumes all risks concerning the product's specifications and salability. In buying production capacity, the buyer's objective is not only to attain production capability but also to acquire such control over it as may be needed to improve the product and the production process. This type of control can be achieved only by negotiation and the voluntary cooperation of suppliers.
- When *tooling and setup costs represent a large percentage of the supplier's total costs.* For many contracts, the supplier must either make or buy many costly jigs, dies, fixtures, molds, special test equipment, gauges, and so on. Because of their special nature, these jigs and fixtures are primarily limited in use to the buyer's contract. The division of special tooling costs between a buyer and a seller is subject to negotiation. This negotiation includes a thorough analysis of future buyer or seller use of the tools, the length and dollar amount of the contract, the type of contract to be used, and so on.
- When *a long period of time is required to produce the items* purchased. Under these circumstances, suitable economic price adjustment clauses must be negotiated. Also, opportunities for various improvements may develop—for example, new manufacturing methods, new packaging possibilities, substitute materials, new plant layouts, and new tools. Negotiation permits an examination and evaluation of all these potential improvements. Competitive bidding does not. What supplier, for example, would modify its plant layout to achieve increased efficiency without assurance of sufficient long-term business to cover the cost involved and assurance of a reasonable profit for the effort?

- When *production is interrupted frequently* because of numerous change orders. This is a common situation in fields of fast-changing technology. Contracts in these fields must provide for frequent change orders; otherwise the product being purchased could become obsolete before completion of production. The ways in which expensive changes in drawings, designs, and specifications are to be handled and paid for are subjects for mutual agreement arrived at through negotiation.
- When a *thorough analysis is required to solve a difficult make-or-buy decision.* Precisely what a seller is going to make and what it is going to subcontract should be decided by negotiation. When free to make its own decision, the seller often makes the easiest decision in terms of production scheduling. This may well be the most costly decision for the buyer in terms of price.
- When the *products of a specific supplier are desired to the exclusion of others.* In this case, competition is totally lacking. Terms and prices, therefore, must be negotiated to prevent unreasonable dictation by the seller.

In all ten of these cases, negotiation is essential; and, in each case, quality and service are as important as price.

THE BUYER'S ROLE IN NEGOTIATION

Depending on the type of purchase, a buyer plays one of two distinct roles in negotiation. In the first role, he or she is the company's sole negotiator. In the second, the buyer heads a team of specialists which collectively negotiates for its company.

The Buyer Acting Alone

For recurring purchases of standard items, regardless of their dollar amounts, the buyer invariably acts alone. Typically, for this type of purchase, a negotiation conference is held in the buyer's office with the supplier's sales manager (the seller's sole negotiator). These two persons alone negotiate all the important terms and conditions of the contract.

A buyer's "solo negotiation" is not limited to periodic formal negotiating sessions. Rather, such negotiations continue on a daily basis with both current suppliers and visiting vendors who wish to be suppliers. Consider several typical examples. A supplier calls on the telephone and informs the buyer that prices are to be raised 20 percent within sixty days. The buyer responds with the thought that production in her company's plant is slack and that a price rise as high as 20 percent could well trigger a "make" decision, in lieu of what is now a "buy" decision. The buyer is negotiating!

A seller's value analyst discovers a substantially less expensive method of manufacturing one of the buyer's products. However, there is one drawback:

an expensive new machine is required for the job. The supplier's sales representative informs the buyer of the discovery. The buyer and an engineer study the concept; it is a good one. The two thank the sales representative for introducing the new idea. At the same time, the buyer explains that his company is financially unable at this particular time to invest in the required new machine. Further, the buyer conjectures that if the seller's company were to purchase the machine, then the buyer without doubt could get his company to reconsider the rejected long-term contract the seller proposed last year. Informal, unplanned negotiations are being conducted.

A salesperson calls, and the buyer says, "I have been thinking about your contract with us. Under the contract, our purchases now total roughly $60,000 per year, primarily for valves. But your company also manufactures a number of fittings that we use. If these fittings were combined with the purchase of the valves, what benefits would your company be able to grant us?" Another informal negotiation is under way.

The preceding year a buyer purchased $300,000 worth of liquid oxygen in individual cylinders from a single supplier. Because of its high dollar value, the buyer began to analyze oxygen usage requirements thoroughly. In this analysis, an interesting fact was discovered. By installing a bulk storage tank at the buyer's plant (at a cost of $160,000) and having the stores personnel deliver the required liquid oxygen to the shops, $70,000 per year could be saved. When the supplier's salesperson called she was informed of the buyer's study and was given the buyer's worksheets for her review and study. Negotiations were under way, and the price of liquid oxygen would soon be reduced.

The Buyer as Team Leader

The complexity of a purchasing contract usually correlates directly with the complexity of the item being purchased. For high-value, technically oriented contracts (such as those developed for the purchase of high-technology products, capital equipment, and much research and development work), the buyer typically is no longer qualified to act as a sole negotiator. The buyer's role, therefore, shifts from that of sole negotiator to that of negotiating team leader. A typical team consists of from two to eight members, depending on the complexity and importance of the purchase to be made. Team members are selected for their negotiating knowledge and their expertise in the technical or business fields needed to optimize their team's negotiating position. Customarily, members are from fields such as design engineering, cost analysis and estimating, finance, price analysis, production, traffic, purchasing, and legal affairs.

In the team approach to negotiation, the buyer usually serves as the leader of the team (and is called the negotiator). In this capacity, he or she functions as the coordinator of a heterogeneous group of different specialists who can be expected to view similar matters differently. As head of the team, the negotiator must weld the team members into an integrated whole. By careful planning, the leader must draw on the specialized knowledge of each team member and combine this expertise with his or her own. To accomplish this, *it is very important that every member of the team be assigned a specific task* and that mock negotiations be included as one of the final steps in team preparation. Mock negotiations normally constitute the best possible insurance to preclude the team's committing *the most costly error of negotiation*—that of the members speaking out of turn and thus revealing their firm's position to the seller's team. In this way, the buyer develops a sound, unified approach to uncover, analyze, and resolve (from a companywide point of view) all the important problems applicable to the contract under negotiation.

THE NEGOTIATION PROCESS

In the broadest sense, negotiation begins with the origin of a firm's requirements for specific materials or services. As discussed in Chapter 6, the ultimate in purchasing value is possible only if design, production, procurement, and marketing are able to reconcile their differing views with respect to material specifications. Buyers must always think in terms of total cost and total value, not in terms of price alone.

Actual two-party negotiation begins with a buyer's requests for proposals from potential suppliers. It develops as the negotiator carefully evaluates these proposals and prepares for discussion of the important issues that may arise in the impending negotiation conference. The negotiation process ends with the resolution of all issues that actually do arise during the negotiation conference.

The negotiation process consists of three major phases: *preparation*, *the establishment of objectives*, and *face-to-face discussions* which result in agreement on *all* items and conditions of a contract, or a decision not to enter into an agreement with the potential supplier.

Preparation

Probably *90 percent or more of the time involved in a successful negotiation is invested in preparing for the actual face-to-face discussions*. The negotiator must: (1) possess or gain a technical understanding of the item to be purchased, (2) analyze the buyer's and seller's relative bargaining positions, (3) have conducted a price or cost analysis (as appropriate), and (4) know the seller.

Know the Item or Service The negotiator does not need to understand all the technical ramifications of the item being purchased. But it is essential that he or she have a general understanding of what is being purchased, the production process involved, and any other issues that will affect quality,-

timeliness of performance, and cost of production. The negotiator should understand the item's intended use, any limitations, and the existence of potential substitutes. The buyer should be aware of any prospective engineering problems which may arise. The negotiator should be aware of the item's procurement history and likely future requirements. Ideally, the buyer will be familiar with any phraseology or customs relevant to the industry.

The Seller's Bargaining Strength   The seller's bargaining strength usually depends on three basic factors: (1) how badly the seller wants the contract, (2) how certain he or she feels of getting it, and (3) how much time is available to reach agreement on suitable terms.

The buyer should encounter no difficulty in determining how urgently a seller wants a contract. The frequency with which the salesperson calls and general market conditions are positive indicators of seller interest. Sellers' annual profit and loss statements, as well as miscellaneous reports concerning backlog, volume of operations, and trends, are valuable sources of information about individual sellers. Publications such as the Department of Commerce's "Economic Indicators," *The Federal Reserve Bulletin*, industrial trade papers, and local newspapers provide a wealth of basic information about potential suppliers and their industries in general.

The less a seller needs or wants a contract, the stronger its bargaining position becomes. The presence of an industry boom, for example, places it in a strong position. On the other hand, when a seller finds itself in a general recession or in an industry plagued with excess capacity, its bargaining position is decidedly weakened.

If a seller learns that its prices are lower than the competition, or learns from engineering or production personnel that it is a preferred or sole source of supply, it naturally concludes that its chances of getting the contract are next to certain. In these circumstances, a supplier may become extremely difficult to deal with during negotiations. In extreme situations, it may be unwilling to make any concessions whatever. When this happens, the negotiator sometimes has only one alternative—to accept the supplier's terms.

When trapped by such circumstances, a negotiator can threaten delay to search for other sources. Such threats are likely to be ineffective, unless the seller knows that alternate sources are actually available and interested in the business. An alternative threat which may be effective when patents are not involved is the threat to manufacture the needed item in the buyer's plant. When made realistically—when the supplier believes the buyer has the technical capability, the determination, and the capacity to make the product— this threat usually gains concessions.

A firm's negotiating position is always strengthened when the company has a clear policy that permits only members of its purchasing department to discuss pricing, timing, and other contractual terms with sellers. Most prenegotiation information leaks that give sellers a feeling of confidence about getting a contract occur in the technical departments of a firm. Such leaks can be extremely costly, and because they are often undetected by general management, they can be a continuing source of profit loss.

Short lead times drastically reduce the buyer's negotiating strength. Conversely, they significantly increase the seller's bargaining strength. Once a supplier knows that a buyer has a tight deadline, it becomes easy for the supplier to drag its feet and then negotiate favorable terms at the last minute when the buyer is under severe pressure to consummate the contract.

The Buyer's Bargaining Strength The buyer's bargaining strength usually depends on three basic factors: the *extent of competition* present among potential suppliers, the *adequacy of cost or price analysis*, and the *thoroughness with which the buyer has prepared* for negotiation.

Intensive supplier competition always strengthens a buyer's negotiating position. Competition is always keenest when a number of competent sellers eagerly want the order. General economic conditions can bear heavily on the extent to which a firm really wants to compete. A firm's shop load, its inventory position, and its back-order position are typical factors that also bear heavily on the ever-changing competitive climate.

When necessary, a buyer can increase competition by developing new suppliers; making items in-house rather than buying them; buying suppliers' companies; providing tools, money, and management to competent but financially weak suppliers; and, above all, hiring highly skilled negotiators.

The Adequacy of Cost or Price Analysis A comprehensive knowledge of cost analysis and price analysis is one of the basic responsibilities of a negotiator. When an initial contract is awarded for a portion of a supplier's production capacity rather than for a finished product, cost analysis becomes vital. In this situation, the negotiator is not prepared to explore with the supplier the reasonableness of his or her proposals until after a comprehensive analysis of all applicable costs has been completed. Cost analysis in such purchases, in a very real sense, is a substitute for direct competition. For follow-on contracts, and for contracts for common commercial items, price analysis is usually sufficient to assure the buyer that prices are reasonable. In the aggregate, *the greater the amount of available cost, price, and financial data, the greater are the buyer's chances for successful negotiation.*

Know the Seller The professional buyer will endeavor to know and understand both the prospective supplier firm and its representatives. Buyers at a leading East Coast firm prepare for critical negotiations by reviewing financial data and articles dealing with their prospective suppliers. The buyers know how the supplier's business is faring, key personnel changes, and so on. This level of preparation pays dividends when conducting face-to-face negotiations!

The Thoroughness of Buyer Preparation   Knowledge is power. The more knowledge the negotiator acquires about the theory and practice of negotiation, the seller's negotiating position, and the product being purchased, the stronger his or her own negotiating stance will be. A negotiator without a thorough knowledge of the product being purchased is greatly handicapped. A negotiator is similarly handicapped if he or she has not studied and analyzed every detail of the supplier's proposal. Whenever feasible, *before requesting bids*, the negotiator should develop an estimate of the price and value levels for the items being purchased. Knowledge of current economic conditions in the market for the product in question is also an essential element of preparation.

Prior to the main negotiating session, negotiators must evaluate all relevant data and carefully assess *their own* and *their supplier's strengths* and *weaknesses.* From this assessment, they develop not only a basic strategy of operation, but also specific negotiating tactics. Alert suppliers readily recognize negotiators who are not prepared. They gladly accept the real and psychological bargaining advantage that comes to them from lack of buyer preparation.

Establishing Objectives

The outcome of contract negotiations hinges on relative buyer-seller power, negotiating skills, and how both perceive the logic of the impending negotiations. Each of these controlling factors can be influenced by adroit advanced planning. This is why *proper planning is without question the most important step in successful negotiations.*

Having prepared for negotiations, the next step is to establish objectives. Negotiation objectives must be specific. General objectives such as "lower than previous prices," "good delivery," or "satisfactory technical assistance" are inadequate. For each term and condition to be negotiated, the negotiator should develop three specific positions: (1) an objective position, (2) a minimum position, and (3) a maximum position. Using the cost objective as an example, the minimum position is developed on the premise that every required seller action will turn out satisfactorily and with minimum cost. The maximum position is developed on the premise that a large number of required seller actions will turn out unsatisfactorily and with maximum cost. *The objective position is the negotiator's best estimate of what he or she expects the seller's actual costs plus a fair profit should be.*

In developing concrete objectives, actual dates are established for delivery schedules, actual numerical ranges for quality acceptance, and actual dollar levels for applicable elements of cost. The major elements of cost which traditionally are negotiated—and for which objective, maximum, and minimum positions are developed—include *quantity of labor, wage rates, quantity of mate-*

rials, prices of materials, factory overhead, engineering expense, tooling expense, general and administrative expense, and *profit.* In addition to determining his or her own position for each major element of cost, the buyer must estimate the objective, maximum, and minimum positions of the seller. Determining the seller's maximum position is easy; it is the offer made in the seller's proposal.

In addition to costs, specific objectives should be established for all items to be discussed during the negotiation, including:

- All technical aspects of the purchase
- Types of materials and substitutes
- Buyer-furnished material and equipment
- The mode of transportation
- Liability for claims and damage
- F.O.B. point
- General terms and conditions
- Progress reports
- Production control plans
- Escalation/de-escalation provisions (if appropriate)
- Incentive arrangements (if appropriate)
- Patents and infringement protection
- Packaging
- Warranty terms and conditions
- Payment terms (including discount provisions)
- Title to special tools and equipment

The Dynamics of Negotiation

Typically, the two opposing positions appear as shown in Figure 15-1. The seller's positions are generally all higher than the corresponding positions of

FIGURE 15-1
Negotiating positions. (*Source:* Paul R. McDonald, *Government Prime Contracts and Subcontracts,* Procurement Associates, Glendora, Calif., 1981, pp. F–1–18.)

the buyer. The closer the two objectives are initially, the easier the negotiations will be. As negotiations proceed, the seller tends to make concessions from its maximum position toward its objective. At the same time, the purchasing negotiator reduces his or her demands, moving from the minimum position toward the objective.[1] Usually, little difficulty arises during this preliminary skirmish. This is not to say that this part of the negotiation process is easy or that it does not take time. Normally, vigorous testing is required to convince each party that the other is actually at his or her objective. Each party attempts to convince the other that he or she has arrived at the objective before this has, in fact, occurred.

As each party approaches its objective, negotiation becomes difficult. The distance between the buyer's objective and the supplier's objective can well be called the "essence" or "heart" of the negotiation. (See Figure 15-1.) Any concession made by either party from its objective position will appear unreasonable to him or her based on the previous analysis of the facts. Changes in position, therefore, must now be the result of either logical persuasion and negotiating skills (entailing further investigation, analysis, and reassessment of the facts) or the pressure of brute economic strength.

It is in the area of objective persuasion that the skillful negotiator stands out. He or she makes progress by uncovering new facts and additional areas of negotiation that permit the supplier to reduce its demands. For example, an analysis of the supplier's manufacturing operations might reveal that if lead time were increased by only one week, the job could be done with fewer machines making longer production runs. This change could substantially reduce the supplier's setup and scheduling costs, thus permitting a price reduction. Additional lead time might be made available by a slight modification in the buyer's production schedule. The cost of making this change could well be much less than the seller's savings from the longer production runs. Thus both parties would profit from the change. It is this type of situation that competent negotiators constantly seek to discover and exploit in their attempt to close the gap between the seller's objective and their own. Such situations have the highly desirable effect of benefiting each party at no expense to the other party.

In some sole-source negotiations, the seller's objective is to maximize its position at the expense of the buyer. In these situations, a continuing relationship is of secondary interest to the seller; therefore, it uses its bargaining strength to maximize price, rather than to achieve a mutually advantageous contract that will lead to continued business. The buyer who senses such a situation should start negotiations by attacking the reasonableness of the seller's cost breakdown, using his or her own prepared cost estimates as the basis for such contentions. In the absence of competition, this is a buyer's most

---

[1] If the negotiator believes there is a possibility of actually achieving the minimum position, he or she should open with a position below this point—*provided such a position can be logically supported.*

logical and most effective plan of action. If the supplier refuses to divulge its cost data, the negotiator has only two available courses of action, both admittedly weak. He or she can appeal to the seller's sense of reason, pointing out the potential negative long-run implications of such actions, or he or she can attempt to fight force with force by threatening to use substitutes, to redesign and manufacture the product. When faced with this type of problem, the negotiator must attempt to bring the supplier's price as close to the objective as possible. In the short run, the buyer usually pays the seller's price. In the long run, the buyer works toward the development of competing sources, substitute products, and compromises with the supplier.

If a seller's negotiation objective is to resolve issues as quickly as possible, employing logical analysis rather than economic bargaining power, it is sometimes reasonable for the buyer to start negotiations by proposing his or her actual objective as the counteroffer to the seller's proposal. In fact, in industrial situations where continuing relationships are the rule, each successive negotiation brings the objectives of both parties ever closer together. Under these conditions, buyers and sellers need develop only their objective positions; there is no need for maximum and minimum positions.

The Four Phases of Face-to-Face Negotiations

Fact Finding During the *initial meeting* with the potential supplier, the professional negotiator and the negotiating team limit discussions to fact finding. Any inconsistencies between the supplier's proposal and the buyer's information are investigated. Fact finding should continue until the negotiator has a complete understanding of the supplier's proposal. Questions of a *how, what, when, who,* and *why* nature are used by the negotiator. Experience has shown that when the negotiator limits this initial meeting to fact finding, a satisfactory agreement normally results with a minimum of hassle and disagreement. During the fact-finding process, the negotiator should gain a better understanding of both the supplier's position and the supplier's strengths and weaknesses. *On completion of the fact-finding process, the negotiator should call for a recess.*

The Recess During the recess, the negotiating team should reassess its relative strengths and weaknesses, as well as those of the supplier. The team then should review and revise its objectives and their acceptable ranges. Next, the team should organize the agenda it desires to pursue when the two teams return to the negotiating table.

All negotiations center on specific issues. One of the difficult tasks of negotiation is to define fully the important issues which are to be included on the agenda and then to be sure that the discussion is confined to these issues. Most authorities believe that the issues should be discussed in the order of their probable ease of solution. With this priority system, an atmosphere of cooperation can develop that may facilitate solving the more difficult issues.

Narrowing the Differences   When the formal negotiations reconvene, the negotiator defines each issue, states the facts (and any underlying assumptions), and attempts to convince the supplier's representative(s) that the negotiator's position is reasonable. If agreement cannot be reached on an issue, the negotiator moves on to the next issue. Frequently, discussions on a subsequent issue will unblock an earlier deadlock.

During this phase of the negotiating process, *problem solving* and *compromise* are used to find creative solutions where both parties win. The buying team's manufacturing engineers may identify a more cost-effective process than the supplier had planned to use. Small acceptable changes in packaging, schedule, or tolerances; offers by the customer to furnish a material or an item of equipment; and payment terms (including possible advance payments) can unblock negotiations to the benefit of both parties.

In most instances, it is possible to reach a satisfactory agreement through the use of these procedures. If a satisfactory agreement cannot be reached, the negotiating team has the choice of adjourning (an attractive alternative for the buyer if another supplier is waiting in the wings) or moving on to hard bargaining.

Hard Bargaining   Hard bargaining, the last resort, involves the use of take-it-or-leave-it tactics. The negotiating team should carefully and professionally review and revise its objectives and, if absolutely necessary, give the supplier the option of accepting or rejecting its final proposal. The experienced negotiator does not bluff unless willing to have the bluff called. Unless a one-time purchase of an item already produced (e.g., an automobile on a dealer's lot) is involved, the wise negotiator avoids having the seller feel that it has been abused or treated unfairly. Such feelings set the stage for future confrontations, arguments, unsatisfactory performance, and possible claims.

Techniques

Negotiation techniques (tactics) are the negotiator's working tools. The negotiator uses them to achieve his or her strategic goals. In the hands of a skillful negotiator, these tools are powerful weapons. In the hands of a novice, they can be dangerous booby traps. Competent negotiators, therefore, spend a great deal of time studying and perfecting the use of these techniques. There are so many negotiating techniques that all cannot be discussed here. Those selected for discussion adequately represent the techniques that have proved to be most important and most effective.[2]

---

[2]Readers desiring a more detailed discussion of negotiating techniques may wish to review such books as Chester L. Karrass's *Give and Take: The Complete Guide to Negotiating Strategies &*

The objective of negotiation is agreement. Once either party adopts the position of "take it or leave it," negotiations break down. Even though agreement is the fundamental goal of negotiation, negotiations occasionally end without agreement. In the short run, reaching no agreement is sometimes better than reaching an unsatisfactory agreement. Generally speaking, however, experienced negotiators seldom let negotiations break down completely. They do not intentionally maneuver or let their opponents maneuver themselves into take-it-or-leave-it or walkout situations.

"Murder Boards" and Mock Negotiations Experienced negotiators frequently finalize their preparation through the use of "murder boards" and mock negotiations.

A murder board consists of senior purchasing, materials management, finance, manufacturing, quality, engineering, and general management personnel. The negotiating team presents its agenda, objectives, and tactics for the forthcoming negotiations. Members of the murder board dissect the negotiating plan in an effort to identify avoidable problems.

Mock negotiations allow the members of the negotiating team to prepare for the negotiation through a simulation of what is likely to occur. Other members of the organization (preferably from general management) play the roles of the supplier's negotiating team members during a simulated negotiation.[3]

Murder boards and mock negotiations enhance the negotiating team's level of preparation. Further, the processes result in general management's being aware of the negotiating team's agenda, objectives, and tactics. Should the subsequent negotiations deadlock, management is in a position to step in and revitalize critical negotiations.

Keep the Initiative The buyer should strive never to lose the initiative automatically obtained when the supplier's proposal is received and reviewed. There is a good deal of truth in the old saying that a good offense is the best defense. The buyer should constantly "carry the game" to the supplier, keep the supplier on the defensive by confronting its representatives with point after point, making the supplier continually justify its position. For example, if the supplier states the cost of materials in dollars, the buyer should ask the seller's representative to justify the figures with a bill of materials, appropriate scrap rates, and a full explanation of the manufacturing processes to be used. The more the buyer bores in and the more pressure he or she maintains, the better will be the buyer's bargaining position. If the

---

Tactics, Crowell, N.Y., 1974; G. I. Nierenberg's *The Complete Negotiator,* Nierenberg & Zeif Publishers, 1986; and J. A. Carlisle and R. C. Parker's *Beyond Negotiation,* John Wiley and Sons, Chichester, U.K., 1989.

[3] See David N. Burt, "Simulated Negotiations: An Experiment," *Journal of Purchasing and Materials Management,* Spring 1982, pp. 6–8.

supplier's position seems sound, the buyer can offer a counterproposal. In either case, the buyer starts with the initiative, and should work hard to retain it.

Use Diversions   On the human side of negotiations, the negotiator who knows the seller personally, or has carefully studied his or her personal behavior patterns (as should be the case), has an advantage. When tempers start to get out of hand, as they occasionally do, the experienced negotiator quickly diverts attention away from the issue at hand. At such times a joke, an anecdote, or a coffee break can be an effective means of easing tensions. This type of diversion is usually more easily accomplished when the participants know what situations are most irritating to the other.

Use Questions Effectively   The wise use of questions is one of the most important techniques in negotiation. By properly timing and phrasing questions, the negotiator can control the progress and trend of the negotiation. A perceptive question can forcefully, yet tactfully, attack the supplier's position. Similarly, the negotiator can effectively defend his or her own position by asking the seller to evaluate certain carefully chosen data the buyer has developed.

The technique of answering questions properly sometimes is as important as the technique of asking them properly. The successful negotiator knows when to answer, when not to answer, when to answer clearly, and when to answer vaguely. Not all questions require an answer. Many questions are asked for which the seller knows there is no answer; therefore, a reply is not really expected.

The correct answer to questions in negotiation is not governed by the same criteria governing the correct answer to questions in most other situations. For negotiation questions, the correct answer is the answer that furthers either the negotiator's short-term tactics or long-range strategy. Labor leaders and politicians are experts at asking and answering questions. Their questions and their answers are made to correlate with their strategic plans (strike platforms, party platforms, and so on). To an uninformed observer, it often appears that the answers given by politicians and labor leaders do not relate to the questions that they are asked. These observations are only partially correct. When answering questions, politicians and labor leaders tell their listeners what they want them to know about their platforms, whether or not the response fully answers the questions asked.

Successful negotiators realize that negotiation sessions are not like the classroom, where precise answers earn high marks. In negotiation, the purpose of questions and answers is not to illustrate to the seller how smart the negotiator is. Rather, it is to ferret out the seller's objectives and to learn as much as possible about how the seller's representatives intend to maneuver to achieve them. For this purpose, precise answers are sometimes the wrong answers. The correct degree of precision is dictated by the particular circumstances of each negotiation.

Use Positive Statements   As with sophisticated questions, perceptively used positive statements can favorably influence the course of negotiations. For example, assume a buyer knows that certain questions will evoke an emotional reaction from the seller. The questions are asked, and an opportunity is created for the proper use of a positive statement. A competent negotiator would say something like this: "I see your point, and I understand how you feel about this matter. Your point is well taken." Contrast the effect of this type of positive response with that of an emotional, negative response in which the buyer tells the seller that he or she is "dead wrong." When a buyer tells a seller that the seller's viewpoint is understood and considered reasonable, even though the buyer does not agree with it, the seller is certain to consider the buyer's viewpoint more objectively.

Machiavelli, in *The Prince*, gave the world some unusually sage advice concerning the use and misuse of positive statements: "I hold it to be proof of great prudence for men to abstain from threats and insulting words toward anyone, for neither...diminishes the strength of the enemy; but the one makes him more cautious, and the other increases his hatred of you, and makes him more persevering in his efforts to injure you."[4]

Be a Good Listener   Generally speaking, salespeople thoroughly enjoy talking. Consequently, buyers should let them talk. While talking, they very often talk themselves into concessions that a buyer could never gain by negotiation. Listening, per se, recognizes a basic need of a seller. Additionally, listening carefully to a seller's choice of words, phrases, and tone of voice, while at the same time observing his or her gestures and other uses of body language, can be rewarding. From observing such actions, a buyer can gain many clues regarding a seller's negotiating position.

Be Considerate of Sellers   A small number of negotiation experts contend that negotiations are best won by negotiators who are as brutal and as arbitrary as possible. Although some evidence supports this viewpoint, it is definitely a minority one.

Unquestionably, there are some purchasing situations in which a merciless frontal assault can be a proper and successful negotiating technique. However, for the vast majority of firms—those that seek profitable, continuing relationships with the seller—a more considerate and reasoned technique is recommended. Buyers lose no negotiating advantages whatsoever by being fully considerate of sellers personally, by letting them save face, and by reasonably satisfying their emotional needs.

---

[4] Niccolo Machiavelli, *The Prince*, Great Books of the Western World, Encyclopedia Britannica, 1982, vol. 23.

Never Give Anything Away   As a matter of strategy, a successful negotiator periodically lets the seller maneuver him or her into accepting one of the seller's proposals. This does not mean that the negotiator gives something away. He or she never "gives anything away." The buyer always expects to get a concession in exchange. On the other hand, the buyer does not feel obligated to match every concession made by the seller. Consequently, in the exchange process, the successful negotiator makes fewer concessions than his or her less successful adversary. By a continuation of this exchange process, a position close to the objectives of both parties is usually reached. Mutual concessions benefit both parties, and a contract so negotiated is *mutually* advantageous; but it is not *equally* advantageous.

Benefits Are Not Divided Equally   In some purchasing circles, a common misunderstanding exists that successful negotiation means an equal buyer-seller distribution of the benefits. While both buyer and seller should benefit from a well-negotiated contract, the benefits are seldom divided 50:50. Traditionally, 60 to 70 percent of the benefits of a typical negotiated contract go to the more skillful negotiator, leaving 30 to 40 percent for the less skilled negotiator.

NEGOTIATING FOR PRICE

Historically, price is the most difficult of all contract terms to be negotiated. Based on its high relative importance and its complexity, negotiation for price will be used as an example to illustrate what is involved in negotiating all the terms of the contract. If the reader understands what is involved in negotiating price, he or she can easily visualize what is involved in negotiating other issues.

When negotiating price, the negotiator must concurrently consider the type of contract to be used. Contract type and the negotiation of price are directly related; hence, they must be considered together.

To assure buying at favorable prices, buyers strive to develop the greatest practical amount of competition. Whenever it is possible, therefore, the initial step for a buyer seeking successful negotiation is to get an adequate number of bids or proposals from among those potential suppliers who are genuinely interested in competing for the contract.[5] In negotiated purchasing, requests for proposals usually ask for not only total price but also a complete breakdown of all attendant costs.

For every negotiated purchase, either price analysis or cost analysis, or both, is required. Which analysis is best to use and the extent of the analysis required are determined by the facts bearing on each specific purchase being

---

[5] The term "bids" is traditionally used in competitive bid purchases. Consequently, bids used in negotiated purchases are sometimes referred to as "proposals," to clearly identify the buy as a negotiated purchase. However, the terms are frequently used interchangeably.

negotiated. Generally speaking, price analysis is used for lower-dollar-value contracts and cost analysis for higher-dollar-value contracts. A discussion of the applicable uses of both price analysis negotiation and cost analysis negotiation follows.

Price Analysis Negotiation

Price analysis negotiation (often referred to simply as "price negotiation") is the most commonly used approach when negotiating for price. Some proponents of cost negotiation disparage price negotiation, referring to it as "unsophisticated" and "emotional." In the many cases where price negotiations are undertaken in an unprofessional manner, such criticism is fully justified. Banging on the table and shouting "I want lower prices" or "I can get it cheaper from B" is certainly not professional price negotiation.

On the other hand, in many specific cases where pricing data are developed and utilized with professional skill, price negotiation can be just as advantageous as cost negotiation, or more so. Compared with cost negotiation, price negotiation has three distinct advantages: (1) negotiation time is shorter, (2) support of technical specialists is seldom needed, and (3) pricing data are relatively easy to acquire.

The traditional sources from which buyers get pricing data are federal government publications, purchasing trade publications, newspapers, and business journals. Competing suppliers are excellent sources of pricing data. They can provide the buyer with price lists, catalogs, numerous special pricing data, and formal price quotations. From these competing supplier data, the buyer can readily determine two very important facts: *the nature of the market* (competitive or noncompetitive) and *the extent of supplier interest* in this particular purchase. As discussed in Chapter 12, historic pricing data and engineering estimates also provide a sound basis for price analysis.

Price Comparison The negotiator's first step in price analysis is to determine the extent of market competitiveness and supplier interest. The second step is to examine in detail the absolute and relative differences existing among the various prices quoted by the competing suppliers. From this examination, a buyer detects that differences in prices among suppliers exist but does not learn the causes of these differences. The search for causes begins in the purchasing department's supplier information file.

The bid prices of the competing suppliers are compared with past prices of similar purchases from the supplier information file. The causes of all significant variations are pinpointed and analyzed. Adjustments are made for changes in factors such as specifications, quantities ordered, times of deliveries, variations which have taken place in the general levels of business activity and prices, and differences which may have resulted from learning experience. After these adjustments are made, the negotiator (sometimes with the help of an engineering estimator or a price analyst) determines whether or not the prices offered are reasonable. From this determination, the negotiator decides on the target price to use for his or her negotiating position.

Trend Comparisons   Historic prices paid for purchases of similar quantities can be analyzed to disclose helpful price trend information. For example, if prices have been increasing, it is reasonable to expect that the seller will attempt to maintain a similar pattern of increase. Hence, by carefully analyzing the reasons for all price increases, the negotiator can structure a bargaining position on the basis of any invalidities uncovered.

Similarly, the negotiator can analyze decreasing prices to determine whether the price decrease is too little or too much. If the buyer determines that the decrease is too large, he or she must determine whether the trend is creating, or is likely to create, quality or service problems in contract performance. If the decrease is too little, then the buyer must determine whether the benefits of improved production processes are being proportionally reflected in lower prices.

Even a level price trend offers opportunities for price analysis. For example, the negotiator may ask whether level prices are justified, considering the many manufacturing improvements which have been made. Did the supplier charge too much initially? Has the supplier's competitive position in the industry changed? If the negotiator's analysis indicates that costs have fallen because of reductions in the supplier's cost for materials or because of improvements in the production processes, his or her negotiating position is clear. The buyer negotiates for pro-rata reductions reflecting these changes.

Cost Analysis Negotiation

As previously stated, price analysis negotiation is more commonly used than cost analysis negotiation. In cost negotiations, each applicable cost element is negotiated individually, i.e., design engineering cost, tooling cost, direct materials cost, labor hours, labor rates, subcontracting, overhead cost, other direct costs, profit, and so on. Cost analysis negotiation (commonly referred to as cost negotiation) is steadily growing in use. It has been used successfully for decades in many large firms such as General Electric, Ford, and Polaroid, and in recent years it has been employed increasingly in small and medium-size firms.

DOCUMENTATION

Personnel turnover and the frailties of the human memory make accurate documentation of the negotiation essential. The documentation must permit a rapid reconstruction of all significant considerations and agreements.

Documentation begins in the purchasing office with the receipt of a purchase requisition and continues with the selection of potential suppliers and their proposals. Documentation of the actual negotiation must be adequate to allow someone other than the buyer to understand what was agreed to, how, and why. Burt, Norquist, and Anklesaria suggest the following format for the documentation of negotiations[6]:

Subject This is a memorandum designed for many readers with different orientations. This section, together with the introductory summary, should give the reader a complete overview of the negotiation, including information such as the supplier's name and location, the contract number, and a brief description of what is being purchased.

Introductory summary The introductory summary describes the type of contract and the type of negotiation action involved, together with comparative figures from the supplier's proposal, the buyer's negotiation objective, and the negotiated results.

Particulars The purpose of this section is to cover the details about what is being bought and who is involved in the procurement. This should be done without duplicating information that was included in the subject section.

Procurement situation The purpose of this section is to discuss factors in the procurement situation which affect the reasonableness of the final price.

Negotiation summary This section shows the supplier's contract pricing proposal, the buyer's negotiation objective, and the negotiation results, tabulated in parallel form and broken down by major elements of cost and profit. Whether these are shown as summary figures for total contract value, summary for the total price of the major item, unit price for the major items, or some other form of presentation depends on how negotiations were conducted. The general rule is to portray the negotiation as it actually took place.

CHARACTERISTICS OF A SUCCESSFUL NEGOTIATOR

The characteristics of successful negotiators should now be clear. These people are skillful individuals, with broad business experience. They possess a good working knowledge of all the primary functions of business, and they know how to use the tools of management—accounting, human relations, economics, business law, and quantitative analysis. They are knowledgeable about the techniques of negotiation and the products their firms buy. They are able to lead conferences and to integrate specialists into smoothly functioning teams. In addition to being well educated and experienced, successful negotiators excel in good judgment. It is good judgment that causes them to attach the correct degree of importance to each of the factors bearing on the major issues. Combining their skills, knowledge, and judgment, they develop superior tactical and strategic plans. Additionally, they consider prob-

---

[6]David N. Burt, Warren E. Norquist, and J. Anklesaria, *Zero Base Pricing*™: *Achieving World Class Competitiveness Through Reduced All-in-Cost*, Chapter 13, Probus Publishing, Chicago, Ill., 1990.

lems from the viewpoint of the firm as a whole, not from the viewpoint of a functional manager.[7]

Fully successful negotiators share three common attributes:

1 All realize that specialized training and practice are required for an individual to become an effective negotiator. Although some people have stronger verbal aptitudes than others, no one is born with negotiating knowledge and skills.
2 All habitually enter into negotiations with higher negotiating goals than their counterparts, and generally they achieve them.
3 All are included, or are destined to become included, among an organization's most highly valued professionals.

CONCLUSION

Negotiation is free enterprise at its very best. In the aggregate, it matches the skills of determined buyers against those of equally determined sellers. Both explore ways to achieve objectives that tend to optimize the self-interest of their organizations. In short, negotiation is a powerful purchasing tool which competent buyers use to achieve maximum value at minimum cost. By rewarding efficiency and penalizing inefficiency, the negotiation process not only benefits the negotiating firms, it also benefits the nation's economy as a whole.

FOR DISCUSSION

15-1 What does negotiation mean in purchasing? Why is it often confused with "hassling" and "price chiseling"?
15-2 "Superior negotiation skills merit superior reward." Do you agree with this statement? Why?
15-3 Enumerate the five major objectives common to all negotiations. Should a negotiation team pursue all objectives while negotiating?
15-4 Under what circumstances should negotiation be used in preference to competitive bidding?
15-5 Compare and contrast the terms "informal negotiation" and "mock negotiation."
15-6 Discuss the three factors which influence a buyer's negotiating strengths and weaknesses.
15-7 Discuss the three factors which influence a seller's strengths and weaknesses.

---

[7] In recent years women have entered the purchasing and materials management profession in increasing numbers. These new professionals have proved themselves capable in all phases of the profession—especially negotiation.

15-8 In the process of negotiation, after both sides reach their negotiation objectives, progress becomes difficult. Why? How are such difficulties resolved?

15-9 "For negotiation questions, the correct answer is the answer that furthers either the negotiator's short-term tactics or long-range strategy." Explain.

15-10 Identify the differences between cost and price negotiation. When should you use cost negotiation? Would you recommend using cost negotiation for certain industries and not for others? Why?

15-11 Describe how the documentation for a given negotiation typically is organized. What purpose does the documentation serve?

15-12 What are the characteristics of a successful negotiator?

15-13 Why is price the most difficult of all contract terms to negotiate?

CASES FOR CHAPTER 15

The Apex Aviation Case, page 710
Bronx Business Machines Corporation, page 720
Muenster Pump Buys a Car, page 765
SDC Corporation, page 803
A Problem of Price, page 791
Campbell Typewriter Corporation (in the Instructor's Manual)
Three Vendors and a Tub (in the Instructor's Manual)
Collier Company II (in the Instructor's Manual)

PART **FOUR**

SPECIAL PURCHASES

16

PURCHASING CAPITAL EQUIPMENT

The purchase of capital equipment differs substantially from the purchase of production materials and supplies. Such items as pianos, pumps, standard electric motors, microcomputers, materials-handling trucks, and office furniture are typical examples of *general-purpose* capital equipment. Things such as power-generating equipment, specialized machine tools, unique production machinery, and chemical processing equipment are examples of *special-purpose* capital equipment, designed for unique applications. Development of specifications for this latter category of capital items usually requires a great deal of interaction between technical personnel in the buying and selling firms. And frequently the effective life of the equipment is determined by technological obsolescence factors.

For accounting purposes most firms classify both categories of equipment as noncurrent assets, which are capitalized and depreciated over the course of their economic lives.

DIFFERENCES IN THE PROCUREMENT OF CAPITAL EQUIPMENT

Nonrecurring Purchases

The purchase of a particular piece of capital equipment typically occurs only once every five to ten years or so. For example, one buyer recently purchased a unique high-temperature electric furnace for use in her company's research and development laboratory. Since the furnace is used only periodically for experimental work, it is very likely that another purchase of this kind of equipment will not be made in the foreseeable future.

On the other hand, a few industrial operations require the use of many identical machines in the production process. For example, in petroleum and chemical processing plants, the product is transported by pipeline throughout most of the production operation. This requires dozens, at times hundreds, of similar pumps which vary only in size and details of construction. To keep capital expenditures at a fairly uniform level from year to year and to minimize maintenance costs, pumps are often replaced on a continuing basis, rather than all at once. Although relatively uncommon, this type of capital equipment purchase assumes some of the characteristics of conventional production purchasing.

A unique feature of most capital equipment purchases is the lead time requirement. While some types of capital equipment are standard off-the-shelf products, many are not. Much production machinery and prime moving equipment is built (at least in part) to operate under specific conditions peculiar to each purchaser's operation. Consequently, manufacturing lead time is usually a matter of months or years. The production of a large steam turbine generating unit, for example, may require negotiating and expediting work substantially different from that normally required in production purchasing.

Nature and Size of Expenditure

An expenditure of company funds for capital equipment is an investment. If purchased wisely and operated efficiently, capital equipment generates profit for its owner. Because it exerts a direct influence on the costs of production, the selection of major capital equipment is a matter of significant concern to top management.

Although capital equipment prices cover a wide range, the purchase of most major equipment involves the expenditure of a substantial sum of money. The purchase price for a piece of equipment, however, is frequently overshadowed in importance by other elements of cost. Since a machine is often used for ten years or more, total costs of operation and maintenance during its lifetime may far exceed its initial cost. Hence, the *total life cost* of a machine, relative to its productivity, is the cost factor of primary importance.[1] Estimating operating and maintenance costs which will be incurred in future years is not easy; frequently these costs vary from year to year. Consequently, discussions involving the choice between several alternative machines often center on the probable accuracy of specific cost estimates.

The timing of many capital purchases often presents a paradoxical situation. Typically, the general supply capabilities of capital equipment producers do not adjust quickly to changes in levels of demand. Thus, because capital equipment purchases are made infrequently and can often be postponed, producers of industrial capital goods frequently find themselves in a "feast or famine" type of business. When a potential purchaser's business is good, it needs additional production equipment to satisfy customers' burgeoning demands. But because other purchasers are in the same situation, the buyer also finds capital equipment prices rising in a market of short supply. Conversely, when a buyer's business is down and additional production equipment is not needed, capital equipment is in plentiful supply, often at reduced prices.

Considerations in Source Selection

When purchasing capital equipment, selection of a supplier is governed largely by four general considerations: (1) operating characteristics of the equipment, (2) engineering features of the equipment, (3) a total economic analysis, and (4) various qualitative considerations.

Operating Characteristics   This is by far the most influential factor in selecting the supplier for a particular production machine. Once the user and appropriate engineering personnel clearly establish the function the equipment is to perform, design and operating capability are paramount in selecting the specific machine to be purchased.

Design and operating features for a given type of equipment can differ

---

[1] This type of analysis is also called *life cycle costing*. The term and the concept were originally developed and refined in military procurement. Subsequently, industry adopted the concept and now it is widely used in most industries.

markedly among the machines available from different vendors. For this reason, the number of vendors willing to produce a machine capable of meeting every aspect of a purchaser's operating requirements is frequently limited. This, of course, is more likely to be the case for specialized equipment than for general-purpose equipment. Nevertheless, this is one reason why a purchasing department usually finds its freedom of source-selection activities constrained considerably in obtaining capital equipment as compared with buying production materials.

Engineering Features   Closely related to the equipment's operating characteristics are its engineering features. These features must be compatible with the buyer's existing equipment, process, and plant layout; they must also be in accordance with standards established by state and federal regulatory agencies such as the Occupational Safety and Health Administration and the Environmental Protection Agency (EPA). A few major engineering considerations are noted below.

- *Specific process capabilities.* Is performance compatible with that of existing machines, thus minimizing process coordination problems? Will use of the new machine produce capacity imbalance problems?
- *Physical size and mounting dimensions.* Will the machine fit into existing available space satisfactorily? Can it be tied in to existing supporting structures without difficulty?
- *Flexibility.* Can the equipment be moved and relocated without excessive difficulty?
- *Power requirements.* Can existing power supplies be used?
- *Maintenance.* Are lubrication fittings and adjusting mechanisms conveniently located? Is any special maintenance required that cannot be handled by existing maintenance programs?
- *Safety features.* Does the machine have any unsafe features? Does it meet OSHA standards, and is its general safety level comparable with that of existing equipment?
- *Pollution characteristics.* Does the equipment perform in accordance with EPA requirements concerning pollution and contamination discharge levels?

The general questions to be answered are: How does this piece of equipment fit in with the existing operation? Will many costly modifications be involved in adapting the equipment to the existing system?

Economic Analysis   After several acceptable machines have been identified, a thorough evaluation of their relative merits is undertaken. The task is a complicated one. An analysis of the major operating alternatives includes a comparative economic analysis of the potential new machines, and also a comparison of each with the alternative of using the existing equipment now in operation. In all cases, the analysis of each machine must relate its total expected life cost to its total expected productivity. The cost analysis is done most commonly utilizing the *life cycle costing* technique (see page 327). These results, in turn, can be expressed using several different measures of profitability.

Although it has serious limitations, the *payback* approach is still widely used throughout American industry. As its name implies, the objective of payback analysis is to determine the number of years a machine requires to pay for itself from additional earnings generated by its increased level of operating efficiency. This is a useful measure for evaluating a potential purchase in light of a firm's liquidity position. However, it must be supplemented with one of the discounted cash flow–based measures that gives a more complete picture of a machine's total profitability over the life of the equipment investment. The *time adjusted rate of return* on investment is one such technique that is commonly used. Among several other widely used approaches is the *net present value method.*[2]

Before the total investigation proceeds too far, a formal proposal justifying the need for additional capital equipment should be prepared for top management. Although the proposal must consist of more than an economic analysis, a complete quantitative analysis showing the potential profitability of the various alternatives should constitute a major section of such a proposal.

Qualitative Considerations Certain qualitative factors concerning potential suppliers are important in making any purchase. However, not all the factors important in selecting sources for production materials weigh as heavily in selecting sources for capital equipment. Capital equipment purchases require a different type of cooperative relationship between the buyer and the seller. It is important, initially, that a supplier be willing to work with the buyer's technical personnel to ensure a good fit of equipment to operating need. After the purchase, the buyer may need help with installation, start-up, adjustment, and so on. In fact, adjustment or calibration may be a continuing need, depending on the type of equipment and the buyer's in-house capability.

At some future date, the buyer may also require a warranty adjustment. Especially important is an assessment of the supplier's policy and cooperativeness with respect to the supply of replacement parts and service for the equipment, particularly later when the equipment is superseded by a new model. These types of factors represent one group of qualitative considerations that a buyer considers in making a capital equipment purchasing de-

---

[2]The reader interested in a detailed treatment of this topic should review any current text dealing with financial management. Particularly good are: Robert N. Anthony, *Management Accounting,* Richard D. Irwin, Inc., Homewood, Ill., 1964, chap. 19; E. F. Brigham, *Financial Management—Theory and Practice,* 3d ed., Dryden Press, New York, 1982, chap. 3; and S. B. Block and G. A. Hirt, *Foundations of Financial Management,* revised ed., Richard D. Irwin, Inc., Homewood, Ill., 1981, chaps. 9 and 11.

cision, with each individual case posing its own unique requirements. Generally speaking, however, the buyer focuses on somewhat different considerations than when a continuous stream of production materials is being purchased.

Another group of qualitative considerations the capital equipment buyer is concerned with are those indicating a vendor's ability to produce reliable equipment that performs in accordance with specifications. This implies the definite need for an assessment of the vendor's technical and production capabilities. As the situation demands, a good buyer uses various approaches and personnel in making such an assessment, including plant visits and technical discussions with the vendor's personnel. However, buyers should not overlook the simple technique of investigating a vendor's reputation among present customers. This is an invaluable source of information that is easy to tap.

Generally speaking, qualitative considerations do not play a primary role in the selection of a supplier for capital equipment. They are usually considered in the final analysis, after the major factors have been weighed. The qualitative factors are the straws that tip the balance one way or the other for the several potential suppliers who rank high on combined technical and economic considerations.

Joint Selection of Equipment

It should now be clear that the final selection of capital equipment should be a joint undertaking by all departments having a legitimate interest in the decision. To facilitate this process, larger firms frequently utilize a buying team composed of representatives from operations, process engineering, plant engineering, finance, and purchasing, depending on the nature of the purchase.[3] In smaller firms, this coordination may be achieved less formally by a series of meetings among the appropriate functional individuals; in this case, purchasing's capital equipment buyer often serves in a coordinating or administrative role. In either case, because capital equipment represents a long-range investment, a general management executive frequently makes the final purchasing decision, based on recommendations from this interdepartmental group.

Because the operations manager is responsible for the efficiency of the total production operation, his or her views logically carry a great deal of weight in the selection of production equipment. Heinritz and Farrell suggest also that the importance of the human element should not be overlooked. They point out that because "the head of the department where the equipment is to be used...has an important interest in the decision, the enthusi-

---

[3]This topic is explored in depth in D. B. Carmody and John O'Shaughnessy, "Interdepartmental Coordination in Buying Capital Equipment," *Journal of Purchasing and Materials Management*, Spring 1979, pp. 21–24.

asm or reluctance of his acceptance may have a direct bearing on the efficiency of the equipment in actual use."[4] Consequently, the operations manager may well choose to bring the appropriate supervisor into the decision also. The technical contribution to be made by process engineering and plant engineering representatives is clearly an important one, for the reasons previously outlined.

The finance department has three primary interests in capital equipment purchases. First, this department usually administers the firm's capital budget; it is therefore concerned with the allocation of funds for the proposed purchase. If the budget contains a provision for such equipment, all is well; if not, a priority question must be resolved. Second, the finance department has the responsibility of deciding how to finance such purchases. Is enough cash available? Can a long-term loan be arranged? Will it be necessary to raise the money through a bond issue? For large purchases, the answers to these questions bear heavily on the final decision. Third, the finance department should review and evaluate the economic analysis of alternative machines. In some firms, the finance department conducts the original analyses; in others, they are made by engineering or purchasing. In any case, the finance department typically administers these activities in connection with its capital budgeting responsibility.

After the technical and economic analyses have been completed, the purchasing department develops and evaluates the qualitative factors relevant to the decision. After the supplier is selected, purchasing handles the negotiations and carries out the conventional purchasing responsibilities.

LIFE CYCLE COST ANALYSIS

How important is the *price* of a new piece of productive equipment? The answer is, it depends. It depends on a number of factors that vary widely with the design and usage of the equipment, as well as the number of years it will be in service (coupled with various economic inflation factors). In addition to the original delivered cost of the machine, its total cost to the owner includes such cost factors as those associated with installation, ongoing adjustment and calibration, energy and labor for operation, routine maintenance, major overhauls, downtime, and eventual disposition of the machine (net cost or salvage value). As a rough rule of thumb, in industry today the delivered price of a piece of productive equipment seldom exceeds 50 percent of the eventual total cost of ownership of the asset.[5]

The price of anything that one buys is important. But in the case of capital equipment, it is usually less important than the sum of all the *follow-on* costs

---

[4]Stuart Heinritz and P. V. Farrell, *Purchasing: Principles and Applications,* Prentice-Hall, Inc., Englewood Cliffs, N.J., 1981, p. 299.

[5]Researchers Leenders and Fearon find that most industrial equipment falls in the 20 to 60 percent range; Leenders, Fearon, and England, *Purchasing and Materials Management,* Richard D. Irwin, Inc., Homewood, Ill., 1989 p. 554.

that eventually accompany the purchase, particularly if the equipment is expected to have a reasonably long life. In any case, the important requirement in capital equipment purchasing is to conduct a life cycle cost analysis to put all the cost factors in the correct perspective. It is not uncommon for the operating and maintenance costs of a less expensive machine to exceed those of a somewhat higher-priced machine to the extent that, in total, the higher-priced machine is a significantly better buy.

Conceptually, the life cycle costing concept is quite simple. It seeks to determine the *total* cost of performing a given function during the useful life of the equipment performing the function. It focuses on the total cost of ownership rather than on initial price.

In practice, however, the concept frequently is not so easy to apply. A number of the anticipated costs are not known with certainty; many will occur in the future, and many will be based on estimates of labor rates, energy costs, and downtime requirements during maintenance and overhaul. The extent to which these costs can be estimated accurately depends on three factors: (1) the experience and sophistication of the manufacturer in making its performance estimates, (2) the buying organization's experience with similar types of equipment, and (3) the sophistication of the buyer's economic forecasting group.

Despite the practical difficulties, in most cases organizations that utilize the life cycle costing concept have learned to make the required estimates with an acceptable degree of accuracy. The procedure followed in conducting a life cycle cost analysis is summarized below.

1 Determine the operating cycle for the equipment—types of operation, routine maintenance, overhaul, sequence, and so on, detailing how the machine functions or what will be done in each step of the cycle.
2 Identify and quantify the factors that affect costs—power consumption and rates at various levels of operation, labor requirements and rates, maintenance requirements and rates, average time between failures, time between overhauls, average downtime cost, and so on.
3 Calculate all costs at current rates and prices.
4 *Project costs to the future dates at which they will be incurred*, adjust for expected inflation or deflation, consider estimated salvage value, and complete the life cycle cost matrix.
5 *Discount all future costs and benefits to their present values.*
6 Sum all costs and benefits to obtain the total life cycle cost, expressed in *present value* terms.

PROCEDURE FOR PURCHASING CAPITAL EQUIPMENT

The major differences between capital equipment purchasing and production purchasing have now been identified and discussed. At this point the entire procedure is outlined briefly to illustrate how the differences fit into the overall decision-making plan.

1 For more than 75 percent of the capital equipment purchases, recognition of the need arises in the using department. Typically, this is in one of the operations departments or in the general management area.

2 Rarely is the need for capital equipment absolute; acquisition can usually be postponed until conditions for purchase become favorable. Although the initial inquiry may come to purchasing in the form of a requisition, more often than not the purpose at this point is only to obtain general information about the equipment in question, not to make an immediate purchase. The purchasing department consequently obtains general sales and performance literature, together with approximate price and delivery information.

3 The using department studies the preliminary information obtained by purchasing and determines the feasibility of pursuing the matter further.

4 If the decision is affirmative, a buying team may be formed. Detailed specifications then should be drawn up jointly by the using and engineering departments, with input from purchasing. Specifications should spell out unambiguously the required design or performance characteristics necessitated by the current operating situation.

As a rule, the user needs to discuss various aspects of the equipment with manufacturers' representatives. A manufacturer's sales engineer can often provide valuable suggestions regarding application of his or her firm's equipment in the user's unique situation. Moreover, in the case of complex applications, the sales engineer frequently offers to make an engineering study as a service to the buyer. This activity normally is coordinated by the buyer assigned to the job.

5 When the investigation is complete and specifications are firm, the purchasing department may take one of two courses of action, depending on the type of equipment being purchased.

If it is possible to do so, the buyer often arranges a side-by-side demonstration, on the buyer's premises, of selected vendors' products that meet the specifications. The purpose is to provide a hands-on comparative testing opportunity for using personnel and members of the buying team. Based on the results of this performance comparison, the team then develops a list of acceptable machines and potential suppliers. Subsequently, purchasing requests formal proposals from the selected suppliers. This approach works well when buying standard products that are transportable. At times, the sequence of the demonstration and bidding activities may be reversed to provide a smaller and more selective demonstration event if matters of practicality or purchasing strategy indicate a preference for this approach.

When buying equipment for which on-site demonstrations are not possible—things such as mainframe computers, industrial drying ovens, and custom designed machines—purchasing initiates a different course of action. In this case, two-step bidding might well be used.

First, technical proposals are requested. After the most attractive bidders have been identified, the buying team typically visits the selected group of potential suppliers to talk with appropriate technical and managerial personnel and to study similar types of equipment in operation at the vendor's facility. Subsequently, the bidding field may be narrowed further and final bids requested. In the event that only one or two vendors can produce an acceptable machine, the buyer may have decided initially to negotiate the purchase.

6 An economic analysis of the various feasible alternatives is made at this point. The analysis can be made by any of the departments involved in the review. Frequently it is made by purchasing or finance, based on operating, technical, and cost information provided by the engineering, using, and purchasing departments.

7 The required facts are now ready for evaluation. In a large organization this is done by the buying team. In some smaller firms it is done informally by the departments participating in the decision. The end result of the evaluation should be the preparation of a written report justifying the recommendation that a certain machine be purchased. Included in the report should be a description of where and how the machine will be used, why it is required, and estimated figures for its utilization and its life. Also included should be cost data for the existing operation and for the several alternatives considered. Financial computations concerning the rate of return on investment (or other similar measures of profitability), together with any qualitative comments from the participants, should constitute the last section of the report.

8 The written report is submitted to top management for a decision.

9 If the decision is positive, the purchasing department proceeds to conclude the purchase.

PURCHASING'S ROLE IN CAPITAL EQUIPMENT PROCUREMENT

At this point, the reader undoubtedly has concluded that the purchasing department plays a distinctly different role in the acquisition of capital goods than it does in the acquisition of production materials. In the procurement of capital equipment, the purchasing department acts to a great extent in a service capacity as a gatherer of information, a process coordinator, a purchasing consultant to management, and finally a contract administrator.

Source of Information

No department is in a better position than purchasing to keep abreast of the general developments occurring in major equipment industries. Through daily contact with both salespeople and current trade literature, alert buyers pick up considerable information of value to operating department managers. In a large company, one buyer may specialize solely in machinery and capital equipment purchasing. A good purchasing department makes a point of regularly relaying information concerning new developments in the capital equipment area to appropriate operating executives.

Once a requisition has been initiated, of course, it is purchasing's responsibility to locate competent vendors and secure the information required by the user in making a preliminary analysis. Suppose the quality control manager, for example, wants to buy an expensive microscope. With his or her knowledge of the market, the capital equipment buyer can easily obtain the basic data needed for analysis. Moreover, a good buyer should be able to arrange a side-by-side display or demonstration of major competitive models so quality control personnel can test and compare them.

Liaison Service

During investigation of various manufacturers' equipment, an operating manager frequently finds it advantageous to discuss technical details with a machine manufacturer's representative. A customary (and sound) practice is for the appropriate buyer to act as a liaison in arranging meetings between potential suppliers and operating departments. As a rule, the capital equipment buyer should sit in on these meetings, or at least keep informed of significant developments. It is his or her responsibility to ensure that no premature commitments are made by line departments; likewise, the buyer must at all times be aware of the current status of all negotiations if he or she is to function effectively in the buyer's role.

In these types of preliminary discussions, as noted earlier, a manufacturer's sales engineer may offer to make a preproposal applications study as a service to the buying organization. Sellers in *some industries* customarily make preliminary technical studies as part of their regular sales efforts. Both parties realize that such vendor participation is entirely voluntary and that the related expenses are those normally encountered in stimulating sales. Selling prices in these industries are set so that the revenue from successful efforts covers those situations where preproposal efforts do not result in eventual sales. In other industries, the cost of preproposal studies is not covered fully by the selling price.

The purchasing department, therefore, should always be cautious with respect to the acceptance of presale engineering work. The buyer naturally wants all the assistance available. But in some cases presale engineering studies can entail excessive costs and place the buyer under obligation to the seller. The wise buyer avoids this kind of obligation. Before accepting a seller's offer for such a study, the buyer should find out how much money is involved and determine whether the offer is consistent with standard practice in the industry. If the costs exceed normal industry practice—yet the study is clearly worthwhile—the buying firm should consider contracting and paying for the study itself. By separating the purchase of the study from the purchase of the machine, the buyer ensures against the incurrence of an unwise obligation.

Specification Development and Bids

One of the advantages of formally establishing a buying team is the fact that more *cooperative* action usually is generated in attacking the buying problem. This can be extremely useful in development of the equipment specifications, particularly when the buyer is genuinely involved. As a part of this involvement, when specifications are nearing completion and invitations for bid are to be issued, a good buyer should also function in the role of an informal auditor. Although technical requirements predominate, the buyer should make every effort to see that specifications are written as functionally as possible. Most users hold biases for and against specific types of equipment. It is not unusual to find pilots who want to fly only McDonnell-Douglas airplanes, or printers who believe they obtain good work only on a Harris press, or machinists who believe only Cincinnati machine tools maintain precise tolerances. Every effort should be made to exclude such personal biases from the specifications. The nature of many capital equipment requirements limits the number of possible suppliers in the first place. This number should not be further reduced by arbitrarily excluding certain types of equipment on the grounds of prejudice alone.

To function effectively in this role, the buyer should have participated in most of the technical discussions between the company's line personnel and the various manufacturers, and he or she must have a basic understanding of the significance of the technical problems involved. The buyer's job is still one of challenging questionable specification inclusions. Ironically, however, a buyer's success in this endeavor depends less on technical knowledge than on skill in understanding and dealing with people. In the realm of technical matters, the buyer is at a disadvantage because he or she is dealing with professionals in this area. Therefore, the long-range approach should focus on an attempt to *gain the cooperation of technical managers*. The buyer must persuade them that unbiased functional specifications serve the company's best interests.[6]

Once specifications are completed, the buyer is responsible for arranging comparison demonstrations and for securing bids from a reasonable number of qualified vendors.

---

[6] Humana Inc. has successfully implemented a unique capital equipment purchasing system that utilizes an interdepartmental panel to develop equipment specifications, evaluate equipment, and select suppliers. The cooperative action achieved in specification development is unusual. For a detailed discussion, see "Capital Equipment Buying—A Joint Decision," *Purchasing World*, January 1981, pp. 86–89.

Qualitative Analysis

Some vendors are more qualified than others. The degree of qualification should be considered carefully by the review team in deciding which machine to buy. Purchasing normally gathers and analyzes such information for the group. The buyer must first determine, usually with engineering assistance, the level of a vendor's *technical* and *production* capabilities. This is of utmost importance.

Second, the buyer must assess the vendor's *capability* and *willingness* to provide any engineering service required during the installation and start-up of the new equipment. This is an extremely important financial consideration when complex, expensive equipment such as steam turbines, numerically controlled machine tools, and so on, is involved. Closely related to this factor is the necessity of training operators. What service is the vendor willing to provide in this area?

Another important consideration is the reliability of a vendor in standing behind its guarantees. Once the equipment is installed, unexpected problems beyond the purchaser's control sometimes add significantly to the total cost of a machine. Finally, what is the vendor's policy on providing replacement parts? When the purchased machine is superseded by a new model, what will be the availability of obsolete parts? The policy of one pump manufacturer, for example, is to produce a small stock of replacement parts for obsolete equipment once every six months. The semiannual production policy of this manufacturer, combined with its low inventory levels, forces some customers to carry unreasonably large stocks of major replacement parts. The other costly alternative for the customer is to risk occasional breakdowns, which might leave a machine out of service as long as three or four months, waiting for the next run of parts.

In practice, unfortunately, such considerations frequently play a minor role in the initial selection of equipment, only to assume major proportions at a later date. It is the purchasing department's responsibility to evaluate potential suppliers in light of these qualitative factors and to bring significant considerations of this kind before the evaluating group for adequate appraisal. After a machine is purchased, the wise buyer works closely with the maintenance department in keeping and interpreting historical records (part by part) of machine performance. Data of this kind are valuable in making similar future analyses.

Bid Tabulation and Economic Analysis

When bids are received, the buyer tabulates them and makes any adjustments necessary so they can be interpreted on a comparable basis by the group responsible for the final recommendation.

As noted previously, the finance department frequently assumes responsibility for conducting the total profitability study, because administration and control of such activities are clearly related to the capital budgeting function. The authors' view, however, is that once management has selected the types of analysis to be used, the purchasing department might well perform the analyses more easily and effectively than the finance department. Such analyses are a logical extension of the purchasing department's bid analysis activities. Clearly, the buyer is familiar with any bid complications. Through his or her involvement in the preceding technical discussions, the buyer should also understand any technical problems involved in estimates for maintenance and operating costs. Thus, one individual with a fairly complete understanding of the total cost situation could perhaps most effectively prepare, interpret, and present the complete package of price, cost, and profitability data for the group's consideration.

Negotiation, Contract Preparation, and Administration

After top management has approved a proposal for the purchase of capital equipment, the buyer assumes his or her customary responsibility for negotiating the final price, delivery, and related terms of the contract. The purchase order or contract should be written with particular care, specifying the responsibility of both parties for equipment performance and postsale activities. Acceptance testing and inspection methods, acceptance timing, machine specifications and performance standards, and guarantee conditions should be clearly stated. Similarly, supplier responsibility for postsale services pertaining to installation, start-up, operator training, maintenance checks, and replacement parts should be spelled out clearly so there is no question about what is expected.

In the event that the purchase involves a lengthy manufacturing period, a special follow-up and expediting program should be developed. This may call for periodic plant visits and in-process inspection of the work. Responsibility for monitoring this activity often rests with the purchasing department.

Viewing the situation in total, purchasing's role in the acquisition of capital equipment assumes a considerably greater staff orientation and a lesser decision-making orientation than is customary in the procurement of standard production materials.

USED EQUIPMENT

A buyer is by no means restricted to the purchase of new capital equipment. Purchases of used machinery, in fact, constitute an important percentage of total machinery sales.

Reasons for Purchasing Used Equipment

A purchaser may consider buying used equipment for several reasons. First, the cost of used machinery is substantially less than that of new equipment.

Analysis of payback or return on investment may well reveal that a piece of used equipment is a better buy than a new machine. Even if this is not the case, a firm's financial position may dictate the purchase of a lower-priced machine. Second, used equipment is frequently more quickly available than new equipment. In some situations, availability may override all other considerations.

A third and very common reason for the purchase of used equipment is that used equipment adequately satisfies the purchaser's need, in which case there is no point in buying new equipment. In cases where operating requirements are not severe, a used machine in sound operating condition frequently provides economical service for many years. In the event that equipment is needed for standby or peak-capacity operation, or for use on a short-lived project, more often than not used equipment can satisfy the need adequately.

The Used Equipment Market

Used equipment becomes available for purchase for a number of legitimate reasons. When a firm buys a new machine, it frequently disposes of its old one. Although the old machine may be obsolete relative to the original owner's needs, it is often completely adequate for the needs of many potential buyers. If significant changes are made in a firm's product design or production process, it may be advantageous to obtain more specialized production equipment. Finally, some used equipment becomes available because the owner lost a particular contract or has discontinued operation altogether.

Whatever the reason, a great deal of used equipment is available and is commonly purchased from one of four sources: (1) used equipment dealers, (2) directly from the owner, (3) brokers, and (4) auctions. In recent years, the majority of these purchases have been made from used equipment dealers who specialize in buying, overhauling, and marketing certain types of equipment. Dealers are usually located in large industrial areas, and, as a rule, they periodically advertise the major equipment available.

Used Equipment Dealers These dealers typically specialize in certain kinds of equipment and sell two types of machines—"reconditioned" machines and "rebuilt" machines. Generally speaking, a *reconditioned* machine carries a dealer guarantee and sells for approximately 40 to 50 percent of the price of a similar new machine. The machine has usually been cleaned and painted, broken and severely worn parts have been replaced, and the machine has been tested under power. A *rebuilt* machine typically carries a more inclusive dealer warranty and sells for perhaps 50 to 70 percent of a new machine's price. A rebuilt machine has usually been completely dismantled and built up from the base. All worn and broken parts have been replaced, wearing surfaces have been reground and realigned, the machine has been reassembled to hold original tolerances, and it has been tested under power.

Sale by Owner   Some owners prefer to sell their used equipment directly to the next user because they think they can realize a higher price than by selling to a dealer. Some buyers also prefer this arrangement. It permits them to see the machine in operation and learn something about its usage history before making the purchasing decision.

Brokers   A broker is an intermediary who brings buyers and sellers together but generally does not take title to the equipment sold. Brokers sometimes liquidate large segments of the equipment of a complete plant. Occasionally, an industrial supply house or a manufacturer's agent will act as a broker for a good customer by helping the firm dispose of an odd piece of equipment which has a limited sales market.

Auctions   Auction sales represent still another source of used equipment. Several types of auction firms are in operation. Some actually function as traders, buying equipment and selling from their own inventory. More common, however, are the firms which simply provide the auction sale service. Their commission is usually somewhat less than a broker's commission. Generally speaking, buying at auction is somewhat more risky than the other supply sources because auctioned machines usually carry no warranty, and rarely is it possible to have the machine demonstrated. In some cases, however, machines can be purchased at auction via videotape or closed-circuit TV; this permits the buyer to see the machine operating in a distant plant.

Cautions in Purchasing Used Equipment

It is difficult to determine the true condition of a used machine and to estimate the type and length of service it will provide. For this reason it is wise to have one buyer specialize in used equipment. Moreover, it is virtually essential to enlist the cooperation of an experienced production or maintenance specialist in appraising used equipment. It is always sound practice to check the reputation of a used equipment supplier and to shop around, inspecting several machines before making a purchase. Whenever possible, a machine should be observed under power through a complete operating cycle. Finally, a prospective buyer should determine the age of a machine. If not available in the seller's records, the age of a machine can be traced through the manufacturer simply by serial number identification. The combined knowledge of age and usage history is a key guide in predicting the future performance of a used machine.

In preparing a purchase order for used capital equipment, care must be taken to include all essential data. In addition to an adequate description of the machine, an order should specify the accessories included, warranty provisions, services to be performed before shipment, and financing as well as shipping terms.

Generally speaking, sellers do not provide service for used equipment after the purchase. All transportation, handling, installation, and start-up costs, as well as risk, are usually borne by the purchaser.

LEASED EQUIPMENT

In addition to the possibilities of purchasing new or used capital equipment to satisfy a firm's requirements, a buyer has a third alternative—that of *leasing* the equipment. In recent years, leasing indeed has become big business. It is now a $120 billion industry whose volume of business has doubled in the last five years. It is estimated that approximately 20 percent of the new office and industrial equipment used in American business today is leased.[7] Generally accepted reasons underlying this trend appear to be the heavy demand for capital in most firms, relatively high interest rates, and the fact that in an inflationary economy depreciation usually fails to produce sufficient funds to replace all the capital equipment that needs replacing.

Types of Leases

If one looks at leases in terms of the basic purposes for which they are used, most fall into one of two categories—operating leases and financial leases.

An *operating lease,* as the name implies, is used by most firms as a vehicle to facilitate business operations. The focus typically is on operating convenience and flexibility. Frequently, a firm has a temporary need for equipment to be used in the office or on a special production or maintenance job. It requires the use of the assets but is not interested in owning them. In some cases, the need stretches beyond the temporary period, but the firm still is not interested in ownership and the risks and responsibilities that accompany it. Equipment obtained by means of an operating lease may fit such a firm's needs well. Most operating leases are *short-term,* for a fixed period of time considerably less than the life of the equipment being leased.

A *financial lease,* in most cases, is used for a very different purpose. While operating equipment is obtained by means of a financial lease, the primary motivation for using this type of lease is to obtain financial leverage and related longer-term financial benefits. A financial lease, relatively speaking, is a *long-term* lease that usually covers a time period just a bit shorter than the approximate life of the equipment being leased. Many financial leases are noncancellable.

[7] R. S. Reichard, "Tax Reform May Spur Leasing," *Purchasing World,* December 1986, pp. 52–53.

Factors Favoring Leasing

The primary potential advantages of leasing are identified and discussed briefly in the following paragraphs.

Operating and Managerial Convenience While there are different types of leasing organizations, most leasing firms industrial buyers deal with are *full-service* lessors. This means that the leasing organization owns the equipment, has its own continuing source of financing, and is prepared to assume all the responsibilities of ownership for the lessee. Hence, the lessee has full use of the equipment and can concentrate on its regular business operations, without having to worry about maintenance, special service, and other administrative tasks associated with equipment ownership. In the case of complex equipment requiring highly specialized technical support, this can become a benefit of major importance.

Operating Flexibility With relatively short-term leases for selected pieces of operating equipment, a lessee is not locked into long-term commitments because of large capital investments. It can maintain maximum flexibility in its operations to respond to changing business conditions and subsequent production requirements. It can use the lease vehicle to meet temporary operating needs with relative ease, and in the same manner it can test new equipment prior to making a longer-term purchasing decision.

Obsolescence Protection Leasing substantially reduces the risk of equipment obsolescence. In many businesses, particularly those using high-tech equipment, some machines become technologically obsolete in a very short period of time. When leasing such things as data processing equipment, for example, an arrangement usually can be made with the lessor to replace or upgrade the old equipment. This can be an extremely important consideration in a highly competitive industry.

Financial Leverage A major advantage of leasing expensive equipment stems from the fact that a leasing decision typically replaces a large capital outlay with much smaller, regularly timed payments. This frees working capital for use in meeting expanded operating costs or for investment in other segments of the business operation.

Viewing the lease strictly as a financing mechanism, generally it also provides a cash flow advantage over a conventional bank loan financing arrangement. Most equipment leases can be stretched over a longer payment period, thus reducing the relative size of the monthly payments.

Balance Sheet Structure In an accounting sense leasing, as compared with a capital equipment purchase, permits the lessee to record the financial commitment in a statement footnote rather than as additional debt on the balance sheet. Consequently, the firm's debt structure as shown on the balance sheet appears to be more favorable than it really is. Although this accounting technicality produces only a cosmetic effect, some lessees view this as an advantage.

Income Tax Considerations If a lease fulfills the Internal Revenue Service requirements for a "true lease," from an accounting point of view lease payments are recorded as an operating expense. Thus, as long as lease payments exceed the value of allowable depreciation (if the asset were owned), an additional tax shield is provided for the lessee. Comparatively speaking, the amount of taxable income is reduced by the difference between the lease expense payments and allowable depreciation expenses. So, if a lessee plans on obtaining this tax benefit, it is important to compare the proposed lease payments with the corresponding allowable depreciation figures (if the asset were owned) over the life of the lease—to ensure that the anticipated positive relationship actually exists.

It is important to bear in mind, also, that the IRS has established rather stringent guidelines to distinguish between a true lease and a lease which is really intended to be a disguised conditional sales contract. Whenever it appears that the actual intent of the parties is simply to use the lease as a financing arrangement for a subsequent purchase of the equipment, no incremental tax benefit is allowed.

A related but separate action, the Tax Reform Act of 1986, has had a significant influence on the lease/buy decision for some firms. The 1986 tax law eliminated the investment tax credit and modified the allowable depreciation preferences, forcing many firms into an alternative minimum tax position. The combined effect of these two provisions has made it more costly, from a tax perspective, for some capital-intensive firms to buy capital equipment. Although the situation is different for each firm, experience to date indicates that the 1986 law has made leasing a more attractive alternative for many firms.

Factors Weighing against Leasing

Cost As a general rule, the primary disadvantage of leasing is its cost. "Margins" are typically higher on leases than interest rates are on direct loans. This is understandable, because in addition to covering financing charges, the lessor must also bear all the risks associated with ownership (including obsolescence and inflation risks). The typical financial lease runs for approximately three-quarters of the equipment's estimated useful life, and monthly fees total approximately 120 to 135 percent of the purchase price.

Control A second disadvantage arises from the fact that the lessor retains control of the equipment. This loss of control often places restrictions on the manner in which the equipment is operated; it also requires that the lessee allow the lessor access to the equipment for inspection and maintenance. There are usually times when such control by the lessor creates inconveniences for the lessee. Closely related to this fact is the possibility that the lessee may have its purchasing prerogatives constrained with respect to the purchase of operating supplies for the leased equipment. A lessor normally wants to have the equipment operated with its own supplies. In the event that use of other manufacturers' supplies could conceivably impair the machine's performance, the lessee usually agrees to such an arrangement.

To Lease—or to Buy?

Cost Comparison Because the cost aspect of leasing is its primary disadvantage, it is imperative for a buyer to make a comparative analysis of the cost to lease and the cost to own. A discounted cash flow analysis of the two alternatives over the life of the lease is the most accurate and straightforward approach to use.

Procedurally, the same approach is used in this analysis as is used in making a life-cycle cost analysis (see page 327). Basically, all cost and savings factors for the lease alternative are identified and quantified—and then projected to appropriate future dates when they actually will be incurred. This produces a cost matrix over the life of the lease. All future costs are then discounted to their present values and subsequently summed to express the total cost in present value terms. The same procedure is followed for the "buy" alternative. Total present value costs can then be compared directly to determine the additional true cost (or saving) associated with the leasing alternative.

The Decision The lease-or-buy decision should be made just like any other sound purchasing decision is made. First, the merits of the alternative products must be assessed relative to the buying firm's functional needs. The total cost of each is then considered in light of the preceding functional analysis. To these factors are added the relevant qualitative considerations that may vary among vendors, markets, economic conditions, and so on. A decision is then made on the basis of the relative cost/benefit assessments. In the case of a lease-or-buy decision, this process can be summarized in the following four steps:

1 Determine the *operating* (including financing considerations) advantages and disadvantages of leasing and of owning. Input from operations, finance, and purchasing is required.
2 Compare the two alternatives and answer the question: From an operating point of view, is leasing the preferred alternative?
3 If leasing is preferable, calculate and compare the *present value costs* of the two alternatives.
4 Make the decision: Are the operating benefits of leasing worth the additional cost?

More often than not, the final decision will center on a determination of whether the extra cost entailed in leasing is justified by the avoidance of the major risks and responsibilities associated with ownership.[8]

CONCLUSION

In most firms capital equipment is not purchased every day—but when it is, such purchases represent important management decisions. As a rule, these purchases are major investments—investments that lead to improved productivity or to the manufacture of more competitive products that increase sales in the marketplace.

The role of the purchasing department is distinctly different in this type of buying activity than it is in production buying. In the procurement of capital equipment, purchasing personnel function in a creative capacity as facilitators, coordinators, contract administrators, and purchasing consultants to management. Specifications must be precise and complete, and they must be written as functionally as possible. Economic analyses should utilize appropriate techniques, they must be thorough, and they must be based on accurate data. The contract must be equally precise and complete. There should be no doubt about installation and start-up responsibilities, performance requirements, test and inspection methods, related postsale responsibilities, and warranties.

The buyer contributes directly to the accomplishment of some of these activities. More important, however, is his or her responsibility to orchestrate the total performance. The buyer's main job is to ensure that everything happens as it should and when it should.

FOR DISCUSSION

16-1 Explain how capital equipment purchases differ from purchases of production materials and supplies.

16-2 Discuss the role the purchasing department plays in capital equipment purchasing.

16-3 Discuss the major factors in selecting a source from which to purchase capital equipment.

16-4 What qualitative considerations relative to supplier capabilities are important in capital equipment purchasing? Compare these qualitative considerations with those important in production purchasing.

16-5 Explain the concept of life cycle cost analysis.

16-6 Outline a procedure for conducting a life cycle cost analysis.

16-7 Why is a *total* economic analysis of alternative machines important in purchasing capital equipment?

---

[8] For a comprehensive analysis of the lease buy question, see W. L. Ferrara, J. B. Thies, and N. W. Dirsmith, *The Lease-Purchase Decision*, The National Association of Accountants, New York.

16-8 Why should a present value analysis be conducted?

16-9 Discuss the reasons why a company might want to purchase a used machine rather than a new machine.

16-10 Discuss the differences between a reconditioned machine and a rebuilt machine.

16-11 What risks are involved in purchasing used equipment? Discuss.

16-12 Is economic analysis applicable in evaluating a used machine compared with a new machine? Discuss.

16-13 Discuss the major types of equipment leases.

16-14 Discuss the advantages and disadvantages of leasing capital equipment.

16-15 Discuss the impact of high interest rates on the lease-or-buy decision.

16-16 What impact did the Tax Reform Act of 1986 have on the typical firm's lease-or-buy decision? Discuss.

CASES FOR CHAPTER 16

Capital Equipment Purchasing, page 724
Pacific Printing Press, page 779
Gotham City Buys Fire Engines (in the Instructor's Manual)
Winsmore Laboratory (in the Instructor's Manual)

17

PURCHASING SERVICES

The procurement of services is an activity of increasing importance. Expenditures on services by commercial firms, not-for-profit organizations, and government increase each year. In some cases, services procurement represents more than 25 percent of the organization's expenditures. Purchased services play key roles in the successful operation of these organizations. In many instances, *the impact of the services themselves on the success of the organiza-*

tion's operation is far greater than the impact of the dollars spent. Services ranging from architectural engineering, promotion and advertising, and the development of software, to the maintenance and repair of production equipment are of critical importance to the operation of the organization. More mundane purchases such as cafeteria and janitorial operations impact the morale of all employees.

Obtaining services is one of purchasing's most challenging responsibilities. In no other area is there a more complex interdependency between the purchase description (statement of work), method of compensation, source selection, contract administration, and a satisfied customer.[1]

THE STATEMENT OF WORK

As is true in the procurement of production requirements and capital equipment, the most critical ingredient to a successful procurement of services is the development and documentation of the requirement—the *statement of work (S.O.W.).* And, as is true with production requirements and capital equipment, *one of the keys to success is the involvement of qualified purchasing personnel at this point in the procurement process.* In fact, professional buyers know that most of their service customers lack training and experience in the development of service requirements or specifications. Accordingly, a buyer can provide invaluable assistance during this phase of the procurement. In many instances, professional buyers invite two or three carefully prequalified potential contractors to aid in the development of the statement of work. Such early involvement aids the customer in fully understanding the organization's needs. At the same time, the potential contractor gains insight into the nature and level of effort required.

The statement of work identifies what the contractor is to accomplish. The clarity, accuracy, and completeness of the S.O.W. determine, to a large degree, whether the objectives of the contract will be achieved. The S.O.W. clearly identifies first the primary objective and then the subordinate objectives, so that both the buyer and seller know where and how to place their emphasis. Those responsible for developing the S.O.W. must ask themselves questions such as: Is timeliness, creativity, or artistic excellence the primary objective?

One of the objectives of writing a statement of work is to gain understanding and an agreement with a contractor concerning the specific nature of the technical effort to be performed. Satisfactory performance under the contract is a direct function of the quality, clarity, and completeness of its statement of work.

---

[1] This material is based on *Zero Base Pricing* ™: *Achieving World Class Competitiveness Through Reduced All-in-Cost* by David N. Burt, Warren E. Norquist, and J. Anklesaria, Probus Publishing, Chicago, Ill., 1990.

The S.O.W. also impacts the administration of the contract. It defines the scope of the effort, that is, what the contractor does and what the buyer receives. The manner in which the scope is defined governs the amount of direction that the buyer can give during the contract's life.

A well-written statement of work enhances the contractor's performance in pursuit of S.O.W. objectives. Before writing it, those responsible must develop a thorough understanding of all the factors that will bear on the project and that are reflected in the S.O.W.

Planning the Statement of Work

A statement of work frequently is described as a document that details a strategy for contractor and buyer accomplishment of the objectives of a project. But before any strategy can be developed, certain basic questions must be answered and understood:

- What are the objectives of the project?
- Where did the objectives come from, who originated them, and why were they originated?
- What is the current status, including resource and schedule constraints, of the effort?
- Based on current status, what is the risk factor associated with the achievement of project objectives?

The planning phase of S.O.W. preparation is aimed at a thorough investigation of the *why* and *what* of the project. The following checklist will assist the program manager and the buyer in this determination.

- Identify the resource, schedule, and compensation constraints for the project.
- Identify all buyer and contractor participation needed for the project, and define the extent and nature of their responsibilities. All buyer support, such as buyer-furnished equipment, materials, facilities, approvals, and so forth, should be specifically stated.
- Challenge the tasks identified, including sequencing and interrelationships of all required tasks. For example, on a janitorial services contract, should the contractor be required to wash (versus completely erase) blackboards every evening or only once a week? On a landscape maintenance contract, should the contractor be required to furnish expendables such as fertilizer? In effect, those responsible should apply the value analysis techniques described in Chapter 26.
- Identify contractor delivery requirements at specified points in time; include details about the type and quantity of any deliverables.
- Identify specific technical data requirements such as plans, specifications, reports, and so on.

Writing the Statement of Work

As a result of a thorough planning effort, the individuals writing the S.O.W. have determined the tasks and details that need to be included. These must now be documented.

Writing a quality statement of work is not an easy task. The S.O.W. must maintain a delicate balance between *protecting the buyer's interests* and *encouraging the contractor's creativity* during both proposal preparation and contract performance. For example, when purchasing janitorial services, some well-intended buyers specify the number of personnel which the contractor must supply, in the rather questionable belief that this provision will guarantee satisfactory performance. But such action blocks the supplier's creativity and generally results in needlessly high prices. The use of a carefully developed S.O.W. which specifies the required performance and procedures for monitoring (inspecting) the contractor's performance allow the contractor to apply its experience and creativity—usually at a significant savings. To further complicate the task, those developing the S.O.W. must remember that it will be read and interpreted by customer and contractor personnel of widely varying expertise.

The following issues deserve special attention on a case-by-case basis. Required provisions may be in either the S.O.W. or special terms and conditions included by the buyer in the request for proposal and the resulting contract.

- *A performance plan.* The contractor must be required to develop a nonsubjective, quantifiable blueprint for providing the services. Staffing, equipment, and supplies should all be identified. After developing the blueprint, all required processes must be identified by the contractor.
- *Quality monitoring system.* The contractor should be required to establish fail-safe measures to minimize quality problems.
- *Personnel plan.* The contractor is required to develop and maintain recruiting and training programs acceptable to the buyer.
- *Performance and payment bonds.* The contractor must provide performance and payment bonds equal to X percent of the value of the contract amount.

SELECTING SERVICE CONTRACTORS

Selecting the "right" source is much more of an art when purchasing services than when purchasing materials. Based on the complexity of many service procurements and the unexpected problems that tend to arise, it normally is prudent practice to select only established, reputable firms. Exceptions may be made occasionally in cases involving promising minority suppliers who have not yet established a "reputation." Unless the potential supplier possesses some truly unique skill or reputation, competition typically is employed. In some service markets, however, experienced buyers find that the competitive process is not completely effective because of the structure of the market. This issue is discussed later in the chapter.

When a large number of potential contractors is available, the buyer and the customer normally reduce this list to three to five firms. The purchasing/ customer team interviews prospective contractors' management, talks with previous customers, and checks out employees through random interviews. The buyer then invites proposals from only the potential suppliers with which the buying firm would be comfortable doing business.

During the evaluation process, emphasis should be placed on the *total* cost and *total* benefits to the buying organization. Assume, for example, that two architect-engineering (A-E) firms are under consideration for the development of plans and specifications for a new building estimated to cost approximately $10 million. Firm X has a reputation of designing functional buildings whose costs are relatively low. Firm Y, on the other hand, has a reputation of designing more elaborate and esthetically more attractive buildings whose costs tend to run about 10 percent more than X's. For the sake of illustration, however, assume that firm X's professional fees tend to run about 12 percent more than Y's. Figure 17-1 illustrates these cost differentials and shows the overriding influence of construction costs in the complete analysis. Hence, in this case, the contractor's design fee is a relatively minor item in the total cost package.

In addition to the traditional concerns about a prospective contractor's financial strength, management capability, experience, and reputation, the area of *technical capabilities* requires special analysis. A recent article in *Purchasing World* identifies the following issues that should be addressed when selecting a contractor for computer maintenance. This list of issues is introduced simply as an example of the depth of analysis required when selecting a contractor for this specialized service.

- Will the contractor maintain *all* the equipment in your computer installation?
- Can the contractor *quickly* correct the problem?
- How close to your facilities is the contractor's field engineering office?
- Does the contractor specialize in your type of equipment?

FIGURE 17-1
Total costs for construction project.

	Firm X	Firm Y
Construction cost	$10,000,000	$11,000,000
Design fee	739,200	660,000
Total cost	$10,739,200	$11,660,000

- Does the contractor have a prescribed schedule of service calls?
- Does the contractor have troubleshooting escalation procedures, skilled field engineers, and ready availability of spare parts?
- If there is any possibility of having to move the computer equipment, does the contractor have proven successful experience moving computers?
- Does the contractor offer equipment brokerage?
- Does the contractor have the technical ability to make low-cost modifications to your equipment? If so, can the firm support the resulting system?
- Will the contractor service refurbished equipment?
- Does the contractor have high hiring standards, require appropriate training, and equip field service personnel with appropriate tools and equipment?
- Does the contractor supply maintenance documentation?
- Will the contractor develop custom products for your special needs?
- Is the contractor flexible in meeting your specific requirements?[2]

The selection of suppliers for repair services depends on the situation. The best way to cope with emergency repairs is to anticipate them. Vehicles, office machines, and plant equipment do break down. Sewer lines do get clogged. In many cases, it is possible, and certainly desirable, to establish the source and the price or dollar rates for such services *before* the emergency occurs.

When purchasing transportation services, consistent on-time pickup and delivery, equipment availability, and service to particular locations typically are more important than price.[3]

Competitive prices should be solicited every two or three years for recurring services. Such action tends to avoid complacency and helps to maintain realistic pricing. *More frequent changes in contractors often cause too many service disruptions.*

PRICING SERVICE CONTRACTS

Procurement authority Louis J. DeRose writes that "the competitive process is not truly efficient in services markets. It is constrained by (three) forces and factors of supply":

- One of the strongest factors influencing competition and prices—a continuing or cumulative supply—is absent.
- Interchangeable services generally are not available due to the personal effort and involvement of the supplier.

[2]"How to Choose a Computer Maintenance Service," *Purchasing World*, August 1987, p. 73.
[3]James R. Stock and Paul H. Finszer, "The Industrial Purchase Division for Professional Services," *Journal of Business Research*, February 1987, p. 3.

• "The supply of services is more easily restricted or restrained than it is for commodities or products."

It is for these reasons, DeRose writes, "that buyers must negotiate service agreements."[4]

Yet there are some situations where competitive bidding is an effective method of determining both source and price. A janitorial services contract for which competition is intense is an example. But in many instances, the authors agree with Mr. DeRose that negotiation often results in better pricing.

Too frequently, the pricing of service contracts is not tailored to motivate the supplier to satisfy the organization's *principal* objective. Once the primary requirement (artistic excellence, timeliness, low cost, and so on) is identified, the buyer must ensure that the resulting contract motivates the supplier to meet this need. When conditions require, the contract should reward good and penalize poor service.

Professional Services

Architect-engineering firms, lawyers, consultants, and educational specialists are representative of the individuals and firms which provide professional services. The professional buyer pays particular attention to the relationship between the price mechanism (e.g., firm fixed price, cost plus incentive fee, fixed price with award fee, and so on) and the contractor's motivation on critical professional services contracts. For example, fixed price contracts reward suppliers for their cost control. Every dollar that the supplier's costs are reduced results in a dollar of additional profit.

Assume that you were selecting an individual or a firm to prepare a fairly complex personal income tax return for a gross income of $125,000. Firm C advertises that it will prepare any tax return, regardless of its difficulty, for a guaranteed maximum of $200. Firm D offers rates of $75.00 per hour. Discussion with a representative of firm D indicates that approximately five hours will be required to prepare your return. If foregone tax savings are considered as a cost, which firm is more likely to provide the service at the lowest *total* cost? The use of firm D will cost an estimated $375 ($75 × 5 hours), or $175 more than firm C. Assuming that C and D had similar hourly costs, it is likely that D would spend about two hours more preparing the tax return. Most individuals with a $125,000 income would pay the extra $175 in hope of offsetting the outlay with a larger tax saving.

Cost-type contracts should be considered when there is significant uncertainty concerning the amount of effort that will be required or when there is insufficient time to develop a realistic S.O.W. Obviously, the dollar amount involved must warrant the administrative cost and effort involved. For

---

[4]Louis J. DeRose, "Not by Bids Alone," *Purchasing World*, November 1985, p. 46.

smaller dollar amounts, a time and materials or labor-hour contract should be considered to avoid contingency pricing. Such contracts require close monitoring to ensure that the specified labor skill is furnished and that the hours being billed are in fact required.

Administratively, it may be impractical to use anything other than a fixed price contract or an hourly rate price for relatively small professional services contracts. Even on larger dollar amounts, the supplier's reputation may allow the use of a fixed price contract. But buyers should be aware of the potential effect of the pricing mechanism on the contractor's performance.

Technical Services

Technical services include such things as:

Research and development	Pest control
Software development	Energy management
Machine repairs	Accounting and bookkeeping
Printing services	services
Advertising and promotion	Payroll services
Heating and air-conditioning	Mailroom services
maintenance	Copyroom and message
Elevator maintenance	services

R&D services normally are purchased through one of two methods of compensation: a fixed price for a level of effort (e.g., fifty days) or a cost plus fixed or award fee. Software development lends itself to cost plus award fee contracts. This approach rewards excellent performance and punishes poor performance while ensuring the contractor that its costs will be reimbursed and at least a minimum fee will be received.

In a competitive market, once a good S.O.W. is available for services such as printing, promotional services, and the development of technical manuals, competition should be employed to select the source and determine the price, using a fixed price contract.

Operating Services

Janitorial, security, landscaping, and cafeteria operations are typical operating services. Experience has shown that obtaining effective performance of such services can be very challenging for administrators. Accordingly, the compensation scheme should reward the supplier for good and penalize it for poor service. Such an approach to pricing greatly aids in the administration of the contract and results in a far higher level of customer satisfaction.

Insurance, plant and equipment maintenance, and anticipated emergency services should be sourced and priced through the use of competition of *carefully prequalified* suppliers. Unanticipated emergency repairs normally are purchased on a "not-to-exceed" time and materials basis (as described in Chapter 14).

CONTRACT ADMINISTRATION

The four keys to successful service contract administration are: (1) a sound S.O.W., (2) selection of the "right" source, (3) a fair and reasonable price, and (4) aggressive management of the contract. The administration of many service contracts can be a very challenging responsibility. The buyer needs to monitor and have a realistic degree of control over the supplier's performance. Crucial to success in this area is the timely availability of accurate data, including the contractor's plan for performance, and the contractor's actual progress. The buyer *must* proactively manage the relationship to ensure success. Chapter 18 describes in detail the actions required to ensure timely, high-quality performance.

CONSTRUCTION SERVICES

The purchase of new facilities is a commitment for the future. Quality, productivity of the new plant, the time required to effect the purchase, and cost all must be considered. Aesthetic requirements, time requirements, and the availability of highly qualified designers and builders all will tend to influence the selection of a purchase method.

There are five common methods of purchasing construction; however, it is unlikely that any one of the five methods will consistently be the proper choice for all building requirements. Figure 17-2 provides a graphic presentation of the various steps involved in each method, from start to completion of a construction project.

Conventional Method

This is the most frequently employed approach to buying building construction in the United States. With this approach, design of the required facility is performed by architects and engineers without the involvement of a builder. Design of the facility is completed before potential contractors are requested to submit bids. Two separate organizations are responsible: one for the design work and one for the construction phase of the project.

Many architects are not noted for being cost-conscious. Nevertheless, the cost factor can be controlled in several ways. A common approach involves employment, on a consulting basis, of a "cost-control architect" who is concerned solely with cost reduction. Naturally, the general architect typically does not appreciate having his or her work reviewed. However, use of a consulting architect undeniably tends to make the primary architect more cost-conscious.

If a consulting architect is not used because of the general architect's sensitivity, alternative methods of cost control are available to the buyer. For ex-

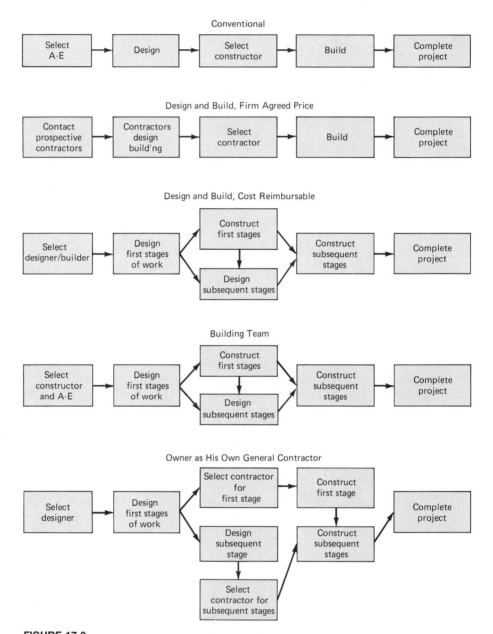

FIGURE 17-2
Sequence of steps involved with alternative methods of purchasing construction. (Source: David N. Burt, "Stretching Your Building Dollar," *California Management Review*, vol. 15, no. 4, Summer 1973, p. 56.)

ample, for major interior furnishings, the architect or interior decorator can be required to specify three manufacturers' products which can be purchased by competitive bids (any one of the specified products being satisfactory).

The actual purchasing can be done by the organization, the architect, or the interior decorator. The three-bid requirement itself assures competitive pricing. As an added bonus, this practice helps eliminate conflicts of interest, unreasonable personal bias, and the specifying of low-volume, proprietary items.

Design and Build, Firm Agreed Price Method

This approach could be described as construction with gratuitous design. The owner determines the basic facility requirements, such as size, temperature, electrical, mechanical, and so on. These requirements become the basis of a performance specification. This specification is furnished to carefully prequalified builders who, with their prospective subcontractors, prepare a bid package consisting of a *design and price proposal*. The purchasing firm awards a firm agreed price contract for construction to the builder whose bid is most attractive.

Design and Build, Cost-Reimbursable Method

With this method, only one contract is awarded for both design and construction. Design is accomplished by architects and engineers employed by the general contractor. Thus, the builder has ample opportunity to influence the design of the required facility. With this approach, construction of a work element (excavation, structural work, and so on) proceeds when the design of the element has been completed. It is not necessary to await design of the total project since one firm is responsible for both the design and the construction phases. This approach is particularly useful when a structure is required within a very short time period and the design and build, firm agreed price method is not applicable.

Building Team

With this approach, the owner retains both a designer and a builder concurrently. In contrast to the conventional method, the builder is retained during the design phase and is expected to contribute information on costs, procedures, and time requirements to the designer. As the A-E completes the plans and specifications for a work element, the builder either accomplishes the work with its own crews or obtains prices from several specialists and awards the work to the qualified subcontractor making the best offer (price, time, and quality considered). As with the other methods, the general contractor oversees and integrates the efforts of the subcontractors.

The Owner as a Contractor

With this method, the owner contracts directly for the various work elements and performs the functions of integrating and controlling that would otherwise be accomplished by a general contractor. Since purchase orders and contracts are awarded on a work element basis, it is possible for construction to proceed prior to completion of the total design phase.

Research conducted by one of the authors on these five methods shows that the conventional method is, by far, the most costly approach to purchasing construction.[5] Savings of approximately 25 percent were found to result when the design and build, firm agreed price method was used rather than the conventional method. Savings of 9 percent resulted when either the design and build, cost-reimbursable or the building team method was used in lieu of the conventional method. Savings of about 5 percent resulted when the owner acted as his or her own general contractor.

The amount of time from first contacting the designer or builder until completion of the facility usually is as important as the price paid. Availability of the required facilities varies significantly with the methods used. On a typical 130,000-square-foot manufacturing plant, 16 months were required with the conventional method; 11.5 months with the design and build, firm agreed price method; 12 months with both the design and build, cost-reimbursable method and the building team method; and 15.5 months when the owner acted as the general contractor.

Professional buyers know that selection of the most appropriate method of purchasing plant facilities can significantly reduce the cost and time required to purchase new facilities. Their early involvement in such projects is a key to saving both time and money.

Construction Purchasing Entails Unique Problems

Construction purchasing is a highly specialized field. Of particular importance is the fact that proper financial, legal, and planning actions must be undertaken to prevent possible losses. For example, an organization sometimes discovers that after completion of a new building it has a mechanic's lien filed against it. In such cases, the organization has typically paid the general contractor, but the general contractor has not paid its subcontractors. Under the law, if a "general" does not pay its "subs," the owner of the building is financially responsible.

The proper financial and legal steps that must be taken differ among states and municipalities; hence, the *specific* steps to be taken must be determined individually in each case. In general, though, the first step that must be taken is to carefully analyze the financial status of all prospective contractors before awarding any contracts. Next, the buyer should consider the desirability of utilizing such protective devices as bid, performance, and payment bonds[6]; liquidated damages contract clauses; and the development of construction

---

[5] Burt, op cit, pp. 54–60.
[6] Some organizations require performance bonds on all construction contracts, at times mistakenly believing that performance bonds per se assure quality performance.

cost estimates by the organization's own engineering personnel (perhaps with the assistance of a specialized consultant). Finally, legal protection is achieved when the organization properly files all required completion and related reports, at the appropriate times, at the appropriate courthouses.

Construction Insurance   Because construction is a high-risk business, the insurance a buyer requires the contractor[7] to carry is very important. All construction contracts should stipulate specific insurance responsibilities. For example, such a contract clause might require the contractor, at its expense, to maintain in effect during performance of the work certain types and minimum amounts of insurance coverage, with insurers satisfactory to the buyer.

In addition, the contract should specify that prior to the performance of any work, the contractor must provide certificates of insurance as evidence that the required insurance is actually in force—and that it cannot be canceled without ten days' written notice to the buying organization. Failure to require any of the foregoing insurance provisions could be very costly.

CONCLUSION

The procurement of services is one of purchasing's most interesting and challenging assignments. Large sums of money are involved. Of equal or greater importance, successful operation of the organization is affected by the effectiveness with which key services are purchased.

FOR DISCUSSION

17-1 Define and discuss your concept of the "procurement of services." How does the procurement of services differ from that of materials?

17-2 Purchases of services are growing faster than purchases of materials. Why is this area growing so fast? What are the implications for purchasing personnel?

17-3 Why should a service be performed by the firm itself? Mention the variables involved in this decision.

17-4 Which purchasing method (negotiation or competitive bidding) should be used for complex or specialized services? Discuss.

17-5 What is a statement of work? Why is the statement of work so important in services procurement?

17-6 Enumerate the elements a buyer should identify in the planning phase of developing a statement of work.

17-7 Identify issues that should be addressed when selecting a services contractor.

17-8 "The competitive process is not truly efficient in service markets." Do you agree with this statement? Why or why not?

---

[7]In the construction business, the supplier is typically referred to as the "contractor."

17-9 When developing a fair and reasonable price, what are the major differences between services and materials contracts?

17-10 In purchasing a professional service, which method of compensation should be selected: a fixed price contract or a cost plus award fee contract? Why? Discuss the advantages and disadvantages of each method.

17-11 Describe the five common methods of purchasing construction.

17-12 The most costly approach to buying construction is the "conventional" method. Why do you think it is the most widely used?

17-13 How could the early involvement approach save money and time when purchasing construction? How about with technical services?

17-14 What types of bonds should be considered when purchasing construction?

17-15 What insurance issues should be considered?

CASES FOR CHAPTER 17

PART **FIVE**

CONTRACT ADMINISTRATION

SUPPLIER MANAGEMENT

KEY CONCEPTS

- Ensuring understanding
- Preaward conference
    Supplier reporting requirements
- Monitoring and controlling project progress
    Gantt charts
    CPM and PERT
    Closed loop MRP systems
- Monitoring and controlling total supplier performance
    Supplier performance evaluation
- Motivation
    Punishment
    Rewards
- Assistance
    Training
    Quality audits and procurement system reviews
    Problem solving
- Supplier surveys
- Partnerships
- Appendix: How Critical Path Scheduling Works

Historically, the post-award phase of procurement has been a weak one in many purchasing operations. Large inventories were available to accommodate quality problems and late deliveries. Multiple sources of supply often allowed the buyer to live with little supplier management. But this mentality cost the buying firm dearly. Shorter production runs under a multiple sourcing policy frequently resulted in higher prices, lower quality, and the receipt of items which were not completely identical. Late deliveries resulted in production disruptions, higher production costs, and broken delivery commitments to the firm's customers.

Just-in-time (JIT) manufacturing creates even more need for professional supplier management. Under JIT, large inventories are no longer available to cushion the results of weak supplier management. JIT requires the receipt of consistently interchangeable items. Tight schedule integration between supplier and customer must be maintained. These forces combine to make buyer-supplier partnerships virtually essential. Such partnerships require the buyer to take a proactive approach to managing the supplier relationship.

Professional supplier management is a vital ingredient in several other settings: defense subcontracts, construction contracts, and the purchase of essential services.

This chapter discusses the many activities which a buyer must perform in order to ensure that the quality specified in the contract or purchase order is received on time.

ENSURING UNDERSTANDING

The foremost prerequisite to successful supplier management is a sound understanding by both parties of all aspects of the program. Early supplier involvement, as described throughout this text, greatly facilitates the development of this understanding.

PREAWARD CONFERENCE

When the dollar magnitude or the complexity or criticality of the work to be performed dictates, professional buyers hold a conference with the prospective supplier immediately prior to award of the contract. The buyer's management team—consisting of the buyer, subcontract administrator or expediter, design engineer, manufacturing engineer, internal customer, quality engineer, and inspector(s), as appropriate—meets with the supplier's team. The issues to be discussed will have been addressed in technical terms in the request for proposal and the proposed contract. The preaward conference is the vehicle the professional buyer and his or her team use to ensure that these provisions are fully understood and implemented. The following items, as appropriate, are addressed:

- All terms and conditions
- Delivery or operations schedule
- Staffing and supervision
- Site conditions, work rules, safety

- Invoicing procedures and documentation (for incentive and cost contracts)
- Materials purchase procedures (for incentive, cost, and time and materials contracts)
- Background checks and security clearances
- Insurance certificates
- Permits
- Possible conflicts with other work
- Submission of time sheets (for incentive, cost, and T&M contracts)
- Buyer responsibilities. Buyer-supplied items such as tools, equipment, facilities, and so on. Timeliness of buyer reviews and approvals for studies, reports, plans and specifications, and so on must be established and accepted by both parties.

Supplier Reporting Requirements

During the preaward conference, arrangements are made for the timely receipt of the following data, as appropriate in a given situation.

- *A program organization chart.* For a large job, the supplier designates its program manager and shows the key members of the organization by name and function. The program manager's functional authority should be clearly defined.
- *Milestone plan.* For a complex project, this plan identifies all major milestones on a time-phased basis, including those of the supplier's major subcontractors.
- *Funds commitment plan* (incentive and cost reimbursement contracts only). This plan shows estimated commitments on a dollar versus month basis and on a cumulative dollar versus month basis.
- *Labor commitment plan.* This plan shows estimated labor loading on a labor-hour versus labor-month basis.
- *Monthly progress information.* This report should be submitted ten days after the close of each month. The report should contain as a minimum:

—*A narrative summary of work accomplished* during the reporting period, including a technical progress update, a summary of work planned for the next reporting period, problems encountered or anticipated, corrective action taken or to be taken, and a summary of buyer-seller discussions.

—*A list of all action items*, if any, required of the buyer during the forthcoming performance period.

—*An update of the milestone plan* showing actual progress against planned progress.

—*An update of the funds commitment plan* showing actual funds committed against the planned funds by time (incentive and cost reimbursement contracts only).

—*A report on any significant changes* in the supplier's program personnel or in the financial or general management structure, or any other factors that might affect performance.

—*Missed milestone notification and recovery plan.* The supplier should notify the buyer by phone within twenty-four hours after discovery of a missed major milestone or the discovery of an anticipated major milestone slip. The supplier should provide the buyer with a missed milestone recovery plan within seven working days after notification.

Such data can be costly to compile and should be required only when it has been determined that their cost and the cost associated with using them to manage an order will result in a net saving or the likely avoidance of a schedule slippage. The subcontract manager, on a case-by-case basis, must determine what level of detail is necessary.

MONITORING AND CONTROLLING PROJECT PROGRESS

Suppliers are responsible for the timely and satisfactory performance of their contracts. Unfortunately, a buyer cannot rely entirely on the supplier to ensure that work is progressing as scheduled and that delivery will be as specified. Poor performance or late deliveries disrupt production operations and result in lost sales. Accordingly, purchasing must monitor supplier progress closely to ensure that desired material is delivered on time. The method of monitoring depends on the lead time or period of performance, complexity, and urgency of the order.

At the time that a purchase order or contract is awarded, the buyer should decide whether routine or special attention is appropriate. On many orders for noncritical items, simply monitoring the receipt of receiving and inspection reports may be adequate. On others, telephone confirmation that delivery will be as specified may be sufficient. (See Chapter 3.) But on orders for items critical to the scheduling of operations, more detailed procedures are in order.

When evaluating a supplier's progress, the buyer is interested in *actual* progress toward completing the work. Data about progress may be obtained from a variety of sources: production progress conferences, field visits to the supplier's plant, and periodic progress reports by the supplier.

In some instances, the supplier is required by the terms of the contract to submit a phased production schedule for review and approval. A phased production schedule shows the time required to perform the production cycle—planning, designing, purchasing, tooling, plant rearrangements, component manufacture, subassembly, final assembly, testing, and shipping.

In many cases, the buyer may include a requirement for production progress information in the request for proposal (R.F.P.) and in the resulting contract. The ensuing reports frequently show the supplier's actual and forecasted deliveries, as compared with the contract schedule; delay factors, if any; and the status of incomplete preproduction work such as design and engineering, tooling, construction of prototypes, and so on. The reports also should contain narrative sections in which the supplier explains any difficulties, and action proposed or taken to overcome the difficulties. In designing the system, the buyer should ask himself or herself, "What is really essential information?" in an effort to prevent the system from becoming a burden instead of a tool of good management.

Production progress reports do not alleviate the requirement to conduct visits to the supplier's plant or the work site on crucial contracts. The right to conduct such visits must be established in the R.F.P. and the resulting contract. On critical contracts, where the cost is justified, it may be desirable to establish a resident plant monitor at the supplier's facility to monitor the quality and timeliness of the work being performed.

When it is determined that an active system of monitoring the supplier's progress is appropriate, the first step in ensuring timely delivery is to evaluate the supplier's proposed delivery schedule for attainability. In their planning and control activities, most suppliers utilize a variety of graphic methods for portraying the proposed schedule, and for then monitoring progress against it. These are useful management tools that can also be reviewed and evaluated by the buying team. These visual presentations are forceful and usually can be updated economically. Two progress planning and control techniques commonly used for important projects and jobs are now briefly discussed.

Gantt Charts

Gantt charts are the simplest of the charting techniques for planning and controlling major projects and the materials deliveries that flow from them. Gantt charting requires that: (1) first, a project must be broken into its elements; (2) next, the time required to complete each element must be estimated and eventually plotted on a time scale; (3) the elements must then be listed vertically in time sequence, determining which elements must be performed sequentially and which concurrently; and (4) finally, actual progress is charted against the plan on the time scale.

In addition to the detailed charts maintained by the supplier, the buyer can also construct a master chart to use in controlling the job. In this case, the supplier is asked to submit weekly or monthly progress data which are posted to the buyer's master chart. Figure 18-1 illustrates a typical Gantt chart of this type.

The Gantt chart, then, portrays the plan, schedule, and progress together in one easy-to-use chart. It shows the status of project elements, or activities, and identifies which are behind or ahead of schedule. Unfortunately, Gantt charts fail to provide the full impact of an activity's being behind or ahead of schedule, and they do not provide sufficient detail to detect some schedule slippages in a timely manner.

As long as the project is not too large or complex, Gantt charts work fine. As the number of *interdependent* activities increases, however, a Gantt chart

Description of Work	Jan.	Feb.	Mar.	Apr.	May	June	July	Aug.	Sept.	Oct.	Nov.	Dec.
Engineering drawings												
Bill of material												
Tooling, etc.												
Raw material proc.												
Raw material rec'd.												
Long-lead proc. parts												
Long-lead parts rec'd.												
Production												
Assembly												
Final insp. and accept.												
Shipments												

Key: planned
actual

FIGURE 18-1
Production schedule and progress chart (Gantt chart).

fails to tell the buyer one important fact he or she needs to know to manage the project efficiently. If slowdowns occur as work progresses on the various parts of the project, is the timing of some activities more critical than others? The answer is yes—and the Gantt chart does not tell the buyer which ones! For every project, large or small, there is one group of interrelated activities that comprise the so-called *critical path;* if any of these activities fall behind schedule, the total project will not be completed on time. It is these potential bottleneck activities that the buyer must manage very carefully. To overcome this Gantt chart deficiency, a computer-based technique called critical path scheduling has been developed to provide this required management capability.

CPM and PERT

Critical path scheduling is a tool that can be used to manage project buying activities, construction projects, and research and development projects, to name just a few. The technique can be used for these and other complex projects of a one-time nature whose magnitude justifies its relatively high cost compared with more conventional methods such as the Gantt chart. It is useful for planning, monitoring, and controlling complex projects composed of a large number of *interrelated* and *interdependent* activities. The critical path approach quantifies information about uncertainties faced by the activities responsible for meeting a predetermined time schedule. The very process of analyzing these uncertainties focuses the manager's attention on the most critical series of activities in the total project—those that constitute the critical path. When these are pinpointed, the manager can develop an appropriate control strategy to optimize the operating results.

When used for controlling contract performance, the posting of progress data permits the buyer to compare actual accomplishments with those planned. He or she can then determine the likely implications of slippages, with respect to critical path time requirements, and work with the supplier to correct or minimize the resulting problems.

A variety of specific techniques have been derived from the basic critical path scheduling concept. The best known of these are *critical path method* (CPM) and *program evaluation and review technique* (PERT). CPM was orginally developed in 1955 by the du Pont and Remington Rand companies for use in coping with complex plant maintenance problems. PERT emerged in 1958 through the joint efforts of the United States Navy, the Booz, Allen & Hamilton consulting firm, and the Lockheed Missile and Space Division in connection with the Polaris weapons program. With the passage of time, PERT and CPM have become very similar in concept. Currently, they differ only with respect to various details of application.

In practice, the application of CPM/ PERT generally is accomplished with a computer program. It uses network diagrams to show time and dependency relationships between the activities that make up the total project. The purpose of the technique is to keep all the "parts" arriving on schedule so that the total project can be completed as planned. Using CPM/ PERT data outputs, the buyer can evaluate possible trade-offs if supplier resources are reallocated in alternative ways to improve the chances of meeting the time schedule. This technique can quickly determine the results of alternative courses of action, thus making a choice of decisions available.

Most important, the CPM/ PERT technique is both a planning and a control tool. The fact that the individual activities of a project are structured into a network requiring time and sequence determination is critically important; it is the basis for all subsequent monitoring and control activity. Use of the technique forces the buyer to conduct this step-by-step planning in advance, and to periodically reexamine the logic of the decisions as the dynamics of the operation unfold.

The mechanics of critical path scheduling are briefly described with an example in the appendix to this chapter.

Closed Loop MRP Systems

Many progressive manufacturers use a closed loop MRP system (as described in Chapter 20) to schedule and control production, inventory levels, and deliveries from outside suppliers. Supplier-furnished data can be used by the individuals controlling the firm's incoming materials schedules as they monitor their system reports. Daily or weekly status reports flow from the supplier to the scheduler, who then inputs the data for the next MRP run. (A growing number of firms link their suppliers' computer-based systems into their own computer system so that real-time data are available to both parties.) If supplier-furnished data indicate that the supplier's delivery dates will result in a disruption of the buyer's schedule, the appropriate scheduler or buyer can take action to modify the supplier's schedule or to adjust the firm's own production schedule, as appropriate.

MONITORING AND CONTROLLING TOTAL SUPPLIER PERFORMANCE

Many progressive buying organizations monitor their major suppliers' performance at both a contract and an aggregate level. This information is used to control a supplier's contract performance, and it is also used during source selection for follow-on procurements to ensure that only satisfactory performers are considered.

Supplier Performance Evaluation

After a major supplier has been selected and the buyer-supplier relationship has begun to develop, it is important to monitor and assess the supplier's overall performance. The purpose is to enhance the relationship and thereby control performance.

In its research study, "Evaluation of Supplier Performance," the National Association of Purchasing Management investigated three types of evaluation plans: the *categorical plan*, the *weighted point plan*, and the *cost ratio plan*. Each of these plans is reviewed briefly in the following pages.

Categorical Plan Under this plan, personnel from various departments of the buyer's firm maintain informal evaluation records. The individuals involved traditionally include personnel from purchasing, engineering, quality, accounting, and receiving. For each major supplier, each evaluator prepares a list of performance factors which are important to him or her. At a monthly or bimonthly meeting, each major supplier is evaluated against each evaluator's list of factors. After the factors are weighted for relative importance, each supplier is then assigned an overall group evaluation, usually expressed in simple categorical terms, such as "preferred," "neutral," or "unsatisfactory." Figure 18-2 portrays a typical supplier performance evaluation form used in the categorical plan. This simple qualitative plan is easy to administer and has been reported by many firms to be very effective.

The Weighted Point Plan Under this plan, the performance factors to be evaluated (often various aspects of quality, service, and price) are given "weights." For example, in one circumstance, quality might be weighted 25 percent, service 25 percent, and price 50 percent. In another, quality could be

Supplier _____   Date: _____

Summary Evaluation, by Department	Preferred	Neutral	Unsatisfactory
Purchasing	_____	_____	_____
Receiving	_____	_____	_____
Accounting	_____	_____	_____
Engineering	_____	_____	_____
Quality	_____	_____	_____

Performance Factors

Purchasing

	Preferred	Neutral	Unsatisfactory
Delivers on schedule	_____	_____	_____
Delivers at quoted prices	_____	_____	_____
Prices are competitive	_____	_____	_____
Prompt and accurate with routine documents	_____	_____	_____
Anticipates our needs	_____	_____	_____
Helps in emergencies	_____	_____	_____
Does not unfairly exploit a single source position	_____	_____	_____
Does not request special consideration	_____	_____	_____
Currently supplies price, catalog, and technical information	_____	_____	_____
Furnishes specially requested information promptly	_____	_____	_____
Advises us of potential troubles	_____	_____	_____
Has good labor relations	_____	_____	_____
Delivers without constant follow-up	_____	_____	_____
Replaces rejections promptly	_____	_____	_____
Accepts our terms without exception	_____	_____	_____
Keeps promises	_____	_____	_____
Has sincere desire to serve	_____	_____	_____

Receiving

	Preferred	Neutral	Unsatisfactory
Delivers per routing instructions	_____	_____	_____
Has adequate delivery service	_____	_____	_____
Has good packaging	_____	_____	_____

Accounting

	Preferred	Neutral	Unsatisfactory
Invoices correctly	_____	_____	_____
Issues credit memos punctually	_____	_____	_____
Does not ask for special financial consideration	_____	_____	_____

(*Cont.*)

FIGURE 18-2
Supplier performance evaluation form, categorical plan.

Performance Factors	Preferred	Neutral	Unsatisfactory
Engineering			
Past record on reliability of products	_____	_____	_____
Has technical ability for difficult work	_____	_____	_____
Readily accepts responsibility for latent deficiencies	_____	_____	_____
Provides quick and effective action in emergencies	_____	_____	_____
Furnishes requested data promptly	_____	_____	_____
Quality			
Quality of material	_____	_____	_____
Furnishes certification, affidavits, etc.	_____	_____	_____
Replies with corrective action	_____	_____	_____

FIGURE 18-2 (Continued)
Supplier performance evaluation form, categorical plan.

raised to 50 percent, and price reduced to 25 percent. The weights selected in any specific situation represent buyer judgments concerning the relative importance of the respective factors.

After performance factors have been selected and weighted, a specific procedure is then developed to measure actual supplier performance on each individual factor. Supplier performance on each factor must be expressed in quantitative terms. To determine a supplier's overall rating, each factor weight is multiplied by the supplier's corresponding performance number; the results (for each factor) are then totaled to get the supplier's final rating for the time period in question.

The following hypothetical case illustrates the procedure. Assume that a purchasing department has decided to weight and measure the three basic performance factors as follows:

Weight	Factor	Measurement formula
50%	Quality performance	= 100% − percentage of rejects
25%	Service performance	= 100% − 7% for each failure
25%	Price performance	= $\dfrac{\text{lowest price offered}}{\text{price actually paid}}$

Assume further that supplier A performed as follows during the past month. Five percent of its items were rejected for quality reasons; three unsatisfactory split shipments were received; and A's price was $100/unit, compared with the lowest offer of $90/unit. Table 18-1 summarizes the total performance evaluation calculation for supplier A.

This procedure can be used to evaluate any number of different suppliers whose performance is particularly important during a given operating pe-

TABLE 18-1
ILLUSTRATIVE APPLICATION OF THE WEIGHTED-POINT PLAN
Supplier A monthly performance evaluation

Factor	Weight	Actual performance	Performance evaluation	
Quality	50	5% rejects	$50 \times (1.00-.05)$	$= 47.50$
Service	25	3 failures	$25 \times [1.00-(.07 \times 3)]$	$= 19.75$
Price	25	$100	$25 \times \dfrac{\$90}{\$100}$	$= \underline{22.50}$
			Overall evaluation:	$= 89.75$

riod. The performance of competing suppliers can be compared quantitatively, and subsequent negotiating strategies developed accordingly. The user should always remember that valid performance comparisons of two or more suppliers require that the same factors, weights, and measurement formulas be used *consistently* for all suppliers.

In contrast to the categorical plan, which is largely subjective, the weighted point plan has the advantage of being somewhat more objective. The exercise of subjective judgment is constrained more tightly in the assignment of factor weights and the development of the factor measurement formulas. The plan is extremely flexible, since it can accommodate any number of evaluation factors that are important in any specific case. Also, the plan can be used in conjunction with the categorical plan if buyers wish to include important subjective matters in the final evaluation of their suppliers.

Cost Ratio Plan   This plan evaluates supplier performance by using the tools of *standard cost* analysis that business people traditionally use to evaluate a wide variety of business operations. When using this plan, the buying firm identifies the *additional* costs it incurs when doing business with a given supplier; these are separated as costs associated with the quality, service, and price elements of supplier performance. Each of these costs is then converted to a "cost ratio" which expresses the additional cost as a percent of the buyer's total dollar purchase from that supplier. These three individual cost ratios are then totaled, producing the supplier's overall additional cost ratio. For purposes of analysis, the supplier's price is then adjusted by applying its overall cost ratio. The adjusted price for each supplier is then compared with the adjusted price for other competitive suppliers in the final evaluation process.

For example, assume that for one supplier the quality cost ratio is 2 percent, the delivery cost ratio is 2 percent, the service cost ratio is -1 percent, and the price is $72.25. The sum of all cost ratios is 3 percent; hence, the adjusted price for this supplier is $[72.25 + (.03 \times 72.25)] = \$74.42$. This is the price used for evaluation purposes vis-à-vis other suppliers.

Although the cost ratio plan is used by a number of large progressive firms, on the whole it is not widely used in American industry. Operationally speaking, it is a complex plan. It requires a specially designed, companywide, computerized cost accounting system to generate the precise cost data needed for effective operation. Consequently, the majority of purchasing departments employing a quantitative type of evaluation rely on the simpler but effective weighted point plan—typically, modified specifically to meet their own unique circumstances.

For these reasons, the cost ratio plan is not discussed in detail in this book. Nevertheless, it is an excellent concept that has the ability to provide the most precise evaluation data of the three plans discussed. For firms using sophisticated, computerized information systems, the cost of designing and implementing the cost ratio plan typically is repaid many times by savings resulting from more precise analysis of supplier performance.

All three of the plans discussed—categorical, weighted point, and cost ratio—involve varying degrees of subjectivity and guesswork. The mathematical treatment of data in two of the plans often tends to obscure the fact that the results are no more accurate than the assumptions on which the quantitative data are based. In the final analysis, therefore, supplier evaluation must represent a combined appraisal of facts, quantitative computations, and value judgments. It simply cannot be achieved effectively by mechanical formulas alone.

MOTIVATION

Two common approaches are used in motivating suppliers to perform satisfactorily: punishment and reward. Many progressive buyers use a combination of both approaches.

Punishment

Quite obviously, the greatest punishment for unsatisfactory performance (if the area of litigation and punitive damages is ignored) is *not* to award contracts for future requirements. This is a powerful motivator, especially during periods when buyers reduce the number of suppliers with whom they do business. A less drastic approach called the "bill back" is especially appropriate when dealing with a "partnership" supplier or a defense contractor. Under the bill back, incremental costs resulting from quality problems or late deliveries are identified and then billed back to the appropriate supplier. Some progressive buyers have increased the motivational effect of the bill back by sending the bill to the supplier's chief operating officer so that he or she is aware of problems within the supplier organization.

Rewards

The biggest reward for satisfactory performance is follow-on business. Additionally, as with raising children or dealing with "significant others," recognition also is a powerful stimulant to future successful performance. Recently, an Arizona purchasing manager divided her suppliers into three categories: outstanding, acceptable, and marginal. She wrote an appropriate letter to the CEO of each supplier firm. The results of her efforts were rewarding. The outstanding group performed even better! Most of the CEOs from the second and third groups requested meetings to discuss what they could do better to earn *an outstanding letter!*

⌐ General Electric's Major Appliance Group in Louisville, Kentucky, publicly recognizes its most successful suppliers. Such suppliers are encouraged to share their recognition with their employees. The employees are encouraged to continue their efforts to improve quality and productivity. Many suppliers reward their outstanding employees with a trip to GE's Appliance Park to see how their products are used (and to visit nearby Churchill Downs, home of the Kentucky Derby).

Each year, the Major Appliance Group selects its 100 "best" suppliers. This selection is based on a combination of service, responsiveness, value analysis suggestions, cost, and related factors. Each representative and CEO attends the Supplier Appreciation Group's Day. Over 50 senior GE managers also attend. Each of the 100 outstanding suppliers receives a plaque acknowledging its status and contribution. GE publicizes this list in appliance and purchasing magazines, to the delight of those listed.

The Ford Motor Company, like GE, believes in recognizing its successful supplier partners. Ford's quality, engineering, manufacturing, and purchasing departments rate their suppliers based on an extensive system survey, defect prevention activities, delivery performance, technical capabilities, and management.

High ratings result in increased follow-on business. But public recognition also plays a big role in motivating suppliers. Ford publicly recognizes its highest-rated suppliers in the *Wall Street Journal* by identifying those suppliers who have received the firm's exalted "Q1" status (see page 407).

ASSISTANCE

Progressive firms have discovered that two types of assistance to suppliers pay big dividends: training and problem solving.

Training

Firms such as Xerox, Texas Instruments, GE, and Tennant have learned the benefits of providing training to their suppliers in the areas of statistical process control (SPC), just-in-time (JIT) manufacturing, and total quality commitment (TQC). These progressive firms recognize that their ability to purchase the required levels of quality, delivered on time, requires supplier firms with competence in these areas. By the time this book is in print, the authors estimate that these and other purchasers also will provide essential training to their suppliers in the techniques of modern purchasing and materials management.

Quality Audits and Procurement System Reviews

As organizations realize their interdependence with their suppliers, they are becoming more proactive in ensuring that their suppliers' quality systems and procurement systems operate effectively. Quality audits are described in Chapter 19.

A supplier's procurement system affects its quality, cost, technology, and dependability. In theory, competition rewards suppliers that have efficient procurement systems with *survival* and *profit,* and it penalizes suppliers with inefficient systems. But such theory may take years to show results. Further, as firms move from reliance on market competition to partnerships, the implications of inefficient supplier procurement systems become even more frightening. The procurement system review provides a framework which a buying firm may follow when reviewing and assisting its key suppliers to upgrade their procurement systems. The review is conducted in a constructive, cooperative atmosphere. Details of this concept are described in the presentation "The Purchasing Manager's Guide to Improved Status, Cooperation, Leadtime, and Staffing," contained in *Freedom of Choice,* published by the National Association of Purchasing Management in 1987.

Problem Solving

Most progressive firms provide technical and managerial assistance to their suppliers when quality and related problems are encountered. Progressive buyers have replaced the attitude "It's their contract and it's their problem" with the knowledge that the buying firm's success is dependent on its suppliers' success.

SUPPLIER SURVEYS

An often overlooked aspect of successful supplier management is the solicitation of supplier feedback. As quality guru Philip B. Crosby writes, "You need to demonstrate your understanding and willingness to clean your own house before asking the supplier to clean his."[1] Crosby suggests soliciting answers from suppliers to the following questions:

- How knowledgeable are our buyers?
- How accurate are our engineering specifications?

---

[1]Philip B. Crosby, "Seven Steps for Producing a Useful Supplier Survey," *Purchasing,* Sept. 6, 1984, p. 126 A31.

This topic is discussed in detail in Chapter 19.

- How clearly do we state our quality requirements?
- How timely are our payments?

The Ford Motor Company utilizes a supplier survey at least once a year. Ford purchasing personnel feel that the feedback obtained has played a significant role in improving supplier relations and in ensuring that high-quality materials are received on time.

PARTNERSHIPS

Experience in recent years demonstrates that the most successful supplier management results when the buyer and the supplier view their relationship as a "partnership." Partnerships are based on mutual interdependency and respect. Supplier partnerships begin with careful source selection during the product design and development process. At this point, the buying firm needs a dependable supplier to provide the required design and technological input if a marketable, profitable product or a satisfactory service is to result. In turn, the supplier needs a responsible customer for its products and services. Professional buyers need the supplier as much as (or more than) the supplier needs them. This interdependence grows as a project moves from design into production. Unexpected problems arise which require a "We shall overcome" attitude by the partners. During production, the buyers and suppliers must mesh their schedules, requiring another phase of cooperation.

Respect permeates the partnership and replaces the adversarial attitude present in too many buyer-seller relationships. It has not been that many years since many buyers treated their suppliers with distrust and contempt. Today, this attitude has been replaced with programs such as GE's "Partners in Progress."

The *ultimate* in partnerships is a vertical integration of buyer and supplier, wherein two independently owned entities pool their resources for as long as the relationship benefits both parties. Lengthy contracts, change orders, and other legalistic and defensive procedures are replaced by one- or two-page memoranda of agreement.[2]

Purchasing professionals have moved a long way from the old adversarial ways of doing business with suppliers. But it will take many years of successful partnerships before this level of vertical integration becomes the norm.

CONCLUSION

Without question, supplier management is a critical and challenging activity. Perhaps the most challenging aspect is the evolution from managing or con-

[2]For additional insight into this issue, see "Reopening the Vertical Integration Case" by David N. Burt and Michael F. Doyle, *Harvard Business Review,* March–April 1989, pp. 190–191.

trolling the supplier to managing the partnership or the relationship. New attitudes and skills are required. As Theodore Levitt wrote in the *Harvard Business Review*, supplier partnerships require the same amount of attention as a good marriage.[3] But the many benefits of successful partnerships make the efforts worthwhile.

FOR DISCUSSION

18-1 What are the possible results of late deliveries of critical materials?

18-2 Does JIT manufacturing call for more or less emphasis on supplier management? Why?

18-3 What is the foremost prerequisite to successful supplier management?

18-4 Describe and discuss the objectives and potential topics for a preaward conference.

18-5 Describe the missed milestone notification and recovery plan.

18-6 What are logical sources of data on the supplier's actual progress?

18-7 What is the simplest progress charting technique? Describe it.

18-8 Describe critical path scheduling. When is it applicable?

18-9 How can closed loop MRP systems aid in controlling a firm's incoming materials?

18-10 Identify and describe three supplier performance evaluation plans.

18-11 How can a buyer motivate suppliers to perform satisfactorily?

18-12 Should industrial firms facilitate the training of their suppliers? If so, in what areas? Why?

18-13 What is the procurement system review? How can it help the buying firm?

18-14 Philip Crosby suggests that we clean our own house before asking the supplier to clean its house. What questions does Crosby suggest the purchasing firm address?

18-15 Describe a supplier partnership.

CASES FOR CHAPTER 18

---

[3] Theodore Levitt, "After the Sale Is Over," *Harvard Business Review*, Sept.–Oct. 1983, pp. 87–93.

APPENDIX: How Critical Path Scheduling Works

Critical path scheduling begins with the identification and listing of all significant activities involved in the project to be planned and controlled. When the list of activities is complete, the sequential relationship between all activities is determined and shown graphically by constructing an activity network (see Figure 18-3a). The network shows the time required to complete each activity, and it explicitly indicates the relationship of each activity to all other activities. Finally, it establishes the sequence in which activities should be scheduled for efficient completion of the total project. Some activities can be paralleled, allowing many different jobs to be carried on simultaneously; other activities must be placed in series to allow step-by-step completion of interrelated tasks. The complete interrelationship of all project activities is the important feature that distinguishes critical path analysis from Gantt and other bar chart planning techniques.

Construction of the network permits determination of a project's *critical path*—the chain of activities requiring the most time for completion from start to finish of the project. Once the critical path is determined, the planner can identify precisely and completely the activities that require close control. He or she can also determine which activities permit the greatest latitude in scheduling and can, if necessary, most easily relinquish manpower to more urgent jobs. An activity network also highlights the activities that can be expedited most effectively in case a stepped-up pace becomes necessary.

Figure 18-3 illustrates the mechanics of network development. This simplified example shows a partial network of the major subcontracted activities involved in the construction of a new laboratory. Engineering and purchasing activities prior to site preparation have been omitted for reasons of simplification. The example shows only the major activities to be completed after the site has been excavated and prepared for the concrete subcontractor.

1 Column 1 (Figure 18-3b) lists the major activities to be completed.
2 Figure 18-3a shows the activities in network form. The required interdependencies and sequencing of operations have been determined and reviewed with the project engineer and the various subcontractors. Each arrow in the diagram represents an *activity* that will be conducted during a period of time. Each circle represents an *event* that will occur at a specific period in time (e.g., the start of an activity and the completion of an activity).
3 Careful estimates of the time required to complete each activity have been made by the respective contractors and are noted next to the appropriate arrows.*

*The PERT technique is often used for jobs whose time requirements cannot be accurately estimated. For this reason PERT requires three time estimates for each activity: (1) t_l = longest time required under the most difficult conditions (expect once in 100 times), (2) t_s = shortest time required under the best conditions (expect once in 100 times), (3) t_m = most likely time requirement. The expected time t_e, the figure actually used on the network, is a weighted average computed as

$$t_e = \frac{t_l + t_s + 4t_m}{6}$$

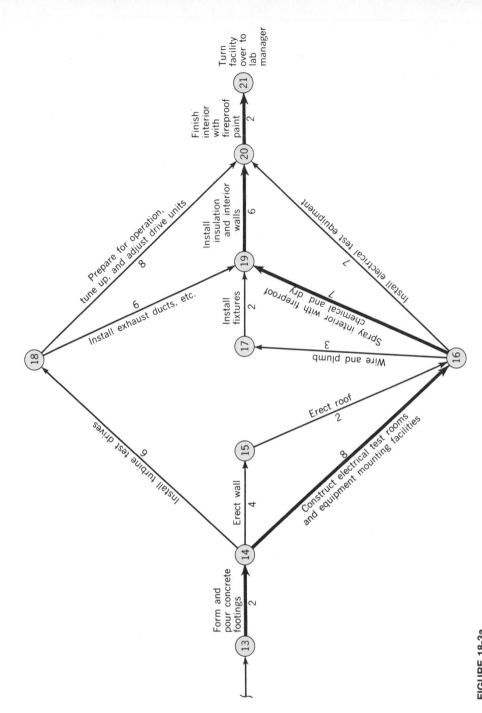

FIGURE 18-3a
Simplified critical path network for subcontracted activities of a laboratory construction job.

376

Activity (1)		Earliest (2)		Latest (3)		Slack (4)
		Start	Complete	Start	Complete	
13–14	Form and pour concrete footings	0	2	0	2	0
14–16	Construct electrical test rooms and equipment mounting facilities	2	10	2	10	0
16–19	Spray interior with fireproof chemical and let dry	10	17	10	17	0
19–20	Install insulation and interior walls	17	23	17	23	0
20–21	Finish interior with fireproof paint	23	25	23	25	0
14–15	Erect walls	2	6	4	8	2
15–16	Erect roof	6	8	8	10	2
16–17	Install electrical wiring and plumbing	10	13	12	15	2
17–19	Install fixtures	13	15	15	17	2
14–18	Install turbine test drives	2	8	5	11	3
18–19	Install exhaust ducts, etc.	8	14	11	17	3
16–20	Install electrical test equipment	10	17	16	23	6
18–20	Prepare for operation, tune up, and adjust drive units	8	16	15	23	7

FIGURE 18-3b
Data for Figures 18-3a and 18-3c.

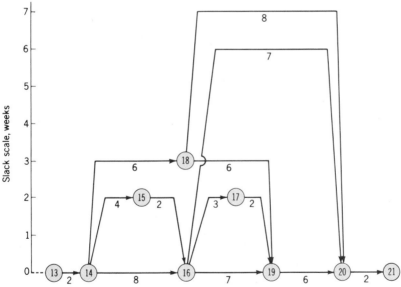

FIGURE 18-3c
Network of Figure 18-3a drawn against a slack scale.

4 The critical path (longest chain of activities) consists of the activities 13-14-16-19-20-21; it will take 25 weeks to finish the project. The critical path is determined by totaling the time requirements for individual activities put together in every conceivable path from start to finish of the project. The critical path is the one requiring the longest

time. Using the given time estimates, it is impossible to complete the project in less time.

5 At this point, the objective is to determine the amount of "slack time" (extra time, or leeway) existing in each of the noncritical paths. This is done by first developing the figures in column 2 (the earliest start and completion dates for each activity) and then those in column 3 (the latest possible start and completion dates for each activity) of Figure 18-3b.

The earliest start and completion date for each activity is determined by starting with the first activity and totaling the time requirements of the various paths through the network. If we say that the earliest start date for 13–14 (the concrete work) is today (the 0 point in time), the earliest completion date for 13–14 is the end of week 2 (0 + 2 = 2). Therefore, the earliest start date for both 14–15 and 14–16, which cannot begin before 13–14 is completed, is the end of week 2. The earliest completion date for 14–16 is the end of week 10 (2 + 8 = 10), and for 14–15 it is the end of week 6 (2 + 4 = 6). The earliest start date for 15–16 is the end of week 6, and the earliest completion date is the end of week 8 (6 + 2 = 8). What is the earliest start date for the electrical wiring and plumbing activity 16–17? Is it the end of week 8 or week 10? Clearly, it is the end of week 10, because the wiring cannot be started until the electrical test rooms and mounting facilities are completed. The analysis continues in this manner through the entire network until column 2 is complete.

The latest possible start and completion date for each activity (column 3) is determined in exactly the reverse manner. Begin with the completion date for the final activity and work backward through the network, determining the latest completion and start dates that can be used for each activity without delaying completion of the project. All activities on the critical path will have identical "earliest" and "latest" dates. This is not true, however, for the noncritical path activities.

The latest completion date for the final painting activity (20–21) is the end of week 25, and the latest start date is the end of week 23 (25 − 2 = 23). Therefore, the latest completion date for 18–20 is the end of week 23, and the latest start date is the end of week 15. Notice, however, that the latest completion date for 14–18 is not the end of week 15. Activity 14–18 must be completed by the latest start date for activity 18–19, which is the end of week 11 (23 − 6 − 6 = 11). This procedure, then, is followed back through the network to complete column 3.

6 The purpose in developing columns 2 and 3 is to determine the amount of *slack time* in each noncritical, or slack, path (column 4). The slack time existing for a particular activity is simply the difference between the earliest start date and the latest start date (or between the earliest completion date and the latest completion date). This important factor repre-

sents leeway which can be used in scheduling the slack path activity most efficiently in light of other demands for facilities and manpower.*

7 Figure 18-3c represents the network in Figure 18-3a drawn against a vertical slack scale. Its purpose is merely to show, at a quick glance, how much slack is available in each slack path activity. Such a chart frequently serves as a good visual planning aid.

The preceding discussion has dealt only with the rudiments of the critical path planning concept. In practice, performance is monitored, and progress data are periodically compared with the original plan. The technique is therefore an effective control device as well as an aid in making future planning decisions as changes in plans occur. The projects to which the technique is applied in practice are often made up of several thousand activities. After the initial network is constructed for such projects, a computer program is written or adapted for use, and the mechanics of preparing and monitoring progress reports are accomplished by computer.

The illustration depicted in Figure 18-3 considers the planning and controlling activities only with respect to the factor of time. Some techniques of critical path analysis add to this the factor of cost. These techniques integrate the two important variables in a single system, permitting virtually total managerial control.

A wise manager always raises two questions about the practicality of any planning or control concept: How accurate is it? and How much does it cost? Like other planning techniques, critical path analysis is no more accurate than the data it manipulates. As for cost, some companies find it profitable; others do not. Generally speaking, the greatest profit potential for such a system lies in its application to projects too complex for adequate planning with bar charts. The basic question a firm must answer is: How important is the ultimate control the system affords? When management puts a price tag on this variable, it then can determine whether or not adoption of the system is likely to be profitable.

Its current popularity indicates that a large number of users find critical path analysis profitable primarily because it forces suppliers to do more planning than they otherwise would do. Numerous governmental and industrial buyers require subcontractors to submit a critical path network (for major events, or "milestones") with their bids on subcontract and construction jobs. Some companies have found that the technique can pay off even without the use of a computer, although it is rare today to find a firm without access to a mini- or microcomputer adequate for the job.

---

*Column 4 indicates that both activities 14–15 and 15–16 have two weeks' slack. Notice that this is an either-or situation. Two weeks' slack cannot be utilized in both activities; two weeks represents the total combined slack for both activities.

CHAPTER **19**

MANAGING FOR QUALITY

KEY CONCEPTS

- Concepts of quality
- Purchasing's role in quality management
    Specification of quality requirements
    Determination of supplier capability
    The current view of quality
    Motivation and control of suppliers
- Quality control concepts
    Process capability analysis
    Statistical process control
    Supplier certification
    Inspection/Statistical sampling
    OC curves and their use
- Industrial applications

Chapter 6 discusses how to determine and how to specify quality. This chapter discusses another major consideration—purchasing's responsibility for managing supplier quality.

As noted in Chapter 6, there are several different views of quality, depending on one's perspective. It is important that the reader understand the

380

significance of these different concepts before proceeding further. Basically, quality can be defined in three ways:

1 In absolute terms
2 Relative to a perceived need
3 As conformance with stated requirements

In *absolute terms,* quality is a function of excellence, intrinsic value, or grade, as determined over time by society generally, or by designated bodies in specialized fields. Hence, most people consider gold to be a high-quality precious metal. In a more utilitarian sense, "prime" beef is generally considered to be among the highest-quality meats in the meat market. While few absolutes endure the test of the ages, for a given period of time in a given culture, most people hold absolute views about the quality of many things.

In business and industrial activities, generally quality is first defined in terms of *relationship to a need* or a function. In these cases the important thing is not the absolute quality of an item, but the suitability of the item in satisfying the particular need at hand. Thus, design engineers, users, and buyers attempt to develop a material specification in which the quality characteristics of the specified material match closely with the quality characteristics needed to satisfactorily fulfill the functional requirements of the job. Consequently, in the *development* of product or material specifications, quality is defined relative to the need.

Once the specifications have been finalized, the specific requirements have been set for those who subsequently work with the specifications. For these people, especially purchasing personnel and suppliers, quality is defined very simply—*conformance with the stated requirements.* A buyer's responsibility, and a supplier's job, is to deliver material whose quality conforms satisfactorily with specification requirements.

The last two definitions of quality, then, are the ones with which this chapter deals. As purchasing works with users and suppliers in the development of material specifications, it is concerned with quality relative to a functional need. In dealing with suppliers' output quality levels, purchasing is concerned with quality in the sense of its conformance to requirements.

As pointed out in several of the preceding chapters, in recent years top management's expectations for the purchasing function have changed markedly. In progressive firms, purchasing's role has shifted significantly from "buying materials" to "managing suppliers." And one of the most important elements in managing suppliers is managing the quality levels of the materials shipped by those suppliers. Once material specifications are firm, purchasing's major responsibility is to ensure that qualified suppliers are selected, and then that they perform consistently at the desired quality levels. The partnering concept discussed in the preceding chapter is one of the approaches that can be utilized to facilitate management of this important responsibility.

PURCHASING'S ROLE IN QUALITY MANAGEMENT

A designer alone cannot impart quality to a product, nor can an inspector inspect quality into a product. Clearly, quality must be *built into* a product. It is the buyer's responsibility to ensure that suppliers possess the ability, the motivation, and adequate information to produce materials and components of the specified quality in a cost-effective manner. In fulfilling this responsibility, a buyer can exert positive control over the quality and attendant costs of incoming material.

Generally speaking, four factors determine the long-run quality level of a firm's purchased materials:

1 Creation of complete and appropriate specifications for quality requirements
2 Selection of suppliers having the technical and production capabilities to do an adequate quality/cost job
3 Development of a realistic understanding with suppliers of quality requirements, and creation of the motivation to perform accordingly
4 Measurement of suppliers' quality/cost performance—and exercise of appropriate control

Purchasing is directly responsible for factors 2 and 3, and it should play a strong supporting role in the first and fourth factors.

Material Specifications

A sound material specification represents a blend of four different considerations: (1) design requirements, (2) production factors, (3) commercial purchasing considerations, and (4) sometimes marketing factors. When dealing with the commercial considerations, purchasing personnel should make the following investigations with respect to quality:

- Study the quality requirements.
- Ensure that quality requirements are completely and unambiguously stated in the specifications.
- Investigate their reasonableness, relative to cost.
- Ensure that specifications are written in a manner that permits competition among potential suppliers.
- Determine whether the desired quality can be built into the material by existing suppliers.
- Ensure the feasibility of the inspections and tests required to assure quality.

For some materials and components, such investigations are relatively simple. For others, they are extremely complex, involving highly technical considerations. Some firms, for example, include "reliability or quality engineers" on the purchasing staff to assist with analysis of the more complex problems. When technical quality problems arise, a reliability engineer and the buyer jointly review the specifications to determine the appropriateness of the quality requirements. Working in a coordinating capacity, they make their recommendations to the design engineer, directing to his or her attention the potential quality problems arising from commercial considerations.

In some cases it also is desirable to involve appropriate designers or application engineers from the supplier's organization in the specifications development process before the specs are finalized. Early cooperative involvement of these individuals frequently provides technical and manufacturing input from the supplier's perspective that is useful in reducing costs or in avoiding subsequent processing and quality problems in the supplier's operation. This type of cooperative activity is becoming more common in progressive buying organizations today. Clearly, purchasing is responsible for planning and coordinating this type of supplier involvement.

Selection of Suppliers

Most firms can minimize their material quality problems simply by selecting competent and cooperative suppliers in the first place. The following paragraphs discuss briefly some of the methods used to achieve this objective.

Product Testing   One practical approach used in determining potential suppliers' quality capabilities is to test their products before purchasing them. The quality of most purchased materials can be determined by *engineering tests* or by *use tests*. Usually such tests can be conducted by the buying firm; when this is not practical, commercial testing agencies can be used.

The object of product testing is twofold: (1) to determine that a potential supplier's quality level is commensurate with the buyer's quality needs, and (2) where feasible, to compare quality levels of several different suppliers. This permits the development of a list of qualified suppliers which the buyer can compare on the basis of the quality/cost relationship.

Buyers frequently utilize their own operating departments for the performance of use tests. It is not uncommon, for example, for a buyer to test several brands of tires on his or her firm's vehicles during the course of regular operations. Although still feasible, use testing of most *production* parts and components is more difficult because tests often cannot be conducted until the buyer's finished product is placed in service. In many cases, though, the buyer's sales force is able to obtain feedback data on operating performance from customers. In such cases, various kinds of use tests can be conducted to compare the performance of different suppliers' components.

Regardless of the method used, purchasing usually needs the cooperation of other departments in setting up and conducting the tests. Consequently, the buyer typically functions as an organizer and an administrator in coordinating the efforts of others.

A word of caution is appropriate, however, for the practitioner unskilled in experimental testing. Test results for products being compared must be obtained through well-designed experiments that permit *valid* comparisons. For example, mileage data on two sets of tires, each taken from a different truck, are not comparable if the two trucks were operated under significantly different conditions. The variables in the testing situation must be controlled to the extent that the results are truly comparable. A "comparison of apples with oranges" is of little value in the decision-making process.

Unfortunately, in conducting use tests without the benefit of controlled laboratory conditions, it may be difficult to generate truly comparable test data. Consequently, experience and judgment play an important role in determining the extent to which test results are comparable and, hence, useful. At times, interpretation of test data may also require a basic knowledge of statistical inference. While many buyers have this background, it is essential to recognize when the help of an experienced statistician is required.

In firms that have testing laboratories for their engineering and research work, the purchasing department has an additional resource to support its quality management activity. Such laboratories take much of the experimental and interpretive burden off purchasing's shoulders. In addition, they are usually equipped to conduct more precise and sophisticated tests with greater speed and ease than use testing allows. An example will illustrate the point. One of IBM's computer-manufacturing plants has an electronic testing laboratory used primarily for research and development work. The laboratory, however, also serves the purchasing department. Before new electronic components are purchased for assembly into IBM products, a sample of each new component is subjected to rigorous tests in this laboratory to determine whether its performance characteristics meet the company's quality specifications.

Firms without testing laboratories frequently use one of the many commercial testing laboratories located throughout the country. A directory of these laboratories, indicating their locations and their types of services, is published annually by the U.S. Department of Commerce.

Proposal Analysis A second point at which purchasing assesses a potential supplier's quality capabilities is in the proposal analysis. Bidders indicate in their proposals, either directly or indirectly, how they intend to comply with the quality requirements of the purchase. The buyer must be especially alert in detecting areas of misinterpretation or possible areas of overemphasis by the bidder that could result in excessive costs. In purchases where quality requirements are critical, the trend today is to *require* bidders to state *explicitly* how they plan to achieve the specified quality level with consistency.

Capability Survey For those bidders whose written proposals survive the buyer's analysis, the next step in evaluating quality capabilities is an on-site capability survey. Because of the time and expense involved, most companies conduct this survey only for their more important purchases and for government contracts requiring it. In inspecting a bidder's facilities and records, and in talking with management and operating personnel, the buyer's investigating team attempts to ferret out answers to questions such as these:

1 What is the firm's basic policy with respect to product quality and quality control?
2 What is the general attitude of operators and supervisors toward quality? Does the bidder utilize quality circles, a zero defects program, or other quality programs that focus attention on the attitudes and responsibilities assumed by each individual for high-quality work?[1]
3 What is the bidder's engineering/production experience and ability with respect to this type of work?
4 Is the bidder's production equipment capable of consistently producing the quality of work required?
5 Exactly how is the bidder organized to control quality, and to what extent does the quality assurance organization receive management support? Does the quality staff report to operations management personnel or to general management personnel?
6 What specific quality control programs, techniques, and test equipment does the bidder employ? Is statistical process control utilized effectively?

These questions make it clear that an effective survey cannot be conducted by a buyer alone; rather, the endeavor must be a team effort. Specialists from design and process engineering, quality assurance, and sometimes maintenance are needed to give professional interpretation to the facts the survey uncovers. The buyer's major responsibility in such an endeavor is to organize and coordinate the efforts of these specialists and to make a composite evaluation of the bidder, considering the findings of all team members.

The Current View of Quality—Motivation and Control

To this point, the discussion has focused on ways in which a purchasing department can contribute to quality assurance *prior* to the placement of business with a particular supplier. The next logical question is: What can be done to ensure suppliers' quality performance *after* they have been added to the firm's supplier base?

During the past decade, U.S. industry's answer to this question has changed markedly. This change was precipitated to a great extent by the quality challenge posed by Japanese industry in world markets during the 1980s. Ironically, as a result of the influence of W. Edwards Deming, the

[1]For two unique discussions about the individual's responsibility for quality, see (1) William Ouchi, "The Q-C Circle," *Theory Z*, Addison-Wesley Publishing Co., Reading, Mass., 1981, pp. 261–268; and (2) Robert M. Smith, "Zero-Defects and You," *Management Services*, January–February 1966, pp. 35–38.

noted American quality expert, Japanese manufacturers maintained extremely high standards for the precision and the performance of their products. They were able to do this primarily because of their ability to control part and component quality at a consistently high level. In working with the Japanese, Deming contended that the vast majority of defective or poor products produced in manufacturing operations are directly traceable to poor-quality input materials—parts and components. These, in turn, in some cases are the result of poorly coordinated design specifications.[2]

Defect Detection System   To control the quality of production materials entering a manufacturing or assembly operation, American industry historically has utilized a defect detection concept. That is, after a batch of items has been produced at one step in the process, the items are inspected to identify the ones that do not meet the design specification. Those that do not are reworked or scrapped, and the good items pass on to the next processing operation. Frequently, though not always, a similar inspection activity is also conducted after this operation, and so on through the entire manufacturing process until a finished product is produced. This concept is depicted graphically in Figure 19-1.[3]

Three basic problems are inherent in the defect detection type of operation. First, there tends to be some duplication of inspection activity, both within the supplier's manufacturing operation and between the buyer's and the supplier's operations. Second, a very large number of items are in-

---

[2]For an interesting article on this subject, see Richard G. Newman, "Insuring Quality—Purchasing's Role," *Journal of Purchasing and Materials Management*, Fall 1988, pp. 14–21.

[3]Figures 19-1 and 19-2 are developed from material in Gordon K. Constable, "Statistical Process Control and Purchasing," *Freedom of Choice*, National Association of Purchasing Management, 1987, p. 15.

FIGURE 19-1
Defect detection concept.

spected. Third, *and most important,* defective items are found only after they are finished (or semifinished)—after the mistakes have been made and after substantial processing costs have been incurred. Hence, the design of such a system makes it inefficient and expensive. And in the interest of cost control and the maintenance of production schedules, there is frequently a tendency to cut back on inspection and to reduce the standards, resulting in the acceptance of some off-spec items. The bottom line is that in many firms using this system, quality levels tend to be inconsistent and perhaps lower than originally planned.

Defect Prevention System   To alleviate the problems inherent in most defect detection systems, Deming proposed the use of a defect prevention system. The idea is to detect the operating (process) problems that produce defective items before many defectives are produced. This approach monitors the output of a process as it occurs and identifies unacceptable process changes soon after they occur, often before any defective items are produced. When an unsatisfactory situation is identified, the process is stopped and the operating cause (tool wear, machine adjustment, operator error, and so on) is determined. Appropriate corrective action on the operating system is then taken to prevent the production of more defectives.

The specific technique used to detect such process changes is called *statistical process control (SPC)*. The theory and the operating details of SPC are discussed on pages 392–396. For the moment it is sufficient to say that in practice the technique is relatively easy to apply and it operates with a high degree of reliability. A defect prevention system utilizing SPC is shown in simplified graphic form in Figure 19-2.

FIGURE 19-2
Defect prevention concept.

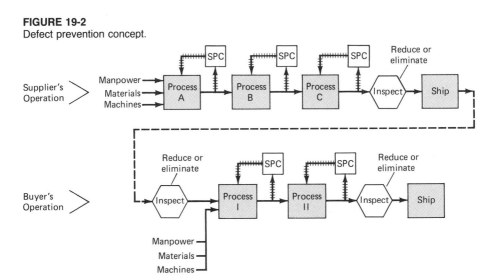

Critique In summary, it is important that a buying organization develop some type of system that monitors a supplier's quality performance. Historically, defect detection systems have been widely used, but they are expensive and results frequently are not as effective as desired. While such systems will continue to be used in some applications, the trend has moved rapidly toward the use of an SPC type of defect prevention system. Philip Crosby summarizes the current attitudes in American industry well in the following statement:[4]

> A prudent company makes certain that its products and services are delivered to the customer by a management system that does not condone rework, repair, waste, or nonconformance of any sort. These are expensive problems. They must not only be detected and resolved at the earliest moment, they must be prevented from occurring at all.

Once an SPC system is in place, benefits of improved quality control capability and reduced costs of quality flow to both the buyer and the supplier. Properly implemented, it should be a win-win situation that tends to improve buyer-seller cooperation and set the stage for a continuing relationship that is mutually beneficial.

Motivation A *cooperatively* developed defect prevention system, including appropriate training by the buying firm of suppliers' personnel, creates a situation that should enhance a supplier's motivation to perform satisfactorily for the buyer. The anticipated prospect of follow-on business in a longer-term continuing relationship normally provides a significant incentive for the supplier to perform well in the quality area.

Appropriate public recognition of exceptional supplier quality performance is another technique that is often used to provide visibility for a supplier who has earned it, as well as a psychological stimulus to continue the good work. The Ford Motor Company's Q1 Preferred Quality Award program is a good illustration of this technique.[5] It is discussed in more detail on p. 407.

The broader issue of motivating suppliers is discussed extensively in the preceding chapter, which deals with the complete realm of buyer-supplier relationships. Motivation in the quality area is an integral part of that total effort.

QUALITY CONTROL CONCEPTS

All buyers should have at least a rudimentary understanding of quality control (QC) systems, statistical process control, and statistical sampling inspec-

---

[4] Philip B. Crosby, *Quality Is Free*, Mentor New American Library, Times Mirror, New York, 1979, p. 106.

[5] James R. Lorincz, "Job-One Is Being Done with Statistical Process Control," *Purchasing World*, September 1985, pp. 34–38.

tion concepts. As pointed out in the preceding section, a progressive firm views its quality control system and the supplier's quality control system as two parts of a single integrated system. The buyer is the middle person in this operation. He or she first must be able to cooperate with in-house quality control people intelligently and creatively in designing and making operating decisions about the firm's QC system. Next, because the buyer is the key communication link with suppliers, he or she must be able to deal with them effectively on a wide variety of QC issues. Recurring matters include things such as additional SPC training requirements for supplier personnel; interpretation of SPC control charts for given orders; the costs associated with use of various sampling inspection plans, and who should bear them; and decisions about the disposition of unsatisfactory product and related cost responsibilities, just to name a few.

For these reasons, this section deals with fundamental quality control concepts as they relate to the things a good buyer should know.

Process Capability Analysis

No operations activity can produce identical results time after time. This is true even for machine-based production processes. Every process possesses some natural variability due to such things as machine part clearances, bearing wear, lubrication, variations in operator technique, and so on. In the language of statisticans, these are "chance" or "common" causes that produce *random variations* in the output. Over time, this natural variability in the output of a process will produce a distribution of outputs around the mean quality level. In many cases this distribution approximates the normal bell-shaped curve. The difference between the two extremes of the curve, the high and low values, is defined as the *natural tolerance range* of the process. As long as the process is properly adjusted and is not affected by any outside nonrandom forces—as long as the process is "in control"—the distribution it produces is predictable, as shown in Figure 19-3.

If a buyer's desired range of quality for a given purchased part is compatible with the natural tolerance range of a potential supplier's production process, the supplier should have little difficulty in providing the buyer with parts of satisfactory quality. On the other hand, when the buyer's required quality range is narrower than the natural capability range of the process, the supplier is bound to produce some unacceptable parts.

Alert buyers recognize the direct economic relationship between their specified quality requirements and the producer's ability to perform consistently at the specified level. In the case of a nonstandard item, the capable buyer, before selecting a supplier, must determine: (1) whether the potential supplier in fact knows what the natural capability range for its production process is; (2) if so, whether the buyer's *desired* range of quality is compatible with the supplier's natural capability range; and (3) if so, how the supplier plans to monitor the process to ensure that is stays in control so that it will

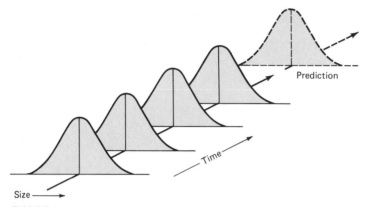

FIGURE 19-3
The output distribution of a process that is "in control."

consistently produce satisfactory output. The following examples should clarify this concept.

In Figure 19-4a, assume that a buyer wants to purchase 100,000 metal shafts 1 inch in diameter, with a tolerance of ± 0.005 inch. Assume further that the supplier has studied its process, stabilized it, and knows its natural capability for this type of job to be 1 inch ± 0.004. Examining Figure 19-4a, the buyer sees that as long as the supplier's process operates normally, every piece produced will fall within his or her acceptable range of quality. In this example, then, if the supplier is able to keep the process in control, this situation appears to represent a sound purchase for the buyer from a quality point of view.

FIGURE 19-4
An illustrative comparison of quality requirements with process capability. (Process frequency distribution curves for shafts are shown.)

Assume now that the buyer wants to purchase 100,000 shafts 1 inch in diameter, with a tolerance of $\pm$ 0.003 inch. Examination of Figure 19-4b reveals that, dealing with the same supplier, under normal operating conditions the production process cannot entirely satisfy the buyer's requirement. Some shafts will be produced with diameters less than 0.997 inch, and some with diameters larger than 1.003 inches. It is important for the buyer to understand this type of situation. Unusable shafts, whether reworked or scrapped, must be paid for. In the long run, it will be the buyer who pays. Assuming that the buyer's requirements cannot be compromised, he or she is faced with two alternatives:

1 Negotiate with the supplier to determine whether the natural range of process capability can be narrowed economically to a point nearer the buyer's requirements.
2 Seek another supplier whose process can meet the requirements more economically.

Process Capability Index   Another way of expressing a process's capability relative to a buyer's specific design requirement is by means of a *process capability index* (PCI). This index is defined as:

$$PCI = \frac{\text{buyer's absolute design tolerance}}{\text{natural capability range of the process}^{6}}$$

A PCI value of 1 indicates that the capability range of the process matches exactly the quality range required by the buyer. A value of more than 1 reveals excess process quality capability, while a value of less than 1 indicates insufficient process capability.

Consider the example in Figure 19-4.

$$PCI(a) = \frac{1.005 - .995}{1.004 - .996} = \frac{.01}{.008} = 1.25$$

$$PCI(b) = \frac{1.003 - .997}{1.004 - .998} = \frac{.006}{.008} = .75$$

In case (a), the PCI = 1.25, indicating that the quality capability of the process exceeds the buyer's requirement. In case (b), the PCI = .75, showing

---

[6] In practice, the natural capability range of the process frequently is *estimated* by taking the mean output quality value ± 3 standard deviations of the output values. In the case of normally distributed output values, this means that the process capability range includes 99.7 percent of the expected population values. In other words, there are 3 chances in 1,000 that the process output will fall outside the estimated process capability range.

Some firms with high precision requirements estimate the natural capability range of a process by using the mean output value ± 4, ± 5, or ± 6 standard deviations. In the latter case, there is approximately 1 chance in a million that the process output will fall outside the estimated process capability range.

clearly that the process is not capable of satisfying the buyer's quality requirement. In the vernacular, for case (*a*) the process is "capable"; for case (*b*) the process is "incapable."

Statistical Process Control

The preceding discussion about the natural process capability range was based on the premise that the supplier could keep the process operating in a stable manner—that is, "in control."

At this point in the discussion, it is necessary to point out that in addition to the random variations which occur naturally in any process, during the course of operation some *nonrandom* variations caused by external factors also occur. At times a machine goes out of adjustment, cutting tools become dull, the hardness or workability of the material varies, human errors become excessive, and so on. When these things happen they usually take the process "out of control." What really happens is that *the quality capability of the process changes because of these unplanned events.* The process output distribution changes. It may spread out, increasing the range; it may shift up or down, altering the mean and the extreme values; or a combination of these things may occur. The end result is that the characteristics of the distribution no longer can be predicted—statistically, *the process is out of control.*

As noted earlier in the chapter, the statistical process control technique has the ability to detect these process shifts due to outside forces, or assignable causes, as they occur. When such changes are detected, the process is stopped and an investigation is initiated to find the cause of the problem. An operator who is familiar with the process and the equipment typically can locate the problem fairly quickly. This technique thus enables the operator to detect the problem, make necessary corrections, and continue operation, with the production of few, if any, defective products.

So, after a buyer locates a potential supplier whose process capability matches his or her needs, the final step in the process is to persuade the supplier to use an SPC system that will keep the process in control and ensure the consistency of the process's output quality.

The following paragraphs discuss the basics of SPC theory and application.

Control Charts   Several different types of control charts are used for different kinds of applications. The most common, however, are the $\bar{X}$ and R control charts for variables. These typically are applied in situations where the quality variable to be controlled is a dimension, weight, hardness number, or other measurable characteristic. Operationally, the two charts are used together. The $\bar{X}$ chart monitors the absolute value, or the location, of the process average; and the R chart monitors the spread (range) of the output distribution, that is, the piece-to-piece variability.

Figure 19-5 illustrates an $\overline{X}$ and an R chart in simplified form. Before the charts are constructed for operating use, *the process must be studied carefully to determine that it is, in fact, stable*—that it is in statistical control. This is usually done by quality assurance and maintenance specialists and often is a time-consuming experimental task. Once the process has been stabilized—its operation is influenced only by natural, random variations—its natural capability range can be determined and process control limits can be calculated.

At this point, the operating procedures are established. Usually the operator will inspect a small sample of output units every 15 minutes or so. Sample size typically runs between 3 and 5 units. The idea is to sample sequentially pro-

FIGURE 19-5
An illustration of $\overline{X}$ and R charts in simplified form.

$\overline{X}$ Chart

R Chart

Subgroup No.		1	2	3					20
Time		8:00	8:15	8:30					
Individual sample measurements in 0.001″	1	999	997	998					
	2	997	1003	1000					
	3	1002	1003	1001					
	4	1004	998	999					
	5	1003	999	998					
Sum		5005	5000	4996					
$\overline{X}$ (average)		1001	1000	999.2					
R (range)		7	6	3					

$\Sigma \overline{X}_{20 \text{ subgps.}} = 20{,}004$

$\overline{\overline{X}} = \dfrac{20{,}004}{20} = 1000.2$

$\Sigma R_{20 \text{ subgps.}} = 72$

$\overline{R} = \dfrac{72}{20} = 3.6$

duced units in a manner than tends to minimize the quality variation within a given sample subgroup, and to maximize variation between the periodic sample subgroups.

The measurements are recorded as they are taken in the upper portion of the table shown below the R chart. (For illustrative purposes, hypothetical shaft dimension data from the example in Figure 19-4 are included in the first three subgroup columns.) The measurements for the *subgroup sample* are then summed and the average, $\bar{X}$, is computed. The range for the subgroup is also determined and entered in the table. After 20 to 25 subgroups have been inspected, enough data are available to provide good estimates of the process average and spread. At this point, an average of the subgroup $\bar{X}$ values is computed ($\bar{\bar{X}}$), and an average of the subgroup R values is computed ($\bar{R}$). The $\bar{\bar{X}}$ value represents the mean value of the average shaft diameter sizes determined in each subgroup; *this is the value used as the process average on the $\bar{X}$ chart.* The $\bar{R}$ value represents the mean value of the range of the shaft diameter sizes found in each subgroup; *this is the value used as the average range on the R chart.*

In most applications, $\bar{X}$ *control chart limits are set at* $\bar{\bar{X}} \pm 3$ standard deviations of the $\bar{X}$ values (3 sigma limits). Parenthetically, the reader should note that the frequency distributions used in constructing control charts are distributions of averages, not distributions of the individually measured values produced by the process. This fact ensures the existence of a normal distribution of control chart values when the process is in control.[7] Thus, the 6 sigma range (±3 sigma limits) of the chart encompasses 99.7 percent of the $\bar{X}$ values that will result from the process operation as long as only natural random process variations are occurring.

The 3 sigma control chart limits can be determined by calculating the standard deviation of the $\bar{X}$ values, multiplying by 3, and subtracting and adding to $\bar{\bar{X}}$. In practice, however, this calculation has been simplified by the construction of a table of constant factors (for various sample sizes) that can be applied to $\bar{R}$ (and $\bar{\bar{X}}$) to obtain the control limit values directly. This can be done quickly and easily.

The same rationale and procedure applies to the construction of R chart control limits. In this case, however, it should be noted that only the upper control limit is of practical significance in operation.

After the control charts are constructed, *as the operation continues data are plotted and the charts are interpreted.* As shown in Figure 19-5, the operator plots both the $\bar{X}$ value and the R value on their respective charts following his or her inspection and computations for each subgroup sample.

In the majority of cases, interpretation of the charts is a relatively simple matter. Any points falling outside the control limits usually indicate the ex-

---

[7] The statistical central limit theorem states that the *means of small samples* tend to be normally distributed, regardless of the type of distribution from which the individual sample values are taken.

istence of nonrandom variation. (If the process were actually in control this would happen only 3 times in every 1,000 subgroup inspections.) The appearance of other nonrandom patterns may also be observed. For example, an unusually large number of points in sequence on the same side of the average line may indicate a shift in the process average or an expansion of the spread. As a rule of thumb, a run of seven points usually indicates an out-of-control situation. Clear-cut trends of points in one direction may indicate a tool wear or adjustment problem. As noted previously, when the operator suspects an out-of-control situation, he or she stops the process and investigates the potential problem.

The Personal "Buy-In"   Statistical process control is not a new concept. Its origins date back to the 1920s when Walter Shewhart, of Bell Laboratories, conceived the idea and first began to experiment with the use of control charts. Subsequently, a significant number of manufacturing firms used the SPC concept during the 1940s and the 1950s. For various reasons, interest in the concept waned and it was not until Deming's work in the late 1970s that it was dusted off, refined, and resold to American industry.

There is one major difference, however, between the way SPC is practiced today and the way it was practiced in the "old days." The difference is personal commitment by the operator using the technique in his or her operation.

In the early days all quality control activities, including SPC, were handled by QC specialists. The quality engineer did the inspection, charting, and so forth—and the operator did the production work. There was little integration of the two activities, and often an adversarial climate developed. Today, the focus is on operator involvement. The operator does his or her own inspecting, recording, and charting. Then the operator interprets the charts and decides what to do. The operator is responsible for the quality of his or her own production. The idea is to give the operator the tools to do the complete job, including quality control, and then stimulate the development of his or her pride in the output of the job.

Training   By now, the importance of training should be obvious. Clearly, all operations people who are going to utilize SPC must be thoroughly trained. One who doesn't understand the concept well is not going to use it enthusiastically or properly. Similarly, supervisory personnel need to understand it equally as well as the operators. Staff support personnel, including buyers, who interface with the SPC function need a different kind of understanding. They need to understand the rudiments of the concept and the applications aspects as they are utilized in their jobs.

Finally, general management personnel must understand not only how SPC works, along with its benefits, problems, and costs to the organization; management must lead the charge. It is management's responsibility to inculcate the defect prevention philosophy into the business life of the organization.

The last point to be made is this: These efforts must be conducted not only in the buyer's organization, but in the supplier's organization as well. And generally it is the buyer's responsibility to see that the supplier's programs are properly designed, conducted, and funded.

Application Limitations   A word should be said about the practical limitations of SPC usage. Although the defect prevention concept is now widely accepted, statistical process control is not a panacea for all quality problems. It works better in some situations than others. It is ideally suited for application in continuous or semicontinuous manufacturing operations. It also works well in some standardized office and clerical operations. From a process point of view, the key is standardized repetitive operations. Consequently, SPC is not well suited to some types of job shop operations, particularly low-volume jobs and those that are not completely standardized. The process itself has to be capable of attaining a stabilized state and then continuing in operation long enough to justify the cost of implementing the SPC system.

Like many other managerial control techniques, the use of SPC is sometimes limited by cost considerations. In some cases, on-line measurement may be very difficult to do and, hence, fairly costly. In other cases involving low-value products, the cost of on-line inspection and charting may exceed the benefits it produces. The decision to use SPC in a given case should be made on the basis of the expected benefits weighed against the cost to obtain the benefits.

Supplier Certification

The concept of supplier certification has been practiced by a number of progressive firms for years. However, the increased emphasis on quality and the renewed interest in SPC in recent years have sharpened the focus on the real values of a certification program. The concept of supplier certification fits very logically with supplier SPC and partnering arrangements.

The certification concept simply recognizes the fact that a supplier's quality control system and a buyer's quality control system are two parts of a larger quality assurance system, and that through integration of the two the total costs associated with quality can be reduced. The objective, in addition to maintaining desired quality levels, is to reduce duplicate efforts in inspection and related QC activities. Certification agreements take many forms, ranging from a simple supplier's guarantee of quality to a formally negotiated document that specifies the responsibilities of both parties for specifications, inspection procedures, SPC applications and training, reporting and correction procedures, and so forth.

Qualification requirements for certification typically are rigorous. They start with a tightened capability survey to ensure mutual agreement on the

QC system the supplier will employ. At this point in the process, the buyer's QC personnel work with their counterparts in the supplier's organization to fine-tune the system and develop the procedures to be used in final inspection. Next, the supplier's output is subjected to periods of 100 percent inspection (often by both parties), and subsequently to periods of sampling inspection during which a predetermined percentage of lots are required to pass.

Once a supplier has gained certification, the buyer's goal is to do very little, if any, inspection of incoming materials. When possible, material is delivered directly to the point of use after the required receiving activities. Periodically, however, the buying organization checks supplier performance in one of several ways: (1) by reviewing the supplier's process control charts for critical manufacturing operations, (2) by using a minimal sampling inspection program, (3) by reviewing test reports from the buyer's laboratories, and (4) by using other similar techniques. Firms that have used certification programs generally have experienced favorable results. Inspection costs typically are reduced, while quality levels usually remain high. Most suppliers take pride in being included on a customer's certification list. They are also aware that good performance places them in a favored position to receive additional business.

Inspection and Quality Control

Even with the increasing use of SPC systems today, most firms maintain a traditional inspection department. Not all of a firm's suppliers use SPC, for a variety of reasons, so traditional incoming inspection capability is still necessary. In addition, some selected operations in both the buyer's and the supplier's plants may still require either 100 percent or sampling inspection. This is particularly true in some cases following certain types of assembly or final assembly operations. In any case, inspection activities are still part of a buyer's world—and for this reason selected basic concepts are discussed in this section.

Receiving and Inspection Procedure   When a purchase is consummated, the receiving and inspection departments both receive copies of the order, which specifies the inspection the material is to receive. When a shipment arrives, receiving personnel check the material against the supplier's packing slip and against the purchase order to ensure that the firm has actually received the material ordered. This is the basis for subsequent invoice/payment approvals. The receiving clerk then inspects the material in a nontechnical manner (looking for shipping damage and so on) to determine its general condition. Finally, a receiving report is prepared on which the results of the investigation are noted. In some cases, no further inspection is required. In the case of more complex materials, a copy of the receiving report is forwarded to the inspection department, advising it that material on a given order has been placed in the "pending inspection" area and is ready for technical inspection.

The inspection department performs the specified technical inspection on a sample or on the entire lot, as appropriate, and prepares an inspection report indicating the results of the inspection. If the material fails to meet specifications, a more detailed report is usually completed describing the reasons for rejection. Rejected material, in some cases, is clearly useless to the buying firm, and the purchasing department immediately arranges with the supplier for its disposition. In other situations, the most desirable course of action is less clear-cut. The purchaser often has three alternative courses of action:

1 Return the material to the supplier.
2 Keep some of the more acceptable material and return the rest.
3 Keep all the material and rework it to the point where it is acceptable.

Cases involving rework are usually sent to a materials review board for study and decision. A typical board is composed primarily of personnel from production, production control, quality, and purchasing. After the board reaches its decision, the appropriate papers are sent to the buyer, who concludes final cost negotiations with the supplier.

Technical Inspection Before a contract or a purchase order is issued, quality control personnel, in conjunction with engineering and purchasing, should decide what type of inspection the incoming material will require to ensure that it meets specification requirements. If the supplier is certified, perhaps no inspection will be required. If the supplier is using SPC in the item's production, it may be sufficient simply to review the supplier's control charts for selected processing operations to determine if further inspection is required. In other cases sampling inspection may be desirable, and in still other situations 100 percent inspection may be required. In all cases, a technical inspection plan should be prepared by QC personnel. Although the practice varies, a strong case can be made for communicating key information from this document to the supplier in the purchase order or a related contractual document.

Economics of Inspection

Whether incoming material actually requires inspection beyond general receiving inspection depends in part on the way in which it is described in the purchase order. If the material is identified by brand name or by commercial grade, visual inspection by receiving personnel is usually adequate. Materials that are described by performance characteristics, by detailed specifications, or perhaps by sample, may well require technical inspection.

Materials purchased to unique specifications invariably have a number of features that are subject to inspection. However, some features typically are more critical than others. Consequently, technical features are commonly classified as "critical," "major," and "minor." Inspection effort, in turn, is allocated in accordance with the criticalness of the feature to be inspected.

When technical inspection *is* required, the decision to use 100 percent inspection or sampling inspection usually is based on two factors: (1) how critical the quality characteristic in question is and (2) the economics of the situation. If absolutely no defective items can be tolerated, 100 percent inspection clearly is required.[8] If some defective items can be tolerated, sampling inspection probably will be used. The statistical sampling approach usually is less costly because it inspects a relatively small number of items. However, every defective item that is missed in the sampling approach, and then enters the buyer's production operation, subsequently generates an operating cost when it has to be repaired or replaced. Consequently, this cost must be added to the cost of sampling inspection to determine the total cost of the sampling alternative. Operating experience usually provides the data required to make the total sampling cost calculation, which then can be compared with the cost of 100 percent inspection in the decision-making process.

The following section on sampling inspection acquaints the reader with the basics of the technique, which in turn will provide greater insight into the various cost factors.

Sampling Inspection   In years gone by, many inspectors attempted to determine the quality characteristics of an entire lot of material by examining a sample from the lot. Then, having considered the results of the sample in light of some arbitrary rule of thumb, they made a decision to accept or reject the entire lot. The difficulty with this approach is that no way exists to predict the soundness of the decision. Sampling, like throwing dice, involves chance. Predictability can be attained only by using the mathematics of probability in developing the sampling plan. Today, literally thousands of such plans have been developed by professional statisticians and are available for business and industrial use.

Conditions for the Use of Sampling   The use of a statistical acceptance-sampling plan is predicated on the existence of certain conditions.

1 Complete accuracy in locating defective parts not conforming to specifications must *not* be required. Since sampling error is always present, no sampling procedure can detect all defective parts. The quality objectives of acceptance-sampling inspection are to establish a control that assures an *acceptable* material quality level *over the long run*.

---

[8] In many types of inspection activities involving human operation or judgment, experience indicates that 100 percent inspection may detect only 80 to 95 percent of the defects present. Consequently, when quality is extremely critical, a second inspection operation may be required.

2 All items in a lot must be produced under identical or nearly identical conditions.
3 Individual items in each lot must be arranged so that a random sample can be drawn without excessive expense. A statistician defines a *random sample* as one in which each item in a lot has an equally likely chance of being selected.
4 The quality characteristic to be measured must be easily definable as being acceptable or unacceptable. Valid results depend on the inspector's ability to make consistent decisions from one unit to the next.
5 Finally, from the standpoint of cost, sampling inspection is most effective when lots of incoming material are reasonably large. The absolute size of a sample influences its effectiveness considerably more than does its relative size. For example, a 10 percent sample of 100 pieces from a lot of 1,000 pieces yields much more protection against accepting an excessive percentage of defectives than does a 10 percent sample of 10 pieces from a lot of 100 pieces.

Attributes and Variables   Acceptance sampling can be conducted on two different bases: (1) by attributes and (2) by variables. It is important to understand clearly the distinction between these two concepts. If measurements of a particular quality characteristic are taken and recorded in terms of the units in which the actual measurements were made (e.g., inches, millimeters, degrees), quality is expressed by "variables." If, on the other hand, a particular quality characteristic is investigated and the record indicates only the number of pieces which met the specified value and the number of pieces that did not, quality is expressed by "attributes." Attributes inspection is an either-or proposition; an item is either *acceptable* or *unacceptable*. The great bulk of inspection done in industry today is conducted on the basis of attributes.

Attributes inspection can generally be conducted more quickly and less expensively than variables inspection. It is typically done using many different types of special "go, no-go" gauges. If, for example, a hole drilled in a piece of metal has a specified diameter of 1.00 inch ± 0.01 inch, this inspection can be made quickly and easily with a special gauge as shown in Figure 19-6. The inspector simply inserts the gauge in the hole. If the 0.990-inch-diameter member does not go into the hole, the hole is too small. If the 1.011-inch-diameter member goes into the hole, it is too large. The small member of the gauge should "go"; the larger member should "not go." Therefore, the inspector's instructions are to accept the piece if only the small member of the gauge goes, but to reject the piece if both members go or if neither member goes.

Lot-by-lot Acceptance-sampling Procedure   For any sampling plan three values must be specified: (1) the number of units N in the incoming lot of material, (2) the number of units n to be inspected in the sample, and (3) the

0.990 in. dia.

1.011 in. dia.

FIGURE 19-6
Go, no-go plug gauge used in attributes
inspection.

maximum number of defective items c allowable in the sample. This latter value is commonly called the *acceptance number*.

The typical procedure of an inspector is as follows:

1 Determine from the purchase order or the inspection plan the applicable sampling plan and lot size.
2 Using this information, refer to the appropriate sampling table to determine the sample size n and the acceptance number c to be used.
3 Draw the sample randomly from the lot.
4 Inspect each of the sample items in accordance with the inspection plan.
5 If c or fewer defectives are found in the sample, the lot is accepted. If more than c units fail to meet specification, the entire lot is rejected.

Use of a single sampling plan has been assumed in the preceding discussion. In practice, a double or a "sequential" sampling plan is sometimes used.

The Operating Characteristic Curve The performance ability of every statistical sampling plan is described by its *operating characteristic curve (OC curve)*. How does a manager know what to expect from a particular sampling plan if it is used for the next six months? This is shown, or can be computed, by examining the plan's OC curve. Figure 19-7 shows the OC curve for the sampling plan with $N = 1,000$, $n = 135$, $c = 3$.

Knowing the size of the lot, and using the mathematics of probability, it is possible to compute the probability that 3 or fewer defectives will be drawn from the lot in a random sample of 135 if there are a known number of defectives in the lot. Figure 19-7 was constructed by first making this probability computation individually for a 1 percent defective lot, a 2 percent defective lot, and so on through a 7 percent defective lot. The probability points were then plotted on the grid, and the OC curve was subsequently generated by connecting the plotted probability points. Using this or a similar technique, mathematicians have developed literally thousands of statistical sampling plans for use under different conditions in business, industry, and the military services.

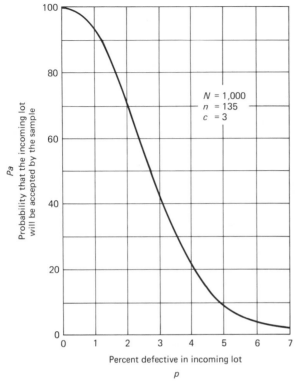

FIGURE 19-7
OC curve for a single acceptance-sampling plan.

What does the curve tell the manager? Simply this: When he or she uses this sampling plan to decide whether to accept or to reject lots of 1,000 widgets, if the incoming lot contains 1 percent defective items, there is a 95 percent probability that the sample will contain 3 or fewer defectives, thus telling the manager to accept the entire lot. There is also a 5 percent probability that the sample will contain more than 3 defectives, thus telling him or her to reject the lot. Stated differently, *over a period of time*, 95 percent of all incoming lots that contain 1 percent defectives will be accepted, and 5 percent will be rejected. Further examination of the curve discloses that the sampling plan will accept 71 percent of the lots containing 2 percent defective products and reject 29 percent. Similarly, it will accept 9 percent of the lots submitted with 5 percent defective items and reject 91 percent of such lots. Thus, the manager knows for incoming lots of every quality level exactly what percentage of them over the long run will pass the inspection operation for entry into his or her own production operation.

The OC curve, in reality, tells the user how well the sampling plan discriminates between good and bad lots. The steeper the slope of the curve, the more discriminating is the plan. Either by increasing the sample size or by reducing the acceptance number, a more discriminating plan with a steeper OC curve can be obtained.

Selection of the Appropriate Sampling Plan   Assume now that a company is buying widgets in lots of 1,000 every week. From past experience it knows that the supplier's process average usually runs around 1 percent (that is, incoming lots contain approximately 1 percent defective widgets). On occasion, however, lots are received containing as high as 8 or 9 percent defectives. As far as the purchaser is concerned, joint opinion of the production, quality control, and other general management executives indicates that lots of widgets containing up to 5 percent defectives can be tolerated in the manufacturing operation. This level of defective incoming parts does not result in excessive production interruptions, rework costs, or similar disadvantages. What, then, is the best way to determine an appropriate sampling plan to use?

Several approaches may be used. One reasonable approach, however, is to ask: What is the poorest incoming quality level that can be tolerated? In this case, management indicates that it does not wish to accept any widget lots that contain more than 5 percent defectives. The analyst, therefore, searches through several books of sampling plans[9] in an attempt to find an OC curve having a *Pa* value of near 0 for a *p* value of 5 percent. After locating several, he or she studies them closely. Unfortunately, it turns out that one has an impractically large sample size. The others, while rejecting nearly all lots with a *p* of over 5 percent, also reject from 30 to 65 percent of the lots with a *p* of 1 percent. These plans are obviously impractical, since the supplier's predominant process average is 1 percent.

Thus, a second important requisite of the sampling plan comes to light. In addition to *rejecting* lots of *unsatisfactory* quality, the plan must also *accept* lots of *satisfactory* quality. The ideal plan in this example would accept all lots with 5 percent or less defectives and reject all lots containing more than 5 percent defectives. Its OC curve would appear as shown in Figure 19-8.

---

[9]Industry uses a wide variety of sampling plans. Two of the more commonly used sources are Dodge and Romig, *Sampling Inspection Table—Single and Double Sampling*, John Wiley & Sons, Inc., New York; and Freeman, Friedman, Mosteller, and Wallis, *Sampling Inspection*, McGraw-Hill Book Company, New York.

The Dodge and Romig tables are designed specifically to minimize total sampling. All plans involve 100 percent inspection of rejected lots; such sampling plans commonly go under the name of *acceptance/rectification plans*. The Dodge and Romig publication includes single and double sampling plans indexed by LTPD.

Sampling Inspection, by Freeman et al., contains plans which are particularly useful in inspecting material coming from statistically controlled production processes. These plans tend to minimize "consumer's risk." This publication includes single, double, and other multiple sampling plans indexed by AQL. An extended and modified version of these plans is available from the U.S. Government Printing Office under the title of *Military Standard—Sampling Procedures and Tables for Inspection by Attributes*.

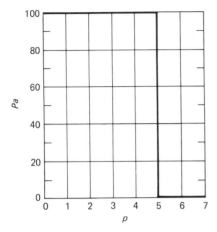

FIGURE 19-8
OC curve for a sampling plan with perfect discrimination between acceptable and unacceptable items, at $p = 5$ percent.

Obviously, then, the sampling plan user cannot have it both ways. The user must usually settle for a compromise on both ends of the curve. Would the firm, for example, be willing to accept a lot containing 6 percent defectives approximately 1 time in 20? And would the firm (and its supplier) be willing to reject a 1 percent defective shipment 1 time in 20? If cost calculations indicate that this would not be prohibitive, the sampling plan represented by the OC curve in Figure 19-7 will do the job. Other less costly compromise curves may be available, and these too should be investigated before a final decision is made.

One final concept should be emphasized. In practice, American industry has selected several points on the OC curve as benchmarks in the design and indexing of sampling plans. The first of these is the p value which corresponds with approximately a 95 percent probability of acceptance (point 1 in Figure 19-9); this is commonly called the *acceptable quality level (AQL)*. The second point is the p value which corresponds to a 10 percent probability of acceptance (point 2 in Figure 19-9); this is commonly called the *lot tolerance percent defective (LTPD)*.

The 5 percent probability of rejecting a supplier's satisfactory shipment (containing only 1 percent defective product) is defined as the "producer's risk" under this particular sampling plan. Likewise, the 10 percent probability of accepting an unsatisfactory shipment (containing slightly more than 5 percent defectives) is the "consumer's risk" under this plan.

HOW INDUSTRY DOES IT

The following paragraphs provide some insight into the quality management activities found in several progressive U.S. firms. The purpose of this section simply is to highlight and summarize key approaches and experiences as they relate to the concepts discussed earlier in the chapter.

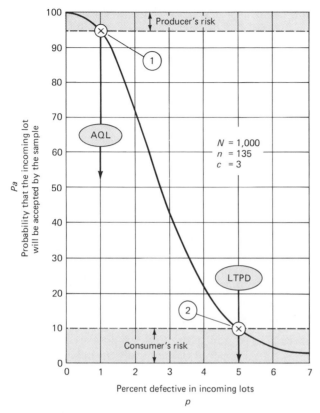

FIGURE 19-9
Illustration of basic concepts: producer's risk, consumer's risk, AQL, and LTPD.

Xerox Corporation[10]

Xerox was the 1985 winner of *Purchasing Magazine's* Professional Excellence in Purchasing award. Xerox utilizes a materials management form of organization in which three geographically based line purchasing units and four specialized staff support units all report to the corporate manager of materials management. One of the four staff units is Materials Quality Assurance. This group works directly with buyers and suppliers to ensure the continued flow of specified quality materials into Xerox plants. Key elements of the operation are discussed below.

   1 In all cases where it is practical, the firm *requires its major part and component suppliers to utilize statistical process control* in their manufacturing

[10]Somerby Dowst, *Purchasing Magazine Medal of Professional Excellence,* Cahners Publishing Co., June 27, 1985.

operations. Xerox quality assurance (QA) staff people assume the responsibility and the cost for training suppliers in the use of SPC and related inspection and QC techniques.

2 To provide continuing follow-up support, *a Xerox QA staffer is assigned to work with each major supplier* (and the appropriate buyer) in helping resolve quality problems. As a rule this QA specialist visits his or her assigned suppliers frequently—from once a week to once a month, depending on the need.

3 Xerox is committed to *a strong supplier certification program.* Approximately 50 percent of the materials purchased come from suppliers that have been certified. In a majority of these cases, materials are not subjected to incoming technical inspection.

   Early in the certification process a number of "concurrence sessions" are held with the supplier. Key factors such as material specifications, tolerances, processing operations, SPC applications, and inspection are explored thoroughly. Both parties must come to an acceptable "concurrence" before the certification process continues.

4 Based on continuing Xerox manufacturing experience, *each supplier receives a monthly report on its quality,* taken from a consolidated report covering Xerox's entire supplier base.

It is clear that this organization is committed to high-quality procurement on a worldwide basis. Its approach, at least philosophically, is one of buyer-supplier cooperation and partnership.

Ford Motor Company[11]

"The quality revolution at Ford falls squarely under the heading of supplier relations." Beginning in the early 1980s, communications with suppliers carried the theme of Ford's new operating philosophy, which, in a nutshell, was "to pursue never-ending improvement in the quality and productivity of products and services throughout the company, its supply base, and its dealer organizations."[12] The key elements of the Ford program are noted below.

1 The first step in the program was to *reduce the number of suppliers* purchasing had to deal with. The base has been reduced over 25 percent since the program started. Presently, approximately 90 percent of Ford's expenditures for production parts for North American operations are concentrated with about 300 suppliers. In addition, Ford relies on *longer-term single-sourcing agreements* in dealing with most of these suppliers.

---

[11] James A. Lorincz, "Job-One Is Being Done with Statistical Process Control," *Purchasing World,* September 1985, pp. 34–38.
[12] Ibid., p. 34.

2 Part of *the longer-term relationship with these suppliers involves them more closely and earlier* in new product planning, design, specifications, and production.

3 Strong *emphasis is placed on supplier use of SPC systems.* Initially Ford *encouraged* suppliers to use SPC, and the company included SPC as a factor in its overall supplier performance evaluation program. Less than two years later, Ford suppliers were *required* to utilize SPC systems in their production operations.

   In implementing this requirement, Ford assumed responsibility for training suppliers' personnel. Today it has conducted or cosponsored over 250 SPC seminars that have trained nearly 10,000 individuals from suppliers' organizations.

4 As noted earlier, another important element of Ford's overall quality program is its Q1 *Preferred Quality Award Program for suppliers.* Suppliers that meet the stringent Q1 requirements are rewarded with public visibility in national news publications. Figure 19-10 is a reproduction of a full-page presentation that appeared in the March 2, 1988 issue of the *Wall Street Journal.* Such suppliers also receive preferential treatment in new part development programs and a preferred position in source selection.

Ford's purchasing function obviously plays an important role in the total corporate quality management effort.

Tennant Company[13]

The Tennant Company's philosophy is that a supplier is responsible for the quality of material delivered to Tennant, and that purchasing is responsible for the supplier's performance. The quality management program of the firm has achieved remarkable results in just a few short years. Major elements and results of the program are summarized below.

1 The process begins with *a rigorous materials and process qualification program* that includes the following activities.
   a All new engineering drawings are reviewed by a "new product development team" which includes both purchasing and quality engineering. Purchasing is responsible for the early involvement of suppliers at this point, if appropriate.
   b Next, prototype and sample parts undergo a thorough inspection by QC personnel.

---

[13] *Tennant Company Supplier Requirements and Information Manual,* Tennant Company, Minneapolis, Minnesota, August 1984; "Tennant Company—Quality in Purchasing," *Purchasing World,* June 1988, p. 36.

THANKS FOR THE QUALITY.

Active Tool & Manufacturing Co.
- Active Industries, Inc.
  Elkton, MI
- Sebewaing Industries Division
  Sebewaing, MI

Ada Metal Products
- C.T. Charlton Group
  Lincolnwood, IL

Aisan Industry Co., Ltd.
- Anjo Plant
  Anjo, Aichi, Japan

Allied-Signal, Inc.
- Bendix Electronics
  Controls Products
  Chatham, ONT., CN

Almco Steel Products Corporation
  Bluffton, IN

BASF AG/Sterling Group
- BASF Corp./Sterling Chemicals, Inc.
  Texas City, TX

The Budd Company
- Wheel & Brake Division
  Ashland, OH

Cirtek Corporation
  Flint, MI

Colonial Rubber Works
  Dyresburg, TN

Color Custom, Inc.
  Warren, MI

Colt Industries, Inc.
- Stemco Truck Products Division
  Longview, TX

Crescive Die & Tool, Inc.
  Saline, MI

Dana Corporation
- Weatherhead Division
  Columbia City, IN

Dexter Corporation
- Dexter Plastics Division
  Grand Prairie, TX

Dow Chemical Company
- Texas Division
  LaPorte Plant
  LaPorte, TX

Edgewood Tool & Mfg. Co.
- Ann Arbor Assembly Corporation
  Ypsilanti, MI

Exxon Corporation
- Exxon Chemical Company
  Baton Rouge, LA

Fawn Plastics, Inc.
  Middlesex, NC

Federal-Mogul Corporation
- Switches, Inc.
  Juarez, MX

Gilreath Enterprises
- Gilreath Mfg., Inc.
  Michigan Division
  Howell, MI

Goetze Corporation of America
- Muskegon Piston Ring Company
  Muskegon, MI

Handy & Harman
- Handy & Harman Automotive Group, Inc.
  Dover Division
  Dover, OH

Hatch Stamping Company
  Chelsea, MI

The Hill and Griffith Co.
  Cincinnati, OH

ITT Corporation/ITT Automotive
- ITT Milrod Metal Products
  Mississauga, ONT., CN

Jason, Incorporated
- Janesville Products
  Norwalk, OH

The Lobdell-Emery Manufacturing Co.
  Alma, MI
  Winchester, IN
- Greencastle Manufacturing Co.
  Greencastle, IN

Magna International, Inc.
- Decoma International
  Rollstamp
  Richmond Hill, ONT., CN
  Vernomatic
  Downsview, ONT., CN

NOK Corporation
- Fukushima Plant
  Fukushima, Japan

Phillips Plastics Corp.
  Phillips, WI
  Medford, WI

Pullman Industries, Inc.
  Pullman, MI

SGS—THOMSON
- Microelectronics, Inc.
  Brianza, Italy

Siemens Corporation
  Regensburg, W. Germany

Sparton Corporation
- Kent Products Division
  White Cloud, MI

Special Machine & Engineering, Inc.
- Grant-Durban, Inc.
  Belleville, MI

Thiem Corporation
- Foundry Materials Division
  Oak Creek, WI

Trinova Corporation
- KMC Division
  Sterling Engineered Products
  Henderson, KY

Walbro Precision Plastics
  Bad Axe, MI

Worthington Industries, Inc.
- Hamilton Plastics
  Mason, OH

Q1

The **Q1** Preferred Quality Award is a special tribute to suppliers who are helping us produce the highest quality American cars and trucks. This is based on an average of owner-reported problems in a series of surveys of '81, '82, '83, '84, '85, '86 and '87 models designed and built in North America.

The companies whose names appear on this page join a select group of **Q1** preferred quality suppliers. To the new recipients, we'd like to say thanks for your time, energy and commitment to make Quality Job 1.

Quality is Job 1.

Ford • Lincoln • Mercury • Ford Trucks

FIGURE 19-10
One approach to recognizing preferred quality suppliers.

c Thorough reliability testing of all new items is then conducted by engineering.

d If all results are positive at this point, the potential supplier's processes are subjected to a thorough process capability analysis.

2 After a supplier has come on line, *all shipments pass through receiving inspection and often through the traditional technical inspection* activities, depending on the supplier's past performance.

3 If quality problems develop, *a "supplier corrective action team" is formed* to monitor the supplier's performance and to work with appropriate individuals in the supplier's firm to identify and correct the problems. Representatives from purchasing, quality engineering, and product engineering make up the team.

4 More recently, Tennant has *initiated an SPC program*, both in-house and in its suppliers' operations. Tennant assumes the responsibility for training its suppliers in SPC techniques.

The results of Tennant's total quality program have been monitored closely. They are indeed gratifying. Tennant has been able to increase its quality levels significantly, and at the same time the firm has reduced its total cost of quality approximately 50 percent. For a number of its component parts, in three years the firm's failure rates have dropped from the 8–9 percent level to the 1–3 percent level. During the same period, Tennant's overall cost of quality dropped from 2 percent to approximately 1 percent, through reduced rework and failure costs, coupled with fewer stockouts and related costs.[14]

CONCLUSION

Purchasing's responsibility is fulfilled only when materials of the specified quality are available and ready for production use—not before. Quality management is a major component of purchasing's supplier management responsibility. Quality failures lead directly to costly difficulties that reduce productivity, profit, and often market share. To preclude such losses, purchasing should participate creatively in the corporate quality management program. To contribute most effectively to the organizational effort, purchasing's role in the program should include: (1) participation in the preparation of specifications; (2) participation in the selection of appropriate quality control, inspection, and test requirements; (3) the selection and motivation of qualified suppliers; and (4) the subsequent monitoring and nurturing of the ongoing buyer-supplier relationship.

The concluding thought for this chapter is expressed well by Philip Crosby:

[14] Ibid., p. 36.

Given the chance to explain quality management to people who will listen, it is possible to make a case for becoming deeply involved. No other action a manager can take will generate improved operations, increased profits, and reduced costs so quickly with so little effort.[15]

FOR DISCUSSION

19-1 Define "quality."

19-2 Discuss the role which the purchasing department should play in a firm's overall quality program.

19-3 Once an order has been negotiated and placed with a supplier, what interest does the purchasing department have in the quality level of the product the supplier delivers? Why?

19-4 What is the purchasing department's interest in its firm's material specifications, as far as quality is concerned?

19-5 How do "use tests" differ from "engineering tests"? What role should the purchasing department play in the handling of use tests? What role should it play in the handling of engineering tests?

19-6 What specific precautions should be observed by the person conducting a use test?

19-7 What can a buyer tell about a potential supplier's quality capability from an analysis of its proposal for a particular job?

19-8 What is a quality capability survey? How is it conducted? What role does the purchasing department play in a capability survey?

19-9 A statement is made in the text to the effect that the buyer is responsible for positively motivating the supplier with respect to quality. What is meant by this statement? What specific courses of action might a buyer take in carrying out the responsibility implied in this statement?

19-10 Buyers frequently visit suppliers at their plants. Is there any reason why a buyer might want to ask a supplier's representative to visit him or her at the buyer's own plant? Explain.

19-11 One large company feels strongly that individual buyers should be responsible for the performance of their suppliers. Accordingly, in the annual merit review for promotion, one of the points on which buyers are evaluated is the performance rating of their suppliers. Discuss the strengths and weaknesses of this policy.

19-12 Generally speaking, what should a top-notch buyer know about his or her firm's quality department? How is this knowledge related to the actual buying job?

19-13 Explain the difference between receiving inspection and technical inspection. What generally determines whether an incoming material

---

[15] Philip B. Crosby, *Quality Is Free*, p. 14.

should be subjected to receiving inspection, technical inspection, or both?

19-14 What is a defect detection system? Discuss.

19-15 What is a defect prevention system? Discuss.

19-16 "In reality, the purchaser usually seeks a practical balance between costs of quality and value of quality." What is your reaction to this statement?

19-17 What is statistical process control?

19-18 What is process capability analysis? How is the natural process capability range determined?

19-19 What is an $\bar{X}$ chart? How is it constructed?

19-20 What is an R chart? How is it constructed?

19-21 Who should be responsible for plotting and maintaining control charts? Discuss.

19-22 Discuss the role of training in SPC implementation.

19-23 What are the basic conditions which must exist before a purchaser can consider the use of sampling inspection in inspecting incoming material? Discuss each condition in reasonable detail.

19-24 Distinguish between variables inspection and attributes inspection.

19-25 What courses of action might the buyer initiate to reduce the total cost of inspection? Discuss each.

19-26 What is an OC curve? Discuss its use.

19-27 "In the long run, all costs of inspection and all costs of producing unusable products are borne by the purchaser." Comment.

19-28 What is "consumer's risk"? What is "producer's risk"? Explain.

19-29 In a medium-sized automobile engine manufacturing plant, all personnel associated with the inspection of incoming materials report to the manager of the purchasing department. Discuss possible strengths and weaknesses of this organizational arrangement.

19-30 Briefly discuss the concept of supplier certification. What possible dangers do you see in the use of this concept by a purchasing department?

CASES FOR CHAPTER 19

Placido Engine Company, page 785
SDC Corporation, page 803
The Case of The Unruly Spider (in the Instructor's Manual)
OCR, Inc. (in the Instructor's Manual)
The Chugalug Problem (in the Instructor's Manual)

PART **SIX**

FUNDAMENTALS OF
MATERIALS
MANAGEMENT

PRODUCTION PLANNING

KEY CONCEPTS

- Fundamentals of production planning
- Modern production planning systems
    Aggregate planning and master scheduling
    Material requirements planning (MRP)
    Capacity requirements planning (CRP)
    Control of shop floor activities
    Management considerations
- Evolution of planning systems
    Closed loop MRP system
    MRP II system
- Impact of MRP systems on purchasing
    Buyer-planner concept
    Vendor scheduler concept
    Contract buying
    Supplier flexibility and reliability
    Relationships with suppliers
- Just-in-time system (JIT)
    The concept
    Applications
    Impact on purchasing

As was discussed in Part One, the production planning and control function is part of the materials management organization in approximately half of those firms utilizing the materials management concept. Regardless of the organizational arrangement, however, the interface between procurement and production planning is extremely important.

One of the major reponsibilities of the production planning group is the determination of timing and volume requirements for materials used in the manufacturing operation. These decisions, along with the communication lead time, have an obvious impact on the purchasing and inventory management operations. If the item has not already been sourced, the thoroughness of the market analysis, the number of sources solicited, the quality of the negotiations, and the total cost of the material are all influenced by the production planning actions. Even if the item has been presourced, supplier scheduling and a host of related quality and logistical issues are affected by the planning decision. For these reasons, it is essential that procurement personnel understand and coordinate effectively with production planning.

Over the past two decades, production planning and control has evolved into a highly specialized and often sophisticated activity. A number of books have been devoted to the technical aspect of the subject.[1] The purpose of this chapter is to examine only the fundamental activities involved in production planning—and to relate them to procurement activities.

THE FUNDAMENTALS OF PRODUCTION PLANNING

The objective of the production planning and control function is to coordinate the use of a firm's resources and to synchronize the work of all individuals concerned with production in order to meet required completion dates, at the lowest total cost, consistent with desired quality.

Historically, all firms conducted their production planning and control activities manually, with the use of a variety of Gantt charts and specialized visual scheduling/control boards. Today, most firms utilize some type of computer-based system to perform essentially the same types of activities in a more comprehensive, semiautomatic manner. Regardless of the specific operating system used, an effective production planning and control operation must accomplish five general activities:

1 Preliminary planning
2 Aggregate scheduling
3 Detailed production scheduling
4 Release and dispatching of orders
5 Progress surveillance and correction

Preliminary Planning After the initial product design and process design work are completed by the respective engineering groups, the preliminary planning work begins. The product's engineering bill of materials is re-

---

[1] Several comprehensive works are: Joseph Orlicky, *Material Requirements Planning*, McGraw-Hill Book Company, New York, 1975; Oliver W. Wight, *The Executives' Guide to Successful MRP II*, Wight Publications Inc., Essex Junction, Vt., 1982; *Material Requirements Planning*, IBM Corporation, undated; J. E. Schorr and T. F. Wallace, *High Performance Purchasing: Manufacturing Resource Planning for the Purchasing Professional*, Wight Publications Inc., Essex Junction, Vt., 1986.

structured for compatibility with the firm's planning system. *For the given product (or special job),* analysts then determine the specific material requirements, standard labor and machine requirements, and tooling requirements. And in the case of most intermittent manufacturing operations, one or more work-flow routings through the shop are determined.

Aggregate Scheduling   The next step in the process is scheduling—first, aggregate scheduling and then, detailed production scheduling. As orders and forecasts are generated, they are matched against and fit in with the facility's overall capability. Aggregate scheduling is simply a first-pass, broad-brush determination that shop capacity—equipment and people— and required materials probably can be made available through careful, detailed scheduling work.

Production Scheduling   The ensuing step is the detailed production scheduling work. The aggregate planning work is broken down into specific product models and configurations, and for each the detailed manufacturing steps are scheduled into specific work centers or on specific machines. Start and completion dates for each operation or set of related operations are assigned, indicating the desired production priorities. Specific material and tooling requirements for the job are determined, as is the specific shop routing for the job.

Release and Dispatching of Orders   The work completed to this point in the process has developed an operating plan. When the order is released to the shop, the plan becomes operational and the order is dispatched from one operating unit to the next until it is complete. One of the key functions in this activity is to review the production priorities established in the prior scheduling activity. Any desired changes can be made at this point.

When the order is released it is accompanied by a packet of paperwork and instructions. The packet typically contains such things as the engineering drawings and perhaps the bill of materials, tooling and material requisitions or computer entry instructions, a routing sheet, and detailed operations instructions for the production people. It may also contain instructions for charging labor and moving the job from one operation to the next.

Progress Surveillance and Correction   The last step in the process is the control function. Progress at each stage of the operation is monitored and fed back to the shop dispatcher and the production scheduler, who compare actual performance with the plan. Significant deviations from schedule typically require some type of corrective action—rerouting, rescheduling, the use of overtime work, and so on. These decisions, if fairly routine in nature, typically are made by production planning and control personnel. If a serious trade-off of resources or priorities is involved, marketing and manufacturing personnel may also enter the decision-making process.

MODERN PRODUCTION PLANNING SYSTEMS

The preceding discussion sketched briefly the fundamental activities that must be accomplished in planning and controlling production operations effectively. In practice, manufacturing firms conduct these activities in a variety of ways—some with great detail and precision, others with less sophistication. As competition in the marketplace has become increasingly keen, however, firms have been forced to meet higher performance standards and to do so cost-effectively. This economic reality, coupled with the availability of relatively inexpensive computing capability, has spawned a new era in production planning. Within just a few years, a progressive firm without a sophisticated, computer-based production planning and control system will be a rarity.

Although numerous different systems are evolving, both as custom designed and standard commercial software packages, most utilize essentially the same basic elements. Figure 20-1 portrays, in flowchart form, the basic operating elements found in most current computer-based production planning systems.

FIGURE 20-1
A basic flowchart for a modern production planning system.

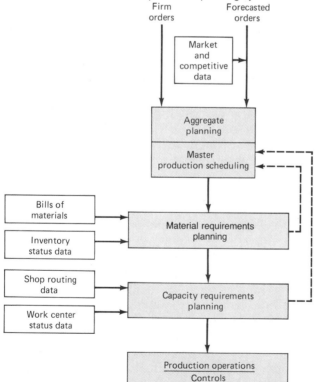

Aggregate Planning and Master Scheduling

The development of a viable aggregate plan and a coordinated master production schedule is the starting point for the use of a detailed computer-based planning system.

The *aggregate plan* is based on the expected receipt of a certain number of orders for a given family of products during the planning period. For the near term, a number of firm orders typically are in hand. As the planners peer further into the future, they use various forecasting techniques to determine an approximate aggregate demand for the product family. The most commonly used forecasting approaches are:

- Bottom-up analysis, utilizing the opinion, judgment, and market surveys of field sales personnel
- Time series analysis
- Exponential smoothing techniques
- Regression and correlation analysis

Forecasting activities typically are conducted or coordinated by a specialized staff group and generally are handled as a responsibility separate from the computerized planning system activities.

Development of the aggregate plan itself is usually a top management responsibility. General management, sales management, and manufacturing management personnel jointly develop the initial version of the plan, based on the known and expected order data.

With the assistance of senior production planning personnel, in most firms the plan is developed for a period of from six to twelve months. To be effective, the schedule must cover a time span that exceeds the cumulative lead time of the finished product. The plan must be firmed up for a reasonable period of time, simply because overall production volume cannot be changed abruptly without incurring significant unplanned costs. Every production volume utilizes a given mix of labor, materials, and equipment. When the output rate is changed, a new optimal mix must be achieved by readjusting the usage rate of the various resources. In the longer term this is possible by replanning the variables—the employment level, the use of overtime, the use of subcontracting, and the variation of inventory levels. In the short run this usually is difficult to do efficiently.

The *master production schedule (MPS)* is developed directly from the aggregate plan—and is the instrument that drives the firm's entire production system. The aggregate plan establishes an overall level of operations that balances the plant's capability with external sales demand. The master schedule translates the aggregate plan into specific numbers of specific products to be produced in identified time periods.

The relationship between the master schedule and the aggregate plan is shown in Figure 20-2. In this hypothetical illustration, an appliance manufacturer's aggregate plan for refrigerator production is shown at the top of

Aggregate Plan for Refrigerators

Month	Jan.	Feb.	Mar.	Apr.	May	June	July	Aug.	Sept.	Oct.	Nov.	Dec.
Number of refrigerators	500	500	600	700	700	800	800	700	600	500	400	400

Master Production Schedule for Refrigerators

Month	Jan.	Feb.	Mar.	Apr.	May	June	July	Aug.	Sept.	Oct.	Nov.	Dec.
Business model												
· Standard	—	100	—	200	—	200	—	150	—	100	—	100
· Heavy duty	—	100	—	100	—	100	—	100	—	50	—	50
Model A												
· Standard	200	100	300	150	300	200	350	200	250	150	150	100
· Deluxe	50	—	50	—	100	—	100	—	50	—	50	—
· Executive	—	100	—	150	—	200	—	150	—	100	—	100
Model B												
· Standard	200	100	200	100	200	100	250	100	250	100	150	50
· Deluxe	50	—	50	—	100	—	100	—	50	—	50	—

FIGURE 20-2
Illustrative relationship of the aggregate plan and the master production schedule.

the figure. (When this plan is added to the firm's aggregate plans for ranges, washing machines, and dryers, the firm's total production capacity will have been utilized for the year.) Note that the master production schedule breaks down the aggregate production of refrigerators into the production of seven specific models, time-phased by quantity per month for the planning period of a year. For example, the 500 units planned in January consist of 200 Model A Standards, 50 Model A Deluxe units, 200 Model B Standards, and 50 Model B Deluxe units. The master schedule for the rest of the year was constructed in the same manner.

The next step in the development of the master schedule is to evaluate its feasibility by simulation, checking the availability and balance of required materials and capacity resources. If bottlenecks or imbalances are encountered, the schedule is modified by trial and error until an acceptable arrangement is found. Many computerized planning systems have this simulation capability built in, as will be seen shortly.

Once an acceptable schedule is determined, its outputs—the volume and timing of the production of specific products—become the inputs required for the subsequent detailed computer planning work that drives the production, inventory, and purchasing operations.

Before moving on to this part of the discussion, however, it is necessary to say just a word about timing and modification of the original plan. The time interval used in master scheduling obviously varies from firm to firm; it depends on the types of products produced, the volume of production, and lead times of the materials used. However, weekly periods are probably most commonly used, followed by biweekly and monthly intervals. So, within the time frame of a six- to twelve-month aggregate plan, the master schedule typically is updated weekly to reflect changing sales demands and perhaps internal problems that require rescheduling. If the system is to work effectively, it is essential that the schedule be updated regularly. After each update, many firms follow the policy of holding the next four weeks' schedule *firm*, providing only modest flexibility for adjustment in the schedule for weeks 5 through 8, and providing considerable flexibility for change in the schedule for weeks 9 through 12.[2]

Material Requirements Planning

Material requirements planning (MRP) is a technique used to determine the quantity and timing requirements of "dependent demand" materials used in the manufacturing operation. The materials can be purchased externally or produced in-house. The important characteristic is that their use be directly dependent on the scheduled production of a larger component or finished product—hence, the term "dependent demand." For example, a refrigerator door is a dependent demand item in the production of a refrigerator.

The material requirements planning and the capacity requirements planning (CRP) segments of the production planning system are the responsibility of the production planning and control group. In practice, the actual number-crunching and paperwork generation usually is accomplished by computer.

Production planning personnel are responsible for structuring and formatting the product bills of material eventually contained in computer memory. The same group is responsible for setting up the part and component inventory status records (perpetual inventory records) that are also computerized. In addition to the current inventory balance, an inventory status record typically contains the timing and size of all open (scheduled) orders for the item, the lead time, safety stock levels, and any other information used for planning purposes. When this preliminary planning work is completed, material requirements for a given time period can be generated.

Although details of the software operation may vary, generally speaking, the MRP segment works as follows. It takes the master production schedule output for a given product and calculates precisely the specific part and component requirements for that product during the given period of operation.

---

[2]Some firms use time frames of five or six weeks rather than four weeks.

This is done by "exploding" the product bill of material (listing separately the quantity of each part required to make the product) and extending these requirements for the number of units to be produced. Since a given part often is used in more than one finished product, the process is repeated for all products. Then all products' requirements for a given part can be summed to obtain the total requirement for the part during the given period of operation.

For illustrative purposes, return to the refrigerator example in Figure 20-2 for a moment. Assume that all the refrigerator models produced, except the Model B Deluxe, use one standard 1-horsepower electric motor. Because of an additional freezing compartment, Model B Deluxe uses two standard 1-horsepower motors. For the month of January, the MRP system would determine that the manufacturing operation requires 550 standard 1-horsepower electric motors.

Returning now to our general discussion of the MRP processing activity, after a part's requirements for the operating period are calculated, the computer compares these requirements with the inventory balance, considering open orders scheduled for receipt, to determine whether a new order needs to be placed.

The output of the MRP system, then, can be the following items:

1 Current order releases to purchasing, with due date requirements.
2 Planned order releases to purchasing for ensuing periods (considering inventory balance, scheduled requirements, and lead time requirements).
3 Current and planned order releases for in-house production, with completion date requirements.
4 Feedback to the master production scheduler, in case operating changes or supplier performance have produced material availability problems.
5 With revised output from the master production schedule, the MRP system will replan and schedule the material requirements.

A more detailed ilustration of an MRP system's operating logic is provided in the following section.

MRP Logic and Format[3]   As utilized today, most versions of MRP act as information processing systems which seek to develop and maintain a set of orders that support the production plan, while simultaneously maintaining inventories within the production system at reasonably low levels. Orders within an MRP system fall into two categories: (1) open orders which have been released but have not yet arrived and (2) planned orders which are developed in anticipation of future releases. As previously noted, each category can contain both purchase orders and shop orders.

---

[3] Based on Daniel J. Bragg and Chan K. Hahn, "Material Requirements Planning and Purchasing," *Journal of Purchasing and Materials Management,* Summer 1982, pp. 18–20. Used with permission of the authors.

The processing logic of MRP centers on the development of a materials planning record for each item. Figure 20-3 illustrates a typical planning record based on the data contained in the master production schedule, bill of materials, and inventory record file shown at the top. The top row of each record shows the "gross requirements," or anticipated usage of the item projected into the future. The second row shows all current "open orders (scheduled receipts)," with each order assigned to the time period in which it is expected to arrive. The "on hand" row projects the inventory balance into the future. This is calculated by determining the impact of gross requirements (planned withdrawals) and open orders (planned receipts) on the inventory balance. The current inventory balance is shown to the left of period 1. The bottom row shows the "planned order releases" for the item, with each order assigned to the time period when it should be released.

The development of the planning record is based on three fundamental concepts which form the essence of the MRP-based approach to materials planning and control. They are:

• Dependent demand
• Inventory/open order netting
• Time phasing

Dependent demand takes the multistage product into account in the planning for individual items. Clearly, the decisions to acquire purchased materials should be based on anticipated production plans. These decisions include both quantity and timing considerations. Dependent demand logic is used to calculate the gross requirements for each planning record. This projected usage includes the planned production of all other products which require the item being planned.

The inventory/open order netting concept is used to develop the "on hand" balance row of the planning record. Efficient use of inventory implies that current stocks should be largely depleted prior to the acquisition of additional inventory. The netting process accomplishes this by allocating current inventory and open orders to the earliest requirements. When the on-hand balance falls below zero, additional stock must be ordered. This process not only signals the need to plan an order but also determines when the order should arrive. This "need date" becomes the due date for the order.

Time phasing utilizes lead time information and need dates. The "planned order releases" row of the planning record shows time-phased orders, whose placement dates are offset from the need dates of the orders by the lead time of the item. Each order, if released in the time period designated by the planned-order row, should arrive exactly at the time it is needed by a following production stage.

Utilization of the three basic concepts can be observed in the simplified illustration of Figure 20-3. The bill of materials diagram shows that item B is a fabricated part that is manufactured using D as a raw material, and that B is used as a component of A. The dependent demand concept is seen in the

Master Production Schedule				
Week	1	2	3	4
Production	100	150	170	130

Inventory Record File			
Item	B	C	D
On hand	100	0	150
Lead time	1	1	2
Open orders:			
Quantity	–	100	170
Due week	–	1	2

Bill of Materials

A
B   C
D

Week

Item A	1	2	3	4
Master production schedule	100	150	170	130

Item B	1	2	3	4
Gross requirements	100	150	170	130
Open orders (scheduled receipts)	–	150 0	170 0	130 0
On hand	100	0	0 −150	0 −170	0 −130
Planned order releases	150	170	130	0

Item C	1	2	3	4
Gross requirements	100	150	170	130
Open orders (scheduled receipts)	100	150 0	170 0	130 0
On hand	0	0	0 −150	0 −170	0 −130
Planned order releases	150	170	130	0

Item D	1	2	3	4
Gross requirements	150	170	130	0
Open orders (scheduled receipts)	0	170	130 0	0
On hand	150	0	0	0 −130	0
Planned order releases	130	0	0	0

FIGURE 20-3
A typical MRP planning record.

gross requirements data; the planned usage of B matches the planned production of A, both in quantity and timing.

The netting process calculations determine the need for additional orders to be planned. For item B, in week 2, 150 units are needed. Since the on-hand quantity of 100 is used to meet week 1 requirements, an order release for 150 units is shown in week 1. Time phasing maintains the timing difference between the planned order and its need date; this is the item's lead time. In this case the lead time is one week. A similar process is used to develop the remaining orders in the "planned order releases" row. Looking at item D, the process is repeated, the only difference being that D is dependent on B.

MRP not only plans for each order, but it also allows the replanning of orders. Replanning is generally necessary when the status of an item is changed due to new information. An example of a status-changing event could be notice of a late delivery. Using item D as an illustration, an open order currently is planned to arrive in week 2. If this order is known to have an altered delivery date of week 3, the current plan should be adjusted (replanned) to reflect this new information. The impact of this change can be traced to every other item by reversing the processing logic and working from bottom to top rather than from top to bottom.

The impact of the shortage also can be reduced by adjusting the orders for the other items. Looking at item B, the planned order release in week 2 is no longer feasible and should be shifted into week 3. The requirement that was to be covered by this planned order can no longer be supported. It should also be shifted into the next week, thus affecting the master production schedule.

Hence, the MRP system generates a complete set of planned orders for all manufactured parts and purchased materials based on the information inputs. Clearly, the validity of the plan produced by the system is dependent on both accurate and timely lead time information from purchasing personnel. At the same time, if system planning is done far enough in advance (and rescheduling activity is kept to a minimum), the advance knowledge about specific material requirements certainly can facilitate planning and conduct of the buying activities.

Capacity Requirements Planning

The next step in the production planning process is capacity requirements planning (CRP). The function of the CRP segment of the process is to convert the shop orders produced by the MRP system into scheduled workloads for the various factory work centers. In addition to the MRP system output, two other sets of data inputs are required to do this: (1) shop routing data and (2) work center status data. These inputs for CRP operation are analogous to the bill of materials and inventory status inputs for MRP operation.

In an intermittent production operation, the manufacture of each product or component requires that a series of specific machine or human operations be performed on the item as it progresses toward completion. These required operations define the "route" the item must travel through the manufacturing facility. Sometimes more than one routing sequence is possible. In any case, one of the required preliminary planning activities is to develop one or more shop routing plans for each product and component produced in-house. In addition to the physical routing plans, standard processing time requirements must be determined for each operation in the sequence—and included in the shop routing data file. In a continuous manufacturing operation, these activities usually are simplified by the design and layout of the production facility.

The work center status data file maintains a perpetual record of the capacity—equipment and human—that is available (and committed) in each of the factory's work centers. Capacity typically is measured in standard man or machine hours per time period.

With shop routing data and work center status data files loaded in computer memory, the CRP system is ready for operation. Recall that during the development of the master production schedule, a preliminary analysis of work center capacity was done prior to firming up the schedule. While this "rough cut" produced approximate data accurate enough for overall scheduling purposes, it is not precise enough for the detailed work-loading job at hand. So—with the MRP-generated current and planned shop order releases now known with certainty for a given time period—a second pass is made. The CRP program first obtains the necessary routing and timing data for each scheduled order—and then checks the appropriate work center status files to determine if the required capacity is available. Frequently the proposed plan does not mesh satisfactorily with the availability and timing of capacity existing in the required work centers. In this case, the CRP activity becomes an iterative process, and replanning continues until realistic work-center loads are developed. The variables that can be manipulated by the system and the planner to achieve a reasonable balance typically include:

- Alternative routings
- Personnel reallocation
- Use of overtime
- Inventory level variations
- Use of alternative tooling
- Use of subcontracting

Occasionally an impossible scheduling situation is encountered. In this case the system communicates to the scheduler the need for selected capacity modification or for a revision of the master schedule. Most of the time, however, a reasonable fit can be achieved. The normal output of the system in these cases is:

1 Verification of the planned orders from the MRP system
2 Work-center load reports that reflect the priorities established by the MRP system

This information subsequently is used in the final stage of the planning and control process.

Control of Production Activities

As the old adage says, "The proof of the pudding is in the eating." The validity and the usefulness of the detailed planning done to this point in the process will now be seen as it is applied to production operations in the shop.

The output of the MRP and CRP systems is transmitted to the manufacturing organization in the form of order releases and a dispatch list. Referring again to Figure 20-3, the planned order releases shown on line 4 of the planning record, when released as the date moves into the current period, officially become the open orders (scheduled receipts) shown on line 2 of the planning record. Before releasing an order, the planner must make one final check to ensure that the priority sequencing of the order is still valid, that capacity is still available, and that materials are available. If all factors are not "go," release may be delayed rather than having the order held up after it is started in the shop.

When an order is released, typically it is accompanied by a packet of materials and instructions required to complete the job. Included are such things as engineering drawings, bills of materials, route sheets, move tickets, materials requisitions, labor charge forms, and so on. Depending on the extent to which the entire system is computerized, some of these functions may be handled through the use of on-line terminals.

The dispatch list, containing a series of order releases, is prepared by the planner and may cover a time period ranging from a day to a week. It goes to the appropriate work center foreman, who schedules his or her machines and people in accordance with the due dates specified for each order on the list.

If daily dispatch lists are used, the foreman generally has little discretion in scheduling the jobs in the work center. On the other hand, if the list covers several days of work or more, the foreman has an increasing amount of latitude in his or her detailed scheduling activities. This provides a better opportunity to maximize the operating efficiency of the work center. Perceptive planning and scheduling by the foreman usually can minimize setup and material move costs and maximize the utilization of equipment and labor. Consequently, it is important that planners coordinate the development of their dispatch lists closely with the appropriate foremen in an effort to optimize both planning control and shop efficiency. A team-type spirit and effort usually produce the best results.

As noted earlier, control is an essential element if the entire process is to work effectively. In most operations this is accomplished at two levels. First, as a job progresses, status and related information is fed back to the planner from either the operator or the foreman on the job. Information reported typically includes order status, anticipated delays, materials shortages, and re-work and scrap data. As appropriate, such feedback occurs either daily or when a job is started and completed. Some firms report only on an exception basis. In continuous manufacturing operations, such reporting typically is done less frequently at predetermined checkpoints in the process. In any case, such information is used by the planner to determine if replanning or other corrective action is necessary to meet the firm's sales commitments.

In addition to order status types of control reports, most systems also require one or more types of capacity control reports. The most commonly used one is an input/output report, typically developed weekly. This type of report usually shows the hours of work planned for a given work center, the number of hours actually worked on the planned jobs, and the difference between the two. Significant deviations from plan can produce obvious problems in the CRP and subsequent scheduling activities. Hence, in most operations, this type of control is essential.

Reporting and monitoring methodology varies among firms. Some are totally computerized, with computer graphics output, while others use a combination of computer and manual communication and charting techniques. The use of Gantt charts and schedule/control boards is still fairly common.

In most organizations, control is also exercised at a second level—personal control right on the shop floor. One or more dispatcher/expediters, usually assigned to the production planning and control group, spend most of their time on the floor visually following jobs through the manufacturing operation. This individual's job is threefold: (1) to ensure the integrity of the job priority plan—that is, that the routing and scheduling instructions for jobs are implemented reasonably; (2) to ensure reasonable capacity control—that is, that the hours scheduled in the various work centers are actually being worked; and (3) to help the operating people solve unexpected planning and scheduling difficulties. As problems arise, the dispatcher/expediter works with the various foremen in helping to resolve them. This person is the planning group's representative on the shop floor. Within reason, he or she has the authority to suggest certain micro planning and scheduling changes that may be able to resolve a problem directly and expeditiously.

To summarize, the production planning activities all come together on the shop floor to initiate and control the production operations. Overall responsibility for *control* of operations usually is vested with the production planning and control manager or the materials manager. In firms without a materials management department, the manufacturing manager is sometimes responsible. The control function usually has both a centralized and a decentralized component. Order release, dispatching, and formal status control are the responsibility of the centralized production planning and control group. Decentralized informal control on the shop floor is the joint responsibility of dispatcher/expediter personnel and the line foremen responsible for the actual production operations. Viewed in another sense, it is the responsibility of the foremen to do the micro work-center scheduling and to run each production operation so that planned completion dates are met. It is the responsibility of production planning and control to keep work flowing through the shop at a steady rate, focusing always on order priority control and capacity control.

Two Management Considerations

It is appropriate at this point to reiterate two important concepts that may have gotten buried in the details of our discussion of the total planning system.

The first concerns the *multilevel nature of the operation of the production planning system.* A review of Figure 20-1 perhaps will recall the fact that for the most part, the aggregate planning and the master scheduling activities are top-management and staff responsibilities. Most activities associated with the material requirements planning and capacity requirements planning activities are primarily the responsibility of production planning and control personnel. Finally, the control of production operations themselves is a joint responsibility of production planning and control personnel and supervisory operating personnel. For a system to function effectively, the coordinated efforts of all three groups are required.

The second concept focuses on the *dynamic nature of the total production planning system.* Although time periods vary for different organizations, a majority of firms utilizing a comprehensive computer-based planning system work from an aggregate plan structured for the coming year. The master schedule subsequently covers the same year's period, but typically it is further delineated by month and by week. Material and capacity requirements are also structured in weekly "time buckets." In order to maintain a current plan that correctly reflects changing sales demands and internal scheduling and capacity constraints, the entire operation typically is replanned on a weekly basis. So the firm, semifirm, and flexible portions of the total operating schedule simply drop the week just past and encompass one new week as replanning occurs each week. Some systems utilize a technique in which only selected portions of the operation that are influenced by changing conditions are replanned; this approach has some obvious logistical advantages. Regardless of the specific technique used, however, the important point is that the dynamic nature of the planning system keeps it current on at least a weekly basis. And from a practical point of view, this is the feature that makes such a system so valuable to a large complex firm operating in a competitive environment.

EVOLUTION OF MRP AND MRP II SYSTEMS

As innovations are accepted and refined in the business world, inconsistencies in the use of terminology and variations of the concept inevitably emerge with the passage of time. Such has been the case with MRP and its subsequent derivatives. The following paragraphs describe briefly the evolution of MRP and its progeny, MRP II.

The computer-based material requirements planning technique found its first significant industrial usage in the early 1970s. Though it became known as MRP, for a number of years it was used primarily to generate orders for parts and materials that related to a specific demand schedule. Later, users found that with some refinement it could be used as a scheduling technique. It could be used to feed back schedule change data and subsequently reschedule existing orders to maintain valid material and shop order dates. Hence, it became a much more valuable tool.

However, from a production planning point of view, MRP still left something to be desired because it was unable to deal with the capacity variable. Before long, though, necessity proved to be the mother of invention, because soon a capacity requirements planning module was developed and linked to the original MRP module. With further development of the master production schedule concept, the bulk of the planning activities shown in Figure 20-1 were integrated into a single planning and scheduling package. Today, with the exception of the aggregate planning and the production operation controls segments, this entire integrated package is identified as a *closed loop MRP system*. Thus, the concept and the terminology have both changed with time.

The last step, to date, in this evolutionary process is an expanded system known as *MRP II—manufacturing resource planning*. This system simply adds two new capabilities to a closed loop MRP system. The most significant addition is the financial interface. This module provides the ability to convert operating production plans into financial terms, so the data can be used for financial planning and control purposes. The second addition provides a new simulation capability that makes it possible for any user of the system to do more extensive alternative planning work. This can be done by asking "what if" types of questions—that is, by modifying an operating variable and receiving a systemwide response to the proposed operating change.[4]

IMPACT ON PURCHASING

Sooner or later, most major manufacturing firms will use some type of MRP-based system as a central component of their production planning system. If present experience is a reasonable indicator of the future, purchasing operations will be affected in the following important ways:[5]

1 Expanded use of the buyer-planner or vendor scheduler concept

---

[4] For an interesting discussion of MRP II development, see Troy Juliar, "Completing the Mix: Materials Management and MRP II," *Purchasing Management*, February 1987, pp. 6–11.

[5] An MRP-type system also generates output that can be utilized easily and effectively as input for an electronic data interchange (EDI) system. Consequently, as EDI operations become more widely used, MRP systems will tend to facilitate their use.

2 Expanded use of contract buying
3 Necessity of greater supplier flexibility and reliability
4 Development of closer relationships with suppliers; possibly more contract administration effort
5 Increased accuracy and timeliness of materials records

Buyer-Planner and Vendor Scheduler Concepts   The very nature of an MRP operation places the planner in close, continuing contact with material requirements and their frequently changing schedules. Typically, the planner has a much more sensitive feel than the buyer for the probable usage pattern of most materials. Consequently, to improve efficiency of the planning-buying activity, as well as communications with suppliers, many firms have used one of several organizational schemes that utilize the planner as the supplier contact person.

The buyer-planner concept is one commonly used approach. This organizational arrangement was discussed in Chapter 5, and will be reviewed only briefly here. In essence, the buyer's job and the planner's job are combined into a single job done by one individual. This person obviously handles a smaller number of items than were originally handled by either the buyer or the planner. The buyer-planner is responsible for determination of material requirements, developing material schedules, making order quantity determinations, issuing all material releases to suppliers, and handling all of the activities associated with the buying function. Thus, in this integrated role, the buyer-planner maintains close contact with various supplier personnel.

Another popular approach is simply to assign to the planner the responsibility for dealing directly with suppliers in releasing and following up materials orders. In this arrangement, the buyer handles all the normal purchasing responsibilities except requirements releases against existing contracts. The planner handles this latter function—and becomes the buying firm's supplier contact on all day-to-day material scheduling matters. Most firms refer to this arrangement as the *vendor scheduler concept.*

In a recent survey of present MRP users, researchers found that approximately 55 percent of the firms utilize the vendor scheduler concept and that 30 percent use the buyer-planner organizational arrangement. Only 15 percent of the firms utilize the traditional pattern of operation.[6] It seems clear that a continued expansion of the use of these two concepts will accompany MRP development in the future.

Contract Buying   Because an MRP system requires the placement of frequent orders for relatively small quantities of materials, it obviously would be inefficient, if not impossible, to make a new buy for every weekly requirement. The alternative, of course, is to place annual or longer-term contracts

---

[6] J. E. Schorr and T. F. Wallace, *High Performance Purchasing: Manufacturing Resource Planning for the Purchasing Professional,* Wight Publications Inc., Essex Junction, Vt., 1986, p. 150.

with suppliers for the required materials—and then simply issue a telephone or an MRP schedule release against the contract, as the production operation requires.

This buying approach is not only required in an MRP-scheduled operation, but as a general rule it is excellent buying practice. It permits more careful purchasing planning and more thorough market and supplier research—and it needs to be done only once every year or two for each material. In addition, such contracts usually produce attractive pricing arrangements and improved supplier relations. This topic is discussed at length in Chapter 25, "Developing and Managing the Buying Plan."

Supplier Flexibility and Reliability   Because of the weekly updating of most MRP systems, coupled with the frequent rescheduling that sometimes occurs, a supplier has to be more than reasonably flexible. Even if a supplier has the buyer's MRP schedule with weekly or biweekly requirements for the next two months, the irregularity of demand and the short notice given on schedule changes present a difficult operating situation for most suppliers. Resolution of the potential problems requires careful cooperative planning and usually some compromises by both parties.

It is obvious that supplier reliability is a must. The buying firm typically carries some inventory, but not as much as in the traditional operating situation since one of the objectives of the system is to reduce inventory levels. Hence, there is much less cushion in the system to handle the problems of late deliveries and off-spec materials.

The bottom line of these two stringent operating requirements is that supplier selection is a critical, yet a more difficult, task.

Closer Relationships with Suppliers   The use of contract buying and the need for unusual supplier flexibility and reliability create an operating situation in which the buyer-supplier relationship must be closer and more cooperative than it might normally be. As discussed in the earlier chapters on sourcing, this type of operating situation requires the ultimate in coordination, cooperation, and teamwork. A mutual understanding of each other's operations and problems is essential in achieving this type of effectiveness. It literally is an informal partnership operation—and it must turn out to be a win-win deal.

The buyer-planner or the vendor scheduler must stay in close touch with the supplier's counterpart on a week-to-week operating basis as far as scheduling and delivery matters are concerned. And the buyer (or buyer-planner) must handle the broader issues of the relationship with appropriate supplier sales and technical personnel on a regular and timely basis.

Materials Records   As one reviews the MRP segment of the production planning system, it is readily apparent that the accuracy of the system will be no better than the accuracy of the data used in its calculations. If the system is to work effectively, records such as specifications, bills of materials, supplier lead times, receiving reports, inventory balances, and so forth must be as near 100 percent accurate as possible.

JUST-IN-TIME PRODUCTION PLANNING

Although originally pioneered by Henry Ford, the just-in-time manufacturing concept has been refined and developed over the past two decades in Japanese industry. The purpose of this recent concerted effort was to improve quality and reduce costs to help Japanese business become more competitive in world markets for selected product lines. The resounding success of the Japanese effort prompted a growing number of U.S. firms to develop and implement modified versions of the system in this country.

The just-in-time concept is considered by many to be a technique used for reducing inventories. In reality, it is much more. The complete JIT concept is an operations management philosophy whose dual objectives are to reduce waste and to increase productivity. It is true, operationally speaking, that the basic theme of the JIT concept is that *inventory is evil*. Inventory is considered to be undesirable for three reasons:

- It hides quality problems.
- It hides production inefficiencies and productivity problems.
- It adds unnecessary costs to the production operation—carrying costs of approximately 25 to 35 percent of the inventory value per year.

Inventories of production materials permit suppliers' quality deficiencies to be covered up and in-process inventories permit off-spec work in-house to be given less attention than it should. This occurs simply because the unacceptable items can be replaced with good items from inventory while those that are unacceptable are being reworked. The same rationale applies to schedule slippages caused by inefficiences in the workplace and in the system itself. The end result, claim JIT proponents, has been a tendency among U.S. managers and their employees to accept mediocre, second-rate work as the norm.

Hence, in an effective JIT application the operating policy is to minimize production and work-in-process inventories by providing each work center with just the quantity of materials and components needed to do a given job at the exact time they are needed. In an ideal situation, each unit of output would be produced just as it is needed at the succeeding work station. In reality, of course, this ideal is not achieved. But, within reason, it is a viable objective in many organizations. Practically speaking, the result is a reasonably continuous flow of small-lot production. At the supply end of the operation, those materials that are procured in a JIT mode are delivered frequently by suppliers in fairly small quantities. Deliveries may range from twice a day to once a week.

Consequently, throughout the entire system, with only minimal inventories on hand to cover for poor-quality materials and workmanship, the focus is on consistently high-quality material and in-process work. Without it, the system breaks down.

To summarize, then, the basic operating plan is to gear production and final assembly as closely to sales demand as possible. Individual production operations are also geared more closely together. This is accomplished either by means of a product-type layout of equipment and work centers,[7] or by means of a material-pull, "Kanban" type of material movement system[8] in a process-oriented layout. Finally, the firm's total production operation, through purchasing, is geared as closely as practical to key suppliers' production operations. So—the characteristic of small-lot flow can be traced through the entire system from a supplier's plant, through the buyer's plant, out into the finished goods distribution system. The actuating element is sales demand, which *pulls* the various stages of in-process work and materials through the complete system.

A JIT Illustration

Figure 20-4 provides a flow diagram of the major production operations in an electronic instrument manufacturing plant, both before and after the firm implemented a JIT system.

The top portion of the figure shows the original operation. After incoming material was received, counted, and logged into the system, it went through a standard visual receiving inspection operation where potential quality problems were detected, and perhaps submitted to quality assurance for further detailed inspection. The next step was to prepackage the materials, parts, and components that would subsequently be used in putting together a given subassembly. This was done for each subassembly produced to facilitate stock picking for the later assembly work. Most production inventories were thus stored in this subassembly kit form. After subassembly operations occurred, subassembly units were then inventoried until later used in a product's final assembly operation. Approximately a week's finished goods inventory for most products was maintained at the plant.

The lower portion of Figure 20-4 shows the dramatic change that occurred

---

[7]A product-type layout is one in which the various types of equipment required to make a given product are arranged adjacent to each other so that operations occur sequentially, in line, from one end of the manufacturing process to the other. An automobile assembly plant is a good example of product layout. A process-type layout groups similar types of equipment together, without regard for the flow of the product being manufactured—e.g., all lathes are grouped together, all boring machines are grouped together, and so on. A traditional job shop exemplifies this type of layout.

[8]A *Kanban material production and movement system* is simply one in which no more than approximately an hour's supply of material is produced in one run in each work center—and the next production run does not occur until the material is called for by the succeeding operation. It is this feature of the operation that produces the *small batch* and *pull-flow* characteristics of the system.

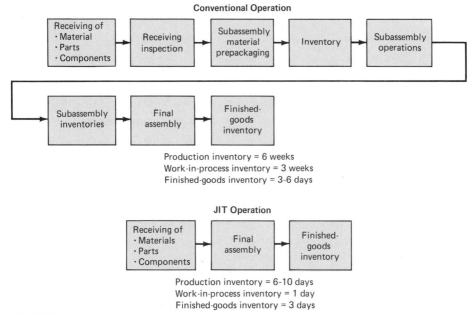

FIGURE 20-4
How JIT was implemented in one U.S. firm.

as a result of JIT implementation. The receiving inspection and quality control technical inspection operations for purchased materials were completely eliminated. The responsibility for incoming quality was placed with the purchasing department and delegated to each supplier organization. This required a reasonable amount of supplier education. In most cases purchasing and QC worked with suppliers to develop and install statistical process control systems in their manufacturing operations. SPC control charts were then required to be submitted with each shipment of delivered material.

The next major change occurred on the shop floor. The facility originally utilized a specialized process-type layout, similar to a large job shop. This was revised to achieve a modified product-type layout. Although the firm produced approximately half a dozen different product lines, enough similarity between products existed to permit the use of several product-flow types of facilities arrangements. This layout permitted the use of an open-type storage system adjacent to the production operations themselves. So incoming materials were delivered directly to the point of use in the shop.

Production scheduling subsequently was based completely on units of finished product, rather than on the production of subassemblies as well. This made it practical to eliminate the subassembly prepackaging and storage activities, as well as the subassembly operations themselves. The firm's closed loop MRP system was still used to generate requirements and overall schedules, but it was necessary to "smooth" the master schedule to facilitate the reasonably continuous, small-lot production. Consequently, the total shop now resembles a continuous manufacturing operation much more than its previous job shop character.

As shown underneath each of the two flow diagrams, inventory levels were reduced greatly. Production inventory was decreased approximately 70 percent, and in-process inventories were dropped from about a fifteen-day supply to a one-day supply. Finished goods inventory was reduced by about 40 percent. Hence, the total float figure declined from approximately fifty days to twelve days—and the firm reports that quality problems have declined noticeably.

In summary, the following elements tend to characterize most successful JIT operations:[9]

1 The JIT concept is most applicable to manufacturing operations that produce a relatively small number of different products in at least a quasi-continuous environment.
2 Product demand must be reasonably predictable, and requirements must be generated accurately. A closed loop MRP system can be used to do this, but typically the master production schedule must be smoothed on a daily basis.
3 Statistical process control typically is used in both the buyer's and suppliers' organizations to ensure tight control of material and production quality. This is vital to the functioning of the low-float, small-volume, relatively smooth-flowing operation.
4 Production operation setup requirements must be able to be reduced to relatively short times. Most firms target for tool changes and equipment setups of less than ten minutes. Without this capability, small-batch and smooth-flow production of different models or different products cannot be accomplished efficiently.
5 Purchasing must be able to reduce materials replenishment lead times. This usually is accomplished by reducing the four major elements of lead time—internal paperwork and ordering time, supplier manufacturing time, transportation time requirements, and incoming receiving and inspection requirements.
6 Successful JIT operation suppliers must be able to be flexible to meet the buying firm's stringent, short-fused material requirements—and they must be reliable to the nth degree.

These considerations lead logically to a discussion of the impact of a JIT system on the purchasing operation.

[9]Several articles and a book that provide good depth analyses of JIT applications are: Chan K. Hahn, Peter A. Pinto, and Daniel J. Bragg, "Just-in-Time Production and Purchasing," *Journal of Purchasing and Materials Management*, Fall 1983, pp. 2–15; A. F. Celley, W. H. Clegg, A. W. Smith, and M. A. Vonderembse, "Implementation of JIT in the United States," *Journal of Purchasing and Materials Management*, Winter 1986–87, pp. 9–15; and P. L. Grieco, M. W. Gozzo, and J. W. Claunch, *Just-in-Time Purchasing: In Pursuit of Excellence*, P T Publications Inc., 1988.

JIT's Impact on Purchasing

Purchasing plays a key role in any JIT operation. Whether a JIT production system works or not depends on how well purchasing does its job in selecting and managing suppliers.

Obviously, it is not practical to procure all materials on a JIT basis. Most successful JIT firms buy from 5 to 10 percent of their individual materials—those that account for 60 to 75 percent of the firm's materials expenditures and those that are space-intensive—in a JIT mode. This keeps the administrative part of the job manageable.

Finding reliable suppliers that are willing to comply with a JIT buyer's stringent requirements typically is not an easy task. Consequently, purchasing usually utilizes two basic strategies:

- A specific plan to reduce the number of suppliers utilized, using single and dual sources in many cases
- Extensive use of long-term contracting

Evaluation and qualification of JIT suppliers clearly is a critical and time-consuming activity.

The very nature of a JIT purchasing operation requires and in fact usually creates a closer, more cooperative relationship between the buying and supplying firms. Hence, from a practical point of view a reduced supplier base is a necessity—and a longer-term contract is the primary incentive that attracts a supplier to consider the arrangement. Only with knowledge of the buyer's long-term requirements schedule can a supplier schedule production and size inventories so that replenishment lead time can be reduced, while simultaneously providing both flexible and reliable service.

As noted earlier, the basic objective of the "partnering" relationship is to reduce costs, improve efficiency, and increase profitability for *both* organizations. The development of scheduling guidelines and parameters, the implementation of SPC quality systems, and the conduct of value analysis work on the purchased items must be done jointly in a team-type environment. To assist in all of these activities, the buyer often makes greater use of *performance specifications* to encourage the supplier to exercise as much creativity as possible.[10]

Reducing the delivering carrier's transportation time is also an important objective. Consequently, suppliers located near the buyer's operation may offer a distinct advantage. The most important strategy in this element of the equation, however, is to work out a longer-term contractual JIT arrangement with a small number of selected carriers. This type of transportation service can be purchased in the same manner material is purchased from a JIT supplier. This topic is discussed further in Chapter 23, "Traffic."

---

[10] For a detailed discussion of the buyer-seller relationship, see: C. R. O'Neal, "The Buyer-Seller Linkage in a Just-in-Time Environment," *Journal of Purchasing and Materials Management,* Spring 1989, pp. 34–40.

A final impact of JIT is seen in the form of a shift in the workload within the purchasing department. The buyer's job now involves more responsibility for contract administration and supplier management than previously. The tight delivery schedules, the emphasis on control of quality and performance, and the joint resolution of problems with suppliers require this. At the same time, the nature of the JIT buying operation now requires less routine, nitty-gritty buying work. In effect, the JIT buyer's job tends to require a broader range of professional and managerial skills than typically was the case previously.

CONCLUSION

The interface between procurement and production planning is an extremely important one. Production planning decisions influence the parameters within which purchasing does its work. At the same time, the effectiveness with which purchasing does its job directly influences the success of the production planning system.

In recent years, with the aid of computerized systems, production planning has evolved into a highly specialized and sophisticated activity. Closed loop MRP systems, MRP II systems, and JIT systems all significantly affect the design and implementation of a firm's purchasing systems. To a great extent, purchasing strategies used in prior years must be modified, and in some cases replaced with new approaches, to create the supply environment required to support and sustain these evolving planning systems.

In this dynamic environment it is imperative that the procurement and production planning functions be developed in close coordination because of the interdependencies they share—and that operationally they be coordinated effectively on a day-to-day basis.

FOR DISCUSSION

20-1 "An effective production planning and control operation must accomplish five general activities." Identify these activities and discuss each briefly.

20-2 What is aggregate planning? Discuss its significance in the production planning process.

20-3 What is the relationship between the aggregate plan and the master schedule?

20-4 Describe how the material requirements planning module works and what it does in a modern production planning system.

20-5 What does the capacity requirements planning module accomplish in a production planning system? Discuss.

20-6 Frequently the proposed production plan does not mesh satisfactorily with the availability and timing of the capacity existing in required work centers. What variables may be manipulated by the planner to achieve a reasonable balance between the proposed requirements and available capacity? Discuss.

20-7 What type of information is transmitted from the formal production planning system to personnel on the shop floor for detailed planning and control purposes? Discuss.

20-8 When an order is released to the shop for production, what materials accompany it? Discuss.

20-9 What is meant by "the multilevel nature of the operation of the production planning system"? Discuss.

20-10 What are the time frames of operation for the various modules (or elements) of a typical production planning system?

20-11 What is a closed loop MRP system? Draw a flowchart and discuss.

20-12 What is the difference between a regular MRP system and an MRP II system? Discuss.

20-13 Identify and discuss the impacts of an MRP system on a purchasing department's operation.

20-14 Describe how the buyer-planner concept works.

20-15 Describe how the vendor scheduler concept works.

20-16 Describe how a just-in-time production system works.

20-17 According to JIT proponents, why are inventories undesirable?

20-18 Identify and discuss the key characteristics of a JIT production operation.

20-19 How does a firm's purchasing operation contribute to the success of its JIT production operation? Discuss in some detail.

20-20 "The interface between procurement and production planning is an extremely important one." What is your reaction to this statement? Discuss in depth.

CASES FOR CHAPTER 20

CHAPTER **21**

INVENTORY MANAGEMENT

KEY CONCEPTS

- Functions of inventories
- Types of inventories
- Analysis of inventories
    ABC concept; 80/20 analysis
    Dependent and independent demand
    Inventory costs
- EOQ concept
    Incremental costs
    Quantity discounts
- Types of control systems
    Cyclical/Fixed order interval system
    Flow control system
    JIT inventory system
    MRP inventory system
    Order point/Fixed order quantity system
    Two-bin system
- Applications and comparisons of various systems

The preceding chapter set the tone for a review of inventory management. The production planning systems just discussed determine to a significant extent the size of a firm's inventories, as well as the types of approaches that can be used in managing them. As the production planning function has become more sophisticated in recent years, so too has its operating twin, inventory management.

440

Several statistics clearly point up the significance of this function. In most manufacturing firms today, inventories constitute the second-largest category of assets shown on the balance sheet, exceeded only by physical facilities and equipment.[1] Inventories frequently account for as much as 30 percent of the firm's invested capital.

A second startling figure is uncovered when one ferrets out and totals the annual costs of carrying a given inventory. While the figure varies considerably from firm to firm, numerous studies made by manufacturing firms and consultants reveal that a typical manufacturer incurs inventory carrying costs of from 20 to 40 percent of average inventory value. This means that a medium-sized firm pays in indirect costs approximately $300,000 per year merely for the convenience of having a million-dollar inventory in its warehouse. This figure is significantly greater than is apparent to the average businessperson.

THE FUNCTIONS OF INVENTORIES

The preceding discussion of the JIT concept highlighted very sharply the disadvantages inventories can bring to a manufacturing operation. In many circumstances, however, inventories do have some redeeming values—they are not all bad. The trick is to obtain the best of both worlds at a reasonable cost.

Generally speaking, inventories make possible smooth and efficient operation of a manufacturing organization by *decoupling individual segments* of the total operation. Purchased-part inventories permit activities of purchasing department personnel to be planned and conducted somewhat independently of shop production operations. By the same token, these inventories allow additional flexibility for suppliers in planning, producing, and delivering an order for a given part.

Inventories of parts and components produced in-house in an intermittent operation decouple the many individual machines and production processes from various subassembly and assembly activities. This typically enables management to plan production runs in individual production areas in a manner which utilizes manpower and equipment considerably more efficiently than if all were tied directly to the final assembly line. In addition, finished goods inventories perform the function of decoupling the total production process from distribution demands, allowing on a broader scale the development of similar efficiencies of production. These inventories also help *balance the firm's supply with the market forces of demand*.

Thus, well-planned and effectively controlled inventories can contribute to a firm's profit. The real problem is to determine the inventory level at which money invested in inventory produces a higher rate of return through these benefits than it would were it invested in some other phase of the business.

[1]D. J. Armstrong, "Getting Things Done: Sharpening Inventory Management," *Harvard Business Review*, November–December 1985, p. 42.

If this problem is viewed through the eyes of various operating department managers, an interesting situation appears. The *marketing manager* tends to favor relatively large inventory stocks to assure rapid assembly and delivery of a wide range of product models. This capability can obviously be used as an effective sales tool. The *production manager* is inclined to go along with the marketing manager, but for quite a different reason. He or she argues for high inventory levels because they allow more flexibility in daily planning; unforeseen problems in producing a given component can be mitigated if productive efforts can easily be transferred to another component for which the required raw materials are on hand. Likewise, a reasonable inventory of the required items *ensures against production shutdowns* due to supplier problems and stock-outs, thus avoiding the incurrence of high production downtime costs. The production manager's arguments reveal the flip side of the arguments favoring JIT.

The *financial officers* of the firm, on the other hand, argue convincingly in favor of low inventory levels. They point out that the company's need for funds usually exceeds availability and that reduced inventories free sorely needed working capital for other uses. They note also that total indirect inventory carrying costs drop proportionately with the inventory level. The *purchasing manager* is the final participant; he or she is concerned with the size and frequency of individual orders. Purchasing favors a policy of placing fewer and larger orders. Unless contractual arrangements with routine delivery-release systems can be worked out with suppliers, fewer and larger orders usually increase the total inventory level. The purchasing manager points out that *large-volume buying often results in reduced purchase prices*, and that it also permits more *efficient utilization of buying personnel* and more effective advance planning for major activities such as value analysis, vendor investigation, and so on.

Thus, it is clear that each departmental executive supports his or her position with legitimate justification. Nevertheless, certain conflicts do exist between the objectives of the various departments. Concepts and techniques useful in analyzing this problem to arrive at sound policy decisions are the focal point of our investigation in this chapter.

DEFINITION OF INVENTORIES

Although inventories are classified in many ways, the following classification is convenient for use in further discussion of the topic:

1 *Production inventories:* Raw materials, parts, and components which enter the firm's product in the production process. These may consist of two general types: (1) special items manufactured to company specifications and (2) standard industrial items purchased "off the shelf."
2 *MRO inventories:* Maintenance, repair, and operating supplies which are consumed in the production process but which do not become part of the product (e.g., lubricating oil, soap, machine repair parts).

3 *In-process inventories:* Semifinished products found at various stages of the production operation.

4 *Finished-goods inventories:* Completed products ready for shipment.

In most manufacturing companies, production and MRO inventories together represent the major segment of total inventory investment.

Let us now place the discussion in perspective. Inventory planning occurs at several levels in an organization and covers various time spans. Our concern in this chapter focuses on the planning and control of production and MRO inventories in a short-run situation, involving weekly, monthly, and in some cases quarterly or yearly decisions. Hence, the discussion assumes that the longer-range activities of sales forecasting, product modification, aggregate planning, and master scheduling have for the moment been completed. Our investigation begins at this point in the planning cycle.

INVENTORY ANALYSIS

The inventory of a typical industrial firm includes as many as 5,000 to 50,000 different items. Initial planning and subsequent control of such an inventory is accomplished on the basis of knowledge about *each* of the individual items and the finished products of which each is a part. Consequently, the starting point for sound inventory management is the development of a complete inventory catalog, followed by a thorough ABC analysis.

Inventory Catalog

After all inventory items have been completely described, identified by manufacturer's part number, cross-indexed by user's identification number if necessary, and classified generically for indexing purposes, some form of inventory catalog should be prepared for use by all personnel.[2] Careful preparation and maintenance of such a catalog pays two important dividends.

An inventory catalog serves, first, as a medium of communication. It enables personnel located in many different departments to perform their jobs more effectively. A design engineer, for example, may have a choice between using either of two standard parts in an experimental design; an inventory catalog quickly tells whether either part is carried in inventory and may be available immediately for use in the experimental work. Suppose the item in question is to be used in large quantities on the production line. If one of the alternative parts is a stock item and the other is not, the engineer knows immediately that procurement time and cost will probably be lower for the part which already is being purchased and used elsewhere in the plant.

---

[2]Most firms have a companywide materials standardization program. The materials included in the inventory catalog should all have been accepted as company "standards." This topic is discussed further in Chapter 7, "Standardization."

As a further example, envision a mechanic who has just removed a faulty bearing from a major production machine that has broken down. Upon examination, the mechanic finds the manufacturer's name and part number stamped on the edge of the bearing. Unfortunately, though, the storeroom clerk cannot help, because that particular bearing is not carried in stock. If the mechanic or a supervisor consults the inventory catalog, however, they may well find that a satisfactory substitute bearing, carried under another manufacturer's part number, is in stock. Proper cross-indexing in the inventory catalog can inform users about common interchangeable parts, a typical situation with many MRO supplies.

A second significant benefit produced by an inventory catalog accrues to the inventory control operation itself. This benefit takes the form of more complete and correct records through the reduction of duplicate records for identical parts. A purchasing department often buys the same part from several different suppliers, under various manufacturers' part numbers. Unless control requirements dictate otherwise, identical parts from all suppliers should be consolidated on one inventory record. A simple situation? Perhaps, but one is amazed to find in highly reputable companies many similar cases in which two or more inventory records bear different numbers for the same part. A carefully constructed catalog significantly reduces the possibility of such problems.

ABC Analysis; The 80–20 Concept

As soon as an inventory is identified and described, the manager must determine the importance and the dollar value of each individual inventory item. This calls for a study of each item in terms of its price, usage (demand), and lead time, as well as specific procurement or technical problems. Without the data provided by such a study, an inventory manager normally does not have enough information to determine the best allocation of departmental effort and expense to the tasks of controlling thousands of inventory items.

A study of several hundred medium-sized West Coast manufacturing firms conducted by the authors reveals the data illustrated in Figure 21-1. This figure shows that in the typical firm a small percentage of the total number of items carried in inventory constitutes the bulk of the total dollars invested in inventory. In the study cited, 10 percent of the inventory items account for approximately 75 percent of the investment, and only a quarter of the items make up approximately 90 percent of the total investment. The remaining 75 percent of the items constitute, roughly, only 10 percent of the inventory investment. While these figures vary somewhat from one firm to another, the magnitude of variation usually is not great. Several similar studies in large corporations have produced strikingly similar results, leading to what some firms call the *80–20 phenomenon* (20 percent of the items account for 80 percent of total inventory investment). Historically, some firms have

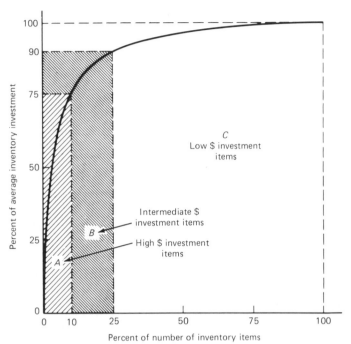

FIGURE 21-1
Graphic analysis of production and MRO inventories.

termed this phenomenon the *Pareto Principle,* based on the law of "the vital few and the trivial many," developed by the Italian economist Vilfredo Pareto around the turn of the century.

Among different companies this type of analysis is known by several different names, *ABC analysis* or *Pareto analysis* being the most common. In practice, such an analysis can be made on the basis of either the average inventory investment in each item or the annual dollar usage of each item. The analysis is easy to conduct once inventory has been properly identified and usage records have been maintained for a complete operating cycle. First, *all items are simply ranked in order of their average inventory investment* (or dollar usage). The total of these values (average inventory investment or annual usage) for all inventory items is then computed. The value of each individual item is next expressed as a percentage of the total. By going down the list and successively cumulating the individual percentages for each item, one can determine which items make up the first 75 percent of inventory investment, the first 90 percent, and so on. If it is convenient to use the three arbitrary classifications noted above, they can be labeled *A, B,* and *C,* respectively, and each inventory item becomes an *A, B,* or *C* item.

The value of such an analysis to management is clear. It provides a sound basis on which to allocate funds and time of personnel with respect to the refinement of control over the individual inventory items. In this sense, control may take several forms. It may be reflected in minimizing purchase cost, in minimizing inventory investment, in minimizing indirect costs associated with inventory, or in utilizing personnel effectively. The concept clearly permeates a number of departmental operations—purchasing, production control, stores, and accounting, for example.

In practice, a never-ending problem is that of adequately planning for handling the thousands of low-value C items. In most cases, availability and reliability for these items is just as important as it is for the A and B items. Even with good purchasing planning, because of the sheer number of C items, low-value nuisance purchases frequently require more time than should be allotted to them. Consequently, they reduce the amount of time available to purchasing personnel for vendor investigation, value analysis, and other creative work involving high-value A and B items. An effective inventory management system must help resolve this problem.

Dependent and Independent Demand

To do the job well, an inventory manager needs one additional bit of information about each of the items in inventory—is the demand (usage) for the item "dependent" or "independent"?

An item is said to exhibit *dependent demand* characteristics when its use is directly dependent on the scheduled production of a larger component or parent product of which the item is a part. Hence, in a plant producing automobile engines the demand for engine block castings is a dependent demand; once the production schedule for a group of engines is established, the planner knows with certainty that one block will be required for each engine. Conversely, the demand for cutting oil used by the machines on the line cannot be calculated accurately from the production schedule and bills of materials; thus, cutting oil is said to have an *independent demand*. Generally speaking, in an assembly or fabrication-type operation, most production inventory items will have a dependent demand, while MRO and similarly used items will have an independent demand.

Although the distinction seems relatively simple, it is important for the inventory manager to know whether an item exhibits a dependent or an independent demand. Certain inventory control systems function more effectively with one type of item than with the other.

COSTS ASSOCIATED WITH INVENTORIES

From a managerial point of view, two basic categories of costs are associated with inventories: (1) inventory carrying costs and (2) inventory acquisition costs. These plus a related variable cost are discussed in the following paragraphs.

Carrying Costs

Carrying material in inventory is expensive. Prior to the recent period of higher interest rates, a number of studies determined that the *annual cost* of carrying a production inventory averaged approximately 25 percent of the value of the inventory. The escalating cost of money in recent years, however, has increased the typical firm's annual inventory carrying cost to a figure between 25 and 35 percent of the value of the inventory. Five major elements make up these costs in the following manner:

1 Opportunity cost of invested funds	12–20%
2 Insurance costs	2– 4%
3 Property taxes	1– 3%
4 Storage costs	1– 3%
5 Obsolescence and deterioration	4–10%
Total carrying costs	20–40%

Let us briefly examine these carrying costs.

1 *Opportunity cost of invested funds.* When a firm purchases $50,000 worth of a production material and keeps it in inventory, it simply has this much less cash to spend for other purposes. Money invested in productive equipment or in external securities earns a return for the company. Conceptually, then, it is logical for the firm to charge all money invested in inventory an amount equal to that it could earn if invested elsewhere in the company. This is the "opportunity cost" associated with inventory investment.

2 *Insurance costs.* Most firms insure their assets against possible loss from fire and other forms of damage. An extra $50,000 worth of inventory represents an additional asset on which insurance premiums must be paid.

3 *Property taxes.* As with insurance, property taxes are levied on the assessed value of a firm's assets; the greater the inventory value, the greater the asset value, and consequently the higher is the firm's tax bill.

4 *Storage costs.* The warehouse in which a firm stores its inventory is depreciated a certain number of dollars per year over the length of its life. One may say, then, that the cost of warehouse space is a given number of dollars per cubic foot per year. And this cost conceptually can be charged against inventory occupying the space.

5 *Obsolescence and deterioration.* In most inventory operations, a certain percentage of the stock spoils, is damaged, is pilfered, or eventually becomes obsolete. No matter how diligently warehouse managers guard against these occurrences, a certain number always take place. With new products being introduced at an increasing rate, the probability of obsolescence is increased accordingly. Consequently, the larger the inventory, typically the greater is the absolute loss from this source.

Generally speaking, this group of carrying costs rises and falls nearly proportionately with the rise and fall of the inventory level. Further, the inventory level is directly related to the quantity in which the ordered material is delivered. When the complete order is shipped at one time, the larger the order quantity, the higher is the *average* inventory level during the period covered by the order. Hence, costs of carrying inventory vary nearly directly with the size of the order quantity. This relationship is illustrated by the CC curve in Figure 21-2.

If a firm has estimated its approximate inventory carrying cost, as a percentage of inventory value, the *annual* inventory carrying costs that would be generated by order quantities of various sizes can be calculated as follows:

$$\left(\begin{array}{c}\text{Carrying cost}\\\text{per year}\end{array}\right) = \left(\begin{array}{c}\text{average inventory}\\\text{value}\end{array}\right) \times \left(\begin{array}{c}\text{inv. carrying cost}\\\text{as a \% of inv. value}\end{array}\right)$$

$$\left(\begin{array}{c}\text{Carrying cost}\\\text{per year}\end{array}\right) = \left(\begin{array}{c}\text{average inventory}\\\text{in units}\end{array}\right) \times \left(\begin{array}{c}\text{material}\\\text{unit cost}\end{array}\right) \times \left(\begin{array}{c}\text{inv. carrying}\\\text{cost as a \%}\\\text{of inv. value}\end{array}\right)$$

$$CC = \frac{Q}{2} \times C \times I$$

where CC = carrying cost per year for the material in question
Q = order quantity for the material, in units
C = delivered unit cost of the material
I = inventory carrying cost for the material, expressed as a percentage of inventory value

Acquisition Costs

Looking at inventory costs in another light, a different set of indirect materials cost factors emerges. These factors all contribute to the cost of generat-

FIGURE 21-2
Relationship of inventory related costs to inventory level (*AC* = acquisition costs; *CC* = carrying costs).

ing and processing an order and its related paperwork. Examples of these costs are listed below and can be thought of as inventory acquisition costs.

1 *A certain portion of wages and operating expenses* of such departments as purchasing, production control, receiving, inspection, stores, and accounts payable—those departments whose personnel devote time to the generation and handling of the order

2 *The cost of supplies* such as engineering drawings, envelopes, stationery, and forms for purchasing, production control, receiving, accounting, and so forth

3 *The cost of services* such as computer time, telephone, fax machines, telegraph, and postage expended in procuring material

When considering this group of acquisition costs, observe that they behave quite differently from carrying costs. Acquisition costs are not related to inventory size per se; rather, they are a function of the number of orders placed during a given period of time.

One simplified example will illustrate this point. Suppose a buyer in the purchasing department receives a requisition for a special fabricated part used in the manufacture of one of the firm's products. Assume further that the part has been purchased before and that price quotations from three or four shops are on file. The buyer first reviews the present inventory situation and probably checks with production control to see if any significant changes are anticipated in future production. Drawings and specifications of the part are then reviewed to refresh his or her memory regarding required tooling and other technical details of the purchase. Next, the buyer reviews the quotations to determine why the order was placed with supplier A last time. Before deciding if supplier A should again receive the order, the buyer must also review supplier performance data. Finally, the buyer decides which supplier should receive the order and subsequently inquires about the firm's current shop loads and any other matters that have arisen during the investigation. It is entirely possible that a price negotiation session may also be required.

In total, the buyer's investigation may require anywhere from an hour to several days. The total cost of the buyer's time to the company will be the same whether the purchase order is written for 20 parts or 200 parts. This process may result in the development of a term contract with the supplier, in which case the buyer's effort is spread over all purchases of the item for the next year or so. If this is not the case, however, the next time the buyer receives another requisition for this part, he or she will go through somewhat the same process, generating almost the same indirect cost for the company.

The largest segment of the acquisition cost element is made up of these types of indirect labor and overhead costs, generated in purchasing and in the other departments that subsequently become involved in handling some activity associated with the purchase. The cost of supplies and services consumed in the placement and handling of an order typically varies directly with the number of orders placed. While these costs are significant, they are considerably less so than the human and related overhead cost figures just discussed. Although the variable acquisition cost per order varies widely among firms, depending on the specific cost inclusions, today the range appears to run from approximately $40 to $100 per order.

If a firm experiences a certain annual usage of an item, the number of orders placed during the year will decline as the individual order quantity increases, thus generating lower *annual* acquisition costs. The experience of numerous firms over the years reveals that this relationship is not linear, but that it follows the approximate contour of the *AC* curve shown in Figure 21-2.

If a firm's cost accounting department can estimate its approximate acquisition cost *per order*, the *annual* acquisition costs that would be generated by order quantities of various sizes can be calculated as follows:

$$\left(\begin{array}{c} \text{Acquisition} \\ \text{cost per year} \end{array} \right) = \left(\begin{array}{c} \text{number of orders} \\ \text{placed per year} \end{array} \right) \times \left(\begin{array}{c} \text{acquisition cost} \\ \text{per order} \end{array} \right)$$

$$AC = \frac{U}{Q} \times A$$

where AC = acquisition cost per year for the material in question
  U = expected annual usage of the material, in units
  Q = order quantity for the material, in units
  A = acquisition cost per order for the material

Economic Order Quantity Concept (EOQ)

If one has to make decisions about managing an inventory, it is useful to understand the behavior of the inventory-related cost factors just discussed. These factors often help a manager determine which items should or should not be carried in inventory, what inventory levels should be carried for specific items, and what order quantities are appropriate for given items.

The latter part of the chapter discusses several types of systems that can be used in managing an inventory. In each case one of the short-term operating questions that must be answered is: How much of the item should be ordered? Among the factors that often enter this decision process is a concept known as EOQ—the notion of an economic order quantity. As its name suggests, this concept holds that the appropriate quantity to order may be the one that tends to minimize all the costs associated with the order—carrying costs, acquisition costs, and the cost of the material itself.

Concentrating for the moment on the first two costs, Figure 21-2 shows clearly that as the order quantity increases, carrying costs rise—and at the same time acquisition costs decrease. To see the total picture more clearly, if carrying costs and acquisition costs are added together over the order quantity range shown on the graph, the total indirect materials cost curve, *TC*, is produced. This transformation is shown in Figure 21-3. The economic order quantity concept simply says that the sum of all the indirect costs associated with inventory will be minimized on an annual basis if the material, for which the graph is drawn, is ordered consistently in the quantity that corresponds with the low point on the *TC* curve. This is the *economic order quantity*.

Note that the low point on the total cost curve coincides with the point at which the carrying cost curve intersects the acquisition cost curve. This makes it easy to develop the basic formula that can always be used to calculate a material's *basic* EOQ. Recall the two simple cost formulas developed for annual carrying costs and annual acquisition costs on pages 448 and 450. These can now be used to develop the EOQ formula.[3]

EOQ occurs when:

$$\text{Annual carrying cost} = \text{annual acquisition cost}$$

$$CC = AC$$

$$\frac{QCI}{2} = \frac{UA}{Q}$$

Solving for Q:

$$Q^2CI = 2UA$$

$$Q = \sqrt{\frac{2UA}{CI}}$$

This formula, then, is the fundamental mathematical representation of the EOQ concept. It can be modified to accommodate numerous special conditions, but in practice it probably finds its most effective application in this form.

Incremental Costs and Stability   Note that the vertical axis in Figure 21-3 is labeled "annual *incremental* costs." It is appropriate at this point to emphasize the fact that the costs which are relevant in making an EOQ analysis are incremental costs. *Incremental costs are those costs that actually change as a result of a particular operating decision.* For example, if the decision to issue more purchase orders during the year actually increases supply and service costs, these are incremental costs. If it requires the addition of a buyer or clerical person to handle the load, the additional payroll costs are incremental costs. *Incremental costs are either variable costs or opportunity costs* that represent a forgone opportunity to utilize an asset in some other productive way.

---

[3]A more straightforward mathematical solution can be obtained using differential calculus: (1) Write the equation for the total cost curve; (2) differentiate the equation; (3) find the minimum value of the function by setting the derivative equal to 0 and solving for Q.

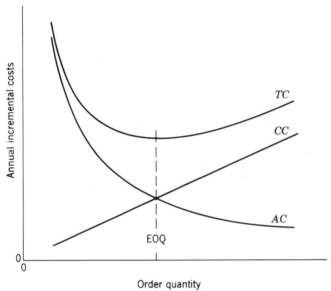

FIGURE 21-3
Graphic representation of the EOQ concept (*AC* = incremental
acquisition costs; *CC* = incremental carrying costs; *TC* = total
incremental costs).

By their very nature, most of the inventory carrying costs discussed are
incremental costs and are reasonably stable. The distinction is less clear when
dealing with inventory acquisition costs. Judgment is usually required in estimating the portion of the human effort that represents a legitimate opportunity cost. In any case, EOQ produces valid results only when the I and A
cost factors are largely incremental, and when the usage and unit cost elements, as well as I and A, are reasonably stable over the operating period.

Material Prices and Quantity Discounts In the discussion of EOQ analysis to this point, it has been assumed that material prices and transportation
costs were constant factors for the range of order quantities considered. In
practice, some situations occur in which the delivered unit cost of a material
decreases significantly if a slightly larger quantity than the originally computed EOQ is purchased. Quantity discounts, freight rate schedules, and
perhaps anticipated price increases may create such situations. These additional variables can also be included in the basic formula, but from a practical
point of view usually they can be handled more easily with a separate simple
calculation.

Using Q computed with the basic formula, such alternative quantity decisions can be made quickly and accurately. By simply comparing annual material cost savings, resulting from the purchase of the additional quantity,
with the additional inventory carrying costs occasioned by the increased pur-

chase, the most economical decision quickly becomes evident. With a limited amount of practice, a buyer can determine in a matter of seconds whether material cost savings exceed carrying costs for the additional inventory.

Other Uses of the EOQ Concept

A final word should be said about *general* usage of the EOQ concept. Even though our discussion has been set entirely in the purchasing environment, the EOQ concept logically has broader application as well.

A very common situation in which the concept is used is the determination of economic production lot sizes in a manufacturing operation. Consider the formula a moment ($Q = \sqrt{2UA/IC}$), and look at the individual factors in light of both the purchasing and the production operations. In converting the formula for production use, the annual usage and carrying cost factors are the same as they were in the purchasing application. The unit cost factor, however, is no longer delivered price; instead, it consists of direct labor and materials and production overhead costs. Production acquisition cost is similar to purchasing acquisition cost, except that production setup cost replaces most of the purchasing and related departmental wage and operating costs.

Buyers should also consider (from a supplier's point of view) the formula in this form when determining lot sizes on term contract purchase orders going to various types of job shop suppliers. A supplier's costs and subsequent product price are obviously influenced by the size and frequency of such orders.

TYPES OF INVENTORY CONTROL SYSTEMS

To this point in the discussion, we have considered background concepts that are useful in formulating fundamental aspects of the plans to manage inventories. The discussion now turns to the specific operating systems that can be used.

Generally speaking, there are four types of inventory control systems in use: (1) the cyclical or fixed order interval system, (2) the JIT approach, (3) the MRP-type system, and (4) the order point or fixed order quantity system. Each system monitors and controls inventory levels. And each system, based on its own unique characteristics, provides the inventory manager with information that helps answer the two basic questions of *when* to order and *how much* to order.

Cyclical or Fixed Order Interval System

The cyclical system, or fixed order interval system as it is sometimes called, is the oldest and simplest of the systems now found in use. Years ago, when most businesses were small and uncomplicated, this control system was used in all types of operations—manufacturing, service, wholesale, and retail. With the exception of one variation called "flow control," the cyclical system is not widely used today except in smaller and medium-size operations.

Operationally, the system works like this. It is a *time-based* operation which involves *scheduled periodic reviews* of the stock level of all inventory items. Looking at it in a manufacturing setting, when the stock level of a given item is not sufficient to sustain the production operation until the next scheduled review, an order is placed to replenish the supply. The frequency of reviews is determined judgmentally and varies with the degree of control desired by management; *A* items might be reviewed weekly (or more often), *B* items monthly or bimonthly, and *C* items quarterly or semiannually.

Stock levels can be monitored by physical inspection, by visual review of perpetual inventory record cards, or by automatic computer surveillance. In most operations, a perpetual inventory record is maintained,[4] either by computer or manually, except in simple flow-controlled shops (which will be examined shortly). As is discussed in the next chapter dealing with warehousing operations, physical stock counts are required once or twice a year to reconcile actual values with book values in all systems utilizing perpetual inventory records.

The first operating question—*when to order*—is answered or controlled by the review dates established by the inventory manager. If material usage has remained reasonably stable, an order (or a release against an order) is usually placed each time the item is reviewed.

The order date decision is also impacted by the quantity previously ordered, so let us consider the second question also—*how much should be ordered?* The quantity to be ordered generally is determined by three factors: the number of days between reviews, the anticipated daily usage during the cycle period, and the quantity actually on hand and on order at the time of the review. One of the primary reasons this system is used is to control high-value items closely and to maintain a relatively low investment in inventory. Hence, the order quantity typically is the quantity required to cover only the ensuing period, with allowance for order lead time. Occasionally a two- or three-period supply is ordered, but not as a rule.

Consequently, as its name implies, the system works in cyclical fashion, with an order typically placed at each review date for a quantity large enough to cover the ensuing cycle plus the order lead time. A small safety stock is generally carried, based on the observed lead time variability. Inventory levels and tightness of control are thus determined by the establishment of the period of the cycle. High-value *A* and *B* items typically are placed on short cycles and *C* items on longer cycles.

This system can be used with both dependent demand and independent demand materials. It works most effectively in an organization that has a

---

[4]A perpetual inventory record for a material controlled in a closed stores system is maintained simply by posting receipts from invoices or receiving reports and disbursements from stores material requisitions or similar withdrawal authorizations. In most firms today, perpetual records are computer-based.

continuous operations function, manufacturing or service, in which demand is fairly stable and can be predicted with reasonable accuracy. Additionally, it is probably the most efficient system to use for independent demand items that experience irregular or seasonal demand and for any items whose purchases must be planned months in advance because of infrequent supplier production schedules. In these cases it tends to keep inventory levels lower than would be possible with the other applicable systems. When used for materials with these characteristics, however, the system must be augmented with a minimum balance figure which signals the need for an early reorder in the case of a sharp usage increase.

To conclude, the cyclical system finds its greatest usage in organizations that have large numbers of independent demand items to control, or in relatively simple process operations where dependent item demand can be projected easily from the production schedule. When used for dependent demand items in an intermittent manufacturing operation, it becomes difficult to determine cycle period demands if many products are involved or if individual items are used in several different products. The bill of materials explosion and time-phasing capabilities of an MRP system must all be handled manually in the cyclical system. As product complexity increases this becomes a virtual impossibility, so historical demand data tends to become the basis for order quantity determination—and this soon leads to unreasonably high inventory levels because of the uncertainties associated with near-term demand. For these reasons, MRP systems have replaced most cyclical systems in intermittent manufacturing operations.

Flow Control System   The "flow control" method of managing inventories is a special variation of the cyclical system. This special method is applicable in continuous manufacturing operations that produce the same basic product in large quantities day after day. Most materials used in such an operation are purchased on term contracts and scheduled for daily or weekly delivery throughout the term. The production cycle is often a day or less in duration, and, in effect, material flows through the plant in continuous streams. Inventory floats consequently can be kept quite low, thus requiring a minimum investment in production inventory.

In such an operation, an open stores system is used for most production materials, and the individual items are stored on the line near the point of use. Stores personnel visually review the level of all material stocks daily and report any imbalances to the purchasing or production control department. Changes in production schedules must be relayed immediately to buyers so that delivery schedules can be revised accordingly.

The Just-in-Time (JIT) Approach

The just-in-time concept was explored in detail in the preceding chapter. It was pointed out there that in total, JIT is an operating management philosophy. Based on that philosophy, a number of specific operating techniques have been developed—techniques for manufacturing operations, for production planning, and for inventory management. Those dealing with inventory management are the products of the JIT decisions made in the manufacturing and the planning areas.

The operating concept of the system is to gear factory output tightly to distribution demand for finished goods, to gear individual feeder production units tightly together, and to gear the supply of production inventories tightly to the manufacturing demand schedule. This means that all inventories in the system, including production inventories, are maintained at absolutely minimal levels.

It should be emphasized at the outset, however, that as a practical matter most firms utilizing the JIT concept do so for no more than 5 to 10 percent of the materials handled by the purchasing activity, regardless of the extent of the commitment in the manufacturing operation. This means that the production inventory items handled in the JIT inventory system are primarily high-value *A* items. All these items are purchased on a long-term contractual basis, with small-volume deliveries scheduled as frequently as once or twice a day up to once or twice a week.

If one were to observe a JIT operation strictly from an inventory point of view, it would look very much like a flow control operation, with material flowing into and through the plant operation in continuous streams. In fact, it functions much like a flow control operation, only more tightly and more stringently controlled. From strictly an inventory point of view, the systems have almost identical objectives. Many JIT materials are delivered directly to the production operation and are stored close to the point of use; others are handled in a conventional closed stores operation.

From a practical point of view, a JIT inventory system is workable only in continuous manufacturing and processing operations or in intermittent operations that produce a small number of standard products and, because of this fact, are similar to continuous operations. Most, if not all, of the materials handled are dependent demand items.

How are the *when* and *how much* questions answered? As discussed in the preceding chapter, the buyer and the supplier work together closely on the matters of delivery volumes and scheduling. The buying firm's production schedule drives the entire process. The detailed production schedule typically is firmed up for one or two weeks at a time, and in more general terms for a month or so ahead. Specific daily requirements for JIT materials can be determined from this schedule and are relayed directly to the contracting supplier. The exact size and frequency of each delivery is worked out jointly in an attempt to minimize the buyer's incremental inventory-related costs and, at the same time, to maintain an efficient and practical operation for the supplier. As a general rule, the buyer does not identify a specific safety stock component in the firm's inventory figure. Depending on the material, the buying firm typically works on an inventory of several days' to a week's supply. As is the case in a flow control system, stores personnel on the shop floor visually monitor stock levels at least daily and communicate potential overage or shortage problems to the appropriate buyer.

To this point, our discussion has covered only the 5 to 10 percent of a firm's production materials that typically are handled by its JIT purchasing and inventory management system. What about the remaining 90 to 95 percent of the items? As a rule, they are handled in the more conventional manner by one of the other standard systems—namely an MRP or an order point system.

Material Requirements Planning (MRP) System

The preceding chapter, "Production Planning," detailed how closed loop MRP systems function as complete production planning and control systems. The material requirements planning module is an integral part of such a system. Through its bill of materials explosion and aggregation process, this element of the system generates on a weekly basis the projected materials requirements for all the finished products included in a firm's updated master production schedule for the coming two- to three-month period.

Taking the projected gross requirements for a given material during the planning period, the logic of the MRP module then calculates the net requirements by subtracting on-hand inventory and any scheduled receipts of the item as production is scheduled to progress through the planning period. This produces a "time-phased" purchase order requirement to be released at a calculated future date. (The reader may wish to review this logic by referring to Figure 20-3 on page 424.)

The inventory that is carried in the system is a function of three factors: (1) the quantity purchased when each order is placed, (2) the purchase lead time specified by the buyer, and (3) any safety stock that is routinely carried. The objective of time phasing the order point is to keep the inventory as close to zero as is practical until the material is actually needed for production. Consequently, using an MRP system, the average inventory levels of most materials are relatively low over the long term.

In the case of some materials, no safety stock is carried. In other cases a one- to two-week supply may be carried as a hedge against uncertainties such as possible fluctuations in demand, variations in supplier lead time requirements, or anticipated scrap or reject rates. Variations in supplier lead time requirements also may be covered by simply extending the lead time figure used in calculating the order release date; in this case safety stock would be reduced correspondingly. These safety stock and lead time hedge values typically are determined judgmentally on the basis of past experience with specific materials and suppliers.

The *when to order* question, then, is answered by the logic of the system. Deciding *how much to order* is in part a judgmental issue. The most common approach, as was the case in the cyclical system, is to order the quantity required during the planning period—the "lot for lot" approach. This method typically tends to minimize the inventory in the system. At times, however, the lot-for-lot approach may produce an order quantity that is too small to be economical. Because of high acquisition costs or production setup costs, order size may have to be larger. In this case, the EOQ or a related least-cost calculation is frequently used to obtain a more appropriate order quantity figure. A number of other decision rules are sometimes used, but those just mentioned appear to be the most common.

The MRP system is designed for use with dependent demand items—that is, production materials. The only way it can handle an independent demand item is by tying such an item's use into a product bill of materials. For production tools and certain other MRO supplies, it is sometimes possible to do this in an approximate way by estimation. But the system's most important use, by far, is with dependent demand materials in an intermittent manufacturing operation. An MRP system can be adapted for use in a continuous or a processing-type operation, but it does not fit such operations well and usually it offers few significant advantages over the other types of systems.

Order Point or Fixed Order Quantity System

The order point system, historically known as the *fixed order quantity system,* is another inventory control system that has been used for years in this country by both manufacturing and nonmanufacturing organizations. The system recognizes the fact that each item has its own unique optimum order quantity, and it is therefore based on *order point* and *order quantity* factors, rather than on the time factor.

Operation of an order point system requires two things for each inventory item:

1 The *predetermination of an order point,* so that when the stock level on hand drops to the order point, the item is automatically "flagged" for reorder purposes. The order point is computed so that estimated usage of the item during the order lead time period will cause the actual stock level to fall to a planned minimum level by the time the new order is received. Receipt of the new order then increases the stock level to a preplanned maximum figure.
2 The *predetermination of a fixed quantity to be ordered* each time the supply of the item is replenished. This determination typically is based on considerations of price, rate of usage, and other pertinent production and administrative factors.

The automatic feature of the system is achieved by maintaining a perpetual inventory record for each item. The computer, or an inventory clerk in the case of a manual system, continues to post all material issues until the balance of an item falls to its order point. At this point the system notifies the appropriate buyer, who replenishes the stock in a quantity that takes the inventory to its planned maximum level. During the course of operation, the ongoing inventory level is thus maintained between the planned minimum and maximum values.

The predetermined order point, then, tells the buyer *when* to order. In most organizations the order point is determined in the following manner: First, basic operating data about demand and lead time must be obtained. Next, a decision must be made about the desired service level. For most materials, most firms target for 100 percent—that is, they don't want to run out of stock before the new order arrives. At this point in the discussion, the process can be described most easily with the use of a simple illustration. Suppose the following data have been determined for a given inventory item:

Purchasing lead time = 1 week (very stable; little chance of variation)

Material usage = 50 units per week, with ±10 percent variation
over the long run

So: Maximum usage during lead time = 55 units
Average usage during lead time = 50 units
Minimum usage during lead time = 45 units

Figure 21-4*a* shows a simplified, or idealistic, inventory movement pattern for the material in question, with the usage rate constant at the maximum level of 55 units per week. Now, if the buyer does not want to run out of stock, at what inventory level should the new order be placed? If lead time is known to be one week, and the *maximum* usage has been determined to be 55 units per week, the new order clearly should be placed when the stock level falls to 55 units. Under these conditions, the new order will arrive just when the stock level reaches zero. So—the order point is 55 units.

Now, what happens when the usage rate runs around 50 units per week, as it does much of the time? The inventory movement pattern shown in Figure 21-4*a* then becomes the dashed sawtooth pattern shown in Figure 21-4*b*. With an order point of 55 units, as long as the *average* usage rate of 50 units per week prevails, the new order will arrive when 5 units (55−50=5) are still left in stock. This brings us to the definition of safety stock. In an order point system, set up as just described, *safety stock* is normally defined as *the maximum lead time usage minus the average lead time usage.* In this case, then, the order point is 55 units and the basic safety stock is 5 units.

In operation, over a period of time, this means that the low point of the inventory pattern sawtooth will occasionally fall to 0 as the new order arrives (55−55=0); and when usage is at its lightest, the low point of the sawtooth will be as high as 10 units when the new order arrives (55−45=10). Most of the time, the low point of the sawtooth will fluctuate between these two extremes, with occurrences concentrated around the

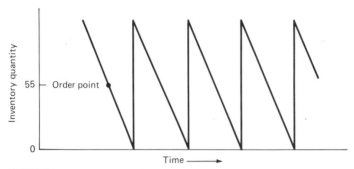

FIGURE 21-4a
Illustrative simplified inventory movement pattern for a given material,
with a maximum usage rate.

FIGURE 21-4b
Preceding movement pattern with an average usage rate, showing
safety stock determination.

safety stock value of 5, which is also defined as the *theoretical* planned minimum. Figure 21-5 depicts this situation hypothetically.

Now that the question of *when* to order has been answered, how does the buyer determine *how much* to order? Any number of decision rules can be used, but the most common approach is to determine the EOQ value. A fixed order quantity system is a natural for EOQ application. The EOQ value can be calculated automatically almost instantaneously with a computer-based order point program. In a manual system, tables of EOQ values can be precalculated and prepared for the near-instantaneous use of inventory clerks. Nomographs and preprogrammed hand-held calculators can also be used easily and quickly. More general decision rules sometimes used by experienced managers are to order a one- to four-week supply of A items, a one- to two-month supply of B items, and a four- to six-month supply of C items.

The major advantages of an order point system are: (1) unlike the cyclical and the JIT approaches, the EOQ concept can be applied easily in this system, so each material can be procured in the most economical quantity; (2) this preplanned approach utilizes the time and efforts of people efficiently—

FIGURE 21-5
Typical inventory movement pattern for a reasonably stable material, with a fixed order quantity.

purchasing and inventory control personnel automatically devote attention to a given item *only when the item requires attention;* and (3) within limits, control can easily be exerted to maintain inventory investment at a target level simply by varying the planned maximum and minimum values.

On the other side of the coin, the system also has some serious limitations.

- The most serious problem in using an order point system stems from the fact that it works on the basis of historical rather than actual demand data. Therefore, the order point cannot be time-phased to correspond with actual demand requirements. This means that over the long term, an order point system almost always produces a higher average inventory level than would a comparable MRP system.
- The system functions correctly only if each of the materials exhibits reasonably stable usage and lead time characteristics. When these factors change significantly, a new order point and a new order quantity must be determined if the system is to fulfill its objectives. Consequently, although it can be adapted, the system becomes costly and cumbersome to operate effectively when applied to materials with highly unstable demand and lead time patterns.

Bearing in mind the advantages and disadvantages just discussed, it is appropriate to note that an order point system can be used equally well with both independent and dependent demand items. In a *dependent demand* manufacturing environment, a time-phased MRP system is far superior to an order point system because of its use of actual demand data and its ability to maintain average inventories at significantly lower levels. However, if it is not practical to use MRP for low-value *C* items, an order point system can be used very effectively, and the increased inventory levels will affect total costs very little. In managing *independent demand* inventories, a well-designed order point system has no peer—it works extremely well.

As pointed out earlier, an order point system is versatile—it can be used in any type of operation from manufacturing to service. For school districts, hospitals, banks, and numerous other service-oriented institutions, virtually all inventory items exhibit independent demand characteristics. And, as one would suspect, order point systems are used in a vast majority of these types of operations.

Two-Bin System   A variation of the basic order point system is found in the operation of the simple two-bin system. The distinguishing feature of this system is the absence of a perpetual inventory record. In practice, the stock is physically separated into two bins, or containers. The lower bin contains a quantity of stock equal to the order point figure. This, typically, is just enough stock (or slightly more) to last from the date a new order is placed until the incoming material is received in inventory. The upper bin contains a quantity of stock equal to the difference between the maximum and the order point figures. At the outset, stock is used from the upper bin; when this supply is depleted, it signals the clerk that the order point has been reached. At this point an order is placed, and material is used from the lower bin until the new stock is received. Upon receipt of the new order, the proper quantities of material are again placed in the two bins.

This method demonstrates very simply the fundamental concept which underlies the basic order point system.

The two-bin method is widely used in all types of operations in handling low-value hardware and supplies whose usage is not recorded on a perpetual record. The major advantage of the method is the obvious reduction of clerical work. Issues do not have to be posted to determine the proper reorder time. Receipts, however, are usually posted to reveal significant changes in usage or lead time. A possible disadvantage of the system in some cases is the requirement of additional storage facilities and perhaps some practical difficulty in keeping the two stocks properly separated.

To generalize, it should be pointed out that none of the systems or their adaptations discussed in this chapter are mutually exclusive. *Several or all of them may be used advantageously for different materials in a single firm.*

SYNTHESIS AND CONCLUSION

Production planning and inventory management activities for the past five years or so have been in a significant state of change. New and evolving systems have spawned new and increasingly sophisticated planning and control capabilities. In some cases, the more traditional inventory control systems have been replaced for certain types of applications—in other cases they have not. Table 21-1 draws together in summary form the most significant applications features of the various systems in use today.

It is becoming increasingly difficult for most firms to control inventories effectively. A major reason for this is that more and more components going into the typical firm's products are being *purchased* as fabricated parts, rather

TABLE 21-1
COMPARISON OF INVENTORY CONTROL SYSTEMS, CHARACTERISTICS AND APPLICATIONS

Type of System/ Characteristics	Order point	Cyclical	MRP	Flow control	JIT
Maintains low inventory level	fair	fair/good	good/excellent	excellent	excellent
Application to items, type of demand	all types; particularly good for independent demand	all types	primarily dependent demand	primarily dependent demand	dependent demand
Application to type of operations	all types of manufacturing operations; particularly good for service operations	all manufacturing operations; service operations	primarily intermittent manufacturing operations, with great product variety	continuous manufacturing operations, with little product variety	continuous manufacturing, with moderate product variety
Demand data used	historical	• actual in simple operations • historical in complex operations	actual	actual	actual
Time-phased order point?	no	• yes in simple operations • no in complex operations	yes	yes	yes
Computer required?	optional	optional	yes	optional	optional
Bill of materials explosion/aggregation capability	no	no	yes	yes	yes
Administrative effort required	minimal	moderate	moderate	heavy	heavy

than being produced in the firm's own shops. This means that the number of inventory items to be managed is constantly growing. And because of the increasingly technical nature of materials today, the number of dollars that may be invested in inventory is growing at an even faster rate than the number of items.

In its daily operation, inventory control should be largely a series of clerical or computerized activities, carried on within a carefully defined and controlled framework. The routinization of the daily operation, however, often camouflages the importance of sound management in this area.

At this point in the discussion, there should be little doubt that the basic responsibility for inventory control should lie with top management. The effects of poor inventory management, unfortunately, are not directly visible on the operating statement as a composite cost of inventory management. Nevertheless, in most organizations these indirect costs, dispersed and hidden throughout the operating statement, can have a significant impact on profit. For this reason, top management should carefully formulate and periodically review the basic policies and operating plans that constitute the framework within which the daily inventory control operation functions.

FOR DISCUSSION

21-1 What function do inventories serve in a manufacturing concern? Discuss both the advantages and disadvantages.

21-2 Managers and firms that promote the use of the JIT concept state in no uncertain terms that "inventories are evil." What is your view of this statement? How does the statement relate to your answer to the preceding question?

21-3 Detail in step-by-step form how you would conduct an ABC analysis of an inventory. As a materials manager in an organization, discuss how you would utilize the results of the ABC analysis.

21-4 Discuss briefly the major features of the cyclical ordering system. What are the primary advantages and disadvantages of the system?

21-5 What is a flow control system? Under what conditions might you consider the use of a flow control inventory management system? What are the advantages and disadvantages in using such a system?

21-6 How does a flow control system differ from a JIT inventory control system? Discuss.

21-7 Explain briefly how the order point system operates. From an operating point of view, what are the major advantages and disadvantages of using an order point system?

21-8 Compare and contrast the use of an order point system with the use of an MRP system.

21-9 Explain how an MRP system operates. How is an MRP system able to keep inventory levels relatively low?

21-10 Under what operating conditions can an MRP system be utilized most effectively?

21-11 What is the economic order quantity concept? Explain the theory underlying the concept.

21-12 Explain what is meant by the terms "inventory carrying costs" and "inventory acquisition costs."

21-13 In making an EOQ calculation, the text states that all costs included should be "incremental costs." Why? Discuss. Define an incremental cost.

21-14 What is "opportunity cost," and why should it be included as an inventory carrying cost?

21-15 Can the economic order quantity approach be used just as easily with all four basic control systems (cyclical, JIT, MRP, and order point)? Explain.

21-16 What is the difference between a dependent demand and an independent demand inventory item?

21-17 How might quantity discounts be considered in making an EOQ computation in practice? Explain.

21-18 In determining a firm's incremental acquisition cost per purchase order, should the salary of the purchasing manager and the senior buyers be included? Explain.

21-19 What is meant by a time-phased order point? Explain.

21-20 Assume that you have just been hired to develop an inventory system for a company which in the past has given little attention to the management of inventories. Prepare an outline of the approach you would use in attempting to carry out this assignment. Discuss each point on your outline in some detail, indicating the information you would need, the problems you would expect to encounter, and any other pertinent factors management would be interested in when evaluating your approach to the problem.

21-21 In an order point system, how is safety stock determined?

21-22 Referring to the example on page 459, what would the order point and safety stock values be if the lead time figure were 1 week ±20 percent?

21-23 List and discuss the chief limitations of EOQ theory.

CASES FOR CHAPTER 21

22

STORES AND RECEIVING

KEY CONCEPTS

- Responsibilities of receiving and stores
- Receiving procedures and control
- Bar coding
- Identification of materials
- Stores systems and procedures
    - Closed system
    - Open system
    - Random-access storage system
- Storing of materials
    - Methods and equipment
    - Automated storage and retrieval system
    - Layout
- Organization

Receiving and storage are important flow control activities in the materials management chain. Regardless of the efficiency with which all preceding materials activities have been conducted, receiving and stores determine the extent to which the operating units will be supplied satisfactorily.

Because the purchasing department is normally responsible for materials until they are ready for use, it is essential that purchasing managers understand the fundamentals of receiving and stores operations. Additionally, in a majority of U.S. industrial and institutional organizations, receiving and stores departments are either placed under the jurisdiction of the purchasing department or grouped with purchasing and related activities in a materials management department.[1] Whether a firm adopts the materials management concept extensively or not, receiving and stores are a vital element in its total materials system. Effective coordination with the purchasing, inventory management, and traffic functions is imperative.

RESPONSIBILITIES OF RECEIVING AND STORES

Receiving and stores operations provide both service and control functions. First, they organize and control the flow of materials into the production operation. Second, the stores organization acts as a custodial and controlling agency. It is responsible for the safety and physical control of a substantial portion of a firm's current assets. And, finally, the existence of a stores operation permits quantity buying and the attendant savings in price, paperwork, and handling.

Specific Responsibilities

The receiving department is responsible for the receipt, identification, and general inspection of all incoming materials. It also notifies the interested individuals of the arrival and condition of the material.

Subsequently, the stores department is responsible for appropriate physical storage of all production materials, some in-process inventory, and most MRO items. In some firms, stores also handles finished goods storage.

The stores manager must develop a system for classifying, marking, and locating all materials so they are readily accessible and, at the same time, protect them against pilferage, unauthorized usage, and unnecessary damage or deterioration. In a closed system, the department must also control physical issuance of material and provide effective service for the operating units.

Cost Implications

Receiving and stores activities *indirectly* influence product costs in several ways. Inventory carrying costs stemming from deterioration, damage, and pilferage of materials, as well as related indirect labor costs, are controllable to a great extent by these managers. Additionally, an alert stores organization can help reduce costs of obsolescence by developing systems to detect slow-moving and inactive materials. Efficient use of scarce storage space can also reduce costs.

---

[1] Harold F. Fearon, *Purchasing Organizational Relationships*, NAPM Inc., Tempe, Ariz. 1988, p. 36.

At the same time, a stores operation typically impacts a firm's *direct* labor costs. Strategically located storage facilities that provide prompt service for operating personnel help reduce the unproductive time of these people. Individuals and machines waiting for the delivery of material add nothing to the productive effort of the organization.

RECEIVING OF MATERIALS

Receiving is essentially a clerical operation. Because many clerical activities are regarded as "routine," however, the importance of the receiving function often is underrated. Only at the receiving desk do the purchasing control documents meet the physical materials themselves. Most problems or errors in a purchasing transaction should come to light during the receiving operation. If the problem (quantity shortage, damaged materials, wrong items shipped, and so on) is not detected and corrected during the receiving operation, the cost to correct the mistake later is always higher. For example, if a shortage is not discovered at the time of receipt, any combination of departments can be drawn into the problem later. Hours are frequently spent trying to determine what "really happened"—and then in rectifying the situation. Thus, hours are required to correct an error that could have been corrected at the receiving desk in minutes.

The *receiving report,* completed upon receipt of a shipment, is the only document a firm has that details the material it actually received. It also contains important supplier information—delivery timing, shipment damage, reject percentage, split shipments, and so on. This document is used as the basis for invoice payment, for continued purchasing negotiation, and for closing the order. Accuracy is therefore essential. Clearly, poor receiving performance can produce costly consequences. For this reason, receiving should be supervised by a person who is reasonably familiar with the physical characteristics of the materials and who is capable of exercising sound judgment in situations where a choice of alternatives must be made.

Receiving Procedure

A typical receiving procedure consists of four steps:

1 *Unloading and checking the shipment.* The number of containers unloaded from the carrier's vehicle is checked against the carrier's manifest (freight bill) to make certain the full consignment has been delivered. All containers are also inspected for external damage; any damage found is inspected by the carrier's representative and noted on the receipt which the receiving clerk signs. Failure to follow this procedure before accepting a shipment can relieve the carrier of all liability, except liability for concealed damage not evident until the container is unpacked.

2 *Unpacking and inspecting the material.* A receiving clerk is held responsible for three verifications. First, he or she checks the material received

against the seller's packing slip and against a copy of the firm's purchase order to verify that the correct items have been shipped. Second, the quantity of the shipment is verified in the same manner. Finally, the clerk inspects the general condition of the material to determine whether any external damage was incurred during shipment.

3 *Completion of the receiving report.* The paperwork system used varies significantly from firm to firm. In some companies a multipart receiving report form is produced as a by-product when the purchase order is generated. When the receiving clerk has finished the inspection, he or she completes this form by recording the quantities of the items received, indicating those that are still open, and noting any other useful information on the form. In other firms that utilize a computerized purchasing/inventory system, the clerk records the receiving data on the receiving report or a short form, from which a data entry clerk keys the data directly into the computer system. The system then updates the order and inventory records and may also generate a receiving report in either hard copy or electronic form.

Regardless of the system used, four operating groups generally require notification that the material has been received: the requisitioner, the purchasing department, the accounting department, and the inspection department if technical inspection is required.

4 *Delivery of the material.* For non-stock materials, the receiving department is usually responsible for delivery—directly or via an internal delivery service. In the case of inventory materials, the practice varies. In some firms the receiving department is responsible for internal deliveries, while in others this function is performed by an internal transportation service. In still others, stores clerks are responsible for picking up their own materials.

Upon delivery of the materials, the recipient customarily signs the receiving report or a delivery receipt, relieving the receiving clerk of further responsibility for the material.

Bar Coding

Anyone who has shopped in a supermarket knows that bar coding is used extensively for product identification in the wholesale and retail food business. Only in recent years, however, has industry used it to any significant extent. Today approximately 20 percent of the country's industrial firms use it in their receiving, inventory control, or work-in-process tracking operations.[2] Although the use of bar coding is still limited in most industrial operations, it is growing. Hence, it is appropriate to introduce the concept briefly at this point in the discussion.

[2] E. J. Walter, "Bar Code Boom Extending through Industry," *Purchasing World,* February 1988, p. 39.

"In its briefest form, a bar code label is simply a unique license plate. This license plate accesses a data file containing information about the labeled object."[3] The size and arrangement of the solid bars and spaces on the label represent the object's part or product number in coded form. When read with a laser scanner, the bars and spaces reflect a light pattern that is converted into electrical pulses that a computer decodes and uses to access the part number's file in its memory.

More than a dozen bar code symbologies are in use today, with four predominating: (1) Code 39, (2) Interleaved Two-of-Five, (3) Universal Product Code, and (4) Codabar. The Interleaved Two-of-Five code is most commonly used in industrial stores and inventory operations, and the Universal Product Code is the standard used in the grocery business. Figure 22-1 provides a sample of each.

If incoming materials shipments are bar coded, the receiving operation in a computer-based purchasing/inventory system can be refined beyond the one just described. The step in the process at which receiving data are entered into the computer system can usually be simplified. The data entry clerk now can access the item's inventory record[4] simply by scanning the bar code, rather than keying the information in manually. This improves both the speed and the accuracy of the operation immensely. If material can be packaged and recorded in standard quantities, the total operation can be refined even more. Some purchasers arrange to have suppliers apply the bar code label to the material or its container before shipment. Others apply their own preprinted labels at the receiving desk, and some generate the labels by computer as the material is being received.

Depending on the nature of a given firm's receiving activities and the design of its computer information system, the potential for improvement of productivity and accuracy can be substantial through development and use of an appropriate bar coding operation.

IDENTIFICATION OF MATERIALS

Stores operations involve the physical aspects of materials handling and storage. From a management perspective, however, the stores manager and the materials manager are concerned first with the design and control of the systems utilized in conducting stores activities. Developing a system for effective identification of materials carried in stores is a major responsibility confronting these managers.

[3] David C. Allais, "Code 49—What Is It? Why Do We Need It?", *Purchasing World*, February 1988, p. 40.
[4] If the original purchase order is also bar coded, the order can be accessed in the open order file as well. Some firms do this to facilitate tracking of the order through the procurement cycle. See Caroline Reich, "Putting Bar Codes to Work," *Purchasing World*, August 1987, pp. 57–61.

Universal
product code

Interleaved
two of five

FIGURE 22-1
An illustration of two commonly used bar codes.

A firm's stock catalog, prepared by the inventory management group, lists and describes every item normally carried in inventory. These descriptions, however, usually are somewhat imprecise and awkward for use in identifying materials during daily operations. Although all standard purchased items can be identified by suppliers' part numbers, different suppliers use vastly different numbering systems. This makes it virtually impossible for a purchaser to develop a satisfactory material identification system based on suppliers' part numbers. Consequently, a firm with a sizable production and MRO inventory is compelled to develop its own numerical identification system for its materials. When the system is complete, the inventory catalog often is arranged and indexed by the *purchaser's own* part numbers, and includes a reference to the supplier's part number for each purchased item. Although the catalog can be cross-indexed in various ways, at a minimum it should be cross-indexed by generic name of the items and perhaps also by suppliers and their part number.

The objective is to develop an unambiguous identification system that facilitates clear internal communication. Ideally, this system should be designed so that it can be used effectively by all departments in the firm. Clearly, the purchasing, inventory control, and stores departments are critical areas where the system must provide consistent and unambiguous identification of materials. If the system can also be integrated with the operations of design engineering, production, and cost accounting, improved communication and simplified clerical activities are almost certain to result.

System Design

Three basic approaches may be used in developing an identification system: (1) the arbitrary approach, (2) the symbolic approach, and (3) the use of engineering drawing numbers. Using the *arbitrary approach,* inventory items are simply assigned arbitrary numbers in sequence as they are added to a stores account. Each item thus has a discrete number, but it bears no systematic relationship to the numbers assigned to related items. For example, two similar pumps or two mating parts may have numbers several thousand digits apart. While this system is used by some firms, if time is to be spent developing a system, a more useful one can be developed with a little extra effort.

The *symbolic approach* to system design is commonly used in American industry. Symbolic systems can be either *numerical* or *mnemonic.* A numerical system assigns a six- to ten-digit code number to each item. The first several numbers usually indicate the classification to which the item belongs, the next several numbers typically indicate the subclass, and the last three numbers are usually uncoded. The following example illustrates the concept:

2	137	019	508
General Class	Generic Class	Subclass	Specific Item Number

This ten-digit code number is one firm's stock number for a ¼- by ¾-inch stainless steel square-neck carriage bolt. The first digit indicates that the item is a purchased part, in accordance with the following general classification:

1 Raw materials
2 Purchased parts
3 Manufactured parts
4 Work in process
5 MRO supplies

The next three digits indicate the generic classification of the item. In this case it is a fastener, code number 137; it might have been a bearing, a pulley, a pump, or an electric motor. All items are generically classified by their nature and carry a number from 000 to 999.

The next three digits indicate the subclass to which the item belongs. In this case, number 019 is a carriage bolt with a square neck. It might have been a machine screw, a rivet, or a nut. All fasteners are subclassified into a class bearing a number from 000 to 999.

The last three digits indicate the specific part number of the item. In this case, all part numbers under 500 designate plain steel, and numbers over 500 represent various alloys; 508 is stainless steel, ¼ by ¾ inch. Other dimensional details can be determined only by referring to the inventory catalog.

This example and similar systems provide a complete and ordered framework within which all materials can be identified uniquely. As a rule, each company devises its own specific system to suit the needs of its own particular materials. A ten-digit number is long and cumbersome; a six-digit system is much easier to use if it provides adequate definition and contains enough unused numbers to accommodate future growth. A few companies structure their systems around finished products rather than generic classification. The subdivision distinctions can be made as fine or as broad as desired. A major factor to consider in these decisions is the value the additional system refinement provides the user.

A mnemonic system functions much like a numerical system. However, it combines numeric and alphabetic notations in its symbols. For example, the preceding carriage bolt might be described this way in a mnemonic system:

P Fa BCS 508

P denotes a purchased part; Fa is a fastener; BCS stands for bolt, carriage, with a square neck; and 508 represents the specific number of the bolt.

Mnemonic systems, particularly where a small number of items are involved, frequently make visual identification easier because they are more descriptive and are often shorter. As more and different types of items are added to the inventory, however, this advantage diminishes because the number of good symbols is limited. Telephone companies encountered this coding problem some years ago. As a result, most have converted telephone calling codes from mnemonic to numeric.

Some firms identify the stock parts manufactured to their own engineering specifications by using the *engineering drawing number* as the part number. This system is effective because it is simple and it directly references the technical data source for the part. Moreover, it simplifies interdepartmental communications because all departments can easily use the same system. On the other hand, the system has the nonsequencing disadvantages of the arbitrary system, and since it covers primarily manufactured parts, a separate system must be devised for many purchased parts.

Physical Identification

Even though a satisfactory identification system is developed, physical identification of materials in the storeroom may still be a problem. The first step in minimizing this problem is to record the storage location of all items in the inventory catalog. When a storeroom is properly laid out, every storage location has a numerical designation. Using a conventional system (non-random-access), each inventory item should be assigned a specific storage location. These locations can be noted in the catalog or in a separate storage locator index so that anyone can locate any material with ease.

Each storage bin should be labeled with its part number. In some cases, an abbreviated description of the item may be helpful. All items that are not readily identifiable on sight should be tagged or marked with the part number by the storekeeper. On nonstandard items, suppliers can frequently mark an item during the manufacturing or shipping operation. Castings, stampings, and forgings are good examples of items that can be marked permanently for little or no extra cost. Some materials, such as steel plate, bars, special bolts, and so on, are difficult to mark, but intercompany groups have made good progress in standardizing identification markings for such materials. One scheme involves the use of a standard color code; the ends or edges of the material are simply marked with the appropriate color to facilitate quick identification.

STORES SYSTEMS

Two basic systems can be used in physically controlling stores materials: (1) a closed stores system and (2) an open stores system. The application of each depends on the nature and requirements of a specific production operation. As a general rule, most firms use one system for certain materials and the second system for others.

Closed System

As its name indicates, a *closed stores system* is one in which all materials are physically stored in a closed or controlled area. Wherever possible, the general practice is to maintain physical control by locking the storage area. As a rule, no one other than stores personnel is permitted in the stores area. Material enters and leaves the area only with the accompaniment of an authorizing document. This system is designed to afford maximum physical security and to ensure tight accounting control of inventory material.

Records In years past, each storekeeper was responsible for maintaining an inventory record for each of the items under his or her control. All receipts and withdrawals were posted on a "bin tag" which eventually became the firm's permanent record of activity for a given material.

Today, virtually all firms maintain centralized perpetual inventory records independent of storeroom stock cards. In most firms these records are computerized. Receipts are posted to the perpetual record from suppliers' invoices or from the firm's receiving reports.[5] Withdrawals from stores are normally authorized and posted from one of three sources. The most common source is the stores requisition, which is made out by the user and signed by an authorized supervisor. Thus, the central record provides a running balance for each major inventory item.

A second commonly used source in continuous and intermittent manufacturing operations is a periodic release (usually weekly) of production requirements. The production scheduling group analyzes and aggregates production schedules for the coming period and forwards a list of the aggregated

---

[5] In some cases, this is done by means of a bar code scanning operation, as described in a previous section.

material requirements to purchasing and stores. This document then authorizes the release of the specified materials from the closed stores operation.

A third source of withdrawal authorization used in job-shop-type operations is the engineering bill of materials. These lists of materials are developed along with the design drawings. After the design engineering work for a job has been completed, production control schedules the job and arranges for the release of the required materials to the shop. Instead of preparing a set of stores requisitions for these materials, production control may simply reproduce the engineering bill of materials and send a copy to stores as the document authorizing release of the materials. For effective use, this system requires clear and complete identification of all materials on the engineering bill of materials. For the materials involved, a single companywide inventory numbering system is a necessity when this system is used.

When the materials required for a job are to be withdrawn from stores over a period of time, using bills of materials as withdrawal authorizations presents a problem. Unless a daily report of withdrawals for the job is prepared, it is difficult for the central inventory record section to keep its records current, because the stores department must retain its copy of the bill of materials until all withdrawals are made.

This problem can be circumvented, however, by using a material apportioning system. Under this system, the bill of materials goes first to the inventory record section, where the total requirement for each material needed on a job is deducted from the current inventory balance. The required amount is set aside, or apportioned (on the perpetual record), so it will not be allocated for use on another job before the current requirement materializes in the shop. When the apportioned material is actually used, the apportioned quantity on the inventory record is charged off to the job. The apportioning system, of course, can be used to assure material availability for specific jobs regardless of the method used to authorize stores withdrawals. The system is widely used among firms with job-shop-type operations.

Every firm uses many low-value inventory items. To maintain a perpetual inventory record for all low-value items may cost more than the control provided by such a record is worth. To obtain a record of approximate usage, it is much cheaper to have the stores clerk record all receipts on a bin tag. To indicate when an item should be ordered, a bin level mark or some form of the two-bin control system can be used. Many firms simply place the reorder quantity of small items in a plastic bag; when the clerk has to use stock from the bag, he or she knows it is time to reorder. This method is frequently used for nuts, bolts, and other low-value hardware. If the accounting charge can be determined at the time an order is issued, the accounting department can pick up the proper distribution code from the purchase order. If not, the accounting department usually develops a method by which the expenditure can be allocated equitably among the users.

Physical Inventory No matter how diligently a storekeeper performs the custodial job or how carefully an inventory control clerk maintains records (computerized or manual), some discrepancy between the actual and the book balances of inventories is bound to occur. The system is operated by people, and people occasionally make mistakes. For this reason, every inventory item should be counted physically and checked against its book balance at least once a year. The books subsequently are adjusted to match the actual count. Most companies create an "inventory short and over" account to absorb such discrepancies; this account is eventually closed into the manufacturing overhead account.

Use of a bar coding receiving/inventory system can reduce the time required to take the physical inventory markedly. If the inventory items or their storage locations have been previously bar coded, the task can be accomplished with a portable laser scanner and hand-held data terminal. The scanner is used to identify the item and the count is entered into the data terminal, which is later uploaded into the computerized inventory system.

From a scheduling point of view, the physical inventory can be conducted in one of three ways:

1 *Fixed annual inventory.* Many companies take physical inventory annually at the close of the fiscal year. This necessitates shutting down the production operation and organizing a special crew for the inventory job.
2 *"Cycle count" or continuous inventory.* At the beginning of each year some firms divide their inventory into fifty-two equal groups and assign one of the fifty-two groups to be physically counted each week. Thus, the physical inventory operation goes on continuously without interrupting the production operation or upsetting storeroom activities.
3 *Low-point inventory.* Some companies take physical inventory irregularly, whenever the stock level of an item reaches its lowest point.

All three methods are widely used; the selection of the most appropriate one depends largely on conditions in each individual business. The fixed annual inventory can be troublesome because it is a major task which must be accomplished in a short period of time. However, it is ideal for seasonal businesses or for businesses that completely close down for an annual vacation or equipment maintenance check.

The cycle count inventory approach has two major advantages. It can be planned and worked into scheduled activities without a shutdown. And it can be conducted in an orderly and relaxed manner, which is conducive to accurate work. It has the additional advantage of early detection and elimination of basic causes of errors that might otherwise continue throughout the year. This approach also facilitates efficient utilization of stores personnel. In many storerooms, withdrawals are heavy early in the day and much lighter later on. Thus, when the stock clerks' normal work slacks off, they always have a backlog of inventory work to do.

The low-point approach minimizes the time required for actual inventory work because of the small quantities of materials involved. However, it has the disadvantage of producing an irregular inventory schedule, which tends to peak the workload for stores personnel.

Finally, before developing the details of any physical inventory method, a company should consult the accounting firm that audits its books. A company must be able to demonstrate to auditing firms, and to local and federal tax officials, that the method finally selected is capable of producing accurate inventory reports.

Storeroom Location   In laying out a manufacturing operation, a layout engineer attempts to develop an efficient work flow that minimizes the transportation and handling of materials. This means that materials should be stored as close to their point of use as is feasible. Hence, the use of decentralized storage facilities frequently reduces manufacturing costs.

On the other hand, the centralization of storage facilities also yields significant benefits. From a managerial point of view, the major advantage of centralization is that it facilitates control of the total stores operation—manpower, materials, space utilization, and equipment. Whenever an activity is divided and conducted as a number of separate subactivities, supervision and coordination of the total operation become more difficult. Up to a point, the larger the storage area, the more efficiently space and equipment can be used. Similarly, a larger operation facilitates the balancing of individual workloads and permits more efficient utilization of personnel.

A firm normally attempts to use both centralized and decentralized locations in its total stores operation. The objective is to secure the major advantages of both approaches to the extent possible in a particular situation. Most plants attempt to centralize as much material as is practical. The result, for example, may be two or three large storerooms strategically located near different manufacturing areas, the exact number depending on the size and nature of the production operation. When possible, heavy or bulky materials that are costly to handle should be stored adjacent to the point of use. For example, in a processing plant it is quite common to find one or two large centralized storerooms handling small production items, packaging materials, tools, and MRO supplies. Located throughout the plant adjacent to the point at which they are used in the process are numerous stacks of large bags and drums containing such things as chemicals and additives.

Open System

The open system represents the second major type of stores system. Its widest use is in highly repetitive, mass production types of operations that exhibit a continuous and predictable demand for the same materials. Most JIT manufacturing systems exemplify this situation.

In plants using the *open stores system,* no storeroom as such exists; each material is stored as close to its point of use as is physically possible. Materials are stored in bins, on shelves, in racks, on pallets, in tote boxes, and so on, much as they would be stored in a storeroom. However, the storage configuration at each work station is arranged to fit the available space. Storage facilities are completely open, and any worker has access to any storage facility.

After material is received, stores personnel are usually responsible for delivering it to the production areas. They are further responsible for working out satisfactory physical storage arrangements with the production supervisors. After the material has been delivered, production supervisors assume responsibility for materials stored in their areas.

The open system is designed to expedite production activities. It places little emphasis on the physical security of materials. In ideal applications, there is considerable justification for this approach because the material is used relatively quickly, and it is not subject to a high rate of deterioration, obsolescence, or theft.

An automobile assembly plant offers the clearest example of an open stores system. Here, daily production is high, and purchased parts and sub-assemblies flow into the plant in a steady stream. For higher-cost, bulky items, deliveries from suppliers may be scheduled several times a day. As a result, average inventory is extremely low relative to plant output. Such systems place unusually exacting demands for close cooperation on personnel in production control, purchasing, and the supplier and carrier organizations.

The open system also places less emphasis on the accounting control of materials. Materials are usually put into production without the use of a requisition or a control document. No perpetual inventory records are kept in an open system. To determine the *actual* usage of a material during a given period, it is necessary to take a physical count of the material at the end of the period and to compare this figure with the similar beginning-period figure, adjusted for material receipts during the period. Hence, accounting charges are determined indirectly rather than directly. As a result, the system provides control over material usage only if it is used in conjunction with an accounting system employing "standard cost" techniques.

To conclude, the open system is most applicable in situations where a repetitive production operation produces standardized products, and in JIT types of operations. Materials handled in an open system should not be subject to pilferage, nor should they be easily damaged. If production requires delicate or pilferable items, they probably should be controlled in a closed storeroom. Generally speaking, an open system is more likely to function successfully if it is not applied to a large number of items. Firms applying such a system to several hundred items typically experience better results than those applying it to several thousand items.

Random-Access Storage System

The random-access storage system is a unique type of closed stores system, used by a relatively small number of large firms. In this system, no material has a fixed storage location. When an item enters the storeroom, it is stored in the first available bin or shelf suitable for its storage requirements. When the item is withdrawn from stores, the storage space is available for any other incoming item having similar physical storage requirements. All materials are thus stored at random locations throughout the storeroom. This means, for example, that a stock of nine 20-horsepower electric motors may be located at nine different places in the storeroom. However, *similar types and sizes of storage equipment* are grouped together. This has the effect of dividing the storeroom into areas of materials that are similar in size and storage requirements.

How does the storekeeper find an item once it has been stored? In a typical system, when an item enters the storeroom a record is created for it in the memory of the system's self-contained computer. This record contains the storage location (each location is numbered) assigned to the item. When a stores requisition is received for an item, an operator can access the item record through a terminal and obtain either a printout or a video screen display showing the item's storage address. In some systems, the item record can also be accessed by the command of another computer—such as one in production planning's system—linked to the storage system's computer. In any case, this sophisticated type of control system makes possible the development of an automated storage/retrieval system—a topic which will be discussed shortly.

The random-access storage system clearly is most adaptable in relatively large operations. It requires a computer-based intelligence system and usually an expensive operating system. The system also has several significant disadvantages. For example, tight physical control of materials may be more difficult to achieve. Stores clerks seldom become familiar with the total stock of any item, simply because they lose the close visual contact they have with their materials in a conventional system. In the event of a storage location input error or a computer malfunction, the item itself may literally be lost for an indefinite period of time. A second drawback is that when a physical inventory is taken, it clearly becomes a major time-consuming project.

On the positive side, if properly designed and operated, a random-access storage system possesses two important advantages. First, it utilizes space much more efficiently than a fixed-location system. In arranging storage facilities, space for a fluctuating inventory level does not have to be left vacant for each individual material. Second, the system provides great flexibility. The same storage facilities can easily accommodate different materials, shifts in inventory mix, and unexpected increases in the stock level of an existing material.

STORING OF MATERIALS

Few things irritate a production supervisor more than an inefficient, poorly organized warehouse. A good layout and good storage methods yield the following benefits:

1 Ready accessibility of major materials, permitting efficient service to users
2 Efficient space utilization and flexibility of arrangement
3 A reduced need for materials handling equipment
4 Minimization of material deterioration and pilferage
5 Ease of physical counting

Methods and Equipment

Planning   Planning is the key to consistent and efficient stores operation. What types and combinations of storage equipment should be used? How should the warehouse be laid out? These are key planning questions that must be answered.

The initial step in answering the first question is to compile a list of information about the materials to be stored. Using a current inventory catalog, the following data should be listed for each item carried:

1 How much space is required to store the item properly?
2 How many units are normally withdrawn at once? Should the item be stored singly, in pairs, in dozens?
3 What is the maximum number of units to be stored at one time?
4 What type of storage facility best suits the item (considering such things as weight, shape, and handling)?
5 What handling equipment is necessary to transport the item?
6 How often is the item withdrawn from stores?
7 Where is the item most frequently used in the production operation?

The numbers and types of storage facilities currently required can be determined fairly definitely if these seven questions are answered for all materials. At the same time, estimates of future needs should be made. By comparing future requirements with current requirements, a solution to the current problem can often be designed to include enough flexibility to permit relatively easy adaptation of the facilities to future needs when that time arrives.

Equipment   Eight general types of equipment are commonly used in storing materials:

1 Pallets and skids
2 Open and closed shelving
3 Cabinets (with or without counters)
4 Bins
5 Stacking boxes
6 Special storage racks
7 Gravity feed racks
8 Outdoor platforms and racks

Figures 22-2 and 22-3 illustrate several storage installations using some of the common types of storage and materials handling equipment.

FIGURE 22-2
A two-level storage facility using a combination of metal shelving, bins, and cabinets. Materials handling equipment shown consists of roller conveyors joined by a belt conveyor. (*Courtesy of Lyon Metal Products Inc.*)

Most industrial warehouses used to be equipped with wooden shelving and storage facilities. Wooden facilities still offer several advantages. Wood is softer than metal and provides safer storage for delicate items which might be dropped or scuffed in the bin. Wooden facilities can also be built to special configurations and can generally be installed quickly and inexpensively.

Wooden facilities are quite inflexible, however, and this causes problems as an operation expands or as storage needs change. To overcome this disadvantage, most companies today use steel equipment of the "knock-down" variety. This equipment is designed so that it can be assembled and reassembled in shelf or bin form in numerous different standardized shapes and sizes. Although steel equipment is more expensive initially, its long-run advantages usually outweigh the additional cost. Its configuration and location flexibility gives steel equipment a major advantage over wooden equipment. Steel equipment has the additional advantages of strength and fire resistance; it is also easy to keep clean.

Automated Warehousing For a growing number of firms, the automated warehouse is now a reality. A combination of the random-access storage concept, highly sophisticated storage/retrieval machines, and a computerized

FIGURE 22-3
Wooden pallets being used to provide efficient storage for heavy, unwieldy industrial valves. The materials handling equipment is a gasoline-powered forklift type of stacking truck. (*Courtesy of the Clark Equipment Company.*)

control system has produced today's *automated storage/retrieval system* (AS/RS).

The storage facility frequently is a 30- to 80-foot high-rise structure, constructed of open steel columns. Typically it is configured into storage cubicles of different sizes and utilizes various types of standardized pallets and containers for storage. Figure 22-4 illustrates two different types of installations. A number of warehouse stock clerks are replaced with automated storage/retrieval machines that are mounted either on captive floor rails or on conventional wheels. The tall, masted vehicles have a lifting platform with a shuttle that stores and retrieves palletized or containerized loads on both sides of the aisle.

These vehicles normally are controlled remotely by a computer, although they can be controlled manually. Hence, this type of operation is simply an extension of the random-access storage concept to include computer direction of mechanized vehicles used in the actual storage and retrieval of mate-

FIGURE 22-4
Automated warehouse installations, using computer-operated, captive-rail storage/retrieval machines.
  (a) Palletized installation. (Note the storage operation in progress.) The materials-handling vehicles in the foreground are computer-controlled "Robocarrier" vehicles. They are precision battery-powered vehicles that "track" a network of guidepath wires embedded in the floor. *(Courtesy of Eaton-Kenway.)*

rials. Operating efficiency can be increased even more by linking the production planning computer system with the AS/RS control computer. In this case, required production materials are automatically located and mechanically "picked" from storage by a computer command initiated by a computer-released production schedule in the production planning department.

In addition to increased operating efficiency, these automated "skyscraper" facilities possess two other advantages. First, they utilize warehouse space (the "cube") exceptionally well, which is welcome news to any financial manager concerned about the cost of buildings and real estate. Second, they drastically reduce warehouse labor requirements and operating costs. The other side of the coin, obviously, is that this equipment requires a large

FIGURE 22-4
(b) Containerized installation. (*Courtesy of Eaton-Kenway.*)

initial investment—and high-volume usage to make it profitable. For these reasons, only a limited number of large firms utilize these systems today.

Storage Methods An important objective of all stores operations is to minimize deterioration and spoilage. It is common practice, particularly when dealing with materials that tend to deteriorate or become obsolete, to issue old material ahead of new material. Numerous schemes can be devised for accomplishing this. A very simple solution, however, is illustrated in Figure 22-5.

Figure 22-5 represents stacked boxes of material. As material is withdrawn, it is taken from the left end of the stack, moving progressively to the right. When new shipments arrive, they are stored on the right. Thus, by moving from left to right, older material is used first, leaving newer material for future use. This technique is commonly referred to as storage for "first-in, first-out" usage.

Special protection is occasionally required for some items. If metal parts are subject to rust or corrosion, they should be stored in dry areas. In some

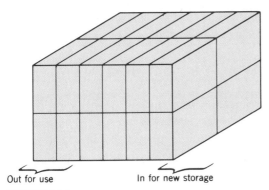

Out for use   In for new storage

FIGURE 22-5
Storage scheme for first-in, first-out usage.

cases, they should be covered with suitable rust-inhibiting compounds. Since dust is harmful to certain items, airtight containers or drawers may be suitable for storage of such items if they cannot be purchased in inexpensive sealed containers.

Some liquids are sensitive to heat and cold; certain granulated materials are sensitive to moisture. Such items should be stored in suitable locations.

Obviously, items subject to pilferage should be stored in locked cabinets or other secure areas to reduce temptation and subsequent losses.

Units of Issue   A warehouse does not always issue a material in the same units in which it is purchased. Steel, for example, is usually purchased in tons or pounds and issued in sheets, bars, or feet. Some boxed materials are purchased by the gross and issued by the dozen. Record-keeping and pricing errors sometimes occur when specific units of issue are not clearly established for such materials.

To avoid possible communication difficulties, the standard unit of issue for a material is usually defined as the smallest quantity likely to be issued. The inventory record should be maintained in terms of the standard unit, and stores requisitions should state withdrawals in the same terms. Errors can be avoided by using the same unit of issue for similar materials. Likewise, units of issue involving calculations, such as square feet or board feet, should be avoided whenever possible. In cases where the unit of issue is not obvious to operating personnel, it should be marked clearly on the stock bin and on the inventory record.

Some items, such as powdered materials, nails, screws, and numerous small items, can be dispensed more efficiently by weight than by actual count. In such cases, weight-to-unit conversion tables should be developed so that records can be maintained in the same units as issues are made.

Layout

Good warehouse layout attempts to achieve five objectives:

1 A straight-line flow of activity through the storage areas with minimum backtracking
2 Minimum handling and transportation of materials
3 Minimum travel and waste motion for personnel
4 Efficient use of space
5 Provision for flexibility and expansion of layout

It is virtually impossible to attain all objectives completely. However, a carefully planned compromise solution can usually satisfy most layout objectives reasonably well.

The initial criteria used in laying out most warehouses are the size, shape, and type of material to be stored. First, items must be analyzed to determine their storage facility requirements—then those with similar requirements are grouped together. From this analysis, the total requirement *for each type of storage equipment* can be determined. Once this determination is made, it can be analyzed in conjunction with a floor plan of the available space. By making scaled templates of the equipment, various arrangements can be simulated on the floor plan until the one that most nearly satisfies the basic objectives is found.

Storage Location Address   A well-worn but appropriate slogan seen in many warehouses is "A place for everything and everything in its place." A "place for everything" can be planned. Keeping "everything in its place," though, is not always an easy job. The development of a good storage location address system provides assistance to those who try to keep everything in place.

There are numerous ways of addressing storage locations. One widely used system is illustrated in Figure 22-6. This system arranges the warehouse in "blocks" of storage units, much as a city is laid out in blocks of houses. Each block is identified by a lateral block letter and a longitudinal block letter. Within each block, every row of shelves is given a number. Each row is divided vertically into columns and horizontally into shelves. A particular bin is identified by reading the letters and numbers in the following sequence: lateral block, longitudinal block, row, column, and shelf.

Blocks and rows should be identified clearly with painted signs. Columns and shelves are always read starting from the lower left corner. Frequently, the shelves are not labeled because shelves are added and taken away from time to time as storage requirements change.

Every item carried in stores thus has a specific storage location address. These location addresses should be listed in the inventory catalog if possible; if not, they should at least be listed in a stores location index.

FIGURE 22-6
A common system used in addressing storage locations.

ORGANIZATION

The stores and receiving jobs are closely related. Therefore, the receiving activity usually is placed under the supervision of the stores manager. As noted earlier, in a majority of U.S. industrial firms, stores either reports to the purchasing department or is grouped with purchasing in a materials management department. There are two strong arguments for such an organizational arrangement:

1 The stores activity is a materials-oriented activity; therefore, it should report to a department whose primary interest and expertise also lie in

materials and supply operations. Supervisory personnel thus will recognize and be equipped to deal with the materials and supply problems encountered in receiving and stores.

2 Receiving is the last step in the material acquisition process, and stores is the last step in the material supply process. From the standpoint of the *total control of materials* these activities should be included with the rest of the materials activities. From an operating point of view, such a materials organization facilitates coordination between the related materials activities. Specifically, it ensures that the relationships between stores, inventory control, and purchasing will receive proper attention, as will the important factor of indirect material costs.

Some firms place the stores activity under the production department. In a few cases, it is placed under a factory superintendent; in others, it reports to the production control manager; and in still others, it reports to the general production manager. Two common justifications for this form of organization are:

1 Production management is responsible for running the production operation smoothly and for meeting product delivery dates. Production should therefore have control of its immediate material supply group to ensure smooth delivery of material to the production work stations.

2 Receiving and stores disbursement activities should not be supervised by the department that buys and authorizes payment for the same materials. Collusion and embezzlement are discouraged when stores and receiving personnel report to a manager outside the purchasing department.

Both preceding sets of arguments are valid, although the authors believe that in most firms, the arguments supporting a materials management structure are significantly more compelling.

In making the organization decision, management's primary concern should be fulfillment of *three basic objectives:* (1) to optimize the effectiveness of the total procurement and supply process by utilizing and coordinating the capabilities of the individual elements of the system, (2) to ensure that materials are in good condition and are available where and when needed to meet operating requirements as scheduled, and (3) to accomplish these objectives and related activities at an optimal cost.

CONCLUSION

Receiving and stores play a more important role than is sometimes recognized in supporting and facilitating a firm's production operations. Receiving is responsible for expeditious receipt and general inspection of materials, as well as for a thorough review and comparison of all relevant documentation with the materials. Stores is responsible for identification and safe, efficient physical handling and storage of materials.

The receiving operation is an important control point in a firm's materials system. This is the only point at which the purchasing control documents actually meet the materials themselves. Subsequently, stores assumes responsibility for the physical care and control of the firm's inventory. Since this material represents from 15 to 30 percent of the organization's total invested capital, this responsibility is a significant one, to say the least.

In addition to the custodial and material control aspects of the responsibility, these functions directly influence costs. The manner in which receiving and stores activities are conducted clearly influences inventory carrying costs and, to some extent, the direct labor costs of production.

FOR DISCUSSION

22-1 "Receiving and stores activities indirectly influence product costs in several ways." Comment on this statement.

22-2 The receiving of material appears to be largely a routine clerical activity. Yet the statement is made that receiving should be conducted by a person who is capable of exercising sound judgment. Discuss.

22-3 Outline and discuss briefly a typical receiving procedure.

22-4 Prepare a complete flowchart for a receiving procedure to be used in a plant where inventory control is handled entirely on a computer. Supplement your flowchart with a brief description of the various documents you use and an explanation of their significance.

22-5 What is a bar code? Explain how a bar coding operation works.

22-6 How can bar coding be used effectively in a materials management operation?

22-7 As bar code usage becomes more widespread, what problems might accompany this development? Discuss.

22-8 Discuss briefly the responsibilities of a typical stores department.

22-9 **a** What problems exist when a company attempts to use suppliers' part numbers in its material identification system?
 b What problems does a company encounter when it develops its own material identification system but develops the system only for its major production materials?

22-10 **a** Explain how a numerical material identification system works.
 b Explain how a mnemonic material identification system works.
 c Devise and explain an eight-digit numerical system which could be used for identifying production materials used in an automobile assembly plant.

22-11 **a** Explain how a closed stores system operates. How is accounting control maintained? Under what conditions should a closed stores system be used?
 b Explain how an open stores system operates. How is accounting control maintained? Under what conditions should an open stores system be used?

22-12 Discuss the use of a perpetual inventory record in both the closed and open stores systems.

22-13 Explain how a random-access storage system works.

22-14 What are the key characteristics of an automated storage/retrieval system?

22-15 Prepare a step-by-step procedure for use in conducting an annual physical inventory of materials. Make rough sketches of any forms required and include any instructions necessary for clerical personnel.

22-16 Describe and discuss the merits of the three scheduling methods which might be used in conducting a physical inventory of materials.

22-17 **a** Discuss the advantages and disadvantages of centralized warehouse facilities.

b Discuss the advantages and disadvantages of decentralized storage facilities.

22-18 Assume that you have been given the responsibility of making a study of an existing warehouse and of taking charge of its reorganization. Outline and explain briefly the approach you would use in planning this undertaking.

22-19 What are the objectives of good warehouse layout? Explain.

22-20 Prepare for your boss a short report summarizing your analysis of the major factors involved in determining how stores and receiving should fit into the company organization.

CASES FOR CHAPTER 22

TRAFFIC

The traffic function, particularly inbound traffic, is an integral part of the materials management function. Traffic's importance is magnified by the fact that, for most firms, transportation cost and service factors significantly affect the total cost of materials. They also influence the efficiency of the production operation and, ultimately, the firm's ability to compete in the marketplace. Current estimates indicate that U.S. industry spends over $350 billion per year for transportation services. By any measure, this is big business.

Managers are concerned not only with their own transportation bill, but also with their competitors' transportation bills. Assume, for example, that steel prices are approximately the same at two different mills. If the first mill can deliver steel for less than the second because it has lower transportation costs, it has a distinct advantage over its competitor. If customers pay the freight charges, the first mill can expect to get proportionately more orders; if the mills pay the freight, the first mill will net a higher unit profit. For this reason, industrial traffic managers must stay attuned to the dynamics of the marketplace and its quasi-regulatory environment.

The traffic function in an industrial firm includes responsibility for four areas of activity:

1 The transportation of incoming shipments
2 The transportation of outgoing shipments
3 Major internal transportation of materials and products on the firm's property
4 Participation in hearings before regulatory agencies, congressional committees, and other governmental bodies on matters affecting the cost and quality of transportation services

The primary traffic issues faced by buyers involve inbound shipments. Hence, this chapter focuses on these issues as they relate to the purchasing function. The chapter pinpoints the things a buyer should understand about traffic to do an effective purchasing job.

Transportation costs can be high; in some companies they average as much as 20 to 40 percent of the product cost. In the steel, lumber, cement, and heavy chemical industries, for example, transportation frequently represents one of the largest elements of total cost. At the other end of the spectrum, in some light manufacturing firms transportation costs sometimes total less than 1 percent of product cost. Electronics and pharmaceutical producers are good examples. Thus, transportation costs vary greatly, depending on the nature of the materials a firm uses. The importance of the traffic management function consequently varies from one industry to another.

Irrespective of cost, transportation *service* is frequently a critical factor in the purchasing process. If shipments fail to arrive when scheduled, serious operating delays may ensue. Moreover, the general efficiency of a total supply program can be affected significantly by the type of cooperation obtained from carriers. On matters of materials handling methods, shipment tracing and expediting, and the allowance of various in-transit privileges, carrier cooperation is essential.

Transportation services should be purchased much as any material or service is purchased. After careful investigation of potential carriers, the selection decision should be based on thorough evaluation of service, quality, and price.

CARRIER SELECTION

A purchaser normally can obtain the option to specify the carrier and the routing to be used in transporting the purchased material. When this prerogative exists, a buyer should view it as part of his or her overall purchasing responsibility. Unfortunately, too many buyers forfeit this profit-generating opportunity by simply noting, "Ship best way."

Shipping Terms

The shipping terms included in a sales contract determine who has the legal right to specify the carrier and the routing. More precisely, shipping terms define the point at which a buyer takes title to the goods. This, in turn, defines who is responsible for payment of freight charges, for handling negotiations with the carrier, and for filing any necessary loss or damage claims. In short, the owner of the material holds all rights and responsibilities that accompany ownership. Numerous terms of shipment can be used, but the most common are:

1 F.O.B. buyer's plant (destination)
2 F.O.B. seller's plant (origin)
3 F.O.B. seller's plant, freight allowed to buyer's plant
4 C.I.F. contracts

The abbreviation *F.O.B.* historically meant "free on board"; legally, the F.O.B. designation defines the point of title transfer. Under the first arrangement, title to the material passes from the seller to the buyer when the carrier delivers the material at the buyer's plant. Because the seller retains ownership of the material during transit, it has the right to select the carrier as well as the responsibility for paying the freight charges. Under the second arrangement, the buyer takes title when the carrier accepts the material for shipment at the seller's plant. In this case, the buyer assumes responsibility for carrier selection and payment of freight charges. The third arrangement is similar to the second, so far as legal liability is concerned; however, the shipper agrees to reimburse the buyer for the freight charges. The fourth type of contract is used commonly in international trade. The abbreviation *C.I.F.* stands for "cost, insurance, and freight"—which means that the contract price includes insurance and freight charges, as well as the cost of the material.[1]

Buying under the terms of F.O.B. seller's plant is common practice today; approximately 90 percent of all shipments are purchased under these terms.[2] Buyers utilizing this approach want control of an order during transit. Many feel that they can do a better job of carrier selection and routing than their

---

[1] C.I.F. rates normally do not include local pick-up and delivery costs.
[2] Ernest Gilbert, publisher of *Inbound Traffic Guide*, "Problems in Purchasing Transportation," NAPM 67th International Purchasing Conference, Los Angeles, Calif., May 10, 1982.

suppliers can. This is frequently true, because many small shippers simply are not properly staffed to make such decisions for all of their geographically dispersed customers. Many purchasers also develop long-term relationships with carriers, just as they do with suppliers. Hence, the routing of each major production material, from various points across the country, is but one element of a total transportation purchasing program which is designed to serve the purchaser's long-range interests. Consequently, the buyer usually wants the prerogative of carrier selection because he or she plans to develop certain types of relationships with specific carriers.

There are situations, however, in which a supplier will be better informed than the buyer about traffic conditions and about the services offered by specific carriers in the supplier's area. In such cases, the perceptive buyer works with the supplier and utilizes the latter's capabilities to the fullest extent.

Some buyers prefer to buy F.O.B. their plant. They reason that by so doing they shift the burden of locating effective carriers to the supplier and do not have to concern themselves with the details of transportation investigations. Likewise, since the supplier has agreed to pay the freight charges, the buyer does not have to worry about costs of transportation. And, finally, in the event that problems arise from shipping damage, the buyer is not responsible for the time-consuming negotiation with the carrier which often ensues. Operating in this manner, the buyer is assured of acceptable carrier performance before he or she pays the supplier. Unfortunately, this type of reasoning contains two fallacies. In the first place, there is no assurance that the supplier will accept the responsibility of finding an "effective" chain of carriers. The buyer, in effect, abdicates his or her responsibility for buying effective transportation service. Second, even though the supplier pays the freight bill, in the long run freight charges are included and passed on to the buyer in the material selling price. Ultimately, the buyer pays the transportation bill and also bears any extra costs resulting from poor carrier selection.

Modes of Transportation

The bulk of U.S. intercity freight traffic is moved by rail, motor freight, water carrier, and pipeline. The railroads have continually lost ground to the motor freight industry since World War II. Today they haul approximately 30 to 35 percent of the country's freight—down 50 percent from 1947—while the truckers haul approximately 40 percent.[3] During the same period freight movement by air has increased at a fantastic rate, but it still amounts to only about 1 percent of all freight moved.

A surprisingly large number of transportation methods are available. Most buyers, at one time or another, utilize a majority of the following methods:

[3]"The Changing Face of Railroading," Consolidated Rail Corporation, *Annual Report*, 1980, p. 5.

1 Parcel post
2 Private parcel delivery service
3 Bus service
4 Air cargo
5 Rail freight, carload (CL) and less than carload (LCL)
6 Motor freight, truckload (TL) and less than truckload (LTL)
7 Freight forwarder
8 Coastal, intercoastal, and inland water freight
9 Piggyback and fishyback
10 Pipeline

Generally speaking, a buyer of transportation finds that methods providing fast delivery cost more than slower methods. For example, a West Coast firm buys heavy machine parts from a firm in Philadelphia. The parts can be shipped by water, by rail, by truck, or by some combination of these methods. If shipment is by truck, delivery time is approximately eleven days. By intercoastal steamship, delivery takes roughly twice as long. Depending on the specific part, however, the water freight rate ranges from 20 to 50 percent lower than the truck rate.

Exceptions to this rule, of course, do exist. A buyer may discover some isolated cases where a faster mode is also cheaper. For instance, for many years the air freight rate between San Diego and San Francisco was less than the rail rate! Other similar exceptions undoubtedly exist.

When approaching a shipping problem for the first time, wise purchasers initially compare rates and delivery times of the feasible alternative shipping methods. Buyers should bear in mind, however, that certain indirect cost factors may be just as important as the freight rate itself. Packaging and crating costs may vary from one mode to another. Also, the size and frequency of shipment is determined by the mode. Consequently, the necessity for warehousing and the cost of maintaining inventory may vary from one mode to another. Clearly, the buyer is concerned with *total costs* influenced by transportation, not direct transportation costs alone.

Parcel Post   Very little industrial freight travels by parcel post. However, this rather expensive service is a relatively fast and convenient method of shipping small packages. The U.S. postal service has placed the following size and weight limits on parcel post shipments:[4]

Weight limit = 70 pounds for all zone destinations

Size limit = 108 inches combined length and girth for
all zone destinations

---

[4] These parcel post limitations were in effect Jan. 1, 1989. They may be changed from time to time by the Post Office Department.

Air parcel post (Express Mail) service is also available for one- or two-day delivery at substantially higher rates. Shipping limits for air service are 70 pounds and 108 inches.

Private Parcel Delivery Service   Privately operated parcel delivery services provide important door-to-door delivery services for packages up to 150 pounds. Most of these firms operate in interstate commerce, although some operate only intrastate or intracity. In recent years private parcel delivery services have grown rapidly in number and size, primarily because of their flexibility and strong service orientation. Typically it is possible to arrange for one- or two-day delivery with these carriers, most of which move their long-haul shipments by air. United Parcel Service and Federal Express are outstanding examples of this type of firm. Business customers have generally responded favorably to the wide range of specialized and custom-tailored services available.

Bus Service   Intercity bus transportation is another method used occasionally for shipping easily manageable packages over relatively short distances. Most bus lines accept packages larger than parcel post size, provided one person can handle them without difficulty. Although this too is an expensive service, delivery is usually fast for distances less than 200 miles because of the numerous scheduled runs between major cities. In an emergency situation the buyer sometimes finds this service to be extremely valuable. Some of its value, however, may be negated by the necessity for local delivery or pickup of the shipment at the bus terminal.

Air Cargo   Although air cargo movements have increased tremendously in recent years, high rates still prohibit regular use of air service for most industrial purchasers. As a general rule, freight rates are approximately twice as high for air cargo as for LCL and LTL movements. The continued development of high-capacity jet freighters, however, may permit further rate reductions in the future.

Because air travel produces a smooth ride compared with other methods of moving freight, it is an exceptionally good way to transport delicate equipment or perishable commodities. Because of this fact, if ground handling is not too rough, packaging and crating requirements for materials may be reduced substantially if they are shipped by air. This cost reduction partially offsets the higher freight rate in some cases.

One selling point emphasized by most air cargo carriers is the fact that the short delivery time afforded by air shipment permits a purchaser to carry smaller inventories. The rationale underlying this point is entirely valid. The final decision, however, still involves an analysis of *total* costs. Each purchaser must make his or her own analysis and determine in which cases a net saving in fact results.

Rail Freight   Rail shipments move as *full carload (CL)* shipments or as *less than carload (LCL)* shipments. For ordinary materials, a CL movement is considered to be approximately 30,000 pounds or more. When hauling a dense commodity such as grain, however, the figure might range from 60,000 to 100,000 pounds. The CL volume is usually sufficient to fill a car, so the car does not have to be opened until it reaches its destination. CL shipments move at a freight rate that is substantially below (in some cases approximately one-half) the LCL rate. As will become evident in the following paragraphs, LCL shipment frequently does not compete favorably with motor freight shipment. For this reason, the volume of LCL shipments is declining for most railroads.

To make effective use of CL movements, the shipper and purchaser should each have conveniently located spur tracks and loading facilities. If a purchaser has to unload a railcar at the freight yard and truck the material to its plant, the cost of double handling frequently makes it less costly to utilize a single truck haul all the way from the supplier's plant. On the other hand, *for LCL shipments,* the rate usually includes pickup and delivery service, provided the shipment moves more than 300 miles.

A railroad's major advantage over its trucking competitors is in the area of long intercity hauls. A railroad must make a huge investment in equipment, rolling stock, and trackage. While its fixed costs are high, its variable operating costs are relatively low. Once a train is loaded and rolling, it costs little more to move it 1,000 miles than to move it 100 miles. Hence, on long hauls, its total operating cost per ton-mile typically is lower than that of its motor freight competitors. For shipments moving less than 1,000 miles, the reverse situation occurs.

Railroads offer CL shippers two privileges that prove extremely valuable in some types of business: (1) in-transit privileges and (2) diversion and reconsignment privileges.

In-transit privileges, generally speaking, give a shipper the right to stop a shipment en route, unload it, perform certain processing operations on the material, reload the processed material, and continue the shipment at the original freight rate (subject to a modest additional charge). The economics of the total operation become clear when one observes that freight rates on processed materials are usually significantly higher than on corresponding raw materials. This means, for example, that a tank fabricator in Kansas City might purchase a car of steel in Chicago, ship it to Kansas City, fabricate tanks from the carload of steel, and then ship the tanks on to a customer in Denver. In doing this under a fabrication-in-transit agreement, the tank fabricator pays almost the same freight rate on tanks shipped from Kansas City to Denver as it paid on the steel shipped from Chicago to Kansas City.

A similar type of agreement allows shippers to delay a shipment and use the railcar as a temporary storage facility until they wish to continue the movement.

Diversion privileges permit a shipper to divert a car in transit to a new destination. This can be a very convenient prerogative when unexpected conditions in a multiplant company call for the shipment of an extra car of material to plant X, rather than to plant Y as scheduled. *Reconsignment privileges* allow the shipper to go a step further; it can also consign the car to a new customer, or consignee, at the same or at a different location. In certain types of businesses these privileges can be used to very definite advantage.

Rail carriers also provide other privileges, for little or no additional cost. One of these services is pickup or loading at two separate points with a single delivery at destination. They also provide for a single pickup with delivery and unloading at two separate points. These privileges can be of particular value to multiplant companies.

Motor Freight In this industry shipments move on either a *truckload (TL)* or *less than truckload (LTL)* basis. TL rates are substantially lower than LTL rates. In contrast with rail freight movement, a load of 20,000 to 30,000 pounds of ordinary material typically makes up a full truckload. The definition of a "full truckload," however, varies somewhat among commodities and among carriers.

Comparison of truck rates with rail rates reveals that, in general, the difference between them depends on the length of the haul and the weight of the load. On movements of less than 1,000 miles, truck rates often are lower than rail rates. On long hauls, however, the reverse typically is true, notably for heavy, low-grade bulk materials.

A point of interest to purchasing personnel centers on the difference between weight requirements for TL and CL shipments. Suppose a buyer is considering shipping a 20,000-pound order by rail, LCL. If truck shipment is feasible, a TL rate probably will apply. In most cases, the TL rate will be considerably lower than the LCL rate. A similar situation may exist when shipment weights are somewhat below 20,000 pounds. The freight bill for a 17,000-pound shipment which is moved and billed as a full truckload may well be lower in total than if it were actually billed as 17,000 pounds and moved at the higher LTL rate.

The most important advantage a truck line possesses over a rail line is its operating flexibility. For short hauls it has no peer. In contrast with a train, a truck is a small, flexible, self-contained unit. It can be loaded easily and less expensively (because less bracing is required) at a shipper's plant. Once on the road, a TL shipment can proceed directly to its destination. It does not have to wait in various classification yards across the country, as a railcar does, to be switched to a new train that moves it over the next leg of its journey. As a consequence, in almost all cases, motor freight delivery is faster than rail freight delivery.

For a short haul of 300 miles an LTL shipment should arrive in a day, while an LCL shipment typically requires three or four days. As the length of the haul increases, the truck advantage becomes less pronounced. Finally, on transcontinental CL hauls delivery performance tends to be about equal. Some of the aggressive railroads now offer improved service, on a limited basis, between selected metropolitan areas having high-density traffic movements. This service takes two forms: (1) fast "hi-ball" freight trains which bypass classification yards and (2) scheduled "merchandise cars" which move immediately on through trains.

Freight Forwarder The operations of rail freight forwarders are designed to provide a service to firms buying materials in less-than-carload lots. For distances over 300 miles, freight-forwarding shipments should normally move much faster than ordinary LCL shipments, closely paralleling CL and LTL delivery service. Freight forwarders' rates, in virtually all cases, are at least as low as LCL and LTL rates, and on long hauls they are usually significantly lower.

A freight forwarder operates much like a broker. The firm accepts only less-than-carload shipments. Such shipments are then combined into a full load and shipped by rail at the CL rate. Thus, the forwarder's operating margin is the difference between the rate the firm charges and the CL rate it pays for shipment. Long hauls are therefore most profitable for the freight-forwarding firm. They frequently permit the firm to reduce its rate below the LCL level and still generate a reasonable profit.

Air freight forwarders operate in much the same way. Some air freight forwarders now offer a combination of air and surface movement for their shipments. These can be used to advantage when direct air shipments are not feasible or when the combination provides advantageous movement at a lesser cost than direct air service.

Coastal, Intercoastal, and Inland Water Freight Domestic shipping lines, operating on inland as well as on coastal and intercoastal waterways, represent one of the earliest forms of American freight transportation. Because of infrequent sailing schedules and relatively slow speeds, water transportation is by far the slowest of all transportation methods. To compensate for slow deliveries, water carriers offer considerably lower rates than their rail and truck competitors.

The federal government considers domestic shipping lines to be a vital part of the American Merchant Marine. It therefore protects their existence in various ways. For example, it legislates protection against competition from more cheaply operated foreign ships, makes capital equipment available at reduced prices, and partially subsidizes the harbors and docking facilities they use. Such actions permit domestic water carriers to remain financially sound and still quote freight rates substantially below competing rail and truck carriers.

Water transportation is frequently used by strategically located firms for moving raw materials, heavy items, and low-value materials, when shipments can be planned well in advance of operating requirements. In computing total shipping costs, the user should be aware that water freight rates do not include pickup and delivery service. The cost of transporting material to and from dockside must be added to the water carrier's quoted rates. Water carriers charge on the basis of weight or volume, depending on which yields the greater revenue. Consequently, shipping costs for bulky, low-density materials, relative to corresponding rail costs, are higher than for high-density materials.

Piggyback and Fishyback   These combination methods of freight transportation made their initial appearance on the commercial transportation scene during the mid-1950s. In both cases the cargo is loaded in truck trailers at the shipper's plant. In using *piggyback,* a truck tractor pulls the trailer from the plant to rail loading yards, where the trailer is placed on a flatcar which holds several trailers. The long intercity haul is then made by rail. At the destination, truck tractors pick up the trailers and deliver them to the purchaser's plant.

This method of transportation actually combines the major advantages of both truck and rail movement. It utilizes the flexibility of trucks on pickup, delivery, and short off-line hauls, and it takes advantage of the railroads' favorable cost and speed performance on long hauls. This method of shipment usually cuts down loading and handling time, and it also frequently results in faster delivery for the purchaser. At times it results in a lower rate, particularly when shipment is made from or to plants without rail sidings.

Fishyback is similar to piggyback, except that it combines the use of truck and water carriers rather than truck and rail. While the main objective of piggyback is to utilize the strong features of both truck and rail movement, the major objective of fishyback is to reduce the extremely high costs of loading and unloading individually packaged items aboard ship. Fishyback replaces the handling of thousands of individual items with the handling of a relatively small number of previously loaded trailers or large standardized containers.

Pipeline   Pipelines are used primarily in transporting petroleum products, chemicals, and water. However, they are also being used increasingly for transporting cereal, coal, and certain ores. Movement of these materials is accomplished by pulverizing the solid material, mechanically suspending it in water, and pumping the solution through a pipeline. Although pipelines of this kind are considered common carriers and are regulated by the Interstate Commerce Commission, they have very specialized uses when viewed as part of the total freight transportation picture.

Types of Carriers

A transportation buyer should be familiar with the basic legal status of the carriers with which he or she deals. The federal government recognizes three types of carriers: (1) common, (2) contract, and (3) private.

Common Carriers   A common carrier serves all customers but carries only the types of freight for which it is certified. Some truck certificates, for example, explicitly exclude specific types of freight, while others include only certain very limited types. The bulk of industrial freight moves by common carrier. The preceding discussion, with the exception of postal service, has dealt with freight movement by common carriers.

Regulation and Deregulation   The Interstate Commerce Act of 1887, although targeted at regulation of the railroads, gives the federal government the right to regulate—in the public interest—almost all common carriers engaging in *interstate* traffic. A host of subsequent legislation reinforces the basic intent and supplements the authority of the original act. Most notable among these additions are:

- *Motor Carrier Act of 1935.* Established trucking industry regulation.
- *Civil Aeronautics Act of 1938.* Established airline industry regulation.
- *Department of Transportation Act of 1966.* Created cabinet-level department (DOT).

All rail, motor, and intercoastal water common carriers are regulated by the federal Interstate Commerce Commission (ICC). Ships in international commerce are regulated by the Federal Maritime Commission (FMC). Prior to deregulation, air common carriers were regulated by the Civil Aeronautics Board (CAB). The regulatory agencies operate under the Department of Transportation, a cabinet-level department of the executive branch of the federal government.

Fundamentally, the regulating agencies do two things. First, they prescribe *a body of operating regulations* which constitute the legal framework within which carriers operate their businesses. The ICC, for example, issues all "certificates of public convenience and necessity." The certificates give truck lines the authority to haul freight in a designated geographic area or over certain specific routes. No truck can operate as an interstate common carrier without a certificate. Second, they act as *controllers of the freight rate structure* to ensure that no carrier charges rates which discriminate against other carriers or against customers. All common carrier rates must be approved and filed with the ICC. Most states have state agencies which function in a similar manner for all carriers engaged in *intrastate* transportation.

During the late 1970s, a strong effort was initiated to *deregulate* the U.S. transportation system. This movement culminated in the passage of four additional legislative acts, all designed to reduce governmental control and promote freer market competition in the transportation industry. The key legislation includes:

1 Air Cargo Act of 1977
2 Staggers Rail Act of 1980
3 Motor Carrier Act of 1980
4 Shipping Act of 1984

In reality, this legislation did not deregulate the industry—rather, it produced a form of "re-regulation." The primary impact on the transportation industry has been fourfold:

1 Carriers in all four modes (rail, motor, air, and water) possess substantially increased flexibility to modify freight rates and services without regulatory intervention.
2 For air and motor carriers, entry into the business and acquisition of specific routes are much easier to achieve.
3 For rail carriers, low-cost federal loans are available to upgrade facilities and equipment.
4 Water carriers have considerably more freedom to enter joint ventures with other carriers, producing unique, containerized intermodal services for inland shippers.

All common carriers now have the ability to adjust freight rates rather freely within a broad range. Rail carriers, for example, are permitted to raise rates up to 175 percent of their variable costs, plus possible additional inflation offsets. Motor carriers and freight forwarders can adjust rates up to 10 percent per year, on the basis of the previous year's rates. Perhaps the greatest benefit of the legislation to motor carriers is the "ease-of-entry" provision for service and routes. Although a trucker still must obtain a certificate of public convenience and necessity, the procedure is greatly simplified. An applicant simply must be able to demonstrate that the firm is "fit, willing, and able" and that the proposed service is responsive to a public need.

From the transportation buyer's point of view, the full effect of deregulation remains to be seen. Clearly, the legislation has produced greater competition—competition among carriers in a single mode and also among carriers in competing modes. Hence, buyers find most carriers to be much more marketing-oriented and more willing to negotiate different types of price and service arrangements. The development of national transportation contracts (with correspondingly reduced rates) for multiplant buyers has become a very profitable alternative.

The element of increased competition cuts both ways. Typically it produces benefits for most buyers located in high-density traffic areas. For buyers located in low-density traffic areas, however, it has produced some negative consequences. Although more carriers are in operation, service to customers on many low-volume, low-profit routes has been curtailed or dropped by a number of carriers. Additionally, a number of weaker and less efficient carriers have felt the brunt of the "survival of the fittest" environment. A dozen or so major carriers and an uncounted number of smaller ones have either closed their doors or experienced bankruptcy.[5]

Contract Carriers   A contract carrier does not provide service to the general public; it operates only under negotiated contractual agreements with

[5]Interesting discussions of the effects of deregulation are presented in T. S. Robertson, S. Ward, and W. M. Caldwell, "Deregulation: Surviving the Transition," *The Harvard Business Review*, July–August 1982, pp. 20–24; John Fitts, "Deregulation Offers Opportunities and Dangers," *Purchasing World*, June 1981, pp. 48–52; and Joseph L. Cavinato, "Buying Transportation," *Guide to Purchasing*, NAPM, 1986, pp. 3–7.

specific customers. Although all contract carriers are regulated by the same agencies as common carriers, generally speaking their regulation is less stringent. Each carrier must obtain an operating permit and also must file a schedule of minimum rates with the appropriate agency.

As a rule, contract carriers have no loading or terminal facilities. Consequently, their operating costs are usually somewhat lower. This also means that, by and large, contract carriers handle only truckload shipments. Unlike the liability of a common carrier, which is fixed by law, the liability of a contract carrier depends entirely on the contractual arrangement made with the customer.

An interesting provision of the deregulation act now permits a contract carrier also to hold a common carrier certificate, and vice versa. Hence, a carrier holding both types of certificates can combine "common" and "contract" loads on the same vehicle.

Private Carriers   Private carriers are not subject to regulation by the ICC. A private carrier transports material that the carriage firm owns. Some industrial firms have thus become private carriers by operating their own fleets of trucks. A common problem such firms encounter in hauling their own production materials, though, is that of running the truck empty on one leg of the trip. Consequently, this type of private carrier generally tries to haul finished goods to customers traveling one way, and production materials to the plant going the other. However, in such an operation scheduling becomes a major problem. Likewise, in the industrial relations area the company may find that it has an additional union—the Teamsters—to deal with. Thus, becoming a private carrier puts the firm in the trucking business as well as the manufacturing business, and it cannot escape certain problems unique to the transportation industry.

Purchasing people need not concern themselves with the plethora of legal details surrounding carrier operation, but they should be aware of the general framework within which carriers operate. Keeping out of legal difficulties in the transportation business is a complex problem in itself. Furthermore, the law holds a shipper equally liable with the carrier for violation of federal transportation regulations. Consequently, it behooves buyers of transportation services to have a general knowledge of the regulatory acts that influence the transportation segment of their responsibilities.

Freight Rates

The structure of freight rates in the U.S. transportation industry appears to be little short of chaotic. Unlike most business operations, the price charged for hauling freight usually does not bear a consistent relationship to the carrier's actual cost of providing the service. The difficulty of allocating operating costs to specific products carried, coupled with the plethora of rates that represent historic precedents, contributes to the inconsistent and confusing rate structure which now exists.

A brief review of the rough-and-tumble era during which railroads were laying the foundation for the nation's transportation system provides a clear explanation of how the complex rate system originated. The miscellany of rates developed during that period were, for the most part, created independently of each other as various needs arose. Little thought was given at that time to the rate structure for the total transportation system. Individual rates were based largely on "what the traffic would bear" and were conditioned by numerous economic and political pressures coming from different areas of the country.

Rates established today are based on cost to a greater extent than in past years. However, the following factors, some of them very subjective, are all considered in present-day rate making, which still appears to be much more an art than an exact science.

- Value of the service to the shipper
- Cost to the carrier of providing the service
- Special services involved, such as transit privileges
- Volume of traffic movement involved
- Rates on similar articles moving under similar conditions
- Rates of competing carriers
- Competitive conditions existing in the *shipper's* industry

Class Rates and Commodity Rates Generally speaking, freight moves under one of two types of rates: (1) class rates or (2) commodity rates. It was originally impossible to establish a rate for every individual commodity shipped. Consequently, similar commodities were grouped in classes, and rates were established for each class of commodity. These rates became known as *class rates*. Commodity classifications have since become standardized to ensure uniform treatment by all carriers. For rail transportation, the *Uniform Freight Classification* is the document used to determine which class rating is appropriate for a given shipment. In the trucking industry, the *National Motor Freight Classification* is the guide used for shipment classification purposes.

A *commodity rate* is a unique rate created for the shipment of a given material in large quantities between specified origin and destination cities. The material must be shipped in CL or TL lots on a continuing basis. Commodity rates normally are significantly lower than class rates—and are established to give special treatment to particular commodity movements that have economic or competitive importance in a certain market.

In practice, although a majority of the *number of shipments* move under a class rate, a majority of the *dollar volume* moves under commodity rates. A transportation buyer who wants to apply for a commodity rate generally proceeds in the following manner:

1 The buyer contacts the major carrier involved, explains the problem, and requests the carrier to initiate a proposal on his or her behalf.

2 If the carrier agrees, carrier representatives prepare a complete proposal for the requested commodity rate and submit it to the standing rate committee of the carrier's cooperative rate-making association.

3 This committee studies the proposal and accepts or rejects it. If the proposal is accepted, the new rate is written and filed with the ICC.

4 If the proposal is rejected, the case can be appealed to an executive group of the rate-making association.

5 If the proposal is again rejected, final appeal can be made directly to the ICC for a hearing of the case.

One thing is clear: Even in today's environment, rate making and commodity classification are extremely specialized activities. It is not uncommon for a well-qualified general traffic manager to call on a specialist for assistance.

Designating Carrier and Route

Not only do freight rates differ significantly between the modes of transportation which might be selected for a given shipment, but, since deregulation, they vary markedly among carriers and among the various routes over which the shipment might move. Hence, to minimize shipping costs, it is important that the right mode, carrier, and routing be designated.

To many transportation buyers, the service factor is a more important consideration than cost in designating a specific carrier and routing. Service offered by different carriers can vary as much as that of different suppliers. In the case of a motor freight shipment, on long hauls a buyer may have the choice of using a dozen or more connecting carriers. Usually, he or she tries to involve as few separate carriers in the move as possible in order to reduce the number of transfers required. When a shipment passes from one carrier to another at the boundary of the first carrier's operating territory, the transfer can be made with varying degrees of efficiency. The time actually lost during the transfer depends on running schedules and transfer facilities of the lines involved.[6]

A city in the Rocky Mountain area, for example, is served by three major motor carriers from Chicago. Because of differences in schedules and facilities at intermediate transfer points, normal delivery times for the alternative carriers range from three to six days. This difference can be quite significant if a firm operates with low inventories or needs an emergency shipment.

On many railroad runs between two points, the carrier can use several alternative routes. There is the fast, direct route, and usually there is a slower,

---

[6]Between New York and Los Angeles there are over 300 possible rail carrier combinations. The number of possible truck combinations from New York to Los Angeles has never been calculated; there are thousands of possibilities.

circuitous route designed to serve communities located off the direct route. So long as the carrier operates both routes, it can move unrouted shipments over either one. However, the railroad frequently sends unrouted shipments via the circuitous route to achieve a better load distribution among its trains. The informed buyer avoids this possibility by specifying the routing to be used.

A final reason for controlling carrier selection involves a principle well understood by purchasing people. If a firm distributes its transportation business among a few selected carriers, in adequate volumes, it is possible to develop very favorable long-term relationships with the carriers. Relationships of this kind can be valuable to the buyer in many ways. When the buyer needs the best service possible for occasional urgent shipments, a favored and friendly carrier is much more inclined to provide the desired service willingly. Likewise, such a carrier is more prone to settle claims promptly and to provide assistance with cost reduction projects.

EXPEDITING AND TRACING SHIPMENTS

When it is imperative that a buyer receive a tightly scheduled shipment by a particular date, he or she may wish to *expedite* the shipment. In these cases, the buyer advises the carrier of the situation *prior* to shipment and requests that arrangements be made for faster than normal movement. Most carriers are willing to expedite shipments if a purchaser requests the service only when really necessary. Like the proverbial boy who cried wolf too often, the buyer who makes frequent and unnecessary use of this service soon finds that the carrier pays little attention to repetitious demands.

Tracing is the process of following a shipment *after* its departure to obtain a record of the various steps of its movement. A purchaser finds that this activity occasionally is required to bring in an overdue shipment; it is inevitable that some shipments become misdirected or lost. In critical situations, tracing is necessary to ensure prompt delivery and continuity of manufacturing operations. Effective tracing work is contingent on a rather detailed understanding of how various carriers handle their freight. In conducting expediting and tracing work, a buyer may simply contact a carrier's general agent and ask him or her to handle the detailed investigation. If the matter is urgent, the buyer may have a traffic specialist from his or her firm also participate in the detailed investigation with the carrier's personnel.

The ease with which a shipment can be traced depends largely on two things: (1) the completeness and accuracy of the shipping information possessed by the tracer and (2) the shipping records maintained by the carrier.

As an example, the following information is helpful in tracing a CL shipment:

- Description of material
- Date shipped
- Car number
- Train number
- Route
- Shipper
- Consignee
- Origin
- Destination

In tracing an LCL shipment, additional information typically required is the number of pieces, weight, waybill number, and the first transfer point for the shipment.

Rail CL shipments can be traced fairly easily because most railroads keep records of CL shipments by car initial and number. *Passing reports* are also maintained along the line, so that a particular car usually can be traced without difficulty from one classification yard to the next as it progresses along its route.

Rail LCL tracing is sometimes difficult. Some railroads keep records of the loading of LCL shipments, others do not. Where records are available, tracing can be accomplished. When no records are maintained, tracing is a nebulous task because of the guesswork involved, and frequently it is impossible.

Freight forwarders usually trace their own CL shipments. Forwarders maintain records which permit them to cross-check any individual shipment to the railcar in which it moved.

Motor TL shipments can be traced quite easily because records are kept on every trailer. A trailer travels directly from origin to destination, with perhaps several tractor changes, and can be traced through its various checkpoints along the route.

Motor LTL shipments, as a rule, can be traced fairly easily. Most truck lines maintain a record of every LTL shipment handled.

Air cargo carriers, for the most part, keep records of individual shipments. When a plane takes off, most carriers teletype its entire manifest, giving individual shipment identification, to the destination stations. Consequently, tracing can usually be accomplished without difficulty.

Water carrier shipments can be located easily because once loaded, they remain aboard the ship until it reaches its destination. The important point, however, is to ensure that the shipment is taken aboard in the first place! Occasionally, cargo is left behind because more material is delivered to the dock than the vessel can carry. In tracing, however, there should be no mystery as to whether cargo was in fact loaded, because the first mate (or a subordinate) is required to sign the waybill when the cargo is actually taken on board.

Private parcel delivery service shipments as a rule can be traced easily. But this capability does vary among firms. Most firms have improved this service markedly in recent years.

Parcel post shipments cannot be traced unless they are registered or insured. The postal service keeps records of individual shipments only when they are registered or insured.

Clearly, the completeness of the shipping records maintained by any carrier determines the ease with which tracing can be accomplished. In those firms that have computerized records systems, tracing is usually a simple matter.

In recent years some carriers, notably the progressive trucking firms, have developed an exceptionally valuable service for key customers. Through a computer terminal located in the customer's office, they provide direct access to their computer information system containing trailer loading, routing, scheduling, and movement data, as well as tariff and classification information. Thus, without leaving the office it is possible for a buyer to trace his or her shipments and compare actual movement with the schedule, to audit the freight bill, and to obtain selected information for management reporting purposes. Other carriers provide the same type of tracing service, though less personalized, by means of an 800-number telephone inquiry.

LOSS AND DAMAGE OF FREIGHT

Shipments sometimes get lost or arrive in damaged condition. Normally, a carrier is legally responsible for a shipment from the time it is loaded aboard the vehicle until it is unloaded at the destination. To obtain a satisfactory settlement for lost shipments, the purchaser should initiate the following procedures: If a shipment does not arrive within a few days of its expected delivery date, the buyer should contact the supplier to determine definitely that the material was shipped—and if it was, also to obtain necessary tracing information. The buyer should then contact the carrier and request that the shipment be traced. If the shipment cannot be located, a loss claim for a specific amount of money should be filed in writing with the carrier. It is mandatory that all claims be filed within nine months after the loss, or they may be disallowed. In the interest of prompt investigation and settlement, the sooner the claim is filed, the better.

Damage

A shipment can incur two types of damage in transit: (1) apparent damage and (2) concealed damage. If a shipment appears to be damaged or partly missing, these facts should be noted in writing before the shipment is accepted. This can be done on the delivery receipt or the freight bill. Generally, the carrier's driver signs the exception on the copy left with the consignee, while the consignee's receiving clerk signs the exception on the copy retained by the carrier. The purchaser should then contact the carrier's freight agent and request him or her to inspect the damage and prepare an inspection report.

Occasionally, damage is concealed and not discovered until a shipment is unpacked. When this happens, the unpacking operation should be discontinued immediately upon detection of damage. The purchaser should contact the carrier's freight agent when the damage is found, in no case more than fifteen days after delivery, and request an inspection of the shipment. The merchandise, as well as the packing material and container, should be left undisturbed for the agent's inspection. Most firms use an instamatic camera to photograph the damaged item in its partially unpacked condition to provide evidence in support of the claim that subsequently will be filed. Claim settlement is dependent on satisfactory determination of the party responsible for the damage. Consequently, it is to the purchaser's advantage to preserve all evidence for the carrier's inspection.

The following data are usually submitted in support of a damage claim filed with a carrier:

- The statement of claim, itemized and submitted on a standard claim form available from the carrier
- The carrier's inspection report
- A certified copy of the invoice indicating the value of the shipment
- The paid freight bill
- The original bill of lading

In the case of concealed damage, a statement from the supplier may also be required.

A claim should always be filed as quickly as practical after the damage is known. The probability of obtaining a favorable settlement usually is greater while the facts of the case are still fresh and clear.

Responsibility for filing a claim rests *with the owner of the material at the time damage occurred.* Consequently, if the damaged material was shipped F.O.B. supplier's plant, the purchaser bears this responsibility. On the other hand, if the shipment was made F.O.B. purchaser's plant, the supplier is responsible for assembling supporting data and filing the claim. In either case, the purchasing firm must do most of the work preparatory to the actual filing of the claim because its personnel discovered the damage and it has possession of the material.

It is very difficult for a claimant, even by resorting to legal action, to recover the full cost of concealed damage from a carrier. A claimant must present evidence that the material was properly packed to withstand the normal rigors of shipment and that the merchandise was in undamaged condition at the time it was delivered to the carrier. A claimant also must show that loss or damage was not sustained after delivery while the shipment was in its custody. These are sometimes difficult matters to prove. The wise buyer, therefore, makes every effort to settle such claims out of court. The development of a good business relationship with carriers and a cooperative attitude in following carriers' regulations for reporting and inspecting damage can pay handsome dividends.

DEMURRAGE

When a purchaser receives a carload of material, the railroad allows the firm approximately two days to unload the car. If the purchaser retains the car beyond the allowable period, the carrier assesses a *demurrage* charge. The reason for such a penalty is clear. A freight car is a piece of productive equipment for the railroad; as long as it sits idle on a customer's siding it produces no revenue.

Straight demurrage charges are assessed in the following manner. After a car is received and properly placed for unloading, the purchaser is given forty-eight hours beyond the next 7:00 A.M. to unload the car. For instance, if the railroad delivers and positions a car at 1:00 P.M. Monday, the purchaser has until 7:00 A.M. Thursday to unload the car. For each day the buyer keeps the car after 7:00 A.M. Thursday, he or she must pay a demurrage charge. Although rates fluctuate with the supply and demand for cars, charges typically run $20 to $30 per car per day for the first week, and $60 or more per car per day thereafter. Saturdays, Sundays, and holidays are considered free days and are excluded from demurrage computations.

If a firm does much purchasing in carload lots, it may wish to enter into an *average demurrage agreement* with the carrier. Under such an agreement, one demurrage debit is assessed for each day one car is held beyond the allowable time period; one demurrage credit is allowed for each car released during the first twenty-four hours of the allowable forty-eight-hour period. Each month the purchaser is billed for the debits in excess of its credits.

Clearly, a purchasing department should consult with the department responsible for car handling and unloading when it schedules carload shipments. Good coordination at this point can produce an orderly flow of cars that does not exceed the manpower and physical facilities available for unloading. Sound planning in this area minimizes congestion on the receiving docks, reduces demurrage charges, and reduces labor overtime costs.[7]

FREIGHT BILL AUDITS

A purchaser of transportation services has the right to audit its freight bills and submit a claim for overcharges within a three-year period after the date of delivery. Most firms find it profitable to audit freight bills. Although such an audit is only prudent business practice, the complexities of freight classifications and rates provide a clue to a more compelling motive for scrutinizing freight bills.

The voluminous and complex commodity classification structure produces literally thousands of rates under which different materials move between different geographical points. It is not uncommon, even for a skilled rate clerk, to make an error in commodity description or commodity classification. This results in an incorrect rate determination. For example, "fiberglass insulating blocks packed loosely in boxes" take one rate, while "fiberglass insulating shapes other than blocks packed loosely in boxes" take another rate. In thumbing through the Uniform Freight Classification, one finds literally thousands of similar cases illustrating even finer distinctions between two classifications. It is, therefore, an understandably common occurrence

[7]While most companies object to paying demurrage charges, at times a boxcar can serve effectively as a rolling warehouse. In certain situations, it may be profitable to pay planned demurrage charges and use a car for storage purposes.

for most firms to receive a significant number of freight bills that are incorrect simply because the carrier's billing department unintentionally applied the wrong rate. If the item is purchased repetitively, errors of this kind may be repeated and a firm's loss compounded.

A firm's freight bills can be audited by its own traffic specialist(s) or by an external consultant. During the last several decades, numerous specialized audit bureaus and traffic consultants have developed profitable businesses by auditing their clients' freight bills on a 50 percent commission basis. Under this system the consultant audits all the purchaser's freight bills free of charge. If incorrect bills are detected, the consultant prepares and processes a claim with the carrier, and the purchaser pays the consultant 50 percent of the net recoverable overcharges. The fact that more than two dozen independent rate consultants operate in the San Francisco area alone attests to the significance of this problem.

TRANSPORTATION STRATEGY AND COST REDUCTION

If one takes a broad view of effective management and cost control in the transportation area, two basic approaches become evident. First, and certainly most important, is the development of a strategy for the buying of transportation—an *integrated* plan for the purchase of transportation services to meet *all* of the organization's major needs. Second is the identification and conduct of the more traditional cost reduction projects that have high payoff potential for the organization.

Purchasing Transportation Services

A statement made early in the chapter bears repeating: "Transportation services should be purchased much as any material or service is purchased." Although the logic of this observation seems obvious, only a minority of the firms in the country actually do it! If a single commodity accounts for even 5 percent of a firm's total cost of materials, its purchase should be handled with thorough research and analysis—that is, professionally. Transportation is just such a commodity for virtually every purchaser in the country.

Until the 1980s, this concept was not easy to implement effectively. Competition was constrained by regulation and, as a result, most carriers simply did not think in terms of developing competitive service-oriented arrangements with their customers. Deregulation changed that. Today virtually all carriers compete vigorously and are interested in negotiating arrangements that are mutually advantageous.

Intelligent purchasing dictates the development of an integrated one- to three-year transportation buying plan. This begins with a macroscopic analysis of inbound (and outbound) materials movements with respect to origin and destination points. After determining the approximate annual tonnage movements between general areas of the country, specific carriers are identified that might be able to handle such movements. From this point forward, the procedure is much like that involved in any vendor evaluation. Subsequently, the top group of carriers is invited to submit proposals for the firm's business on a contractual basis for the next several years. Specific factors considered in the carrier evaluation process are:

1 Financial stability and profitability
2 Equipment capability
3 Number and location of terminals and break-bulk centers
4 Percentage of shipments that would have to be interlined
5 Average transit times between the major origin and destination areas
6 On-time performance record
7 Various elements of service available
8 Cooperativeness in working on service improvement and cost reduction projects
9 Effectiveness of the tracing system; direct access to the computer information system via buyer's terminal
10 Claims to freight bill ratio performance record
11 Claim settlement ratio performance record
12 Shipping rates for the contract period

The number of carriers required is then determined, depending on the buyer's tonnage movement configuration. If the geographic configuration permits, normally two or three carriers are used for the contract period! And the business is divided among them in a manner that produces optimal incentives for performance.

In most cases, the closeness of the buyer-carrier relationship produces improved understanding, cooperation, and reliability of service. In virtually all cases, the rates are significantly lower than they would have been working on an order-by-order basis. In the case of contracts with motor carriers, rate discounts of 25 to 50 percent are reported consistently.[8]

Project-Oriented Cost Reduction Possibilities

A skilled traffic specialist can contribute substantially to the reduction of delivered materials costs. In addition to the freight bill auditing program discussed earlier, four types of projects should be considered: (1) the use of unique multimodal shipping arrangements, (2) freight reclassification studies, (3) commodity rate investigations, and (4) pool car arrangements.

Multimodal Arrangements Since the advent of piggyback and fishyback, buying organizations have devised innumerable unique cost-saving

---

[8]R. S. Reichard, "Discounts and Price Shading Continue," *Purchasing World*, April 1988, p. 28.

intermodal arrangements. Some firms have even found that a combination of rail and barge carriage is advantageous for selected coast-to-coast runs.[9]

One innovative arrangement, possible only in a relatively deregulated environment, is reported by the Ball Corporation.[10] Ball is an eastern manufacturer of glass, among a wide variety of other products. One of the key ingredients in glassmaking is soda ash, a dense, bulky commodity produced primarily in southwestern Wyoming. Because of the product weight, shipping distance, and shipping volume, the soda ash transportation cost was a significant element in Ball's final product cost.

Ball's initial cost reduction effort was targeted at the one railroad geographically positioned to serve the soda ash supplier. Unfortunately, after extensive attempts Ball was unable to negotiate a satisfactory shipping rate with the railroad. Subsequently, however, joint efforts with the supplier produced a unique solution to the problem. The soda ash is now hauled, under contract, by a truck line from the supplier's plant to another railroad located approximately 200 miles distant. With the use of a newly renovated transfer station, the soda ash is transferred to the cars of the second rail line, which hauls it to the Ball plant. Even with the double handling and the unusual expenses involved, Ball was able to generate an attractive cost saving on the total arrangement—a product of creativity and buyer-supplier-carrier cooperation.

Reclassification Projects   The numerous, closely related commodity classifications which have been devised for rate-making purposes present a fertile field for cost reduction investigation. Because many items shipped do not fit neatly into a single classification, the elements of interpretation and judgment play a significant role in the final assignment of a classification number to a given item. Similarly, the method in which a material is packed influences the risk involved in transporting it and, consequently, the classification to which it is assigned.

An alert rate specialist frequently is able to negotiate the reclassification of certain materials into lower-rated classes. Ironically, this can often be accomplished merely by revising written descriptions of materials or by slightly modifying packing methods.

For example, one traffic manager in a small plant was successful in getting a regularly purchased casting reclassified as a lower-rated material. Upon investigation, he discovered that several different classifications were applicable to the casting; the classifications differed only with respect to the way in which the casting was crated. By eliminating only one board from the original crate, the lower-rated classification was fully applicable. This was done,

[9]S. A. Reese, "Cargo: How to Get It from There to Here," *Pacific Purchasor*, September 1987, pp. 20–24.
[10]Peter J. Walters, "The Purchasing Interface with Transportation," *Journal of Purchasing and Materials Management*, Winter 1988–89, p. 23.

and the reclassification was approved by the carrier. The savings on this simple project amounted to more than 10 percent of the transportation cost.

Commodity Rate Investigations

As noted previously, commodity rates exist as exceptions to class rates and are usually lower than class rates. Quite often, however, no commodity rate exists for the particular item a purchaser ships from a given city. If shipments are repetitive and the volume is reasonably large, or if economic or competitive reasons justify it, the purchaser should negotiate with a carrier in an attempt to obtain a commodity rate. It is sometimes possible, too, for several small buyers to consolidate their regular shipments of like materials and attain a volume sufficient to justify the establishment of a commodity rate.

The case of a large San Francisco firm illustrates the point. Although the firm purchased a large number of castings from a Chicago foundry, the volume was not sufficient to justify the establishment of a commodity rate. Consequently, the traffic manager studied the casting requirements of other manufacturers in the area. Fortunately, he found several that patronized Chicago foundries. By coordinating their plans, he and the traffic managers from the other firms worked out a shipping schedule which permitted them to combine shipments of similar castings to attain a large and consistent volume. A subsequent rate negotiation yielded a commodity rate for these shipments which was 40 percent below the previously paid class rate.

In a more widely publicized case, one large California winery, unable to negotiate what it considered to be a satisfactory commodity rate on East Coast shipments, designed and built a ship for the sole purpose of shipping its wine in bulk. This action gave the winery a significant shipping cost advantage over its competitors. However, as often happens with innovations, the loss of this large traffic movement prompted the railroad to establish a lower commodity rate for the remaining California wineries, to forestall further traffic losses.

Quite apart from the consideration of rates, the additional costs of special handling and packing required for transportation of fragile or unusual items can be excessive. In the case of frequent, large-volume shipments of such items, a buyer may find it profitable to modify the design of a conventional railcar (or trailer) for exclusive use in shipping this material. Through negotiation, the carrier or the supplier may agree to provide this service at minimal or no cost.

Pool Car Arrangements

It is also possible for several buyers to consolidate their requirements for dissimilar items into one single shipment. The individual buyers' small shipments would each ordinarily move under LCL class rates. By combining the small shipments, however, it is often possible to move the *pooled* shipment under a lower CL class rate. Cost-conscious transportation specialists make a point of knowing about other firms that patronize suppliers located in the same areas and are quick to take advantage of pool car opportunities. At the same time, alert suppliers should know about the availability of pool cars. This is one situation about which the seller may have better transportation information than the purchaser.

PURCHASING'S ROLE

Two things are clear. First, the typical buyer who has a basic understanding about the buying of transportation is in a position to do his or her job in a more enlightened manner. Second, the buying of transportation is a specialized task best handled by a buyer trained in the specialty.

The purchasing department and the traffic department must work together. Their most important task is to jointly establish their firm's strategy with regard to the basic plan for buying transportation, shipping terms and conditions to be utilized, and supplier development activities. Wise buyers consult frequently with traffic specialists on matters of carrier designation and routing; they also request estimates of realistic delivery times and costs via different methods when either is critical. Additionally, buyers must coordinate their efforts with those of traffic personnel with respect to expediting and tracing activities, the filing of loss and damage claims, and the scheduling of major incoming carload shipments. Finally, where appropriate, buyers and traffic specialists should work together in identifying and conducting transportation cost reduction projects.

CONCLUSION

Many people are not aware of the keen competition that exists in the transportation industry. Truck, rail, air, and water carriers all compete vigorously for tonnage. Deregulation has made it possible for carriers in the same mode to compete much more actively for business on the basis of a variety of innovative price and service options. Contract carriers utilize only a schedule of minimum rates; hence, buyers often can save money by competitive bidding or negotiating with these carriers as well as common carriers. Progressive buyers understand the potential of this market and take full advantage of its competitive nature.

FOR DISCUSSION

23-1 "The traffic function is an integral part of the materials management function." Do you agree? Discuss.

23-2 What should be the operating relationship between purchasing and traffic?

23-3 "Transportation services should be purchased much as any material or service is purchased." Analyze and discuss this view.

23-4 What is the significance of the shipping terms (F.O.B. terms) which appear on a purchase order issued by the buyer?

23-5 Some firms prefer to buy F.O.B. supplier's plant. What do you see as the major arguments for and against this policy? Discuss.

23-6 When a buyer specifies the method of transportation to be used in shipping an order, he or she has at least a dozen different choices in some cases. List and discuss the significant factors the buyer should consider when viewing the possibility of shipping by each of the following methods:
a Parcel post
b Intercity bus service
c Air cargo

23-7 Answer question 23-6 with respect to the following methods of transportation:
a Freight forwarder
b Intercoastal or inland water freight
c Piggyback and fishyback
d Pipeline

23-8 Recognizing that there may be many specific exceptions, if you were to state a general rule, under what conditions is it usually most advantageous to use rail freight, and under what conditions is it usually most advantageous to use truck freight?

23-9 List and discuss the major types of carriers as viewed by the federal government for regulatory purposes.

23-10 Which federal regulatory agency has jurisdiction over the activities of each type of carrier listed in answer to question 23-9?

23-11 What is the significance of the Staggers Rail Act of 1980? Of the Motor Carrier Act of 1980? Of the Shipping Act of 1984?

23-12 From a buyer's point of view, what has been the impact of the government's deregulation activities?

23-13 It has been said that in many cases there appears to be little logical relationship between the freight rates in effect for different commodities. What are some of the general reasons which might help to explain this situation?

23-14 What is the difference between a class rate and a commodity rate? Explain.

23-15 Is it very likely that a shipper will ever be billed incorrectly for the transportation service rendered by a carrier? Explain.

23-16 **a** Define the term "expedite."
b Define the term "trace."
c Under what conditions might a shipper or a purchaser engage in either of these activities?

23-17 Outline step by step the procedure you would use in developing an integrated transportation buying plan for your firm.

23-18 In what way might a manufacturing firm employ the services of a traffic consultant or an audit bureau? Explain.

23-19 Outline in detail a receiving procedure which a firm might use to ensure proper handling of lost and damaged shipments.

23-20 a Define the term "demurrage."
  b Explain the different types of demurrage agreements under which a firm may operate.

23-21 Discuss in detail the various things a firm might do to reduce its transportation costs.

23-22 What is purchasing's role in the traffic function? Explain.

CASES FOR CHAPTER 23

SURPLUS MATERIALS

PROBLEMS AND OPPORTUNITIES

For most people, surplus is not an inspiring topic. It may bring to mind thoughts of old pup tents, mess kits, gas masks, and other military paraphernalia. Even industrial surplus seems to imply mistakes in overprocurement, wasteful production processes, and inefficiencies in general. To make matters worse, surplus is often associated unglamorously with junk heaps. Consequently, surplus is seldom considered an exciting business activity, and it rarely receives the management attention it deserves. This is regrettable, because the total cost of production is the sum of the costs of labor, materials, and overhead *minus* any return from the successful sale of all kinds of surplus materials. Profits are maximized only when all elements affecting cost are fully controlled.

Profit Opportunities

In spite of the lack of glamour associated with surplus materials, effective disposal of surplus can be very profitable. For example, a large aircraft manufacturer recently increased its annual revenue from surplus sales by over $980,000 after reorganizing and refining its approach to surplus disposal. Similarly, a large oil company recovered $286,000 the first year it reprocessed sludge and sediment that was formerly discarded as valueless. Several years ago Monsanto Chemical Company restructured its surplus equipment disposal program, which is a full-time activity for one of its purchasing groups. The firm's experience to date is that "on average, the return on investment [in this program] is ten to one."[1]

Environmental Problems

In the 1970s, the United States determined it should reclaim the purity of its air, water, and living environment. The reduction or elimination of the causes of pollution and the conservation of natural resources became major national objectives. These objectives impinged directly on the materials manager's responsibilities for recovering idle investment from capital surpluses and for recycling surplus materials back into economic channels. Thus the image and the scope of surplus operations, and the materials manager's responsibility for this activity, changed perceptibly.

Because minerals constitute such a significant part of the overall environmental and natural resources problem, they will be discussed in the following paragraphs to bring the surplus problem into focus from a macroscopic point of view.

Strategic Materials Problem

Most Americans are concerned about the energy problem and understand the environmental problem; however, they do not seem to comprehend the

---

[1] C. C. Lewis, "Monsanto Chemical's Purchasing Is Smaller and Stronger," *CPI Purchasing*, August 1987, p. 31.

strategic minerals problem. This lack of understanding is regrettable, because this problem has far more serious implications than the energy problem. To function as an industrial society, the United States *must* have thirty-six strategic minerals. The country is presently dependent on foreign sources for twenty-two of these minerals. To make matters even more serious, a high percentage of our imports of many of these strategic metals come from Russia and South Africa—hardly the most reliable sources of supply. In 1980, 92 percent of the chromium consumed in the United States was imported. Other critical materials imports include: tantalum and manganese, 97 percent; cobalt, 93 percent; platinum group, 88 percent; nickel, 77 percent; and tungsten, 50 percent. *In comparison, oil imports totaled only 42 percent.* In the face of such circumstances, the necessity to conserve and reuse scrap metal is clear.[2]

Recycling Benefits

Consider the critical facts depicted in Table 24-1.[3] Recycling steel, aluminum, lead, zinc, and copper scrap, compared with processing virgin ores, results in energy savings averaging 76 percent. In an era of energy shortages, this is indeed a desirable source of savings.

In addition to energy savings, recycling yields many other desirable benefits. For example, when 1,000 tons of steel are produced from recycled scrap rather than from virgin ore, the following benefits accrue: 6.7 million gallons of water are saved, because water usage is reduced from 16.6 million to 9.9 million gallons; 104 tons of air pollution effluents are avoided, because pollutant discharges are reduced from 121 tons to 17 tons; and 2,754 tons of mining wastes are avoided, because these wastes are reduced from 2,828 tons to 63 tons.[4]

In its totality, therefore, *recycling reduces energy requirements, reduces gaseous and solid pollutants, and conserves raw materials.*

Conflicting National Objectives

The federal government wholeheartedly supports and encourages beneficial processes such as recycling. However, laws enacted prior to 1970 to achieve *different* objectives are temporarily thwarting the full implementation of environmental and conservation legislation. For example, trucks transport much freight that could be transported equally as economically by less polluting, less fuel-consuming railroads. Scrap iron is being exported, while at the same time less desirable virgin iron ore is being imported. Since virgin

---

[2]"Strategic Minerals: The Invisible War," *Reader's Digest,* February 1981, pp. 81–85.
[3]*Phoenix Quarterly,* Institute of Scrap Iron and Steel, Summer 1981, p. 9.
[4]U.S. Environmental Protection Agency, *Report to Congress on Resource Recovery,* April 1973, p. 12. See also *Phoenix Quarterly,* Institute of Scrap Iron and Steel, Fall 1980, p. 10.

TABLE 24-1
ENERGY SAVINGS AVAILABLE THROUGH METALS RECYCLING AND INDUSTRY RECYCLING TARGETS

Metal	Level of scrap recycling 1976, tons[a]	Energy required to produce 1 ton of metal from primary ore, kwh/ton	Energy required to produce 1 ton of metal from scrap, kwh/ton	Energy savings, kwh/ton	Energy savings, %	Recycling targets		
						Actual % recovered material used in reference year—1976[b]	Final target 1987: % of industrial output[b]	Actual % recovered material used in 1980[c]
Aluminum	1,446,000	51,379[d]	2,000[d]	49,379	96	32	35	29
Copper	1,425,000	13,532[d]	1,726[d]	11,806	87	47	50	58
Iron/steel	41,144,000	6,481[e]	1,784[e]	4,697	74	38	41	42
Lead	670,000	7,910[f]	3,176[f]	4,734	60	51	60	66
Zinc	180,000	19,044[g]	7,031[g]	12,013	63	33	36	37

[a]Charles L. Kusik and Charles B. Kenahan, *Energy Use Patterns for Metal Recycling*, U.S. Bureau of Mines, IC8781, 1978.
[b]U.S. General Accounting Office, *Federal Industrial Targets and Procurement Guidelines Programs Are Not Encouraging Recycling and Have Contract Problems*, EMD-81-7, Dec. 5, 1980.
[c]U.S. Bureau of Mines data; Institute of Scrap Iron and Steel calculation.
[d]J. C. Bravard, et al., *Energy Expenditures Associated with the Production of Recycle of Metals*, Oak Ridge National Laboratory, ORNL–NSF-EP-24, November 1972.
[e]U.S. Environmental Protection Agency, *Report to Congress on Resource Recovery*, Midwest Research Institute, Economic Studies in Support of Policy Formation on Resource Recovery, 1972.
[f]Personal communication, J. A. Rathjen, U.S. Bureau of Mines.
[g]Personal communication, V. A. Cammarote, U.S. Bureau of Mines.

iron ore moves at less than half the freight rate of scrap iron over the nation's rail system, the rate structure encourages use of the product least desirable from ecological and energy points of view. Tax benefits are paid for depletion allowances of virgin ore to encourage discovery and production; no similar benefits are paid to encourage the increased use of environmentally and economically preferable scrap metals. Similarly, in the Mining and Minerals Policy Act of 1970, the government states its desire to "develop an economically sound and stable domestic mining industry." At the same time, the government thwarts this objective by withdrawing from exploration and mining large areas of public lands. The Department of Commerce estimates that presently 65 percent of government lands are now closed to exploration and mining.[5]

Congress is aware of these conflicting laws, and changes are in process. During the reconciliation period many opportunities will be created for competent materials managers. They will have continuing opportunities to integrate more profitably a firm's goals of increased conservation, improved environment, and increased dollar return from recovery of surplus materials.

Related Problems

The purpose of this chapter is to discuss the specific surplus responsibilities of materials managers. Overall surplus materials problems, however, go far beyond the responsibilities of materials managers. Important illustrations include problems such as balancing the cost of environmental, health, and safety regulations against the nation's need for critical minerals; weighing the benefits of nuclear energy against its possible dangers; and developing a foreign policy designed to preclude the pitfalls of foreign supply disruptions and price fixing.

Of lesser but still significant importance are tangential surplus problems, such as the disposal of hazardous materials, the control of toxic substances, and the need for insurance to protect firms from pollution accidents. Although materials managers do not have direct responsibility for the types of surplus problems illustrated above, an understanding of these macroscopic problems can help them in solving their specific surplus problems.

PRIMARY SOURCES OF SURPLUSES

Industrial surpluses are defined as those materials which are in excess of a firm's operational requirements. Surpluses typically originate from three primary sources: (1) scrap and waste; (2) surplus, obsolete, or damaged stocks; and (3) surplus, obsolete, or damaged equipment. Each is discussed in the following paragraphs.

---

[5]"Strategic Minerals: The Invisible War," *Reader's Digest*, February 1981, pp. 84–85.

Surplus from Scrap and Waste

Surpluses from production processing are inevitable. Not all production materials are wholly consumed in most manufacturing processes; frequently, a residue is left. For example, one company stamps disks from copper strips. From this operation, at least 15 percent of the copper left cannot be used elsewhere in the firm's operations. This excess, called *scrap,* must be disposed of as surplus. It is impossible to eliminate this type of surplus; however, by intelligent planning and effective production controls it can be minimized.

Surpluses also result from the inefficient use of production machinery, carelessness, and poor purchasing. This type of surplus is called *waste.* Effective management does everything possible to keep waste at a minimum.

Obviously, the least costly method of controlling surplus of all types is to eliminate it at the source. This is why cost reduction programs that eliminate surpluses before they occur are so profitable.

The largest single category of salable surplus material is scrap metal.[6] Nationwide, the estimated value of this scrap is well over $16 billion. Because of its high dollar value, the disposal of this large quantity of scrap is a significant element in the nation's economy. Scrap metal is also an essential material in the operation of one of the nation's largest industries—the steel industry.

The proper recovery and disposal of scrap from *precious metals* is a growing source of profit and conservation. These metals are especially important today because of their increasing rates of usage by the electronics, precision instruments, health care, photography, and chemical industries.

By comparing its results with those of other firms doing similar work, a firm can determine with reasonable accuracy the standard scrap rates for its production processes. When actual scrap rates vary from predetermined standards, or when learning experience does not reduce scrap losses, corrective action should be taken. Scrap losses should decrease with learning for the same reasons that production times decrease with learning. The learning curve concept, as discussed in Chapter 13, also applies to scrap rates. The curve that portrays the relationship between scrap rates and time is called the *efficiency curve.* It is based on the theory that scrap losses will decline at a predictable percentage rate as the work force gains experience in manufacturing any specific product. Like the learning curve, the efficiency curve can be used as an effective negotiating tool.

Surplus from Obsolete or Damaged Stocks

It is unreasonable to expect that sales forecasting and planning will always be absolutely accurate. In cases of overanticipation, material excesses above ac-

---

[6]Traditionally, the word "scrap" is used to mean ferrous metals that are suitable for resmelting to produce iron and steel products. The word "metals" is used to identify surplus nonferrous materials.

tual requirements inevitably result. An automobile company, for example, may predict that consumers want seats of real leather, for which they will be willing to pay an extra charge. Time may prove, however, that most consumers in fact prefer fabric or imitation leather, at no extra charge, thus leaving the manufacturer with a surplus of real leather that must be disposed of.

Changes occur constantly in the designs and specifications of fast-moving technological products. As a consequence, obsolete products and their parts constitute a continuing source of surplus materials. Production planning normally takes place well in advance of the date production actually starts. At any time prior to the beginning of the manufacturing operation, either technical or product changes can completely alter the schedule of materials required for any specific production run. Even after production begins, changes in highly technical items often make some materials in inventory obsolete. The ease with which technological advancement can generate surpluses is highlighted by the single fact that in many firms today over 50 percent of the products they sell did not even exist ten years ago.

Excessive forward buying is another common source of surplus materials. Some firms forward-buy only under specific economic circumstances; others forward-buy as a matter of routine company policy. Regardless of the reason for using this method of buying, it entails the hazard of surplus generation from obsolescence, deterioration, or excessive inventory.

Planned overbuying and overproduction represent still other sources of surplus stocks. Some firms, such as machinery and automobile manufacturers, produce more parts for specific models of equipment and automobiles than they may sell because of what is called the *life of type problem*. Frequently, it is more economical for an automobile manufacturer to produce an oversupply of certain replacement parts for new cars while the production line for those cars is in operation (and pay for their storage for as long as the manufacturer accepts the responsibility of furnishing replacement parts for this model) than it is to pay the high start-up costs entailed in reestablishing production facilities for the same parts some years later.

Any warehousing operation, regardless of how efficiently it is controlled, also accumulates some surpluses from breakage, deterioration, and errors in record keeping.

Surplus from Obsolete or Damaged Equipment

All machine tools and equipment at some point in their life become surplus for one of two primary reasons: They wear out, or they become technologically obsolete. In today's rapidly advancing technological world, major machine tools seldom wear out; more frequently they are replaced because they have become technologically obsolete.

In addition to machine tools and plant equipment, most firms also have a large capital investment in office equipment and in the physical plant itself. Competent management makes every practical effort to extend the life of the firm's capital equipment as long as possible, but ultimately, because of obsolescence, breakdowns, the introduction of new products, or new methods of production, replacement of all capital assets—even buildings—becomes mandatory.

Materials Management Ferrets Out Surpluses

Progressive materials management departments do not wait passively for production or some other department to declare equipment surplus. Rather, in cooperation with the other departments, they review company operations with the objective of determining if any capital equipment should be declared surplus. Suppose, for example, that a firm operates sixteen large truck-mounted cement mixers. Analysis discloses that the firm can operate efficiently with fifteen. One mixer is declared surplus and is sold. This action produces two kinds of benefits: It reduces depreciation, taxes, and operating costs—and it increases profits.

Part-time operations are especially fruitful areas for the identification of surplus equipment. For example, Stanford University found that the Stanford Press, which operated its presses and ancillary printing machines only 20 to 30 hours per week, could not compete with printing shops which ran their machines 60 to 120 hours per week. By purchasing their printing from firms that operated their equipment full-time, the university not only reduced the costs for its printed materials, it also generated cash from the sale of printing equipment that was no longer needed.

Inventories are another prime source for generating surpluses. For example, when old equipment is taken out of service, some of the repair parts stocked solely for that equipment remain in inventory. Additionally, dead inventory stock accumulates for a variety of other reasons as the dynamics of a firm's operations and its product lines change. In many firms, surpluses such as these go undetected. Progressive materials managers, however, develop programs that facilitate their speedy identification and disposition.

ORGANIZATION FOR MANAGEMENT OF SURPLUS

Salvage and Reclamation Departments

Nearly all manufacturing firms (large and small) and many nonmanufacturing firms should have a salvage and reclamation (S&R) department. Depending on the quantity and value of the salvageable material involved, the department can operate full- or part-time from either a salvage yard or the department head's desk. Many small firms, unfortunately, fail to establish a salvage department simply because they believe their volume of surplus does not justify a full-time operation.

Industry loses millions of dollars annually by neglecting salvage and reclamation programs. For example, a large electrical company, by reorganizing its S&R department, recently increased its yearly savings by over 20 percent to roughly $1,200,000. A large university started a salvage program and had sales of over $200,000 and savings of over $130,000 in the program's first year. A bank created additional profits of over $95,000 per year by correctly salvaging its wastepaper. Many other firms could benefit similarly, but they fail to recognize the profit potential of salvage and reclamation programs.

The basic charge management gives to its S&R department is to ensure that surpluses are disposed of with optimum profitability. To accomplish this, *all* of a firm's surplus materials should be handled by its S&R department.

Assume that an obsolete motor-generator is to be disposed of. If there were no salvage yard, the S&R department head would dispose of the equipment "as is." If there were a salvage yard, the first determination to be made would be whether the machine could be sold as an operating machine, either in its present condition or after some minor repair work was done.[7] If it could not be sold as an operating machine, the second determination would be to decide on the economic feasibility of disassembling it and segregating it into its component parts and/or into its various kinds of metals, such as copper, steel, or aluminum. The component parts of some used machines can be valuable either for stock purposes or for sale. If the decision is against disassembly, the machine would be sold "as is" for its scrap metal value. Each of the alternatives will produce a different net revenue. Selling the machine in operating condition *usually* produces the greatest return, while selling it "as is" for scrap produces the least. Some firms with high dollar value surpluses include in their S&R departments recycling or recovery equipment, such as balers, shredders, and metal separators.

How to salvage materials can sometimes be a challenging analytical exercise. A university, for example, had an old chapel organ to sell. Unfortunately, the market for used organs of this vintage was almost nonexistent, and the high bid was $10,000. The surplus and salvage manager thought the organ could be sold for more. Further analysis proved he was right. For $3,000, the organ was disassembled into its component parts. The tin from the pipes was sold for $30,000; the remainder of the organ was sold for $3,200.

Overall company salvage expense frequently can be reduced greatly by preplanning and instituting simple operating procedures. For example, sorting surplus metals by type can often be accomplished inexpensively simply by providing suitably marked containers *at the point of accumulation*. This easy procedure increases scrap value. For example, if high-carbon-steel cutting tools are mixed with less expensive grades of metal scrap, the money realized from selling the mixed scrap as a single lot will be considerably less than that which would result from selling the cutting tools as one lot and the remainder of the scrap as another. To simplify sorting of this type, barrels of different colors can be used for different kinds of scrap metals. Similarly, surplus

---

[7]Major repairs generally are best left to dealers who specialize in repair work.

paper, cardboard, and similar surplus materials should be segregated during accumulation by using the method that will bring the highest selling price.

The S&R department handles all three kinds of surplus: scrap, surplus stock, and surplus equipment.

Materials Management and Purchasing Departments

The materials cycle is not complete until all materials are disposed of in the most productive manner. Consequently, surplus disposal is a basic function of the materials management department. In a large firm not having a materials manager, but having high dollar surpluses, the head of the S&R department traditionally reports to the plant manager. In the majority of firms not having either a materials manager or an *independent* S&R department, the responsibility for surplus disposal usually is assigned to the firm's purchasing department.

Why is this odd responsibility assigned to purchasing? Usually, no other department in the firm is as well qualified to perform the task. The professional and managerial skills required for a successful disposal operation are also required to do a good job of buying. No other department of a firm is as concerned with or as informed about materials, their markets, and related operating practices as the purchasing department.

The purchasing department routinely buys a large variety of raw materials, component parts, and equipment. It has knowledge about who makes these materials, what other firms use them, how they are used in its own firm, and how much they cost. This is the precise knowledge needed to sell surpluses of these materials successfully. Also, a relatively large number of buyers in the metal industries regularly buy some form of scrap or other surplus material for their own manufacturing purposes. The vice president for materials in one of the nation's largest steel companies told the authors that he considers the purchasing of scrap metal to be the *key profit responsibility* of his purchasing department. In this and similar situations, purchasing personnel are particularly knowledgeable about the markets in question. Daily contact with industry representatives, coupled with the reading of purchasing and trade journals, keeps them informed of surplus trends in a variety of markets. Additionally, buyers frequently sell a significant portion of their firms' surpluses back to the suppliers from whom they were purchased.

DISPOSING OF SURPLUS PROFITABLY

When material is declared surplus, the materials management, purchasing, or S&R department, as appropriate, is informed. Following this action, disposal is made by one of seven methods:

1 Use within the firm
2 Return to the supplier
3 Direct sale to another firm
4 Sale to a dealer or broker

5 Sale to employees
6 Donations to educational institutions
7 Some combination of the preceding methods

Use within the Firm

At a well-known multiplant pump company, lists describing surplus materials and equipment available for use within the firm are circulated to all divisions. If no request for use is forthcoming from U.S. divisions, the lists are sent to the firm's overseas subsidiaries.

After restructuring and refining its surplus equipment disposal program, Monsanto Chemical discovered an interesting phenomenon. It found that its single largest customer for surplus equipment was its own engineering purchasing group, which supports the design and modification of production operations in all of the firm's domestic and foreign plants.[8]

At a large automobile manufacturing company, the disposal of fixed assets for all U.S. plants is the function of a three-person staff in the central office. When a surplus develops, it is the responsibility of the local plant manager to inform his or her division manager. The latter contacts all divisional facilities to determine whether the equipment can be used. If it cannot be used within the division, the matter is referred to the three-person disposal staff in the central office. This staff then initiates a companywide screening program that sometimes involves overseas divisions as well. If the screening steps fail to turn up a user, the local plant is given authority to sell the equipment as surplus.

Use within the firm is always the most profitable form of surplus disposal. For relatively new equipment this type of disposal realizes 100 percent of the original cost, whereas returns to suppliers typically yield 80 to 90 percent of original cost, and sales to dealers and brokers only 10 to 40 percent.

Return to Suppliers

If the surplus material cannot be used within the firm, the return-to-supplier method of disposal is generally the next best method. Suppliers typically allow the return of both new and used surpluses as a courtesy to good accounts. Salable materials returned from inventory are traditionally accepted at original cost, less a nominal restocking charge. Since different firms have different levels of technical requirements, suppliers can frequently resell even obsolete inventory items at full price.

Scrap metals can sometimes be returned to suppliers, depending on the size of the buyer's account, the metal involved, its degree of contamination,

[8]C. C. Lewis, "Monsanto Chemical's Purchasing Is Smaller and Stronger," *CPI Purchasing,* August 1987, p. 31.

and the current economics of the scrap market. When scrap is scarce, many suppliers routinely require the return of scrap as a precondition of further sales. Particular attention should be paid to the so-called exotic metals, which include most nonferrous metals, alloy steels, and tool steels. Usually these metals can be sold to the supplier at prices much higher than are attainable in the open market.

Supplier policies regarding the return of used equipment to the manufacturer or dealer from whom it was purchased vary widely with the economics of the used equipment market and the sales policies of manufacturers.

Selling to Other Firms

Some companies sell surplus materials and equipment directly to other firms. Sales of equipment to other firms depend primarily on the condition of the equipment, pricing considerations, and the availability of similar equipment from other sources. Equipment sales made directly to a user typically result in a better price than sales made to dealers or brokers.

Sales of production surpluses are most profitable when the surplus of one company is the raw material of another. For example, if a firm can sell its waste paper back to the paper mill, it generally will get the highest price and cause the least pollution.

Selling to Dealers and Brokers

Surplus dealers and brokers (referred to as "dealers") constitute an excellent outlet for surplus materials. When a firm advertises surplus materials for sale, dealers often respond. Transactions with dealers are usually "where is, as is," and most of the time they are for cash. Surplus machine tool dealers, for example, operate in two ways: by auction, which usually involves selling a plant's entire equipment inventory; or by purchase of small lots. For auctions the dealer receives a commission and seldom does more to the equipment than show it to bidders. For small lot transactions, however, the dealer pays the owners cash, then often reconditions or rebuilds machine tools before selling them. Normally, it is not profitable for the original owner to recondition equipment before selling it.

Although cooperative action among purchasing people to sell surplus materials is rare, such a situation does exist among members of the Cleveland Association of Purchasing Management. This group has a surplus commodity service available to its members. Purchasing and materials managers send their lists of surplus commodities to the association office. The association approves the list, writes a covering letter, reproduces both, and distributes the information to all its members.

Interplay among dealers is more widespread than among purchasing associations. Through the Machinery Dealers' National Association, its members have what amounts to a single inventory pool. One dealer, for example, may have a customer for equipment not in its stock, but by knowing what other dealers have on hand, the first dealer can make a sale from another dealer's inventory. All dealers learn what other dealers have on hand from an equipment listing that is published periodically by the association. Association members find such a reciprocal arrangement advantageous, because even the largest dealer cannot stock everything.

Selling to Employees

Many firms make it a practice to sell both the products they manufacture and their surpluses to their employees. If the surpluses are the result of over-stocking or obsolescence and the materials are in new or good condition, or if they are odds and ends of scrap desired by do-it-yourself employees, this can be a satisfactory method of disposal. On the other hand, if the surpluses are not in fully satisfactory condition, such sales, regardless of their attractive prices, can create resentment in employees toward their employers. Used automobiles can be an especially dangerous item of equipment to sell to employees.

Because of the numerous potential disadvantages involved, many sophisticated firms will not sell *used* surpluses (especially equipment) to their employees. Besides possible dissatisfaction, selling to employees often entails excessive paperwork, and it always involves an administrative burden in an effort to ensure complete impartiality among employees. High administrative costs have caused some firms to set minimum dollar amounts for sales to employees. Other firms, to avoid administrative costs, give their employees surplus materials having only a nominal value.

Donations to Educational Institutions

Federal and state tax laws in some cases can create another profitable basis for disposal of surplus materials: giving them away. At the present time, colleges and schools acutely need machine tools and other types of industrial materials for instructional use. Although recent tax laws have reduced the tax benefits allowed for gifts to educational and other nonprofit institutions, desirable benefits sometimes still exist. Because the applicable tax laws and regulations are complicated, before making large gifts potential donors should consult their tax advisers to determine exactly what benefits are available.

Contractual Considerations

Generally speaking, the following contractual considerations apply to the three major categories of materials that are sold as surplus.

Scrap metals, depending on existing economic conditions, are best disposed of by either a short- or a long-term contract made with a local scrap dealer. The dealer getting the contract should be selected after an investigation of at least three dealers. Because of the breadth of scrap market activities, a purchasing department should generally experience little difficulty in interesting three or more capable dealers who will compete vigorously for the business. Also, the highly competitive nature of the scrap business usually keeps the variation in bid prices within a narrow range. Local dealers have an operating and transportation advantage over more distant competitors; also, they can provide more frequent pickups and more personalized contract service. Published market prices are available for many varieties of scrap, and these prices are frequently used as the bases for long-term contract prices. Bid prices are normally used for short-term contract prices.

Surplus stock that cannot be returned to the supplier is best disposed of by sale to jobbers or secondhand dealers. Such sales are most frequently made on a competitive bid basis, and competition for these materials is usually keen.

Surplus equipment typically can be disposed of most effectively by obtaining competitive bids from dealers. However, on occasion negotiation is used. Intense competition is traditionally developed after a firm acquires a select group of dealers who are interested in bidding for its surplus equipment on a continuing basis. Fixed prices to dealers are satisfactory when a selling firm is sure of the equipment's fair selling price. Auction is frequently used as a quick and convenient method of disposing of large quantities of equipment. Occasionally, advertisements in trade journals or trade papers prove effective in selling this category of surplus.

BUYING SURPLUS MATERIAL

Purchasing departments not only *sell* surplus material, at times they also *buy* it. Purchasing managers often can find real bargains by shopping among surplus dealers. These dealers can supply almost anything—from transistors to molding machines. The wide range of surplus goods now available to those looking for good buys is best illustrated by the yearly displays at the Institute of Surplus Dealers Trade Show. Exhibitors' booths are filled with an impressive variety of power tools, packaging materials, grinding wheels, pressure-sensitive tapes, electronic parts, and a multitude of other products.

The Advantages

Most surplus dealers stress low price as their main selling point; however, a few extol the advantages of *immediate availability*, which is often an even more valuable advantage to a buyer. A company building a prototype product, for example, can often pick up suitable material immediately from a surplus dealer, whereas it might have to wait weeks or months to get the same material new.

Purchases of surplus equipment may also represent sound buying decisions in the following situations:

- When the equipment is to be used infrequently, such as for standby service
- When the equipment fills a one-time need
- When the equipment is to be used for maintenance, pilot, or experimental work
- When the equipment is to be used by students or apprentices
- When the buyer's firm is not able to finance new equipment

Specialized Dealers

The rapid increase in the variety and volume of surplus products has led naturally to the emergence of an increasing number of specialized dealers. Alben Packaging Corporation, for example, specializes in the sale of surplus paper and packaging materials. Specialists in hydraulic parts, nylon rope, bearings, marine supplies, machine tools, and many other fields are replacing those dealers who formerly sold everything.

Even some dealers who specialize, however, still handle a wide range of materials. A few dealers, such as The Tunnel Machinery Exchange, stand ready to equip an entire plant. "If you want to set up a factory to manufacture fluorescent light fixtures," an executive of Tunnel has said, "Tunnel Machinery Exchange can supply presses, molding machines, office equipment, typewriters—everything you need."

Knowledge of Markets Required

Surplus material purchases typically offer buyers significant cost savings. When buying technical products whose design is subject to rapid change, however, knowledge of the market and expected market trends is mandatory. In mid-1981, for example, *Purchasing World* reported the advantages of purchasing used computers.[9] Just two months later a *Wall Street Journal* article reported that "used computers may not be much of a bargain if prices of new ones continue to dive."[10] In the article, Adolph Monosson, board chairman of American Used Computer Company (the largest used-computer dealer in the U.S.), predicted that sales for used computers would peak in 1983, then drop precipitously. He stated that advancing technology would soon drive the price of new computers down so fast that used equipment would no longer be an attractive alternative. Rapidly changing conditions, illustrated in the two articles cited above, emphasize the fact that the effective purchase of used technical products requires perceptiveness, analytical skill, and accurate market data—it is no business for a novice. Likewise, buying new designs and models of the same products requires similar capabilities.

---

[9]"Used Computers: A Cost-Saving Alternative," *Purchasing World*, July 1981, pp. 57–79.
[10]"Used Computers," *Wall Street Journal*, Sept. 17, 1981, p. 1.

Where to Find Surplus Dealers

Buyers looking for a dealer—either for buying or selling—can contact the New York office of the Institute of Surplus Dealers. This office lists all members and their various specialties.[11] Two regional associations can provide similar information: the Associated Surplus Dealers in Los Angeles and the National Surplus Dealers Association in Chicago. The Institute of Scrap Iron & Steel, Inc., in Washington, D.C., can supply a list of dealers who buy and sell all types of ferrous metals.[12] The Machinery Dealers National Association has a free *Buyers Guide* which lists surplus and salvage dealers throughout the United States.[13] Twice a month, the *McGraw-Hill Equipment Bulletin* provides a listing of used, surplus, and rebuilt equipment which has been advertised for sale in twenty-five magazines.[14]

CONCLUSION

Materials for U.S. industry originate from three basic sources—*domestic, foreign,* and *surplus.* To the extent practical, surplus is the preferred source since it provides so many unique advantages. Examples are reduced costs for transportation, processing, and energy; reduced emissions that form gaseous and solid pollutants; and reduced usage of new materials. Consequently, surplus materials always should be well managed, and they should be used whenever it is feasible to do so.

Although mineralogists do not agree precisely when the earth's key mineral supplies will be exhausted, they do agree that the supply is finite, and that at some future dates the various supplies will be exhausted. The seriousness of this situation was highlighted by President Reagan's warning in 1982: "It is now widely recognized that our nation is vulnerable to sudden shortages in basic raw materials."[15] Assuredly, so serious a situation dictates that the United States develop policies that specifically address this national problem.

New *domestic materials policies* are needed to replace current policies that tend to be conflicting and counterproductive. Transportation costs, health costs, safety costs, environmental costs, land preservation costs, and so forth, should be evaluated in terms of the nation's total materials requirements and its ability to pay for these requirements. Only such an evaluation can reconcile the total cost and noncost factors impinging on the nation's overall raw materials problem.

New *foreign materials policies* are needed to secure the nation's supply of critical minerals from foreign sources. Industrial and military analysts alike

[11]Institute of Surplus Dealers, 254 Manhattan Avenue, New York, NY 11211.
[12]Institute of Scrap Iron and Steel, 1627 K Street N.W., Washington, DC 20006.
[13]Machinery Dealers National Association, Box 19128, Washington, DC 20036.
[14]*McGraw-Hill Equipment Bulletin,* Box 900, New York, NY 10020. Single copies free.
[15]White House speech, Feb. 19, 1982.

recognize that secure foreign sources of many raw materials are essential to assure the nation's economic prosperity, its future economic growth, and its national defense.

Because both the industrialized and the developing nations are using increasing quantities of scarce minerals, the world has become engaged in a resources struggle. As the seriousness of this struggle becomes more clearly recognized, and as new scarce materials policies are implemented, additional opportunities will open up for progressive materials managers. By development of timely conservation-oriented programs that maximize the value of surpluses bought and sold for their individual firms, materials managers can make a genuine contribution. They can increase corporate profits, contribute to the reduction of U.S. dependence on foreign sources for materials, reduce the balance of payments deficit, and contribute to continuing national prosperity.

FOR DISCUSSION

24-1 Explain why surplus materials are important to the individual firms that create them.

24-2 What impact can surplus materials have on the national economy?

24-3 What effect does a well-managed surplus materials program have on the environment?

24-4 Explain why metals are so important to a modern industrial society.

24-5 What impact do U.S. international relations have on the answer to the preceding question?

24-6 If recycling scrap metal reduces energy requirements, reduces pollution, and conserves raw materials, why then in some cases is virgin ore smelted in place of available scrap?

24-7 What department in most companies do you feel is best qualified to handle surplus disposal? Why?

24-8 Some observers say that the sales department is the logical place to locate the scrap disposal function. Discuss.

24-9 Discuss how surplus materials are created in the U.S. economy. Can these surpluses be controlled?

24-10 How does national economic planning relate to the effective utilization of surplus materials?

24-11 Explain why some companies engage in planned overbuying, thus possibly creating a disposal-of-surplus problem.

24-12 What are some of the problems in attempting to use surplus material throughout a large multiplant company?

24-13 If you were the purchasing manager for the prime contractor for a Mach 3 commercial airliner, what thoughts would you have about the disposal of scrap metals that will be used in this 2,000-mile-an-hour plane?

24-14 Explain why some purchasing managers follow scrap prices with such great interest.

24-15 Explain and discuss the traditional ways most firms dispose of scrap.

24-16 Discuss the advantages and the possible hazards of buying surplus capital equipment.

24-17 Discuss the impact you think the world's increasing scarcity of raw materials will have on the management of surpluses in the 1990s. Discuss the additional opportunities this impact will open to materials managers.

24-18 Assume that you are the manager of a large firm's reclamation and salvage department. Outline in general form the plan you would use in deciding how to dispose of surplus capital equipment after it comes to your department for handling.

24-19 Referring to the preceding question, outline a general plan for handling and disposing of scrap metal from the production shops.

24-20 Discuss the principal surplus materials problems which materials managers can do very little to solve.

CASES FOR CHAPTER 24

Back Bay University, page 710
Erie Machine, Inc., page 737

SEVEN

GENERAL MANAGEMENT
RESPONSIBILITIES

CHAPTER **25**

DEVELOPING AND MANAGING THE BUYING PLAN

KEY CONCEPTS

- Reactive and proactive purchasing
- The annual operating plan
    The materials budget
- Volume and timing decisions
    Stable markets
    Unstable markets
    Timing of purchases
    Buying policies: Buying to requirements; Forward buying; Hand-to-mouth buying
- The annual buying plan
    Purchasing research: Demand analysis; Market analysis; Vendor analysis
    Buying plan objectives
- Buying strategy
    Contract buying
    Small orders
    The "in-between" materials
    Hedging
- Strategic materials planning

The first purchasing agent's position was created to provide a service for the people managing the primary operating functions of the firm. In time, the buying activity became a specialized, then a professionalized, staff function. Until the last decade or two, however, the job of most buyers in the purchasing department began when they received a purchase requisition from one of the operating units. In other words, the purchasing function typically operated in a *reactive* manner. When a materials need arose, purchasing reacted to it.

Today, progressive purchasing departments operate differently. Most organizations have learned that a majority of their materials needs over the course of a four- to twelve-month period can be determined in advance with acceptable accuracy. Not all materials needs can be forecast, but many can. Hence, most purchasing managers and their senior buyers develop an annual buying plan for their key materials when it is practical to do so. Included in this plan is the use of a variety of volume buying and longer-term contracting techniques. Thus, progressive purchasing departments are *proactive*—that is, they make things happen. In this case, they prepare a flexible "game plan" before specific materials needs arise.

The development and management of these plans is the subject of this chapter.

THE PLANNING APPROACH

The Firm's Annual Operating Plan

In preparation for each new fiscal year most firms construct a firmwide *annual operating plan.* A forecast of the scope and magnitude of key operating activities is the starting point for development of the plan. In a manufacturing firm this is the *sales forecast*—which usually consists of a total annual figure that is further divided into quarterly and monthly estimates by product line. The sales forecast is then translated into an aggregate production plan and master schedule, taking into consideration finished-goods inventory levels as well as desired in-process inventory levels for specific items. For obvious reasons, near-term forecast data can be converted into a production schedule with more accuracy, for shorter time periods, than is possible when the planners peer farther into the future.

All materials planning subsequently flows from the preliminary master production schedule. Likewise, operating plans at the group and departmental levels emanate, in a more general way, from this same source. Planning work to this point sets the stage for the budget planning which follows. Figure 25-1 diagrams this general process in terms of the generation of a simplified organization budget.

The Materials Budget   The basic materials budget, then, is a product of the sales forecast and a planned volume of production. Since sales forecasts are rarely completely accurate, though, actual production levels inevitably deviate from planned levels. When deviation occurs, the basic budget is in error for those items whose costs vary with the level of production—namely, direct materials and labor requirements. This unavoidable situation has led most companies to adopt some form of flexible budgeting. The *flexible budget*

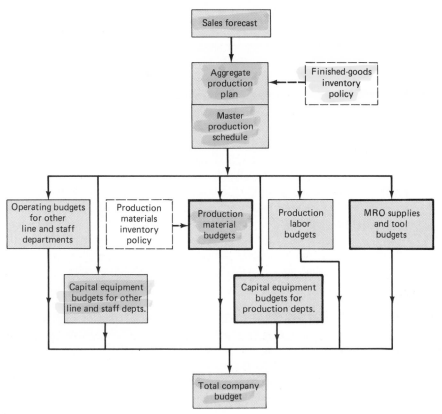

FIGURE 25-1
Major constituents of a total company budget.

makes use of supplementary data which adjust variable costs in accordance with the production level actually experienced.

Since the materials budget is based on an estimated level of production, preparation of a *detailed* annual materials budget is practical only for those products whose sales can be forecast reasonably accurately, or for materials that are used in a variety of products whose aggregate demand can be forecast. This means that many companies find it impossible to develop a materials budget for the full year ahead, and that others may be able to budget only selected key materials (perhaps JIT and Class A inventory items). Nevertheless, whenever possible, most materials departments find it profitable to develop a materials budget in terms of both units and dollars.

When the preliminary production schedule is available, it can be converted into a materials budget with the use of the appropriate product bills of material. Conversion simply entails an extension of materials requirements for each product, followed by a consolidation of individual material requirements. At this point the budget is expressed in units. Conversion of units into dollars is normally accomplished by applying either standard cost data or estimated cost figures.

When a materials budget is to be expressed in terms of dollars, the purchasing manager is normally called on to supply the budget department with two types of information: (1) estimates of material *prices* during the coming year and (2) plans for the specific *timing* of purchases. This information gives the finance department the necessary data to draw up a realistic schedule of cash requirements for each operating period.

In purchasing, reasonably precise knowledge of materials requirements over an extended period of time facilitates forward buying and permits the advantageous use of contract purchasing and blanket order purchasing techniques. Quantity discounts also can be utilized more effectively. Inventory investment, and its associated risks, likewise can be reduced by advance planning of requirements. *Materials budgets provide maximum purchasing lead time.* This benefit permits the careful selection of qualified suppliers, negotiation without the pressure of deadlines, and a better chance to obtain maximum value for each dollar spent. Additional lead time also produces savings by the use of routine rather than premium transportation, by a reduction in expediting costs, and by a smoothing of the purchasing workload. Supplier relationships can be improved and costs can be reduced because time is available to mesh purchasing requirements with the supplier's production schedule more effectively.

The next step in the process is the development of a detailed *annual buying plan* for each major material or category of materials. Before discussing this topic, however, it is first essential to review the nature of volume and timing decisions.

Volume and Timing Decisions

Volume and timing decisions are influenced by a number of factors, including the type of market in which the purchase is to be made. The first significant variable is the stability of the market.

Stable Markets Materials purchased in stable markets are the multitude of standard, off-the-shelf industrial products, supplies, and hardware (e.g., standard electric motors, pumps, valves, bearings, chemicals, tools, nuts, bolts). In the long run, in a reasonably competitive economy the general forces of supply and demand tend to determine the price levels at which these standard products will be sold. In conducting daily business, however, a buyer is more concerned with short-run market conditions. And, in the short run, shelf prices of these materials are relatively insensitive to the general forces of supply and demand. In the short run, about the only way a buyer can influence the prices he or she pays for these types of items is through some type of volume buying arrangement that permits a supplier to reduce its production or distribution costs.

Nonstandard components and materials, which constitute a substantial portion of most manufacturers' purchases, represent a special situation. Many nonstandard items are bought from numerous small machine shops, foundries, and similar job-shop producers. Consequently, the supply of these items adjusts fairly quickly to the general level of demand. As far as the buyer is concerned, the result in most cases is a reasonably stable supply and price situation. Because of the number and the flexibility of suppliers, the price a buyer pays for such materials is determined largely by the effect of his or her unique demand on the suppliers' costs of production.

Unstable Markets Unstable markets exhibiting substantial short-run fluctuation of the supply and price factors exist for numerous raw materials. Typical examples of such commodities are crude rubber, copper, tin, zinc, lead, scrap iron, burlap, wool, cotton, hides, wheat, flour, and vegetable oils. The supply of such raw materials is frequently influenced by political forces, weather conditions, actions of speculators, and similar unpredictable factors. As a result, the short-run prices of such commodities may be extremely sensitive to the general forces of supply and demand.

In most cases, the market is supplied by a large number of producers, and the buying action is conducted by a large number of relatively small purchasers. This means that the actions of an *individual buyer* have little effect on the equilibrium price in the market. The market price of such commodities often varies substantially from week to week and month to month, as is indicated by recent price charts for several commodities shown in Figure 25-2.

Timing of Purchases When considering the timing of purchases, buyers are interested first in assuring their firms an *adequate supply* of material and second in acquiring the material at an *optimal price*, considering quality and service requirements. As a general rule, timing is not a critical matter from either point of view when the purchase is made in a market that tends toward price stability. There are exceptions, of course. For example, a buyer always tries to anticipate general price increases arising from wage and other cost increases in his or her suppliers' industries. Likewise, the buyer keeps a close eye on the level of general demand for key suppliers' products. If general demand for a particular supplier's product increases sharply, a temporary shortage may develop until demand again tapers off or until production capacity has increased to satisfy the increased level of demand.

Timing is a much more important matter when a purchase is made in a market that tends to be unstable. Careful observation and analysis of market conditions are essential if buyers hope to satisfy their price and supply objectives. Although buyers cannot influence the *market price*, they can, by their timing of purchases, control to some extent the *price they pay*.

In recent years, demand for certain raw materials, and the products derived from them, has tended to increase more rapidly than supply. This phenomenon has frequently produced periodic shortages and an increase in the

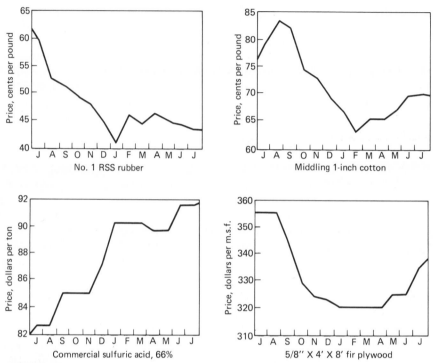

FIGURE 25-2
Illustration of commodity price movements for selected commodities.

number of materials markets that are characterized by periodic instability. Expansion of multinational business activity and international purchasing, coupled with the volatility of some foreign political environments, has tended to compound the problem of market instability. This situation is particularly evident in markets heavily affected by countries located in the Middle East, Latin America, and Africa. Hence, the timing of purchases made in a growing number of these markets has become increasingly important—a situation which likely will continue into the foreseeable future.

Buying Policies Related to Volume and Timing In a broad sense, a buyer can utilize one of two basic buying approaches: (1) purchase according to current known requirements, or (2) purchase primarily according to supply market conditions. If the first approach is used, the purchasing schedule is based strictly on the volume of the firm's current needs and largely disregards the behavior of the market in which the purchase is made. If a buyer adopts the second policy, in addition to considering anticipated needs he or she bases purchase timing decisions, in part, on the behavior of the market. In this case, two types of buying activity can be employed—(1) hand-

FIGURE 25-3
Buying policies in approximate relation to time.

to-mouth buying and (2) forward buying. Each type of buying activity is discussed briefly in the following paragraphs.

Buying to requirements, as the name implies, is a buying policy designed to cover only a firm's materials requirements that are definitely known. Although the time coverage varies from firm to firm for obvious reasons, a period of from one to three months is most common in practice. Most firms use a rolling production forecast that is translated into a firm schedule on either a monthly or a quarterly basis. Buying to requirements generally is the most conservative of the various alternatives and is considered by many firms to be the soundest approach when dealing in a market involving price risks.

Forward buying is the practice of buying materials in a quantity exceeding specified current requirements, but not beyond the actual foreseeable requirements. Even though not known with precision, it is reasonably certain that a longer-term production need for the material does exist. Any purchases beyond this point fall into the speculative buying category. Forward buying can be used in stable markets or in unstable markets where prices appear to be rising. One potential hazard in forward buying, however, is the possible price risk involved, depending on the volatility of the market in which the purchase is made. Intelligent forward buying clearly requires a careful professional analysis of numerous market factors. The buyer must also consider the additional inventory carrying costs and the attendant tie-up of working capital that accompany forward-buys, unless contractual arrangements can be made for the supplier to carry part of the inventory.

Hand-to-mouth buying is the practice of buying material to satisfy current operating requirements in quantities smaller than those normally considered economical. As the term indicates, the production operation literally exists on a hand-to-mouth supply of materials. This buying policy is used primarily in an unstable market that is falling or in situations where demand for specific items may decline or terminate on short notice, for any number of reasons. This approach is *unlike* a small-delivery JIT operation that is based on a longer-term contractual arrangement. When employing a hand-to-mouth buying policy, each purchase is contracted separately at the current material price.

Because of the many variables involved in any specific buying situation, from a precise timing point of view there is no clear-cut definition of the dividing lines between the individual buying policies discussed. However, in order to place these policies in some concrete time perspective, they are defined in a general way as shown in Figure 25-3.

The Annual Buying Plan

After a preliminary materials budget has been developed for the coming year, buying plans are then developed for the same period. A precise buying plan should be structured for *each major material or category of materials.*

Demand Analysis   For dependent demand materials, the annual demand for each can be estimated by aggregating the requirements of all products using the given material. For independent demand materials and MRO items, an approximate annual demand figure can be estimated based on prior usage and expected plans for the coming year. At this point, an all-inclusive ABC analysis should be conducted to quantify with reasonable accuracy the high-value materials for the coming year's operation. As a general rule, the 80-20 phenomenon holds for most organizations. That is, approximately 80 percent of the firm's purchase dollars will be expended in buying approximately 20 percent of the materials the firm uses.

Buying plans should be constructed for most materials, but for obvious reasons, it is particularly important that plans for the top 20 percent or so of the materials be developed using careful detailed analyses. The 80 percent of the materials that account for approximately 20 percent of the firm's expenditures typically are grouped by general classifications and a plan is made for each group of similar items.

Market Analysis   The next step in making a buying plan is to assess the market in which the item will be purchased. Since a buyer's major *initial* concerns are availability and price, the anticipated supply and demand factors, along with their expected stability, must be reviewed. The results of this analysis can be compared with the buyer's estimated quarterly demand requirements to determine whether any potential supply problems exist. At the same time, potential changes in the pricing situation can be estimated by comparing supply-demand data and data from general economic forecasts with comparable data from the preceding period. Such an analysis should disclose the likely impact of capacity utilization and cost factors on suppliers' pricing actions.

Vendor Analysis   The next level of the analysis focuses on specific vendors in the market. At this point in the process, the objective is to review generally the past performance of current suppliers to determine whether any significant problems exist. At the same time, a *general* review of other potential suppliers can be done to determine whether any particularly attractive possibilities should subsequently be investigated more closely. The result of such an analysis can lead to several possible courses of action:

- Current suppliers are completely satisfactory, and no further analysis is required.
- Current suppliers are not completely satisfactory, so a subsequent search for one or more new suppliers should be undertaken.
- The material in question should be submitted for a value analysis study to determine whether specification modifications are possible, to the extent that effective sourcing of the item can be simplified.

Purchasing Research   These analyses required for the preparation of a buying plan—demand analysis, market analysis, vendor analysis, and perhaps value analysis—are, in effect, fairly specialized types of purchasing research work. Operationally they can be accomplished in several ways. Some firms' purchasing departments include these activities as part of a senior buyer's job. In these organizations, each buyer does his or her own purchasing research work for the materials he or she handles. In a majority of the more progressive firms, however, this purchasing research work is assigned to a group of staff specialists who are specifically trained in these activities.

In most firms, in recent years individual buyers have tended to purchase an increasing number of varied items. And, in many cases, these are complex items produced by more complex manufacturing processes. Consequently, many firms have found that the mounting pressure of daily buying activities tends to require an increasing amount of the individual buyer's time, leaving him or her without adequate time to conduct all the necessary purchasing research investigations. Instead of simply adding more buyers to the department, many firms have resolved the problem by creating a staff of purchasing research specialists to assist the buyers. This approach, it is claimed, solves the problem more efficiently, because it ensures time for adequate depth research and it eliminates duplications of research effort.

Buying Plan Objectives and Target Modes of Operation   Chapter 2 discussed various purchasing and materials management objectives and noted that they are developed for use at three different levels—managerial activities, functional operations, and detailed buying plan development. This section discusses the third level—those detailed objectives and operating targets that are formulated as a part of the buying plan *for each major material.*

In developing a buying plan, objectives and target modes of operation should be established within each of the broader functional objectives of the department. The following series of questions are classified in this manner and can be used as a checklist in developing the plan.

To Develop Effective Suppliers

1 Is the supplier base reduced to the lowest practical level?
  How many suppliers should be used? Multiple source? Single source?
2 Should an ongoing collaborative relationship be developed with the supplier?
3 How important is it that the supplier be a low-cost producer?
4 Are there any unique service requirements?
5 How important are reliability and cooperativeness?
6 How important are transportation costs and services?

To Buy Competitively

1 Should the purchase be competitively bid? Should it be negotiated?
2 Should the material be purchased on a term contract?
  What is the preferred contract period?
3 Are short-term supply-demand shifts important?
  Should hand-to-mouth or forward buying be used?
4 What price is being paid? What should be the target price in the new buying period?
5 What value improvements should be sought in the new buying period?
6 Should a life cycle cost analysis be made?
7 What terms of payment are preferred?

To Optimize Material Availability and Investment

1 Should a JIT purchasing arrangement be developed?
2 What should be the average inventory level target?
  What should be the target service level?
3 Are storage capacity constraints a problem?
4 Should systems contracting, blanket orders, or petty cash buying methods be used?
5 Should a supplier stocking plan or a consignment buying plan be used?

To Buy Quality Effectively

1 Does the material specification fit the need effectively?
  Is the specification as flexible as is practical?
  Should purchasing be involved in firming up the specification?
2 Is the specification compatible with the supplier's capability?
  Should the supplier be involved in firming up the specification?
3 Should SPC be used?
  Should quality assurance personnel work with the supplier's quality assurance people in developing the QC/inspection system?
  Should statistical sampling be used? Which plan?
4 What value improvements should be sought in the new buying period?

To Coordinate Effectively with Users

1 Does this item require further standardization work?
2 Do items 1 and 2 from the preceding quality objective require further coordination with using departments?
3 Is further liaison required with the user during the new buying period?

In developing the various elements of a new material buying plan, whenever a buyer makes a change from the preceding buying plan, a brief written discussion of the reason for the change is appropriate. This type of justification forces the buyer to rethink the analysis to verify its correctness—and the document also should explain clearly to the authorizing manager the rationale for the proposed new course of action.

Finally, it should be noted that in most cases the specific objectives and modes of operation for the annual buying plans will be somewhat different for each material. The markets, the suppliers' capabilities, and the characteristics of the materials and their usage are all quite different. Consequently, it is reasonable to expect that the key elements of the buying plans will also be different.

BUYING STRATEGY

A buyer's basic elements of strategy for managing each material are embodied in the various buying plans developed. Additionally, from a *departmental perspective,* the purchasing management team must develop an overall strategy for handling its buying responsibilities *in the aggregate.* As a general rule, this strategy includes three elements:

1 *Contract buying.* Most firms typically attempt to develop annual or longer-term contracts with suppliers for materials that represent 60 to 80 percent of the firm's annual purchasing expenditures.
2 *Minimizing small orders.* A well-managed firm attempts to minimize the number of small orders placed.
3 *Managing the "in-between" materials.* Good management attempts to optimize value relative to total cost for those medium- and lower-value materials that are purchased primarily in response to requisitions from inventory and operating departments.

Contract Buying

Properly used, contract buying can yield a number of significant benefits. The major advantages flow from the continuing collaborative relationship that can be developed with the supplier during the contract period. Such a relationship facilitates the development of improved control of material quality and costs as well as delivery and service arrangements. A long-term agreement also usually produces a significantly better pricing arrangement than is possible for shorter-term, smaller-volume purchases.

From an internal managerial point of view, term contracting has several important advantages. Since the supplier review and selection effort is undertaken only once every year or two, the buying organization can utilize a review team of specialists to conduct a comprehensive, detailed investigation of the market and individual potential suppliers. Thus, both efficiency and effectiveness are improved. Likewise, paperwork is reduced and ongoing ordering efficiency is increased.

Term contracting clearly can be utilized most effectively in markets that are reasonably stable and predictable. Although an incentive or cost-type contract is sometimes used, typically such agreements are structured with a firm fixed price contract or a fixed price with escalation/de-escalation clause type contract. Contract buying is used for as many of the high-value items as is practical, simply because it can provide a more manageable, cost-effective buying situation. Many of the progressive firms target approximately 80 percent of their dollar expenditures for contract buying.

Minimizing Small Orders

Ironically, in many otherwise well-managed purchasing departments small orders account for a disproportionately high percentage of the purchase orders placed. It is not uncommon to find half of the orders issued to be for purchases of less than $250. This type of purchasing activity is extremely inefficient. It is a poor use of clerical time and an even poorer use of buyers' time. Consequently, perceptive managers develop a buying strategy that minimizes this type of operating situation.

A number of techniques can be used to reduce the volume of small orders to a practical level. Many firms use systems contracting and blanket orders effectively to reduce both the required purchasing and clerical effort and, at the same time, improve price and service performance. Petty cash purchases and special low-value "field order" or "short order" forms can also be used to accomplish similar results. And in some cases, frequently used low-value items can be placed in inventory and easily pay for their additional carrying costs. Chapter 3 discusses these and other small-order management techniques in detail.

Managing the "In-Between" Materials

Many B and some C category materials do not possess a stable enough demand to warrant the use of contract buying, or the markets in which they are purchased are too unstable to make contract buying practical. In the case of these materials, purchases are usually made in response to specific purchase requisitions. Sometimes requirements contracts, systems contracts, or blanket orders can be used to improve buying effectiveness, but more commonly each buy is made on an individual basis.

If a buyer determines that a rising or a falling market clearly exists, hand-to-mouth buying and forward buying strategies might be used, as shown in Figure 25-4.

By using a forward buying strategy during a rising market, the average price actually paid on the cycle upswing *should be significantly less* than the average market price during the period. If hand-to-mouth buying is used on the downswing, the average price paid *will approximate the average market price* during the period, if the purchase intervals are fairly short.

On the other hand, if a buyer's strategy is to *minimize price risk* during the entire cycle—particularly in an unpredictable market—a hand-to-mouth strategy in both up and down periods will tend to produce an average price paid that is close to the average market price during the complete cycle. This situation is portrayed in Figure 25-5.

Hedging

When purchasing raw materials and commodities, hedging is another technique used to *minimize the risk associated with fluctuating market prices*. However, the technique can be used only in buying materials for which an organized commodity exchange exists.

An organized commodity exchange is a marketplace where a particular commodity is bought and sold in substantial quantities. At many of the exchanges, both "cash" transactions and "futures" transactions take place. A *cash transaction,* as the words imply, involves a current exchange of cash for the physical commodity. A *futures transaction* involves a current purchase or sale, at a quoted price, for which the physical commodity will be delivered at a specified date in the future. With the passage of time, the current cash price for a commodity and its futures price often fluctuate together, approximately

FIGURE 25-4
Timing purchases to take advantage of market action: forward buying in a rising market; hand-to-mouth buying in a falling market.

Price

J F M A M J J A S O N D J F M A M J J A S O N D J

Time

FIGURE 25-5
Timing purchases to minimize price risk: hand-to-mouth buying in both rising and falling markets.

paralleling one another.[1] It is the futures transaction that is essential in a hedging operation.

If the reader refers to the market section of the *Wall Street Journal*, or a similar financial publication, he or she will find a listing of the numerous commodity markets. Futures markets operate for many of these commodities, such as cotton, cocoa, coffee, sugar, hides, rubber, wool, and various metals, grains, and oils.

For the industrial buyer, hedging is a technique that can provide protection against market price declines during the period when his or her firm is processing a raw material preparatory to selling it in another form as a finished product. With this financial worry removed, the manufacturer is free to concentrate on normal production and sales activities.

For example, suppose a chocolate manufacturer has signed a contract to sell a large candy manufacturer ten carloads of refined chocolate syrup each month for the next year. The contract stipulates that chocolate syrup will be sold at a price based on the market price of raw cocoa *at the time of delivery of the chocolate syrup.* What happens to the chocolate manufacturer, then, if it buys raw cocoa at $0.26 per pound, and one month later, when it delivers the refined chocolate made from this cocoa, the market price for raw cocoa has fallen to $0.21 per pound? The firm has to sell the refined chocolate at a lower price than was intended when the cocoa was purchased. Consequently, the chocolate manufacturer's profit margin is reduced, or perhaps entirely elim-

---

[1]The most important single factor to the hedger is the difference between the cash price and the futures price, commonly called the *basis.* In a completely competitive situation where supply and demand are in balance, the futures price would be expected to exceed the cash price by the total cost of carrying the commodity in storage until the future date. Because supply and demand typically do not remain in balance long for free market commodities, the difference between futures and cash prices is influenced considerably by the way buyers evaluate present and anticipated supply-demand conditions. This explains why the basis for a given commodity varies with time, reflecting something less than a parallel relationship between the movement of the cash and the future prices.

inated. To protect against such an occurrence, the manufacturer might choose to engage in a hedging operation. Such a hedge would consist of the following market transactions:

1 First, the firm *buys raw cocoa* in the cash market. At the same time, it *sells a futures contract* in the futures market for the same quantity of raw cocoa, to be delivered shortly after it expects to sell the refined chocolate. (Note that the firm does not own any cocoa at this time which it could deliver at this future date.)

2 At the time the firm *sells the refined chocolate,* it also *buys a futures contract for cocoa* to cover the futures contract it originally sold and would soon have to deliver.

The protection offered by the hedge is based on the premise that should raw cocoa cash market prices drop during the manufacturing period (resulting in a reduced selling price for chocolate), futures prices will also drop proportionately. Thus, although the producer takes a loss by selling its chocolate at a reduced price, it makes an approximately equal profit by covering its futures contract at a similarly reduced price. Bear in mind that in this example the selling price of chocolate maintains a constant relationship to the purchase price of raw cocoa. An important prerequisite to the use of hedging requires that the purchaser's finished product be sold in a market where prices move approximately parallel to the prices of the purchased raw material. These concepts are illustrated numerically in the following simplified example and in Figure 25-6.

Cash activities	Futures market activities
January 15: Cash market *purchase* of 100,00 pounds of *raw cocoa* at $0.26/pound = 100,000 × $0.26 = $26,000	**January 15:** *Sells* a March *futures contract* for 100,000 pounds of raw cocoa at $0.275/pound = 100,000 × $0.275 = $27,500
January 15 to February 15: Purchaser incurs manufacturing costs (*including normal profit*) of $0.43/pound = 100,000 × $0.43 = $43,000	
February 15:* *Sells refined chocolate* (equivalent of 100,000 pounds of cocoa) to customer at $0.64/pound = 100,000 × $0.64 = $64,000	**February 15:** *Buys* a March *futures contract* for 100,000 pounds of raw cocoa at $0.225/pound = 100,000 × $0.225 = $22,500
Net gain on manufacturing activity = $64,000 − ($26,000 + 43,000) = − $5,000	*Net gain* on activity in March futures cocoa market = $27,500 − 22,500 = + $5,000

*The raw cocoa market price has dropped $.05/pound since January 15. Had it not dropped, refined chocolate would have sold for $0.69/pound on February 15.

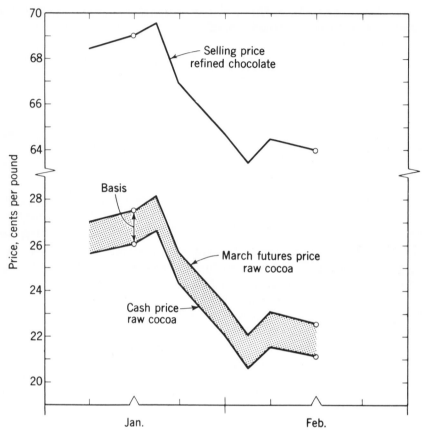

FIGURE 25-6
Simplified illustration of a perfect hedge.

So—while the chocolate manufacturer lost $5,000 on its manufacturing activity because of the 5 cent/pound drop in cocoa prices, it was able to offset this loss with a $5,000 gain by hedging in the futures market, thus preserving its normal profit margin on the sale of the refined chocolate. Had the price of cocoa risen from January 15 to February 15, the situation would have been reversed. The firm would have shown an extra profit in its manufacturing operation because of the price increase, but it would have suffered a loss on its futures transaction; thus, the firm would still experience no net gain or loss as a result of fluctuating market prices.

The preceding case is a simplified example of a perfect hedge, which, to reiterate, is based on two assumptions:

1 The selling price of the buyer's finished product will move exactly parallel to the cash market price of its major raw material.
2 Futures prices will move exactly parallel to cash market prices.

In practice, these conditions exist only imperfectly. The degree of perfection found in the relationship depends largely on specific market conditions and on the characteristics of each specific seller's market. The hedger nearly always gains or loses *some* money on a hedging transaction because the spread between futures and cash prices and the spread between product selling price and material purchase price both vary somewhat with time. However, this by no means invalidates the technique. Provided the relationships show reasonable stability, hedging can in many cases provide good protection against the risk of *wide* price swings. To use hedging successfully, buyers must be skilled enough to estimate the magnitude of possible gain or loss through "basis" variation. Their decision to hedge (or not to hedge) rests on a comparison of this factor with an assessment of the probable magnitude and direction of cash market price fluctuations.

STRATEGIC MATERIALS PLANNING

Strategic planning is concerned with the development of a firm's plans for its long-term material requirements, as contrasted with its plans for foreseeable, near-term requirements. Strategic planning focuses management's attention on long-term competitiveness and profitability, rather than on short-term bottom-line considerations.

Until a decade or so ago, conventional corporate planning wisdom held that a firm's long-range planning cycle began with an analysis of its products, its markets, and its competition—and then worked back through the various operating and staff departments, as shown in Figure 25-7a Historically, purchasing or materials management departments seldom participated in this process until the long-term plans were firm and subsequently translated into annual operating plans. This process worked satisfactorily as long as materials were readily available at competitive prices. In recent years, however, scarcity of some resources, intensive worldwide competition, and increasing international and environmental uncertainties have produced a marked change in this approach.

Many firms now find themselves faced with a significant list of critical materials that may not be readily available at competitive prices in the years ahead. Consequently, it is necessary to identify the potentially critical materials early in the planning process—and to analyze each issue thoroughly enough to determine whether a serious problem does in fact exist. In many firms this situation has led to a modification of the corporate long-range planning process, as shown in Figure 25-7b. The process now begins as it did originally, but it brings together almost immediately both *product demand* and *material supply* considerations, recognizing the respective dynamic market environment of each.

The unique characteristic of strategic materials planning is its focus on the impact that *changes in the external environment* might have on the firm's materials needs and procurement policy. Dr. Robert Spekman's generalized

FIGURE 25-7
Simplified models of information flows in the corporate strategic planning process. (a) Traditional
model. (b) Model including materials planning.

model of the strategic procurement planning process highlights the significance and the interactive nature of this characteristic. (See Figure 25-8.)[2]

Strategic materials planning involves both economic and technical investigations. On the domestic and relevant foreign scenes, forecasts of general
economic (and political) conditions are made, and studies of specific industries and commodity markets are undertaken. Price trends and technological
developments in industries producing interchangeable materials are studied
in an attempt to forecast future conditions in competitive industries. These
forecasted conditions are then related to the firm's future needs. This type of
analysis permits an assessment of current purchasing policy and points up
the possible need for changes which may require careful advance planning.
Technical investigations dovetail into two major programs which frequently

[2]Robert E. Spekman, "A Strategic Approach to Procurement Planning," *Journal of Purchasing
and Materials Management*, Winter 1981, pp. 2–8.

FIGURE 25-8
A model of the strategic procurement planning process.

are conducted on a companywide basis—*value analysis* and *make-or-buy analysis*.

The end product of a strategic materials planning investigation can take three forms:

1 Agreements with one or more suppliers to provide agreed-on materials requirements for specific future time periods—i.e., mutually satisfactory long-term contractual arrangements. (This may require mutual support for the development of additional supplier capability.)

2 A decision to phase out the use of a given material and replace it with a more satisfactory or more easily obtainable material. This decision clearly must be coordinated with a preliminary value analysis study to determine its feasibility, and likely will be followed with more detailed value analysis work.

3 A decision to make the item in-house, eliminating dependence on suppliers and external conditions, which may be excessively difficult if not impossible to control.

CONCLUSION

Procurement planning stands at the heart of our purchasing operation: without it, all of our efforts would be opportunistic, and we almost certainly would overlook important opportunities to contribute to company profitability.[3]

This statement was made by an experienced purchasing executive, in a new job assignment, after successfully transforming his new firm's purchasing department from a reactive to a proactive operation. In a broad sense, it serves as a testimonial to the purpose of this chapter.

In developing a department's buying strategies and its annual buying plans, a perceptive manager generally will employ most of the buying objectives, policies, and techniques discussed in this chapter. And although planning is both an art and a science, skill in properly blending the use of these management tools in practice is acquired only through experience as one gains familiarity with specific materials and markets.

FOR DISCUSSION

25-1 What is planning? Discuss.

25-2 What role does the purchasing department play in a company's budgeting procedures?

25-3 What is meant by the terms "stable market" and "unstable market"? List six materials that are purchased in each type of market. Explain why the price of rubber fluctuates substantially, while the price of steel in the short run fluctuates very little.

25-4 Discuss the significance of the timing of purchases. (Include a discussion of the factors which affect the timing of purchases.)

25-5 What is forward buying? Explain.

25-6 What are the major reasons for forward buying? Discuss each briefly.

25-7 What is hand-to-mouth buying? When would you use it?

25-8 What is meant by the term "buying to requirements"?

25-9 What is an annual buying plan? Why is an annual buying plan used?

25-10 Assume you are a buyer for a firm that produces the ore used to make a high-value industrial chemical. The firm operates a large hard-rock mine one-quarter of a mile under ground. It uses large quantities of various structural steel members and steel "roof bolts" to keep the mine tunnels safe and open for traffic.

Describe in detail the steps you would go through in making an annual buying plan for structural steel and roof bolts.

25-11 "All good buyers engage in purchasing research." Explain.

25-12 Why do some companies find it desirable to institute a formal purchasing research program? Explain.

---

[3]Frank L. Bauer, "Managerial Planning in Procurement," *Journal of Purchasing and Materials Management*, Fall 1977, pp. 3–8.

25-13 Why is annual or longer-term buying used? What are the advantages? What are the potential problems?

25-14 In developing a two-year contract for a major material used in your firm's operation, which types of contracts might be used? Discuss.

25-15 Explain how a hedging activity is conducted.

25-16 What is the "basis"? Why is it important in a hedging operation?

25-17 In a commodity market, what is the maximum value a futures price will reach relative to its corresponding cash price? Explain.

25-18 Identify a type of manufacturing organization that could benefit significantly from having a hedging specialist in its purchasing department. Discuss.

25-19 How does strategic materials planning differ from other purchasing planning techniques? Why is it used?

25-20 What benefits might a firm expect to receive from the use of strategic materials planning?

CASES FOR CHAPTER 25

VALUE ANALYSIS/ ENGINEERING

WHAT IS VALUE ANALYSIS?

Approximately twenty-five years ago, the *Reader's Digest* published an article entitled "The Biggest Thing Since Mass Production." The article described how dramatic dollar savings were produced for consumers and taxpayers by a new industrial technique called value analysis. In reality, this "new" concept had its genesis during the war years of the early 1940s. During the intervening years acceptance of the concept grew. By the mid-1960s, value analysis was established as the cornerstone of most purchasing research and cost reduction programs in major manufacturing firms. Since that time, enthusiasm for the concept waxed and waned, until material shortages and volatile prices associated with the 1973–1974 energy crisis again highlighted its profit potential. Today, nearly three-quarters of all American industrial firms have a formal value analysis program in operation.[1]

During World War II many critical materials and components were difficult to obtain, and most manufacturers were required to specify numerous substitutions in their design and production activities. Harry Erlicher, then vice president of purchasing for the General Electric Company, observed that many of the required substitutions during this period resulted not only in reduced costs but also in functional product improvement. Consequently, Mr. Erlicher assigned to L. D. Miles the task of developing a systematic approach to the investigation of the *function/cost* aspect of *existing* materials specifications. Larry Miles not only met this challenge successfully, but subsequently pioneered the scientific procurement concept General Electric called "value analysis."

In 1954 the U.S. Navy's Bureau of Ships adopted a modified version of General Electric's value analysis concept in an attempt to reduce the cost of ships and related equipment. In applying the concept, the Navy directed its efforts primarily at cost avoidance during the initial engineering design stage and called the program "value engineering," even though it embodied the same concepts and techniques as GE's value analysis program. In an operational sense, however, the two terms typically are used synonymously in industry today—only the timing differs. Hence, throughout this book the term "value analysis" is used, and it carries the same conceptual meaning as the term "value engineering," except for the practical matter of timing.

The techniques of value analysis represent a potentially powerful set of tools which can be used by management in controlling materials costs. The fundamental objective of all value analysis activities is the procurement (or manufacture) of materials representing the "best buy" in terms of the *function* to be performed. In this sense the idea is not new; it is synonymous with a longstanding objective of good purchasing. The unique feature of current value analysis programs, however, lies in the systematic and thorough approach used in attaining this objective. Only after widespread publicity of Miles's original work did a significant number of firms make a concerted, systematic effort to engineer unnecessary costs out of the parts used in their products.

---

[1]Somerby Dowst, "Buyers Say VA Is More Important Than Ever," *Purchasing*, June 26, 1986, p. 64.

For many firms, the value analysis effort represents a significant part of their purchasing research activity. Much of the effort devoted to value analysis closely parallels the activity involved in the interdepartmental development of material specifications. The major differences are in the depth of the analysis and in the timing. Interdepartmental development of material specifications, like the Navy's value engineering application, focuses on new specifications developed at the engineering design stage. On the other hand, in most value analysis applications, management attempts to coordinate the talents of personnel in engineering, operations, and purchasing in conducting a meticulous investigation which usually leads to improvement of *existing* rather than new specifications.

Although different companies stress different variations of the fundamental idea, *two general conceptual tools are basic to the operation of a value analysis program:*

1 Design analysis of the required material
2 Cost analysis of the required material

Design Analysis

Design analysis entails a methodical step-by-step study of all phases of the design of a given item in relation to the *function* it performs. The philosophy underlying this approach is not concerned with appraisal of any given part per se. Rather, the appraisal focuses on the function which the part, or the larger assembly containing the part, performs. This approach is designed to lead the analyst away from a traditional perspective which views a part as having certain accepted characteristics and configurations. Instead, it encourages the analyst to adopt a broader point of view and to consider whether the part performs the required function both as effectively and as efficiently as possible. Both quality and cost are objects of the analysis.

One technique many firms use in analyzing component parts of a subassembly is to dismantle, or "explode," the unit and then mount each part adjacent to its mating part on a pegboard or a table. The idea is to demonstrate visually the functional relationships of the various parts. Each component can thus be studied as it relates to the performance of the complete unit, rather than as an isolated element. Analysis of each component in this fashion attempts to answer four specific questions:

1 Can any part be *eliminated* without impairing the operation of the complete unit?
2 Can the design of the part be *simplified* to reduce its basic cost?
3 Can the design of the part be changed to permit the use of simplified and less costly *production methods?*
4 Can less expensive but equally satisfactory *materials* be used in the part?

When viewed in this manner—from the standpoint of composite operation and cost—possibilities for making component design simplifications are frequently more apparent than is possible under the original design conditions. This in no way reflects unfavorably on the work done by the design engineer. The discovery of such potential improvements is simply the product of an analysis with a substantially broader orientation than that possessed by the original designer. An organized value analysis study usually utilizes a number of individuals with different types of background, experience, and skill impossible to combine in the person of a single designer. Resulting design changes often permit the substitution of standardized production operations for more expensive operations requiring special setup work. In some cases, considering the volume of parts to be produced, an entirely different material or production process turns out to be more efficient than the one originally specified.

The specific manner in which a value analyst approaches the problem of design analysis is a highly creative matter which differs from one analyst to another. Each possesses unique analytical abilities and develops unique patterns of thought. Some companies, however, require analysts to follow several general approaches which are designed to stimulate and organize their efforts. Those commonly used are (1) the value analysis checklist, (2) the functional cost approach, (3) the use of brainstorming, and (4) the use of suppliers.

The Value Analysis Checklist Most companies develop some type of checklist to systematize the value analyst's activity. Literally hundreds of questions and key ideas appear on these lists. Some of them are highly specialized for particular types of products. Illustrative of the more general questions is the following checklist suggested by the National Association of Purchasing Management.[2]

First, determine the *function* of the item, then determine:

1 Can the item be eliminated?
2 If the item is not standard, can a standard item be used?
3 If it is a standard item, does it completely fit the application or is it a misfit?
4 Does the item have greater capacity than required?
5 Can the weight be reduced?
6 Is there a similar item in inventory that could be substituted?
7 Are closer tolerances specified than are necessary?
8 Is unnecessary machining performed on the item?
9 Are unnecessarily fine finishes specified?
10 Is "commercial quality" specified? (Commercial quality is usually most economical.)
11 Can you make the item more cheaply in your plant? If you are making it now, can you buy it for less?

---

[2] *Basic Steps in Value Analysis,* a pamphlet prepared under the chairmanship of Martin S. Erb by the Value-Analysis-Standardization Committee, Reading Association, NAPM, Tempe, Arizona, pp. 4–18.

12 Is the item properly classified for shipping purposes to obtain lowest transportation rates?

13 Can cost of packaging be reduced?

14 Are suppliers being asked for suggestions to reduce cost?

In using this or similar checklists, the analyst evaluates the component under investigation with respect to each item on the checklist. When a question is found to which the answer is not entirely satisfactory, this becomes a starting point for more detailed investigation. The checklist focuses the analyst's attention on those factors which past experience has proved to be potentially fruitful cost reduction areas.

The Functional Cost Approach An additional question which appears on some checklists may be worded something like this: "What does it cost to perform the function done by this part?" or "Does the importance of the function to be performed justify the cost of performing it?" The idea underlying such a question is extremely broad and actually constitutes a separate approach to value investigation.

As value analysts in a particular industry gain experience, they quickly establish benchmark costs for performing certain functions characteristically encountered in their industry. For example, it may cost approximately x cents to join two pieces of metal of given sizes if the joint is to perform under conditions of mild vibration. On the other hand, it may typically cost approximately y cents to make the same joint if it must perform under conditions of excessive vibration. In another case, a manufacturer may find that on the average it costs z dollars to circulate coolant through a totally enclosed motor of a given size, under certain operating conditions.

The important point is this: After analyzing certain types of equipment day after day, good value analysts learn in a general way approximately what it costs to perform certain functions. As these kinds of data are accumulated, costs of particular functions appearing on new jobs can be compared with historical benchmarks. If the cost seems excessive, the analyst investigates further to determine the reason. The cost may well be justified due to differences between the new unit and past units on which benchmarks were based. If this does not appear to be the case, the analyst continues to search for a lower-cost method of performing the function.

For some parts, comparative analysis of similarly processed items may highlight unusually high-cost items. For example, formed or fabricated metal parts typically cost less per pound as the weight of the part increases. For all similar fabricated parts, an analyst might construct a graph on which the weight of each piece is plotted against its price per pound. Any items not conforming reasonably well with the resulting curve would be good candidates for more detailed analysis.

One important feature of this general approach is the idea of comparing current performance with typical past performance. A second and perhaps more important feature of the approach is the concept that the cost of performing a function must be reasonably proportionate to the value of the function itself.

The Use of Brainstorming A third technique which is sometimes used in conjunction with either of the preceding approaches is called brainstorming.

Brainstorming is a process designed to stimulate creative thinking. A group of people meet for the purpose of generating ideas useful in solving a particular problem. Emphasis is placed on the free-wheeling generation of ideas, which are recorded as soon as they are made. During this period no one in the group evaluates any ideas, since the objective at this point is to develop spontaneous and positive ideas. The theory underlying this approach to problem solving recognizes that many of the ideas spontaneously generated are completely infeasible. However, the theory holds that some of these ideas trigger thoughts from others in the group that lead to different and often very useful ideas. During a period of sixty minutes as many as several hundred ideas are sometimes recorded. Even if only several workable ideas emerge from the session, a good chance exists that one or two can be developed into a satisfactory solution to the problem.

The potential use of this technique for approaching value analysis problems should be apparent. Once the facts of a problem are thoroughly defined and understood, some companies call on several representatives from the appropriate departments to participate in a brainstorming session. After the session, the resulting ideas are analyzed for feasibility and for cost. The promising ideas are subsequently turned over to an analyst for further development.

Some companies utilize this technique as an integral part of the total value analysis procedure, although not every firm subscribes to extensive use of brainstorming. Some feel that in certain cases a greater number of practical ideas frequently can be generated with the expenditure of fewer man-hours by permitting analysts to work independently.

The Use of Suppliers An increasing number of major manufacturing firms subscribe to the idea that the primary responsibility of the purchasing department is to manage "outside manufacturing"—that is, in a general way to help plan and to coordinate the relevant manufacturing and quality activities of the firm's suppliers. This fundamental concept implies the development of a continuing long-term relationship with major suppliers. Some buying firms view this situation as a "partnership venture" with the supplier, as discussed in Chapter 19.[3] Functioning in this type of environment, suppliers frequently prove to be extremely valuable assets in a firm's total value anal-

---

[3] The value analysis "partnership" concept was strongly recommended fifteen years ago by Mr. Donald Lyons, vice president for purchasing, Manville Corp., and by Mr. Robert Giczewski, director of purchasing for Western Electric Corp., during *Purchasing Forum—'75*, sponsored by the Purchasing Management Association of Denver at Colorado State University, July 21, 1975.

ysis effort. One firm, for example, found that a majority of its value analysis savings came directly from suggestions of suppliers who had been asked to participate in its value analysis program.[4]

Perhaps this fact is not too surprising. After all, as a rule, a supplier knows more about the product and its potential capabilities than do most of the firm's customers. A supplier's technical knowledge, combined with broad experience in applying its product to hundreds of operations, frequently qualifies the firm to participate in most companies' value analysis programs.

A supplier's assistance can be enlisted in two ways: (1) by informal participation and (2) by participation in a supplier workshop. When using the informal approach, a firm usually has numerous high-priority value analysis projects exhibited on display boards, with all parts completely identified and tagged as to current cost. The purchasing executive invites current and potential suppliers to study particular exhibits for the purpose of offering possible cost reduction or quality improvement suggestions for items each might furnish. If a supplier can provide a lower-cost item that performs satisfactorily, or if it suggests feasible design modifications which permit the use of a lower-cost item, the firm is rewarded with additional business.

A similar approach is used by some firms when they ask suppliers to bid on an item. A simple supplier value analysis checklist is included with the specifications in each bid request. As illustrated in Figure 26-1 suppliers are encouraged to utilize their creativity and experience to obtain a competitive edge in the bidding process. If the checklist reveals bidders who use different production methods and different materials, or have similar low-cost proprietary products, chances are maximized for the generation of unique cost-saving ideas.

A second approach entails the use of periodic, formally organized supplier workshops. A group of perhaps fifty technical and managerial representatives from suppliers' firms is invited to the purchaser's plant for a one- or two-day workshop. The sessions typically include an introduction to the purchaser's new products, general company plans and their effects on suppliers, basic buying policies, and selected major value analysis problems. An important segment of the program is a tour of the buyer's production facilities. Here top-level supplier representatives have an opportunity to see how, where, and why their products are used by the purchaser. Additionally, suppliers can be requested to study specific value analysis exhibits, as is done in the informal approach.

An enhancement of this approach was used by General Motors' Oldsmobile Division. As part of the program, the division hired a consulting firm to present a "how to do it" supplier seminar in value analysis. What

---

[4]D. W. Dobler, "A Study of Materials Management and Its Problems in Small Manufacturing Businesses," unpublished doctoral dissertation, Stanford University, Stanford, Calif., 1960, p. 128. For an interesting discussion of this topic, see also Larry Miles, "Dynamic Vendor Programs: They Work!", *Purchasing World*, August 1984, p. 58.

SUPPLIER CHECKLIST FOR VALUE ANALYSIS STUDY

Part name and number _____

Estimated annual usage _____

Buyer _____

Questions	Yes	No	Recommendations

Do you understand the part function?
Could costs be reduced by relaxing requirements:
  ■ Tolerances?
  ■ Finishes?
  ■ Testing?
  ■ By how much?			

Could costs be reduced through changes in:
  ■ Material?
  ■ Ordering quantities?
  ■ The use of castings, stampings, etc.?
  ■ By how much?			

Can you suggest other changes that would:
  ■ Reduce weight?
  ■ Simplify the part?
  ■ Reduce overall costs?			

Do you feel that any of the specifications are too stringent?			
How can we help alleviate your greatest element of cost in supplying this part?			
Do you have a standard item that could be substituted for this part?			

Other suggestions? _____

_____

Supplier _____ Date _____

Address _____

Signature _____ Title _____

Additional comments may be added on the back of this sheet.

FIGURE 26-1
An illustrative value analysis checklist used to stimulate supplier participation in the value analysis program. (Source: *Lea Tonkin, "No Purchasing Department Is Too Small for Value Analysis,"* Purchasing World, *June 1982, p. 87.*)

purchasing management was saying to its major suppliers was: "We want all the help you can provide. Here are the functions we need, the way our customer wants them. Here are the value analysis methods to help you maximize your capabilities to meet our needs." Guidance was specific. "Always improve quality. When possible improve costs."[5] The results from Oldsmobile's first seminar of this type were rewarding—first-year cost reductions totaled approximately $1 million. And the company expected the greatest benefits in the years ahead.

It should be emphasized that solicitation of supplier assistance in a value analysis program is based on the premise that creative suppliers will be compensated for their efforts by receiving additional business or by sharing in the cost savings they help generate. Most companies find either approach to supplier participation profitable. In the case of the supplier workshop or seminar, improved supplier relations frequently emerge as a bonus benefit.

Cost Analysis

It is no secret that many manufacturers do not base the selling prices of their products entirely on costs. In some cases, the complexities of multiproduct cost accounting make it virtually impossible to determine the exact cost of producing and marketing a specific product. In other cases, firms may follow a variable-margin pricing policy, whereby the markup on certain types of products is greater than on others. Still other firms may follow the industry leader in establishing product prices.

Whatever the reason, industrial buyers realize that many of the prices they pay do not accurately reflect the cost of the product. Moreover, unless the buying firm has real clout and substantial knowledge of production costs, in some cases it may not know whether its buyer is in fact paying a fair price. As far back as 1928, C. F. Hirshfeld, then chief engineer of the Detroit Edison Company, advocated the practice of cost analysis to assist the buyer in this quandary.[6] The concept was subsequently adopted widely throughout the automobile industry. Elsewhere it received only sporadic support until the value analysis movement again spotlighted its potential value.

As currently practiced, cost analysis involves the investigation of a supplier's probable costs of producing a given product. The analyst constructs estimated elemental costs for materials, labor, manufacturing overhead, and general overhead. When totaled, these figures represent the theoretical total cost incurred by an efficient producer. An experienced analyst, with the use of wage data, material price lists, and various industry time standards, can determine a total theoretical cost which reasonably approximates the actual cost. To this figure is added a reasonable profit margin. Although the calculated price is not exact, it provides the buyer with a powerful negotiating tool. By using this calculated price as a target, a buyer can place a selling firm in a position of having to point out any errors in the development of the figure, or else justify its own quoted price with supporting cost data.

[5]Larry Miles, op. cit. p. 58.
[6]C. F. Hirshfeld, "Engineers in the Purchasing Department," *Mechanical Engineering*, vol. 50, no. 11, November 1928, pp. 848–849.

As the reader now knows, the use of cost analysis is not confined to value analysis work. Its basic use is in negotiating an original price. In recent years, however, cost analysis has become an extremely useful adjunct of value analysis, playing two major roles:

1 Cost analysis is conducted for currently purchased items whose costs appear excessive. In such cases, the information developed from cost analysis is used as a basis for further price negotiation with the supplier.
2 Cost analysis also serves as a means of locating high-cost parts which should be subjected to design analysis. During the course of a cost analysis, some high-cost elements are frequently isolated for the first time. Subsequent design analysis often leads to specification and production modifications and ultimately to reduced costs.

The Value Analysis Study

Let us take a moment at this point to draw together the foregoing discussions in a simple procedural model of the typical value analysis study. Although many companies have developed well-organized formal analysis programs, it should be obvious now that value analysis studies can be conducted formally by organized groups or informally by individuals such as buyers, engineers, production personnel, and so forth. In either case, the *elements* of the study are the same. Obviously, the depth and breadth of the analysis are influenced by the size and composition of the team making the study. Figure 26-2 illustrates in simplified form the elements of the overall value analysis study.[7]

Examples of Value Analysis

The following examples illustrate the types of modifications and savings that value analysis can produce.

Production Parts and Assemblies   While analyzing the components of a particular small motor, the value analyst for an electric motor manufacturer questioned the construction of the belt guard. The guard, shown in Figure 26-3, was a two-piece assembly made of expanded metal and sheet steel. The expanded metal was blanked to shape and then hand-welded to a metal frame which had also been blanked to shape. After studying the part and its functional requirements, the analyst recommended an equally suitable guard which could be completely produced from sheet metal in a single press-forming operation. The new guard was subsequently adopted and produced

---

[7]This model is based on a discussion of the value engineering job plan in *Value Engineering,* prepared by the Value Engineering Department, Lockheed-Georgia Company, Lockheed Aircraft Corp., pp. 12–15.

Elements of the study | Activities of the study

FIGURE 26-2
A generalized procedural model of the value analysis study.

Original belt guard | Modified one-piece belt guard

FIGURE 26-3
A belt guard before and after value analysis.

at a cost of approximately 20 percent of the cost of the old guard. Thus, a design change permitted less expensive material as well as less costly production methods to be used, producing an annual saving on this simple item of approximately $25,000.

The part shown in Figure 26-4 illustrates how another very simple design change permitted the realization of a substantial saving in both material and production time. This part, which looks something like a bolt with a flat cir-

FIGURE 26-4
A value-analyzed machine part.

cular head, is a rotating machine part. The grooved stem must fit precisely with its mating parts. When the part was originally designed, stringent tolerances were specified for both the head and the stem. This design requirement dictated that the part be machined from larger bar stock the size of the head. Consequently, a large amount of stock was wasted in the lengthy machining process. An investigation of the part's function, however, revealed that the head tolerances could be loosened considerably without affecting the operation of the part. This meant that a less costly production method could be used. It was possible to produce the part by first cold-heading a piece of bar stock the size of the smaller stem and then performing the required finishing machining operations. Cost of the added operation was more than offset by material, labor, and time savings.

Figure 26-5 shows how Walter Kidde & Company applied value analysis to a small, relatively simple assembly. Note that cost savings were obtained using three different approaches:

1 Elimination of the dual-mounting screw configuration and the left- and right-hand coupling reduced cost through *design simplification.*
2 Changing the cover from a brass stamping to molded plastic reduced cost through the *use of less expensive material.*
3 Substitution of a pulley machined from bar stock for the pulley machined from a casting further reduced cost through the use of *less costly manufacturing methods.*

Additional examples of production parts which have been value-analyzed are shown in Figure 26-6.[8]

Packaging Some firms' products and production operations afford very little opportunity to value-analyze production parts. Consider, for example, a

---

[8]For a detailed discussion of these value analysis techniques, see the classical value analysis text by Lawrence D. Miles, *Techniques of Value Analysis and Engineering,* 2d ed., McGraw-Hill Book Company, New York, 1972, chaps. 3 and 4.

FIGURE 26-5
A value-analyzed assembly. After going through two cost reduction studies, the assembly (used to direct steel cable through an angle-top) was value-analyzed with these results: Left- and right-hand coupling was eliminated (bottom); cover was changed from brass stamping to plastic; special tapping operation was eliminated by using one captive screw to hold cover (tapped hole was made concentric with body recess); pulley was made as a screw machine piece rather than a machined casting, and held captive to the body to ease field installation; only one assembly was used for two sizes of cable; specialty suppliers with high-speed equipment were used. Costs on the unit dropped 60 percent; annual savings are approximately $35,000. (*Reprinted with the permission of* Purchasing *magazine.*)

steel mill or a plant producing automobile batteries. Companies of this type use very few production parts. Moreover, the value analysis potential of those parts that are used is restricted because of technical constraints imposed by the requirements of the process or the finished product. Even so, it is amazing to see how companies of this type locate problems *outside the pro-*

HOW VALUE ANALYSIS SLASHES COSTS

Weights mounted on a rotor ring were curved to match the ring curve. Did it need this feature? No. Using a straight piece, the cost dropped from 40¢ to 4¢.

40¢   4¢

Field coil supports were machined from stock, but the original design blended nicely into a casting operation. The change resulted in lowering the cost from $1.72 to 36¢ each.

$1.72   36¢

This insulating washer was made from laminated phenolic resin and fiber. Machined from individual pieces of material, it cost $1.23. A supplier with specialty equipment now fly-cuts the parts, nesting them on full sheets, at 24¢ each.

$1.23   24¢

Standard nipple and elbow required special machining to fit a totally enclosed motor. Casting a special street "L" with a lug eliminated machining and a special assembly jig. The cost dropped from 63¢ to 38¢.

63¢   38¢

An insulator costing $4.56 was originally porcelain, leaded extra heavy. Now molded from polyester and glass, it is lighter and virtually indestructible. New cost: $3.25.

$4.56 $3.25

FIGURE 26-6
Examples of value analysis producing spectacular cost reductions. (*Reproduced with the permission of* Business Management *magazine, formerly* Management Methods *magazine.*)

duction area which lend themselves to value analysis. The general field of packaging is an extremely fruitful area in many companies.

The nail-making department of one of the United States Steel Corporation's division plants provides a good example. This division originally

(a)   (b)

FIGURE 26-7
Box design before and after value analysis.

shipped its nails to customers in wooden kegs. Value analysis of the packaging method produced a seven-part corrugated-cardboard box that did the job better than the keg and saved the firm over $500,000 per year. Subsequent analysis of the seven-part box resulted in the use of a two-part box which saved the company an additional $118,000 per year.[9]

A second very simple example occurred some years ago in a number of companies that packaged their products in light cardboard boxes (e.g., breakfast food, sugar, and soap producers). Originally, on the top and the bottom of the box the closure flaps completely overlapped each other, as in Figure 26-7a. When many firms analyzed the functions the box performed, they found that the strength provided by a full overlap was not required. Consequently, many redesigned their containers to provide only a partial overlap, as shown in Figure 26-7b. Such a simple modification as this in some cases reduced a firm's cardboard requirement by 5 percent, saving hundreds of thousands of dollars because of the large quantity of boxes used.

Broader Applications When firms first started using value analysis, the original emphasis was almost entirely on applications to parts and subassemblies in manufacturing operations. Fundamentally, however, the value analysis concept really defines a creative, systematic thought process that can be applied to problem solving in a wide variety of areas. Hence, over the years, as one might suspect, value analysis has been applied to a broad range of activities and procurement-related problems outside the manufacturing area. Applications range from the design of operating systems to the procurement of services and transportation. The following cases illustrate the point.[10]

When one firm began planning a new warehouse, a major element for analysis was the type of racks and shelving to be used. The original plan

[9]*Cost Reduction through Value Analysis: Conference Leader's Guide*, prepared by the Purchasing and Industrial Engineering Departments, Columbia-Geneva Steel Division of United States Steel Corporation, section on Shipping and Handling Applications.

[10]Edward J. Walter, "Value Analysis—It's Not Just Parts," *Purchasing World*, February 1988, pp. 31–38.

called for conventional closed shelving and cabinets. An analysis that focused on the storage functions to be performed revealed that in many cases, open wire grid racks and shelving would do the job very well. So, the final plan developed was for an ultramodern facility that included both open and closed storage equipment, based on specific functional needs. The results were: (1) a substantial saving in initial equipment costs; (2) simplification of fire sprinkler system requirements and a considerable reduction of the system cost; and (3) most important, reduction of insurance premium costs by more than $100,000 per year because of the reduced fire hazard that resulted from the modified plan.

In another case, purchasing officials from the State of New Mexico applied value analysis effectively to a systems problem. Several state agencies periodically mailed large numbers of a variety of standard documents to state residents. Processing, mailing, and postage costs were high. A value analysis team, including operating personnel, a buyer, a systems analyst, and an equipment supplier, studied the entire operation from a functional point of view. The result of their efforts was a modified system that now saves the state in excess of $250,000 per year. Major operating changes included: (1) redesign of many of the forms and a significant reduction in the number of forms utilized; (2) production of a number of the forms on the in-house computer output mailing system, as opposed to purchase from a commercial printer, reducing material, inventory, and mailing preparation costs; and (3) program changes in the computer-operated mailing system that permitted the insertion of several documents going to the same address in one envelope, thus reducing supply, labor, and postage costs.

In all types of applications, micro and macro, the focus is on *function*. How can the function be performed at the specified quality level, at the lowest total cost?

CONDITIONS CONDUCIVE TO VALUE ANALYSIS

A broad view of American industry reveals vast differences among its thousands of production operations and among the myriad products manufactured. Because of these differences, value analysis holds considerably more cost reduction potential for some firms than for others. Generally speaking, the factors discussed in the following sections determine the usefulness of the value analysis concept to a particular organization.

Design Analysis

Design analysis can be used to greatest advantage under the following conditions:

1 Design analysis is predicated on the assumption that material specifications can be changed. Therefore, the first condition of application requires that a firm's material specifications *not* be tied down rigidly by its

products or operations. The greater the flexibility in the specifications, the greater is the potential value of this technique.

2 A design analysis program can be most easily supported when a firm produces, on a recurring basis, a large number of different products. Further, the probability of finding untapped cost reduction areas is greater when each of these products is made up of a large number of complex components.

3 Greatest benefits accrue when a material is used in large quantities, either by virtue of a high rate of usage in one product or a lesser rate of usage in each of several products.

4 The opportunity to effect significant changes is greater when product designs have not been highly refined by similar analyses during earlier stages of development. Thus, if specifications are originally developed by the use of extensive interdepartmental participation or by computer-assisted design, opportunities to produce savings through subsequent design analysis are reduced. Conversely, when a product design is modified frequently, opportunities for savings usually increase.

5 From the value analyst's point of view, a nonstandard item presents more lucrative possibilities for design change than does a standard item whose design has been refined by its manufacturer.

6 The technique is most applicable to a product on which a single design change can be effected without altering the performance of a large number of other components of the product.

7 The chance for profitable design change on a given product increases as the availability of alternative production materials increases.

Cost Analysis

When strong price competition exists between suppliers, competitive forces tend to keep prices in line with costs. Under these conditions, most suppliers have value-analyzed their own products, and cost analysis by the purchaser usually uncovers very few high-cost components. The buyer therefore finds cost analysis most effective when dealing with nonstandard materials or with standard materials whose markets do not exhibit rigid price structures. Likewise, greatest benefits accrue to a buyer when dealing in large quantities of materials.

ORGANIZATION AND ADMINISTRATION OF VALUE ANALYSIS

When a company initially decides to establish a value analysis program, it must answer two questions: (1) Who should be responsible for developing, leading, and controlling the program? (2) What devices should be used to facilitate communication and coordination between the various departments included in the effort?

There are no pat answers to these questions. The more clearly top-level executives understand the total value analysis concept, the more clearly they realize that value analysis should really be everybody's business. In one sense, value analysis is a state of mind—a way of looking at business life. Maximum potential can be realized from a value analysis program only if everyone in the plant is value-conscious, and then only if management properly taps these potential resources. Consequently, while sound organization is essential to the success of a value analysis program, the total effects of organization per se are not as far-reaching as those stemming from the successful creation of value-conscious attitudes among employees.

It is not surprising, then, to find extreme variation among companies in their organization for value analysis. Because of product and operational differences, each firm's need for value analysis differs. Consequently, each company may choose to emphasize certain aspects of value analysis and largely neglect others. This decision may, in turn, influence the subsequent decision concerning administrative policy. If a firm elects to concentrate on cost analysis, for example, there probably will be a strong inclination to center authority for the program in the purchasing department, because of purchasing's extensive role in this activity. On the other hand, if design analysis is the focal point of the program, the engineering department may logically play the more dominant role in its development and promotion.

Studies of current practice indicate that among firms with successful value analysis programs, three basic organizational approaches are most common: (1) the specialized staff approach, (2) the committee approach, and (3) the staff training approach.

Specialized Staff Approach

The most widely used type of value analysis program among large companies is one built around a group of highly trained value analysts who function in a staff capacity. In some situations the analysts constitute a separate staff agency reporting to a general management executive; occasionally, the group reports to a top-level engineering design manager. Most frequently, however, the value analysis staff is attached to the purchasing department.[11]

In some cases purchasing administration of the program simply can be traced to the fact that the purchasing department was largely responsible for initiating value analysis. Aside from this, two important factors underscore the logic of such an arrangement. First, *every buyer must be a value analyst in his or her own right.* Formal value analysis is simply an extension of the job every buyer should do when placing an order. Since the basic nature of the value analysis function ties in closely with the purchasing function, a close organi-

---

[11]See the classical study by Stanley S. Miller, "How to Get the Most out of Value Analysis," *Harvard Business Review*, January–February 1955, pp. 123–132; and L. S. Miles, *Techniques of Value Analysis and Engineering*, 2d ed., McGraw-Hill Book Company, New York, 1972, chap. 8.

zational relationship for administrative purposes logically follows. Second, *the purchasing department is normally the most cost-conscious department in a company as far as production materials and components are concerned.* Its objectivity in evaluating the cost and performance of materials is usually unencumbered with the biases and goal conflicts which often hamper some departments that are totally performance-oriented. It should be noted that this factor also supports the argument for the independent status of value analysis, that is, assignment of the function directly to a general management executive.

In any case, in the specialized staff approach, most detailed analyses and recommendations are made by the staff analysts. This requires cooperation and assistance from buyers and design engineers. Any specification changes, however, are normally negotiated by the buyer and the engineer, based on the analyst's recommendations. While the manager of value analysis has no direct authority to enforce any staff recommendations, he or she does have a certain amount of indirect leverage. This leverage evolves from the fact that the recommendations are made by impartial and qualified analysts who frequently are also experienced engineers. Added to this is the fact that the value analysis staff usually enjoys a close relationship with higher management.

One medium-sized manufacturing plant which uses the specialized staff approach finds that a background in both purchasing *and* engineering or production is ideal for a value analyst. In this firm it takes a new analyst approximately six months to produce cost savings that exceed his or her salary. After approximately a year, however, the firm reports that most value analysts produce at least five times their salary in savings annually.

The General Electric Company, where value analysis originated, continues to be one of the acknowledged leaders in the field. In describing the General Electric program, Larry Miles states that GE has found the specialized staff approach to be the most successful method of operation.[12] Westinghouse Electric Corporation and the Ford Motor Company also conduct similarly designed programs. During the early years of its program's operation, in one year alone, Westinghouse effected savings totaling more than $7.5 million.[13]

The Committee Approach

A second approach used in both large and small firms involves committee administration of the value analysis program. The committee approach, or some variant of it, predominates among smaller firms.

A typical value analysis committee is usually composed of four to eight

---

[12]Lawrence D. Miles, "Purchasing Productivity Improvement through the Use of Value Analysis," NAPM 67th International Purchasing Conference, Los Angeles, May 11, 1982.
[13]For an interesting discussion about the early development and implementation of a value analysis program in one of America's giant corporations, refer to A. H. Phelps, "Westinghouse Cost Reduction," *Purchasing*, June 1951, p. 108.

people, including senior representatives from areas such as operations, engineering, purchasing, marketing, and general management. The committee may be headed by a senior functional representative, frequently from purchasing or general management, or by a full-time "value coordinator" assigned to the top management staff.

In most companies, the suggestions for projects to be analyzed may come from any department. One firm requires each department head to submit ten potential value analysis projects to the committee every month. Another firm solicits suggestions from all employees, tying this activity into its broader employee suggestion system, which provides financial awards for those whose suggestions are developed into actual cost-saving operations.

However the suggestions are acquired, the value analysis committee then reviews them and selects the promising ones for detailed analysis. At this point, the committee approach often differs radically from the specialized staff approach. In many committee-administered programs, the detailed value analysis work is conducted by operating personnel in the participating departments. It is not uncommon for a project to be assigned jointly to a buyer, a design engineer, and a production supervisor. Analysis is done individually and jointly until the group is ready to submit the results of its study to the value analysis committee for review and decision.

Use of the committee approach does not prohibit the use of specialized value analysts. Many firms use the committee approach, however, because they consider it to be an ideal way to develop a team approach to value analysis. Consequently, they often prefer to involve as many operating personnel as possible in the detailed analytical work. The obvious bonus accruing from such involvement is that each operating participant becomes a better value analyst, carrying this ability and attitude back to his or her daily work in design, production, or purchasing.

Thus, the committee acts as the authority and the coordinating medium for the total value analysis program. A potential weakness of this approach, so far as the total program is concerned, sometimes lies in a committee's inability to elicit support and cooperation. Consequently, for successful operation, a committee-oriented program must have active management support, a strong committee chairperson, and a clear-cut operating procedure which facilitates the enforcement of decisions.

The Staff Training Approach

The philosophy underlying the staff training approach to value analysis grows out of the same idea that leads some companies to involve operating personnel in detailed value analysis work. Companies subscribing to the staff training approach believe that value analysis yields maximum benefits only when it is practiced by all key operating personnel. Consequently, this approach aims primarily at developing an understanding of the concept and a working knowledge of techniques among most professional and operating personnel responsible for specifying, buying, and using production materials.

The value analysis organization in this case consists of a small staff group which reports to general management. The activities of this group focus on value analysis training. The group is responsible for developing a total value analysis training program and for conducting individual value analysis training sessions. In one company, forty hour-long training sessions are conducted for small groups of participants. An individual's initial training experience is followed up every year or so with a short refresher session in which new techniques and ideas are demonstrated, discussed, and practiced.

Most companies adopting this approach have no staff groups of specialized value analysts. To achieve value analysis cost savings, they rely entirely on a continuous training program and on the individual application of this training by participating personnel in all departments, particularly engineering, purchasing, and operations.

To supplement the staff training approach and the committee approach, some companies publish a monthly "value analysis bulletin" which has the following goals:

- To create a cost-conscious attitude on the part of employees and to develop a team spirit in the approach to value analysis.
- To give examples of successful value analysis projects to employees so they can see "how to do it."
- To give recognition to individuals who have submitted good ideas.

It is sometimes difficult to obtain employee acceptance of such a publication. If done successfully, however, it can produce outstanding results because it strikes at the heart of all cost reduction program goals—*individual* motivation.

Quality Circles The quality circle concept is a natural vehicle to use in implementing the staff training approach. Hailed by the Japanese as one of the keys to that nation's exploding productivity, quality circle activity is a broadly based application of Theory Z participative management. Its objective is extensive involvement of all employees in making company decisions that affect them, the workplace, and company productivity.

Each quality circle typically consists of approximately a dozen people who work together in any area of the organization—from the production line to the front office. Participation is voluntary, and groups usually meet once or twice a week for one to two hours; each group selects its own leaders. Topics for discussion and investigation cover any company matter of concern to group members—work procedures, material problems, environmental issues, and so on. Circle members study, plan, and solve their problems together as a team. When necessary, specialized expertise or staff assistance is provided by management.

Clearly, this broadly based "people-management" concept and the basic philosophy underlying value analysis both hold one important common goal: *individual concern* and *individual motivation* that lead to *group pride* and cohesive *group action*. Logically, then, some companies have found that value analysis training and value analysis projects integrate effectively with their ongoing quality circle activities. Of those firms that have embraced the quality circle concept, not all have linked it with value analysis. Some who have, however, report outstanding results. F. A. Boyle of Honeywell, for example, reported annual savings in excess of $1 million in his firm.[14]

Reporting Value Analysis

A firm should determine the magnitude of the savings generated by each dollar it invests in its value analysis program. Such a control measure obviously is useful to management. Most firms therefore develop a reasonably complete cost reporting system.

Some organizations go even further. They tabulate and sometimes publish value analysis savings for each department and each individual. Through this increased visibility they attempt to promote the value analysis program and stimulate increased value analysis effort throughout the organization.

There is considerable difference of opinion, however, concerning the use of reporting systems that detail departmental or individual savings. While some firms find that publication of such data serves as an effective incentive for their individual employees, others find just the opposite. Those opposed maintain that in many cases the credit for a value analysis saving cannot clearly be given to one or even several individuals. They contend that many people usually contribute to the final solution. This view is supported by the fact that some firms have experienced employee dissatisfaction resulting from inequitable recognition and an occasional inflation of savings favoring certain analysts or departments. Nevertheless, it is generally agreed that some form of personal guidance and encouragement is helpful in motivating the individuals involved. This means that the reporting system must provide enough detail to apprise a supervisor of the general acceptability of each individual's value analysis performance.

Value Engineering

As currently practiced in U.S. firms, value analysis techniques typically are most widely used in programs designed to engineer unnecessary costs out of *existing* products. A growing number of firms, however, are wisely attempting to engineer unnecessary costs out of *new products* during the planning and engineering design stages. The early supplier involvement concept fits

---

[14]Lawrence D. Miles, "Principles of Value Analysis," *Purchasing World*, May 1982, p. 26, and June 1982, p. 58.

well with this type of operation. This application typically is called *value engineering*, reflecting the original use of the term by the Navy in 1954.

The concept finds its widest use in companies that produce a limited number of units of a very expensive product and in companies that mass-produce products requiring expensive tooling. In these types of companies, value analysis of an item already in production is often impractical because it is then too late to incorporate changes in the product economically. In manufacturing certain electronic instruments used in missile guidance systems, for example, the production run is often so short that it precludes the effective use of value analysis after production has been initiated. In fact, the Federal Acquisition Regulations now stipulate that most major defense procurement contracts must be subjected to value engineering studies prior to initial production. A somewhat different situation that produces similar operating results is found in firms mass-producing major household appliances. For example, in manufacturing the housing panels on appliances such as refrigerators and ranges, once the design is fixed and the dies are purchased, it is normally too costly to change them, even though value analysis studies might subsequently disclose design inefficiencies.

Value engineering utilizes all the techniques of value analysis. In practice, it involves very close liaison work between the purchasing, production, and design engineering departments. This liaison is most frequently accomplished through the use of various purchasing and production coordinators, who spend considerable time in the engineering department studying and analyzing engineering drawings as they come off the drafting boards. Once coordinators locate problem areas, value analysis techniques are employed to alleviate them.[15]

CONCLUSION

Value analysis is a significant element in most firms' purchasing research activities—and it possesses tremendous profit-making potential. However, if its potential is to be realized, those responsible for administration of the value analysis program must adopt a broadly based management point of view. This is essential because value analysis is a companywide activity whose purpose is to optimize returns to the *total* business operation.

In practice, the value analysis activity cuts across numerous functional lines of authority. For this reason, the activity must be organized and administered with care. Varying historical traditions and orientations in different firms may point to different administrative approaches. In its most basic form, the administrative problem becomes one of *human relations and motiva-*

[15]For a complete discussion of this topic see D. W. Dobler, "How to Get Engineers and P.A.'s Together," *Purchasing*, Aug. 12, 1963, pp. 55–58; P. V. Farrell, "Purchasing and Engineering," *Purchasing World*, November 1980, pp. 48–51; and D. N. Burt, *Proactive Procurement*, Prentice-Hall Inc., Englewood Cliffs, N.J., 1984, chap. 2.

tion more than anything else. In a broad sense, value analysis is simply a unique way of looking at business life. Management must not overlook the fact that, in the long run, it is the attitude of the participants that largely determines the degree of success achieved by any program. Value analysis concepts must be *understood, accepted,* and *practiced* by a majority of the various functional specialists involved in the program if such a program is to be fully effective.

As industrial technology advances, during the years ahead an increasing number of larger firms will utilize robotics and computer-assisted design and manufacturing devices. As higher levels of analytical capability are built into these devices, resulting product designs will become more efficient at the outset than is generally the case today. Hence, some value engineering capability will, in effect, be transferred to the automated design process. The anticipated result is that this evolutionary trend gradually will reduce the need for detailed value analysis of product design as it is practiced today. Consequently, as we move into the next century, the value analysis emphasis in some firms will likely shift toward cost analysis and more broadly based conceptual applications.

FOR DISCUSSION

26-1 Do many firms use value analysis? Discuss.

26-2 Discuss the basic objectives of value analysis.

26-3 What is cost analysis, and how is it used in a value analysis program?

26-4 What is design analysis, and how is it used in a value analysis program?

26-5 What would you say to a disgruntled design engineer who does not want to participate in your firm's value analysis program because he or she believes it infringes on the prerogatives of design engineering?

26-6 "Value analysis is more of a human relations and motivation problem than anything else." Discuss this statement.

26-7 Discuss the specific techniques used in design analysis.

26-8 Dismantle a desk stapler (or similar convenient object) and value-analyze it. Before starting, outline the total procedure to be followed, the records to be kept during the process, and the report to be submitted on completion of the analysis. For all parts, estimate costs as closely as possible, using data in your library and data which may be available from local businesses.

26-9 Experiment with brainstorming by value-analyzing a multipart object in this way: Six people form one group and work jointly, using the brainstorming technique, in value-analyzing the object. Six other people form a second group. Each of these individuals will value-analyze the same object by himself or herself. After finishing, these six individuals will meet and select the best of the individual solutions. Each group should prepare a report on its job. At a class meeting, the two groups will review their activities in detail and present their findings. The class will then compare and evaluate the two approaches. See question 26-8 for procedural details.

26-10 Why can suppliers be helpful in value analysis programs? How can they be used? Does this use of suppliers in any way violate your concept of good business ethics?

26-11 Suppose you have decided that you would like to involve some of your key suppliers in your firm's value analysis program. As the purchasing manager, prepare a plan for this project that you would submit to your boss for approval.

26-12 Earlier in the book, the concept of early supplier involvement was discussed. Operationally, how does this relate to value analysis?

26-13 Suppose you are the purchasing manager for a small manufacturing firm. How would you determine whether or not a value analysis program might pay off in your plant? Outline your investigation in step-by-step fashion, and discuss.

26-14 Referring to question 26-13, suppose you thought that value analysis would be profitable. Prepare a proposal to submit to the general manager attempting to convince him or her that the firm should establish a value analysis program. Detail the type of program you suggest, stating any assumptions you wish to make about the company and its products.

26-15 Discuss the advantages and the disadvantages, as you see them, of each of the organizational approaches used in implementing a value analysis program.

26-16 In your opinion, what are the advantages of locating a value analysis program in the purchasing department for administrative purposes? What are the disadvantages?

26-17 What is value engineering? How does it differ from value analysis?

26-18 What are quality circles? How do quality circles relate to value analysis?

26-19 How can value analysis be used in a nonmanufacturing organization?

CASES FOR CHAPTER 26

CHAPTER **27**

PURCHASING'S ROLE IN NEW PRODUCT DEVELOPMENT

KEY CONCEPTS

- Purchasing's role in designing and developing new products
  The investigation phase
  The development phase
  The production phase
  Engineering change management
- How to expand purchasing's role
  Design or project teams
  Materials engineers
  Co-location
- Buyers who interface successfully with engineers

In progressive firms, the design of new products now is conducted by a team representing a number of functional areas. Product planning, design engineering, reliability engineering, purchasing, manufacturing engineering, quality, finance, and field support all are represented. The turnaround of many troubled manufacturers during the 1980s was the result of replacing departmental walls with teamwork among those who should be part of the design process. Purchasing is moving to earlier involvement in the new product development process because of the important contributions which it can make in the areas of quality, cost, and market availability. This early involvement commonly is referred to as *early purchasing involvement (EPI).*

The lack of effective, cooperative teamwork among divisions frequently has been accompanied by cost overruns, quality problems, and major scheduling problems. These, in turn, adversely affect development and production times and impede early recognition of problem areas. Results often have included extensive redesign, rework, and retrofit operations. Ultimately, the absence of teamwork results in products which are a continuing burden to the firm's long-term competitiveness.

The desired levels of quality and reliability must be engineered into the item at the design stage. Improved quality leads to benefits in both the external and internal worlds. Industry now recognizes that higher product quality can lead to increased market share. Internally, improved quality leads to less test, less rework, and less scrap, resulting in improved productivity and job satisfaction. In turn, lower costs and higher profits result.[1] Additionally, purchased materials which are virtually defect-free are a prerequisite to the successful implementation of just-in-time manufacturing.

This chapter addresses three key issues: (1) the process of designing and developing new products, with emphasis on purchasing's role in the process; (2) several approaches to increasing purchasing's role in the new product development process; and (3) a description of buyers who interface successfully with engineers during the new product development process.[*]

DESIGNING AND DEVELOPING NEW PRODUCTS

The Investigation Phase

The design of new products begins with the investigation phase, as portrayed in Figure 27-1.[2]

Define New Product Marketing scans the firm's environment for unfulfilled wants and needs. Those needs which are compatible with the firm's mission and objectives become candidates for new product development. These potential products are analyzed for risk and reward before entering the design and development process.

Purchasing's Role in Identifying New Components and Technologies One of a buyer's key responsibilities is to acquire, assimilate, digest, and

---

[1]David Garvin of Harvard University, in an article entitled "What Does Product Quality Really Mean?", writes that "in the American air conditioning industry companies with the highest quality were five times as productive, when measured by units produced per man-hour of assembly-line direct labor, as companies with the poorest quality." *Sloan Management Review*, Fall 1984.

[*]Sections of the material in this chapter are from *Zero-Base Pricing™: Achieving World Class Competitiveness Through Reduced All-in-Cost*, by David N. Burt, Warren E. Norquist, and J. Anklesaria. The material is used with the permission of the authors and of their publisher, Probus Publishing, Chicago, Ill.

[2]The authors gratefully acknowledge the assistance of Richard Y. Moss II, reliability engineering manager, Hewlett Packard Corporation, in the development of this section. Additional, more detailed information on the reliability aspects of the design process may be found in chap. 9, "Engineering in Reliability" by Mr. Moss, contained in the *Reliability Handbook*, edited by W. Grant Ireson, McGraw-Hill Book Company, New York, 1988.

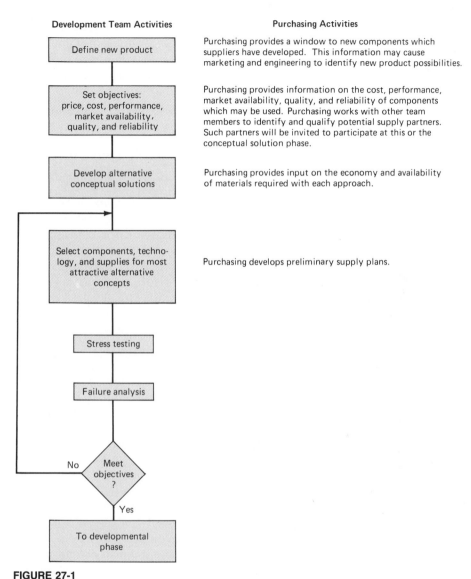

FIGURE 27-1
The modern design and development process, investigation phase. (Source: *Burt, Norquist, and Anklesaria,* Zero-Base Pricing: Achieving World Class Competitiveness Through Reduced All-in-Cost, *Probus Publishing, Chicago, Ill., 1990.)*

share information concerning new or forthcoming developments in the supply markets for which he or she is responsible. Interviews with present and potential suppliers, visits to suppliers (with emphasis on their research and development and production activities), attendance at trade shows, weekly reviews of relevant literature, and discussions with colleagues at Purchasing

Management Association meetings help the buyer remain current. Through such activities, the buyer will become aware of new products and new technologies which may be of interest. This information may help product managers in marketing and senior design personnel responsible for identifying and developing new products. While being careful to screen out inappropriate information, the buyer should share potentially attractive information with marketing and engineering.

Statement of Objectives   Next, a statement of needs, desires, and objectives is established. Needs are based on marketing's perception or knowledge of what customers want, balanced against the company's objectives and resources. Needs that are potentially compatible with the firm's objectives (profit potential, sales volume, payback period, and so on) and resources (personnel, machines, and management) are considered for development. Product objectives, including performance, price, quality, and market availability, are then established and become the criteria that guide subsequent design, planning, and decision making. The well-informed buyer is the key source of information on the cost, performance, market availability, quality, and reliability of supplier-furnished components which may be used in the new product.

Development of Alternatives   Alternative ways of satisfying these needs, desires, and objectives should be developed and then evaluated against the criteria.

There is an unfortunate tendency to proceed with the first approach that appears to meet the need, although less obvious alternatives may yield more profitable solutions. Alternative approaches should be evaluated on the basis of suitability, producibility, component availability, economy, and customer acceptability.

Suitability refers to technical considerations such as strength, size, power consumption, capability, maintainability, and adaptability. Engineering has primary responsibility for these issues.

Producibility is the ease with which a firm can manufacture an item. In the past, designs needed to be changed to accommodate the firm's or its suppliers' ability to produce the item economically. Problems arose when the needed changes were implemented. Early manufacturing engineering involvement in the design is needed to ensure the producibility of items made internally.

Component availability is the time at which components are available, while *component economy* describes the price of the item or service. Component availability and economy are the responsibility of purchasing.

Customer acceptability is defined as the marketability of an item to potential customers.

The selection of components, technologies, and suppliers for the most attractive conceptual solutions is a complex process. At progressive firms such as G.E., Hewlett-Packard, and the Ford Motor Company, the selection process is a team effort, with design engineering providing the majority of the staffing and the team leadership.

Developing Alternative Conceptual Solutions

Often, an engineer has a need that must be filled—a power transmission gear ratio, a structural component, a capacitance, a memory requirement. This need can usually be met in more than one way, yet many times the engineer may not be aware of the options available. In this case, a buyer can supply suggestions. A gear, for example, might be machined of bronze or steel, die cast in aluminum or zinc, molded from plastic, or formed by powder metallurgy. All of these options may meet engineering's constraints while offering a wide range of cost, availability, and reliability choices.[3] Purchasing and potential suppliers can provide information on the economy and availability of the materials and subassemblies to be purchased under each approach.

Early Supplier Involvement (ESI)   As practiced by leading firms today, early supplier involvement is a component of an early purchasing involvement program. With ESI, suppliers are carefully prequalified to ensure that they possess both the desired technology and the right management and manufacturing capability. Thus, the technological benefits of early supplier involvement can be obtained, with due consideration to the commercial aspects of the relationship—the best of both worlds.

When a component or subsystem is to be developed by an outside supplier under an ESI program, normally two or three potential suppliers will be requested to design and develop the required item. Potential suppliers are given performance, cost, weight, and reliability objectives and are provided information on how and where the item will fit (interface) in the larger system. These potential suppliers must develop quality plans during the design of the item to ensure that the item will be producible in the quality specified. Selection of the "winning" supplier is a team effort, with purchasing, design engineering, reliability engineering, product planning, quality, manufacturing, finance, and field support participating. Performance, quality, reliability, and price are all considered during the selection process.

Early purchasing and supplier involvement can reduce the well-known start-up problems that occur when the design and the supplier's process capability are poorly matched. Ideally, supplier suggestions will be solicited and the matching of design and manufacturing process will take place during the investigative phase of the design process. "The technical support suppliers provide in the early stages of design is a critical—some say *the* critical—

---

[3]Jim Esterby, "Design Stage Is the Best Time to Prevent Quality Problems," *Purchasing*, Dec. 8, 1983, p. 78A1.

factor in squeezing the material costs out of a product, improving quality, and preventing costly delays."[4]

Quality Planning The early involvement of quality engineers allows advanced quality planning to begin in a timely manner. Quality standards are developed to ensure that what is being designed is producible at the quality specified. Specifications for test equipment and procedures are developed. Required test equipment is carefully selected and purchased. The firm's and its potential suppliers' quality management systems are reviewed to ensure that once production commences, defect-free materials result.

Materials Catalog The selection of components is greatly facilitated by the availability of an internal current catalog of items and sources which have been carefully prequalified. The use of such a catalog simplifies the design engineers' job while simultaneously supporting materials management's efforts to standardize the items used by the firm.

As was seen in Chapter 7, there are many hidden costs associated with an unnecessary variety of production items or purchased components: excess paperwork; short, needlessly expensive production runs; higher inventory costs; higher unit costs of small quantities of purchased materials; additional order processing costs; higher inspection and materials handling costs; additional quality problems; an increased probability of stock outages; and field support problems. The use of standard materials, standard production processes, and methods resulting from standardization programs can greatly reduce the time required and the cost of designing and producing an item.

The selection of technologies is a complex issue due to the inherent cost/benefit tradeoffs and functional orientations present. Engineers are eager to incorporate the latest technology. The marketplace often richly rewards those who are first with improved performance; therefore, there is a strong case for incorporating new technology or processes before they are perfected.

But the cost of such action can be very high. Not only does such an approach result in a proliferation of components to be purchased and stocked, but it frequently results in the use of items whose production processes have not stabilized. Quality problems, production disruptions, and delays frequently result. Engineering, quality, purchasing, and manufacturing personnel *must* ensure that both the costs and the benefits of advanced developments are properly considered. The design team's objective should be to design new products to the sophistication level of the customer, not to the state of the art.

Stress Testing and Failure Analysis Once candidate component and subsystem items have been identified, they are subjected to stress testing

---

[4]Marilyn J. Cohodas, "Make the Most of Supplier Know-How," *Electronics Purchasing,* July 1988, p. 38.

and failure analysis. Failures are caused by failure mechanisms which are built into the item, and then activated by stresses. Studying the basic stresses and the failure mechanisms they activate is fundamental to the design of effective reliability tests. The correct design approach is to find and eliminate the fundamental causes of failure. This means that the most successful stress tests are ones that result in failures. Successful tests are also ones that are tailored to look for particular failure mechanisms efficiently, by selectively accelerating the tests.

Every failure has a cause and is a symptom of a failure mechanism waiting to be discovered. The tools of failure analysis are both statistical and physical; used together, they are a potent means for detecting the often unique fingerprint of the underlying source of the failure.

The Development Phase

In this phase of the design process, as illustrated in Figure 27-2, breadboard and hardware prototypes are developed so that the design team may conduct tests on the integrated system in an effort to eliminate performance and quality problems. During this phase, approaches are reviewed in detail for feasibility and likely risk. Efforts are taken to reduce risk to acceptable levels by developing and testing prototypes for high-risk items.

Prototypes The first complete prototypes of the new product are designed, built, and tested. Documentation such as materials lists, drawings, and test procedures is created. It is not unusual to repeat this phase more than once, perhaps building the first prototype in the laboratory to test the design and the second generation in manufacturing as a test of the documentation. The design should not exit this phase until a prototype has met all the design goals set for it, although it may not be possible to demonstrate the reliability goal because of the small number of prototypes available to test.

Design Reviews The design review is the point at which the new design can be measured, compared to previously established objectives, and improved. Purchasing participates in design reviews and provides information on the effect of specifications and the availability of items that are standard production for, or are inventoried by, suppliers. The buyer must ensure that the specification or other purchase description is complete, unambiguous, and provides necessary information on how items furnished under it are to be checked or tested. The buyer should be satisfied that the purchase description is written in terms relevant to and understandable by potential suppliers.

Quality Maps For firms not adopting the team approach to new product development, engineering should develop a *quality map*—a description of the detailed design logic required to achieve the desired quality. This design

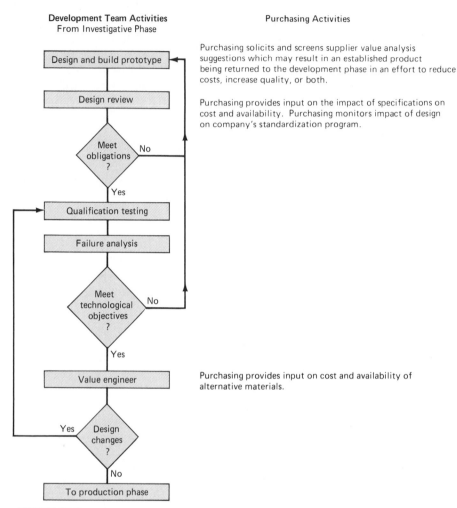

Development Team Activities
From Investigative Phase

Purchasing Activities

Purchasing solicits and screens supplier value analysis suggestions which may result in an established product being returned to the development phase in an effort to reduce costs, increase quality, or both.

Purchasing provides input on the impact of specifications on cost and availability. Purchasing monitors impact of design on company's standardization program.

Purchasing provides input on cost and availability of alternative materials.

FIGURE 27-2
The modern design and development process, development phase. (Source: *Burt, Norquist, and Anklesaria,* Zero-Base Pricing: Achieving World Class Competitiveness Through Reduced All-in-Cost, *Probus Publishing, Chicago, Ill., 1990.)*

logic starts with each desired end-product characteristic. It then identifies the characteristics of purchased materials and process steps that collectively contribute to building the desired attribute into the product. The quality map shows engineering, manufacturing, and purchasing specialists how the customer's expectations will be fulfilled. The process of putting the product designer's logic into the form of a quality map serves several purposes. It allows purchasing specialists to comment on the probability of obtaining the desired level of quality in purchased materials. It also allows quality assurance to review the design logic. This review ensures that the quality specified by marketing will result if the firm's suppliers and manufacturing all comply with the design criteria.[5]

Qualification Testing   Qualification tests are conducted on the prototype equipment. There are two different types: (1) margin tests and (2) life tests. *Margin tests* are concerned with assuring that the threshold of failure—the combination of conditions at which the product just begins to malfunction— is outside the range of specified conditions for the product's use.

Life tests are intended to find patterns of failure which occur too infrequently to be detected by engineering tests on one or two prototypes. These tests differ from margin tests primarily in the number of units tested and the duration of the test.

Failure Analysis   The stress testing and failure analysis techniques described in the investigation phase are applied to the prototype.

Meet Objectives?   The design team determines whether the prototype meets the objectives established in the investigation phase. If the prototype fails this analysis, it reenters the design process and a new or upgraded prototype is developed.

Value Engineering   Prior to releasing a design to production, it should be reviewed to engineer out unnecessary costs through the application of the techniques described in Chapter 26.

The Production Phase

Manufacturing and Production Plans   In the production phase, as shown in Figure 27-3, the manufacturing plan and the procurement plan (frequently in the form of a bill of materials) are finalized. As a result of its early involvement in the design and specification development process, purchasing also should be able to develop contingency plans that will satisfy the firm's needs if the first source doesn't work out. The appropriate plans are now formalized and implemented.

Make-or-Buy Analysis   The make-or-buy issue should be addressed for all new items which can be either purchased or produced in-house. Every job release and every purchase request implies a decision to make or to buy. Purchasing plays a key role in the make-or-buy process by providing information on the cost, quality, and availability of items, as discussed in Chapter 8.

---

[5]Unfortunately, the use of quality maps or similar procedures is a rare exception. In effect, those responsible for design seem unwilling to take the time to do it right the first time. But much more time and money are required to correct the errors which occur during production, errors which would have been detected during the development and review of a quality map.

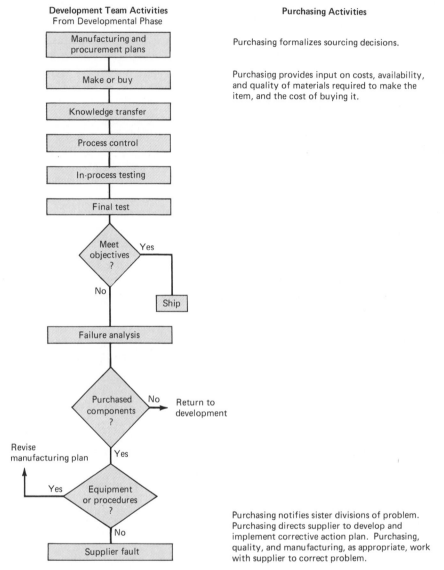

Development Team Activities
From Developmental Phase

Purchasing Activities

Purchasing formalizes sourcing decisions.

Purchasing provides input on costs, availability, and quality of materials required to make the item, and the cost of buying it.

Purchasing notifies sister divisions of problem. Purchasing directs supplier to develop and implement corrective action plan. Purchasing, quality, and manufacturing, as appropriate, work with supplier to correct problem.

FIGURE 27-3
The modern design and development process, production phase. (Source: *Burt, Norquist, and Anklesaria,* Zero-Base Pricing: Achieving World Class Competitiveness Through Reduced All-in-Cost, *Probus Publishing, Chicago, Ill., 1990.)*

Knowledge Transfer Manufacturing engineering applies experience from similar projects and new developments from other manufacturers to the production process. Manufacturing engineers also work with suppliers to share new and improved production techniques.

Process Control Contrary to popular opinion, the design is not finished when the transfer from development to production takes place—quite the contrary. Unfortunately, changes at this stage of product development are very costly and tend not to be evaluated with the same thoroughness as the original alternatives. Finding a quick fix typically is the order of the day, preferably a fix that does not require extensive retooling or scrap. Still, there are some legitimate reasons why changes in the design occur after release to production. For example, there may be phenomena that occur so infrequently that they are not discovered until a large number of products are manufactured. Another reason for changes at this point is that with the pressure to develop new products in a shorter time, *concurrent design* is often practiced. This means that a new manufacturing process is developed simultaneously with a new product using that process, rather than sequentially. This is a risky approach, but one that is gaining popularity because it saves time and results in earlier new-product release.

When manufacturing problems arise, whether in the buyer's or the supplier's manufacturing operations, there is a tendency to look for a quick fix. One type of solution is to adjust the manufacturing process to minimize the problems, rather than to change the design. Perhaps this approach is taken because the process documentation is internal and not shipped to the customer along with the product. More likely, such changes in manufacturing processes are made because the process is under the jurisdiction of production and consequently the change does not require design engineering's approval. This approach can create problems. The situation can deteriorate to the point where there is a customized process for each product—nothing is standard—and the process is out of control most of the time. When design rules and process parameters are both being varied at the same time, the situation quickly becomes too complex to understand or control, and quality suffers. The correct solution is to optimize the process, get it under control, and keep it that way. Then the designs can be modified so that they fit the standard process, producing stable and predictable yields day after day.

In-Process and Final Testing There are two objectives for in-process testing: (1) to eliminate defects before much value is added to the product and (2) to adjust or calibrate the performance in some way. Final product testing ensures that the item meets its performance objectives.

Every failure has a cause and is a symptom of a failure mechanism waiting to be discovered. For example, if failure analysis identifies a purchased component as the source of the failure, further analysis is required to determine whether: (1) faulty equipment or procedures are to blame or (2) the problem resides with the supplier. Failure analysis also may identify a latent defect in the product's design, requiring redesign.

Engineering Change Management

Any changes in components or the product itself may have profound effects on its cost, performance, appearance, and acceptability in the marketplace. Changes, especially at the component or subassembly level, can have a major effect on manufacturing. Unless changes to the configuration of an item or its components are controlled, manufacturers may find themselves in trouble. They may possess inventories of unusable raw materials or subassemblies. They may possess materials that require needlessly expensive rework to be adapted to a new configuration. Or they may produce an end item that will not meet the customer's needs. Uncontrolled changes generally mean that quality and reliability requirements have been compromised without appropriate retesting.

Engineering change management, a discipline which controls engineering changes, has been developed to avoid such problems.[6] How often engineering change management is required is a matter of managerial judgment. But for most modern technical items, engineering change management is a necessity. In some cases, it will be imposed on the manufacturer by the customer. Using this approach, changes are controlled and recorded. Marketing and all activities involved in the purchase, control, and use of purchased materials are told of any proposed changes to the item's characteristics. These organizations then comment on the effect of the proposed change. Such control and coordination is especially important when production scheduling and the release of purchase orders are controlled by a material requirements planning system.

There are many ways to organize an engineering change management group. Ideally, an engineering change management board is established with engineering, manufacturing, marketing, production planning, inventory management, and purchasing represented. When a materials management organization exists in the firm, a senior representative of production planning and inventory control is a logical candidate to chair this board. It is crucial that purchasing and the function responsible for materials control be involved in the review of proposed engineering changes for three reasons: (1) to provide input on the purchased materials implications of a proposed change, (2) to discuss the timing of proposed changes in order to minimize costs associated with unusable incoming materials, and (3) to be aware of forthcoming changes so that appropriate action can be taken with affected suppliers.

Adherence to this or a similar design process is key to the firm's success in the development of new products. Product quality, cost, and availability all must receive proper attention. Engineering, manufacturing, marketing, quality assurance, and purchasing all have vital roles to play in the design process.

---

[6]Engineering change management controls the changes to a product's design—specifically, its form, fit, and function.

HOW TO EXPAND PURCHASING'S ROLE

This chapter has described the design and development process with early purchasing involvement. In too many firms, the design engineer attempts to address not only the technical and functional issues of design and development, but also manufacturing considerations, marketing implications, and the procurement considerations of economy and availability. Many of these individuals enjoy interacting with suppliers both on technical and commercial issues. And most believe that they are serving their employer's best interest—even when making sourcing and specifications decisions that turn out to be suboptimal in the long run.

Purchasing personnel have their work cut out for them. They must develop and maintain cooperative relations with engineering *that protect the profitability of the firm*. Early purchasing involvement is an essential ingredient of the program to maximize a firm's profitability.

Purchasing personnel must understand the orientation and dedication of the typical design engineer. Obviously, an ability to speak the engineer's language is very helpful. In a study conducted by one of the authors, it was found that purchasing personnel who think in the same manner as engineers have a much higher success rate when dealing with engineers than do other individuals. Such thought processes can be identified through established testing procedures.[7]

Whenever feasible, purchasing personnel should provide advice on the commercial implications of designs under consideration in a positive and constructive manner. When the advice is accepted, the resulting estimated cost avoidance should be publicized in a manner to bring credit and recognition to both the engineer and the buyer. Buyers must learn to co-opt their engineering counterparts by providing value and service. Purchasing then is seen as a partner which takes care of business problems, thereby allowing engineers to concentrate on technical issues. Several successful approaches to obtaining the desired level of purchasing input during the design process now are described.

Design or Project Teams

When the importance of a project or program warrants, a dedicated project team is the ideal means of ensuring early purchasing involvement.

Materials Engineers

Individuals with an engineering background are good candidates for buying positions whose responsibilities require involvement with design engineer-

---

[7]See "Personal Factors in the Purchasing/Engineering Interface" by J. Anklesaria and David N. Burt, *Journal of Purchasing and Materials Management*, February 1988.

ing. Some purchasing organizations divide buying responsibilities into two specialties: (1) materials engineering and (2) the buying activities of sourcing, pricing, and negotiating. The material/liaison engineer is responsible for coordination with design engineering, for prequalifying potential sources (usually with the assistance of quality assurance), and for participating in value engineering and value analysis.

Co-Location

This approach calls for the placement of members of the purchasing staff in locations where design engineering and development work is done. These individuals are available to assist design engineers by obtaining required information from prospective suppliers and advising designers on the procurement implications of different materials and suppliers under consideration.

BUYERS WHO INTERFACE SUCCESSFULLY WITH ENGINEERS

The buyer is the key to successful early purchasing involvement in the new product development process. Management directives, policies, and procedures supporting early purchasing involvement all help. But it is only when design engineers realize that the early involvement of a professional buyer is a productive asset, and not a nuisance, that EPI makes its full contribution.

The buyer who recognizes the importance of being involved early in the process can acquire the necessary skills and knowledge to be seen and accepted as a contributor. Courses in the development and interpretation of engineering drawings, as well as in a wide variety of technologies, can be taken via correspondence or night school programs. Sales personnel love to talk and will gladly help a willing listener gain technical insight into their products. Visits to suppliers' operations provide further insight and understanding.

CONCLUSION

The design and development of new products is one of a firm's most crucial activities. Profitability and even survival are affected. Purchasing has major contributions to make during this process. A number of successful firms involve purchasing upfront, because of contributions it can make in the areas of quality, cost, and market availability.

FOR DISCUSSION

27-1 Discuss the turnaround of manufacturers in the 1980s referred to in the text and the role early purchasing involvement played in this effort.

27-2 Explain marketing's role in new product development.

27-3 Explain purchasing's role in new product development.

27-4 How can early supplier involvement facilitate proactive manufacturing?

27-5 What is the importance of a statement of objectives in the product development cycle? What role can purchasing play?

27-6 Why is it important that quality standards and materials catalogs be available at the onset of the design process?

27-7 What are some of the pitfalls that can arise from the incorporation of the latest technologies in a product design?

27-8 Describe the components of the development phase, as outlined in the text. What role can purchasing play?

27-9 What is a quality map?

27-10 How can firms not adopting the team approach to new product development benefit from developing a quality map?

27-11 Describe the components of the production phase, as outlined in the text. What are purchasing's responsibilities?

27-12 Discuss the objectives of in-process testing and the benefits of failure analysis.

27-13 What is engineering change management and how might this discipline constructively affect manufacturing?

27-14 Name the three principal reasons why purchasing must be involved in engineering change management.

27-15 Describe three approaches to expanding purchasing's role in new product development.

27-16 How might you, as a manager, bridge the communication gap between technical and nontechnical employees in a manner that provides a productive workplace and respect for all involved?

CASES FOR CHAPTER 27

CHAPTER 28

APPRAISAL, CONTROL, AND REPORTS

KEY CONCEPTS

- Control concepts
    - Problem prevention
    - Problem detection
    - Postaction control process
- Appraising and controlling procurement performance
    - Problems in controlling purchasing
    - A basic approach to purchasing control
    - The purchasing management review
    - Controlling buying effectiveness
    - Controlling procurement efficiency
    - Buyer models
- Guidelines for development and use of control systems
- Reports to management

How do managers know when their departments are performing satisfactorily? How do they know whether departmental objectives are being achieved? On what basis do they set priorities in allocating resources to improve performance? This chapter deals with the answers to these questions. Appraisal and control of operations is the last step in the management process.

CONTROL CONCEPTS

Experienced managers know that two approaches should be used in performing the control phase of the management job—*problem prevention* where possible, followed with a *monitoring system that detects problems* that slip through the prevention net.

Problem Prevention

Problem prevention, or *preaction control* as some call it, is standard operating procedure for all airline pilots. Before the airplane leaves the ground, engines, alternators, pumps, various operating systems, and other vital pieces of equipment are tested to ensure that they function as they should. *The control mechanism is built into the procedure* before the action occurs. Similarly, in a purchasing operation, a number of problem prevention techniques are built into the department's operating policies and procedures. A few of the more common ones are listed below.

1 Each buyer is authorized to commit the firm to a limited number of dollars per purchase order. Beyond that limit, supervisory approval is required.
2 Competitive bidding between at least three bidders may be required on all orders in excess of x dollars, and between at least five bidders on all orders in excess of y dollars.
3 Policy may require that a job be negotiated if certain specified conditions exist.
4 Policy may require that for certain types of purchases all suppliers must utilize an SPC system.
5 The methodology for conducting a vendor process capability analysis may be specified in one of the firm's procedures.

Thus, this means of preventive control through the use of carefully constructed policies and procedures is designed to facilitate correct or effective action by purchasing personnel *the first time*. This approach, coupled with appropriate training, supervisory guidance, and motivation, is perhaps a manager's most effective control technique. In the preceding chapters of the book, a wide range of these concepts has been presented. By design, the first twenty-seven chapters have established the foundation for preaction control.

Problem Detection

The second, and most visible, segment of a manager's total control responsibility is the postaction control operation. The purpose of a *postaction control* system is to *monitor performance* and to *detect any problems*—some of which are bound to occur in a dynamic operating system in which human judgment and supplier behavior are but two of the variables. As soon as problems are detected, the system should provide for corrective action quickly to minimize nonstandard operation or output. This type of after-the-fact control process consists of four activities:

1 Establishing a workable *standard* of performance
2 Developing procedures that *feed back* actual performance data to the manager
3 *Comparing* actual performance with the standard and *evaluating* the results
4 Taking *corrective action* when necessary

Of the four activities, establishing a realistic standard that is accurate and readily accepted by operating personnel usually is the most difficult. Performance variability is the culprit. Although output standards can be set fairly easily for repetitive jobs, as job duties become varied and require more creativity, determination of a workable standard becomes increasingly difficult. Similarly, in establishing standards for material prices, the uncertainties associated with the market and with suppliers' cost structures obviously introduce problems of estimation that can be difficult to handle with accuracy.

This chapter focuses on the development and implementation of postaction control systems in purchasing and materials operations.

APPRAISING AND CONTROLLING PROCUREMENT PERFORMANCE

In developing a system to monitor and control the performance of a purchasing or a materials department, the logical starting point is to study the objectives of the department. Aggregate departmental objectives should be broken down by major material category or by buying group because, as noted in Chapter 25, different objectives frequently are established for the handling of different materials. Once the performance objectives—those relating to quality, price, quantity, timing, supplier relations, and so on—are clear, the critical activities where control is most important can be determined.

Problems in Controlling Purchasing Performance

When an analysis of these detailed objectives is made in a typical purchasing department, it reveals one unfortunate fact. Most of the critical control points lie in a single activity—the buying activity. As a rule, a given commodity buyer's job encompasses a number of extremely variable activities. Additionally, a buyer's performance in most of these areas is hard to measure in quantitative terms. Hence, the very nature of the purchasing function makes it unusually difficult to establish meaningful performance standards. Consequently, the development of a reliable control system is not an easy task.

Several examples illustrate the problems involved. Suppose a manager attempts to control the quality of a cast-steel valve purchased repetitively by a particular buyer. What performance standard can be used? Probably the most feasible quantitative standard is the percentage (or number) of valves rejected per month by the inspection or the operating department. Thus, if the supplier's rejection rate remains at or below the established standard, this fact would seem to indicate that the buyer has selected a valve and a supplier that satisfy the using department's requirements. So far, so good. However, is this accomplishment the extent of the buyer's responsibility? Who knows whether it might have been possible for the buyer to locate a more satisfactory valve (considering the quality of the valve related to the function for which it is used)? If the buyer had studied the user's need more carefully, and if he or she had investigated the valves of additional suppliers, it is possible that a more suitable valve might have been found. By far the most important part of the buyer's performance results from his or her ability to go beyond the simple purchase of a valve whose quality is "satisfactory."

In the preceding example, the factor of price is clearly interrelated with the factor of quality. Suppose the manager also wants to control the price paid for the valve. By studying the market it is probably possible to establish a target (or standard) price for the type of valve selected by the buyer. However, how meaningful will this standard be? Does it reflect the fact that a valve of lower quality and lower price might be acceptable? Does it reflect the potential price reduction the buyer might have obtained by using a detailed cost analysis in negotiating with the supplier? Does it reflect the pricing improvement that might have been gained from more skillful grouping of commodities or timing of purchases? A perceptive observer can ask many such questions which tend to place the validity of the price standard in doubt.

Assume, further, that the manager wants to control departmental operating costs. As part of this objective, he or she wants to set a standard time (or cost) that a buyer should expend, on the average, in processing a purchase request. Again, the important question is: How can a standard that will be useful for control purposes be determined? At what level should the standard be set so that it does not deter a buyer from making a thorough prepurchase investigation of specifications and potential suppliers? To compound the problem, time requirements vary widely for making different types of purchases. This situation makes it even more difficult to establish an effective "average time" standard.

The preceding examples highlight one cardinal point. Although it is usually possible to establish quantitative standards for purchasing performance, in many cases the real accuracy, and hence the validity, of the standards may never be known. *Consequently, control systems based on such standards may be much less precise and meaningful than their quantitative character would indicate.*

The intangible nature of purchasing's primary responsibilities often prohibits the direct measurement of purchasing accomplishment. Most standards and measurements therefore focus on secondary factors that are indirect indicators of true accomplishment. The secondary factors that can be measured (e.g., quality rejection rate and price paid) are useful in determining *trends* of performance. In appraising the absolute level of accomplishment, however, secondary factors may or may not be useful. The validity of each factor must be assessed in each specific case; it varies with materials, markets, and suppliers.

A Basic Approach to Purchasing Control

Because of the difficulties encountered in developing precise purchasing control systems, many companies have adopted a fairly broad approach to the evaluation and control of their purchasing activities. Such an approach includes three different types of assessments:

1 *A qualitative assessment of a number of broad managerial responsibilities—a management review.* This assessment includes factors such as the capabilities of personnel; the soundness of the organization structure; scope of the purchasing job; purchasing plans, policies, procedures; and so on. The theory underlying the use of such an evaluation is that these factors control the *potential* level of a department's performance; as such, they are useful indirect indicators of performance.

2 *An appraisal of buying effectiveness.* Buying effectiveness is defined as the degree of success experienced in achieving a firm's primary buying objectives. To evaluate this success, attempts are made to establish performance targets (standards) for the measurable *secondary* factors that relate to *primary* buying objectives. Recognizing that a single factor may not provide an accurate indication of creative buying performance, most companies develop a cross-check by measuring several factors that relate to the same primary objective. For example, buying performance relative to the price objective can be checked from two standpoints: (1) Actual prices paid can be compared with target prices, and (2) targets for cost savings resulting from negotiation and from value analysis can be established and actual savings compared with these targets. Thus, two measurements provide a cross-check on the same primary objective—price. A similar approach can be used in evaluating buying performance relative to each of the other basic objectives.

3 *An assessment of purchasing efficiency.* "Effectiveness" in buying and "efficiency" in buying are two distinctly different elements. Control of efficiency involves evaluation of work loads, personnel utilization, operating costs, and processing times as related to specific volumes of purchasing operations. Clearly, a purchasing executive wants to achieve a high degree of operating efficiency—*but not at the expense of buying effectiveness.* The latter element offers far more opportunity for cost savings than the former.

The Review—Appraising Managerial Performance

The broad appraisal of managerial effort is, in essence, a management review of the purchasing operation. Because of the subjectivity involved in this kind of evaluation, it usually can be conducted most effectively by someone outside the purchasing department. Individuals normally called on to conduct such reviews are private consultants, staff systems specialists, staff management engineers, and internal staff auditors. This does not mean that purchasing management should not make such evaluations. On the contrary, to improve the operation, purchasing management should continuously ask itself the same types of questions that management consultants ask.

The areas investigated and the types of questions raised during the evaluation are similar to those discussed in the first ten chapters of the book. Without repeating the details, the list that follows outlines the general areas of inquiry.

1 *Scope of the purchasing function.* How important does management consider the purchasing activity in the firm's total operation? Is purchasing properly located in the organizational hierarchy? Does purchasing participate in the formulation of policies on forward buying, JIT, and inventory levels? To what extent does purchasing participate in make-or-buy decisions, in the materials standards program, in the value analysis program, in the quality management program?

2 *Evaluation of purchasing managerial personnel.* Are purchasing managers adequately qualified? Do they fully understand the economic and business intricacies of their company and industry? Are they qualified administrators? Do they have adequate knowledge of relevant materials and manufacturing processes? Do they have adequate knowledge of the suppliers and markets with which they deal?

3 *Organization.* Does purchasing have a complete and current organization chart? Is all purchasing activity centralized in the purchasing department? Have clear lines of responsibility and authority been established? Is sufficient authority delegated along with responsibility? Are the operating activities logically grouped for purposes of functional operation, coordination, and control? Has the department developed adequate job descriptions and employee qualifications for its jobs? Is adequate organization planning being done to meet future needs?

4 *Personnel.* Do employees' qualifications match job requirements? Are adequate selection criteria used in hiring personnel? What job training is given personnel? What professional development training is afforded and required of personnel? What planning and preparation are done for the advancement and replacement of personnel? Are compensation levels adequate to retain competent personnel? Is the employee turnover rate reasonable?

5 *Policies.* Is a well-defined basic purchasing policy, outlining purchasing responsibility and authority, well known and accepted throughout the company? Is a well-developed policy manual in use? What policy has been adopted regarding purchasing research activities (economic research, commodity research, systems research)? Do buyers concentrate time and effort on materials proportionate to their respective dollar-volume values? Is adequate advance materials planning done to permit effective purchasing and term contracting? Do satisfactory policies exist concerning forward buying and speculative purchasing? Do satisfactory

policies exist for the following activities: new supplier identification, supplier evaluation and selection, use of competitive bids, use of negotiation (cost analysis and price analysis), and vendor relations? Have satisfactory policies been developed concerning terms of purchase, routing of shipments, SPC and types of inspection (and coordination with suppliers), and the use of single and multiple sources?

6 *Procedures.* Have all procedures been automated to the extent reasonably possible? Is a well-developed procedure manual in use (simple, clear, complete)? Have procedure flowcharts been developed? Are all forms well-designed, simple, and effective? Are procedures in operation that effectively coordinate purchasing with using departments, the data processing division, inventory control, receiving and stores, traffic, engineering (as regards value analysis work), and inspection? Are adequate procedures used to handle rush orders and small orders? Are sound procedures in existence for such activities as negotiation, competitive bidding, supplier selection, and order follow-up? Are complete procedures available for controlling the receiving activity and for handling loss and damage claims? Do adequate stores procedures exist for receiving, storing, and disbursing materials? Have procedures been developed for evaluating capital equipment purchase alternatives? Are sound procedures used in managing inventory, in determining ordering quantities, and in determining safety stock levels?

7 *Records and reports.* Are adequate records maintained to facilitate effective purchasing (emphasis on commodity records and supplier records)? Do operating records contain necessary data for control purposes? What reports are submitted to purchasing management to facilitate managerial control by exception? How frequently are such reports submitted? What reports are submitted to top management?

The first two areas, *scope of the purchasing function* and *evaluation of managerial personnel*, are vital to the long-range health of the purchasing organization. However, development and changes in the first area, and to some extent in the second, are conditioned heavily by a firm's management philosophy—and typically occur rather slowly. On the other hand, the other five areas are tightly interwoven with the department's short-term operation. Consequently, in progressive organizations a systematic evaluation of the first two areas usually occurs every three to five years, with the latter five areas receiving more frequent reviews—perhaps every one to two years.

Controlling Buying Effectiveness

In most cases, a manager needs feedback on at least a monthly basis, and frequently more often, to do a good job of controlling buying effectiveness. The operating situation is dynamic, and corrective action or a change in strategy usually should be accomplished fairly quickly. In addition, an *annual re-*

view of the effectiveness measurements is also useful as a foundation for the development of the ensuing year's buying plan.

A number of different performance factors can be measured to provide a basis for appraising and controlling buying effectiveness. The factors differ in importance among companies, depending on the nature of the business and the materials purchased. Most firms, therefore, do not use *all* the measures discussed in this section. Similarly, to pinpoint certain problems more precisely, some firms find it desirable to divide certain individual measurements into several more detailed measurements.[1] Each firm selects a managable number of measurements that are tailored to its particular needs.

In the following discussion, measurement factors are classified according to the primary purchasing objectives whose attainment they help achieve.

Controlling the Timing Factor A purchasing department's first responsibility is to support the firm's line operations. The following measurements indicate how effectively this responsibility is fulfilled.

1 Percentage of overdue orders. To provide more direct control, a weekly or more frequent list of overdue orders can be reported.
2 Percentage of stock-outs caused by late deliveries.
3 Number of production stoppages caused by late deliveries.
4 Actual expediting expense compared with budgeted expediting expense.
5 Premium transportation costs paid.

Targets (standards) against which most of these measurements are compared are based on historical performance and subjective assessments of possible improvement. An initial categorization of these data by material classification usually provides an adequate basis from which subsequent control action can be taken.

Controlling Quantity and Inventory Investment Closely related to the preceding measures of operations support effectiveness are the following three measures:

1 Percentage of stock-outs caused by underbuying or poor JIT performance
2 Number of production stoppages caused by underbuying or poor JIT performance
3 Actual stock supply "service level" compared with a target service level figure

---

[1]One of the most comprehensive studies conducted in recent years was funded by the National Science Foundation and conducted by three professors from Michigan State University. For a good in-depth discussion of purchasing measurement and control, see R. M. Monczka, P. L. Carter, and J. H. Hoagland, *Purchasing Performance: Measurement and Control*, Michigan State University Graduate School of Business Administration, Research Division, 1979.

Other measurements useful in controlling the quantity factor are:

4 A chart showing target and actual inventory levels in the aggregate and by major material classification. This chart is most useful when supplemented with a chart showing inventory turnover rates (annual material usage divided by average inventory) for the same material classifications. When analyzed together, these charts point up imbalances between inventory carrying costs and material acquisition costs.

5 A report of "dead stock" materials in stores, resulting from overbuying. The report should be classified by major material classes, listing the items in each class and their respective dollar values.

6 A list of supplier stocking arrangements that have been negotiated and an estimate of resulting inventory savings.

Controlling Prices Paid for Materials The following techniques provide a cross-check on the reasonableness of prices paid for materials.

1 Target prices should be established for most major materials. Prices actually paid can then be charted against the target figures to display any significant differences. Targets commonly used are:

- Historical prices, adjusted for inflation and other relevant factors
- Standard cost figures developed jointly by accounting and purchasing personnel
- Producer prices (wholesale) and commodity prices published by the Department of Labor and the Department of Commerce
- GSA prices for MRO and office purchases, published by the General Services Administration

2 A materials budget, utilizing standard price data, can be used to achieve the same result. However, the preceding technique provides a more direct measurement which can be interpreted more easily and more quickly.

3 A firm can develop its own weighted average "price paid" indexes for major classes of materials. If developed on a comparable basis, these indexes can be charted against various national commodity price indexes such as the Producer Price Index (PPI) published by the Bureau of Labor Statistics. Such comparisons reveal cases in which a firm's materials costs may be rising or declining more than market prices during an inflationary or deflationary period. Viewed over time, the *trend* of the buyer's own weighted index can also provide useful control information.[2]

4 Periodic cost savings figures can be charted individually for savings arising from such activities as negotiation, cost analysis, volume buying,

---

[2]The General Motors Corporation's use of price targets and Bureau of Labor Statistics price indexes to provide an independent measurement of purchasing performance is discussed in an excellent article by its director for international trade. See Patrick L. Hanafee, "Use of Price Indexes in MRO Buying," *Journal of Purchasing and Materials Management*, Spring 1981, pp. 2–9.

long-term contracting, value analysis design changes, value analysis material changes, supplier suggestions, changing suppliers, packaging improvements, and transportation cost reduction projects.

The development of accurate figures for such projects frequently poses a problem because of the variables involved. Numerous individuals and departments sometimes contribute to the solution of a single problem, making it difficult to allocate credit for the savings fairly. Also, questions often arise concerning the magnitude of savings figures and the validity of the time period used in computing repetitive savings. For these reasons, it is wise to have a separate auditing group coordinate the development of the actual figures. The credibility of the effort depends on the credibility of the figures.

Further, if cost savings data are used to compare the performance of one buyer or buying group with another, usually they must be adjusted to reflect differences in the *potential* for cost savings between those people or jobs being compared. For example, there is usually more opportunity to generate major cost savings when buying specially designed production components than when buying standard office supplies.

5 Gains and losses from forward-buying activities should be reported periodically to determine forecasting effectiveness. Again, a major problem is the determination of a standard figure to use as a basis for comparison. Typically, prices actually paid during a period are compared with the average market price during the period. While this is a feasible approach, in reality it produces only approximate savings figures. A more precise approach would compare prices paid with prices that would have been paid had the conventional buying schedule been followed. However, this approach requires more clerical effort than typically can be justified.

6 A report of the percentage of purchase orders that are issued without firm prices provides another basis for controlling materials costs.

All the preceding measurements can be classified and subclassified in various ways to pinpoint responsibility for the problems they reveal. The most useful initial classification, however, is by major material groupings—then perhaps by buyer, using department, and supplier.

Controlling Material Quality   The following measures are most commonly used to monitor buyers' and suppliers' performance in the area of quality.

1 Once material specifications have been established, the most direct measure of quality performance is the percentage or number of delivered materials that are rejected by the inspection and operating departments.

2 Another measure is to track the number of suppliers that have achieved and maintained a "certified supplier" status with the buying firm.

3 For firms utilizing statistical process control, it is useful to track the number of suppliers using SPC, the number of individual SPC applica-

tions per supplier, and the number of quality problems detected when reviewing suppliers' SPC control charts in inspection.

4 To check on the improvement of quality specifications, a record can be maintained showing the number and type of design changes and material changes resulting from joint value analysis work. A record of supplier involvement in these activities can also be maintained.

Controlling Source Reliability   The following measurements can be used to indicate the reliability of major suppliers:

1 Reports dealing with percentage of late deliveries and percentage of rejected items can be further analyzed and classified by supplier.
2 Percentage of orders on which incorrect materials were shipped.
3 Percentage of orders on which incorrect quantities of materials were shipped.
4 Percentage of orders on which split shipments were made.
5 Some firms combine these and other measurements, by means of a formula, into a single supplier rating which is published and used for control purposes. This approach is discussed in detail in Chapter 18.
6 To provide close control of single-source suppliers of nonstandard materials, a periodic report should be made summarizing for each supplier the percentage of rejected materials, the percentage of late deliveries, and the dollar volume of business handled.
7 The quality of transportation service offered by various carriers can be appraised partially by maintaining records of transit times, damaged shipments, and carrier suggestions for quality and cost improvements.

Controlling Supplier Relations   This intangible factor is extremely difficult to control because of the numerous nebulous activities that combine to shape suppliers' opinions. However, a periodic supplier survey is useful and probably is the most common method used to monitor performance in this area. The survey typically is conducted by means of a mail questionnaire. Although responding suppliers normally remain anonymous, various techniques can be used to relate responses to material classifications or to buyers for control purposes. The following questions appear on one firm's questionnaire:

1 Are your sales representatives always received in a friendly, courteous, businesslike manner by our purchasing personnel?
2 Are your personnel kept waiting in our reception room longer than is necessary?
3 Do our buyers devote full attention to the interview, with only a reasonable number of distractions?
4 Are you allowed a sufficient amount of time in each interview?
5 Are our buyers eager to hear your suggestions and ideas?

6 Are you urged by our buyers to develop new ideas and methods that will help both firms cut costs?

7 Do the buyers with whom you do business have a satisfactory knowledge of the items they purchase?

8 Do you believe that our buyers are concerned excessively with price considerations?

9 Do you consider our buyers' negotiation techniques to be satisfactory?

10 Are our buyers overly critical of your products and services?

11 Do you believe that our buyers all have high ethical standards?

12 How could we make better use of your firm's know-how and experience?

13 Do you always receive fair treatment in your dealings with our purchasing personnel?

14 Do we place too many rush orders with you?

15 Do we expect only services that are reasonably justified?

16 How would you rate our purchasing department as compared with other firms' departments with which you are familiar?

17 With which buyers do you normally come in contact?

18 We would appreciate any additional comments or suggestions.

Controlling Internal Coordination A purchasing department can partially determine how successfully it coordinates its efforts with those of other departments by evaluating the effectiveness of certain joint activities (e.g., the joint development of materials standards with users, joint value analysis investigations with engineering, joint establishment of order quantities with production control). Unfortunately, these assessments tend to be somewhat haphazard and difficult to make. Moreover, they cover only a few isolated cases out of the many potential possibilities for coordination.

Consequently, many purchasing departments now conduct periodic surveys of the departments with which they interface to supplement their own subjective assessments of performance in this area. By means of a biennial questionnaire, one firm asks its using departments the following questions:

1 Does the purchasing department regularly provide you with a list of estimated lead times for the items you use?

2 Do you believe that the buyers who handle your requirements know enough about the key items to make intelligent purchasing decisions?

3 Is the quality of material the purchasing department obtains for you always suitable for your needs?

4 Does the buyer who handles your requirements occasionally visit your department?

5 Is he or she familiar with the operations of your department?

6 Does he or she assist you in planning your materials requirements?

7 Does he or she keep you informed regarding delays, estimated delivery dates, and so on, for materials that you have requisitioned?

8 Does he or she periodically bring a supplier's representative to your department to discuss cost-saving proposals?

9 Are you always treated in a friendly, courteous, businesslike manner by purchasing personnel?

10 Do you believe that purchasing personnel are taking advantage of cost-saving ideas and recommendations of suppliers?

11 Do you think that purchasing personnel continually urge suppliers to develop new methods and ideas that will help you cut your costs and improve your operations?

12 Do the materials you requisition usually arrive on time?

13 How often do the buyers arbitrarily change the quality specifications on your purchases without consulting you?

14 How long does it take, on the average, for the stores department to fill your requisition for items that are carried in inventory?

15 Additional comments and suggestions.

The success of interdepartmental coordination is evidenced by the extent to which using departments follow published purchasing policies and procedures. To check on this phase of coordination, some firms periodically have buyers formally evaluate using departments' performance on such matters as unauthorized negotiations with vendors, cooperativeness in reducing materials costs by changing specifications and suppliers, allowance for sufficient purchasing lead time in planning requirements, correctness and completeness of requisitions, and so on.

When used together, the preceding three techniques provide a reasonably good measurement of purchasing's performance in the area of coordination with its internal customers.

Composite Audit of Buying Performance   To supplement the use of selected techniques from the preceding lists, some firms continually audit a small random sample of completed purchase orders or contracts in each major material classification. Such an audit typically is conducted on a weekly basis and entails a careful evaluation of total buying performance. Each order or contract reviewed is scrutinized closely to determine whether the buyer (1) used the appropriate method of purchase, (2) conducted a thorough price analysis, (3) consolidated order requirements advantageously, (4) handled bids properly, (5) selected the supplier wisely, (6) devoted sufficient value analysis effort to the order, and (7) obtained the appropriate quality of material.

When conducted on a continuing basis, such an audit frequently detects newly developing problems more quickly than do the other techniques using aggregate measurements. Moreover, the psychological effect of the audit usually stimulates buyers to higher and more consistent levels of performance.

The Value of Statistical Trends   Valid and accurate *absolute* standards are difficult to determine for many of the preceding measurements. Even so, most firms find it helpful to *compare present performance with past performance.* Although a firm has no assurance that past performance occurred at an optimal level, such a comparison does indicate the *trend* of performance and serves as a basis for setting priorities and developing plans for future improvement. In addition, graphing each measurement over a period of time is an excellent method of portraying performance to facilitate quick visualization and comprehension of progress.

The need for careful interpretation of the preceding statistical measurements cannot be overemphasized. Many of the performance measures are interrelated in such a manner that improvement of one factor may contribute to poorer performance of another factor (e.g., the relationship of material quality measurements and delivery time measurements in the case of certain materials or suppliers). Further, the behavior of numerous operating variables such as production demands, departmental workloads, suppliers' problems, and so on significantly influences short-run performance. The purchasing manager must look behind the statistics carefully to determine their true meanings and significance.

Controlling Procurement Efficiency

Every purchasing manager wants to achieve a high degree of buying effectiveness and, at the same time, utilize the department's resources as efficiently as possible. A number of measurements can be used as guides in controlling departmental efficiency, but they must be used in a very general way. Too much emphasis on efficiency can easily decrease buying effectiveness. The challenge is to determine the optimal level of operating efficiency that still permits personnel to do a thorough, proficient job of buying. Because this problem can never be solved completely, few *absolute* standards of efficiency are used in practice. Purchasing management customarily compares *trends* of efficiency measurements with *trends* of effectiveness measurements in an attempt to determine the optimum combination which yields a maximum net purchasing profit.

Buying Efficiency Although many different statistics are used to reflect buying efficiency, some combination of the following measurements is most common. Most of the measurements can be broken down by buying group, by buyer, and by commodity, as is most useful for control purposes.

Workload Measurements

1 *Number of noncontract purchase orders issued per period* (and per working day). Useful related information is:
   - Number of new requisitions per period
   - Number of open contracts requiring administration
   - Number of blanket order releases per period

2 *Purchasing processing time report.* Many firms periodically sample the orders issued to determine the percentage of purchase requests processed in one day, two days, three days, and so on. This report provides data useful in detecting imbalanced workloads and purchasing bottlenecks. Moreover, it provides another indication of purchasing service to the using departments.

3 *Number of new long-term contracts per period.* This is an extremely important statistic for purchasing management. First, as discussed in Chapter 25, it indicates the extent to which the department has engaged in studying major materials needs and has developed commensurate long-term buying plans to meet those needs. Second, the technique reduces total buying time requirements and subsequently the aggregate departmental workload. Total value of all term contracts should also be expressed as:

- A percent of total dollars purchased per period

4 *Number of purchase orders placed against long-term contracts per period.* This statistic, coupled with the blanket order release figure, indicates the extent to which such negotiated arrangements are used to reduce buying time. An additional useful statistic is:

- The percent of total number of orders placed per period

5 *Average number of dollars expended per purchase order per buying group.* Changes in this value provide an indication of buyers' abilities to control low-value purchases. More important, when used in conjunction with the average number of purchase orders issued per day, this statistic helps a manager plan *workloads* and *staffing requirements* as operating conditions change.[3]

6 *Incidence of purchase order value.* Every month (or quarter) some firms sample the orders issued to determine the percentage of orders for purchases under $50, the percentage of orders for purchases between $50 and $100, $100 and $500, and so on, for the various value classifications they find useful. When possible, it is usually useful to categorize the data also by material classification and by supplier.[4]

These data are extremely useful to purchasing management. They provide specific information required for controlling the allocation of buying time, for initiating standardization projects, for initiating stock level changes, for developing more effective consolidation of require-

---

[3]The experience of several governmental purchasing units reveals that on the average their buyers process between 1.7 and 2.2 requisitions per buyer per hour. For a detailed discussion, see Joseph L. Howard, "How to Evaluate Your Purchasing Shop," *Golden West Purchasor*, July 1979, p. 14.

[4]In automated records systems, a complete tabulation of summary data can be obtained inexpensively as a by-product of normal operation.

ments, and for making more effective use of blanket orders, petty cash purchasing, and so forth.

7 *Number of rush orders issued per period.* Although this statistic cannot be completely controlled by buyers, it indicates to some extent how effectively rush order control procedures preserve buying efficiency. The number of rush orders also indicates how satisfactorily the routine system is working. Additional useful information is:

- Percent of total number of orders placed per period
- Premium transportation costs incurred

8 *Number of change orders issued during the period.* In addition to measuring the stability of design characteristics and demand, this statistic also partially measures the thoroughness with which original buying activities are conducted. Obviously it is a workload measure, as well.

Social Responsibility Measurements

1 *Dollar purchases to small businesses per period*
2 *Dollar purchases to minority businesses per period*

These two measurements are useful for two reasons. First, if the buying firm does business with the federal government, it probably will be required to supply these data as part of the contractual agreement. Completely apart from government contracting requirements, many firms have made commitments of social responsibility to place certain volumes of business with small and minority-owned firms when it is practical to do so. Hence, data provided by these measurements can be utilized directly in such programs.

Departmental Operating Cost Measurements

1 *Purchasing department operating costs per period.* Most firms use a departmental operating budget categorized by nature of expenditure (salaries, travel, telephone, and so on) and by work group. Actual expenditures can thus be expressed in several ways:

- Actual expenditures versus budgeted expenditures
- Operating cost as a percent of material purchase expenditures
- Operating cost as a percent of the firm's operating budget
- Operating cost per purchase order issued

2 *Number of purchasing employees.* This figure may be expressed as:

- A percent of the organization's total number of employees

3 *Employee turnover rate per period.* The following formula typically is used:

$$\frac{\text{Number of terminations per year}}{\text{Average number of departmental employees}} \times 100$$

The statistics included in the first two operating cost measurements have very little meaning by themselves.[5] They vary as much as several hundred percent from one firm to another. It is their *trends* over time that are important to management from the standpoint of control. When their trends are carefully analyzed in conjunction with the trends of other efficiency and effectiveness statistics, they can provide a good indication of the relationship between departmental cost and such factors as business volume, materials quality, and total materials costs.

General Information

1 *Purchases per year* in dollars
2 *Company sales per year* in dollars
3 *Dollar purchases ÷ dollar sales* = percent per year

It is useful for purchasing management to know what percent of the firm's sales dollar is expended for materials—and what variations occur from year to year. As was discussed in the first chapter of the book, this statistic provides some insight into the potential impact purchasing can exert on a firm's net profit. Indirectly, too, it provides a clue to the level of departmental budget support that might be justified.

Efficiency of Personnel   The following techniques and records are helpful in controlling performance in this area.

1 *Performance standards for clerical jobs.* It is entirely feasible to develop performance standards that are acceptable to employees for the repetitive jobs in purchasing, receiving, stores, and inventory control.[6] Although most standards for such work are not as precise as factory standards, they can nevertheless be used very effectively in controlling the volume of clerical performance over the period of a week or longer.[7]
2 *Study of time utilization for nonrepetitive jobs.* Although satisfactory performance standards (for the volume of work done) can rarely be developed for jobs requiring creative intellectual activity, a manager can take a step in this direction which definitely facilitates control. The work habits of

---

[5]Good buying efficiency in terms of cost per purchase order may in reality represent only a decrease in the dollar amount of each purchase order and an accompanying increase in the number of purchase orders issued. Similarly, a reduction in the cost of committing each purchase dollar may merely be the result of spending more than necessary for some of the items purchased.

[6]Of the numerous available techniques, work sampling and predetermined standard data are the most commonly used today for determining clerical performance standards.

[7]During the past few years, a large insurance firm (with an increasing workload) has reduced the number of clerical jobs in its 3,500 district offices by approximately 35 percent. It has achieved this $5 million annual saving solely by refining procedures and systems and by establishing standards for repetitive clerical jobs.

buyers and managers (including the chief purchasing executive) should be studied periodically to detect inefficiencies in their patterns of activity.

A work sampling study, for example, can accurately reveal to a buyer the proportion of his or her time devoted to the various activities of the job. Such data may well indicate that too much time is being spent on relatively inconsequential matters. This awareness perhaps would call for a reallocation of his or her time. It might also lead to a study and modification of various office and paperwork systems that tend to require the buyer to perform in this manner. In fact, inefficiency in a purchasing office frequently is due more to the use of inefficiently designed systems (management's responsibility) than to ineffective or lackadaisical performance by employees.

3 *The use of models for staffing purposes.* Based on specific operating experience, today growing numbers of firms are developing fairly precise workload models for buyers with different types of responsibilities. The objective is to develop a series of models that establish a standard workload for each type of buyer in the organization. The quantitative data required in the model usually are determined jointly by buyers and managers, based on past experience and judgmental estimates. As the departmental workload expands or contracts, then, the aggregate figure can be divided by the standard workload for a given type of buyer to determine the number of buying positions involved. One firm's buyer models are reported in *Aljian's Purchasing Handbook* and are outlined for illustrative purposes in Figure 28-1.[8]

Receiving and Stores The key measurements used in planning workloads and controlling efficiency in receiving and stores are noted below.

1 *Average number of incoming shipments received daily.*
2 *Average time required to receive and process an incoming shipment.*
3 *Average number of stores requisitions processed daily.*
4 *Stores loss, obsolescence, and damage report.* A periodic report listing damaged, obsolete, and lost items (traced to stores activities) is helpful in appraising the efficiency of storage methods and handling procedures.
5 *Periodic personal inspection of storage areas.* The stores operation should be inspected periodically to ensure that materials are properly marked, easily located, and adequately stored and protected. Such an inspection also permits an appraisal of safety procedures and general housekeeping practices.

---

[8]Paul V. Farrell and George W. Aljian, *Aljian's Purchasing Handbook,* McGraw-Hill Book Company, New York, 1982, pp. 27–22.

MODEL 1 BUYER	
Buys:	• New subcontracted systems, new forgings, new castings.
Assumptions:	• Buyer has 5 to 7 years experience, is working on systems or parts with 30 weeks lead time, and is buying for 3 programs.
Workload:	• Buyer can handle 25 active part numbers and 3 new requisitions per week.

MODEL 2 BUYER	
Buys:	• State-of-the-art products with special testing and data requirements.
Assumptions:	• Buyer has 3 to 5 years purchasing experience, is working on parts with 24 to 30 weeks lead time, and is buying for 5 programs
Workload:	• Buyer can handle 75 active part numbers and 5 new requisitions per week.

MODEL 3 BUYER	
Buys:	• Special parts made to customer specification without special testing.
Assumptions:	• Buyer has 2 or more years experience, is working on parts with 8 weeks lead time, and is buying for 10 programs.
Workload:	• Buyer can handle 340 active part numbers and 30 new requisitions per week.

MODEL 4 BUYER	
Buys:	• Standard parts.
Assumptions:	• Buyer has 1 or more years experience, is working on parts with 3 weeks lead time, and is buying for 15 programs.
Workload:	• Buyer can handle 450 active part numbers and 100 new requisitions per week.

FIGURE 28-1
Illustrative buyer models for workload/staffing estimates.

Guidelines for Development and Use of Measurement and Control Systems

At this point in the discussion, it is appropriate to summarize a few key guidelines that are important in the development and implementation of purchasing measurement and control systems. The following seven guidelines are a synthesis of the experience and judgment of a number of practicing managers over a decade or so of experimentation, failures, and successes.

1 Performance measurement systems are a tool of good management—not a substitute for it. The effectiveness of the system will not exceed the perceptiveness and the sensitivities of the managers operating it.

2 A measurement system should be designed to support the individual buyer in doing a better job. Correspondingly, the buyer should participate in designing the system and in establishing the standards that affect him or her.

Communication is vital in implementing an effective operating system. The system must be clearly understood by all who use and are affected by it.

3 The degree of sophistication of the system should be based on the specific needs of the organization. As long as the system provides the major information required for control—the simpler the better.

4 The cost of a measurement and control system should be balanced against the management value of its output. When the cost of an incremental unit of output exceeds its usefulness, the system should be redesigned and cut back to the point of equilibrium.

5 The measurements of efficiency and effectiveness must be separated. Efficiency measures reflect the resource utilization of the department and tend to be quantitative in nature. Effectiveness measures focus on how well people do their jobs and often involve subjective assessments to some extent. While efficiency is important, buying effectiveness offers far more opportunity for improved organizational performance.

6 A small number of precise measures typically are more useful than a larger number of less precise approximations. Validity and accuracy are essential for effective use of the results.

7 Systems that measure past performance are of value primarily in providing information and experience that can be used for improvement in the future. Thus, the most effective systems are found in an environment that provides a positive stimulus for the buyer to use the output of the system constructively.

REPORTS TO MANAGEMENT

The measurements discussed to this point provide purchasing management with the detailed data required to appraise and control purchasing activities. The purchasing executive, in turn, should summarize the most significant features of this information in periodic reports to top management. Reports for top management should serve two purposes. First, they should provide *new* information that management can use in controlling company operations and in planning future company activities. Second, reports should keep management informed about key purchasing operations, and they should apprise management of purchasing's contribution to the total company effort.

Consequently, purchasing reports to management should take two forms. The first is a monthly (or biweekly) report containing the following type of information:

1 *A summary of general business conditions* in the major markets the company patronizes
2 *A list of specific price increases or decreases* for the major materials purchased
3 *A summary of trends in lead time requirements* for major materials
4 *A list of materials that may be in short supply* and a statement of purchasing's strategy for coping with each individual problem

This report is designed to inform management of conditions in the materials area that potentially could have a serious impact on the company's total operation.

The second report, usually issued quarterly (or monthly), apprises management of matters dealing primarily with purchasing performance and administrative programs. Typically, it contains the following kinds of information:

1 *A summary of how well purchasing has performed* during the period. This summary should include indications of both purchasing effectiveness and purchasing efficiency. In the section on effectiveness, it is usually desirable to summarize supplier quality and reliability improvements and cost savings resulting from negotiation, value analysis, and so forth. The summary figure for savings may be reported as a percentage of total annual purchasing expenditures.
2 *Selected but very brief operating statistics* that are useful to management. Typically, the following items are included: number of purchasing department employees and department operating cost, number of purchase orders issued during the period, number and value of outstanding contracts, and total dollars committed during the period (usually broken down by major material classifications).
3 *A brief discussion of department status and problems.* This section should summarize progress made on projects and undertakings previously reported. It should also point up existing problems in the materials function and indicate what action is being taken to alleviate them.
4 *Future plans.* Plans for significant procurement projects and administrative activities should be summarized to provide clear communication with management on matters which management may want to coordinate with other plans.

Reports to top management should contain only timely information that is of definite value to the recipient. Functional managers at times have difficulty in discriminating between the data they need to appraise and control performance of their departments and the data management needs to appraise and control the operations of the total firm. Whenever possible, data should be presented graphically to facilitate interpretation. The objective of management reports is to present key departmental data in concise form so that they can be quickly and clearly understood.

CONCLUSION

Performance evaluation and control constitute the last step in the management process. No matter how well the preceding planning and procurement work may have been done, much of it can be rendered largely ineffective if the control element fails to function well. Failure may result from a poorly designed system or from poor execution by management.

During the past decade, control of the procurement function has become even more important than it was previously. Competition has become keener for most firms as a result of increasing pressures from the cost-price squeeze. Additionally, the cost of materials, as a percent of total product cost, continues to increase for most organizations. Compounding these problems for some firms are volatile markets and prices that create planning difficulties and periodic materials shortages. These three factors have combined to make thorough evaluation and tight procurement control an absolute essential for many organizations.

The silver lining of these ominous clouds is the fact that most firms now have a computer-based information system for their procurement operations. If planned properly when the system and the database are designed, it is possible for a computer-based system to "massage" a large amount of data and produce numerous timely performance evaluation reports. Hence, despite the fact that purchasing is innately difficult to control, more thorough and less expensive control can be achieved under these conditions.

FOR DISCUSSION

28-1 Define and discuss the use of preaction control.

28-2 Define and discuss the use of a postaction control system. What are the objectives of postaction control?

28-3 What general criteria should a manager use in determining the points at which to control the performance of his or her organization? Explain.

28-4 "Establishing a realistic performance standard against which to compare actual performance is usually the most difficult part of the control process." Explain this statement.

28-5 List and discuss the major problems involved in controlling purchasing performance.

28-6 Explain the difference between purchasing efficiency and purchasing effectiveness. Which is more important? Explain.

28-7 Is a management review of the purchasing department useful in controlling purchasing performance? Explain.

28-8 How does the use of a JIT system affect a purchasing department's control system? Explain.

28-9 How can Producer Price Index data be used in the development of a purchasing performance control system? Explain.

28-10 How does a supplier's use of an SPC system affect a buyer's traditional quality monitoring system? Explain.

28-11 Assume that as a purchasing manager you have just received a production report which indicates that your department has caused an excessive number of material stock-outs and an excessive number of production stoppages due to materials shortages. Outline in step-by-step fashion exactly how you would proceed to correct the situation. What additional facts must you know? Discuss.

28-12 Develop three additional questions that could be used advantageously on the supplier relations survey questionnaire shown in the text.

28-13 Develop three additional questions that could be used advantageously on the departmental internal coordination survey questionnaire shown in the text.

28-14 Why is it difficult to appraise purchasing efficiency?

28-15 How would you develop a buyer model for use in making purchasing department staffing estimates? What problems would you expect to encounter?

28-16 What problems arise in establishing value analysis cost-savings targets (or standards) for buyers? What problems arise in administering such a control program? Discuss.

28-17 Assume you are a purchasing manager. Outline how you would proceed to establish and place in operation performance standards for the clerical personnel in the purchasing office. Discuss not only what you would do but also the problems you anticipate and how you would overcome them.

28-18 Develop a reporting system for the materials manager of a steel-fabricating firm (employing 110 people) to use in reporting to the company president. Design the system completely, including forms and any explanations required.

28-19 What impact does utilization of a computer have on a manager's ability to evaluate and control purchasing operations?

CASES FOR CHAPTER 28

The Centennial Company, page 727
Eagle Machine Company, page 736
Golden Buffalo, Inc., page 742

CHAPTER **29**

LEGAL CONSIDERATIONS

- The Uniform Sales Act
- The Uniform Commercial Code
- Status of an agent
- The purchase contract
    Offer and acceptance
    Consideration; Competent parties; Legality
- Inspection and rejection rights
- Title
- Warranties
- Order cancellation and breach of contract
    Liquidated damages
- JIT contracts
- Arbitration
- Honest mistakes
- Patent infringement
- Restraint of trade laws
- Product liability and purchasing
- The buyer's responsibility

In professional life most purchasing professionals seldom, if ever, become involved in litigation. Yet their daily activities are subject to two major areas of the law—the law of agency and the law of contracts. A purchasing manager acts as an agent for his or her firm. Legally, this relationship is defined

623

and governed by the law of agency. When a purchasing manager buys materials and services from other firms, each purchase involves the formation of a purchase contract. Should a serious disagreement arise between the purchaser and the supplier, the dispute would normally be settled by a court of law or, if the contract provides for arbitration, by an arbitrator. In either case, the dispute would be resolved in accordance with the law of contracts.

A purchasing manager's basic responsibility is to conduct the firm's procurement business as efficiently and expeditiously as possible. Buying policies and practices are therefore predicated primarily on business requirements and business judgment, rather than on legal considerations. As Professor Dean Ammer has aptly stated, "A highly legalistic approach is both unnecessary and unprofitable." From a business standpoint, contractual disputes can normally be resolved much more effectively and with less cost by negotiation. A lawsuit almost always alienates a good supplier. Additionally, the outcome of any court case is usually uncertain; otherwise there would be little need for court action. Litigation is also costly, even in the event of a favorable decision. The total cost of legal fees, executive time diverted to the dispute, and disrupted business operations is seldom recovered from damage awards. For these reasons, in settling disputes, most business firms utilize litigation only as a last resort.

The fact that a purchasing executive tries to avoid litigation, however, does not mean that he or she can overlook the legal dimensions of the job. On the contrary, a basic knowledge of relevant legal principles is essential to success. Unless a purchasing manager understands the legal implications of his or her job—and actions—legal entanglements are almost certain to crop up from time to time.

The purpose of this chapter is to review briefly some of the principal legal concepts as they relate to a purchasing professional's responsibilities. The chapter does not attempt to provide a complete discussion of these concepts. Most purchasing people should acquire some depth in the field through selected studies in commercial law.

DEVELOPMENT OF COMMERCIAL LAW

Historically, each state developed its own body of statutes and common law to deal with the problems prevalent in its particular spheres of activity. This ultimately led to the creation of a series of commercial laws that varied widely from state to state—a situation that obviously produced difficulties for businesses involved in interstate commerce.

In an attempt to promote uniformity among the laws applicable to business transactions, the American Bar Association created a committee known as the National Conference of Commissioners on Uniform State Laws (NCCUSL). The assignment of this group was to codify (i.e., set forth in writing) the laws applying to various business transactions. Its first product was the Uniform Negotiable Instruments Law, followed by the Uniform Stock

Transfer Act, the Uniform Conditional Sales Act, the Uniform Bills of Lading Act, the Uniform Warehouse Receipts Act, and the Uniform Sales Act.

The work of purchasing professionals has been influenced most heavily by the Uniform Sales Act, which contributed substantially to the uniformity of laws affecting sales and contracts. Unfortunately, however, in practice the act still left much to be desired. It permitted each state considerable latitude in applying its own laws of contract, and decisions on legal interpretations still varied widely among state courts. Moreover, only about three-quarters of the states adopted the Uniform Sales Act.

Recognizing the need for modernization, and noting the sporadic adoption of the act in the face of increasing interstate trade, the NCCUSL joined with the American Law Institute in the early 1940s to formulate a new uniform code. The resulting code, entitled the *Uniform Commercial Code* (UCC), was published in 1952; refined versions of the code followed, with the most recent being published in 1978. Although the UCC deals with a wide range of commercial problems, Article 2 deals specifically with sales.

A fundamental difference between the UCC and the Uniform Sales Act lies in the basic underpinnings of the acts themselves. The Uniform Sales Act determined many rights and obligations of contract parties on the basis of title; that is, such decisions depended heavily on which party had title to the material. The UCC, on the other hand, determines rights and obligations on the basis of fairness and reasonableness in the light of accepted business practice. Thus, the code is geared more closely to the needs and circumstances found in daily business operations.

Today, the UCC has been adopted by all the states except Louisiana.[1] It has effectively eliminated a majority of the important differences that existed between the commercial laws of the various states and has also provided new statutory provisions to fill many of the gaps in the prior laws. It should be noted, however, that the code is silent on some matters covered by earlier laws. Consequently, unless superseded by provisions of the UCC, earlier laws dealing with matters such as principal and agent, fraud, mistakes, coercion, and misrepresentation continue in effect and supplement the provisions of the code.

Topics treated throughout the rest of the chapter therefore reflect the provisions of the UCC where applicable, as well as the provisions of earlier laws not displaced by the code.

BASIC LEGAL CONSIDERATIONS

Status of an Agent

In the legal sense, an *agent* is a person who, by express or implied agreement, is authorized to *act for* someone else in business dealings with a third

---

[1]Louisiana has enacted only parts of the UCC.

party. Regardless of the job title, this is precisely what purchasing managers and buyers do. A "purchasing agent" is not a legal party to his or her business transactions, but rather serves as an intermediary. In this capacity, the law requires the agent to be loyal to the employer (the principal) and to perform his or her duties with diligence, dedication, and capability. Because the purchasing agent has agreed to act for the benefit of the employer, the law permits the employer to hold its purchasing agent personally liable for any secret advantages gained for himself or herself or for any aid given to competitors.

The authority under which a buyer functions is granted by the employer. Since the law requires him or her to operate within the bounds of this authority, it behooves every buyer to know as precisely as possible the types of transactions in which he or she can and cannot legally represent the firm. In practice, the amount of authority delegated to buyers varies significantly among companies. Hence, it is difficult for sales representatives to know the exact limits of a particular buyer's authority. Consequently, under the law, a buyer operates under two types of authority—*actual authority* and *apparent authority*. Although a salesperson may not know the buying agent's actual authority, if both act in good faith the sales representative can reasonably assume that the buyer has apparent authority comparable with that of similar agents in similar companies.

The significance of "apparent authority" becomes evident upon examination of a buyer's legal liability. For example, if an agent acts outside his or her actual authority but within what can reasonably be inferred as his or her apparent authority, the seller generally can hold the agent's firm liable for the agent's action. However, the firm, in turn, can legally bring suit against the agent for acting beyond the limit of his or her actual authority. On the other hand, if an agent exceeds the limits of both his or her actual and apparent authority, a seller usually cannot hold the firm liable, but may be able to hold the agent personally liable for the action. In both of these situations, however, if the seller knows at the time of the act that the agent is exceeding his or her authority, the seller generally has no legal recourse against the agent or the firm.

Just as purchasing professionals occupy the legal status of buying agents for their firms, sales representatives similarly hold the status of selling agents for their firms. Buyers and purchasing managers, however, usually are classified as *general* agents, while salespeople typically are classified as *special* agents, having somewhat more restricted authority. Consequently, in most cases a *salesman or saleswoman* does *not* have the authority to bind a company to a sales contract or to a warranty. The courts usually hold that, unless otherwise stated, as special agents sales representatives have authority only to solicit orders. It is important that buyers recognize this fact. On important jobs, to ensure that a legally binding contract does in fact exist, a buyer should require acceptance of the order by an authorized company officer, normally one of the supplier's sales managers who customarily serve as the company's general agent for this purpose.

The Purchase Contract

Although a legalistic approach to purchasing is in most cases unnecessary, every buyer nevertheless must protect his or her company against potential legal problems. The buyer's major responsibility in this regard is to ensure that each purchase contract is satisfactorily drawn and legally binding on both parties. To be valid and enforceable, a contract must contain four basic elements: (1) agreement ("meeting of the minds") resulting from an offer and an acceptance; (2) consideration, or mutual obligation; (3) competent parties; and (4) a lawful purpose.

Offer and Acceptance   When a buyer sends a purchase order to a supplier, this act usually constitutes a legal offer to buy materials in accordance with the terms stated on the order. Agreement does not exist, however, until the supplier accepts the offer; when this occurs, the law deems that a "meeting of the minds" exists regarding the proposed contract. In the event that a buyer requests a quotation from a vendor, the vendor's quotation usually constitutes an offer. Agreement then exists when the buyer accepts the quotation.

Under the Uniform Sales Act, the law required acceptance of an offer in terms that were identical with the terms of the offer. The UCC, however, eliminates this stringent requirement. The code states that "conduct by both parties which recognizes the existence of a contract is sufficient to establish a contract or sale although the writings of the parties do not otherwise establish a contract." The code also recognizes suppliers' standard confirmation forms and acknowledgment forms as a valid acceptance, *even if the terms stated thereon are different from the terms of the offer.*

When the terms of an acceptance differ from the terms of the offer, they will automatically be incorporated in the contract unless one of three conditions exists: (1) They materially alter the intent of the offer, (2) the offeror objects in writing, or (3) the offer explicitly states that no different terms will be accepted. What happens when an offer and an acceptance contain *conflicting terms,* and yet none of the preceding conditions exist? All terms except the conflicting terms become part of the contract, and the conflicting terms are simply omitted from the contract. This provision of the code substantially clarifies the legal position of many such purchase orders. Moreover, as a consequence, it is clear that a wise buyer should carefully review the terms contained in a supplier's acceptance.

The code contains another important provision relating to the acceptance of an offer to buy. It recognizes as valid the communication of an acceptance in "any manner and by any medium reasonable to the circumstances." Consequently, when a supplier receives an order for the purchase of material for immediate delivery, it can accept the offer either by prompt acknowledgment of the order or by prompt shipment of the material. The code thus permits *prompt supplier performance* of such proposed contracts to constitute acceptance of the offer. The contract becomes effective when the supplier ships the material.

A hitherto longstanding principle of commercial law stated that an offer could be revoked by the offeror at any time before it had been accepted, regardless of the time period stipulated in the offer. The UCC has changed this principle with respect to the purchase or sale of goods. The code states that a *written* offer to buy or sell material must give the offeree assurance that the offer will be held open for the time period stipulated in the offer. If no time period is stipulated, the offer can be assumed firm for a "reasonable" period of time, not to exceed three months.

This provision of the code has significant implications for industrial purchasers and their potential suppliers. Purchasers can use vendors' quotations in making precise manufacturing cost calculations and rely on the fact that the quotations cannot be revoked before a certain date. Without the code, no such assurance existed. On the other hand, this provision prevents a buyer from canceling an order, without legal obligation, prior to vendor acceptance. An offer to buy, like an offer to sell, must also remain firm for a stated or a reasonable period of time. To maintain firm control, it is now doubly important that the buyer state in the order the length of time for which the offer is valid (or the date by which acceptance of the order is required).

Consideration   In addition to a meeting of minds, a valid contract must also contain the element of obligation. Most purchase contracts are bilateral; that is, *both parties* agree to do something they would not otherwise be required to do. The buyer promises to buy from the supplier certain material at a stated price; the supplier promises to deliver the material in accordance with stated contract conditions. The important point is the *mutuality of obligation*. The contract must be drawn so that each party (or promisor) is bound. If both are not bound, in the eyes of the law neither is bound. Hence, no contract exists.

A buyer is confronted with the practical significance of the "mutual obligation" concept when he or she formulates the terms of purchase. The statements regarding material quantity, price, delivery, and so on, must be specific enough to bind both the buyer's firm and the supplier to definable levels of performance. In writing a blanket purchase order for pipe fittings, for example, it is not sufficient to state the quantity as "all company X desires." Such a statement is too indefinite to bind company X to any specific purchase. However, if the requirement were stated as "the quantity company X uses during the month of March," most courts would consider this sufficient to define X's purchase obligation. It is also prudent to qualify such a statement by indicating approximate minimum and maximum levels of consumption.

Similar situations arise in specifying prices and delivery dates. Some companies, for example, occasionally issue unpriced purchase orders. Aside from the questionable wisdom of such a business practice, a legal question concerning the definiteness of the offer also exists. From a legal standpoint, the question which must be answered is: Under existing conditions, can the price be determined precisely enough to define the obligations of both parties? The UCC provides more latitude in answering this question than did the Uniform Sales Act. The code specifically says that a buyer and a supplier can make a binding contract without agreeing on an exact price until a later date. If at the time of shipment a price cannot be agreed on, the code includes provisions by which a fair price shall be determined. On such orders, however, a buyer should protect his or her firm by noting a precise price range or by stating how the price is to be determined.

Competent Parties   A valid contract must be made by persons having full contractual capacity. A contract made by a minor or by an insane or intoxicated person is usually entirely void or voidable at the option of the incompetent party.

Legality of Purpose   A contract whose purpose is illegal is automatically illegal and void. A contract whose primary purpose is legal, but one of whose ancillary terms is illegal, may be either void or valid, depending on the seriousness of the illegality and the extent to which the illegal part can be separated from the legal part of the contract. The latter situation may occasionally have relevance for buyers. Such would be the case, for example, if a material were purchased at a price which violated restraint of trade or price discrimination laws.

The Written and the Spoken Word   Buyers should be aware of several basic concepts concerning the construction of a contract. Contrary to common belief, a contract is not a physical thing. It is actually a relationship which exists between the parties making the contract. When a contract is reduced to writing, the written document is not in fact the contract; it is simply evidence of the contract. Hence, a contract may be supported by either written or oral evidence. In most cases, courts hold an oral contract to be just as binding as a written one, although it may be substantially more difficult to prove the facts on which an oral contract is based. However, the law requires some types of agreements to be in writing. In the case of sales transactions between qualified "merchants,"[2] for example, the UCC specifically states that when a selling price of $500 or more is involved, the contract must be

[2]Section 2-104 of the UCC defines a "merchant" as one who deals in goods; one who holds himself out as having particular skill in the subject matter; or one who uses a person who holds himself out as having such knowledge or skill. Hence, it is generally held under this broad definition that almost every person in business, including a purchasing officer, is a "merchant." Even a person not in business may be classified as a "merchant" if he or she employs a purchasing officer or broker.

reduced to writing to be enforceable.[3] In the event an oral contract between a supplier and a buyer is later confirmed in writing, the *written confirmation* is binding on both parties if no objection is raised within ten days.

Hence, it is important to note that when a contract is reduced to writing, the written evidence supersedes all prior oral evidence. The courts generally hold that a contract expressed in writing embodies all preceding oral discussion pertinent to the agreement. Generally speaking, this means that a buyer cannot legally rely on a supplier's oral statements concerning a material's performance or warranty unless the statements have been included in the written agreement. Consequently, from a legal standpoint, a buyer should consider carefully the content of his or her oral negotiations with a supplier and ensure that all relevant data to be included in the contract have been reduced to writing. The buyer should also be aware that courts have ruled that written or typed statements take precedence over printed statements on the contract form, should conflicting statements appear in the document.

Finally, in signing a written contract, a buyer or purchasing manager should specifically indicate on the document that he or she is acting in the capacity of an agent for his or her firm. This avoids any possible misinterpretation as to the identity of the parties making the contract. Moreover, all data to be included as part of the contract should appear above the agent's signature. Courts have ruled that data appearing below the signature are informational only and not part of the contract.

SPECIAL LEGAL CONSIDERATIONS

Inspection Rights

If a purchaser has not previously inspected the material purchased to ensure that it conforms with the terms of the contract, the law gives him or her a reasonable period of time to inspect the material after it is received. If the purchaser raises no objection to the material within a reasonable period of time, he or she is deemed to have accepted it. In court decisions on this matter, it has been largely industry practice which sets the standard for "reasonable" time.

Rights of Rejection

A purchaser has the right to reject material if it does not conform with the terms of the contract. If an overshipment is received, the purchaser can either reject the complete shipment or reject the quantity in excess of the contract. When a buyer does not wish to accept wrongly delivered material, he

---

[3]Prior to enactment of the UCC, the Statute of Frauds required contracts relating to personal property, for which neither delivery nor payment had been made, to be in writing if the value of the sale exceeded a specified amount; this specified amount varied widely among states.

or she is required only to notify the supplier of this fact, describing specifically the nature of the defect or default. The buyer is not legally bound to return the rejected material. However, the buyer's firm is obligated to protect and care for the material in a reasonable manner. If the buyer neither returns the material nor notifies the supplier of rejection within a reasonable period of time, however, the buying firm is then obligated to pay for the material.

Title

From a legal point of view, the question of which party has title to purchased materials is normally answered by defining the F.O.B. point of purchase. In the case of an F.O.B. origin shipment, the buying firm becomes the owner when the material is loaded into the carrier's vehicle. When material is shipped F.O.B. destination, the supplier owns the material until it is off-loaded at the buyer's receiving dock. A complete discussion of this matter is presented in Chapter 23, "Traffic."

Warranties

The UCC identifies four specific types of warranties:

1 Warranty of title
2 Implied warranty of merchantability
3 Implied warranty of fitness for a particular purpose
4 Express warranty

When a supplier agrees to sell a particular item the firm implies that it (or its principal) has title to the item and hence has legal authority to sell it. This is the *warranty of title.* The supplier also implies that the item is free from defects in material and workmanship—that it is at least of "fair average quality." This means that the item meets the standards of the trade and that its quality is appropriate for ordinary use. This legal provision is the *implied warranty of merchantability.*

Another implied warranty a buyer *may* receive under certain circumstances is an *implied warranty of fitness for a particular purpose.* If a buyer communicates to a supplier the requirements the purchased material must satisfy, and subsequently relies on the skill or judgment of the supplier in selecting a specific material for the job, the material usually carries an implied warranty of fitness for the stated need. This assumes that the supplier is fully aware of the buyer's need and knows that the buyer is relying on guidance from the supplier's personnel. Hence, it should be amply clear why buyers must insist that purchase orders and related material specifications be written clearly and completely.

If a supplier accepts a purchase order without qualification, descriptions of the material included on the order form—model number, size, capacity, chemical composition, technical specifications, and so on—in fact become an *express warranty*. The supplier warrants that the material delivered will conform to these descriptions. Additionally, vendors frequently make express warranties for their products in sales and technical literature. Such warranties typically refer to the material's performance characteristics, physical composition, appearance, and so on. If a buyer has no way of determining the facts of the matter and consequently relies on such warranties, the supplier normally is held liable for them. The buyer should also recognize that an express warranty nullifies an implied warranty to the extent that it conflicts with the implied warranty (with the exception of an implied warranty of fitness for a particular purpose).

Numerous variable factors influence the extent to which a buyer can rely on an implied warranty in a specific situation. The knowledge and conduct of both buyer and seller, as well as the specific conditions surrounding a transaction, are taken into consideration by the court in resolving a dispute over warranty. Generally speaking, if a buyer acts in good faith and has no knowledge of conditions contrary to an implied warranty, the law holds a supplier liable for such implied warranties, unless otherwise stated in the contract.

Recent legislation[4] has tended to increase warranty protection for buyers by strengthening and expanding the liability of manufacturers and sellers with respect to warranty performance. A buyer should recogize, however, that the UCC permits a seller to exclude or modify the implied warranty for a product. A supplier can do this by including a *conspicuous* written statement in the sales contract. Statements commonly used to accomplish warranty exclusion are: "This item is offered for sale 'as is,'" or "There are no warranties which extend beyond the description on the face hereof." Interestingly, in several states such warranty disclaimers have been declared to be contrary to public policy—and, hence, invalid. As a general rule, however, a prudent buyer adopts a caveat emptor attitude in verifying the warranty protection he or she actually has in any given purchase.

Order Cancellation and Breach of Contract

If a supplier fails to deliver an order by the delivery date agreed on in the contract, or if it fails to perform in accordance with contract provisions, legally the supplier has breached the contract. The breach usually gives the purchaser the right to cancel the order. In addition, the purchaser can sue for damages if he or she wishes. In practice, the latter right is infrequently exercised because a more effective settlement can usually be negotiated directly with the supplier. Nevertheless, under the law, a buyer may be able to re-

[4]The Consumer Product Safety Act and the Federal Warranties Act, as well as the UCC.

cover damages if injury is actually suffered as a result of a breach of contract. In the case of delivery failure, if the buyer subsequently purchases the material elsewhere, damages are generally limited to the difference between the contract price and the price paid the new supplier. If the material is not available elsewhere, actual damages may be difficult to determine. In any case, the courts usually follow the general rule of attempting to place the injured party in the same financial position he or she would have been in had the contract not been breached.

When no specific delivery date is stated in a contract, the law requires the supplier to deliver within a reasonable period of time. What the buyer thinks is a reasonable period of time may or may not coincide with what the supplier or the court deems to be a reasonable period of time. Hence, in such a situation, a buyer may be on uncertain ground if he or she decides to cancel an order because of nondelivery and subsequently places the order with another supplier. The buying firm may or may not have the legal right to do so. The desirability of including a specific delivery date in the contract thus becomes amply clear.

Situations sometimes arise that compel a buyer to cancel an order before the supplier is obligated to supply the material. In making such a cancellation, the *buyer* breaches the purchase contract. This act legally is termed *anticipatory breach,* and it makes the purchaser liable for any resulting injury to the supplier. If the cancellation results in no real injury to the supplier (as is often the case with orders for standard materials), the supplier can collect no damages. On the other hand, if the cancellation leaves the supplier with semifinished goods in its shop, the firm frequently does suffer injury. In such cases, if the in-process material is salable, the purchaser is usually held liable for the difference between the prorated contract value and the market value of the in-process material. If the material is not salable, the purchaser's liability usually covers the supplier's costs prior to termination plus a reasonable profit[5] on the contract.

Liquidated Damages Provision   If it is evident at the time a major contract is drawn that breach of the contract would severely injure one or both parties and that damages would be difficult to determine, it is wise to include in the contract itself a termination or liquidated damages provision. Such provisions stipulate *in advance* the procedures to be used in determining costs and damages. In some cases, specific damage payments are stated. For example, if the contract is for the purchase of power-generating equipment to be used on a large construction project, the date of delivery may be critical for the purchaser. Perhaps installation of the equipment must precede other important phases of the construction work. If the project is delayed by late delivery of the generating equipment, the purchaser might well incur heavy

---

[5]A "reasonable profit" generally is calculated using the same profit margin (percentage rate) as was included in the original contract.

financial losses. It is therefore normally sound practice on such a contract to include a liquidated damages clause that requires the supplier to pay the purchaser damages of x dollars per day for late delivery. It is essential, however, that the damage figure specified be a reasonable estimate of the probable loss to the buyer, and not be calculated simply to impose a penalty on the supplier. Courts generally refuse to enforce a penalty provision.

A termination or liquidated damages provision represents prior agreement by both parties on the ground rules to be followed in case the contract is breached. If such a breach actually occurs, the provision minimizes the possibility of misunderstandings and the generation of ill will between the two firms.

JIT Contracts

Because just-in-time purchasing and manufacturing operations are somewhat unique, they occasionally generate unexpected legal difficulties. The most common problems are reviewed briefly in the following paragraphs.

The major factor a buyer should keep in mind is that in most cases a JIT purchasing agreement requires different levels of supplier performance than the supplier typically has been used to. Consequently, it is important that communications be clear and complete. This includes oral discussions prior to the purchase, as well as the final written documents. Requirements for quality, quality control, delivery scheduling, inventory levels, and any other key factors should be spelled out in unequivocal terms, so there is little opportunity for misunderstanding that might lead to litigation.

Consider the following illustration. Assume that a buyer and a supplier have been doing business satisfactorily for several years. During the past year, approximately one-third of the shipments from the supplier arrived a week or so late, but the buyer accepted them without serious complaints. In the eyes of the law, these acceptances by the buyer may well have set a precedent which *waives the buyer's rights* to timely delivery on future contracts—not good for a new JIT contract. What must the buyer do to regain his or her rights? The two legal requirements are:

1 Give explicit written notice to the supplier.
2 Provide the supplier a reasonable period of time to gear up to meet the new delivery requirements.

With respect to the timing of design or configuration changes, the contract should always specify the minimal lead time, in terms of days or weeks of material usage, that the supplier will accept prior to supplying the modified material. Both parties should know what the supplier's planned inventory levels are so the firm is not likely to be left with an unusable stock of items built to the buyer's specifications. By the same token, the two must also agree on the minimum practical lead time requirements for a delivery lot size increase or an accelerated delivery schedule.

The point is that JIT systems must be able to respond quickly to demand changes because of their tight scheduling and low inventory characteristics on the buyer's side. These requirements for flexibility must be built into the purchase contract to the extent possible. Although meshing the buyer's needs with the supplier's capability may be difficult, it is these issues that should be discussed ahead of time, agreed on, and stated in the contract.

Inspection and acceptance is another area that can pose problems. Many JIT shipments are delivered directly to the point of use, without first going through incoming inspection. In many cases, detection of non-conforming items does not occur until some time later, after the item has entered the production process. If no provision for this situation is made in the contract, legally the material may be considered to have been accepted when delivered. Consequently, this modified operating procedure should be detailed clearly in the contract. A satisfactory time frame for acceptance and the responsibility for subsequent rework costs should be stipulated.

In structuring JIT purchase orders and contracts, common sense tells the buyer to be conservative and to include ample detail about these unique issues in the contractual documents.

Arbitration

Serious contract disputes are a rarity in the lives of most purchasing managers. But, in a complex business operation, they do arise from time to time. When a dispute does arise, after doing the appropriate "homework," the first step in the resolution process is to discuss the problem with the supplier. Happily, most disputes are resolved at this step through negotiation and compromise. In most cases, the executives involved want to avoid further confrontation simply because it is too time-consuming and too costly.

In the event a satisfactory solution cannot be worked out by the two parties, however, two alternatives remain. They can go to court, or they can employ an impartial arbitrator to settle the dispute. In the latter case, a professional arbitrator will hear testimony and study evidence from both sides, then make an impartial decision based on the facts. This alternative is the one usually chosen because it is much faster, less expensive, and produces less visibility and fuss outside the organization. In the settlement of commercial contract disputes, litigation is usually the last resort.

To avoid the possibility of future litigation on an important contract, buyers sometimes include in the purchase order an arbitration clause. The clause simply says, in effect, that any dispute arising out of the contract will be settled by arbitration, and that both parties will be bound by the decision. Normally, administration of the matter is handled through the American Arbitration Association. If upheld by law, this is an easy and convenient mechanism to use in establishing in advance the ground rules to be followed in the event a serious dispute arises.

To ensure that the ruling of an arbitrator will be legally binding, before preparing the order the buyer should seek assistance from the firm's legal counsel on two points. First, state statutes must be reviewed to determine whether the states in question do in fact have such legal provisions (most, but not all, do). Second, wording of the arbitration clause must be developed carefully in consonance with the state law and guidelines of the American Arbitration Association.

Honest Mistakes

When an honest mistake is made in drawing up a purchase contract, the conditions surrounding each specific case weigh heavily in determining whether the contract is valid or void. As a general rule, a mistake made by only one party does not render a contract void, unless the other party is aware or should be aware of the mistake. To affect a contract, the mistake usually must be made by both parties. Even then, not every mutual mistake invalidates the contract.

Assume, for example, that a vendor intends to submit a quotation with a price of $260. Through an error, the price is typed on the quotation as $250 and is so transmitted to the buyer. In such cases, courts have held that if the buyer accepts the offer, without knowledge of the error, a valid contract exists. The magnitude of the error is deemed insufficient to affect agreement materially. On the other hand, if the $260 price were incorrectly typed as $26, the court would probably hold that a competent buyer should recognize the error, and if one party knows or should know of the other's error, the contract is void.

Mutual mistakes concerning matters of opinion usually do not affect a contract. Neither is a contract affected by immaterial mutual mistakes about matters of fact. However, a mutual mistake concerning *matters of fact that materially affect agreement* usually renders a contract void. Assume, for example, that a buyer and a vendor agree on the sale of specific machinery. If, unknown to either, the machinery has been destroyed or for some other reason is not available for sale, the contract is void.

Generally speaking, a buyer should not assume that a mistake, however innocent, will release his or her firm from a contractual obligation. In the majority of cases, it will not do so. A prudent buyer employs all reasonable means to minimize the possibility of committing contractual mistakes.

Patent Infringement

The law gives a patent holder the exclusive right to manufacture, sell, and use the patented device for a specified number of years. A purchaser who engages in any of these activities during the period of patent protection, without permission from the patent holder, is guilty of patent infringement and can be sued for damages by the patent holder.

Buyers frequently have no way of knowing whether their suppliers are selling patented materials with or without authorization from the patent holder. If a purchaser unknowingly buys an item from a vendor who has infringed the patent holder's rights, the purchaser is also guilty of infringement if the firm uses the item. To protect against such unintentional violations, most companies include a protective clause in their purchase orders which states that the seller will indemnify the purchaser for all expenses and damages resulting from patent infringement. Clauses of this type do not prevent the patent holder from suing the user. If properly stated, however, they can require the seller to defend the user in such legal proceedings and can give the user legal recourse to recover any resulting losses from the seller.

Infringement suits are rare in the normal course of business activities. However, one area where most manufacturing firms frequently encounter potential infringement problems is in the maintenance of productive equipment. In some cases, a complete machine is patented, but its individual parts are not. In other cases, individual parts are patented. In cases where the individual part is not patented, the owner of the machine usually has the right to make a replacement part or to have it made by a vendor. When the individual part is patented, however, this cannot be done legally without permission from the patent holder.

On the other hand, if the owner of a patented machine wishes to rebuild the machine substantially, such activity is not considered within the range of normal maintenance and repair activity. To accomplish a rebuilding job, the owner must either have it done by the patent holder or obtain the patent holder's permission to do the job himself or herself.

Restraint of Trade Laws

The *Robinson-Patman Act* is a federal statute designed to prevent price discrimination that reduces competition in interstate commerce. Generally speaking, the act prevents a vendor from offering the same quantity of a specific material to competing buyers at different prices, unless: (1) one buyer is offered a lower price because his or her purchases entail lower manufacturing or distribution costs for the supplier, or (2) one buyer is offered a lower price in order to meet the legitimate bid of a competing vendor.[6]

It is important that all buyers be familiar with the detailed provisions of the act, because it also makes it *unlawful for any buyer knowingly to induce or receive a discriminatory price*. Thus, if a buyer accepts a price that he or she knows is in fact discriminatory, the buyer violates the law to the same extent as the supplier. The act does not prevent a buyer from seeking legitimate

---

[6]A third condition also permits the offering of a discriminatory price—namely, one in which the marketability of goods is affected. Seasonal goods or those approaching obsolescence or deterioration fall into this category.

price concessions. It is imperative, however, for a buyer to ensure that any price concessions gained are in fact justifiable under the act.

Nearly every state also has its own price discrimination legislation applicable to intrastate transactions. Since these laws vary widely from state to state, each buyer should likewise be familiar with the regulations in his or her state.

Product Liability and Purchasing

Product liability is the responsibility held by manufacturers and downstream sales organizations to pay for injuries to users (or bystanders) caused by defective or unreasonably hazardous products. During the past several decades court decisions and interpretations of legal theories have produced a marked change in the legal environment surrounding such issues. Not only are business firms now placed at greater risk—so are their purchasing departments.

Two things, for the most part, have acted as catalysts to produce the sensitive situation that exists in this area today. The first was a decision handed down by the California Supreme Court in 1963. The decision concluded that "a manufacturer is *strictly liable* when an article he places on the market, knowing that it may be used without inspection, proves to have a defect that causes injury to a human being."[7] The practical result of this decision was that to obtain legal redress an injured user had to prove *only* that the product was defective and that it caused the injury. The earlier requirement that the manufacturer be proved negligent was eliminated. Since then, a majority of the states have followed the precedent set by the California court. Additionally, over the years the strict liability concept has been extended to cover all goods, not just consumer items.

The second major occurrence was the gradual elimination of the longstanding requirement for "privity of contract" in product liability cases. Originally, if an injured user sued the manufacturer on the grounds that it had breached the product warranty, the user was required to have a purchase contract directly with the manufacturer. Since this often was not the case, the elimination of this requirement facilitated the user's access to the courts for recovery. Subsequently, court interpretations frequently extended liability also to the wholesalers and retailers of the manufacturers' product. Thus, the injured party could seek redress at any point in the manufacturer-distribution chain.

For professional purchasing people, the bottom line of this evolutionary pattern of events is very clear—and important. Product liability suits have literally skyrocketed during the past decade. Most manufacturing and distribution firms now assume a much greater potential risk than in earlier years.

[7]*Greenbaum v. Yuba Power Products, Inc.*, California Supreme Court, 1963.

Whether a buyer is purchasing a chemical compound for use within the organization, or buying component parts that go into the firm's finished product, he or she often has a magnified responsibility to safeguard the interests of the firm. This requires an added emphasis on the following activities:

1 Initial supplier investigation—with respect to quality capability, quality control, and reliability.
2 Purchase order or contract preparation—with respect to clear and complete communication of specification, operating, and safety requirements, as well as test and inspection procedures.
3 Coordination with quality control and inspection personnel—to ensure jointly that adequate procedures are being used. Further, the buyer must ensure adequate coordination between the QC personnel of both firms on problem issues.
4 In the case of potentially hazardous materials—clear communication to all users within the organization of information dealing with warnings, safety measures, usage instructions, and so on.
5 Documentation for all the preceding activities. Even though the buyer's performance may have been first-rate, it is imperative that the purchasing and QC records *show clearly* what was done, and that it *was* done prudently and well.

In summary, from a materials point of view, purchasing managers assume an added responsibility to minimize the exposure of their firms to potential product liability litigation.[8]

CONCLUSION

The purpose of this chapter is to alert buyers and potential purchasing professionals to the most basic legal considerations that relate to the purchasing function. Yet there is danger in doing this. No author can briefly accomplish this objective without simplifying the issues. And such simplification may at times leave the reader with an incomplete understanding which lulls him or her into a false feeling of security.

Even though adoption of the UCC by all but one of the states creates greater uniformity among state commercial laws than ever before, it is unreasonable to assume that interpretations of the laws by the various states will not vary. Only time can reveal how significant such variations will be. Moreover, the interpretation of circumstances surrounding each specific case weighs heavily in the analysis of that particular case. These factors virtually defy a definite and unqualified analysis of a legal controversy by anyone who

---

[8]For a thorough analysis of purchasing's responsibility in the area of product liability, see R. J. Adams and John R. Browning, "Purchasing and Product Liability," *Journal of Purchasing and Materials Management*, Summer 1989, pp. 2–9.

is not a highly skilled professional in the legal field. Heinritz, Farrell, and Smith state the matter cogently in saying that "the layman who tries to be his or her own lawyer has a fool for a client."[9] Perhaps the most important function of this chapter is to underscore the fact that purchasing professionals should seek sound legal counsel whenever potential legal problems arise.

Just as a lawyer is expected to exhibit skill in extricating his or her client from legal entanglements, so a purchasing executive is expected to exhibit skill in avoiding legal controversies. A purchasing manager must understand basic legal concepts well enough to detect potential problems before they become realities. At the same time, the most powerful tool he or she can utilize to avoid legal problems is skill in selecting sound, cooperative, and reliable suppliers. Vigilance in this area of responsibility minimizes the need for legal assistance.

FOR DISCUSSION

29-1 What is product liability?

29-2 What has been the impact of the legal aspect of product liability on purchasing activities? Discuss.

29-3 "A highly legalistic approach to purchasing is both unnecessary and unprofitable." Comment on this statement.

29-4 It has been said that the purchasing manager who tries to be his or her own lawyer has a fool for a client. If this is true, why do purchasing professionals study commercial law? Discuss.

29-5 Discuss the legal responsibilities of a buyer to his or her firm. To what extent are buyers liable for their actions?

29-6 Purchasing professionals and sales representatives are both "agents" for their respective firms. Is there usually any significant difference in the authority they possess as agents? Explain.

29-7 List and discuss the four essential elements of a contract.

29-8 When a purchase (or sales) contract is created, what specific actions constitute the "offer" and the "acceptance"? Explain.

29-9 What is the Uniform Sales Act? Discuss.

29-10 What is the Uniform Commercial Code? Discuss.

29-11 What is the legal status of a purchase order which has been accepted by a vendor who used an acceptance form containing terms that conflict with the terms stated on the purchase order? Explain.

29-12 Would the answer to question 29-11 be different if the Uniform Sales Act were still in effect? Explain.

29-13 What is meant by the term "mutuality of obligation"? What is its significance for normal purchasing transactions?

29-14 What inspection rights does a buyer have? Explain.

[9]Stuart Heinritz, Paul Farrell, and Clifton Smith, *Purchasing Principles and Applications,* Prentice-Hall, Englewood Cliff, N.J., 1986, p. 291.

29-15 Under what conditions can buyers reject materials they have purchased?

29-16 Discuss the warranty protection buyers have when they make a purchase.

29-17 What are a buyer's legal rights and obligations when canceling an order if:

a The supplier has failed to make delivery by the agreed delivery date?

b The delivery date is three weeks in the future?

c No delivery date has been specified on the order?

29-18 Discuss "liquidated damages" in relation to purchase contracts.

29-19 What is a warranty? What warranties usually accompany the purchase of production materials and equipment?

29-20 In what ways are JIT contracts different from contracts for the purchase of materials used in a traditional purchasing system?

29-21 What factors should a buyer pay particular attention to when preparing a JIT purchase order or contract?

29-22 Why might a purchasing manager be interested in arbitration? Discuss.

29-23 How do "honest mistakes" affect purchase contracts? Discuss.

29-24 How can a purchaser infringe the rights of a patent holder?

29-25 Discuss the significance of the Robinson-Patman Act for the professional buyer.

CASES FOR CHAPTER 29

ETHICAL AND PROFESSIONAL STANDARDS

> **KEY CONCEPTS**
>
> - Professional purchasing ethics
> - Professional purchasing practices
>   1978 proposed update of N.A.P.M. standards
>   Avoiding sharp practices
>   Competitive bidding
>   Negotiation
>   Sales engineering work
>   Samples
>   Personal purchases
>   Treating salespeople with respect
>   Substandard materials and services
>   Authority to direct changes
>   Gifts and gratuities
> - Management responsibilities
>   Written standards
>   Ethics training
>   Personnel responsibilities; Conflict of interest
>   Professional training

Ethics are the guidelines or rules of conduct by which we aim to live. Organizations, like individuals, have ethical standards and, frequently, ethics codes. The ethical standards of an organization are judged by its actions, not by pious statements of intent put out in its name. The *character* of an organization is a matter of importance to its employees and managers, to those who do business with it as customers and suppliers, and to those who are considering joining it in any of these capacities.

Marks and Spencer, the highly regarded U.K. retailer, is an example of an organization whose character is held in high regard. Some years ago, when the British pound had declined in value, Marks and Spencer reopened a contract which it had with a U.S. supplier, Burlington Mills, to see whether Burlington was making an adequate profit. A Burlington official commented that this was the first time in Burlington's history that a customer had been concerned over the effect of unforeseen economic events on Burlington's ability to make a profit. Marks and Spencer's *character* undoubtedly makes it a highly desirable customer!

One of the classic dilemmas facing management at all levels of any organization is the issue of "time focus": Do we focus on the short run or the long haul? Recent events on Wall Street demonstrate that expediency may be rewarding in the short run, but not in the long run. Dr. Clarence Walton, professor of ethics and the professions at the American College, adds, "Studies have indicated that companies which adhere to a set of ethical standards are healthier in the long run."[1]

Gary Edwards, executive director of the Ethics Resource Center of Washington, D.C., states, "Surveys show that corporations are paying more attention to the institutionalization of ethics within their organizations. This is happening, in part, because they've become aware of the *enormous costs of unethical activity*—in fines and penalties, in increased government regulations, and in damage to their public image. But they also believe that ethical behavior is good business."[2]

PROFESSIONAL PURCHASING ETHICS

We live and work in a highly competitive market economy with emphasis on results. There is pressure for sales, pressure to compromise, pressure to succeed in an environment of both internal and external competition, and pressure resulting from government mandates. The *pressures* which the marketplace exerts on purchasing departments and on individual buyers make it essential that top management, purchasing managers, buyers, and all other members of the procurement system recognize and understand both the professional and ethical standards required in the performance of their duties.

The foreword to the National Association of Purchasing Management (N.A.P.M.) Standards of Conduct, officially adopted in June 1959, portrays the critical role of ethics in the purchasing profession:

---

[1]"Greater Concern for Ethics and the 'Bigger Backyard,'" *Management Review*, July 1986, p. 28.
[2]Gary Edwards, quoted in "Is Ethics Good Business?" by Abbey Brown, *Personnel Administrator*, February 1987, p. 67.

...If there is such a thing as a profession as a concept distinct from a vocation, it must consist in the ideals which its members maintain, the dignity of character which they bring to the performance of their duties, and the austerity of the self-imposed ethical standards. To constitute a true profession, there must be ethical tradition so potent as to bring into conformity members whose personal standards of conduct are at a lower level, and to have an elevating and ennobling effect on those members. A profession cannot be created by resolution, or become such overnight. It requires many years for its development, and they must be years of self-denial, years when success by base means is scorned, years when no results bring honor except those free from the taint of unworthy methods.

The 1959 N.A.P.M. Standards of Conduct have served three useful functions:

1 They have had an educational effect by providing members with guidelines to the ethical behavior which experience had found to attract and justify the public's confidence.
2 The guidelines have narrowed the areas of uncertainty and doubt for those in the profession.
3 The guidelines have served as a visible standard that professionals can use to support their decisions.

These 1959 Standards of Conduct are the basis of modern purchasing ethics. During the thirty-odd years since these standards of conduct were advanced, new challenges have arisen. We now address professional purchasing standards.

PROFESSIONAL PURCHASING PRACTICES

1978 Proposed Update of N.A.P.M. Standards

In 1978, the Twin City Purchasing Management Association conducted research which led to the development of a list of modifications to the original N.A.P.M. standards. Interestingly, the study recommended that the basic structure and intent of the original standards remain intact. The suggested revised standards are detailed in their entirety below:[3]

- To consider, first, the interests of your company in all transactions and to carry out and accept its established policies insofar as they are consistent with other N.A.P.M. standards. [Note: This is what a *genuine agent* is supposed to do. An agent puts the organization's interest first.]
- To be receptive to competent assistance from your colleagues and to be guided by such assistance without impairing the dignity and responsibility of your office.
- To obtain the maximum ultimate value for each dollar of expenditure in an open and competitive manner.

---

[3]Richard E. Trevisan, "Developing a Statement of Ethics: A Case Study," *Journal of Purchasing and Materials Management*, Fall 1986, p. 11.

- To strive consistently for knowledge of the materials and processes of manufacture and to establish practical and ethical methods for the conduct of your office.
- To subscribe to and work for honesty and truth in buying and selling, and to denounce all forms and manifestations of commercial and government gratuities.
- To accord a prompt and courteous reception to all who call on a business mission.
- To respect, honor, and enforce your obligations and to ensure that obligations to you and your concern be honored, consistent with good business practice.
- To assist fellow purchasing managers in the performance of their duties.
- To cooperate with all organizations and individuals engaged in activities designed to enhance the development and standards of the purchasing profession.
- To promote the acceptance of good purchasing standards within your company, with your suppliers, and within the general business community.

Avoid Sharp Practices

The eighth item in N.A.P.M.'s 1959 Standards of Conduct reads, "Avoid sharp practices." Section 4.7 of the N.A.P.M. *Guide to Purchasing* reads, "The term 'sharp practices' is typically illustrated as evasion and indirect misrepresentation, just short of actual fraud." These unscrupulous practices focus on short-term gains and ignore the long-term implications for a business relationship. "Some examples of sharp practices are:

- A buyer talks in terms of large quantities to encourage a price quote on that basis. However, the forthcoming order is smaller than the amount on which the price was based. The smaller order does not legitimately deserve the low price thus developed.
- A large number of bids are solicited in hope that the buyer will be able to take advantage of a quotation error.
- Bids are obtained from unqualified suppliers whom the buyer would not patronize in any case. These bids are then played against the bids of responsible suppliers in order to gain a price or other advantage. The preparation of bids is a costly undertaking which deserves buyer sincerity in the solicitation stage.
- A market is misrepresented by a buyer who places in competition the prices of seconds, odd lots, or distress merchandise.
- An attempt is made to influence a seller by leaving copies of bids, or other confidential correspondence, where a supplier can see them.
- A concession may be forced by dealing only with "hungry" suppliers. The *current* philosophy is that a purchase order should create a mutual advantage with a price that is fair and reasonable.
- Obscure contract terms of benefit to the buyer's firm are buried in the small type of contract articles.
- A buyer may take advantage of a vendor who is short of cash and who may seek only to cover his/her out-of-pocket costs. Such a situation poses a di-

lemma, since the vendor may be saved from borrowing at a disadvantage and may look upon such an order as a blessing!"[4]

Acurex Corporation adds the following ten items to N.A.P.M.'s list of practices to be avoided:[5]

- Allowing one or more suppliers to have information on their competitor's quotations and allowing such suppliers to requote
- Making statements to an existing supplier that exaggerate the seriousness of a problem in order to obtain better prices or other concessions
- Giving preferential treatment to suppliers that higher levels of the firm's own management prefer to recommend
- Showing bias against suppliers whose salespeople attempt to reach other company departments directly rather than going through purchasing
- Canceling a purchase order for parts already in process while also seeking to avoid cancellation charges
- Allowing personalities—liking for one sales representative and dislike for another—to enter into the supplier selection process
- Getting together with other buyers to take united action against another group of people or a company
- Lying to or grossly misleading a salesperson in a negotiation
- Allowing a supplier to become dependent on the purchasing organization for most of its business
- Obtaining discounted prices from suppliers for employees, if the supplier does not understand that employees are benefiting from the discounted prices; obtaining discounted prices only for selected employees

While many of these practices were once commonplace, Dr. Felch notes that they are now replaced by a philosophy which holds that mutual confidence and integrity are far more desirable ends than the short-term gains obtained through willful misrepresentation.

Competitive Bidding[6]

Purchasing professionals respect and maintain the integrity of the competitive bidding process. They:

- Invite only firms to whom they are willing to award a contract to submit bids.
- Award the contract to the lowest responsive, responsible bidder. If the buyer anticipates the possibility of awarding to other than the low bid

---

[4]Robert I. Felch, "Proprieties and Ethics in Purchasing Management," *Guide to Purchasing*, N.A.P.M., Oradell, New Jersey, 1986, p. 4.7–3&4.

[5]Trevisan, op. cit., p. 13.

[6]Much of the discussion included from pages 646–649 is based on material in N.A.P.M.'s *Guide to Purchasing*, section 4.7: "Proprieties and Ethics in Purchasing Management," authored by Dr. Robert I. Felch in 1986. Specific footnotes are utilized where appropriate.

der, then he or she notifies prospective bidders that other factors will be considered. (Ideally, these factors will be listed.)
- Keep competitive price information confidential.
- Notify unsuccessful bidders promptly so that they may reallocate reserved production capacity.
- Treat all bidders alike. Clarifying information is given to all potential bidders.
- Do not accept bids after the announced bid closing date and time.
- Do not take advantage of apparent mistakes in the supplier's bid.
- Do not "shop" or conduct auctions for low prices. This practice is common in the construction industry. General contractors frequently will pit potential suppliers against one another in an effort to reduce prices, with little concern for the supplier's costs. The unfortunate result frequently is a contract wherein the supplier cuts corners in order to avoid a loss.

On the other hand, it *is* ethical for the buyer to work with the low bidder in an effort to identify possible areas of savings. Such identified savings allow the potential supplier to reduce its costs and its bid.

Negotiation

Professional buyers maintain high ethical standards during negotiations.

- Competitors are informed of the factors which will be involved in source selection.
- All potential suppliers are given equal access to information and are afforded the same treatment.
- Professional buyers strive to negotiate terms which are fair to both parties. They do not take advantage of mistakes in the supplier's proposal.[7]

Sales Engineering Work

A question may arise concerning how much presale engineering work the purchasing firm can receive without incurring a legal or moral obligation to the technical representative's organization.

This issue must be addressed *before* any possible problem arises. The responsible buyer needs to determine the amount of "free" sales engineering work that is common in the particular industry. (This so-called free work is a selling expense that must be absorbed by purchasers of the supplier's products if the supplier is to remain in business.) If the cost of an engineering study that appears to be especially desirable exceeds normal industry practice, the purchasing firm should pay for the study. If a free study is offered, wise buyers ensure that neither they nor their firm will be under any obliga-

---

[7]Felch, op. cit., p. 4–5.

tion to purchase the proposed material or equipment. *It is considered to be unethical for the buying firm to use the resulting study as the basis for competition.*

Frequently, a buyer will invite two or three qualified suppliers to submit technical proposals and then negotiate price and other terms with those potential suppliers whose technical approaches are acceptable. When such an approach is employed, the purchasing firm's buyers *and engineers* must exercise great care not to transfer one potential supplier's technical concepts to another supplier.

Samples

Many potential suppliers offer, even push, the acceptance of samples. When a sample is accepted, professional buyers ensure that appropriate tests are conducted in a timely manner. The potential supplier then should be informed of the test results and suitability of the item in meeting the buyer's needs.

Personal Purchases

It is estimated that about one-third of all company purchasing departments make personal purchases for company officials or employees. This appears to be a misuse of trade discounts to obtain prices significantly below retail. There are several logical consequences of this practice:[8]

- A buyer incurs an obligation to the seller who makes such a concession.
- When a purchase is unsatisfactory, the purchasing department can become involved in distasteful negotiations at the expense of its reputation.
- The practice entails obvious administrative costs to the company.
- Several state legislatures have passed laws prohibiting the practice of buying for company personnel.

Treating Salespeople with Respect

As noted earlier, the use of courtesy and consideration by purchasing departments can influence the effectiveness of supplier relationships, and it clearly produces overtones in the area of professional standards of conduct.[9]

- Salespeople should not be kept waiting for protracted periods of time, and appointments should be meticulously kept. The power that is attached to the patronage position of a buyer must not be abused so that the long-run interests of the buyer's company will be advanced.
- A mutually effective policy is for purchasing personnel to see every salesperson on his or her first call.

[8]Felch, op. cit., p. 6.
[9]Felch, op. cit., p. 7.

Substandard Materials and Services

When substandard materials or services are received, two proprieties should be observed:[10]

1 The supplier should be given prompt notice.
2 Negotiations for adjustments should be carried out through the agency of the purchasing department concerned.

Authority to Direct Changes

When a new, complex, technical product is initially produced by a supplier, design engineers may demonstrate their natural professional interest by visiting the supplier's plant during design and the early stages of production. Sometimes, initial production operations reveal a technical oversight or an opportunity for design improvement. Product engineers may direct or encourage the supplier to make design or specification changes. The need for concurrent changes in the contractual agreement may be overlooked.[11]

- Such engineering changes can prove to be embarrassing if they are not concurrently attended by the buyer and seller through appropriate contract and financial changes. The buyer is clearly placed at a disadvantage when he or she must resolve an after-the-fact engineering change.
- Good supplier relationships and control by a purchasing department can be maintained only through discipline and understanding on the part of both engineers and buyers. Top management attention may be required.

During the preaward meeting discussed in the chapter on supplier relations, the professional buyer ensures that the supplier and the buying firm's design and quality personnel recognize that only the buyer may make changes in the contract. Nonpurchasing members of the procurement system properly are concerned with receiving technically acceptable materials and services. Unfortunately, such individuals frequently ignore the commercial ramifications of such changes. When it appears desirable to interpret or change the technical requirements under a contract, the buyer should be present to ensure that ethical as well as scheduling and commercial issues are properly addressed.

Gifts and Gratuities

The guidelines contained in the N.A.P.M. 1959 Standards of Conduct apply today more than ever. There is nothing that can undermine respect for the purchasing profession more than improper action on the part of its members with regard to gifts, gratuities, favors, and so forth. People engaged in pur-

---

[10]Felch, op. cit., p. 7.
[11]Felch, op. cit., p. 7.

chasing should not accept from any supplier or prospective supplier any substantive gifts or favors. All members of the procurement system must decline to accept or must return any such items offered them or members of their immediate family. The refusal of gifts and favors should be done discreetly and courteously. Possible embarrassment resulting from refusal does not constitute a basis for an exception.[12]

The term "gifts, gratuities and favors" includes, but is not limited to, money, credits, discounts, seasonal or special occasion presents, edibles, drinks, household appliances and furnishings, clothing, tickets to sporting events and theaters, dinners, parties, transportation, vacations, travel or hotel expenses, and various forms of entertainment. In any case, where the return of a gift is impractical for some reason, disposition should be made to a charitable institution, and the donor informed of the disposition.

Personal business transactions with suppliers or prospective suppliers should be scrupulously avoided. Personal loans must not be accepted from such companies on any basis. Offers of hospitality, business courtesies, or favors, no matter how innocent in appearance, can be a source of embarrassment to all parties concerned.

The purchasing firm's representatives should not allow themselves to become involved in situations where unnecessary embarrassment results from refusal of a hospitality or a business courtesy from suppliers. Generally, the best policy is to decline any sort of favor, hospitality, or entertainment in order to *ensure that all relationships are above reproach at all times.*

Clearly, all situations require the use of common sense and good judgment. For example, acceptance of company-provided luncheons during the course of a visit to a supplier's plant located in a remote area certainly is reasonable. Likewise, the acceptance of supplier-provided automobile transportation on a temporary basis where other means are not readily available is a reasonable course of action for a buyer, expeditor, or inspector to take.

Purchasing personnel may ethically attend periodic meetings or dinners of trade associations, professional and technical societies, or other industrial organizations as the guest of a supplier, where the meetings are of an educational and informative nature, and where it is considered to be in the professional interest of the buyer-seller relationship. However, the repeated appearance of an individual at such regularly scheduled meetings, as the guest of the same company, is the type of situation which should be tactfully avoided.

The simple casual lunch or cocktail with a supplier's representative typically is merely a normal expression of a friendly business relationship, or frequently a timesaving expediency. It would be prudish to raise any serious question on this score. The individual, himself or herself, is in the best posi-

---

[12]Minor modifications have been made in the original text to reflect application to all members of the procurement system and to recognize the role of women in procurement and marketing.

tion to judge when this point has been exceeded. Any breach of ethics can be rationalized. But members of the procurement system can avoid embarrassment or possible unethical behavior by asking, How would this look if reported in the company newsletter? It is the desire to continue to talk shop or to resolve a business issue that accounts for most buyer-supplier lunches. Since the buying firm's prestige also is involved, *there is good reason why an adequate expense account should be available to the buyer.* This permits him or her to reciprocate in picking up the bill for lunch! It is a small price to pay for maintaining a position free from any taint of obligation.

"There's No Such Thing As a Free Lunch."   Mike Darby of the Purchasing Management Association of Silicon Valley recently addressed the issue of free lunches.

The person who came up with this quote many years ago was probably a materials manager. There are many pro's and con's about buyers going to lunch with their suppliers. I don't propose to advocate one or the other, but I would like to point out some ideas that may help you to make up your own mind.

First and foremost in my mind is, *WHY* would a company want to spend some of its dollars that would normally flow directly to the bottom line to have me join them for lunch? I've asked this question of many suppliers. Some of the answers I've received include: "I have to take somebody to lunch every day, and it might as well be somebody I like"; "If I take you to lunch, then my lunch is free also"; "It will give us an opportunity to get to know each other better." These are all good answers, some of them more honest than I expected.

When I asked the same question of the buyers, the answer changed slightly. 'We may need this supplier in the future, and I want to develop a close relationship with him'; 'We have some serious problems to discuss'; 'This will give me a good opportunity to negotiate a better deal with them.'

Whatever the justification, the bottom line to me gets down to this. The supplier is willing to commit some of his profit dollars to this form of entertainment in *the belief that it will help him generate more profit in the future.* He may be in hope that the relationship he is building will help sustain him in your company through rough times, such as poor delivery performance or bad quality. He may be expecting to increase his prices, and a friend will never complain about a small change in price. He may ask you to lunch expecting that the slight social obligation he has just obtained from you may be paid back by getting another crack at a quote, first look at a new drawing, etc. Or he may join you for lunch hoping to obtain some information that will be useful to him in future negotiations.

All the above tend to add up to a one-sided deal, favoring the supplier and putting the buyer in the position of having to be very careful. Let's face it, the sales force of the supplier is being paid to perform a service to the supplier, and this is a good tool for him to use. He gets your undivided attention for a good hour or so, to use as he sees fit. Remember, it's impolite in our society to refuse to answer a question. A question as simple as "How's business?" provides the supplier with important information as to its market share within your company, business trends, and helps to set his expectations in future negotiations. It's also very difficult as a buyer not to show a slight amount of favoritism toward the supplier that you had lunch with last Friday. Should he ask, "Where do I stand on that quote, and what do I need to do to get the job?", it gets difficult to be firm and say no to such a request.

Now before I get blasted out of the water for being one-sided, let me say that there are times when a business meal is appropriate. If you have a supplier in from out of town, and your business discussions extend through lunch or past business hours, a meal is probably appropriate. In this circumstance, I like to use the Host rule—If the meeting is in your territory, then you should be the host. If you are visiting the supplier's territory, then he can be the host. Make it fair and equitable, and the supplier loses any advantage he might have held from an obligation point of view. Remember, an obligation is in the mind of the person who received the favor. If, because of the manner in which you handle your conduct, there was no potential for a favor, then there can also be no obligation.

As a buyer, picking up the check can quickly change a supplier's expectations, and as such is a very useful negotiation tactic. If he thought he had a contract in the bag, he suddenly begins to think that he may not be as secure as he thought. It also sends the message that you too are a professional and certainly not an easy target.[13]

Mature purchasing people know that they are quickly classified among the sales fraternity by the amount of entertainment they expect or will accept. Salespeople usually speak with real respect of the buyer who pays his or her share of entertainment expenses. The purchasing expense account is the most effective answer to this ethical problem.

Traditional Sales Techniques Many purchasing personnel feel that any form of gratuity (lunches, pens, calendars) constitutes a conflict with ethical standards. Others—in fact, the majority, according to N.A.P.M. studies—consider these items traditional sales tools. They do not, therefore, believe that such gratuities are offered with the expectation of favorable consideration.[14]

There are two common ways of controlling the acceptance of these kinds of gifts. The first is by placing a dollar limit on what can be accepted. In this case, a purchasing department may have a stated policy of refusing any gratuity with a value in excess of, say, $10. Such policies provide a very simple, measurable guideline as to how a buyer should decide acceptance.

The other common policy is to forbid acceptance of any gratuity the buying firm is not in a position to reciprocate. Thus if a firm's buyers accept sales promotion items such as pens or planning calendars, they should be in a position to reciprocate with similar items from their own firm.

Cultural Ramifications Executives of many foreign suppliers expect that buyers will exchange gifts with them. Such action is an accepted part of many foreign cultures. Some buyers encounter situations where refusing a

[13]*Pacific Purchasor*, November–December 1988, p. 11.
[14]Michael H. Thomas, "Know Where You Stand on Ethics," *Purchasing World*, October 1984, p. 90.

gift would interfere with the development of relations prerequisite to consummating a successful transaction. In such cases, professional buyers *report* the situation to their superiors and arrive at a solution that may include acceptance *and* a reciprocal gift.[15] If a buyer hides his or her action, he or she automatically knows that the action is unethical.

MANAGEMENT RESPONSIBILITIES
Written Standards

Management's first responsibility is to develop a set of written ethical and professional standards applicable to all members of the organization's procurement system. Purchasing supervisors, buyers, expediters, design engineers, manufacturing engineers, quality assurance personnel, maintenance supervisors, receivers, and accounts payable personnel all must accept these standards. These standards should address the topics discussed in this chapter.

Ethics Training

Professional purchasing managers, with the *assistance of top management* and their colleagues in other functional areas, ensure that appropriate personnel receive periodic training with respect to the organization's ethical and professional standards. Such training cannot address all issues. It can, however, increase the sensitivity of those attending. All members of the procurement system must respect their roles as agents of their employer and must represent the best interest of their organizations. Subsequent to such training, many organizations require the attendees to sign *a statement to the effect that they have taken the training and understand and will honor the standards.*

Management's Personnel Responsibilities; Conflict of Interest

As part of the hiring process, professional purchasing supervisors should always obtain detailed information on applicants' previous purchasing experience, performance, and reputation. They should also determine if an applicant, or an employee, has a lifestyle beyond his or her means or has possible conflicting outside interests.[16]

Managers are aware that buying from a firm in which the buyer has a significant financial interest almost always creates a conflict of interest. Since some buyers learn a great deal about a supplier's profitability, they may be sorely tempted to make investments that would create such conflicts. Profes-

---

[15]Somerby Dowst, "Taking the Mystery Out of Conflict of Interest," *Purchasing,* Sept. 11, 1986, p. 70A1.

[16]Bernard Fried, "Criminalization of the Procurement Process," *Freedom of Choice,* N.A.P.M., Tempe, Arizona, 1987, p. 113.

sional managers ensure that these types of activities do not occur. An Illinois corporate director adds, "It's the responsibility of each level of supervision to constantly observe employee lifestyle, check logs on visitors, and particularly investigate suppliers used with any frequency."[17]

Bernard Fried, vice president and government operation general counsel, Unisys Corporation, recommends several additional managerial actions:[18]

- Rotate buyers.
- Scrutinize single sourcing closely.
- Avoid excessive engineering-directed purchases.
- Limit signature authority.
- Rotate blanket purchase agreements among different companies and validate prices periodically.
- Advise suppliers to use the company's hot line to report any wrongdoing in the firm's business practices.
- Prevent the release of advance information.
- Avoid release of competitors' information.
- Avoid tailoring specifications to favor a specific subcontractor.
- Obtain written agreements from selected personnel to prevent their employment with the firm's suppliers for a specified period after leaving the firm's employ.
- Ensure that suppliers maintain an effective fraud, waste, and abuse awareness program.
- In engineering, the firm should ensure that technical exchanges with subcontractors are closely monitored to prevent: (1) the lessening or waiving of technical requirements or (2) the providing of technical assistance to one subcontractor over another.
- Quality assurance should ensure that inspections are conducted by qualified, trained personnel, and that inspection standards are adequate. Waived, delayed, poor, or false inspections can be fraud indicators. So can a very low rate of rejections or deficiency reports.
- Maintain an open and free atmosphere that allows and encourages employees to report code violations without fear of reprisal. They will do this if they honestly believe that top management is genuinely committed to it.

A few progressive organizations have established an internal or external ombudsman who can be contacted with impunity on ethical issues. Once accepted, the practice works well.

Doyle Selden, president of Selden Associates, suggests greater utilization of postpurchase audits as desirable safeguards. Mr. Selden writes, "When every buyer knows that his or her purchases will be audited, there is a built-in safeguard tending to assure ethical purchasing."[19]

---

[17]Amy J. Rogers, "How Purchasing Execs View Taking Gifts from Suppliers," *Purchasing*, Feb. 14, 1985, p. 23.
[18]Bernard Fried, op. cit., pp. 112 and 116.
[19]Doyle Selden, "Ethics, An Additional Look," *Purchasing Management*, December 1988, p. 41.

Professional Training

Professional purchasing managers should ensure that their personnel receive training on current thinking and techniques in the areas of requirements development, source selection, pricing, cost analysis, negotiation, and supplier management, as well as ethical and professional standards.

The vast majority of buyers and their supervisors in U.S. firms are dedicated and conscientious people. Accordingly, it is almost shocking to see how little high-quality training many of these individuals have received. Procurement system reviews conducted by the authors indicate that the majority of buyers are being asked to perform tasks for which they have received little current training, including training in the area of ethical and professional conduct.

CONCLUSION

Buyers and other members of the procurement system who deal with present and potential suppliers must recognize their responsibilities as agents. An agent has very special authority and responsibilities in the eyes of the business world and the legal community. An agent must represent the best interest of his or her employer.

FOR DISCUSSION

30-1 Define "ethics."

30-2 How are the ethical standards of an organization judged?

30-3 To whom is the character of an organization important?

30-4 Why is Marks and Spencer a highly desirable customer?

30-5 What are the costs of unethical behavior?

30-6 What is the relationship between ethics and true professionalism?

30-7 Define and describe "sharp practices."

30-8 Is it ethical to allow one or more suppliers to have information on their competitors' quotations and to allow such suppliers to requote? Discuss.

30-9 What is meant by the term "shop"? Is such action ethical?

30-10 Is it ethical for the buyer to work with the low bidder in an effort to identify possible areas of savings?

30-11 Describe three ethical guidelines to be followed during negotiations.

30-12 What are the ethical implications of purchasing departments' making personal purchases for company employees?

30-13 How should substandard materials and services be handled?

30-14 How should the authority to direct purchase order or contract changes be controlled?

30-15 What are the ethical implications of gifts, gratuities, and favors?

30-16 Should buyers have expense accounts?

30-17 What is management's first responsibility in the area of ethics? Personnel responsibilities?

30-18 What is the role of an ombudsman?

CASES FOR CHAPTER 30

Laxtec, Inc., page 751
Collier Company I, page 728
Hardy Company, page 743
Worldwide Industries (in the Instructor's Manual)
Dynaflight, Inc., California Division (in the Instructor's Manual)
Hy Tech (in the Instructor's Manual)

PART **EIGHT**

INSTITUTIONAL AND GOVERNMENT PURCHASING

PURCHASING FOR INSTITUTIONS

KEY CONCEPTS

- Differences between institutional and industrial purchasing
    Control of budgets
    Early purchasing involvement
    Conflicts of interest
    Inspection
    Backdoor selling
    Reciprocity
- Teachers and scientists
- Public and private institutions
- Application of principles
    Centralization
    Cooperative purchasing
    Price
    Personnel
    Organization
- Government research contracts
- Special considerations
    Insurance
    Construction and furnishings
    Stores
    Auxiliary functions

The U.S. economy can no longer be considered predominantly a "production economy." By spending more for *services* than for *goods*, the United States has become the world's first nation having a service economy. Because the national demand for services continues to rise faster than the demand for goods, the economy is becoming increasingly service-oriented.

This chapter focuses on purchasing for education and health care institutions—two fast-growing service industries. Most of what is said, however, applies to all other types of institutions, such as penal institutions, art galleries, and libraries. When educational institutions are discussed, the emphasis is on colleges and universities. Because the purchasing operations of these institutions cover the entire spectrum of educational buying, a discussion of purchasing at this level also includes the purchasing considerations of elementary and secondary schools. Purchasing differences which exist among schools are generally ones of degree, rather than substance.

Buying for institutions is big business![1] Schools and hospitals[2] are a large segment of the U.S. economy. Their economic size alone makes them important. In 1987 the cost of U.S. education at all levels exceeded $282 billion.[3] Medical services are growing at an even faster rate than education. In fact, medical services now represent the nation's fastest-growing industry. In 1986 the cost of health care was just over $458 billion.[4]

Every principle of good purchasing discussed in the preceding chapters applies fully to purchases made for institutions. All buying activities—whether industrial, governmental, or institutional—have one cardinal objective: to obtain the maximum value for each dollar spent. There is no separate group of principles for institutional buying. In comparison with industrial purchasing, however, institutional purchasing places different emphasis on some of the factors of good purchasing. This chapter examines these differences.

DIFFERENCES OF EMPHASIS IN INSTITUTIONAL AND INDUSTRIAL PURCHASING

Control of Budgets

Parkinson's law on budgets states that "expenditures will always rise to exceed income." This "law" applies to many business operations; however, it is especially applicable to institutions, where the determination to control expenditures is not as strong as it is in industry. Until recently, it was easier for schools to raise tuition rates and for hospitals to raise room and service rates than it was for industrial companies to raise the selling prices of their products. Consequently, in many cases institutions have not been motivated to control purchasing costs in the same way as competitive industrial organizations. It appears, however, that this situation has changed. The federal gov-

---

[1] For institutions, the cost of materials and business services (including construction costs) averages 20 to 30 percent of total cost, rather than approximately 60 percent, as is the case for industrial firms. Nevertheless, the opportunity for cost savings is still an important one.

[2] The term "hospitals" in this discussion is used generically to include many types of medical institutions, such as clinics, convalescent homes, nursing homes, and similar health care facilities.

[3] U.S. Bureau of the Census, *Statistical Abstract of the United States: 1988*, p. 119.

[4] Ibid., p. 88.

ernment and individual taxpayers alike are increasingly concerned about the high cost of education and medical care. This concern has been forcefully communicated to hospital and school administrators. As costs for these services continue to rise, Congress is directing a larger portion of its investigatory time to these areas of expenditure. Congressional investigations, in turn, invariably result in closer control over the expenditures of government funds—which represent a significant portion of total educational and medical resources.

Savings Purchasing savings are as valuable to institutions as they are to industry. In industry these savings increase profits and, therefore, increase a firm's capability to survive competitively. In education and health care, purchasing savings permit a college or hospital to further pursue its goals of better education, better patient care, better physical facilities, better salaries, and so on. Because most purchasing savings recur year after year, such savings can be viewed much like a gift to an institution's endowment fund. For example, a major university recently achieved purchasing savings of approximately $640,000. With its endowment income generated at roughly an 8 percent earning rate, the $640,000 recurring saving is equivalent to an endowment gift of $8,000,000 ($640,000/0.08 = $8,000,000). Stated differently, each $1 saved by wise purchasing has the same budgetary effect as a $12.50 gift to the institution's endowment fund.

Early Purchasing Involvement

The gains from purchasing's early involvement in the specification of requirements are especially important to institutions, because an institution purchases a much broader spectrum of materials and services than does the average industrial firm. Although most teachers, researchers, and physicians are exceedingly knowledgeable about their professional specialties, they are not always equally knowledgeable about the principles of procurement for research, instructional, and medical equipment. Unfortunately, early purchasing involvement is the rare exception in many institutions. These well-intentioned professionals typically specify their purchase requirement by brand name. Too frequently, they conduct *all* the discussions with the prospective supplier. Their focus normally is on the technical and performance aspects of the item. Few users have the orientation or requisite skills to investigate the commercial aspects of a procurement. As a result, the institution commonly pays more than if a qualified buyer were involved early during the development of the requirement. Such early involvement allows the buyer to assist his or her customers in selecting the most appropriate *and* nonrestrictive purchase description. The buyer should be involved with the user in the initial discussions with prospective suppliers of equipment, supplies, or services. The user (physician, teacher, researcher, or administrator) should focus on the performance aspects of the procurement, while the buyer focuses on the commercial issues.

For example, assume that a chemistry professor or a medical biologist wants to acquire a complex new microscope. The purchasing department can help by arranging for demonstrations of competing microscopes or scintillation machines from several major manufacturers. This is something that the users typically cannot accomplish by themselves, simply because they do not have the time or the economic leverage to do so. The microscope buyer learns much about many types of microscopes. He or she knows (or can learn) which models are competitive, who sells them, and which distributor has the best facilities for servicing them. Additionally, the buyer can discuss technical and marketing changes with all manufacturers' representatives. On the other hand, even constant users of microscopes make only infrequent purchases; therefore, they normally do not keep up with the many advancements of all major manufacturers. Because the purchasing department buys many things in addition to microscopes from the same distributors of scientific equipment, it usually can obtain a superior response in terms of sales effort, timing, and price.

When it comes to the purchase of unique or seldom-purchased capital equipment, the technical competence of the customer must be relied upon heavily. The purchasing staff can help by working with the user well "upstream" in planning the procurement. Purchasing can help with the economic problems of capacity, prices, and obtaining favorable terms and conditions in general. A professional buyer is sensitive to the importance of introducing to the purchasing process special terms and conditions concerning such things as warranties, responsibility for installation, responsibility for site preparation, follow-up maintenance, maintenance response times in case of problems with equipment, and so on. It is very important that these items be discussed *before* the purchase and that the understandings between the institution and the supplier be put in writing. Such action makes the supplier's responsibilities clear and makes enforcing them much more routine when the purchase and delivery take place. Obviously, this is particularly important in the case of high-dollar-value procurements, procurements which are very complex with regard to installation, calibration, and maintenance, or procurements which extend for a considerable period of time into the future. Institutions, in general, tend to be weak in this respect and tend unnecessarily to place blind faith in the good intentions of the supplier and the assurances of the sales representative, thereby placing the institution in some jeopardy of having little recourse if performance is not satisfactory.

For example, in the purchase of high-speed computer memory units, a competent university purchasing specialist was able to combine his skills effectively with the technical know-how of a systems analyst and the operating experience of a professor. The professor wanted to purchase memory units that would increase the capability of his computer-assisted instruction project. Among the problems included in this procurement were funding of the purchase, possible contract cancellation at no cost, deferred delivery of some units, and an option to increase the number of units at the original price approximately one year later. The purchasing specialist entered the procurement picture as soon as the requirement was known. He prepared the request for proposals, sent it to six major firms, participated in the evaluation of the proposals, negotiated with the two firms whose proposals were most favorable, and suggested in detail a possible basis for the manufacturers' financing of the sale. The contract award ultimately was made on the basis of the quality of one manufacturer's product, together with the consideration of its responsiveness to the nontechnical aspects of funding and to other desired contractual provisions. The final unit price, a six-digit figure, was approximately 15 percent below the best quotation among the other five initial competitive proposals.

Conflicts of Interest

Conflicts of interest in institutional purchasing are probably more critical than those in industry. Medical scientists and college professors control millions of research dollars flowing from the government and philanthropic foundations. These individuals, in addition to teaching and conducting research, frequently serve as consultants to industrial companies. Such companies in turn often work on projects similar, if not identical, to those the scientists work on in connection with their research grants. Additionally, some of these same people serve on boards of directors of still other companies that have similar types of research projects. Such relationships can raise many delicate questions of propriety. Consider, for example, patents and royalties. Who owns the patents to and who gets the royalties from a product developed by a consulting professor or researcher while working under a government research contract or grant? Is it the professor, the government agency, or the firm for which he or she is consulting? To confuse a situation that is already vague, various agencies of the federal government (the Departments of Energy, Defense, Health and Human Services, and Education) answer these questions differently!

In his book *The Closed Corporation—American University in Crisis*,[5] James Ridgeway discusses many questions of this type. Ridgeway points out that the number of professors involved in industry as consultants and directors is growing; an increasing number of dealings between business institutions and university officials has caused an increasing number of conflicts of interest; professors and scientists increasingly are using their prestige as scholars to advance the interest of specific firms, industries, and governmental organizations. Such situations tend to make the individuals involved biased, rather than objective, in their views. In such cases, conflicts of interest can easily follow.

[5]Published by Random House, New York, 1968.

To further compound matters, few institutions have developed clearly defined and effective policies concerning conflicts of interest. Many, however, now are beginning to do so. Congress historically has demanded tight controls in areas where public expenditures are high, and private foundations are now starting to examine very closely the ethical implications of their grants. An important current issue with respect to conflicts of interest is Medicare regulations. These regulations are very specific in banning any payment which may be perceived as a kickback encouraging use of a particular facility by Medicare patients. This is becoming a very touchy issue in such matters as joint ventures between hospitals and physicians for operation of freestanding facilities.

Inspection of Materials and Services

Schools and hospitals have a more difficult problem inspecting purchased items than do industrial organizations. A large university, for example, deals in nearly every field of human knowledge. This requires the purchase of practically the entire range of materials, services, and products developed by humans. The huge range of incoming materials, therefore, makes centralized inspection practically impossible. Too many different kinds of inspectors and too much expensive inspection equipment would be required to perform the function at reasonable cost.

In most universities and medical centers, therefore, receiving departments inspect only for bulk quantity and outward evidences of physical damage. The inspection for unit quantity, quality, and compliance with specifications typically is made by the individual who originated the request for the material. When desired, the receiving department can, of course, inspect for general stores-type or common-use items. Inspection is much less of a problem at hospitals where there normally is a central receiving and stores function for hospital supplies.

Backdoor Selling

Controlling the visits of sales personnel is considerably more difficult in schools and hospitals than it is in industry. Most physicians, scientists, and professors are extremely individualistic and tend not be organization-oriented. This fact, at times, creates vexing problems in establishing and enforcing effective business procedures. Coupled with this, the physical layout of most institutions compounds the problem. For example, most industrial concerns have a reception room, and visitors cannot get past this area without clearance. Such is not the case in most colleges and hospitals; here visitors are free to roam. For these reasons, and also because controls can seldom be accomplished by fiat in an academic, scientific, or medical environment, the purchasing department must use the techniques of persuasion to convince its internal customers that using proper purchasing procedures is to their advantage.

Naturally, there are many situations in which such individuals have a genuine need to talk with sales representatives. Indeed, as noted previously, institutions must rely on the technical competence of their physicians, academicians, and scientists to develop specifications and to recommend suppliers in those instances where the item to be purchased is highly unique or complex. In such situations, the purchasing staff should do everything possible to bring competent sales personnel (generally sales engineers) and the institution's technical personnel, together.

Controlling sales representatives properly involves scheduling them in accordance with two commonsense alternatives: (1) Those who, from an institutional point of view, can be utilized most effectively in the purchasing department should be handled there; and (2) those who can be utilized most effectively by appropriate technical personnel should be assisted in establishing such relationships.

Reciprocity

In theory, reciprocity should be easier to control in institutions than it is in industry; in practice, this often is not the case. Trustees, donors, and alumni on occasion bring great pressure on institutions to purchase a particular company's products or services. Normally, such pressures should be resisted. By its very nature, a school or hospital has nothing to sell back to its potential suppliers. Therefore, when a potential supplier says, "Give me your business because I gave you a donation of $10,000," he or she could in effect be saying, "I really did not want to give you $10,000, but some unstated lesser amount." If the business the donor demands for his or her firm yields a profit in excess of $10,000, then the donor is actually asking the institution to give him or her a gift.

This obviously is a different situation from the typical scenario surrounding industrial reciprocity. There the objective of reciprocity is, in theory at least, for the buyer and the seller to reach an agreement on an exchange of business that is mutually beneficial. The preceding discussion of reciprocity is not meant to imply that donors cannot be good suppliers. They certainly can be. In fact, when they are willing to compete on the basis of quality, service, and price, they can be the very best suppliers. It is only when they are not willing to compete freely that their motives become suspect. Leading institutions deliberately separate, by policy and procedure, purchasing from any development effort involving gift giving. Buyers are in a better position to do their job if they can say they have no knowledge of gifts—from whom received, or dollar amounts. At the same time, the development effort benefits from being able to say that it has no connection with purchasing or any influence over purchasing decisions.

TEACHERS AND SCIENTISTS

Teachers and scientists are a valuable national resource. They have no counterparts in industry. Scholars work in industry as well as in the academic world, but when they do, they usually change their orientation. Ph.D.s or M.D.s who work at universities are usually more concerned with their own professional accomplishments than with those of the institution. If offered significantly better laboratories, teaching conditions, and assistants at another institution, frequently they will accept the offer. This is not to imply that such individuals are not loyal to their institutions. Typically, however, their loyalties are first to their professions, and second to their schools. This is the reverse of expected loyalty priorities in the business world.

During their tenure at any firm, business executives' loyalty must be first to the firm and then to their profession; otherwise, neither the executives nor the firms can be fully successful.[6] If any single, basic business function in a firm (finance, purchasing, personnel, production, engineering, and marketing) fails to perform satisfactorily, the firm as a whole suffers. Business managers, therefore, cannot achieve optimum individual success unless they cooperate and become team players. This is not true for academics. Scientists and teachers can be entities unto themselves. They can succeed or fail individually, without regard to the success or failure of the institutions that employ them. In addition, they are usually less motivated by material rewards than are their colleagues in industry. Typically, it is intellectual and peer recognition that inspires scientists and researchers to do their best.

Working successfully with this kind of person requires different appeals and techniques from those used in industry. Nevertheless, these professionals are concerned with getting the greatest possible mileage from their research and teaching dollars. The purchasing department that proves its ability to help them achieve this goal will be welcome as a member of *their* team.

DIFFERENCES BETWEEN PUBLIC AND PRIVATE INSTITUTIONS

There can be notable differences between the purchasing responsibilities of public and private institutions. Some public schools and hospitals are completely free from political purchasing constraints. Such freedom, however, is not typical; rather, most public institutions are highly constrained by governmental regulations in their operations. Private institutions, on the other hand, are usually free to use their economic power in the way they deem most desirable.

A primary objective of most public and private institutions is to create goodwill for the institution. Goodwill is achieved when the public feels as-

---

[6] "Loyalty" as used in this statement is not meant to imply that business people would be disloyal by leaving a firm. As a matter of fact, a typical business career includes employment in three or four different firms.

sured that an institution treats all interested parties impartially. To satisfy such diverse institutional groups as alumni, trustees, donors, business firms, and governmental agencies, a private institution has no rational alternative but to buy without favoritism—just as public institutions are required to do by law. The difference between purchasing for public and private institutions is not a matter of concept; rather, it is a matter of how the concept of buying without favoritism is implemented. Political pressures frequently cause public institutions to carry otherwise sound concepts to ridiculous extremes. For example, public institutions are often forced to use competitive bidding in situations where negotiation would produce both lower total costs and better service.

APPLICATION OF BASIC PRINCIPLES IN INSTITUTIONAL PURCHASING

Centralization of Purchasing

In a large research-oriented institution, the broad scope of technical effort and the complete lack of departmental routine in many situations make it difficult to centralize purchasing. To complicate matters further, universities tend to spread themselves over large physical areas. (A wit once defined a university as a "collection of colleges and schools connected more or less by inadequate plumbing.")

It is difficult to coordinate widely separated organizational units under any circumstances; in an atmosphere of academic freedom, it is especially difficult. In an academic environment, very few things can be accomplished by edict. Consequently, it is extremely difficult and generally unwise to attempt a total centralization of the institution's purchasing activities. Nevertheless, the centralization benefits described in Chapters 1, 2, and 5 are as valid in an institutional setting as in a business setting. Competent institutional management, therefore, should strive to achieve centralization of the purchasing function to the greatest degree practical.

Purchasing authorities estimate that a well-run centralized purchasing operation can achieve savings of 10 to 15 percent compared with a decentralized operation. Additionally, centralized purchasing allows suppliers to give institutions better service, as well as better prices, because their expenses are reduced. Specifically, their sales representatives have fewer people to call on, fewer orders have to be serviced, fewer invoices have to be prepared, fewer shipments have to be made, fewer financial records have to be kept, and so on.

Cooperative Purchasing

When properly guided, cooperative institutional purchasing can be beneficial. Many colleges and universities have affiliated with the Educational and Institutional Cooperative Service, Inc. (E&I), an activity of the National Association of Educational Buyers, of Woodbury, New York. This national organization provides many useful services to its members. Because of the nominal cost of affiliation, a college or university cannot prudently take the financial risk of not joining E&I. Even one small purchase against any E&I contract may result in savings well in excess of the small affiliation fee. Purchase Connections, a subsidiary of Health Resources Institute of Los Angeles, and M.D. Buyline of Dallas, Texas, offer purchasing assistance to hospitals. M.D. Buyline focuses on high technology and diagnostic equipment. It helps hospital personnel determine their needs and then provides additional support throughout the procurement.

A number of hospitals have also formed regional purchasing cooperatives. These cooperatives sometimes engage in regional service ventures such as laundries. Successes of regional ventures have been proportional to the skill with which the cooperatives have been conceived and managed. There is no doubt that savings result from the effective, cooperative grouping of economic power and professional talent. However, many cooperatives fail because they are ill conceived, poorly managed, and too small to reap the benefits resulting from large-dollar-volume contracts. Also, on many occasions large institutions can purchase at lower-than-cooperative prices, especially when they are located in metropolitan areas close to supplier distribution points.

Price

Until rather recently, many suppliers granted special prices to institutions, especially to schools and hospitals. Suppliers used to feel it was their philanthropic and patriotic duty to help these institutions financially. However, that was when the institutional market was small and financially unimportant. The present market has changed. Today, most suppliers view the institutional market as large, choice, highly profitable, and deserving of their best sales effort. To obtain fair prices in such a market, institutions must have buyers and materials managers who have the knowledge and intellectual capacity to negotiate effectively with their highly competent sales counterparts.

Institutions, as a group, continue to violate one of the basic principles of good purchasing—that of *not disclosing prices.* Many small institutions (especially hospitals) waste their time and money trying to improve their prices by making price comparisons with other institutions. This practice frequently penalizes the efficient institution while seldom helping the inefficient one. No rational sales representative will offer a price concession to a buyer who he or she suspects will disclose this fact to other buyers, who in turn would soon pressure the sales representative for the same low price. Institutions should follow the pricing practices set forth in Chapters 12 and 13. These are the only effective practices for achieving good pricing.

Personnel

Despite their rapid growth thus far, many schools and hospitals have lagged behind industry and government in recruiting the most competent purchasing personnel. Historically, institutional salary levels have been lower than industry's. As they "grew up," hospitals and schools were considered places of service that primarily attracted employees who were not materially oriented. For example, nurses are paid less than senior secretaries, and college professors' salaries usually are lower than those of some of their recent master's-level graduates working in industry. The salaries for purchasing personnel tend to be similarly low. Fortunately, institutional salaries are now becoming more competitive.

There is no need for institutions to deceive themselves about purchasing salaries. Good purchasing results primarily from professional competence. Determining the best combination of quality, service, and price is the result of actions such as effective negotiation, value analysis, supplier analysis, cost analysis, and price analysis—all actions requiring a high level of professional competence.

Organization

Where a purchasing department is located within an entity's organizational structure greatly influences the department's ability to function optimally and to influence the decision-making process within the entity. As discussed in Chapter 5, a large percentage of industrial purchasing managers report directly to the chief executive of their companies or to a senior vice president. In government, purchasing invariably reports to the chief executive officer of the unit to which the purchasing department is attached. Institutions have routinely placed their purchasing departments too low in the management structure. Hospitals particularly have been guilty of this error. Undoubtedly, this is another reason why some hospitals have experienced difficulty in attracting top purchasing talent.

The pursuit of and the administration of government research contracts frequently entail organizational problems that also lead to ineffective procurement performance. Traditionally, one organizational unit of the university (often called "research administration") is charged with the responsibility of negotiating the university's research contracts with the government. Another organizational unit (the purchasing department) is responsible for negotiating the subcontracts for all goods and services purchased from outside suppliers with funds from the government. Close coordination between these two university offices—research administration and purchasing—is essential to ensure that the funds allocated under various government research contracts are: (1) handled properly within the constraints of government procurement regulations, (2) expended properly in accordance with the terms of the contract, and (3) processed expeditiously to accomplish the institution's goals. In practice, such coordination frequently does not exist. Too often, the two organizational units even report to different functional heads. Consequently, many universities fail to gain the benefits which can result from an effective organization of their total government research procurement/ contracting effort.

GOVERNMENT RESEARCH CONTRACTS

Government research contracts and grants are a major source of income for a research-oriented institution. Such contracts generally entail a highly sophisticated procurement activity. Any research effort can require complex negotiation, plus the preparation and management of complex contracts. Government research can be even more complex because it involves increasingly severe constraints. As a contractor with the United States, an institution must comply with government regulations and undergo a periodic government review of its purchasing system. Often, this review is made under the auspices of the Department of Defense. The Federal Acquisition Regulation (FAR) requires a review of an institution's purchasing techniques when "the procurement work being done is complex and the dollar value is substantial."

It is highly desirable for an institution to get its purchasing techniques approved by the government. Without such approval, the government will examine each subcontract involving government funds. FAR states: "Reliance upon a contractor's approved procurement system will usually obviate the need for reviewing and consenting to individual subcontracts."

Educating purchasing personnel in the specifics of government purchasing is extremely important. An institution can best satisfy government requirements for good purchasing by hiring personnel with recognized competence in the field of government procurement. Also, as discussed earlier in this chapter, institutions can optimize their benefits from government contracts if all institutional operations regarding government contracts are coordinated and controlled by a single organizational unit.

SPECIAL CONSIDERATIONS

Insurance

Institutions are concerned with a large variety of activities, ranging from the operation of small electrical shops to the operation of huge linear accelerators. Also, colleges and hospitals are concerned with the physical presence of large and diverse groups of people, including faculty, staff, students, patients, and a continuous stream of visitors. For these reasons, the insurance requirements for institutions are normally more complex than those for industrial operations.

Purchasing insurance involves the application of the same principles used to purchase other services and commodities. The first procedural step—and the critical one—is to prepare a list of exactly what categories of insurance are needed. Competent brokers or agents (the suppliers) can assist in this step. Specifically, they can caution institutions not to overlook their unusual and unique risks. For example, a college should insure against the risk of a chartered airplane crashing with its football team aboard. In the event of such a tragedy, claims far in excess of the insurance carried by the airline would result.

After an institution's insurance needs have been determined and listed, an effective broker or general agent can assist the institution in developing competition between appropriate underwriters. Competition for insurance coverage is not confined to price alone; traditionally, reliability and service are more important than price. Hence, in evaluating insurance agents and brokers, an institution must consider not only their ability to assist in selecting the correct coverage, but also their capability to help in settling claims quickly and inexpensively.

Construction and Furnishings

New construction and remodeling programs at medical and educational institutions constitute a significant part of their total expenditures. Furthermore, because construction costs are currently rising at a rate considerably above the average of other operating costs, these costs could become even more significant in the future. The interested reader is encouraged to review the section on procurement of construction in Chapter 17.

Purchasing of Interior Furnishings When possible, it is profitable for an institution to buy interior furnishings—such things as chalkboards, classroom and office furniture, carpets, drapes, laboratory equipment, and scientific instruments—directly from manufacturers. If such items are purchased through an architect, a general contractor, or a contract furnisher, the institution frequently pays higher prices. Prices can be as much as 40 percent above those at which the institution can purchase the items directly; typically, the middleman's markup ranges from 10 to 40 percent. Not only will the institution save on markups by purchasing directly, but since most institutions are tax-exempt, they will save a substantial amount of sales tax also.

Naturally, when an institution's purchasing department contracts for the interior furnishings of a building, additional but financially rewarding work results. The methods of delivery and installation are particularly important in this context. The delivery and installation responsibilities and coordination should be very carefully spelled out in the purchase order.

Interior designers are primarily concerned about the appearance of the institution on opening day. And clearly this is important. Frequently, however, they are not very sensitive to the ongoing operational needs of the institution. One small example: Designers frequently specify custom fabrics primarily on the basis of style and appearance; often, however, such fabrics are very difficult to replace in case of damage or stain. Both the buyer and the user must be sensitive to the designer's orientation, but they must also ensure that the issues of maintenance and serviceability are addressed.

One category of interior furnishings deserves special mention. Typically as much as 90 percent of the total demand for educational office, classroom, and library furniture occurs in the summer and early fall months. Consequently, significant savings can result when orders for such furnishings are placed as far as possible in advance of desired delivery dates. Furniture manufacturers can schedule the production of long lead time orders at times when factory workloads are light. This makes it possible for such manufacturers to price on a marginal cost basis (as discussed in Chapter 13) and for institutions to receive the ultimate in good pricing. One college saved over 30 percent ($305,000) on the cost of furniture for its new married-student housing unit by placing its order eight months in advance of the date the furniture was actually needed. This saving was realized despite payment of five months' commercial storage charges.

Stores

Institutions have the same reasons as industry for carrying items in inventory—economy and service. Economy results from savings made through quantity buying with its resultant savings in paperwork, handling, and prices. Service results from having items immediately available. Stores items provide a buffer between fluctuations in demand and changes in lead time; thus they protect an institution's using department against uncertainty and delay. As discussed in Chapter 21, it is important to avoid carrying duplicated brands of the same functional item, because of the additional costs of maintaining the items in inventory and the additional cost of maintaining adequate safety stocks. This is a particularly important function in hospitals and one which ordinarily receives a good bit of attention.

In addition to economy and service, the modern university campus and some hospitals have engendered another very practical reason for having a stores system: congestion. If materials were to be delivered by suppliers as needed to each using department, most institutions would increase their traffic congestion substantially.

Hospitals must have access to immediate emergency reserves of patient-care materials. Loss of life cannot be risked because of such inevitable business failures as strikes, transportation breakdowns, and fires. However, this does not mean that the hospital itself must stock all the required emergency supplies in its own storerooms. Quite the contrary; suppliers can stock many medical supplies for the hospital in their storerooms. The specific items the hospital needs to have stocked, together with their exact quantities, must, of course, be determined in advance. The materials so determined can be included as a legal requirement in the procurement contract. The supplier thus becomes legally bound not only to have these materials on hand, but also to earmark them solely for the hospital making the purchase.

Under this concept of supply, the supplier's stores system literally becomes an extension of the hospital's stores system. Additionally, this concept usually permits the hospital to achieve its reserve supply protection at much lower warehousing costs than by using its own storerooms.

The concept just discussed clearly is not limited to medical supplies. It is equally applicable to maintenance, repair, and operating supplies items and to virtually any type of laboratory supplies.

Auxiliary Functions

Many institutions find it organizationally desirable to group their auxiliary purchasing functions—traffic, receiving, delivery, and surplus—together in what can appropriately be called the "purchasing services division" or the "materials management department."

Traffic   Many institutions, as contrasted with industry and government, do not have a traffic specialist. Outgoing shipments are small in number, and incoming shipments are usually consigned F.O.B. the institution. Nonetheless, at the appropriate stage of its development, every institution should consider the advantages of having a traffic specialist. Such an individual is responsible for processing its freight bills for payment (which by law must be paid within five days) and for initiating settlement of its freight claims. In all likelihood, this individual will generate cash savings greatly exceeding his or her salary. In addition, improved traffic and damage claims service will result. For example, one institution's traffic manager, after checking the classification guide for a shipment, challenged the carrier on the classification of a $10,800 shipment. As a result of this challenge, the classification was changed from "electronics" to "radio repair parts mounted on a truck or trailer." The bill was reduced from $10,800 to $4,460, a saving of $6,340.

Receiving   Because institutions do not have production schedules to meet, they sometimes underestimate the importance of the receiving function. Poor receiving can produce costly consequences for institutions, just as it can for industry. Receiving is a critical control point in an institution's materials system. It is at the receiving dock that the paperwork directing the flow of purchased materials and the physical materials themselves meet for the first time. At this meeting, if the receiving function is performed correctly, any existing discrepancies will be uncovered. Errors are easily corrected at this time. If they are not corrected then, however, the cost to correct them later is certain to be higher. This is why the importance of the receiving function should not be underestimated.

Delivery   Many of the materials received by purchasing from outside suppliers and all materials requisitioned from stores must be delivered to using departments. To the extent possible, the delivery of these two categories of materials should be combined into a single, integrated delivery system. Mail and other items to be delivered to using departments can also be included in this delivery system if such action prevents duplication of effort.

Failing to plan ahead for their materials requirements is a common shortcoming of many institutional departments. To compensate for this lack of planning, many departments frequently want immediate delivery of all materials they requisition, especially stores items. Putting all other aspects of the problem aside, institutions simply cannot afford the cost of making continuous deliveries. Schools, especially, can support only a "reasonable" delivery system, not an "express" delivery system. Each school must determine for itself what is reasonable. This is not always easy to do. Sears, Penney's, and other similarly successful retailers have found a weekly delivery schedule to their customers to be satisfactory. Some successfully managed industrial firms now operate on a weekly delivery system, for operating supplies, from stores to various shops in their plants. At one time, all these companies thought that daily deliveries were essential for customer and production scheduling satisfaction. There appears to be no reason why institutions should not pattern their delivery systems along industrial lines.

Surplus and Salvage In institutions, surplus and salvage sales usually are not given the importance industry accords these activities. Institutions, however, are generating larger and larger surpluses of increasing value. One university's surplus and salvage section recently returned over $240,000 in cash to the university. Nearly all of this money came from sales that formerly had not been made, or from sales of materials and equipment that formerly had been made to employees for a token payment. Without a formalized surplus and salvage program, institutions tend to sell surplus materials to employees and friends on a subjective rather than a business basis. The salvage of metals can be a source of significant revenue. Precious metals sometimes can be salvaged from old computer equipment, and such things as silver can be extracted from photographic and X-ray processes. Old film, and the extraction of silver from the chemicals used, can be especially attractive sources of revenues for some institutions.

It is often possible to use surplus items, which have relatively little value, as trade-ins for new purchases. The trade-in is really just a discount, but some suppliers would prefer to document the discount as a trade-in rather than to have a straight discount, which might create problems for them with other customers or with their suppliers.

CONCLUSION

Most purchasing savings available to industry are also available to institutions such as schools and hospitals. To attain these benefits institutions must take four actions:

1 Hire enough people to perform the purchasing job well.
2 Compete with industry for competent purchasing personnel.
3 Provide a stimulating environment in which the people hired will be motivated to do excellent work.
4 Ensure adequate training and advanced education.

Schools and hospitals must understand what industry has understood for a number of years—money spent intelligently for good purchasing is not an expense, it is an investment!

FOR DISCUSSION

31-1 Explain what a service economy is, and discuss two fast-growing service industries in the U.S. economy.

31-2 Explain why early purchasing involvement in developing specifications is as important for colleges and hospitals as it is for industrial firms.

31-3 Discuss why conflicts of interest can be more critical in educational and medical purchasing than in industrial purchasing.

31-4 Why is inspection of materials and services sometimes so difficult in universities and hospitals? Explain.

31-5 Explain why reciprocity can take a different form in institutions than in industry.

31-6 What is the most common organizational problem in institutional purchasing? Explain.

31-7 Discuss how the orientation of teachers and scientists who serve in an academic environment differs from that of those who serve in industry. What unique problems does an academic orientation create for purchasing? Discuss.

31-8 Discuss the difficulties of centralizing purchasing in large, research-oriented institutions.

31-9 Explain why pricing for institutions has changed greatly in recent years.

31-10 Explain why materials management progress in institutions usually appears much more advanced than it really is.

31-11 Insurance for institutions can be very important for many reasons. Discuss briefly as many of these reasons as you can.

31-12 Discuss the major problems of institutional purchasing in the area of interior furnishings.

31-13 Why do institutions operate storerooms? Do required stores stocks have to be physically located at the institution? Explain.

31-14 Discuss the primary auxiliary functions normally associated with institutional purchasing. Why are they important?

31-15 Most purchasing savings available to industrial firms are also available to institutions; to attain these benefits, an institution usually must take four actions. Name and discuss these four actions.

31-16 Specifically, how can formalized surplus and salvage programs help institutions?

CASES FOR CHAPTER 31

GOVERNMENT PURCHASING*

*Appreciation is expressed to Larry L. Smith, dean emeritus of the School of Systems and Logistics at the Air Force Institute of Technology, for his invaluable assistance in updating this chapter.

- Government specifications and quality
    Design specifications
    Performance specifications
    Quality of government-purchased items
- Mechanics
    Volume of paperwork
    Award lead time
    Contract administration
    Disputes
    Remedies
- Code of ethics

The purpose of this chapter is to acquaint the reader with government purchasing and in particular the federal procurement system. The first part examines some management aspects of government procurement and highlights some differences between government and industrial purchasing. The discussion then outlines some key federal procurement legislation to show some sources of the processes' complexity. The third part of the chapter examines some specific practices of the government contracting process, including types of contracts, special approaches, contract administration, and remedies.

SIMILARITIES AND DIFFERENCES

The same principles which govern private contracts apply to government contracts. Both instruments are a promise or set of promises for which the law provides a remedy if breached. The legal elements of the enforceable private and government contract are also the same, namely: legal capacity of the parties, mutual assent, consideration, lawful purpose, certainty of terms, and being in a form provided by law. Similarly, both government and industrial purchasing are concerned with buying the right quality, in the right quantity, at the right price and time, and from the right source. While the principles are the same, the process is sufficiently different to be worth examining. The following paragraphs highlight some of those differences.

Size

The first thing that catches the eye of the student of government contracting is its sheer magnitude. The numbers are overwhelming. In fiscal year 1987, almost $200 billion, or 18 percent of the federal budget of $1,100 billion, was spent through the contracting process.[1] This was done through more than 22 million contract actions, ranging from complex weapon systems to paper and

---

[1]The *Budget of the United States* for Fiscal Year 1989, page 6g–7, reports the actual expenditures for fiscal year 1987. The *Federal Procurement Data System Standard Report* for the fourth quarter of fiscal year 1987 reflects total federal procurement expenditures on page 2.

pencils. An examination of the expenditures by major federal departments shows that nearly 80 percent of the almost $197 billion in contracting actions was obligated by the Department of Defense (see Table 32-1.)

The volume of business done with major federal government contractors is another indicator of size. In fiscal year 1987, the top 100 federal contractors were the object of some 90,000 procurement actions with a sum of more than $110 billion. The top 10 contractors (by total dollars) are major weapon system or subsystem suppliers. Together, they account for some $52 billion. In order of their ranking by dollar share these contractors are: McDonnell Douglas, General Dynamics, General Electric, Lockheed, Martin Marietta, General Motors, Raytheon, United Technologies, Boeing, and Rockwell International.[2]

The inherent nature of the goods purchased by the Department of Defense (DOD) assures a skewed distribution of contract dollars. (See Table 32-1.) Major weapon and space systems account for many millions or billions of dollars each. Few firms have the manpower, physical capacity, and technological virtuosity required to participate in the research, definition, and production cycle of major weapon and space systems. As a result, there are substantial barriers to both entry into and exit from the markets for major weapon and space systems. Therefore, it should not be surprising that names such as General Dynamics, United Technologies, McDonnell Douglas, Boeing, and General

[2]Ibid., p. 14.

TABLE 32-1
FEDERAL CONTRACT ACTIONS AND DOLLARS BY EXECUTIVE DEPARTMENT*

	Reported actions (000)	Percent of total actions	Reported dollars (000,000)	Percent of total dollars
Total federal government	22,300	100.0	197,276	100.0
Executive Department				
Agriculture	1,198	5.4	2,179	1.1
Commerce	128	0.6	430	0.2
Defense	15,301	68.6	155,385	78.8
Education	7	—	159	0.1
Energy	35	0.2	13,944	7.1
Health and Human Services	867	3.9	1,520	0.8
Housing and Urban Development	15	0.1	116	0.1
Interior	533	1.4	1,486	0.8
Justice	605	2.7	934	0.5
Labor	29	0.1	531	0.3
State	19	0.1	326	0.2
Transportation	274	1.2	1,587	0.8
Treasury	163	0.7	780	0.4

*The data in this table were extracted from the *Federal Procurement Data System Standard Report* for Fiscal Year 1987, published by the Federal Procurement Data Center in Arlington, Va.

Electric appear year after year in the roster of firms obtaining the largest portion of DOD dollars.

While concentration of economic power is a fact of current U.S. industrial life, no other economic concentration is as great as that represented by the top defense contractors. Also, no other economic block of comparable size sells only or primarily to one customer. The economic and political power potential of this group of concentrated sellers interacting with a single buyer is one which requires constant vigilance. Former President Eisenhower highlighted the importance of this unique situation in his now-famous farewell address as President:

> Now this conjunction of an immense military establishment and a large arms industry is new in the American experience. The total influence—economic, political, and spiritual—is felt in every city, every state, every house, every office of the Federal Government. We recognize the imperative need for this development. Yet, we must not fail to comprehend its grave implications. Our toil, resources, and livelihood are all involved; so is the very structure of our society.[3]

State and Local Government

State and local governments also have great purchasing power in the aggregate. The *Statistical Abstract of the United States* reflects some 83,200 governmental bodies that possess the power to spend.[4] That same publication goes on to indicate that state and local purchases of goods and services have grown from $119 billion in 1970 to $504 billion in 1986. It is interesting to note that this amount is more than twice the size of federal procurement expenditures.

Diversity

Another characteristic of government procurement is the diversity of the item or service purchased. Federal government purchases range from the mundane to the exotic—from pencils and paper to supersonic aircraft, sophisticated missiles, and space vehicles. The largest dollar value of military and space purchasing is for technical items involving extensive research and development. Roughly 75 percent of federal government purchasing by dollar value is for complex major weapons and space systems, and 25 percent is for civilian-type commodities. On the other hand, in state and local governments, purchases are usually limited to civilian-type commodities, construction, and services. Interestingly, the largest single expenditure of local governments is for construction contracts.

---

[3]President Dwight D. Eisenhower, farewell address, 1961.
[4]U.S. Bureau of the Census, *1988 Statistical Abstract of the United States,* 108th ed., Table No. 433, "State and Local Government Receipts and Expenditures in the National Income and Product Accounts, 1970–1986."

Unfortunately, ethical problems are all too common in state and local government procurement. One cannot read the newspaper for long without reading of unethical or questionable purchasing practices in state and local government. For example, a judge and four present or former commissioners of a Texas county were indicted recently for allegedly "violating state law by failing to seek bids for purchases of more than $5,000, or by making 'component purchases'—breaking up a large purchase so the individual purchases did not exceed $5,000."[5]

Sovereignty

The concept of the government as a sovereign power also distinguishes government from the commercial contracting processes. As a sovereign power, the government can change the procurement rules through statute, executive order, or regulation. It can write and require contract clauses, sometimes extraneous to the instant contract purpose. Further, in limited areas, the government can change the terms of a contract at any time. Of course, the procedures provide for an equitable adjustment, but the government reserves the right of contract change. The free market contracting process would have the buyer and seller negotiating as power equals. But the student of economics knows that purchasing power, size, technical knowledge, and skill often favor one contracting party over the other. Size, purchasing power, and sovereignty give the skilled government buyer great power in the contracting process.

Regulations

The decision-making processes of government agencies are governed by regulations. The *Federal Acquisition Regulation (FAR)* is the primary regulation for use by all federal executive agencies in their acquisition of supplies and services with appropriated funds. The FAR system has been developed in accordance with the requirements of the Office of Federal Procurement Policy Act. *The FAR is a compilation of all the laws and policies governing the federal procurement process.* Sources of these rules include statutes, executive orders, comptroller general decisions, attorney general opinions, agency boards of contract appeals decisions, and federal court decisions. While agencies may supplement the FAR, such additional rules are supposed to be limited to those necessary to implement the regulation's requirements within the agency.[6]

---

[5]*Fort Worth Star-Telegram*, Dec. 11, 1988, section 1, pp. 1 and 21.
[6]The Federal Acquisition Regulation is published under the joint auspices of the Defense Department, the General Services Administration, and the National Aeronautics and Space Administration. It is a living regulation, being frequently changed through the publication of Federal Acquisition Circulars.

Sources of Funds

Important differences between industrial and government purchasing result from the source of funds used for purchases. At all levels of government, taxes paid by citizens and businesses or debt are used to purchase required supplies and services. Thus, there is no profit and little cost control incentive to generate funds for ongoing operations. In executing their roles as funds stewards, both the legislative and the executive arms of government promulgate procedures to carefully control funds expenditures. These procedures give government buyers *considerably less flexibility* than their industrial counterparts have. For example, fixed budgets often stop the government buyer from taking advantage of quantity discounts and long-term contracts. Similarly, the rigid requirement for competition and resulting long lead times usually keep the government buyer out of the quick-sale marketplace. The rules for competition frequently have been blamed for award to the low bidder who may provide an inferior-quality product. Thus, the contracting process using public funds is probably not as efficient as its commercial counterpart using funds from hard-won prior sales.

Public Review

The expenditure of public funds properly attracts the interest of every taxpayer. This results in open government records and files as well as contracts subject to review by many audit activities. The process is supposed to be conducted in full public view and all actions are a matter of public record. In contrast, the commercial buyer's requirements, sources, specifications, bid requirements, and prices paid are privileged information.

Socioeconomic Programs

Following directly from the source of funds issue is the inclination of taxpayer representatives to utilize the government purchasing process to accomplish social or political ends. Such laws as the Buy American Act may restrict the government buyer from purchasing the lowest-price items that meet the requirements. Rules that require purchases to be shipped on U.S. carriers often conflict with selection of the lowest-cost carrier. Rules requiring awards to small or so-called disadvantaged businesses usually add to the instant price of contracts so awarded. In his study of socioeconomic goals through the procurement process, Richard Hampton cataloged fifty-two separate programs that add complexity and cost to the federal government contracting process.[7]

---

[7]Richard J. Hampton, "Achieving Socioeconomic Goals through the Federal Procurement Process," doctoral dissertation, George Washington University, 1981.

Conservatism

The individuals managing and performing the purchasing function in almost all government purchasing activities are motivated by a merit promotion system rather than a profit-oriented promotion system. It is difficult to reward the innovative and risk-taking government buyer. As public officials, these people are subject to public censure. More than one authority has referred to the buyer's environment as a goldfish bowl wherein everyone can see everything. Seldom does one hear about the commercial buyer who made a big mistake. But federal government procurement errors make daily headlines. Coupled with the general philosophy promulgated in the Federal Acquisition Regulation that if an action is not specifically permitted, then it is prohibited, the government buyer is motivated to be conservative in every decision.

One can trace important differences in government versus commercial purchasing over time through key legislative actions. The pace of those actions has accelerated as the procurement budgets of the federal government agencies have grown to their enormous peacetime levels. It is useful to examine some of those key laws over time to gain a perspective of the legislative branch's influence over the federal procurement process.

KEY LEGISLATIVE ACTIONS

History

The first law dealing with government procurement in the United States was passed by Congress in 1792. Under this law, the Departments of War and Treasury were given responsibility to make purchases and contracts in the name of the United States. In 1795, a purveyor of public supplies was established in the Treasury Department to act as the government's purchasing manager. In 1798 a separate Department of the Navy was established, and Congress declared "that all purchases and contracts for supplies and services for the military and naval services of the United States should be made by or under the direction of the chief officers of the Department of War and Navy respectively."

Considering the historic interest of Congress in the profits of contractors, it is interesting to note that the first procurement abuses in government arose from the activities of congressmen. They used their influence and offices to secure government contracts for their friends and for the firms with which they were associated. This situation resulted in an 1808 law which required a clause in every government contract to stipulate that no member of Congress might benefit therefrom. This clause is still required; it is now known as the "Officials Not to Benefit" clause.

In the early days of the republic, the conduct of both public officials and private business managers left much to be desired. Graft and favoritism in the award of government contracts were commonplace. Incoming administrations investigated the activities of the former administration. The political party out of power kept a watchful eye on the activities of the "ins." Congress soon concluded that the most effective way to prevent procurement abuses was to require that government purchases be made by competitive bids. To implement this conclusion, Congress passed the Procurement Act of March 3, 1809.

The Procurement Act of 1809 established a general requirement that formal advertising be used in the procurement of supplies and services for the government of the United States. Over the next fifty years, a series of additional acts extended and sharpened the requirements for formal advertising and financial security from bidders for ensuing contract performance. Subsequently, most state, county, and city governments adopted the same principles that are incorporated in federal government procurement legislation.

Competitive bidding,[8] with relatively few exceptions, served the federal government effectively and adequately for well over 100 years. The increasing complexities of a rapidly growing technology, however, combined with a dollar volume of purchases undreamed of in the past, caused the competitive bidding system to break down (almost to the point of collapse) at the beginning of World War II. As a result of this breakdown, negotiated purchasing frequently was substituted for competitive bidding. Local government procurement was not affected by this circumstance; states and cities do not have the technical problems inherent in federal government procurement.

Buy American Act

One of the most basic and well-established statutory decision rules in the award of government contracts concerns whether or not the item required is produced in the United States. Purchasing items produced within national borders provides an economic incentive for maintaining follow-on production capability. The argument proceeds that such follow-on capability may be vital in times of war, when foreign sources may be inaccessible or undependable. The Buy American Act of 1933 was passed to foster and protect American industry, American workers, and invested American capital.

The Buy American Act generally requires that the federal government buy for public use only raw materials mined or produced in the United States, and only manufactured items which are made in the United States, "substantially all from" materials or items mined, produced, or manufactured in the United States. However, the act has several important exceptions: the general requirement is inapplicable if the items to be purchased are not available domestically in commercial quantities of good quality, or if the cost of the

---

[8]"Formal advertising" and "competitive bidding" over the years grew to be synonymous terms. Actually, competition can be effected in either the formal advertising or the negotiation method of purchasing. The primary difference is that in formal advertising the competitive bids are the last step in price determination, whereas in negotiation they are only the first step.

domestic items is "unreasonable," or if the head of the department otherwise determines it to be in the public interest to waive the requirement.

After World War II, the government faced the problem of returning to peacetime operations and peacetime procurement. To prosecute the war effectively, the rules for government purchasing had been temporarily liberalized. The question raised in 1946 was what rules should apply now that peace had been restored. The war and its realignment of world power produced permanent changes in the mission and responsibilities of the U.S. government. The nation's armed forces were destined to remain at roughly ten times their prewar size. These forces, spread throughout the entire world, would need vast quantities of supplies and equipment to support them. In addition to changes in size and responsibilities, constantly changing technology also complicated and enlarged the scope of postwar government purchasing. Returning to the limited provisions of prewar purchasing legislation was simply out of the question. But what should the new procurement policy be?

After protracted study to determine the best course of action, Congress in 1947 passed the Armed Services Procurement Act.[9] Later in the same year, it passed Public Law 152, which granted the General Services Administration and other federal purchasing agencies permission to negotiate contracts under specific circumstances.

The Armed Services Procurement Act

The Armed Services Procurement Act accomplished two major objectives. First, it established workable procurement policies for periods of national emergencies. Either the President or the Congress can put these policies into immediate effect when either thinks the nation is threatened. Second, the law recognized that *negotiated procurement* is a required method of purchase in peacetime as well as in wartime.

Small Business Act: Set-Aside and Non-Set-Aside Procurement

It is the desire of Congress that small business should receive a fair share of the government's procurement dollar.[10] Procurement requirements selected

---

[9]This act, now codified as chapter 137, title 10 of the United States Code, is quite short. It is implemented within the Department of Defense by the *Federal Acquisition Regulation,* a ponderous volume of over 3,000 pages, including appendices. In addition, the Army, the Navy, and the Air Force each have their procurement regulations which, in turn, implement the DOD regulations.

[10]A *small business* is defined in general terms as a firm independently owned and operated, not dominant in the field in which it is bidding, and having total dollar receipts, depending on the industry, below an amount specified by the Small Business Administration. There are special definitions, including number of employees, tailored to the peculiarities of specific industries, e.g, construction, dredging, petroleum, and small arms.

as having small business application are of two types: those assigned solely to small business and those divided between big and small business.

If previous experience indicates that there are enough small firms interested in and capable of performing any given procurement, that procurement can be assigned to small business only. Theoretically, the government might pay premium prices for materials purchased in this manner, since big business could conceivably supply such materials at lower prices. Although sufficient evidence is not available to support a definite conclusion that higher prices are paid, enough real and circumstantial evidence does exist to support a logical suspicion that higher prices probably are paid. Consider the following example of existing evidence. Contrary to instructions, big business firms on occasion unwittingly bid on purchases set aside solely for small business firms. In these cases, the prices bid by the larger firms invariably are lower than those bid by competing small firms. Consider an example of existing circumstantial evidence, which stems from a research study (of numerous small-business contracts for repairs to major weapon systems) in which one of the authors participated. The prices paid under many of these contracts were compared with the prices paid to big business for similar contracts. In many instances, the prices paid to the small business firms appeared to be substantially higher than those paid to big business firms for similar purchases. Conclusive research studies, based on incontrovertible evidence, seem highly desirable in this important area of government purchasing.

If the total quantity to be purchased is too large for small business alone, but small business can handle part of it, the procurement is divided. Divided requirements are portioned on a set-aside and a non-set-aside basis. The non-set-aside portion is solicited by free, competitive advertised procurement. All small business firms wishing to be considered for the set-aside portion must bid with big business on the non-set-aside portion. When award prices for the non-set-aside portion are known, the small business concerns are given the opportunity of matching them, i.e., small business can have the set-aside portion of the contract at the same price paid for the non-set-aside portion. As awards to small and big business are made at identical prices, the government does not pay a premium price for materials or services purchased in this manner.

Office of Federal Procurement Policy Act

In 1972, Congress created a Commission on Government Procurement to review all facets of government procurement. The commission concluded its work by making a number of far-reaching recommendations to Congress. In 1974, Congress responded by enacting Public Law 93-400, which established the Office of Federal Procurement Policy (OFPP), under the Office of Management and Budget (one of the most powerful agencies in the federal government).

The initial mission of OFPP was to implement the recommendations of the Commission on Government Procurement. In 1979, to broaden the authority and responsibilities of OFPP, Congress amended Public Law 93-400 with Public Law 96-83. The combined effect of both laws is to give OFPP a mandate to develop a uniform procurement system for the federal government, giving consideration to the dissimilar program activities of the executive agencies.

One important product of the Office of Federal Procurement Policy was a 1982 proposal for a Uniform Federal Procurement System.[11] The proposal examined many of the recommendations for reform submitted by a Congressional Commission on Government Procurement, the Presidential Blue Ribbon Defense Panel, and numerous General Accounting Office reports and congressional hearings. Specific recommendations promised a simplified and more responsive system, expanded competition, and enhanced work force professionalism. Many of the suggested improvements have been implemented and continue to affect the way the government carries out its purchasing function.

Truth in Negotiations Act

The Department of Defense purchases large numbers of unique or partially unique products or weapon systems. These items frequently are being manufactured for the first time; therefore, the normal economic factors of supply and demand seldom create a competitive price environment for them. Because of the unique technical skills required to manufacture these items, or because of the nature of a particular product, there is frequently only one acceptable supplier. As a result of a lack of market competition, prices have to be determined from extensive negotiations—negotiations which are based on analyzing previous costs of similar items or projections of future costs extrapolated from known costs. The critical cost data controlling these negotiations are invariably provided by the contractors. These firms are naturally much better informed than the government concerning the specific cost patterns of the products they manufacture. Purchases of these unique-type items represent many billions of dollars (roughly one-third of the DOD total). Consequently, it is possible for these purchases to provide dishonest, misinformed, or inefficient contractors an opportunity for making excessive profits by simply overstating their cost and pricing data.

To help overcome this undesirable situation, in 1962 Congress passed Public Law 87-653, better known as the Truth in Negotiations Act. This act was designed to place the government buyer in a more equal bargaining position with the contractor (who in the past held all the trump cards on cost).

---

[11]"Proposal for a Uniform Federal Procurement System," Executive Office of the President, Office of Management and Budget, Office of Federal Procurement Policy, Washington, D.C., February 1982.

The act established the requirement that for noncompetitive negotiated contracts of over $100,000, contractors must furnish the government buyer complete, accurate, and current data on appropriate costs. Additionally, the act requires contractors to certify that, to the best of their knowledge and belief, all data furnished are current, accurate, and complete. Last, the act provides that all applicable contracts must contain a clause requiring readjustment of the contract price whenever it can be shown that the contracting data were noncurrent, inaccurate, or incomplete and thus found to be defective. A contract can be renegotiated if a case of defective pricing can be proved.

Competition in Contracting Act

In 1984, the Competition in Contracting Act (CICA) was passed by Congress. This act amended the three principal statutes that prescribed authorized methods of forming government contracts (the Armed Services Procurement Act of 1947, the Federal Property and Administrative Services Act of 1949, and the Office of Federal Procurement Policy Act of 1974). As now amended by CICA, the basic statutes emphasize the requirement that government agencies promote the use of full and open competition in the procurement of property and services. Prior to enactment of CICA, the two basic government procurement procedures were formal advertising (sealed bids and award to the low bidder without discussions) and negotiation.

The law provided seventeen authorized exceptions to the requirement for the use of formal advertising. Extensive documentation and levels of approval were required for permission to use many of the exceptions. Wehrle-Einhorn reports that "of the $146.9 billion in contracts awarded in fiscal 1982 (for amounts exceeding $10,000), 54% was spent in noncompetitive negotiation. The justification most frequently invoked (56.1% of sole-source expenditures) was that competition is impracticable."[12]

Before enactment of CICA, the statutes were thought to have two important shortcomings: First, they did not treat negotiation as a legitimate competitive procurement procedure; second, the statutes did not adequately restrict the use of noncompetitive negotiation. Under CICA, agencies are required to use competitive procedures, whether by soliciting sealed bids or requesting competitive proposals, unless a statutory exception allows the use of noncompetitive procedures. The new statute also strengthened the requirements for justification, approval, and notice, in order to safeguard against unnecessary sole-source contracts. In addition, it required the appointment of a *competition advocate* in each procuring activity to enhance accountability and further increase the emphasis on competition.

The federal government buyer may now award contracts listing noncom-

---

[12]Robert J. Wehrle-Einhorn, Esq., editor and principal author, *Government Contract Law*, 10th ed., United States Air Force, Air University, Air Force Institute of Technology, School of Systems and Logistics, Wright-Patterson Air Force Base, Ohio, June 1988.

petitive procedures under one of seven exceptions to competitive procurement. They are:

1 The property or services needed by the agency are available from only one responsible source or a limited number of sources and no other type of property or service will suffice.
2 The agency's need for the property or service is of such unusual and compelling urgency that the government would be seriously injured unless the agency is permitted to limit the number of sources.
3 It is necessary to award the contract to a particular source in order to maintain an essential industrial or research capability in the United States, or to achieve national industrial mobilization.
4 The terms of an international agreement or treaty with a foreign government, or the written directions of any foreign government which is reimbursing the government for the cost of the property or services, have the effect of requiring the use of noncompetitive procedures.
5 A statute expressly authorizes or requires that the procurement be made through another agency or from a specified source, or the agency's need is for a brand name commercial item for authorized resale.
6 The unrestricted disclosure of the agency's needs would compromise the national security unless the agency is permitted to limit the number of sources from which it solicits bids or proposals.
7 The head of the agency determines that it is in the public interest to waive the requirements for competition and notifies the Congress of this determination thirty days before award of the contract.

Before a contract is awarded without the use of competitive procedures, the contracting officer must prepare a written justification, certify it accurate and complete, and, in escalating face value amounts, have it approved by higher authority. Needless to say, with such pointed motivation to complete every possible procurement action, the percentage of competitive awards has increased. The fiscal year 1987 *Federal Procurement Data System Standard Report* cited earlier shows that 57 percent of the dollars were awarded competitively after CICA as compared to 45 percent of the dollars before CICA. But as with so many fixes to complex processes, there is a negative side to the change. Some requiring activities are experiencing increased lead times because contracting officers are taking longer to effect procurements under the new procedures. Many complain that they must obtain competition for competition's sake. Procurement professionals agree that the present legislation places a disproportionate emphasis on price, with little concern for a supplier's past performance. And many in government and the defense industry point out that the government's obsession with competition flies in the face of the proven benefits of single-source partnerships, as practiced by the procurement leaders of the commercial world.

The process of spending tax dollars to acquire supplies and services for the federal government is clearly under the great influence of the legislative, executive, and judicial arms of the government. The resulting procurement process can be viewed as commercial purchasing plus all those special processes and procedures needed to cope with such complexities as public perception, social and economic side objectives, and weapon system procurement. It is now useful to examine a few of those special processes and procedures.

SOME SPECIFIC GOVERNMENTAL PROCUREMENT PRACTICES

Labor Surplus Program

The Labor Surplus Program provides special consideration to firms in areas designated as having labor surpluses by the Labor Department. Essentially, all purchases exceeding $25,000 are screened to ensure that portions of selected purchases are set aside for suppliers in labor surplus areas. A firm that is a small business and is also located in a labor surplus area gets top priority in a set-aside purchase.

Value Engineering

As was discussed in Chapter 26, the concept of value engineering is a powerful way to improve product design and reduce costs. Have bright people look at an item, carefully define its purpose, and then find ways to improve one or more aspects of the product to reduce costs while still accomplishing the intended purpose. The federal procurement system includes contractual ways to motivate contractors to reduce the cost of producing the items it buys through the use of value engineering. It has been found that even designs that have worked well for years can be significantly improved. The trick is to focus attention on improvement. Two approaches to harnessing the value engineering technique are described in the FAR: Contractors may (1) voluntarily suggest methods for performing more economically and share in any resultant savings or (2) be contractually required to establish a program to identify and submit to the government methods for performing more economically.

The voluntary approach motivates the contractor to use its own resources to develop and submit value engineering change proposals (VECPs). The contract provides for sharing the savings and paying the contractor's allowable development and implementation costs if a VECP is accepted. On contracts for supplies and services, the sharing base for savings is normally the number of affected end items on contracts of the office accepting the VECP. The sharing rates (government/contractor) vary with the type of contract and type of savings. For example, the sharing rate on an instant firm fixed price contract would be 50-50, as it would be on concurrent or follow-on savings. The sharing arrangement for a cost reimbursement contract would be 75-25

(75 percent to the government, 25 percent to the supplier) for the instant, concurrent, and follow-on savings. Contracts with incentive sharing arrangements provide for VECP sharing ratios to be related to the profit or fee adjustment formula. Under this voluntary approach, the VECP costs are paid from the accrued savings. Therefore, costs to the government do not increase.

The second approach to harnessing the power of value engineering is a mandatory program in which the government requires and pays for a specific value engineering program effort. The contractor must perform value engineering of the scope and level of effort required by the government's program plan and included as a separately priced item of work in the contract schedule. Except in architect-engineer contracts, the contractor shares in savings on accepted VECPs, but at a lower percentage rate than under the voluntary approach. Fixed price contract sharing ratios are typically 75-25 and cost reimbursement contract sharing ratios are 85-15. The objective of this value engineering program requirement is to ensure that the contractor's value engineering effort is applied to the areas of the contract that offer opportunities for considerable savings.

Contracting officers are instructed to include an appropriate value engineering clause in most solicitations where the resulting contract is expected to exceed $100,000. Thus the VECP's potential benefit is institutionalized across the government purchasing system. It is obvious that savings are affected by the speed with which government personnel process the change proposal. The technical evaluation and administrative approval processes often prevent any savings from being realized on short-run instant contracts. Some contractors have been discouraged from participating further under the voluntary program because the government moved too slowly to take advantage of their good ideas.

Life Cycle Costing

In the mid-1960s, the DOD introduced the life cycle costing (LCC) approach to procurement. LCC takes into consideration the total cost of a product over its useful life, not just the purchase price. Under this concept, DOD considers likely maintenance costs, as predicted by reliability and maintainability estimates, and/or test data and other costs of ownership in the award decision. For example, aircraft tires are bought on a cost per landing basis, thus motivating suppliers to build better tires. Similarly, traveling wave tubes are bought on a cost per hour of operation basis. The resulting improvements in the tubes have brought down the cost of ownership. The logic of LCC is compelling. It is simply basic, effective purchasing—the kind which many industrial firms use routinely. Unfortunately, government purchasing managers have not utilized LCC extensively because money to "pay more up front to get more value later" simply has not been available.

Risk and Type of Contract

As seen in Chapter 14, the concepts of risk and risk sharing are central to choosing the type of contract for the needed items or services. One might characterize risk as any possibility that an item would perform inadequately (*technical risk*) or cost more than planned (*cost risk*). The government usually wants the seller to assume all of the technical and cost risk. But in very complex procurements with high risk factors, it may be necessary to share risk through some contractual arrangement other than the fixed price contract.

Developing major weapon systems is a case where fixed price contracts normally are inappropriate. New weapon systems are often at the leading edge of technology in order to provide operators an advantage over a potential enemy. Military specifications often stretch current capability in such parameters as speed, power, maneuverability, altitude, depth, and range. Accordingly, since the needed capability has never before been designed or built, the amount of effort required to accomplish the task is uncertain. The technical risk is high. It follows that when the technical risk is high, the risk of cost overrun is also high. Someone has to pay for bringing new technology to fruition.

It is possible to use a fixed price contract to buy a new weapon system, but such an approach has drawbacks. The most obvious drawback is price. The supplier normally would have to add large contingency sums in the price to protect against possible catastrophic cost overruns associated with high-risk projects. Such risk-contingent sums may be so high that the fixed price contractual vehicle is unaffordable. Then the two parties might be advised to share the risk through some type of cost reimbursement and/or incentive contract. Risk sharing would allow the supplier to lower the contingent sums needed to protect against unforeseen difficulties in completing the project.

One might argue that a competitive environment would drive hungry suppliers to assume the technical and cost risk without including contingent sums in the fixed price. Under competition, contractors would be motivated to bid low on the system development contract with the hope of recovering losses due to technical problems (if any) on follow-on sole-source production contracts. Indeed, it was argued that this phenomenon occurred in the 1950s and 1960s, with resulting political and economic unpleasantness. In an effort to place a ceiling on total system costs, the government developed a contract vehicle instrument called Total Package Procurement, a fixed price contract for both development and production of a major weapon system. It was supposed that this type of contract would harness the forces of competition while shifting the weight of risk assumption to the supplier. The Air Force's procurement of the C5A aircraft is an example of the approach. The disadvantages of Total Package Procurement were found to outweigh the advantages. In his book on defense management, Ronald Fox advances two reasons: (1) The Department of Defense introduced or allowed numerous changes in the programs, thereby obscuring any incentives for cost control and accountability for cost growth; and (2) the DOD was either unwilling or unable to enforce the fixed price contracts.[13] The concept is no longer used in system acquisition. More conventional wisdom holds that it is best to match the type of contract with the risk involved in the project.

Chapter 14 introduced the principle that as technical (and cost) risk increases, the buyer and seller should use a contractual vehicle that permits increased risk sharing. Obviously, the level of risk assessment is a subjective matter and therefore selecting the type of contract is one of the elements to be negotiated by the contracting parties. In the past ten years, the government has regularly used the entire range of contract types discussed in Chapter 14. But under CICA, the use of fixed price instruments has increased. Page 17 of the fiscal year 1987 *Federal Procurement Data System Standard Report* indicates that the percentage of dollar awards using fixed price contract actions increased from 48 percent before CICA to 80 percent after CICA. It appears that the emphasis on increased use of full and open competition has resulted in increased use of the fixed price contract arrangement.[14] It was not so long ago that cost-type contracts comprised more than 40 percent of total dollar purchases. Also, during the past fifteen years, top DOD officials have successfully implemented a new dimension in DOD purchasing—the use of advanced business management techniques (i.e., a rigorous, tough-minded, quantitative approach to decision making). These techniques provide, first, for unprecedented *preplanning* in weapons development and, second, for close observance of each stage of a major contractor's progress, from design through production. By requiring contractors' cost and schedule control systems to meet specified criteria, the DOD is increasingly able to monitor a supplier's production efficiency and production costs. As a result of this DOD capability, suppliers tend to analyze, to innovate, and thus to become capable of producing an increasing number of high-quality products at fixed prices.

For example, in purchasing a nuclear-powered aircraft carrier, it took the Naval Sea Systems Command and the Newport News Shipbuilding and Dry Dock Company nine months of preplanning to formalize a contract. To permit the cost calculations required to use a fixed price incentive contract, 4,500

---

[13]J. Ronald Fox, *The Defense Management Challenge, Weapons Acquisition,* Harvard Business School Press, Boston, Mass., 1988, p. 43.

[14]Many procurement professionals believe that fixed price contracting is being misapplied in today's environment. The transfer of risk to development programs such as the Advanced Tactical Fighter results in the competing teams (Lockheed, General Dynamics, and Boeing, form one team, while Northrop and McDonnell Douglas form the other) assuming great and possibly excessive cost risk. Informal discussions with defense contractor executives reveal that DOD's obsession with fixed price contracting may have at least two undesirable effects: (1) Many potential suppliers are choosing not to bid on projects which they are technically competent to perform. This loss of competition well may result in higher costs to the DOD. (2) "Winning" defense contractors may, in fact, be big dollar losers. As we know from our experience in the private sector, the threat of such losses has negative impact on quality, schedule, and overall performance.

individual cost centers were isolated. Preplanning in this purchase rewarded both the government and the supplier. The cost of the carrier to the government was roughly 8 percent below the target price, and the profit to the supplier, as a result of its efficiencies, was well above that originally estimated.

As a result of its effort to shift from cost to fixed price contracts whenever possible, DOD achieved a reduction of "sole sources" for many repair parts. Repair parts were separated from their sole-source equipments and identified either by design specifications or by their original manufacturer's description. The separation of parts from equipment and the use of commercial identification permitted competition. This in turn produced price reductions that averaged 25 to 50 percent.

The paramount advantage of firm fixed price contracts and incentive contracts is that a contractor's profit is not a predetermined amount which remains unchanged regardless of how well or how poorly it performs the contractual obligations. Rather, under these contracts, profit is an amount which varies proportionally to the contractor's efficiency or inefficiency. This method of determining profit illustrates the essence of the competitive free enterprise system: the reward of profit balanced against the risk of loss, and how profit motivates production efficiency.

The DOD has not solved the basic problem of what type of optimum contract to use in purchasing major weapon systems. In fact, this is a problem which can never be fully solved. The primary responsibility of the nation's largest buyer is to *defend* well—to *buy* well must come second. Unfortunately, there are times when these two responsibilities are not totally compatible and, hence, are not both fully achievable.

GOVERNMENT SPECIFICATIONS AND QUALITY

Design Specifications

A design specification provides a complete description of the item wanted. It also lists the composition of the materials to be used, their size, shape, and usually their method of fabrication. Any competent manufacturer having the specifications and the required equipment can make the item. When a purchaser develops its own design specifications, it avoids the duplication of development work by the bidders. Additionally, the use of such specifications permits wide competition among firms not having the scientific or engineering staffs to do their own product development work. Further, design specifications permit formal advertising as an appropriate method of purchase because bidders can quote on exactly the same item.

During a *seller's market*, buyers usually, but not always, get reasonable prices on materials purchased by design specifications. Profits are generally fair, and both efficient and inefficient producers get orders.

During a *buyer's market*, the situation usually changes. Bidding on design specifications becomes extremely keen. In order to be low bidder in such a market, few firms are able to quote prices which permit the recovery of total cost, much less include a profit. Competition sometimes forces suppliers to quote prices that cover all out-of-pocket costs, and only as much overhead costs as they think they can get while obtaining the award. Economic survival forces normally disinterested firms to seek government business. Although this system of purchasing does assure the lowest possible prices to the government, it also creates problems. When faced with tight contract prices, suppliers naturally take every possible measure to minimize costs (and sometimes losses).[15] Ethical manufacturers are stimulated to operate as efficiently as possible. Less scrupulous suppliers have an incentive to cut every possible corner on quality. Industrial purchasers can avoid this latter problem of less desirable suppliers by a careful preselection of prospective suppliers, but government procurement personnel cannot.

The government is sometimes criticized for its use of elaborate and detailed specifications. Up to a point, such criticism is valid. However, the government is now attempting to move away from the use of these kinds of specifications and to utilize specifications that are based on performance or existing commercial standards. Unfortunately, this effort can never enjoy more than limited success, because detailed specifications are the natural outgrowth of the sealed bid method of purchase and its overemphasis on the lowest price. To be the low bidder, sealed bidding practically challenges marginal manufacturers to find and exploit loopholes in government specifications. As these manufacturers are successful in their search, the practice is detected, and the loophole is closed. This process breeds a sequential cycle of evasion and detection which generates increasingly detailed specifications.

Performance Specifications

A performance specification expresses the buyer's requirements in terms such as capacity, function, or operation. Under this type of specification, the details of design, fabrication, and internal structure are left primarily to the option of the supplier. For common equipment such as automobiles, tractors, and trailers, performance specifications permit competition between manufacturers already having products available in the commercial market. Each manufacturer's equipment can differ in design specifications, yet still compete under the required performance specifications. For most standard commercial products, each manufacturer is tooled up to make equipment to its own design. The cost of changing this tooling to permit equipment to be

---

[15]One of the authors is familiar with an example that illustrates this point. The Navy gradually converted almost all its shipboard lighting from incandescent to fluorescent. A series of lighting fixtures were developed, tested, and completely described by drawings and specifications. The initial purchase price for a 4-foot fixture was $40 per unit. Unit costs were successively reduced over a six-year period (during which time raw material prices were gradually increasing) to $36, $32, $28, $24, and finally to a price of $16.75 for a quantity of 20,000. An audit of production costs on this last contract showed that tooling, direct labor, and material costs alone amounted to $17.12 per unit.

manufactured to government design specifications would be a needless waste. It is more logical for Caterpillar, J. I. Case, and John Deere to compete on performance specifications than it is for the government to design a tractor and then pay the high prices that would attend nonstandard production.[16]

Performance specifications are used almost exclusively in the initial procurement of major weapon systems, since no commercial designs are available for such products. In using performance specifications for weapon systems, the principal problem is to select a supplier who is technically, managerially, and financially qualified to design and manufacture the product required.

Quality of Government-Purchased Items

In government purchasing, it is essential that specifications be developed with great care and completeness to obtain materials of the desired quality. However, some quality characteristics are extremely difficult to define precisely. For example, how sharp is "sharp"? How free of defects is "reasonably free of defects"? Or where does a "minor defect" end and a "major defect" begin? How can such qualities be measured? These questions illustrate why writing specifications is so difficult.

In industry, suppliers have a strong incentive to interpret specifications in a way that is fully satisfactory to the buyers. If a supplier's product turns out to be unsuitable for the purpose intended, the supplier knows the buyer is free to take its future business elsewhere. This ability motivates a rational supplier to take the initiative in clarifying questionable specifications or to make adjustments when failures do occur. For example, a household furnishings contractor recently supplied the draperies for a plush new apartment house in San Francisco. A few weeks after installation, the draperies shrank 9 inches. The apartment-house owner asked the contractor for a replacement. The contractor made the same request to the textile mill that manufactured the cloth. The mill initially refused, explaining that the cloth was not preshrunk because the specifications did not call for preshrinking. The contractor admitted the mill was technically right, but implied that if the mill stood on this "technically right" position, future business relationships could be affected. The contractor contended that the mill, as a capable supplier, should have known that preshrunk cloth is a necessity for foggy areas such as San Francisco, regardless of any omission in the specifications. The mill subsequently replaced the drapery material.

The government, on the other hand, is normally not free to take its business elsewhere as a result of such experiences. In similar situations involving

---

[16]A typical exception to this general rule is the purchase of military trucks. These trucks, even though purchased to detailed military specifications, are obtained at low prices because of their great volume.

the government, a contractor can, and often does, contend that its product meets the specifications and that it is a fully reliable supplier. The supplier disclaims any responsibility for its product not being serviceable, maintaining that its responsibility does not extend beyond meeting the specifications. Suppliers challenge the government to prove otherwise. The government's usual recourse to such experiences is to redraft the specifications in the hope that next time there will be no loopholes. In the absence of being able to prove clearly that the contractor has not met the specifications, the government must accept delivery of the product, and keep the supplier on the bidders' list as a qualified supplier in good standing.

Despite the government's difficulties in preparing foolproof design specifications, the conclusion should not be drawn that the government routinely gets cheated on quality. The government's cost of inspection to enforce compliance of quality, under a system that lets sellers choose the buyer rather than vice versa, is obviously high. On the other hand, the quality of many government specifications is attested by the fact that private industry accepts many of these specifications as its own standard of quality. On a product-by-product basis, many GAO and DOD studies show that the prices the government pays and the quality it receives are usually satisfactory—in most cases, both compare favorably with those of private industry. Generally speaking, most industrial purchasing managers can learn much about the difficult art of specifications writing from their government counterparts, who must truly be experts in this field.

MECHANICS

Volume of Paperwork

Critics frequently suggest that the government reduce the size of its paper volume (red tape). "With each F-18 jet fuselage that Northrop turns out, it creates 16,295 pages of manufacturing paper work. Since the F-18 program began, it has generated enough paper to equal the height of the Empire State Building."[17] It is true that for large purchases the government frequently uses 12,000 sheets of paper in situations where industry would use less than 100. It must be remembered, however, that in a typical year roughly 90 percent of all government purchases (by number) are under $10,000, and these purchases are made in essentially the same manner as industry would make them.

A common item such as paint can be used to illustrate the paperwork involved in a typical commodity-type purchase of large dollar value. For such a purchase, the government would use sealed bid purchasing. The *invitation for bids (IFB)* would consist of at least three parts: cover sheet, mandatory

---

[17]Ralph Vartabedian, "Northrop Pioneers Efficient, Paperless F-18 Assembly Line," *Los Angeles Times*, Monday, Oct. 31, 1988, part IV, p. 1.

clauses, and a schedule. On the average, these three parts would require ten to twelve pages. If special instructions were necessary, the number of parts and pages would increase.

Part I, the cover sheet, gives potential suppliers broad general information such as the name of the buying agency, where to send the bids, and the time of bid openings. Part II includes the mandatory clauses commonly called "boilerplate." These clauses are those required either by statute or by executive order (the examination of records clause, Buy American Act, the Eight-Hour Law, and so on). Part III, the schedule, sets forth the most important part of the invitation. It includes specifications, quantities, delivery dates, delivery locations, marking and shipping instructions, inspection instructions, and so forth. Invitations for bids (remember, each set has roughly ten to twelve pages) are normally prepared in sets of three or four (thirty to forty-eight pages) per bidder.

For large procurements, IFBs are usually sent to all firms on the bidders' list. The bidder gets one to three sets, depending on the issuing agency or department. Customarily, for supply-type items, only 15 to 20 percent of the bidders respond. This means 80 to 85 percent of those on the bidders' list choose not to participate in any specific procurement. The question naturally arises: Why then send IFBs to the entire list? The answer: For large purchases, it is cheaper and more efficient to do this than to attempt selectivity.

For small purchases, government buyers can send IFBs to a selected group of bidders—provided the list is rotated in such a manner as to assure equal opportunity eventually to all bidders. For common items with many manufacturers, such as paint, the bidders' list frequently consists of 500 or more firms. To attempt to use a selected group from such a list for a large purchase would be unsuccessful, harrowing, and costly. The national publicity given to procurements over $10,000 would quickly inform the omitted vendors that they did not receive an invitation to bid. Almost in unison, with self-righteous indignation, they would demand an opportunity to participate. The purchasing officer would have no alternative but to grant their requests, and most likely the purchasing officer would have to postpone the bid opening to do so. In many cases, he or she would also have to write letters explaining why the vendors did not get a bid form in the first place. Most government buyers have only to suffer such an experience once to learn the wisdom of overusing rather than underusing the bidders' list.

After the awards are made, the paper mill again starts grinding. Multiple awards are commonplace, and each award produces a need for at least fifty copies of each contract. Inspectors, receiving personnel, inventory managers, supply managers, and finance officers must all be provided with copies.

On occasion, shortcuts to paper usage are achieved. Nonetheless, when it comes to paper consumption, the government procurement system stands guilty as charged. It does use considerably more paper than industry uses to process similar purchases. Nonetheless, in recent years the government has made noteworthy progress in reducing its annual purchasing administrative costs by many millions of dollars. These savings have resulted from actions such as reducing the size of solicitation packages, reducing the number of solicitation packages sent to vendors, referencing required clauses rather than detailing them in their entirety, not furnishing solicitation packages to requesting firms that obviously do not have a technical capability to perform the contract, and using the master solicitation technique (distributing to firms on a one-time basis any clauses, certifications, representations, and requirements that are repeated in solicitation after solicitation).

What about pricing for purchases involving high paper usage? The government generally gets excellent pricing for its large purchases. It is a statistical truth that the larger the number of bidders solicited, the greater is the probability of obtaining a lower price. For this reason, an industrial buyer increases his or her number of bidders for large purchases, but seldom uses more than six to eight bidders. The increased cost of dealing with a much larger number of bidders would ordinarily offset the advantage of a slightly lower price.

Award Lead Time

Total procurement lead time includes administrative lead time. Therefore, total lead time for requisitioners can be reduced either by improving administrative scheduling or by carrying larger inventories of materials in stock.

As insurance against national emergencies, the military services must carry large inventories of many strategic items. No one questions the necessity for these inventories. However, perceptive government critics do question whether the government always differentiates wisely between "strategic military items" and "common items." Strategic items have to be carried in inventory; common items do not. They are kept in inventory out of choice, not necessity. The critical question is: Cannot the needed reserves of common items be carried more economically in the nation's regular distribution channels than in government warehouses? The DOD recognizes this problem, and its recent policy guidelines favor a greater use of commercial facilities. To resolve this problem, one critical question must be answered: In the event of a national emergency, would the nation's storekeepers sell the needed common items to the DOD, or would they hoard the materials for the higher prices they know are certain to come? This is another important problem area in which sufficient evidence is not available to draw reliable conclusions. In-depth research in this area could be helpful in directing national policy.

A representative example can illustrate the lead time problem. Suppose a government purchasing agency receives a requisition for a large quantity of hand tools for delivery at twenty-five different locations. The specifications are clear, and bidder interest is keen. Sealed bid purchasing is therefore mandatory. The total quantity, however, cannot be solicited by an invitation for bids. A portion of the total must be set aside for later negotiation with labor surplus areas or small business. Two weeks are needed to develop the IFB and determine the percentage of set-asides. The bids are in the hands of all the suppliers for four and a half weeks. One week is needed to abstract the bids and select the tentative low bidders (multiple awards would be almost a certainty). One to two weeks are needed to check the competency of those bidders who were successful but who had not had a previous contract with the buying agency. Another week is required to prepare the contracts.

A DOD contracting officer would be fortunate indeed if he or she could process a large advertised procurement for hand tools in less than sixty days; ninety days would not be uncommon. For cost and competitive reasons, private enterprise could not tolerate such a long lead time for the routine purchases of hand tools, or anything else. It is conservatively estimated that industry would process this purchase in less than fourteen days, using fewer than 75 sheets of paper. The government would use over 12,000 sheets.

Lead time is another phase of purchasing in which government and industry differ. Here again, the government, for other than business reasons, has added additional costs to its purchasing operation. It should be understood clearly that without restraints government buyers could purchase hand tools just as quickly and economically as industrial buyers, and with just as few pieces of paper. Government buyers are fully knowledgeable concerning the hand tools industry and low-cost producers in the industry. In *emergencies* and by using *negotiation,* government buyers do purchase supplies with the same speed as industry.

Contract Administration

Once the contract is awarded, all parties have agreed to perform in accordance with the contract terms and conditions. Too often, purchasing or sales activities will consider that the job is done when the deal is closed. In recognizing this human propensity, the FAR provides for sixty-one different tasks to be performed as needed in administering public contracts.[18] In fact, the magnitude of the responsibility in the Department of Defense is such that a separate activity, the Defense Contract Administration Services (DCAS), part of the Defense Logistics Agency, was formed to administer contracts let by all defense activities. The *purposes* of this action were to: (1) provide specialized assistance through field offices located at or near contractor establishments, (2) avoid or eliminate overlapping and duplication of government effort, and (3) provide more consistent treatment of contractors. In some instances, such as in small purchases or research contracts, the purchasing activity retains administration responsibility rather than assigning it to DCAS. Under the Defense Plant Cognizance Program, the service with the majority of the work in a contractor's facility retains contract administration responsibility for all defense contracts in the plant.

[18]See Part 42 of The Federal Acquisition Regulation.

Contract administration activities include such functions as inspecting or assuring quality; making transportation arrangements; monitoring delivery schedules and expediting; monitoring contractor use of government property; modifying the contract; administering payment provisions; and closing defaulted, terminated or completed contracts.[19] Many government contracts provide for inspection and acceptance of the product or service at the source, with subsequent transportation a government responsibility. Government inspectors typically examine a sample of the shipment and accept or reject the entire shipment based on the sample. The transportation people in the contract administration office (CAO) will use the great purchasing power of the government to obtain most favorable rates on shipping. The goods usually are then moved on a government bill of lading.

Industrial specialists in the CAO monitor contractor delivery forecasts to make sure the goods will arrive when needed. Sometimes it is necessary to issue amended shipping instructions to divert products from the original destination to the point of use. Industrial specialists also are skilled at expediting partial shipments in order to obtain early delivery when needed. These contractual changes require formal contract modifications which are negotiated and executed by the administrative contracting officer (ACO).

Government contracts sometimes provide for the contractor to use government-owned materials, tools, equipment, and even factories. In these instances, property administrators from the CAO make sure the taxpayer's interest in the property is protected.

The administrative contracting officer is the leader of the government contract administration team. The ACO is the only person (other than the procuring contracting officer) who may legally commit and obligate the government to changed contract terms and conditions. The ACO carries out such functions as negotiating forward pricing rates for the benefit of all buying activities, negotiating new terms and conditions for contract changes, and certifying contractor eligibility for payment. The ACO accomplishes all contract closeout functions per the contract and is responsible for processing any claims, disputes, and appeals that might arise during contract performance.

Disputes

A dispute sometimes arises between the government and a contractor which the parties cannot resolve by negotiation. In that case, the disputes clause of government contracts (based on the Contract Disputes Act of 1978) provides a legal framework for resolution. The disputes process starts when a contractor files a claim with the contracting officer (CO). The CO then has sixty days to render a decision or give a date by when a decision will be made. The

---

[19]Harry Robert Page expands on postaward activities in Chapter 12 of his 1980 book *Public Purchasing and Materials Management,* published by D.C. Heath and Co., Lexington, Mass.

CO's decision is final unless the contractor appeals or files a lawsuit. The contractor may appeal to the agency Board of Contract Appeals for relief from the decision within ninety days of the ruling date. Alternatively, the contractor may file a lawsuit for relief with the Court of Claims within twelve months of the decision. In any event, the disputes clause of the contract requires that until a decision is rendered, both parties shall comply with the CO's decision and proceed diligently to perform the contract.

Remedies

The government also has available a number of remedies that it may apply during or even after contract performance. A number of them are discussed here. The government contract may be terminated for default (failure to perform). Further, the defaulted contractor may be liable for damages and/or reprocurement costs. The government also may terminate a contract for its convenience. A clause inserted in government contracts permits the CO to stop the work in whole or in part and settle with the contractor at the point of termination. Of course, in contrast to termination for default, under a termination for convenience the government expects to equitably compensate the contractor for effort expended. Complex termination actions are usually referred to an experienced termination contracting officer (TCO) for resolution.

The government may debar, suspend, or declare ineligible an errant contractor to make sure that contracts are awarded only to responsible bidders. Firms or individuals may be excluded (debarred) from government contract awards for a defined period. A suspension of a contractor is used by the contracting officer when immediate action is necessary to protect the government's interest pending formal proceedings such as those used in debarment. Finally, a contractor may be declared ineligible to receive contract awards for up to three years for violating a statute which provides for such action.

The Truth in Negotiations Act, which was discussed in a prior section, provides for contractors to certify that the pricing data submitted with a contract proposal are current, complete, and accurate. If it subsequently is found that a price paid was excessive because one or more of the certifications were false, the contracting officer may reduce the contract price to eliminate the effect of the contractor's error. Further penalties are provided if it is found that the error was intended to mislead the contracting officer.[20]

Statutory remedies are available if a government contractor submits a false

---

[20]In 1988, Sundstrand Corporation settled a suit for defense contracting fraud with an agreement to pay the government $127.3 million in a plea agreement. See "How Sundstrand Stole Millions," *Register Star*, Rockford, Ill., Oct. 16, 1988, p. 1A. It should be noted, however, that most major defense contractors have established ethics programs which are showcases for U.S. industry.

claim such as an inflated invoice. Both civil and criminal remedies are provided.

The contract changes clause provides the government with the vehicle to amend any contract administratively. By terms of the clause, the contractor is bound to proceed with the changed terms and conditions. Subsequent equitable adjustment of the contract is prescribed by the clause.

CODE OF ETHICS FOR GOVERNMENT SERVICE

Department of Defense Directive 5500.7, dated May 6, 1987, contains the following code of ethics for employees of the U.S. Government.

Any person in Government service should:

1 Put loyalty to the highest moral principles and to country above loyalty to persons, party, or Government department.
2 Uphold the constitution, laws, and regulations of the United States and of all Governments therein and never be a party to their evasion.
3 Give a full day's labor for a full day's pay; giving earnest effort and best thought to the performance of duties.
4 Seek to find and employ more efficient and economical ways of getting tasks accomplished.
5 Never discriminate unfairly by the dispensing of special favors or privileges to anyone, whether for remuneration or not; and never accept for himself or herself or for family members, favors or benefits under circumstances which might be construed by reasonable persons as influencing the performance of Governmental duties.
6 Make no private promises of any kind binding upon the duties of office, since a Government employee has no private word which can be binding on public duty.
7 Engage in no business with the Government, either directly or indirectly, which is inconsistent with the conscientious performance of Governmental duties.
8 Never use any information gained confidentially in the performance of Governmental duties as a means for making private profit.
9 Expose corruption wherever discovered.
10 Uphold these principles, ever conscious that public office is a public trust.

The Packard Commission

This group of distinguished individuals recently reviewed the government procurement process. The following were among the commission's recommendations:[21]

1 Development of a code of business ethics and conduct addressing problems and procedures applicable to defense procurement

---

[21]Calvin Brusman, *Pacific Purchasor*, November–December 1988, p. 18.

2 Enforcement of effective internal contractor controls to ensure compliance with the code
3 Adaptation of an internal auditing system to monitor compliance with the code
4 Oversight of the code by an independent committee

A recent letter from the government advised defense contractors to increase the surveillance of their employees' relations with subcontractors in regard to subcontractor kickbacks. The letter stated that in the future, monitoring contractors in this area would be done by means of the Contractor Purchasing System Review (CPSR) to determine whether the contractor's internal policies include the following safeguards:

- Published standards of conduct and business ethics policy for buyers
- Approval by higher management of purchases over $25,000 prior to procurement finalization
- Periodic rotation of buyers' purchasing assignments
- A management program to interview suppliers to determine if they are aware of any irregularities or questionable conduct by company buyers
- A hot line or similar mechanism to contractor management (outside of the purchasing chain) to be used by employees and suppliers to report possible wrongdoing
- A policy requiring the reporting of unethical conduct to the government and subsequent restitution of any resulting gain[22]

CLOSING REMARKS

Government contracting is clearly bound by more rules than is commercial purchasing. The necessity to guard the public interest as well as the peculiar needs of government dictate such rules. As the process grew, Congress found it necessary to pass laws governing many aspects of government procurement. Some of these laws have social, political, and/or economic purposes, rather than just governing the purchasing function. Out of these laws, peculiar needs, and special rules grew some special procedures that guide the government contracting officer in his or her actions.

Harold Brown and James Schlesinger, both former secretaries of defense, wrote a provocative set of recommendations which appeared in the September 14, 1988, issue of the *New York Times.* The following is extracted from this article.

Recent indications of widespread misconduct by a network of Defense Department employees and consultants reinforced popular impressions of serious problems in the Pentagon.

[22]Brusman, op. cit.

Project managers need to be given greater authority for day-to-day management—and to be held accountable for bringing in effective weapons, on time and within budget. Intervening levels of bureaucracy should be reviewed and reduced.

It is particularly important to regain control of the so-called requirement process, which establishes the designs of new weapon systems. Design specifications should be made more realistic and less detailed, permitting industry greater flexibility to solve design problems. Cost should be given higher priority in deciding among competing needs. In some cases, we gain a marginal increase in performance only at an exorbitant price of delays, reduced reliability, or higher unit cost. In other cases, costs are inflated by adherence to "military specifications" when commercial standards for common items of equipment would be sufficient.

We should also consider integrating the acquisition system, creating a single organization staffed by civilians and military officers from each service. A radical change like this, however, should be developed, evaluated and—assuming it holds up to closer scrutiny—implemented by the Defense Department itself. The imposition of such an organization through legislation would guarantee failure.

Meanwhile, Congress has been so concerned with reforming the Pentagon that it has neglected its own role in military management. We hesitate to prescribe to Congress, but the legislature must include its own procedure if any scheme of reform is to make a difference.

Some in Congress already support a shift to a biennial military budget, a move that would impart far greater stability in military planning and management. But the majority resists such a change for fear of losing leverage over decisions by the executive branch. But there are ways that Congress can budget biennially without giving up any real power. One is a "Budget Adjustment Act" for the off-budget year that would cover controversial weapons but not routine military matters. Congress also should simplify its elaborate budget, authorization, and appropriation processes so as to consolidate committee jurisdictions, thus reducing the number of times that decisions are revisited.[23]

FOR DISCUSSION

32-1 What are the characteristic attributes of firms which serve as government contractors?

32-2 Discuss the "grave implications" which former President Eisenhower referred to in his farewell address.

32-3 Name the primary regulation for use by all federal executive agencies in their acquisition of supplies and services.

32-4 Explain why the contracting process using public funds is probably not as efficient as its commercial counterpart using funds from hard-won sales.

32-5 In what way might the practice of public review adversely affect the government's procurement process?

---

[23]Harold Brown and James Schlesinger, "Hippocrates in the Pentagon," *New York Times*, Sept. 14, 1988, p. A31.

32-6 What two major objectives did the Armed Services Procurement Act accomplish?

32-7 Why would government accept bids from small business when circumstances demonstrate that big business often prices lower?

32-8 Discuss the set-aside and non-set-aside bases of procurement and their applications.

32-9 Describe the mission of the Office of Federal Procurement Policy (OFPP).

32-10 What purchasing conditions prompted Congress to enact the Truth in Negotiations Act?

32-11 Which three principal statutes did the Competition in Contracting Act (CICA) amend?

32-12 List the seven exceptions in which the federal government could award a contract using noncompetitive procedures.

32-13 Why would the government encounter difficulties taking advantage of life cycle costing?

32-14 What are some of the disadvantages of total package procurement?

32-15 Describe the conditions of a buyer's and a seller's market with respect to government contracting.

32-16 Why does sealed bidding prevent the government from complete liberation of "specification mania?"

32-17 Why do performance-type specifications leave the details of design, fabrication, and internal structure primarily to the option of the supplier?

32-18 Describe the three sections of an IFB.

32-19 In what ways has the government made noteworthy progress in reducing its annual purchasing administrative costs?

32-20 What is the function of the Defense Contract Administration Services branch of the Defense Logistics Agency?

32-21 Describe the process of a dispute resolution between the government and a contractor.

32-22 Identify some of the remedies which the government can seek when faced with an errant contractor.

32-23 Briefly describe the highlights of the Government Code of Ethics.

CASES FOR CHAPTER 32

Dynaflight, Inc., California Division (in the Instructor's Manual)
Black Motor Company (in the Instructor's Manual)
Hydrosub's Unfloatable Amphibious Assault Vehicle
    (in the Instructor's Manual)
Gotham City Buys Fire Engines (in the Instructor's Manual)
Naval Operating Base, Arkladelphia (in the Instructor's Manual)
Springfield Purchases a Garbage Truck (in the Instructor's Manual)

CASES FOR STUDY AND ANALYSIS

AAA, INC.

On March 1, 1989, All American Aluminum (AAA) authorized the expenditure of $81 million to modernize its sheet mill facility located in Evansville, Indiana. Because of this modernization's strategic importance, a very tight timetable was established—2½ years for completion of the project. Top managers within the company stated that the schedule, *not cost*, was to be given top priority. Marketing projections estimated that $1.2 million in lost opportunity would be incurred for every month this project went beyond its scheduled completion date. Senior management indicated that additional funding was available if needed to keep the project on schedule.

The company did not have in-house engineering resources to complete a project of this magnitude within the allotted timeframe. A project team of twelve AAA engineers was established to provide key technical direction and overall management, while the bulk of the design work was to be contracted out. Of these twelve engineers, ten were located at the plant site in Evansville and two were located at the company headquarters in Stubenville, Ohio.

In early April, a group consisting of two engineers and a senior facilities buyer visited prospective engineering companies to determine which firm was most capable of handling this project. Each firm was evaluated on three major points:

1 Quality of engineering expertise

This case was developed by Pat Craychee, Tim Murphy, Peter Andrade, David Kraylow, and Bruce Gray under the direction of Professor David N. Burt.

2 Number of engineers that could be made available for the project (sub-contracting would not be allowed)

3 Ability to coordinate with the AAA project team (located primarily in Evansville)

Each company visited was given an outline of the project, including scope of work, conceptual design requirements, and the project team's engineering man-hour estimate. Each firm was requested to submit a proposal outlining how it would handle the project.

Four firms appeared to have the quantity and quality of engineering capability required. Consequently, the final decision was based on which firm AAA felt could best coordinate with its project team in Evansville.

Comstock Engineering was selected to do the job. Although its price and quality were only average, Comstock was considered the best choice because it had offices in both Stubenville and Evansville. It was thought that offices in both locations would reduce the potential for coordination problems.

Comstock maintained that the project could be best handled by its larger office in Stubenville, with Evansville providing only those services that required work at the plant site. AAA disagreed, and stated that any contract award would be contingent on the following conditions:

1 All engineering services were to be managed out of the Evansville office. This would require Comstock to relocate a project manager and two project engineers to the Evansville office.

2 All project management services (planning, scheduling, material control) were to be done out of the Evansville office.

3 The engineering design services (electrical, mechanical, and civil) for certain portions of the project must be done out of the Evansville office. This constituted approximately 60 percent of the design required for the entire project.

4 Prior to placement of the order, Comstock must identify key personnel—the project manager and three project engineers (electrical, mechanical, and civil).

These conditions required the addition of fifteen people to the thirty people already in Comstock's Evansville office. Comstock agreed and submitted the names of the key personnel, which in turn were accepted by AAA. An order, including the noted conditions, was issued to Comstock on a cost plus percentage basis with a cap of $3.3 million. The order was dated April 18.

A chronological sequence of subsequent events is noted below.

- *May 1*—Comstock communicated to AAA that three of the four key personnel would not agree to transfer to the Evansville area.
- *May 15*—Comstock suggested that since the key personnel would not transfer to Evansville, the project should be managed from its Stubenville office.
- *May 20*—AAA rejected Comstock's offer. It was learned that Comstock had just finished a very large project in its Stubenville office and would

have to lay off personnel if no work could be found. AAA believed this to be the motivation for Comstock's suggestion.

- *May 25*—Comstock suggested that the project be managed with personnel currently located in the Evansville office.
- *June 15*—AAA accepted Evansville personnel as temporary management only and applied pressure to Comstock to resolve the issue.
- *July 1*—As the scope of work became more defined, it became apparent that electrical engineering man-hours would be double the number estimated by the AAA project team.
- *August 1*—Comstock submitted the names of three people to fill the vacant management slots. AAA accepted one, but rejected the other two as unqualified. The most important position, project manager, was still unfilled.
- *August 15*—AAA was unsatisfied with the scheduler assigned to the project and requested that he be removed. Comstock agreed and replaced him with its best scheduler. The new scheduler was located in Evansville on a temporary basis. Comstock asked that AAA pay for his temporary living expenses.
- *September 1*—It was determined that the civil engineering man-hours required would only be one-third the number estimated by the AAA project team. Comstock claimed that it had adjusted its schedule to accommodate this work and hence was overstaffed with civil engineers.
- *September 1*—Comstock communicated to AAA that it was having difficulty staffing the Evansville office with a sufficient number of electrical engineers. The people within the company were refusing to transfer, and outside recruiting efforts were unsuccessful.
- *September 7*—Comstock requested that the bulk of the electrical engineering work be transferred to its Stubenville office. AAA rejected this request.
- *September 15*—Although the Evansville office was understaffed and overloaded, Comstock was forced to lay people off in its Stubenville office.
- *September 17*—Comstock was still unable to staff its Evansville office with sufficient electrical engineers. It requested that the electrical engineering schedule be extended. AAA did not agree to this.
- *September 21*—AAA verified that Comstock was actively trying to recruit electrical engineers for its Evansville office. However, AAA also discovered that Comstock had submitted a bid for another electrical engineering job, which would conflict with the AAA project.
- *October 1*—By this time, five months had passed without a project manager, and the electrical engineering schedule was slipping badly. Comstock claimed that these problems could be eliminated by transferring the bulk of the engineering work to its Stubenville office. AAA claimed that these conditions were made very clear in the contract and must be adhered to.

AAA has scheduled an internal meeting for October 2 to determine whether to cancel the contract with Comstock.

1 How could AAA have avoided the problems it experienced with Comstock?

2 What are the potential implications of the type of contract AAA used? Discuss.

3 How could AAA have improved its approach to sourcing in this case?

4 What should AAA do now? Discuss.

THE APEX AVIATION CASE

The Apex Aviation Company, with annual sales of $600 million, is a leading supplier of mechanical subsystems to the aviation industry. The firm is in a highly competitive industry, being one of four firms that supply approximately 80 percent of all mechanical subsystems to aircraft manufacturers. Typically, Apex receives a functional or performance specification from an aircraft manufacturer for a subsystem or component from which it designs the required item or subsystem. Due to the cyclical nature of the aviation industry, Apex frequently subcontracts for the manufacture of items, which are then assembled in its own plants.

Recently, Apex received a follow-on order for 100 landing gears. The initial order had been for 50 landing gears, delivery of which was completed three months ago. As a result of heavy plant loading, and following a review by the Apex make-or-buy committee, it has been decided to have the machining of the aluminum outer cylinder struts subcontracted, using aluminum ingots supplied by Apex.

The procurement has been assigned to Mr. Raymond of the purchasing department. Mr. Raymond has sent requests for proposals (RFP) to a number of qualified vendors. Copies of the design specification accompanied the RFP. The RFP calls for a delivery schedule to commence six months after award of the contract. Initial deliveries are to be scheduled for two struts per month, with subsequent delivery quantities increasing until all units are delivered over a period of thirty-nine months.

The roles for Richard Raymond, buyer for Apex, and Ralph Hawk, President of Hawk Manufacturing Co., are contained in the Instructor's Guide.

BACK BAY UNIVERSITY

Back Bay University is a large private university with a distinguished faculty. Enrollment at Back Bay currently is 12,000 students, of whom 6,200 are enrolled in the university's five outstanding graduate schools.

Ms. Sharon Davis has been the director of Back Bay's purchasing department for six years. Her department consists of twenty-two employees and is responsible for the purchase of supplies, services, and equipment that total $36 million. On one of her recent tours of the campus, Ms. Davis noticed a janitor outside the dental school loading used x-ray film, some fairly heavy small cartons, and some floor sweepings into a trash container.

Ms. Davis decided to conduct an informal survey into how the university disposed of its surplus material. In talking with the machine shop foreman, she learned he was selling the shop's scrap metal to a salvage firm. He used the proceeds for the annual shop picnic.

Administrative services disposed of surplus furniture by selling it to interested members of the Back Bay staff on an informal basis. The proceeds were donated to the woman's auxiliary at the university hospital. Surplus scientific and research equipment was either stored in a larger barn or sold to interested faculty. The proceeds were used to purchase research supplies.

1 What arguments are there in favor of a formal salvage program at Back Bay University?
2 What arguments are there in opposition to such a program?
3 Assume that a salvage program is to be implemented. Which department at the university should be responsible for it? Why?
4 Develop an implementation plan for such a salvage program.

THE BIG D COMPANY

The Big D Company of Dallas, Texas, was a family owned, conservatively managed company. For over forty years the company enjoyed slow, steady growth in reaching its current employment level of just over 200. All expansions were financed entirely out of earnings. As the company grew, its operating procedures were periodically re-examined and modified to cope with the complex problems that accompany growth. The company developed, manufactured, and sold metering and flow control devices used in the chemical industry. Recently, as a result of declining profits, management was considering the advisability of installing a more formal system for controlling its cost of materials.

The company's product line contained about forty items, ranging in size from gauges and simple fittings to large flow meters weighing up to 150 pounds. Most of these were made in a number of different models and sizes, so that the total number of separate products was about 300. About half were standard models whose design had not changed greatly in the last ten years; others were subject to considerable technological change; a few involved special features for different customers, sometimes being made of special alloys to resist corrosive action of certain chemicals. Some of the more complex items were supplied with or without certain fittings and refinements. The company's position in the industry depended on its ability to keep ahead of its competitors in design, quality of product, customer service, and price—roughly in that order.

Reprinted by permission of Prentice-Hall, Inc., from *Selected Case Problems in Industrial Management* (2d ed.), by Holden, Shallenberger, and Diehm.

It was the responsibility of the purchasing manager to obtain the castings, materials, and parts indicated. Castings were purchased in the exact quantity required for the manufacturing order. For the most part, the same was true as to bar stock, plate, and similar materials. On the highly standard material sizes, more than enough for one order might be purchased, and in most cases full lengths would be ordered, rather than the exact fraction required. On odd sizes of expensive alloys, the exact amount would be purchased even down to the inch. Standard nuts, bolts, studs, pipefittings, and similar items were usually bought in standard commercial lot quantities, but even here the quantities did not greatly exceed immediate requirements, and frequently even these items were bought by the piece. Molded plastics and special fittings or stampings were sometimes bought in excess of immediate needs, especially when costs of small lot procurement were prohibitive. The purchasing manager did not alter the quantities shown on the make-and-buy sheet without discussion with the superintendent.

When materials began to come in, they were checked off the make-and-buy sheet and taken to the storeroom, to the production floor, or, if they were finished parts, to assembly.

Little attempt was made to schedule work to the shop, and the machine shop foreman was free to work on any manufacturing orders on which materials had been received. It was up to him to keep his staff and machines busy and to meet the estimated completion dates. As parts were completed, they moved on to assembly, where they were placed in the tote box with other parts accumulated against that order. When all parts were completed, assembly could take place. Finished units were placed in stock in the shipping room or were shipped out immediately against orders.

Completion of the lot was not posted to the sales and production record until the entire lot was finished. Inasmuch as some units were often assembled well in advance of the completion of the entire lot, the sales and production record frequently indicated earliest delivery as some time in the future when, in fact, completed units were in storage on the shipping room shelves. In this way sales had been lost to competitors who quoted earlier deliveries. Other sales had been lost because in setting estimated completion dates the superintendent usually allowed himself more time than was necessary for ordering, machining, and assembly.

The company had no formal inventory control system. No record was kept of raw materials, purchased parts, or manufactured parts on hand. An informal tabulation of finished goods, the sales and production record, was maintained for each item. This showed the balance on hand, the amount currently being manufactured, orders received, customers' names, and dates of shipments made. It also showed the minimum stock balance and the standard manufacturing quantity. These had been determined at a top management level, taking into consideration past sales of the item, the time required for a production run, manufacturing economies, potential obsolescence, storage space available, and the financial resources of the company. In the last year, the minimum stock balance and the manufacturing quantity on most items had been revised upward because of a substantial increase in volume, delivery delays, and more frequent manufacturing runs. The company felt that about three to four runs per year was about right for each item. A typical manufacturing run required about nine to twelve weeks, most of which was consumed in obtaining castings. Actual processing in the plant required two to four weeks. Recently, it was found that jobs were frequently sold before completion and a second lot started before the first lot was finished. Currently, about fifty to sixty shop orders were initiated each month.

As customer orders were received, they were posted to the sales and production record. When such orders reduced the balance on hand and in process to the predetermined minimum, a notice of depletions was prepared, showing the balance on hand and the standard manufacturing quantity. This notice was sent to the plant superintendent.

Big D did not have a formal production planning and inventory control activity. The plant superintendent, in determining the exact quantity to manufacture, was guided by the previously set quantities but consulted informally with the engineer, development, sales, and finance departments before each run. He then made out a make-and-buy sheet showing for the item in question the various parts required, the shop print numbers, the materials from which the parts were made, the quantity of each part required per completed unit, and the estimated completion date.

The make-and-buy sheet was forwarded to the assembly foreman, who checked off for each part the quantity of that part which had been accumulated from overruns on previous orders. No records were kept on such accumulated parts. The parts were stored in bins in the assembly department, and those counted out against the make-and-buy sheet were separated in a tote box against the time when that order would be assembled.

The make-and-buy sheet was returned to the plant superintendent, who edited it to determine whether certain parts should be made or ordered in larger quantity than required for that particular order. Where parts were interchangeable, he might also consolidate them with other orders. The plant superintendent was familiar with the manufacturing process and set-ups involved, knew the price breaks on materials, and had a general knowledge of probable future demand. Before forwarding the make-and-buy sheet to the purchasing manager, the superintendent entered an estimated completion date, which in turn was posted to the sales and production record.

The traffic function was performed by the plant superintendent's secretary. Receiving and warehousing were performed by three young employees who were more or less under the control of the superintendent. Normally, when an incoming shipment arrived, the foreman would oversee its receipt. Purchasing reported to the plant superintendent.

Certain executives felt that the company should establish a more systematic control over raw material, manufactured and finished parts, and finished goods inventories. They pointed to the orders lost, the waste of purchasing and producing in small quantities, delays in production and assembly occasioned by absence of materials and parts, and losses by misplacement, breakage, and pilferage. These concerned officials also felt that Big D might be able to make significant savings through a systematic control of surplus and salvage. Two of the officials expressed concern over the amount of money spent on transportation. No survey had been made to evaluate potential savings in these areas since no records were kept. Inventory losses could not be measured. Pilferage was probably negligible, because the only items having real intrinsic value (thermometers and similar components) were kept in a locked cabinet by the assembly foreman. Transportation costs were estimated to be 12 percent of the cost of purchased material.

Those who opposed changing the inventory control procedure pointed out the risks of obsolescence in any inventory accumulation, and, more importantly, the amount of funds that might be tied up in inventory and the space that would be necessary if substantial stocks of materials, parts, or finished assemblies were to be built up. They resisted the introduction of changes in the areas of production planning and control, receiving, warehousing, and traffic. They also pointed out that other uses of company buildings, equipment, research, and development would yield greater returns.

1 What specific action should the company take in the area of inventory control? Support your proposal with an analysis of its strengths and weaknesses.
2 What is your reaction to the argument of those who oppose tighter controls?
3 How would your recommendation in answering question 1 differ if this company were making a single product?
4 How does the inventory control problem change as the company's overall volume of business increases?
5 Do you think that Big D could benefit from the establishment of a materials management operation? If so, what functions should it include?

THE BIG "O" COMPANY

The Big "O" Company manufactures large hydraulic units. One of the most difficult items to manufacture is the hydraulic cylinder. The cylinder housing is fabricated from a malleable iron casting. The housing is machined to close tolerances, and the slightest discrepancy in either material or machining means a total loss. Machine cycle time on a typical housing is approximately sixteen hours.

For several years, castings had been purchased from the Macon Foundries in Georgia. Macon had been a Big "O" supplier for many years, and during that time it produced thousands of castings at acceptable quality levels. Eight months ago, however, when its founder and president, George Chapel, died, Macon announced that it was discontinuing foundry operations.

The purchasing department at Big "O" undertook a search for new sources. At first, few suppliers could be found who were either capable or willing to meet the exacting specifications and tolerances required. Ultimately, however, three foundries were selected and invited to submit bids on 4,000 castings.

The low bidder, at $76.17 a unit, was the Barry Foundry of Muncie, Indiana. Barry was a small concern with a good reputation for doing quality work and fulfilling every delivery promise. Barry was given a purchase order for the full 4,000 units, with the stipulation that Big "O" approve the first 100 units.

Within two weeks the first 100 castings were received. They were subjected to initial inspection and then dispatched to the floor for machining. In the words of the shop foreman, "They machined like butter." Barry was told to proceed with the entire order and a four-month delivery schedule.

It was about this time that problems began to develop in the shop. Some hard castings had damaged both grinding wheels and cutting tools. Also, cracks from casting porosity appeared on newly machined surfaces and slots. Although these conditions were not present in all castings, they occurred in a sufficient number to warrant action. It was determined that quality standards tighter than those of the existing procurement standard would be required. All suppliers were to be notified immediately.

Accordingly, the buyer contacted Barry and told the supplier to stop production of castings to the old standard, advising that new specifications were now being developed and would be issued within the next two days. To the buyer's shock, he learned that Barry had completed all 4,000 castings. Having had approval on the first 100 units, Barry established production on a continuous-line basis and turned out castings at a fast, steady rate. Because the order called for deliveries to extend over the next four months, Barry was holding the castings and shipping them in accordance with the schedule. To meet the new procurement standard, it was obvious that Barry would either have to scrap all the old castings and produce new ones, or undergo an expensive process of reannealing.

1 What are Barry's legal obligations in this matter?
2 Comment on the fact that Barry had already produced the full order quantity of 4,000 well in advance of actual delivery requirements.
3 What does the buyer do now?

BLOZIS COMPANY

The Blozis Company was a manufacturer of highly technical equipment. The $16 million gross sales of the company consisted primarily of units designed to customer specifications by the engineering department and produced on a job-shop basis by the production department. The engineering department also designed highly complex control equipment of general industrial application to be sold by the Blozis Company on an off-the-shelf basis.

The purchasing department consisted of the purchasing manager, a buyer, and two clerks who handled typing and filing. Although many of the items purchased were of a highly technical nature, the purchasing manager had no technical training. Through the years, he had picked up a fair grasp of the engineering terminology used in the field, but had made no attempt to keep up with the specialized design problems of the company. The buyer was a woman who was known in the trade as "hard-boiled but big-hearted" and was generally considered a competent general supplies buyer. Without great ingenuity, the buyer also successfully handled technical items if detailed specifications were supplied by engineering or production.

An expediter was attached to production. He formerly had been one of the technicians in the production shop and had picked up some technical training in the Army. Because he could understand verbal descriptions of items needed by engineering and production, these groups often contacted him on ordering problems before submitting a requisition to purchasing. He frequently would suggest substitute components that could be drawn immediately from the stock room; or he would convert the oral description into a commercial specification, type a requisition, and submit it to purchasing. The expediter had two primary responsibilities: to pick up rush orders and to supervise the stock room. He spent about 50 percent of each day picking up items at nearby suppliers, at truck terminals, or airports, or carrying materials to subcontractors, to platers, or to various carriers for shipment. In the stock room, a clerk kept up the facilities, issued supplies to engineering and production personnel, and kept stock records. The clerk reported to the expediter, who reviewed the stock records, prepared requisitions for items at their reorder points, and disposed of items that were turning too slowly or had deteriorated.

Frequent problems had arisen when suppliers claimed long overdue payments on materials that had been received by the Blozis Company. In these cases it always developed that someone had forgotten to make up a receiving report. Since purchasing only passed bills for payment after receipt of the receiving report, several sizable discounts had been missed and the company had been substantially tardy in meeting the net date on several bills. In these cases, the expediter was always sure that the item had come over the receiving dock, and the receiving clerk was just as sure that the expediter had brought it into the plant in the back of his station wagon.

A particularly unfortunate incident had occurred when two special micrometers disappeared within the plant after the Blozis Company had waited six months to receive them. The supplier could prove receipt by the bill of lading signed by the receiving clerk. The receiving clerk claimed the expediter had picked up the micrometers on the receiving dock to carry them to the engineers as quickly as possible. The expediter claimed he had never seen the micrometers. Both the production and plant maintenance managers had backed their respective men to the fullest. No disciplinary action had been taken since there were no signatures on the receiving reports to prove either case.

The expediter periodically typed up purchase orders for rush items. In other cases he picked up the desired items and informed the suppliers that they would receive "confirming orders" from the Blozis Company purchasing department. When the expediter forgot to ask purchasing for a confirming order, the purchasing department was occasionally distressed to be processing invoices for which it had no corresponding orders. Some suppliers were also mildly petulant when a promised purchase order was not forthcoming. Although suppliers had been warned not to honor an order from the Blozis Company unless it bore the purchasing manager's signature, it was considered poor business to penalize the suppliers who had honored the expediter's request in good faith. Consequently, purchase orders were often made up to match invoices if the material had obviously been received from the supplier.

The president liked to operate "informally" and allowed anyone in the company to initiate requisitions. The only approval signature required on orders up to $10,000 was the purchasing manager's. Orders over $10,000 required the president's approval on requisitions, but, in practice, all orders for more than $10,000 were approved by the president either in the materials budget or the capital budget long before requisitions were made out.

The president had heard something of the micrometer incident from his brother, but had dismissed the whole matter as "one of those unfortunate interdepartment squabbles." However, when his engineering manager and his production manager began to complain of the difficulties of staying within the materials budget, he looked further into the matter. In subsequent talks with both men he drew up the following summary list of complaints:

1 The managers did not know what materials were being charged to their departments until the monthly accounting statement came out.
2 The engineering and operating personnel were not notified when materials came in unless the expediter dropped the material on the desk of the requisitioner.
3 The purchasing department was entirely too slow in processing orders. It took almost a full day just to get the order to the telephone.
4 The purchasing department did not understand technical specifications, and the expediter was being overworked by handling all technical orders.

The president presented these complaints to the purchasing manager and asked him for a solution.

1 If you were the purchasing manager, what recommendations would you have made?
2 At what points does this purchasing department exhibit weak control over (a) materials and (b) overall purchasing performance?
3 How could these weaknesses be corrected?
4 What activities should the expediter be responsible for in this organization?
5 What is the purchasing department's responsibility in establishing and interpreting technical specifications?

THE BOARDROOM

In June 1989, Tom Dewey, purchasing manager for Builder's Bank, Inc.'s (BBI) New York office, wanted to resolve a set of problems arising from the purchase of eighty chairs for the executive boardroom.

GENERAL COMPANY BACKGROUND

BBI was a large international bank with operations throughout the world. It had recently purchased an office building and had hired the well-known architect Peter Tropper to do the major design and renovation plans.

THE PURCHASING DEPARTMENT

The purchasing department in the New York office was responsible for all local purchases, in addition to a few major purchases for the international offices. The bank did not have an approved supplier list; an invitation to bid was an indication that the potential supplier was considered qualified.

BUILDING RENOVATION

The architectural firm of Peter Tropper was hired to redesign the entire building, including the selection of furniture. Once the design was completed, a working group, including the president and vice president, had approved the design, including selection and color for all major furniture. The purchasing department did not participate in this process.

In June 1988, Peter Tropper sent a specification sheet to the purchasing department for all purchases, which included model number and manufacturer. Suppliers would bid on the same manufacturer, with no substitutions allowed. Although the department had the option to split the order between suppliers, Tom Dewey decided to order through a single source.

In late June, the working group asked Tom Dewey to submit a budget of what the bank would have to spend to complete the renovation during fiscal 1989. Therefore, in early July, Tom Dewey submitted a request for proposal (RFP) to ten vendors, all of which responded.

When the bids were received in mid-August, the working group reviewed the bids and rejected them as being too high. The working group and Peter Tropper agreed to a scaling down of the work proposed. A week later, Tom Dewey sent new specifications to the same ten suppliers, of which eight responded. The low bid on the RFP was $1.3 million, submitted by ABCO furniture, a large local furniture dealer. In September, the working group authorized Tom Dewey to purchase major furniture and the chairs for the executive boardroom totaling $400,000.

CHAIRS FOR THE BOARDROOM

Among the items on the RFP were eighty leather chairs for the executive boardroom. These chairs had a single pedestal and a fixed jury base, which would not allow the chairs to rock or swivel. Twelve of the chairs, costing $1,500, required installation in concrete, with the remaining sixty-eight chairs, costing $1,300 each, having bases that could be installed on wood flooring. The RFP made no mention of installation.

In February 1989, ABCO Furniture informed Tom Dewey that the chairs were ready. Since the boardroom was still under construction, he arranged to have ABCO store the chairs, with the agreement that he honor the invoice in March. The invoice was paid in late March and ABCO stored the chairs until they were delivered on the morning of April 22, 1989.

When the chairs were delivered, the construction manager talked with Peter Tropper regarding installation. The construction manager told Tom Dewey that the architect had said he would give detailed drawings regarding installation of the chairs, although the drawings had not been received. When Tom Dewey asked Peter Tropper about the problem, Peter indicated that Purchasing, having bought the chairs, was responsible for installation. Peter Tropper also stated that he had informed Purchasing, by letter in late March, that Purchasing was responsible for installation.

At the instruction of Tom Dewey, ABCO hired a local installer to install the chairs. The installer had seen neither the chairs nor the boardroom before. The installer arrived late on the 22d and discussed the installation procedure with the construction manager. They concluded that they would use expansion bolts in the concrete and wood screws in the platforms. Both the construction manager and the installer agreed that long lag screws could not be used since the platforms were elevated, with electrical conduit underneath.

After installing a few chairs on the morning of April 23d, the installer and construction manager concluded that the wood screws would not hold. Since the chairs were rigid, the smallness of the diameter of the base was insufficient for the torque applied to the base when the chair was used. Since no adequate support was designed into the floor when the room was remodeled, other support alternatives had to be evaluated.

The construction manager contacted the field representative of Peter Tropper and explained the problem. Peter Tropper indicated that toggle bolts were required. As a check on the architect, the construction manager called the furniture manufacturer in Pennsylvania. The call provided no additional information. The manufacturer's service representative stated that since they were not directly involved, they were unable to make suggestions. The representative did state, off the record, that the base was too small for the chair.

The installer, even after installing the toggle bolts, discovered that the chairs were still coming loose. In addition, the expansion bolts, installed in the concrete, would also eventually work loose. However, with the upcoming board meeting on May 6, 1989, the construction manager and installer agreed that the chairs could be used temporarily. The supplier, after discussing installation costs with the installer, told Tom Dewey that the current bill for setting up the chairs would be around $4,000. However, for the installer to do the job correctly would cost an additional $15,000.

The May 6 board meeting went smoothly, although many board members noted the instability of the chairs. In June, the executive directors expressed concern over the need to fix the chairs—and quickly. However, Tom Dewey's frequent discussions with Peter Tropper had yielded no results.

The installer billed ABCO Furniture at the end of May. In late June, Tom Dewey received a bill from ABCO for the installation of the chairs, and a copy of the invoice received by ABCO from the supplier. Tom Dewey recognized that BBI had not allowed for any additional installation costs and wondered what the best way to resolve the problem would be.

1 What alternatives are open to Tom?
2 What is the best course of action now?
3 Who is responsible for the present situation?
4 What should Tom have done to avoid the present situation?

BRONX BUSINESS MACHINES CORPORATION

The Bronx Business Machines Corporation (BBM) was in the process of developing a new, smart personal computer. The first working prototype was planned for release in ten months. The design-to-cost objective was $600 for the 5,000th unit, with a planned production run of 1 million units.

A thorough make-or-buy analysis had been conducted. One of the more costly items studied in the make-or-buy analysis was a radically new input/output (I/O) device. The design-to-cost analysis allocated $100 per unit for the device. The make-or-buy analysis concluded that BBM should buy the

I/O device. Based on limited experience with similar but less sophisticated devices, it was estimated that contractual development costs would be in the range of a half million dollars.

Due to staffing problems, June Oster (a newly promoted procurement manager at BBM) was handling the procurement of the R&D work. She had

---

EXHIBIT 1 TIGERTRONIX CORPORATION
Skunk Hollow, Arkansas

---

1 April 1989

Ms. June Oster
Procurement Manager
Bronx Business Machines Corp.
32 White Plains Avenue
New York, New York 10036

Dear Ms. Oster:

We are pleased to submit our proposal for development of a smart input/output device. If we are able to begin work by April 15, we will be able to provide two prototype models by February 1, 1990.

We understand the confidential nature of the work and agree not to release any data to individuals not employed by your company.

We have submitted the cost breakdown data you requested. The total of our projected costs and profit is $621,000. We will be pleased to answer any questions you may have, while being sensitive to the time constraint under which we both are working.

In the interest of time, we are willing to enter into a cost reimbursement production option with a target cost of $100 per unit for the first 10,000 units of production. With this cost history, we then would be in a position to enter into a firm fixed unit price contract based on our production experience with these first 10,000 units.

Very sincerely,

Ron Cox
President

Attachment: Proposal

ATTACHMENT
ESTIMATED R&D COSTS

Engineering

4,000 hours @ $30/hour	$120,000

Supervisory

600 hours @ $50/hour	30,000
SUBTOTAL	$150,000
Overhead 250%	375,000
G&A 10%	15,000
SUBTOTAL	$540,000
Profit	81,000
TOTAL	$621,000

contacted five firms that had the capability of developing the I/O device. Two firms declined to participate in the project. The third indicated that it would be delighted to proceed with the development on a no-cost basis, provided that BBM would purchase a minimum of 100,000 devices. Production costs for these units would be based on a fixed price redeterminable contract, with the ceiling price to be negotiated on completion of the R&D portion of the work.

Ms. Oster received proposals for the R&D work from the remaining two firms. One appeared to be either a get-rich-quick proposal or a courtesy bid (she was not sure which—and really did not care) of $1 million. The other proposal was from the Tigertronix Corporation of Skunk Hollow, Arkansas. Tigertronix had been founded five years before by four engineers who had worked together at a large electronics firm in Beaverton, Oregon. The new company had expanded to 450 employees, had sales of $50 million, and enjoyed an excellent reputation in the I/O industry.

Ms. Oster met with Freddie Ready, vice president of marketing at Tigertronix, to discuss development of the new I/O device. She indicated BBM's desire to pay for the development so that it would own any patents and data rights, including procurement specifications. Ms. Oster also indicated her desire to enter into an R&D contract which included a fixed price incentive option for production. BBM would retain the right to complete the production work. Obviously, the R&D supplier would have good insight into the costs and nuances of production.

On April 1, Tigertronix submitted a proposal. (See Exhibit 1.)

1 If you were Ms. Oster, what action would you take? Why?

BROTHERS MOWERS

In 1958 the Stanley brothers pooled their efforts and experience to form Brothers Mowers. The company began with production of a single hand mower. The business has grown to include a full line of manual and motorized mowers and motorized gardening equipment including blowers, hedgers, and rototillers. Despite its growth, the company has remained virtually family-run; relatives and family friends have held important positions within the organizational structure. The company has never been an industry leader or even a top competitor. Yet it has managed to provide an adequate profit and retain its independence.

In January 1990, the company was given a shock. Uncle Phill, the head of procurement for the past 22 years, died unexpectedly from a heart attack early in the month. Rod Stanton, a graduate of the University of San Diego, was hired later in the month to replace Uncle Phill as the new procurement director. On his arrival, Rod observed that late supplies sometimes caused breaks in production. He also saw that rework and scrap seemed excessive. Rod figured he had three to four months to "clean up" the procurement function before the increased demand during the winter months became a burial rather than a harvest.

The corporate managers at Brothers are graying, and more new hires are expected. Employees are skeptical of, if not averse to, changes. They fear the company will lose sight of its family origins. The employees are comfortable with the current situation, and the corporate managers were satisfied with Uncle Phill's operation of the procurement function.

Rod Stanton saw an opportunity to clean up the procurement process. Brothers Mowers' limited use of standardized parts prompted Rod to review the numerous routine orders placed with suppliers. Rod found that many of the suppliers had been used for ten to twenty years and were directly linked to one product or model. He sensed that efficiencies that could be gained by using fewer suppliers of standardized parts. Realizing his relative newness at the company, he was cautious not to suggest anything he couldn't support. Discussions with his cousin, Sam, who had worked in engineering for five years, indicated that minor redesign of each product line would allow utili-

This case was developed by Mark A. Sonna and Susanne Thieback under the direction of Professor David N. Burt.

zation of many more standardized parts. Although this approach would be contrary to the current practice of ordering nonstandardized parts for specific models within each line, Rod realized that it would create an opportunity to decrease the variety of parts ordered as a result of the design simplification.

One month after assuming his new position, Rod now has a meeting with the department heads to review his first month on the job. Rod has what he feels are some valuable suggestions. He believes that design modifications are required to utilize simplification and standardization techniques; however, he realizes that his suggestions may fall on deaf ears because of the change-resistant nature of the company.

Rod seems to be in a sensitive position. What suggestions would you offer him in response to the problems he anticipates?

1 How can Rod suggest solutions to problems when the people whose co-operation he needs don't realize that the problems exist?
2 How can Rod get engineers to redesign a whole line of products when sales are healthy?
3 How can Rod propose changing from trusted suppliers of ten to twenty years to new suppliers of standardized products?

CAPITAL EQUIPMENT PURCHASING

In November 1989, James Sampson, manager of central purchasing, Celebrity Electronics Group, in Somerville, California, wondered what action to take. Supplier quotations had been reviewed for a vacuum chamber and significant differences existed among the four finalists.

CELEBRITY BACKGROUND DATA

Celebrity was a manufacturer of electronic equipment, systems, and components for markets in the United States and other countries. In 1988, sales and revenues were $6.2 billion, with net earnings of $321 million.

The company was organized into sectors, groups, and divisions, with essentially a decentralized management structure.

The Celebrity Electronics Group specialized in the research, development, and production of advanced electronic systems and equipment for the U.S. Department of Defense, NASA, and commercial users, both domestic and offshore. The Communications Division, Radar Operations Division, and Strategic Electronics Division, which made up the Group, each had a separate organization for purchasing production material. Because all operations were located in the greater Los Angeles area, a central purchasing organization bought capital equipment, new construction, maintenance, repair, and operating supplies.

For major capital equipment procurements, the manager of central purchasing and representatives from finance, quality assurance, and the test equipment facility organization made up a source-selection team. The team, under the leadership of the manager of purchasing, was responsible, according to procedure, to evaluate supplier proposals, select a supplier, and prepare an appropriate justification memorandum recommending the supplier.

An appropriation request was reviewed by the local general manager and his staff and, based on current approval levels, forwarded to the corporate offices in Los Angeles, California, for approval by a committee of senior corporate executives.

NEW FACILITY PROCUREMENTS

A new, large facility was to be constructed in the Somerville area to provide production capability for new projects. Central purchasing was deeply involved in purchasing equipment for the facility.

One important item was a thermal vacuum chamber, 10 feet in diameter, capable of simulating the vacuum, heat, and cold of deep outer space. The specifications were developed for this custom walk-in chamber by Celebrity engineers, and were within current technological understanding and capabilities. The chamber would test components and systems that would be sent into outer space. In addition to the 10^{-14} atmospheres vacuum, the chamber had to cycle between the extremes of heat and cold that hardware is subjected to in the deep space environment.

Because of the extreme vacuum involved, the speed in achieving the vacuum was important since the energy cost to operate the chamber increased rapidly as the time increased. There were also safety considerations. A catastrophic failure of the chamber could cause severe personal injury as well as heavy damage to the building.

The chamber had to be delivered in 14 months after release of the order. Beyond that point, construction of the building would have progressed to the extent that the chamber could not be installed before the building's last wall was completed. If delivery were late, construction would be halted on the building. It might be possible for work-around construction to continue in such a case, but additional costs would be involved.

SUPPLIER DATA

On receiving the specifications for the chamber, James Sampson prepared a request for bid for ten potential suppliers. Based on various input and evaluations, the list was pared to five companies. (The following table lists the suppliers' proposals.)

Supplier	Location	Quotation in 000's	Delivery
A Rayard Air Products Co.	Peabody, MA	$1,101.5	14 Months
B MRT Engineering Inc.	Chicago, IL	1,051.1	14 Months
C Houston Chambers Co.	Houston, TX	561.8	12 Months
D Engineered Environments	Danbury, CT	No Bid	
E The Wiston Group	San Diego, CA	1,008.0	14 Months

Each of the suppliers reportedly had successfully constructed chambers similar in design and requirements to the one Celebrity was purchasing.

The evaluation team studied the technical proposals at some length. The Rayard submission was very complete and included photos of similar installations. The pump-down time was forecasted to be slightly better than the others. The MRT Engineering proposal was technically sound. Their conditions of sale, however, provided the customer little recourse in the case of late delivery. Six years earlier they had been five months late on a delivery of a critical system to Celebrity.

The Houston Chambers Company's technical proposal was not complete and could not be fully evaluated. Some team members questioned whether the supplier understood the specifications or had been unable to develop the full details in time for the proposal. The low price was also a concern.

The Wiston Group proposal had arrived somewhat late and seemed hastily prepared. Its technical proposal offered no advantages or disadvantages. It was technically less detailed than the Rayard Air Products proposal.

The evaluation team had been impressed with the presentation and completeness of the Rayard proposal. James Sampson was concerned about the spread in the pricing and the fact that a qualified supplier had not bid. He wondered if he should have the team probe further.

One thing was clear; in two weeks, a request for appropriation with a supplier recommendation was supposed to be submitted to the general manager. It would take four or five days to prepare. If construction were delayed, Sampson estimated added construction costs could run from $5,000 to $10,000 a day.

1 Outline in step-by-step fashion the actions you suggest James Sampson take in handling this matter. Discuss the significance of each.

A CASE OF TOO MUCH HELP

Nancy O'Leary, senior buyer at the Northfield Unified School District purchasing department, sat reflecting on a purchase requisition (P.R.) she had just received. The P.R. called for 1,000 model 2001 classroom arm chairs, manufactured by the Twinsburg Chair Company. The P.R. was requested by Betsy Burns, instructor, and authorized by Rudolf Rupp, principal. Sufficient funds and the budget class were cited. A copy of a sales agreement for the chairs was attached. The price was $120 per chair, F.O.B. Northfield. Nancy reviewed three other chair suppliers' catalogues and learned that nearly identical chairs were available F.O.B. Northfield at prices ranging from $40 to $43.

Nancy called Betsy Burns and asked whose idea it was to specify the Twinsburg chairs, mentioning that this chair was nearly three times as expensive as three comparable chairs. Betsy responded in her Georgia drawl, "Why, Nancy, darlin, the superintendent's cabinet decided that at last week's meeting. They said that they wanted the best there was for our young people."

Nancy thanked Betsy for the information. Based on past experiences with the superintendent's cabinet, she knew that it would be futile to get authorization to buy the less expensive chairs. In a resigned manner, she called the Twinsburg rep and requested him to visit her to discuss the terms of the purchase.

Something did not seem right...but Nancy seemed powerless to do anything about it.

1 What courses of action are open to Nancy?
2 What are the advantages and disadvantages of each?
3 Write a policy for the school focusing on early purchasing involvement.

THE CENTENNIAL COMPANY

The Centennial Company manufactured small electrical appliances for the consumer market. Its major product line consisted of several models of electric shavers for both men and women. The shaver division generated over 90 percent of the firm's annual sales, which ran at approximately $30 million last year.

Several years ago the company introduced a new shaver model that proved to be extremely successful. The model utilized a new microscreen-type head that produced an extremely close shave. During the design stage of the new product, the marketing department had conducted an extensive consumer survey to determine exactly what style and color combinations best suited the market for this innovative new product. The style finally selected was an extremely modish plastic case with a sleek futuristic contour.

From a cost and pricing point of view, the new product fit the company's basic operating strategy very well. Over the years, Centennial had become known as a manufacturer of low-cost, high-quality products. The firm typically priced its products 15 to 20 percent below its major competitors. This pricing policy was made possible, in part, because Centennial was basically a design-and-assembly-type operation that purchased a majority of its parts and components in large volumes from specialty manufacturers and supply houses. Centennial's production facilities were highly automated so that its labor cost was relatively low; last year, material costs ran approximately 65 percent of net sales.

During the past six months, Centennial's material costs had been increasing at a level significantly higher than the Producer Price Index for finished nonconsumer goods. Indirect labor costs and overhead also had also begun to increase. Consequently, the firm's profit margin and its return on investment had begun to drop off noticeably. Several members of the firm's top management team thought that Centennial should reconsider its basic pricing policy. The possibility of a 5 to 10 percent price increase was being contemplated. The vice president for sales, however, resisted a price increase because he thought it might erode the low-cost, high-quality image the firm had developed in the marketplace. The result, he thought, could well be a significant loss of economy-minded customers.

Each of the Centennial department managers was asked to consider possible approaches to the resolution of the cost-price squeeze issue and also to prepare a brief report on possible cost cutting/productivity improvement measures that could be undertaken in their respective departments. The manager of the purchasing department was asked in his report to pay particular attention to the matter of material costs and efficient utilization of departmental personnel.

1 As a purchasing manager, what is your responsibility concerning top management's knowledge and expectation of the purchasing operation?
  a What performance data should management have been receiving?
  b What information is necessary to control material costs?
2 What types of suggestions might the purchasing manager make in his report that would be worth exploring? Making several reasonable operating assumptions (also assume the current profit margin is 5 percent), quantify the estimated results from a profitability point of view.

COLLIER COMPANY I

The Collier Company is a large electrical manufacturer. Recently, a new division of the company was started, and entirely new facilities were required. In equipping the new plant, it was decided that for certain subassembly operations it would be desirable to have production employees seated at high stools instead of standing at their work benches. Eight hundred and fifty employees were to be so seated in the new plant.

After investigating many possible stool designs, the plant engineering department and the personnel department agreed on a certain style of stool that was easily described to the trade as "Carter's 816 or equal." Bids were requested by purchasing from most major fabricators of this type of item, and bids from nine suppliers were received more than ten days before the announced closing date.

Several days before the final bid date these suppliers started to call the purchasing manager to see how they ranked. The purchasing manager answered their questions honestly with phrases like:

"You are not low bidder, but you are fairly competitive."

"You are not low bidder. You are way out of line."

"You are presently low bidder, but others seem to be revising their bids."

By April 23, the day originally chosen to close bidding, every supplier except vendor C had submitted at least one revised quotation. (See Exhibit 1.) In most cases, the prices quoted were substantially below the initial bids.

Late in the afternoon on April 23, two suppliers asked for special permission to make a final bid on April 24. Since these two firms had been satisfactory suppliers of the Collier Company for years, the purchasing manager was anxious to give them any opportunity to keep their facilities operating in the depressed conditions that then characterized their industry. He gave them a special extension of one day. By the next afternoon, the purchasing manager had heard from three more firms who wanted the same privileges as the two concerns who had rebid. Firms kept asking for special extensions or equal bid privileges until the purchasing manager finally said to all who called that May 7 was the last day he would entertain bids. On May 7 several suppliers asked for special permission to bid late and were refused. Vendor C still had not called in to change its original bid.

By May 7, the purchasing manager felt that all the firms were bidding at less than their total costs in order to keep their facilities operating at the highest possible volume in this slack period. He also felt that further price adjustments would be negligible. However, not wanting any vendor to go out of pocket on the order, the purchasing manager asked the plant engineers to make a cost estimate on the chairs. The engineers estimated costs as follows:

EXHIBIT 1
UNIT PRICES QUOTED BY VENDORS

	Original bid	April 23 bid	May 7 bid
Vendor A	$55.92	$41.10	$34.08
Vendor B	44.70	37.50	31.62
Vendor C	39.48	39.48	39.48
Vendor D	45.36	35.88	30.06
Vendor E	43.86	38.58	31.98
Vendor F	38.70*	37.92	29.88*
Vendor G	39.00	35.40*	30.60
Vendor H	42.78	39.60	31.50
Vendor I	48.60	41.34	33.18

*Indicates low bid.

Labor	$12.00
Materials	13.62
Overhead: 150% of direct labor	18.00
Total cost (excluding profit)	$43.62

Having satisfied himself that all vendors were making some contribution to overhead at the quoted prices, the purchasing manager awarded the order to vendor D, who had done business with the Collier Company in the past and was considered one of the best fabricators in its field.

On May 9, two days after *making the award*, the purchasing manager heard from both vendor C and vendor F.

Vendor C was extremely angry that he had not been told of the acceptance of new bids. He said that he would write a letter to the vice president of material requesting a review of this "entire deplorable situation." The purchasing manager informed vendor C that reasonable follow-up on the latter's part would have given him any information available to other potential suppliers. Vendor C was not at all satisfied with this answer and again expressed his intention to contact the vice president of material.

Vendor F asked why the purchasing manager had requested bids at all if his "mind had been made up all along." Vendor F said that the order should have gone to the lowest bidder who could provide the object desired. He said he could meet the specifications and could deliver to any schedule vendor D could meet. He demanded the order, and, when the purchasing manager informed vendor F that "final selection of the supplier is entirely my province," the vendor raged that he would "spread the word to the trade" and would write the Collier Company president, who "should know of such favoritism and incompetence." The vendor stated that he suspected that money had passed hands for this order.

The purchasing manager was upset by these calls and did not enjoy his supper on May 9.

1 What suggestions might you have made in the purchasing manager's handling of this matter?
2 What would you recommend that he do now?
3 To what extent would you concur in the purchasing manager's belief that suppliers should at least be allowed to recover direct costs?
4 Who do you feel should have received the order?
5 What are the weaknesses inherent in the competitive bidding process?
6 Should this purchase have been negotiated? Discuss.

DONLEY BROTHERS

The Donley Brothers Company had encountered the problem of latent defects in some of its purchased castings. Being latent, the defects did not show up until after machining had taken place at Donley Brothers. This group of failures greatly irritated the manufacturing boss, who declared that "repairing those darn castings is eating up all our profits."

When the defects were discovered, the rough casting had to be taken off the machine, the defect chipped out, repair welded, and the casting remachined when possible. Even with this process, almost 12 percent of the incoming castings ended up as scrap. Actually, 1,140 raw castings had to be purchased and machined in order to produce 1,000 good machined ones. The raw castings cost $600 each from either of two suppliers. Worse than the costs associated with rework and high scrap rates were the continual changes in production scheduling necessitated by a machined casting not being available as scheduled. These changes were costly because they required shop personnel to tear down the job they were working on and set up a new job. Marketing was constantly complaining about the firm's inability to meet delivery commitments for the finished machinery that incorporated the castings. Marketing claimed that many sales were lost as a result of this failure.

George Donley, the production manager, and Terry Donley, the vice president for marketing, asked Bob Donley, the purchasing manager, to investigate the costs involved in purchasing finished machined castings. If finished castings were purchased, the responsibility for finding hidden defects would be that of the supplier. Such action would encourage the supplier to improve the casting quality. Donley Brothers would accept and pay only for finished, usable castings.

The internal cost of machining each incoming rough casting and repair welding and remachining it, as necessary, was approximately $312 per casting. This figure included $156 of direct labor and $156 of overhead. The accounting department estimated that overhead, which was 100 percent of direct labor, consisted of 50 percent variable and 50 percent fixed costs. No estimate was available on the cost of disrupted production schedules and operations.

Bob approached all his major suppliers of castings in an attempt to generate interest for the supply of finished machined castings. Only one supplier, Akron Foundry, showed genuine interest. Of major concern to all the foundries was the $120,000 to $160,000 investment necessary to set themselves up to machine the raw castings. Akron was willing both to invest in the necessary machines and to guarantee delivery of up to 150 units per month—provided Donley Brothers would contract with it as a sole source for the castings for the next three years. The price per casting would be $1,000 the first year, with an annual increase or decrease in price tied to an appropriate economic index.

Bob was faced with the problem of deciding whether to recommend contracting with Akron Foundry for finished castings, continue as in the past buying rough castings, or developing a more attractive alternative. The Donley machine shop was currently operating at 90 percent of capacity, but it was not possible to make a reliable estimate of what would happen in the next few months, let alone the next three years. The decision of whether to

buy finished castings was of major dollar importance to Donley Brothers because the firm used at least 1,000 finished castings per year and anticipated
that this usage would continue for each of the next five years.

1 Should Bob Donley contract with Akron Foundry for finished castings?
2 Would there be any dollar savings by contracting with Akron Foundry if
the Donley Brothers' machine shop were operating at full capacity?
3 What are the dangers involved if Akron Foundry becomes a single source
for Donley Brothers' castings?
4 Who is responsible for the make-or-buy decision?
5 What other suggestions can you make for improving the situation at
Donley Brothers?

THE DUTZEL DIESEL CASE

Jack Haley, a senior buyer for the Dynamite Truck Company, was confronted
with an interesting predicament—and possibly a trip overseas. Rising gaso-
line costs and increased foreign competition had caused the management at
Dynamite Truck to develop a new truck powered by an air-cooled diesel engine.

From bumper to tailgate, the new vehicle was designed as a full-
performance diesel truck. It was heavy-duty throughout: frame, suspension,
brakes, axles, and steering. It was built to endure. Under normal operating
conditions, the new truck, using an efficient air-cooled diesel engine, was designed to yield 18 to 20 miles per gallon. The warranty was for 100,000 miles
or two full years, whichever came first.

Jack had been actively involved in the development of the new truck. He
provided the Dynamite engineers with information on the availability and
cost implications of various materials, components, and subassemblies under
consideration. From a technical, cost, availability, and service point of view,
the diesel engine was the most crucial item to be purchased for the new
truck.

Jack obtained technical data on four air-cooled diesel engines that appeared to satisfy Dynamite's requirements. Two of the manufacturers of
these engines were located in Europe, one in Japan, and one in the United
States.

Discussions with the program manager indicated that from a technical
point of view, each of the diesel power plants was acceptable. Accordingly,
all four manufacturers were invited to submit bids. The request for bids stipulated an estimated requirement of 10,000 engines per year for each of the
next three years.

The date specified for the close of the bidding period was Friday, June 13.
All four firms submitted bids by the established date. Dutzel Diesel of
Gailsdorf, the Federal Republic of Germany, was the low bidder with an

F.O.B. destination price of $14,263 for the first year, and a standard price escalation clause for the second and third years. The second lowest bidder was a U.S. firm, the Great American Diesel Company. Its price bid for the first year was $16,287 per engine. The price for the second and third years contained the same economic escalation clause as Dutzel's bid.

Jack sat contemplating a course of action. He wondered if the $2,024 per unit price differential required to buy the U.S. engines could be justified. He also wondered about the necessity of a trip to Gailsdorf to perform a survey on Dutzel prior to awarding the contract.

1 Do you believe that foreign purchasing is destined to give purchasing managers and buyers an increasing number of problems? Discuss.
2 What is the easiest way for buyers to start making foreign purchases?
3 If you were Jack, how would you decide this issue?

DYNAMIC AIRCRAFT

The Dynamic Aircraft Company was recently awarded a multibillion dollar contract for a new high-performance aircraft. This project required the use of new materials in many areas of the aircraft. The aircraft incorporated a state-of-the-art concept known as fly-by-wire.

Among the conventional materials no longer useful were many of the types of wire used in the electrical systems of aircraft. Fortunately, however, the electrical wire manufacturers had been brought in on the problem at an early date so that, before long, many of them could offer for sale a standard stock electrical wire capable of withstanding unusually high temperatures.

One leading electrical wire firm, Advanced Wire of Chattahoochee, Georgia, had developed a ceramic-coated wire. Other wire sources had tackled the problem in different ways. The representatives of all these companies were anxious to demonstrate their products to the engineering departments of the aircraft companies.

The engineers at the Dynamic Aircraft Company, a large airframe manufacturer, were quite favorably impressed with Advanced Wire's ceramic-coated wire. They knew from previous experience that Advanced Wire had a reputation as a quality supplier of electrical wiring for the aircraft industry. Believing that Advanced's wire was the highest quality obtainable, the engineers specified it on the bill of materials.

Bill Marshall bought wire and related items for the Dynamic Aircraft Company. An experienced buyer, Mr. Marshall had a reputation for being conscientious and knowledgeable concerning the commodities that he purchased. When the requisition came to him to buy Advanced's ceramic-coated wire, he immediately wondered why Advanced Wire had been designated as a sole source. From his experience in buying wire, he knew Advanced to be a high-cost producer. Moreover, he always attempted to follow the Dynamic Aircraft Company policy of dealing with more than one source whenever possible.

Believing that engineering may have been "sold a bill of goods" by the Advanced sales representative, Mr. Marshall decided to telephone the engineering department to learn what specifications governed the wire in question. Mr. Marshall did not want the engineer he was telephoning to think that, despite the fact that the current instance was typical of a number of similar instances, he was in any way censuring him for specifying Advanced Wire as a sole source. The engineer explained that the wire was of a special nature, designed to withstand extremely high temperatures. He also said that Advanced's wire was the highest quality obtainable and that in his judgment, it should be purchased to fill the current need.

Mr. Marshall pointed out to the engineer that there were many thousands of types of electrical wiring. He said that all of these types were made according to some sort of specification—either military specifications, wire industry specifications, or specifications established by the purchaser. Mr. Marshall also said that a rule of the Dynamic Aircraft purchasing department required a buyer to know about any governing specifications before issuing a purchase order. After a few more minutes of conversation, the engineer said that he would attempt to locate the governing specifications and send them over to Mr. Marshall.

In the meantime, Mr. Marshall got in touch with the local representative of Advanced Wire to request samples of its ceramic-coated wire and price quotations. When the quotations were submitted. Mr. Marshall felt that once again Advanced's prices were higher than those of the industry in general. Yet he realized that this particular wire might well be a more expensive item to manufacture as a result of its ceramic-coating feature.

Several days later, Mr. Marshall received the specifications for the wire. The specifications were of the military standard type and listed the performance requirements that the wire was to meet. They said nothing about whether the wire was to have a ceramic coating. Accordingly, Mr. Marshall solicited quotations from the other qualified suppliers and asked that samples be submitted to him that would meet the performance requirements of the specifications.

Five other suppliers submitted samples and price quotations. On receipt of the samples, Mr. Marshall forwarded the samples, along with Advanced's sample, to the production development laboratory of Dynamic Aircraft for analysis and evaluation. The production development laboratory was under the direction of Dynamic Aircraft's inspection department and was separated both physically and organizationally from the engineering department.

A week later the report of the production development laboratory was in Mr. Marshall's hands. The samples submitted by the six suppliers had undergone exhaustive tests, particularly with regard to their ability to withstand high temperatures for prolonged periods of time. One of the suppliers was eliminated from consideration when its product failed to meet performance specifications. The other five samples, including Advanced's, were found to exceed minimum performance requirements, and at extremely high temperature ranges the ceramic coating of Advanced's sample made it superior to the others.

With regard to the weight of the samples (another important consideration), Advanced's wire was found to be heavier than the others. Furthermore, the conductivity characteristics of Advanced's wire were rated as inferior to the other samples, although all the samples exceeded the minimum performance requirements and were rated as acceptable. On the abrasiveness test, Advanced's wire was found to be slightly less durable than the other suppliers' samples but, nevertheless, acceptable.

These laboratory findings tended to confirm Mr. Marshall's belief that the engineering department had been sold a bill of goods in specifying Advanced as the sole supplier. The samples submitted by four of the other suppliers had met the governing military specifications and in some ways were superior to Advanced's. While Advanced's wire withstood higher temperatures, Mr. Marshall saw no need to pay a premium price for it since the wire supplied by the other suppliers met the specifications that engineering had submitted to him. With regard to price, the Easternhouse Electric Company was the lowest bidder and Advanced was the highest. The high and low bidders compared dollarwise as shown in Exhibit 1 on the quantities to be purchased.

The delivery schedules required by Dynamic Aircraft posed no particular problem since all five of the qualified suppliers seemed capable of meeting required delivery dates.

The laboratory report and the price quotations were then sent by Mr. Marshall to the engineering department, along with a request that the purchasing department be authorized to place the order with any company that could meet the military specifications.

The engineering department refused Mr. Marshall's request, maintaining

EXHIBIT 1

Size	Advanced price (per 1,000 ft)	Eastern-house price (per 1,000 ft)	Quantity to be purchased (in 1,000 ft)	Advanced total price	Eastern-house total price	Difference in total price
20 gauge	$ 55.20	$ 21.00	100	$ 5,520.00	$ 2,100.00	$ 3,420.00
12 gauge	102.00	50.40	70	7,140.00	3,528.00	3,612.00
10 gauge	124.60	76.90	120	14,952.00	9,228.00	5,724.00
8 gauge	243.60	129.60	40	9,744.00	5,184.00	4,560.00
4 gauge	399.90	248.40	20	7,998.00	4,968.00	3,030.00
Totals				$45,354.00	$25,008.00	$20,346.00

that Advanced was the only company that could manufacture wiring that would meet the requirements of Dynamic's engineering department. The engineers stated further that since Advanced had been the first company to develop this particular wire, the purchase order should be placed with it. In conclusion, they reiterated their claim that Advanced had a superior product that would justify any price differential.

1 If you were Mr. Marshall, what action would you take now?
2 Should Mr. Marshall have challenged the engineering department's specification of Advanced's wire?

EAGLE MACHINE COMPANY

The Eagle Machine Company has fallen on bad times. Eagle, a maker of specialty restaurant equipment, has sales totaling $72 million, but sales are declining while costs continue to increase. If things continue in this direction, Eagle soon may have to close its doors.

At a special management meeting, the president lays it on the line! He demands that the firm break even in the remaining quarter of the year. For next year, he calls for profits of 5 percent, a 20 percent increase in sales, and deeper cuts in labor, material, and overhead. Later in the day, the president calls Sally Stone, director of purchasing, in for a discussion.

"Sally, I want you purchasing people to carry the ball at the start of this game. We can't get sales moving for six months. But you can improve your housekeeping—and Eagle's profits—right away. Just think what you can do to that chart! Every penny you save is profit! So take a close look at what you buy. I don't care how you make your savings—by negotiations, inventories, imports, anything. But put the screws on tight—right away!

"Start with inventories, they're sky-high. So get together with manufacturing on a 10 percent cut! We've got $12 million worth of materials stashed away around here, and a 10 percent cut would save at least $300,000 a year in carrying charges. At the same time, get your payroll and operating expenses down 10 percent. That's in line with our companywide cutback. I know this hurts, Sally, because you've got some mighty fine people here in purchasing, but we can't be sentimental these days. Our overhead has got to come down—or we're dead!

"I'm having an executive committee meeting in one week. Have your plans ready by that time! We're betting on you, Sally. You've got to get us out of the hole. I know you can do it."

Sally Stone starts a review of her purchases, which total $43.2 million per year. Eagle buys a wide variety of materials, ranging from a few pounds of rare metals to sizable quantities of sheet metal. A big part of the dollar volume is in nonferrous castings, forgings, stampings, fasteners, and subassemblies.

Her department consists of Sally, three buyers, and four clerks. Salaries, fringes, and expenses come to $370,000 a year. The purchasing department is responsible only for buying and expediting; the manufacturing manager handles production, inventory control, receiving, and traffic. Sally reports to the president, as do other department heads.

Sally learns from inventory control that raw stock inventory is $12.2 million. The marketing manager controls finished goods stocks.

Sally wonders how she can deliver the cost reduction and still keep her department and supplier relations in shape for the long pull.

1 What actions should Sally take to reduce inventories by 10 percent?
2 What dangers, if any, are there in reducing inventories?
3 In what ways could the cost of goods purchased be reduced?
4 What position should Sally take on the president's plan to reduce the purchasing payroll by 10 percent?
5 Develop a list of arguments in support of, and another list in opposition to, the introduction of a materials management organization at Eagle.

ERIE MACHINE, INC.

Erie Machine, Inc., is a small machine shop that derives the bulk of its business from large- and medium-sized copy machine manufacturers. The major part of Erie's work is building prototypes from rough blueprints. From time to time, production runs have been undertaken; however, Erie's machines, layout, and space do not lend themselves to line production.

In the ten years of its life, Erie Machine, Inc., has grown continuously. Employment has increased from 35 to 282 employees, and the company is very successful. A new treasurer, Ray Grabit, has just been hired. Ray, a young man seven years out of college, is full of new ideas and questions. One of the questions bothering him is the company's method of disposing of its scrap metal.

Because of its type of specialized manufacturing, Erie Machine does not use a large quantity of metal. However, it does use several types including iron, steel, Monel, lead, copper, and brass. The total usage of all types generates about 12 tons of scrap per year. Roughly 10 percent of this total is brass and copper.

At the end of each day the metal scrap, together with wood and paper waste, is placed in a trash bin. The bin is emptied by the Lake Erie Sanitation Engineering Company three times a week.

Ray is curious about this procedure. Could the company realize some value by salvaging and selling its scrap?

1 Would a small quantity of metal be worth the trouble of setting up a good procedure to handle it?
2 If so, who should be responsible for managing such surplus material?

FOUR SQUARE LUMBER MILL*

Jon Johansen was the supplies buyer at Four Square's Valdosta plant. One day he sat examining a traveling requisition (TR) card for ten carborundum saw blades. The specified blade was made in Switzerland and obtainable through a mill supply house in Birmingham at a cost of $225 each, F.O.B. Birmingham. Jon observed on the TR that some 110 blades were ordered a year. The requisition specified that no substitutes were permitted. Even so, Jon decided to see if any money could be saved through alternative sourcing. He contacted two of his better mill supply sources to see what they could do.

Both suppliers indicated that the Dipson 412 blade was every bit as good as its Swiss counterpart. Based on an annual purchase of eighty or more blades, one supplier quoted a unit price of $112.50 per blade. (The second supplier's price was $115.00.) Both prices were F.O.B. Valdosta.

Jon then contacted Sam Sharpe, the foreman of sawing operations at Four Square. Jon explained the potential savings and asked Sam to give the American blade a try. Sam was certain that the Dipson blade would not stand up to the Swiss blade. After several minutes of trying to convince Sam of the desirability of buying the Dipson 412, Jon said that he thought that they really should give it a try. Sam left in a good humor saying, "O.K., but I know it won't work."

Jon ordered ten Dipson blades. He included a provision that any unused blades could be returned for credit if the Dipson did not prove to be equal to the Swiss blade. Two days after the blades arrived, Sam entered Jon's office. Sam was grinning from ear to ear, holding a saw blade in each hand. Both blades were burned as a result of the excess heat generated during the cutting operation. Jon was convinced that the boys in the yard had treated the blades unfairly to ensure that they would fail.

1 What could Jon have done to avoid this situation?
2 What should Jon do now?

FRICH TURBO ENGINE COMPANY†

Mr. Fingold, a buying supervisor at the Frich Turbo Engine Company, was responsible for the purchase of valves and other items for low-pressure assemblies in the company's engines. He had handled numerous valve procurements and had found that the designs were subject to considerable variation. He had found it useful, therefore, whenever he was required to initiate

---

* Copyrighted by the Purchasing Agents' Association of Connecticut, Inc. Reprinted by permission.
† Copyrighted by Harbridge House, Inc. Reprinted by permission.

procurement of a new design, to make an estimate of the probable cost of the item from historical costs of similar equipment and from his own wide experience with machine shop practice and with conditions in the industry. He found that this method enabled him to question vendors' cost estimates effectively and to negotiate good prices even on initial procurements, with a corresponding saving in subsequent purchases of the same item.

In February, Mr. Fingold received a purchase request for 10,000 low-pressure valves of a new design. The engineering department was proud of the new design, which called for a valve made largely of stamped parts to replace an older type of valve that had involved a number of casting and machining processes. The last procurement of the old valve in November had been at a unit price of $2.64, and it was anticipated that substitution of the new process would result in a considerably lower unit price.

Mr. Fingold realized that prospective suppliers for the procurement would include a group different from his usual suppliers and decided for that reason to make an extremely careful estimate of the probable cost. After performing research and analyzing the processes and materials to be used, he arrived at a figure of approximately $1.74 per unit as a reasonable price for the item, made up as follows:

Material	$0.448	
Direct labor	0.344	
Manufacturing overhead	0.516	(assumed to be 150% of direct labor)
Tooling	0.192	
General and administrative	0.0752	(assumed to be 5% of total cost)
Profit	0.1576	(assumed to be 10% of total cost)
Selling price	$1.7328	

Meanwhile, requests for proposals were sent out to eighteen companies. The closing date for submission of proposals was set at May 1. By the middle of April, Mr. Fingold had received thirteen proposals, of which nine were in the range from $1.84 to $2.08 per unit, while the other four ranged from $2.32 to $3.04. Mr. Fingold was pleased with the indication that his estimate had "pegged" the low range of quotations. As each of the quotations came in, he examined each vendor's cost breakdown with a view to points for questioning and negotiation. Between April 20 and 23, however, two more companies submitted proposals. One of these, the Bayfleet Machining Company, quoted a unit price of $1.232, and the other, the Union Stamping Company, $1.488. Mr. Fingold was surprised, to say the least, at these low figures, and was inclined to think that they represented unrealistic estimates. On investigation, however, he found that both vendors were large, well-established metal forming companies with good reputations for satisfactory performance on previous contracts. The cost breakdowns for the two low proposals are reproduced below.

	Bayfleet Machining	Union Stamping	Mr. Fingold's estimate
Direct material	$ 0.344	$ 0.408	$ 0.448
Subcontracted parts	0.080	—	—
Direct labor	0.288	0.400	0.344
Manufacturing overhead	0.296 (103%)	0.304 (76%)	0.516 (150%)
Tooling	0.104	0.232	0.192
General and administrative	0.064 (6%)	0.024 (2%)	0.0752 (5%)
Profit	0.056 (5%)	0.120 (9%)	0.1576 (10%)
Selling price	$ 1.232	$ 1.488	$ 1.7328

1 What factors might have caused the variance between Bayfleet's quotation and Mr. Fingold's estimate? Between Bayfleet's quotation and Union's quotation?

2 In light of your answer to the above question, what conclusions can you draw concerning (a) the reliability and usefulness of cost estimates made by the buyer, and (b) the value to be gained from the comparison of one vendor's quotation with that of another?

FUTRONICS, INC.

In July 1989 Steve Hastell, purchasing manager of Futronics, Inc., was studying the replacement of the company's central office stores by an outside service. Futronics, located in Lexington, Massachusetts, was in the midst of a corporate overhead reduction program. As part of this program, Steve had been assigned the task of reviewing opportunities in outside sourcing for in-house services. He was expected to report on the central stores issue at the next program meeting in three days.

FUTRONICS' COST REDUCTION PROGRAM

Futronics was a $2 billion firm with sales in consumer products and government systems and services. It enjoyed high overall growth until fierce competition flattened sales and decreased profits sharply two years ago. By mid-1989, corporate cost and overhead reduction efforts were widespread. The purchasing department sought savings by increasing emphasis in existing areas as well as by participating in corporatewide cost reduction team programs. The central stores operation came under review when two outside firms approached Steve's department with initial proposals to replace Futronics' stores operation with their own inventory and delivery service.

Copyrighted by the National Association of Purchasing Management. Reprinted by permission. This case was written by Joseph L. Cavinato during one of the NAPM-sponsored case writing workshops.

CENTRAL STORES

Central stores at Futronics was created in the middle 1950s when a corporatewide study revealed that large savings would result from bulk buying and distribution of stationery and all other supplies. A central group was formed to serve Futronics' twenty-one area sites. While it represented an increase in manpower, facility, and delivery expenses, large savings resulted through reduction in individual office inventories, mass buying, and decreased purchase order expenses.

By 1989, central stores served forty-two area sites from a warehouse in Lexington. Annual throughput was about $900,000 and the average inventory was valued at $140,000. Over 500 items were stocked. A catalogue of items was updated and distributed every six months. Four people worked in the operation: two as pickers, one order entry clerk, and one to wrap, label, and load trucks. Activity was slightly seasonal, with peaks occurring in December with demand for calendars and at the end of quarter budget periods for other items. The cost of the personnel and space was about $200,000 per year. Deliveries were made on a daily basis with a corporate truck that handled corporate mail and other interplant movements. These deliveries were made to the building docks or reception areas. Corporate stores were part of Corporate Administrative Services, which also included food service contracting, security services, and personnel.

Service complaints in the form of lengthened order times (e.g., specific letterhead stationery took three to four weeks, while other items required ten to fourteen days) were common. It also took a long time for stores to implement the acquisition of new items. Post-Its, for example, were not added until five months after they were on the market. Split deliveries also were common. Up until this time it was generally believed by Steve and his boss that the economies of this system were still better than any other alternatives, but this conclusion had never been verified.

OUTSIDE SERVICES

The idea of investigating outside stores services arose in June when two firms approached Steve's shop with general proposals. These proposals coincided with a top-management mandate in May for all departments to seek and implement reportable savings by year end. Steve heard through outside contacts that other firms in the Boston area were reducing both expenditures and overhead costs by these means.

By June, Steve had in hand initial proposals from Litton, Boise-Cascade, L. E. Muran, Bay State Office, and New England Supply. The initial information provided by the suppliers included:

1 Sample catalogues
2 Price lists
3 Ranges of costs for certain delivery/volume configurations

A line item analysis by Steve's assistant showed that about 90 percent of the 500 currently stocked items would be available at less cost. On the average, the promised savings would be about 6 percent. Furthermore, the suppliers' proposed catalogues included about 600 items each.

All five firms sought three-year contracts with options for renewal. The firms would provide their own specially printed catalogues in unique binders. Order cycle times were promised to be no longer than ten working days, including specially printed letterheads. Deliveries would be made directly to each secretary. The use of special preprinted order forms with the most common items was suggested in all proposals.

Steve, his manager, and others in the review group had some concerns about the outside service idea. These ranged from the uncertainty and risk of the idea to the reduced control over the process. Questions arose over the profit to be made by the outside firms. Greater mass buying power gave these firms pricing advantages. Steve did notice, however, that overhead transparencies, an important item to Futronics, were priced in the $39–45 range in the proposed catalogues. Futronics currently enjoyed a better price of $23 per box. All the proposed contracts would lock in Futronics for three years. The four people in central stores either would be redeployed to other jobs in the company or laid off. One of these four people was physically handicapped and worked in a wheelchair.

DEADLINE

Steve's job was to develop an analysis of the concept behind the initial proposals and to recommend dropping the idea or requesting complete proposals. He felt that by this time there might be political momentum to adopt the idea of outside sourcing and elimination of Futronics' central stores. He wanted to make sure the review group would not compare the worst features of the current situation to the best of the proposed ones. His deadline was the next meeting of the corporate cost reduction team, three days hence.

1 Assume you are Steve Hastell. Prepare an analysis and report on this issue for presentation at the next program meeting.

GOLDEN BUFFALO, INC.

Ruben Gomez is the purchasing manager of Golden Buffalo, a publisher of text books. Golden Buffalo's sales were $45 million last year. Ruben's department purchases paper, printing equipment, and office and printing supplies. From time to time, it contracts for the printing of a Golden Buffalo book. Purchasing reports directly to the general manager. Ruben attends all weekly management meetings along with the manager of marketing, the director of operations, the director of acquisitions, and the finance manager. These weekly meetings are more or less "bull" sessions. Apparently, the general manager, George Zinke, is satisfied with the operating results and the information picked up in the meetings.

The purchasing department consists of Ruben, three buyers, an expediter, and three clerks. Department salaries and operating expenses run about $280,000 per year. Purchasing spent $18 million last year.

Ruben recently attended a National Association of Purchasing Management seminar where he became impressed with the need to market purchasing's contribution to the well-being of the organization. This need for marketing was emphasized when the speaker reported on two incidents wherein purchasing managers had seen their department reorganized under manufacturing. The speaker maintained that both purchasing managers were competent. The major problem appeared to be that they had failed to publicize their department's contributions to their firm's success. Even before returning from the seminar, Ruben began to wonder what information he should report and how he should report it.

1 What information should Ruben Gomez report to his fellow managers at the weekly meetings?
2 What information should Ruben report directly to the general manager?

HARDY COMPANY

The Hardy Company manufactures small electrical appliances, including electric shavers, electric mixers for the home, blenders, and irons. The company had recently introduced a new line of electric shavers for women. In the product design stage of the new product, the sales department had conducted an extensive marketing research survey to determine exactly what style-color combinations best suited the market for this new product. The style finally selected was an extremely modish plastic case with an entirely new shape of cutting head.

Unfortunately, no commercially available fractional horsepower motor could be fitted into the desired style of case. It was, therefore, necessary to have a supplier develop the required motor.

The vice president of purchasing of the Hardy Company, Mr. Monaghan, discussed the problem with the sales representatives of several of Hardy's best motor suppliers. One of the persons contacted was the sales vice president of the Centennial Electric Company, which had been one of Hardy's suppliers for years and was known to have one of the best developmental groups in the small motor field. In his conversation with Mr. Monaghan, the

Copyrighted by the Purchasing Agents' Association of Connecticut, Inc. Reprinted by permission.

Centennial Electric vice president expressed confidence that his firm could do the job, and he even roughed out a proposed method of attacking the problem.

Mr. Monaghan and the engineering manager were so impressed by the approach of the Centennial Company, as compared to presentations of the other companies contacted, that it was decided to award the development work to Centennial. In setting up the contract for this development work, it was discovered that the Centennial Electric Company had a rigid policy of billing separately for developmental services only on government contracts. For all other work, the Company recovered development costs through sale of the motors developed. Consequently, the shaver motor was developed by Centennial on a "no charge" basis simultaneously with the product design work at Hardy. Centennial was very cooperative and made several modifications to the original design specifications. Finally, ten handmade motors of the final design passed rigorous quality control checks by Hardy engineers. These motors were also provided on a "no charge" basis.

A purchase contract was then placed with Centennial Electric for the first production run of 100,000 units. The price of the motors was slightly above the price of a standard motor of equivalent horsepower ratings, but Mr. Monaghan felt that the differential was certainly not enough for Centennial to recover the entire development cost over the run of 100,000. He knew that Centennial had also made a sizable additional investment in special tools, dies, and fixtures for this motor.

The shaver was a great success and another 100,000 units were produced in the first year. Centennial had been given the order for these motors on a proprietary basis when it quoted a price equal to the price of standard motors of the same horsepower rating. A blanket order of 150,000 units for the second year's production was also awarded to Centennial without competitive bids.

When the contract for the third year's production was being considered, sales representatives of four different companies requested the right to bid on motors for the shaver. One salesman was very indignant and said that his company had been discriminated against all along and that he knew that his company could make a better motor for the job and sell it for less than Centennial's price. Although Mr. Monaghan felt that Centennial had done an excellent development job and was providing good service on the contract, he wondered how long he should allow Centennial to have this business on a proprietary basis. He was certain Centennial's price was not substantially out of line, but he was not at all certain that Centennial had recovered all of its investment in development, tools, dies, and fixtures.

1 Do you feel that the purchasing of this motor was properly handled? How would you have handled it?
2 Should the Hardy Company have solicited competitive bids on this item?
3 What would you do if you were in Mr. Monaghan's position now?

HOLY CROSS HEALTH CARE, INC.

BACKGROUND

Holy Cross is the largest health care provider in the Pittsburgh area. It has over 1,100 beds and numerous outpatient clinics spread throughout the city. This dominant size has been achieved through extremely rapid growth during the past three years. All buildings are new or have been recently remodeled to meet state and federal safety requirements.

Current market conditions are extremely competitive. Contributing factors include: an increasing number of patients without health care coverage, a growing number of HMOs (Health Maintenance Organizations), and recent funding cutbacks by government and insurance companies. Technological advances have had a major impact as well, with each hospital seeking to obtain the most up-to-date equipment. State-of-the-art equipment is a major factor in attracting and maintaining a pool of qualified doctors who admit their patients for care. In spite of a growing population, all major area hospitals are feeling the cost/revenue crunch due to the number of organizations competing for a relatively limited amount of revenue.

Holy Cross is one of two area hospitals performing heart transplants. Although it is a nonteaching organization, the hospital encourages new procedures and readily acquires state-of-the-art equipment.

SUPPLIES

Holy Cross previously had utilized a JIT process in obtaining supplies. As the organization grew, problems of stock-outs and shortages plagued operations as demand outstripped the supply system.

Twenty suppliers were dealt with on a regular basis, but the majority of supplies were purchased from only five firms, usually at substantial quantity discounts. Further complications resulted when all but one major supplier relocated to Philadelphia, frequently extending delivery times to over seven days. Management decided that new procedures and personnel were needed to solve these continuing problems.

JOE JONES

One management tactic had been to establish an off-site warehouse for medical supplies. Joe Jones had been hired as the warehouse manager overseeing seven young high school graduates as stockroom personnel. A typical day consisted of $100,000 worth of supplies coming into the warehouse, with approximately 80 percent being distributed within the Holy Cross system. Several things accounted for the remaining $20,000 of supplies. Employee theft

This case was written by Alex Miskiewicz and Lisa Wiethorn under the direction of Professor David N. Burt.

was a problem, though Joe had no idea how extensive. Other area hospitals frequently ran out of supplies and came to the warehouse, paying a 5 percent markup. Finally, some supplies were delivered damaged and were returned to the manufacturer.

When Joe first started working for Holy Cross, only 800 different items were delivered to the hospital. As the hospital grew through the acquisition of other institutions, the supplies used by the new facilities were kept in use following acquisition. An examination of warehouse inventory revealed over 20 different brands of tape, as well as duplication of a number of other items. Over 6,000 items were now stocked in the warehouse. Joe's only guidelines were to prevent shortages by keeping the warehouse adequately stocked, and to screen for items that were slow movers (those not used at least once in 30 days). A computer system was used to monitor inventory levels and to project reorder points for frequently used items. Periodically, Joe scanned a computer-generated master inventory list (nearly 5 inches thick) to identify materials not used within a thirty-day period. These items were then reported to the materials management coordinator, who acted as a liaison with the Joint Standards Committee.

The warehouse items were delivered to each facility in bulk on an "as required" basis.

JOINT STANDARDS COMMITTEE

The Joint Standards Committee consisted of twenty-five members from all the major departments of Holy Cross. (See Exhibit 1.) Several members had been on the committee since its inception and attended the monthly meetings regularly. Others found the meetings too time consuming and attended only when the discussions had a direct impact on their department. The committee exercised final approval prior to deleting an item from the master supply list, but this action was seldom taken. Political interests prevented committee members from effectively controlling the exploding growth of the warehouse.

SUPPLY PROCUREMENT

New items were added to the master inventory list by hospital staff, who submitted a request form to the purchasing department. The request form contained a brief description of the item and the intended use. These forms often were generated following visits from sales representatives to the various hospitals and doctor's offices within the Holy Cross system. Such requests frequently included specifications unique to a given sales representative's product, complete with all necessary ordering information conveniently included. Since the numerous requests were rarely for high dollar amounts, purchasing tended to rubber stamp the majority of these requests to keep the medical personnel happy and to expedite the paperwork.

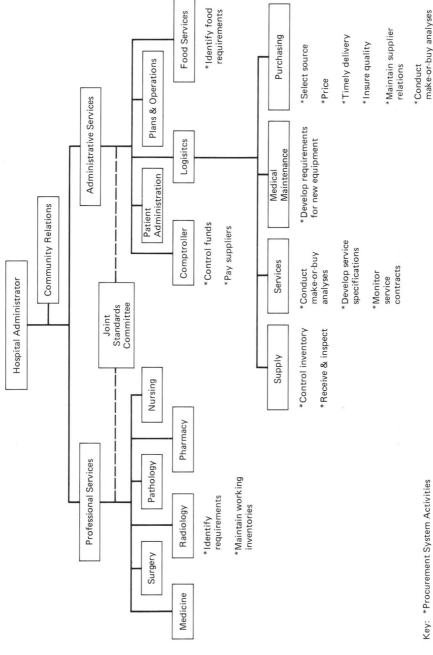

Key: *Procurement System Activities

EXHIBIT 1
Holy Cross organization structure.

To avoid political friction, the Standards Committee rarely raised any questions about the requests.

Joe had little time beyond his daily routine but felt that the current supply system was not the best fit for the needs of the hospital. He wanted to come up with some major cost saving ideas to present to top management before being handed one that didn't include him.

1 Identify the major issues that need to be addressed in this situation.
2 What additional information would be useful in developing a solution to the materials management problems at Holy Cross?
3 Assume you are engaged as a consultant in this case. Prepare an outline for a report to management including:
   a A definition and analysis of the problems.
   b Suggested solutions for each of the problems.
   c Recommendations and suggested guidelines for implementation.

JULBERG, INC.

Julberg, Inc., was a manufacturer of computer output microfilm (COM) devices. These devices transfer data from a computer directly onto microfiche storage and retrieval systems. Banks and insurance companies were the principal users of COM. Julberg was the leading firm in this market, and sales were $150 million per year. Its product line included ten different models of processors, ranging in price from $75,000 to $500,000.

The purchasing department at Julberg was responsible for purchasing approximately 20,000 different parts needed to manufacture the firm's processors. Mechanical parts, tubes, resistors, transistors, and keyboards were typical of the items purchased. The department consisted of fifteen buyers, five purchasing services clerks, and the purchasing manager. The buyers' experience ranged from two to thirty years with varying levels of education. The younger members of the department had degrees in business or engineering while the senior buyers had less education. Several of the senior buyers had worked their way up from manufacturing, receiving, and inventory control. The purchasing manager possessed an M.B.A. and three years of purchasing experience. Previous to this job, he had held a supervisory position in inventory control. His current job required him to oversee the day-to-day functioning of the department and to perform some purchasing duties.

Under the present manual system, considerable time and effort were required to perform supplier selection and price analysis activities. Ideally, information would be gathered on potential suppliers' past performance, including their prices, their ability to meet delivery dates, and their history on

This case was developed by Julie Goldberg of the University of San Diego.

quality (based largely on the number of defective parts received per shipment). In order to compile this historic data, the buyer would have to go through several file cabinets and manually combine separate reports from purchasing, receiving, inspection, and the stockroom. Often, if a decision on a source had to be made in a hurry (the normal situation at Julberg), the buyer would rely on his or her memory.

At the present time, due to the heavy workload, such detailed analyses were the rare exception. Very little research on alternate suppliers and little negotiation were taking place. Further, most purchases were being made using Julberg design specifications. There simply was no time or resources available to study the material specifications and perhaps search for alternative materials, as a good value analysis–oriented buyer should do. The purchasing manager believed that the present procedures were resulting in material costs that were approximately 10 percent higher than should be the case. (An outside consultant offered the observation that the firm was paying 25 percent more than it should for its purchased material.)

One bright day in January, after a careful analysis of potential cost savings, Julberg's parent corporation decided to purchase and implement an on-line microprocessing system for the materials functions at all of its subsidiaries. This data processing and storage system would aid management in decision making. Furthermore, the system would automate routine, repetitive tasks. For example, if a buyer wished to place an order for a part, he or she could have the computer list all the firms that had previously supplied the item. The computer would rank the suppliers' past performance based on price, ability to meet delivery schedules, and history of percentage rejects.

To develop this database, purchasing, receiving, inspection, and stockroom personnel at each subsidiary would enter data regarding the price and status of all purchases as well as information resulting from receipt, inspection, and issuance of ordered material, into the computer databank through the use of a microprocessor (a "smart" terminal). Such a terminal would serve as an input/output device, with the capability of editing input and formatting output data. The database then would be available instantaneously to all individuals requiring it. Purchasing, as a by-product of preparing the purchase order, would input data via the department's microprocessors into the computer data system. In effect, each such input would be the basis for developing a new data file. Purchasing's input would include the name and address of the supplier, the purchase quantity, price, and accepted delivery date. When the ordered material arrived, receiving would enter the date and quantity of material received. Inspection would check the material for compliance with purchasing specifications and enter the number of acceptable parts into the database through its microprocessor. The stockroom would record the fact that the parts were available for distribution to manufacturing.

Robert Hanson, the purchasing manager, was charged with the responsibility of overseeing the implementation of the new system. Both the hardware and software had been purchased by Julberg's parent company from the EZ Computer Company of Chicago. In early September, Mr. Hanson, together with the chiefs of receiving, inspection, and stores, flew to Chicago for an intensive week of instruction on the new system. They all returned eager and enthusiastic to get the system implemented. Mr. Hanson felt confident that the new system would cut materials costs by at least 10 percent.

During the time the team was in Chicago, rumors began flying concerning potential implications of the computerized system. None of the purchasing personnel had much experience or training in the use of computers. Previously, several individuals had worked in other companies that were in various stages of computerization. These employees spoke of the problems that had occurred during the changeover from manual to computerized purchasing. "That is one of the reasons why I finally left," recalled one of the younger buyers. He continued, "I never trusted the information the computer gave me. It seemed like the receiving and inspection departments were never up to date in entering the latest data about shipments into the computer."

A week after returning from the training session in Chicago, Mr. Hanson called a meeting of all purchasing personnel to inform them about the new computer-based system. He began by outlining some of the functions the new system would perform. He continually emphasized that the system would free the buyers from much routine paperwork and give them time to get out and talk with their users and suppliers, research their purchases, find substitutes, and negotiate with suppliers. The buyers appeared to be bewildered as Mr. Hanson talked about the new tasks they would be performing with the aid of the computer. They seemed totally lost when he used terms like "on-line," "CRT," "query the database," and "end-user." Mr. Hanson ended the meeting by saying that management expected the buyers to be able to reduce the prices paid by Julberg by 10 percent as a result of being freed from routine clerical tasks.

The purchasing manager was completely unprepared for the ensuing reactions. "Well, I for one sure would not like a machine telling me who to buy from," said one buyer. "I do not want to have to call a supplier I've been dealing with for years and tell him, 'Sorry, my computer tells me not to buy from you anymore.' So much for supplier relations!" Another buyer who had worked in the purchasing department for twenty years said, "What's wrong with the way we've been doing things? All management has ever wanted us to do was to get parts ordered and delivered on time. And now they want us to research materials, to go out and talk with our customers, and to become negotiators! I have no interest in such activities. It sounds to me like this computer is trying to put me out of a job!"

The chiefs of receiving, inspection, and stores were waiting to see Mr. Hanson when he returned to his office. Phil Woods, chief of inspection, said, "I just had a meeting with my staff to tell them about the computer and our new system. Boy, were they unenthusiastic. It seems they feel that they should not have to change the way they do their jobs in order to put data into a computer for your guys in purchasing. They're happy with just filling out all the old forms."

Sid Brown, chief of receiving, said, "Yeah, my people are afraid that they are going to become slaves to a machine."

Robert Hanson sat speechless, feeling the walls close in. The smart terminals would be arriving in three weeks. Suddenly, he did not feel at all well.

1 What weaknesses are evident in the present materials system?
2 How can these weaknesses be minimized or eliminated by the use of a computer-based operating system? Develop a plan.
3 What is the basic problem confronting Robert Hanson?
4 What should or could Mr. Hanson have done to improve communication with his subordinates?
5 How could the material personnel's resistance to the computer be overcome?

LAXTEC, INC.

COMPANY BACKGROUND

Laxtec, Inc., is a subsidiary of a Texas-based company that manufactures surveillance cameras. Laxtec's main function is to manufacture the motor and arm that rotates the cameras. Laxtec is located in Illinois.

Laxtec, Inc., has no individual ethical regulations, nor does it have an ethics team within the organization. Laxtec's parent company, however, has an ethics staff within corporate headquarters that deals with questions of ethics for its employees. The corporate headquarters does not take an active part in exercising ethics requirements in its subsidiaries due to staff limitations.

SITUATION

Laxtec has been directed by its parent company to manufacture a new arm that will rotate 360 degrees instead of the present 180 degrees.

Since Laxtec is operating near full capacity and cannot extend its resources to design and manufacture the special motor and control unit needed for the 360-degree specification, it has decided to subcontract this project.

Knowing that there were only a few companies that would be able to design and manufacture the arm, Peter Ferdenzi, president of Laxtec, instructed Larry Morris, director of procurement, to inform the bidders that there were many companies bidding for the contract. This would insure that the bids received were competitive.

This case was developed by Brian Kopf and Debbie Sinopoli under the direction of Professor David N. Burt.

One out-of-town bid and three local bids were received. Mr. Ferdenzi called Larry into his office to discuss them. Larry told Mr. Ferdenzi that the out-of-town bid from Aster Company appeared to be the most favorable. But Mr. Ferdenzi told Larry to discard it because he wanted to subcontract the motor within the area to enhance business and social relationships with the community. Out-of-town contracting would only cause friction among the workers. The out-of-town bids, explained Mr. Ferdenzi, were simply to obtain pricing information.

Larry looked over the remaining bids and explained that Prextel was the next best choice, then Gordon, Inc., and lastly Tomos Corporation. Larry was familiar with the Tomos Corporation and told Mr. Ferdenzi that it had been involved in questionable business activities and was being investigated by the local authorities.

Mr. Ferdenzi looked sternly at Larry when he heard the Prextel bid was the best and told Larry to discard it. Mr. Ferdenzi's ex-wife was the director of the research and design team at Prextel and relations between the two were difficult, to say the least.

Finally, Mr. Ferdenzi agreed to award the bid to Gordon, Inc. Mr. Ferdenzi told Larry to negotiate the specifics with Gordon. Mr. Ferdenzi also told Larry to delay notifying the other bidders of the award until two weeks after production had started with Gordon. In this way, it would not be necessary to listen to the other suppliers "beg" for more consideration.

Negotiations between Gordon and Laxtec were finalized and production started. A problem arose within the second week, however, when Laxtec's quality representative noticed that the materials being used were not of the quality standard stated in the contract.

Larry immediately called a meeting with Gordon, Inc. During the meeting it became apparent that there was a lack of honesty in the development of Gordon's bid. Further, Gordon's attempt to use substandard materials was an attempt to increase profit. Larry realized that Laxtec could not rely on Gordon, Inc. He stated that he would cancel the contract based on fraud. Gordon, wishing to avoid any litigation and bad publicity, agreed and passively backed out.

Luckily, at Mr. Ferdenzi's direction, Larry had not notified the other bidders of the award to Gordon. Larry met with Mr. Ferdenzi again and recommended that Prextel be awarded the contract. Mr. Ferdenzi refused and ordered Larry to meet with Tomos and negotiate a contract.

THE DILEMMA

Larry called Chuck Moore, president of Tomos, for a meeting the next day. Chuck knew that if Laxtec wanted him to negotiate a contract, it must be in desperate need of someone. Accordingly, Chuck told Larry that a donation to the Tomos pension fund would make things much smoother in the negotiations. Larry brushed the comment aside and finalized the meeting time.

Larry told Mr. Ferdenzi about the pension fund. Mr. Ferdenzi simply shrugged his shoulders and told Larry to pay Chuck since it was essential to have Tomos accept the contract.

Larry was unsure of what to do. In his last two jobs, he had refused to participate in similar activities and was fired on both occasions. That was when he was single. Now Larry had a house and two children to support.

1 Is it ethical to:

- Tell suppliers that there are many bidders?
- Delay telling unsuccessful suppliers of an award?
- Void a contract on the basis of dishonesty?
- Allow companies to bid even though they would not be considered for the contract (out of towners)?
- Refuse to award on the basis of personal relationships?

2 How important is it to have written procedures dealing with ethics in a company?

3 What should Larry do?

LION INDUSTRIES

In early 1986, Lion Industries was awarded a $1 billion ten-year contract by the Boeing Aircraft Company. The contract stated that Lion was to provide specific engine components for the CF680C2 engine. The engines were to be used on the Boeing 747 and 767 aircraft.

The award was important for several reasons. First, it provided an opportunity to participate in what was anticipated to be a contract with significant follow-on potential. That potential was extremely important to Lion in its efforts to stabilize the cyclical nature of its commercial aircraft revenues. Additionally, Boeing represented approximately 32 percent of Lion's business. A sound performance by Lion would help solidify a strong business relationship.

The major assembly being supplied by Lion was the propulsion system casement, or nacelle. Part of the assembly consisted of a titanium precooler duct, used to direct the hot engine exhaust out of the engine into the atmosphere. Titanium was specified, since it functions well when subjected to high temperatures, as well as being lightweight.

However, titanium also possesses characteristics that make it difficult to work in manufacturing. It requires superordinate heat to get the metal from its elastic to its plastic state. The duct was made by using "hot form" technology. The process entails the application of heat to the metal such that it

This case was developed by John Araneo, Paul Beelman, Tom Donnelly, and Yuki Marsden under the direction of Professor David N. Burt.

would assume the contour of the master tool. The manufacturing problem was to ensure that a sufficient amount of heat was applied for a sufficient duration. If the process was not exact, the metal would not assume the desired contour, because as it cools it tends to rebound to its original state. Additionally, the assembly, after "hot forming," must be welded. Titanium is difficult to weld. The welding environment must be purged of all atmospheric gases; otherwise, the integrity of the fusion would be jeopardized.

Lion performed a make-or-buy analysis on the duct shortly after receipt of the contract. For many years, Lion had the reputation of being a leader in sheet metal forming. However, Lion's production personnel privately stated that they "wouldn't touch" the precooler duct due to its "tricky" titanium configuration. The decision was made to competitively bid the project.

The duct was to be made according to Lion's drawing specifications. On reviewing these drawings, a number of sources declined to bid. Only two suppliers, Polytek and Sennes, submitted proposals for the part. The bids, F.O.B. Lion plant, were as follows:

	Unit Price	Non-recurring	Lead Time	Location	Union
Polytek	$4,500	$300,000	52 wks ARO	Grand Rapids, MI	UAW
Sennes	$6,500	$500,000	52 wks ARO	Moorpark, CA	AFL-CIO

Preaward surveys were performed on both suppliers. The source selection team, comprised of personnel from engineering, finance, quality, and purchasing, chose Polytek as supplier on the basis of submitting the low bid (as the two suppliers appeared to be fairly equal in other key areas of concern). Due to the excessive nonrecurring charges, Polytek was to be the single source of the item.

Due to the complexity of the unit, some problems were anticipated. Lion's production requirements called for only one unit per month through fiscal year 1988, to allow Polytek a lengthy developmental period before going into actual production. However, beginning January 1989, the production rate would be increased to six per month.

The initial units, as anticipated, had numerous quality and producibility problems. In spite of this, however, Lion was able to fulfill its commitments to Boeing through fiscal year 1988, primarily due to the low production rate. Various Lion engineering and quality personnel regularly visited Polytek to advise and instruct Polytek personnel, yet no real headway was made. Quality problems persisted, although the supplier contended that the problems were temporary in nature. However, months of "coaching" by Lion engineering failed to correct these inadequacies.

In October 1988, it became apparent that the supplier lacked the ability to produce at the rate of six per month, which Lion had promised to Boeing beginning in January of 1989. Polytek simply could not progress from the developmental phase to the production phase. A team of Lion employees, representing purchasing, engineering, and quality, were sent to the Polytek plant to review the situation and make recommendations. The team found that Polytek's basic tooling philosophy for manufacturing the parts was at fault. The errors were of sufficient magnitude to require rework, but it was agreed that Polytek did not have sufficient production expertise. Further, quality procedures were being circumvented. It also became clear that Polytek was having difficulty in supporting other customers, primarily due to quality and producibility problems.

Lion was less than three months away from being in a position where it could not support delivery requirements to Boeing due to lack of availability of the precooler ducts. Purchasing scrambled to identify options. Sennes was still interested in the program, but refused to shorten its lead time or decrease its $500,000 nonrecurring charge. In addition, the earliest it could supply units would be November 1, 1990.

The sentiment internally at Lion had shifted somewhat since 1986. While stating that the configuration was a troublesome one resulting in many uncertainties, production personnel felt that the duct could be made at a unit cost of $5,000. Nonrecurring expenses would total $400,000, and the duct could be supplied at a rate of six per month in 40 weeks. The general consensus among nonproduction personnel was that these projections were ambitious and overly optimistic.

Lion purchasing once again solicited additional suppliers, but none showed interest in the design. The options seemed to be fairly clear—and very limited.

The buyer, Harvey Smidlapp, was perplexed by the situation. He had been given the assignment of reviewing the possibilities and providing a recommendation for upper management within forty-eight hours. Harvey wondered if it was possible to support Boeing's needs. And he wondered how he could best protect his company's liability and cost in doing so.

1 How should the buyer approach the situation with Polytek?
2 Should the company consider alternate sources of supply? Discuss.
3 What corrective actions would you recommend to preclude another occurrence of this situation?

MAINE-BARNES, LTD.

Maine-Barnes was a successful small firm that had carved out a profitable niche in the electronic office products field. A proposed new line of sophisticated professional calculators currently posed some manufacturing problems for the firm because of limited shop capacity. Josh Purdy, the firm's purchasing director, was asked to investigate the possibility of subcontracting one of the components to an outside source—and then to prepare a make-or-buy recommendation for the general manager.

Maine-Barnes was located near Boston in the heart of a high tech manu-facturing community. The firm's success was due primarily to its ability to produce high-quality specialty products designed for particular professional uses by engineers, architects, medical researchers, financial analysts, and so on. Product technology in the field was undergoing continual change. As a result, product prices had dropped markedly during the past two years, and competition in the market was keen and fast paced.

The proposed line of new calculators was designed to be highly price com-petitive. Consequently, the units were powered by a permanent rechargeable battery. This meant that each unit was sold with a small plug-in recharging unit. Although the recharger increased the initial cost of the unit somewhat, the user realized significant operating cost savings during the life of the product. In addition to an attractive life-cycle cost, Maine-Barnes was bank-ing on several unique proprietary design features of the calculator and the recharging unit to generate a high demand for the new product line. Unfor-tunately, the new design features were not patentable.

Despite the general manager's optimistic views for the new product line, the marketing manager was unable to forecast demand for the new units with what he considered to be a comfortable level of accuracy. Because of competition and rapidly changing technology in the industry, he was not willing to forecast first-year sales of more than 50,000 units. If the line was well received, he estimated that approximately 100,000 units could be sold in each of the two succeeding years.

Maine-Barnes had grown steadily during the past five years and was now operating near its manufacturing capacity. The shop manager cautioned that addition of the new calculator line would stretch the operation to its limit. In fact, further analysis revealed that the shop could handle no more than 75,000 new calculator units per year—and this was without producing the companion recharger units. If Maine-Barnes were to produce the recharger units too, it would have to invest approximately $84,000 in new equipment. The life of the equipment would be approximately twelve years. For tax pur-poses, however, the Internal Revenue Service would permit it to be depreci-ated over a seven-year period.

As a result of the preceding analysis, Josh Purdy requested bids from three former suppliers for the new recharger unit. All three were known to be competent and reliable; their bids are summarized below.

Bids on the Recharger Unit ($ per unit)			
Purchase qty.	Eastern Mfg.	Boston Electrical	D & A Mfg.
50,000	$8.15	$7.45	$7.82
75,000	7.68	7.12	7.45
100,000	7.06	6.79	7.10

In response to Josh's inquiry, all three firms indicated an interest in discussing the possibility of a three-year, single-source contract. All were willing to discuss bid prices further if a three-year deal could be worked out.

After reviewing the bid figures, Josh discussed the possibility of making the recharger in-house with the shop manager and the firm's chief cost accountant. Several days later, Josh received the following estimated cost data from the controller's office.

In-House Unit Costs to Make the Recharger	
Direct labor	$1.50
Materials	3.00
Factory overhead (110% direct labor)	1.65
Factory cost	6.15
General administrative and selling expense (10% factory cost)	.62
	$6.77 per unit

Notes:
  1 Materials cost includes a 20 percent internal material handling cost.
  2 Factory overhead is estimated to be 35 percent variable and 65 percent fixed.

After studying the cost estimate, Josh was not certain that it was complete. For example, he wondered why an allowance of 15 percent had been made for scrap material but none for labor. He was also puzzled about the overhead figures. The controller indicated that there would be no reduction in overhead if the new equipment was purchased—and that the amortization of the new equipment would constitute an additional expense.

Josh was also aware that the firm's labor contract expired in several months. In the past, subcontracting work to outside suppliers had always been a sensitive issue with the union, although wage rates seemed to be particularly important this year.

1 What factors should Josh consider in conducting a make-or-buy analysis for this product?
2 Prepare a comparative cost analysis of the make/buy alternatives. Which cost elements should be investigated particularly carefully? Discuss thoroughly.
3 Prepare a complete report for the general manager, including the details of your analysis—and your recommendation.

MAZDA ELECTRONICS

Dennis Kwok had been with Mazda Electronics for twelve years, rising from a junior quality control officer to vice president, operations. He had seen the company grow as a manufacturer of monitor screens used in electro-cardiometers. In 1986, Mazda produced and sold about 200,000 units of its current model, the ME1001, at an average price of $150 per unit. The firm operates on a net margin of 5 percent and is in a marginal tax bracket of 50 percent.

A few months ago, Dennis met with Jackie Brown (V.P., marketing) and her marketing research group. Jackie indicated that a recently incorporated medical group was interested in installing 1 million electrocardiogram monitors over the next five years if the screens and frames could be supplied at an all-in-cost of $100 per unit.

Dennis shared this news with Larry McDonald in the engineering R&D department. Larry called back with some exciting news. Engineering was confident that a new model under development, the ME2001, would meet the buyer's specifications and could be manufactured at a variable production cost of $65 per unit provided it could use a special plastic frame designed by Burton Plastics, Inc.

Burton had approached Mazda's engineers with a prototype of a 9-inch supertough frame coated with a special chemical that made the frame more elegant and economical. Burton could manufacture 20,000 such frames per month, starting within three months, and offered a price of $30 per unit F.O.B. Mazda's plant, provided Mazda agreed to use the new frames exclusively for the next five years. This price of $30 per unit was incorporated in the $65 per unit variable cost estimate by engineering for the ME2001. The firm's cost accountant, Dirk Hageman, estimated that if 200,000 units of the ME2001 were sold, the allocation for fixed general, administrative, and marketing expenses of $4 million per annum would add approximately $20 to the cost per unit. This was based on the assumption that the ME1001 would be discontinued, which would have to be the case, since Mazda did not have the plant capacity to produce both the ME1001 and ME2001 simultaneously.

Dennis decided to call a meeting before a final decision was made on whether to replace the ME1001 with the new low-cost ME2001 model. He invited Jackie Brown, Larry McDonald, Patrice Regnier from manufacturing, and Jeff Meltzer of purchasing. Everyone seemed enthusiastic about the new low-priced model, which would also be the first of its kind in the market. Jeff, however, was not too happy that Burton would be the sole source of supply for the supertough 9-inch frame. As a former QC officer, Dennis expressed his concern about the quality of the new frame. On previous occasions he had experienced many unpleasant situations with exciting low-cost

This case was developed by Jimmy Anklesaria and David N. Burt of the University of San Diego.

developments that had failed to meet quality standards over long periods of use. Components that appeared to function well initially would then, for no apparent reason, develop defects that sent the whole process out of control. In his opinion it would take at least a year to effectively test the new component and stabilize the process. Jackie wasn't sure Mazda could wait that long. If it didn't sign the five-year contract with the medical group within six months, chances were that someone else would develop a monitor screen and frame for less than $100 per unit.

Patrice agreed with Dennis and indicated that there was a 10 percent probability that considerable testing and rework might be required by the production department if Mazda's quality standards were to be maintained. In the event the low-cost frame turned out to be defective, the cost of rework would turn the estimated profit contribution into a loss. More disastrous was the possibility that promised delivery dates might not be met. As a result, current sales, customer goodwill, and future business could suffer.

At the end of the meeting, Dennis was in a predicament. There were so many unanswered questions. And a decision on whether or not to proceed with the ME2001 had to be made.

1 Should Mazda Electronics proceed with the low-cost ME2001, incorporating the new frame developed by Burton Plastics, Inc.? Explain.
2 Who should be involved in the decision-making process? Who is ultimately responsible for the decision?
3 What additional information would you require if you were in Dennis Kwok's place?
4 What other issues related to this problem are of concern to purchasing and materials management?

MICROCOMP, INC.

Microcomp, Inc., is a rapidly growing manufacturer of microcomputers, located in the Silicon Valley of California. Since the company was incorporated in 1979 it has experienced an average annual growth in sales of 24 percent. The latest development in its product line is the MCD86, a 16-bit microcomputer that requires state-of-the-art microprocessors. Suppliers of microprocessors included Wedge Computers, Inc., Baker Bros., Synergistic Technologies, and La Playa. While Baker had just entered the market, Synergistic and La Playa had been in existence for over a decade, producing a range of computer peripherals. The firm expected to purchase its annual requirement of 100,000 microprocessors from Wedge Computers, Inc., which had recently developed a new microprocessor, the WC 8000. The main feature of the WC

This case was developed by Jimmy Anklesaria of the University of San Diego.

8000 was that it reduced the number of chips necessary to process signals from three to one. This made it more cost effective than most competing brands and also enhanced the marketability of the MCD86.

Jeff Neuber, the purchasing manager, had been with Microcomp since its incorporation ten years ago. Because of the critical nature of the product, Jeff decided to personally coordinate the preaward survey and participate in the negotiation process. To him, the preaward survey was a mere formality and he was not particularly excited about it. In his opinion, there was really nothing to interfere in negotiating a contract with Wedge Computers. Nevertheless, Jeff realized that such an analysis was an essential step in preparing for negotiations. He decided to seek the assistance of Art Traynor, production manager, Ray Zogob from industrial relations, Shannon Richey from finance, and Christine Bugelli, a senior buyer. The group visited the supplier's facilities in Palo Alto and met with their respective counterparts. The next day, Jeff sent out a memo to each of these persons requesting their individual opinion on the Wedge contract. (See Exhibit 1.)

A week later Jeff received the various responses. (See Exhibits 2, 3, 4, and 5.) He was not surprised by what Art, Ray, and Christine had to say. But Shannon's observations worried him. He took a look at the Balance Sheets (Exhibit 6) and the Income Statements (Exhibit 7) that Shannon had sent him. Although Jeff was not a finance person, he could see that the figures were not as rosy as one would have them appear to be. (For industry averages see Exhibit 8.) What would happen if Wedge ran into a cash shortage during the term of the contract? Suppose lenders were not willing to advance more money to the firm? First, that company's suppliers would not be paid on

EXHIBIT 1
INTEROFFICE MEMO

TO: Art Traynor, Ray Zogob, Shannon Richey, Christine Bugelli

FROM: Jeff Neuber, Purchasing Manager

SUBJECT: Preaward survey

We are about to enter into a contract with Wedge Computers, Inc., for the purchase of 100,000 microprocessors per annum over the next three years. Before entering into the final negotiation stage, I would appreciate your comments on the ability of Wedge to fulfill the terms of this contract, which you know is very important to us.

Please report back to me within a week. You will find copies of relevent documents pertaining to Wedge Computers with my secretary, Sandi Harrod.

EXHIBIT 2
INTEROFFICE MEMO

TO: Jeff Neuber, Purchasing Manager

FROM: Art Traynor, Production Manager

SUBJECT: Wedge Computers

I have examined the documents available on file and sent a team of engineers to the Wedge plant. In my opinion, the firm is fully equipped to satisfy our demand over the next three years. I was particularly impressed with the new equipment installed at a cost of about $5 million. This will increase Wedge's capacity from 400,000 to around 600,000 units per year. The production and quality control systems appear to be adequate, and I believe the firm should have no difficulty meeting our specifications.

time. Would they continue to supply the required raw material in that case? And what if the banks decided to foreclose on the loan secured by the new equipment? These were most disturbing thoughts. What appeared to be an open and shut case was now turning out to be a nightmare. And Jeff had just another week to make the final decision.

EXHIBIT 3
INTEROFFICE MEMO

TO: Jeff Neuber, Purchasing Manager

FROM: Ray Zogob, Industrial Relations

SUBJECT: Wedge Computers

Thanks for soliciting my opinion on the Wedge deal. As far as industrial relations are concerned, the management of Wedge seems to enjoy a cordial relationship with its employees. To the best of my knowledge there is no history of labor unrest in the company. Just last month management increased wages by 8 percent and offered a wide range of incentives to all categories of employees. The employees are not organized and there is little possibility that they will be in the near future.

EXHIBIT 4
INTEROFFICE MEMO

TO: Jeff Neuber, Purchasing Manager

FROM: Shannon Richey, Financial Analyst

SUBJECT: Wedge Computers

I have studied the Income Statements and Balance Sheets of Wedge Computers, Inc., from 1981 till 1985 and wish to make some observations that I hope will be of use to you.

—Sales have grown rapidly from $18.7 million in 1981 to $43.1 million last year. This indicates an average annual growth of 23.21 percent.

—Gross margins have remained close to 20 percent, but I am a bit worried about the decline in the net income after taxes in 1985. While most companies in the industry work on an average net margin of 7 percent, Wedge has failed to meet this figure so far.

—In the past year the firm has spent over $5 million on plant expansion, which I understand has been financed by a $3 million 14.5 percent loan from a local bank. Wedge will need to make five payments of $772,380 each year from January 1, 1987. The balance has been financed through the sale of ten-year 12 percent bonds.

—I am very concerned about the dramatic increase in accounts receivable, which have grown from $2.6 million in 1981 to $21.5 million in 1985. I checked with other companies in the industry and understand that it is an industry practice to allow sixty-days credit to valued customers like us.

Overall, in my opinion Wedge may have some cash flow problems in the near future. The company is heavily leveraged and may find additional borrowing difficult and very costly. I don't know why it is not able to collect money from its customers. I would proceed with caution if I were in your position. Let me know if you need any further information or explanation.

EXHIBIT 5
INTEROFFICE MEMO

TO: Jeff Neuber, Purchasing Manager

FROM: Christine Bugelli, Senior Buyer

SUBJECT: Wedge Computers

In response to your memo of June 21, 1986, I have no hesitation in recommending Wedge Computers, Inc., as a supplier of microprocessors for the next three years. We have studied the bids of three other firms and Wedge's bid of $103 per unit is 10 percent below the next lowest bidder. We investigated the sources of raw material used by the company and are confident that the firm has an adequate source of silicon wafers enhanced with aluminium oxide, which are the main raw materials used by it. I was very impressed with the procurement system at Wedge and especially by the purchasing manager, Richard Cleary, who has a proactive approach to purchasing. The new machines have been installed and are really great. Let me know how the negotiations go. We can't afford to lose this potential source.

EXHIBIT 6
WEDGE COMPUTERS, INC.

Balance Sheets as of December 31 (Dollar amounts in thousands)

	1981	1982	1983	1984	1985
Cash	533.90	1232.00	1736.40	2328.70	594.30
Accounts receivable	2640.00	4686.50	5788.40	15749.70	21500.00
Inventories	2340.30	3379.80	6993.20	3914.30	5590.50
Total current assets	5514.20	9298.30	14518.00	21992.70	27684.80
Land, buildings, equipment	2253.50	2439.50	7364.60	8003.40	13370.20
Less: Accumulated deprcn.	544.00	650.00	1211.30	1687.10	2747.10
Net fixed assets	1709.50	1789.50	6153.30	6316.30	10623.10
Investments/advances	1165.60	28.90	232.30	462.00	633.60
Other assets	488.50	376.60	837.50	1132.00	937.80
Total assets	8877.80	11493.30	21741.10	29903.00	39879.30
Accounts payable	1540.80	2134.60	4140.20	2791.00	6239.20
Notes payable—banks	300.00		1000.00		2000.00
Accrued taxes, interest	674.30	1437.70	1900.70	1941.20	1507.70
Current sinking fund	77.00	173.90	324.30	382.50	512.50
Total current liabilities	2592.10	3746.20	7365.20	5114.70	10259.40
Long-term debt:					
From banks	2186.70	2059.70	1777.20	9000.00	12000.00
Bonds			5162.60	4649.50	7170.40
Total liabilities	4778.80	5805.90	14305.00	18764.20	29429.80
Preferred stock	1757.20	2432.20	2392.50	2347.50	2254.30
Common stock & surplus	2341.80	3255.20	5043.60	8791.30	8195.20
Total liab. & net worth	8877.80	11493.30	21741.10	29903.00	39879.30

EXHIBIT 7
WEDGE COMPUTERS, INC.

Income Statements for the years ending December 31, (Dollar amounts in thousands)

	1981	1982	1983	1984	1985
Net sales	18675.90	23400.20	30563.70	38396.40	43140.10
Cost of goods sold	15500.90	18914.70	24119.50	30416.80	34331.70
Gross profit	3175.00	4485.50	6444.20	7979.60	8808.40
Gen. & admin. exps	1817.20	2134.10	2499.30	2853.60	4350.70
Depreciation & amortzn	263.20	185.90	377.60	584.20	1089.60
Interest charges	199.80	212.70	410.60	881.60	1791.50
Earnings before taxes	894.80	1952.80	3156.70	3660.20	1576.60
Taxes	443.50	1051.60	1671.20	1875.20	788.30
Net income after taxes	451.30	901.20	1485.50	1785.00	788.30

EXHIBIT 8
WEDGE COMPUTERS, INC.
Selected Financial Ratios

	Industry Average
Current ratio	2.13
Quick ratio	1.18
Inventory turnover	6.95
Average collection period	60.00
Fixed asset turnover	12.35
Total asset turnover	5.75
Debt ratio	0.50
Debt-equity ratio	1.00
Times interest earned	10.00
Gross profit margin	0.22
Net profit margin	0.07
Return on investment	0.09
Return on equity	0.25
Average stock price	N/A
Earnings per share	1.37
Price earnings ratio	N/A

1 Calculate the key financial ratios and comment briefly on each one.
2 Based on the information provided in the case, do you think Jeff Neuber is justifiably worried?
3 What problems would you anticipate with the Wedge contract?
4 What additional sources could Shannon Richey use in order to assess the financial position of Wedge Computers?
5 Are there any disadvantages to using financial ratios in a preaward survey?
6 What specific action would you recommend? Would your recommendation be different if Wedge's price were only 1 or 2 percent lower than another supplier's?

MUENSTER PUMP BUYS A CAR

This is a negotiation role-playing case regarding the purchase of a company car. The case provides a negotiating experience that is both educational and fun. It offers students an opportunity to test their negotiating skills born from insight, analysis, and an understanding of the strengths, weaknesses, and objectives of both the buyer and seller.

In this case, each member of the class participates. Half the members are assigned the role of the buyer, the other half the role of the seller. Negotiations are one on one.

The role each student is to play will be assigned in class. Each student playing the buyer will be given the specific information that is known to the buyer at the time negotiations begin. Similarly, each student playing the seller will be given the information known to the seller at that time.

After passing out the role-playing information, the instructor will advise the class how to proceed with the negotiations.

THE MUENSTER PUMP COMPANY

The Muenster Pump Company has manufactured high-quality agricultural pumps for over forty years. The firm's only plant is located in the small midwestern city of Muenster. The company is Muenster's largest employer. Bob Dorf, president of the firm, is the grandson of Emil Dorf, the founder. Bob and his family, along with all key personnel, live in or near the city of Muenster. Cordial relations exist between the firm and the city officials.

Since its founding, the firm has always been as self-sufficient as possible. Shortly after setting up business, Emil Dorf established a foundry to cast pump housings and related items. Today, the foundry provides virtually all of the required pump housings.

Bob's cousin, Terry, is the purchasing manager for Muenster Pump. After graduating from State University, Terry worked as a buyer at a large appliance manufacturer in the southwestern corner of the state. But after two years of life in the big city, Terry returned to Muenster. Bob was delighted to have Terry back in town. He established the position of purchasing manager by consolidating the buying functions previously performed by himself and other members of the firm. As seen in Exhibit 1, Terry reports to her Uncle Ned, who is the vice president for manufacturing.

Terry is an aggressive and conscientious buyer. Materials costs have come down from 60 percent of the cost of sales to 50 percent in the two years since she assumed responsibility for purchasing.

Recently a representative of Union Foundry, a firm located in the southeastern part of the state, called on Terry. The rep was aware that Muenster Pump made its own cast pump housings. But he claimed that new developments in casting pouring allowed his firm to offer extremely attractive prices.

EXHIBIT 1
The internal organization of the Muenster Pump Company.

Terry requested a price on the L-1012 casting housing, Muenster's most popular size. The L-1012 represents 60 percent of Muenster's demand for casting housings. The pump that incorporates the L-1012 is sold to distributors for $500. Within a week of the meeting, a letter arrived from Union Foundry, quoting a price of $90 F.O.B. Muenster. Delivery was promised in 120 days after receipt of the first order. Thereafter, delivery would be made in sixty days after receipt of an order. Minimum orders were established as 100 units. Terry contacted two other foundries and obtained quotations for the L-1012 housing. The prices were $94 and $98 F.O.B. Muenster.

Terry met her Uncle Ned, discussed her findings with him, and asked how much it cost Muenster to produce the casting housings internally in its own foundry.

Ned Dorf was not at all enthusiastic about Terry's efforts in this area of the business. He said, "Terry, I appreciate your interest and efforts at reducing cost. But a lot more is involved here than meets the eye. We produce a quality housing that is not equaled in the industry. It's one of the primary keys to our success! Furthermore, we can respond to requirements much quicker than those city boys."

Terry responded, "Ned, let's assume that all your doubts could be overcome. How much does it cost us to make the housings?" Ned replied, "Terry, there is something else involved. We have sixteen men working in that foundry. If we stop making our own housings, we'll have to close down the foundry. And there's no other place in the firm where these men could work."

At this point, Terry thought that discretion would be the better part of valor. She thanked her Uncle Ned for the information and returned to her office.

Later that day, her cousin Bob stopped by. In the ensuing conversation, she learned that the L-1012 housing cost Muenster about $180. Total overhead at Muenster was calculated to be approximately 200 percent; hence, direct costs for materials and labor for the housings would be about $60. Approximately 70 percent of the overhead is for fixed costs such as depreciation, taxes, and executive salaries.

1 What other information would be useful in arriving at this make-or-buy decision?
2 Who should take part in the make-or-buy decision process?
3 What role should purchasing play?
4 How should the noneconomic factors be evaluated?
5 Should Muenster make or buy its casting housings?
6 What do you think of the organizational structure at Muenster?

NATIONAL COMPUTERS

Tom Jones, manager of purchased materials at the National Computers plant in San Diego, is introducing what the company has termed a "supply line management (SLM) strategy." Long-term goals of the SLM system include reducing production costs, improving product quality, and increasing the overall performance of the plant. The mission statement of supply line management is "to provide the lowest total cost of purchased materials" to the San Diego facility—and "to continuously improve product quality, supplier responsiveness, and delivery predictability of purchased materials." The following objectives were set forth by SLM:

- Develop long-term agreements on 95 percent of purchased material part numbers. Target date: 4th Quarter 1990
- Reduce core supplier base to 125. Target date: 4th Quarter 1990
- Target 100 percent of critical suppliers for "Early Supplier Involvement." Target date: 4th Quarter 1988
- Reduce part number base by 40 percent. Target date: 4th Quarter 1990
- Maintain in-house quality levels at fewer than 500 defective parts per million (PPM). Target date: 4th Quarter 1990
- 90 percent of purchased parts to be certified. Target date: 4th Quarter 1990
- Maintain on-hand direct materials inventory at less than $10K. Target date: 4th Quarter 1990
- Maintain on-time delivery greater than 95 percent. Target date: 4th Quarter 1990
- Maintain planned order late starts at less than 3 percent. Target date: 4th Quarter 1990

- Maintain reschedule left/right at less than 7 percent. Target date: 4th Quarter 1990
- Reduce the largest supplier repeat lead time to four weeks. Target date: 4th Quarter 1991

Out of all the stated position objectives, Tom believes reduction of the part number base by 40 percent to be the least attainable. He thinks that *convincing the engineering department* will prove to be the most important step in achieving the desired reduction—and therefore in achieving the objectives of supply line management. Tom understands that improved communications between the departments are necessary. Attached is a memo sent to the director of operations and the director of hardware engineering, explaining the need for part number reduction and subsequent target performance measurement. (See Exhibit 1.)

EXHIBIT 1

Intracorporation Memo

      Date: February 19, 1988

        To: P. A. Why, Acting Director, Operations; R. W. Hart, Director, Hardware Engineering

    From: T. R. Jones, Manager, Purchased Materials Management

Extension: 2111

    Subject: PURCHASED MATERIAL INVENTORY

The primary drivers of purchased material inventories are:

—The number of part numbers
—The lead time to obtain part numbers
—Schedule fluctuations
—On-time delivery

My concern is that total coordination does not exist to maximize the effectiveness of our materials inventory plan. At inventory meetings, the presentations represent what we are doing to specifically address existing purchasing inventory problems.

To ensure that we are maximizing our improvement potential, the following is recommended:

EXHIBIT 1 (*continued*)

1. Part Number Reduction

Today we have $4.4M of purchased material in inventory, consisting of approximately 4,500 active part numbers ($1,000/part number). The foundation of part number reduction is part number standardization. Larry Lempke's group is attacking this impressively with two people involved part time; however, new part numbers still are being added daily.

Engineering controls need to be established to totally address part number reduction. When new part numbers are added, other part numbers need to be reviewed for deletion.

Target Performance Measurement needs to be implemented for engineering. It should include:

a. Part Number Reduction Objectives. Recommended objectives for target commodities are as shown.

Commodity	Active P/Ns	Targeted reduction	Current inv. dollars
Active electronic	617	25	1,262,339
PCBs	279	25	724,681
Passive electronics	1275	250	662,833
Interconnect products	340	75	446,232
Sheet metal/plastics	785	50	244,833
Wire assemblies	214	25	207,820
Hardware/fasteners	664	140	202,052
Packaging	96	10	37,284
Tools/molds/castings	N/A	N/A	N/A
TOTALS:	4270	600	3.8M

b. Part number targets for new products.

It is recommended that engineering report part number additions and deletions monthly.

Long-term part number reduction objectives are as follows.

ACTIVE PART NUMBERS:	YE88	YE89	YE90
	3700	3200	2800

2. Lead Time Reduction

Today lead times for unique parts are as shown (A). Targeted performance measurement for existing unique parts has been established (B) in purchasing. These lead times include one week for P.O. generation and signoff, supplier lead time, plus one week for receipt and processing to production.

EXHIBIT 1 (*continued*)

	(A) Current lead times (wks)	(B) Lead time targets—YE88 (purchasing)	(C) Future lead times (engr. targets)
Twisted pair wire	12	10	6
Back panels	12	10	6
Card cages	14–16	10	6
AWW	14	10	6
Sheet metal	9–15	10	6
PCBs	10–12	10	6
Wire assemblies	9–14	10	6
Plastic	8–12	10	6
Power supplies	14–22	12	9

For future production requirements, it is recommended that engineering implement target performance measurement for unique products as shown (C). Design attention with early supplier involvement can significantly contribute to further lead time reduction. Our long-term lead time objective for YE90 is *4 weeks*.

1 What specific techniques and methods should Tom use to convince engineering to reduce part numbers?
2 What kind of evidence should he use to support his case?
3 What suggestions could he give engineering to facilitate the reduction in part numbers?
4 Outline in general terms an overall inventory management program for National Computers.

NATIONAL MACHINE AND ELECTRONICS

Early in 1989, Michael Phillips, C.P.M., purchasing director for National Machine and Electronics (NME), met with his company's president at the president's request to discuss reducing materials costs. In considering all possible alternatives, Mike knew that offshore sourcing appeared to offer interesting opportunities. The meeting centered on NME's historical position as a buyer

Copyrighted by the National Association of Purchasing Management and the School of Government and Business Administration, George Washington University. Reprinted by permission. This case was written by Lee Budress during one of the NAPM-sponsored case writing workshops.

only of domestic products, and concluded with Mike receiving authorization to explore the cost-saving potential of offshore sourcing.

NATIONAL MACHINE AND ELECTRONICS (NME)

NME is a division of a worldwide conglomerate that specializes in precision machined products and aerospace electronics. While largely government and defense oriented, NME has one commercial aviation electronics division among its fifteen autonomous operating groups. Total sales for NME during 1986 were approximately $2.5 billion, with over $1 billion being spent by the purchasing departments of the various groups.

The NME purchasing function is divided among the fifteen autonomous divisions. Each has its own purchasing department, which reports to division management but adheres to corporate policies and procedures. There is a relatively small corporate purchasing staff concerned with corporate policy and common goods and services.

THE COST REDUCTION OBJECTIVE

To maintain its competitive position, NME needed to explore all possible ways to reduce costs. In addition to analyzing and working with its domestic suppliers, Mike believed it was necessary at this time to begin considering offshore sources.

OFFSHORE SOURCING

Until 1989, NME had only purchased offshore as part of an offset/countertrade requirement. The other exception was the Commercial Aviation Electronics (CAE) division, which had been acquired in 1986 as a means of diversifying NME's electronics markets. CAE not only had been buying from foreign sources but had established a factory in Singapore to source and manufacture one of its product lines.

CAE's offshore experience began before being acquired by NME. At first, parts were purchased from Singapore and other East Asian sources. These parts were then assembled in this country. Soon CAE began to buy assemblies in East Asia, and finally all factory operations were shifted to their own Singapore facility.

When Mike contacted each of the other divisions' purchasing managers, he was surprised to discover that each one had a collection of horror stories of past foreign purchasing attempts and was unwilling to try again. Most of these stories centered around problems of communication, quality control, credibility, and understanding.

Mike again contacted the CAE purchasing manager to discuss details of the Singapore operation. Not only did the Singapore factory build a product line, but the Singapore purchasing department sourced components for that product line from throughout East Asia. Initial cost savings from first buys (including engineering, test fixtures, and other startup costs) ranged from 10 to 18 percent. Subsequent purchases yielded savings in the 25 to 40 percent range compared to domestic sources. Quality and delivery problems were minimal.

Following that conversation, Mike wondered what he might do next.

1 What choices does Mike have for starting an international sourcing program?
2 What are the advantages and disadvantages of each?
3 Would NME benefit from an international procurement office in Asia?

NATIONWIDE TELEPHONE

BACKGROUND

Nationwide Telephone has been a manufacturer of quality low-cost telephones since 1982. The firm has based its business strategy on automation, fast deliveries, and reliable service. Nationwide is one of the first low-cost telephone manufacturers still producing and selling telephones in the United States. Competition, especially from the Far East, has made this an increasingly difficult endeavor.

The most important segment of Nationwide's sales has been the promotional "Gift with Purchase" market. Magazine publishers currently compose Nationwide's largest customer base. Positive growth has been forecasted in the promotional incentive market for the next five years. To meet market demand, Nationwide manufactures two models of telephones in a variety of colors.

The firm's plant is located in Nogales, Arizona. The plant was built near the major sources of supply, which are in Mexico. Nationwide procures all its components from Mexico except for the plastic items. The plastic components are purchased in the local domestic area. Nationwide has ruled out the use of a maquiladora,* due to the highly automated nature of its production process. As a capital-intensive firm, Nationwide also concluded a maquiladora was not a feasible alternative because of the increased risks of having its equipment in a foreign country.

Roger Stoga is the president and founder of the company. He has an engineering degree from Michigan Tech and an M.B.A. from Purdue University. He attributes Nationwide's ability to stay competitive to two factors: (1) automating its process and (2) procuring highly labor-intensive materials in Mexico.

This case was developed by Bruce Asbaugh and Sandra Sarmiento under the direction of Professor David N. Burt.

*Maquiladora plants are located in northern Mexico. Basically, foreign materials are imported duty free, processed (using low-cost labor), and then returned to the county of origin without customs duties being imposed either in Mexico or the county of origin.

The plant employs only twenty people, of which twelve are responsible for the actual assembly work. With the help of automated assembly machines, Nationwide has been able to meet market demand and keep labor and manufacturing costs down.

PURCHASING

Steven Young is the sales and purchasing manager. He employs two buyers, Jan Newman and Bill Bush. Jan has been with the company for a little over a year and is a graduate of Arizona State University. She has a strong background in price analysis. Bill is the eldest and most experienced member of the Nationwide staff. He is expected to retire later this year. Jan purchases all the electronics and wire harnesses, while Bill concentrates his efforts on the plastics and hardware.

PROCUREMENT SYSTEM

The manufacturing process is highly dependent on timely deliveries from its suppliers. Local sourcing is used to assure prompt delivery and to keep supplier lead times short. Procurement focuses its efforts on maintaining a small supplier base.

The driving force of the procurement system is to obtain low-cost, high-quality materials as a means of staying competitive. As a standard procedure, purchasing prepares annual recosting reports of its suppliers. Currently, requests for quotations are sent to potential suppliers to compare with the current supplier's prices. The buyers are to sort through the various bids and choose the lowest one submitted to use as a basis for negotiating future part pricing.

DEVELOPING SITUATION

Over the last six months, Roger has been noticing a drop in sales, while expenses have begun to increase. A careful evaluation of production costs revealed a recent increase in the plastic component prices. Since plastic components account for 40 percent of the telephone's cost, the rise in price significantly impacted profit.

Plastic components are made by injection molding. Injection molding is a process whereby a thermoplastic material, usually in pellet form, is heated to its melting point. The melted material is then pushed into a mold via an injection molding machine and held in the closed mold while it is cooled into a solid shape. The solidified part is ejected from the mold and the process begins again.

On further investigation, Roger noticed Nationwide is sole-sourced by one injection molder in the local area, ABC Plastics. Nationwide has been purchasing solely from ABC since it consistently submitted the lowest bid. Quality and delivery have been generally good.

Roger called Steve into his office to discuss the situation. Roger said to Steve, "As you are aware, our sales this quarter have been weak and expenses have been increasing. I have gone through our material price sheets and noticed plastic part prices have been steadily increasing. Why is that?" Steve replied, "Bill has made me aware of the problem, but he has not been able to determine the cause of the price changes. He has stated that 'ABC refuses to divulge any cost information.'" Roger firmly said, "We have to understand what the problem is and get it fixed now!"

Steve was pondering his options and alternatives to solve this problem. He knew if he did nothing to rectify this situation quickly, Nationwide would not be able to price its telephones competively.

Steve also knew that Jan had been successful in obtaining price reductions; therefore, Steve decided to ask Jan to work with Bill to develop an action plan to get the escalating plastic material prices under control.

1 What type of analytical tools can be used by the purchasing group to determine the right price?
2 How could Nationwide's purchasing department have prevented the price escalations?
3 How does the competitive condition of the plastic component industry impact the use of price analysis?
4 What kind of resistance might Jan encounter from Bill? How can Bill help facilitate the pricing analysis process?
5 What are some of the costs/benefits of continuing to source from the same local suppliers?

NORTHEASTERN EQUIPMENT COMPANY

The Northeastern Equipment Company manufactured goods for the consumer, government, and industrial markets. The company was organized on a divisional basis according to product lines. Each of the four division managers reported to the executive vice president, as did the personnel director and controller. Each division manager was expected to operate his division as a separate business on a profitable basis. (See Exhibit 1.) Each division occupied a separate building containing its entire production facility, home marketing office, and so on. The divisional plants were all within a 15-mile radius of the executive offices where the president, vice president, personnel department, and accounting department were housed.

THE TEST EQUIPMENT DIVISION

The Test Equipment Division manufactured electrical and mechanical test equipment for industrial, government, and laboratory use. The products of the division fell into two broad classes: relatively inexpensive mass-produced

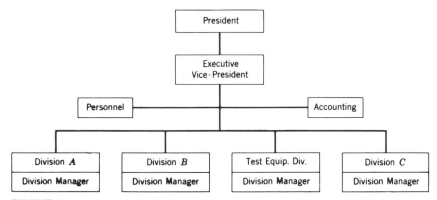

EXHIBIT 1
Northeastern Equipment Company organization chart.

units and expensive highly engineered units that were manufactured on a low-volume or single-unit basis. Manufacturing, therefore, was placed under two foremen: one who was responsible for low-volume or "specialty products" and another who was responsible for the high-volume or "mass production" items. These two groups were supported by a metal shop and a machine shop, each of which was responsible for fabrication of subassemblies for both the specialty products group and the mass production group. (See Exhibit 2.)

PURCHASING—TEST EQUIPMENT DIVISION

The purchasing manager, who was very competent and had twenty years' experience in production, engineering, and purchasing, reported to the production manager because the division manager felt that the purchasing manager's primary function was to "see that production had what it needed when it needed it." The production manager was held responsible by the division manager for keeping all production costs in line.

On the other hand the marketing manager exercised functional authority over the purchasing manager on all specialty products. These products, which were frequently large equipment installations such as automation devices and communication systems, were normally made on a job shop basis to customer specifications. Success in the sale of these products depended on the ability of the division to produce efficiently to tight customer specifications and to deliver more quickly than competitors. The marketing manager, therefore, could specify brands and suppliers for component parts, and he frequently negotiated directly with suppliers and supplier salesmen prior to placing an order through purchasing. The purchasing manager had repeatedly tried to eliminate these direct contacts between the marketing manager and the suppliers since several expensive duplicate orders and contract complications had arisen as a result of purchasing's not being properly consulted or informed.

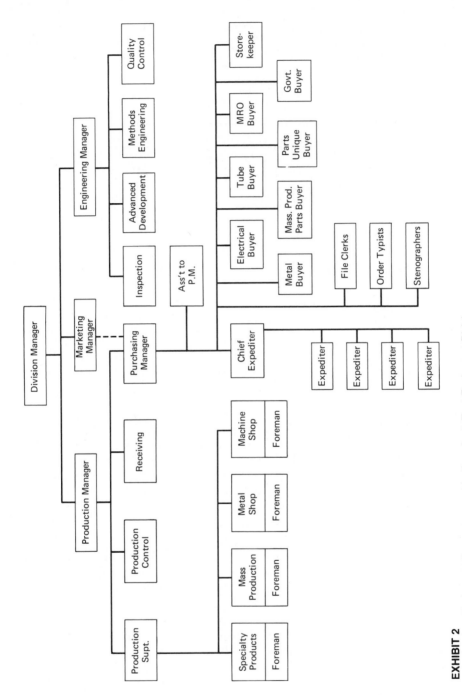

EXHIBIT 2
Northeastern Equipment Company organization chart, Test Equipment Division.

As a result of his resistance to the marketing manager's activities, the purchasing manager and the marketing manager were hardly on speaking terms. Whenever the marketing manager did want purchasing assistance, he always went to the assistant to the purchasing manager. This individual was a very competent engineer and former lawyer and was known to be able to obtain excellent cooperation from all suppliers. Because of frequent favors asked by the marketing manager in expediting and straightening out orders, the assistant to the purchasing manager had only one other set of assigned activities. These duties were keeping up with special features of government contracts in process or negotiation, government regulations concerning procurement, and government liaison.

The internal organization of purchasing is shown in Exhibit 2. The metal buyer bought castings, bar, plate, and extruded stock for the four production groups. His responsibilities included all basic metals and alloys that were to be further fabricated in the division. The electrical buyer bought meters, wire, resistors, capacitors, and all similar fabricated electrical parts, except tubes, for both the specialty products and mass production sections. The mass production parts buyer bought all fabricated parts for the mass production section, other than electrical parts including tubes. The tube buyer bought cathode ray and miscellaneous tubes for both production sections. These tubes ranged in unit price from a few cents to $8,000, some being off-the-shelf items and others special development jobs. The parts unique buyer bought all fabricated parts other than electrical parts and tubes for the specialty products section. The MRO buyer handled all operating and clerical supplies for the entire division.

The government buyer handled subcontracts and purchase orders placed under government prime or subcontracts. Government work was handled by both production sections and accounted for 40 percent of the division's sales. Because government work was carried on in the production section simultaneously with civilian orders, and because many parts were interchangeable, the government buyer only placed orders for parts unique to government orders. For standard items that would be included in government orders, he merely ensured that the other buyers included proper clauses in the orders they placed. The government buyer worked closely with the assistant to the purchasing manager, with the marketing department, and with all other buyers. He was well thought of by the entire division and handled government contract materials with a minimum of friction.

The storekeeper kept all records on preproduction inventories and supervised the stock clerks in the various storerooms of the plant. The expediters helped the buyers by following up on material orders until they were received in the plant and by picking up rush orders, and so on, on request. Once materials were drawn from stores they became the responsibility of the production foreman who had drawn them from stock. Because some materials went directly from boxcars into production, rather than through stores, the receiving department was placed under the production manager. Inspection was performed by engineers assigned to the job by the engineering manager upon request by the purchasing manager. There was no full-time inspection department.

The Test Equipment Division had been operating at a low profit ratio for several years. Inventories of raw materials, goods in process, and final inventories were turning slowly, and orders were being lost because of high quoted prices and slow deliveries. A new division manager was appointed to clear up the situation.

1 What would you recommend the new division manager do to make the materials management operation more efficient?
2 What could be done to make purchasing operations more efficient?

THE OAKLAND SCHOOL DISTRICT

Gene Smith, purchasing manager for the Oakland School District, has just completed an analysis of his purchasing paper workload. His staff, consisting of an assistant, two buyers, a clerk, and a stenographer, had complained of the steadily growing number of orders that the department had to process. The school district had expanded to include another high school and two vo-tech schools during the last several years. This expansion, plus normal growth, had created a workload in which 31,164 purchase orders (exclusive of changes and adjustments) were placed, spending $5,405,678 with 1,296 suppliers. Another breakdown Gene developed showed that 15.2 percent of the suppliers received 82.5 percent of the dollar volume purchased.

A further analysis revealed that the average value of all orders placed was $482.21, and that 35 percent of them ranged between $30 and $100 and totaled 2.8 percent of the total dollars spent annually. In fact, 23 percent of the purchases were for less than $30 and added only 0.35 percent to the dollar volume. Purchase orders were evenly spread throughout the year, running about 2,600 per month.

One cause for the numerous orders, he told the district director for operations, was "daily need for rubber stamps, small equipment parts, special laboratory supplies, fluorescent tubes, MRO supplies, and other miscellaneous items." In Gene's words, "the school district seemed to be like a custom job shop type operation." In addition, the various departments wrote an excessive number of requisitions for purchasing because they needed detailed records for their files, which are required by the stringent district accounting control policies.

Gene had asked Harry Flint, the controller, to reduce some of the documentation required. He was told that "it's necessary to have proper records to control expenses, and the extra orders are not extra expenses because you would be on the payroll anyway."

Mr. Flint also pointed out that the stores supervisor, who initiated many of the orders, was following present district policy to keep only very active inventory items in stock and to make direct purchases of all others. Both the controller and the stores supervisor were under the treasurer's office, which in turn reported to the district superintendent.

Another problem was the unpredictable number of change orders issued by maintenance and by the district engineer's office. These modifications involved changes in quality specifications, actual amount delivered, and date of delivery originally specified by users or by inventory control. Accounting insisted that it would not approve invoices that did not completely match a confirmed purchase order or its supporting changes. During the past year, 5,678 change orders had been issued, of which 2,946 had been due to relatively minor variations.

Smith knew that local suppliers and distributors had complained of the burden of small orders and that some were considering a minimum charge of $40 per order. After further investigation, he concluded that small orders were not economical for either the buyer or the seller and had asked the accounting office and stores to help him solve this problem. But neither would suggest to his boss, the district treasurer, any change in policy or procedure. Smith's boss, the director for operations, also reported to the district superintendent and had expressed interest in trying to update the growing organization's management methods.

1 Identify the basic issues and management problems that Smith should consider in trying to improve the situation.
2 What additional information should Smith attempt to obtain?
3 How would you suggest Smith solve these problems?

PACIFIC PRINTING PRESS

Ron Wise, purchasing manager at the Poway Unified School District (affectionately known as P.U.), entered his office to find Terry Donley, shop instructor, and another gentleman reading copies of *The Journal of Purchasing and Materials Management*. Terry introduced his companion, Mr. Wilbur Segerson, sales manager of Pacific Printing Press. Terry then produced a set of papers and said that he would like Ron to firm up a verbal agreement he had made last month with Pacific for a new $50,000 press for the shop.

Mr. Segerson picked the conversation up and said, "The firm-up is a mere formality. Work has already begun on the press. You are really lucky that Mr. Donley gave us the go-ahead last month. Otherwise, there would have been no chance that you would have had the press in time for the opening of your new shop this fall."

Mr. Wise thanked Mr. Segerson for his input and then requested that he and Mr. Donley be excused for a few moments. Ron then escorted the shop instructor to an empty office. "I know that this project is a rush job and that the appropriation has already cleared the principal's cabinet, Terry. But we haven't even received the specifications yet so we can go out for bids, much less write a purchase contract."

Terry countered with, "There wasn't time or need to get bids. I had checked with all suppliers who had a display at the trade show I attended in Las Vegas early last month. In my opinion, Pacific Printing Press has the best equipment available. In addition, their price is competitive and they will meet my schedule!"

This was not the first instance of trouble with purchasing's customers. It had happened before over capital equipment items, as well as other operating materials. However, Ron thought that his policy manual had settled the procedure with both his own school personnel and with outside vendors and suppliers. He wanted to maintain good relations with his customers and with his suppliers, but he wondered what to say in this instance.

1 What are the basic issues in this case?
2 Outline an approach that might have been used to handle this procurement more effectively.
3 What should Ron Wise do now?

THE PEACH COMPUTER COMPANY

Donald Bright, purchasing manager at the Peach Computer Company, was preparing for a meeting to be held that afternoon. The meeting concerned the construction of a new $6 million, 120,000-square-foot building to be located near Dayton, Ohio. The principal issue to be discussed, and hopefully resolved, was what method of specification the firm should use in the purchase of its new building.

When the requirement for the building first arose, the plant engineer at Peach advocated the use of a design firm as the desired method of developing the specifications. Such firms were employed successfully by Peach on seven previous construction projects it had completed during the past five years. Under this approach, a design firm, traditionally referred to as an architect-engineer or simply A-E, is retained to develop the detailed plans and specifications for the new building. These specifications are identical in concept to the materials and method-of-manufacture specifications used in the manufacturing industry to purchase manufactured goods. After they are developed and approved, the construction plans and specifications in sequence become (1) the basis for solicitation of bid prices from qualified construction firms, (2) the cardinal part of the resulting construction contract, and (3) the standard against which inspections are performed.

Don had conducted some preliminary discussions with members of the Dayton Purchasing Management Association regarding the cost for A-E services. He learned that the fees for local projects similar to his were averaging 8 percent of estimated construction cost. This percentage was in line with Peach's experience on its own projects.

One of the members of the Dayton chapter with whom Don talked suggested that he read an article in an issue of the *California Management Review (CMR)*. The article, entitled "Inflation, Recession, and Your Building Dollar," dealt with the purchase of building construction. Don learned that several alternative approaches to purchasing building construction were available. One approach particularly appealed to him. It provided for the use of performance specifications. Such specifications, instead of describing the building item by item in terms of its physical properties, describe in words the building's intended function, i.e., how large it must be; how well lighted, heated, and cooled it must be; its longevity; its operating costs; and so on. After the performance description is developed, it is used to solicit from qualified bidders a package proposal that includes (1) a design approach, (2) a firm agreed price, and (3) a guaranteed completion date.

The *CMR* article documented that when properly used, performance specifications for buildings can result in a significant savings in both dollars and time. Additionally, the article data revealed that when this method is correctly used, a considerable savings in both the cost and the time required to complete the project is a reasonable expectation. Furthermore, the article indicated that the buyers of buildings purchased under this method have experienced approximately equal satisfaction with their buildings as those who used A-E's.

In preparation for the afternoon meeting, Don decided to develop lists of advantages and disadvantages for each of the two approaches he was considering. After an evaluation of both lists, Don expected to be able to make a formal recommendation as to which method he thought Peach should employ.

1 Should Don get any additional information? Explain.
2 Discuss the inherent advantages and disadvantages of using performance specifications.
3 Discuss the inherent advantages and disadvantages of the plans and specifications method of describing quality.
4 Assuming that Don's investigation and analysis indicates that both methods are practical for use by Peach, discuss which approach Don should recommend.
5 Explain why one method will require more active involvement on Don's part than the other approach.

PEGASUS TECHNOLOGIES

In June 1990, Linda Wang, procurement specialist for Pegasus Technologies, Phoenix, Arizona, and three teammates were responsible for recommending which of four potential suppliers should receive a purchase order for the next year's requirement of 11-inch color monitors. The monitors were expected to be of exceptional quality, with extra high resolution. Pegasus was recognized as a well-established manufacturer of mainframe computers. More recently, the company had expanded its product line to include personal computers. The latest in this line of products was the PT 9000, a high-quality personal computer with two disk drives and an optional hard disk drive.

In its nearly three decades of operation, Pegasus had grown from a single product manufacturer with annual sales of around $250,000 to a multiproduct $5-billion firm. The company has always had a reputation for high quality. Funds have never been compromised where research and development is concerned.

In order to facilitate the sale of the PT 9000, it was decided that the computer would be sold as a package together with an 11-inch color monitor and a printer. While Pegasus manufactured its own CPU, printer, and keyboard, the firm intended to buy the 11-inch color monitor from one of the four potential suppliers. It was estimated that the demand for the next year would be in the region of 1 million monitors. Forecasts indicated that this demand was expected to grow at an annual rate of 20 percent over the next three years. In order to maintain a uniform quality, the company policy was to use a single source of supply as far as possible.

In determining the supplier for the color monitor, Linda was assisted by the following persons, who brought a varied line of expertise to the source selection team:

- *Arno Berg*, the senior engineer, had been with the company for fourteen years and currently was its R&D chief. He held an engineering degree from a Norwegian university and an M.B.A. from the University of San Diego.
- *Kevin Rice*, financial analyst, had recently joined Pegasus after moving from Los Angeles, where he worked for three years with Pasadena Financial Corporation. He held an M.B.A. from UCLA.
- *John Harper*, quality assurance, had been with the company for eight years. He had an engineering degree from MIT and had a reputation for being a very tough man when quality was in question.

The responsibilities of the team included:

1 Identifying potential suppliers.
2 Preparing a brief comparative statement of the key suppliers.

This case was developed by Jimmy Anklesaria of the University of San Diego.

3 Developing a brief analysis of each potential supplier.
4 Recommending the supplier with whom the order should be placed. This recommendation was to be made to a corporate-level review board.

After a preliminary review, including visits to all potential suppliers and a detailed review of their facilities, equipment, management systems, and purchasing departments, the team had narrowed the list of potential suppliers to four manufacturers:

1 *Reese Corporation,* the largest manufacturer of color monitors under consideration, with annual sales of about $6.5 billion. The firm had been in existence since 1956 and was the industry price leader. Recently management had indicated that the company would not be interested in any order of less than $500 million per annum. This decision was made after Reese had put in a bid for the Pegasus contract. Reese's price was $245 per unit.

2 *Capozzi Manufacturing,* a fairly large and highly reputed manufacturer of computer equipment, including color monitors. With sales of nearly $2 billion, more than half of which were through the sale of monitors, the firm was the second largest of its kind in the area. Its price was $250.

3 *Kruger Corp.* had recently entered the market with a new range of color monitors. In its short life of four years, Kruger had established a reputation for quality and innovation. Kruger maintained that its success was largely based on heavy R&D expenditures. The firm quoted a price of $275 per unit.

4 *Payne Industries,* the smallest of the four potential suppliers, looked attractive since it quoted a price of $240, which was about 4 percent lower than Reese or Capozzi and 14 percent below that of Kruger. If selected, Payne would devote almost all of its production capacity to the Pegasus contract. Industry experts viewed the company as one of the most promising and dynamic new corporations in the industry.

Since the estimated contract was for about $250 million, Linda was aware of the critical nature of the decision. She had to turn in the team's recommendation within a week.

1 Briefly analyze the data provided in Exhibit 1 (on page 784) for each of the four potential suppliers. (Compare the figures with industry averages where necessary.)
2 Based on the information contained in Exhibit 1, which potential supplier looks most attractive? Why?

EXHIBIT 1
COMPARATIVE FINANCIAL AND OTHER DATA ON POTENTIAL SUPPLIERS

	Reese	Capozzi	Kruger	Payne	Ind. avg.
Previous year's sales (in millions)	6548.00	1850.05	593.70	253.80	
Net fixed assets (in millions)	1091.80	212.90	75.80	20.63	
Current stock price	$63.77	$55.98	$32.98	$11.63	
Price earnings ratio	18.50	6.45	7.15	34.5	12.00
Liquidity ratios:					
Current ratio	1.89	2.12	2.56	1.78	2.19
Quick ratio	1.14	1.02	1.28	0.99	1.08
Activity ratios:					
Average collection period	29 days	26 days	28 days	37 days	30 days
Inventory turnover	12.65	12.34	11.96	18.25	12.50
Fixed asset turnover	6.00	8.69	7.83	12.30	5.80
Profitability ratios:					
Gross profit margin	16.8%	15.8%	15.4%	13.8%	14.6%
Net profit margin	9.48%	6.78%	7.35%	8.6%	6.57%
Return on equity	16.6%	18.6%	12.8%	18.7%	N/A
Return on investment	14.56%	14.75%	8.7%	12.5%	14.2%
Debt ratio	0.14	0.5	0.45	0.65	0.5
Times interest earned	16.8	8.5	9.6	2.6	6.0
Other data:					
R&D expenditure					
(as a % of sales)	2.30	4.67	8.29	5.5	3.9
Installed capacity	97%	95%	88%	85%	N/A
Production efficiency	102%	91%	95.1%	97.3%	N/A
Sales growth (3 years)	8.2%	11.67%	18.82%	32.1%	N/A
Price quoted	245.00	250.00	275.00	240.00	

THE PERILS OF PRESUMPTION

This is the sad story of Tom Rogers, purchasing manager of the Buzzy Tool Company, who found out that a little knowledge is a dangerous thing. His company makes do-it-yourself power tools. After its president went on a cost-cutting rampage, Tom desperately embraced value analysis.

Tom set up a lobby exhibit that showed the most important components and subassemblies that Buzzy Tool bought. Sales representatives were invited to come up with better ways of making these repetitive items. Whenever visiting suppliers showed interest in this new potential market, Tom gave them the following clues, "Fellows, we used to make a lot of these items ourselves. But our business grew so fast that we eventually had to farm them out. We're satisfied with present designs and quality, but our potential is such that we now are shopping around in all directions for new suppliers, designs, price—everything."

The fancy Drill-A-Thon drew most attention. Made of castings, stampings, and turnings, it had been designed and turned over to a supplier before purchasing became a separate profit center under the president.

Three firms promptly came up with proposals. The first company said, "Tom, the ABC Company can give you a really swell price if you accept plastics instead of metal. Quality will be tops."

The second company said, "Our engineers at XYZ Company have figured out a way to use fewer parts. You know what a cost saving that will be!"

The third company said, "Tom, we at PDQ Company feel your best bet is to do your own assembling again. We'll supply the parts and give you a rock-bottom price because, as you know, we can make all kinds of economies on a big, continuing order."

Tom then got a hot telephone call from the sales vice president of his present supplier, Dandy Products, Inc.: "Tom, I think Dandy Products has a right to get upset when you put an assembly we've been making a long time up for grabs—without even giving us a chance to discuss the situation with you. What do you think a newcomer could possibly offer you? You know we've tried to get your people to talk value analysis time and again. No soap. Now all of a sudden everybody is invited to the party. We understand your product better than anybody else. How about giving us a chance to put our know-how together with any ideas you have floating around and come up with a price—and a job—that you can depend on?"

Then the chief design engineer came in, "Say, Tom what's all that stuff you have rigged up out there in the lobby? Is it true that you have a bunch of unknowns fooling with the Drill-A-Thon design? Don't tell me you've got some of those plastic peddlers trying to cheapen our merchandise! Over my dead body!"

Tom saw that he was in the middle of a four-way crossfire, from his president, who wanted a 5 percent cost reduction, his company's design experts, who were uneasy about outside interference, would-be suppliers who were eager to re-engineer Drill-A-Thon to fit their own shops, and his current supplier, who could count on considerable loyalty throughout Buzzy Tool.

1 How can Tom start a sound value analysis program?
2 How should he inform the suppliers who can be genuinely helpful in this program?
3 What should Tom tell Dandy Products?

PLACIDO ENGINE COMPANY

It was four o'clock on Friday afternoon and Ronald Penson, senior buyer of castings for the Placido Engine Company of Detroit, Michigan, had just finished a telephone conversation with an upset supplier. It was the fourth such call Ronald had received in response to a letter he had sent to his magnesium castings suppliers concerning a severe corrosion problem. All four had told Ronald that they could not adhere to his request without a significant increase in their costs.

THE PLACIDO ENGINE COMPANY

The Placido Engine Company was a division of the General Products Corporation, a $2 billion company that enjoyed a worldwide reputation for quality and leadership in aviation, aerospace, and industrial products. In its nearly four decades of operations, Placido had built more than 45,000 gas engines for a wide variety of commercial, industrial, and military applications. While the most significant part of Placido's sales was in the commercial and general aviation markets, the company was attempting to move toward a balance between commercial and military sales.

THE EXECUTIVE CORROSION TASK FORCE

Last summer, Placido started receiving complaints from its customers concerning corroded gear boxes on engines. The problem was significant and serious enough to warrant the attention of Fred Thompson, senior vice president of the company. In order to resolve this problem and find a permanent solution, Fred created an Executive Corrosion Task Force. This task force immediately solicited inputs from purchasing, quality assurance, manufacturing, engineering, production control, materials, and the Magnesium Corrosion Task Circle* for suggested solutions to the corrosion problem, as well as recommendations for implementing suggested programs. The Executive Corrosion Task Force was under extreme pressure from Fred Thompson to take immediate steps to resolve the corrosion problem.

CORROSION-FREE MAGNESIUM CASTINGS

On investigation, it was determined that a large part of the corrosion problem centered in the Turbo 110 engine and its magnesium castings. It was also found that a significant proportion of these castings were already corroded on receipt from Placido's suppliers. However, instead of rejecting these castings, quality assurance was processing them through for rework. The basis for this action was the need for parts to meet production schedules. It was believed that the delay encountered by rejecting unacceptable castings would be more costly than the cost of reworking them internally.

The task force decided that this process of reworking unacceptable castings was no longer desirable and directed the purchasing department to take

---

*The Magnesium Corrosion Task Circle was established in 1981 to deal with the general problem of magnesium corrosion. It was part of Placido's reliability circles program.

immediate steps to ensure that corrosion-free magnesium castings were received by Placido. As a first step in this direction, the purchasing department was further instructed to notify its castings suppliers that strict adherence to the previously issued Mil Spec-M-3171 and the cleaning and corrosion prevention procedure prescribed by Placido would now be required. Failure to meet these specifications would result in rejection of unacceptable castings or, in cases where Placido elected to reprocess unacceptable castings in lieu of rejection, the supplier would be debited for the cost of the reprocessing work involved.

The responsibility for notifying the castings suppliers of this decision fell to Ronald Penson, who was the senior buyer for castings for Placido. Given the urgency of the situation and the political sensitivity of the issue, Ronald thought it best to send a letter to his current magnesium castings suppliers immediately. (See Exhibit 1.)

EXHIBIT 1
LETTER SENT TO CASTINS SUPPLIERS CONCERNING CORROSION-FREE CASTINGS.

An intense corrosion prevention program for magnesium castings has recently been undertaken at Placido Engine Company. An integral part of this program is the assurance that castings are corrosion free on receipt of shipment from our suppliers. Your strict adherence to Mil Spec-M-3171 and the following is requested:

CLEAN & CORROSION PREVENTION PROCEDURES PER MIL SPEC-M-3171 AND AS FOLLOWS:

- After penetrative inspection, following heat treat, castings will be alkaline cleaned and hydrofluoric acid pickled.
- After hydrofluoric acid pickle, castings to chrome pickle treatment, rinse and bake to dry at 250°F ± 25°F.
- Dip castings in 7220 rust oil B and package for shipment.
- Package to ensure castings do not come into contact with each other, subsequently rubbing away protection.

The responsibility to deliver corrosion-free magnesium castings per casting drawing, engineering blueprint, or M.O.T. is placed with you, the supplier. Failure to do so necessitates an immediate rework at Placido to stop the corrosion process that may ultimately scrap parts. The cost incurred for the rework will be passed on to you in the form of a debit initiated by an Inspection Transfer Report (I.T.R.). The I.T.R. will also have a negative effect on your quality rating.

Your support in this effort is imperative. Please forward the aforementioned procedure to the appropriate personnel in your company.

EXHIBIT 1 (*continued*)

Direct any questions regarding processing to Robert Dear, Quality Assurance Engineer, (405) 876-1241.

Thank you.

Ronald Penson
Senior Buyer

RP:rr

cc: Executive Corrosion Task Force members

NEGATIVE REACTIONS FROM SUPPLIERS

Ronald was not prepared for the quick and negative responses he received from his suppliers. The general sense of the comments from the suppliers was that they were already properly treating the castings to prohibit corrosion and that they disagreed with the procedure Placido was requiring. Furthermore, they all told Ronald that if they were required to follow the procedure prescribed by Placido, it would be necessary for them to expend considerable amounts of time to retool their current processes and to purchase new equipment. These actions would result in substantially higher costs in producing the castings, which would be passed on to Placido.

Ronald was now facing a serious dilemma and was not sure what to do. One thing was certain. He had to act quickly, as Fred Thompson was demanding an immediate solution to the corrosion problem.

1 Define and discuss the basic issues in this case.
2 What should Ronald Penson do?

THE PRETTY CLEAN CAPER

Sol Levowitz, president of the SLI, which grosses around $200 million a year, and Harvey Goldberg, president of Pretty Clean Detergent, Inc., are long-time sailing mates. One day while sailing, Sol brought up the subject of price discrimination. "Say, Harvey, have you heard that the Justice Department is really getting tough on price discrimination? Only last week, Hotdog Equipment got tagged for giving some customers a special break on standard components."

"Yeah, I heard about that," Harvey replied. "Anyone who does special favors to hold customers these days is really foolish. We've put it squarely on the line for our marketing manager—any funny stuff in pricing and we'll drop you like a hot potato."

Sol: "Sure, but that's only half the story. Do you know that your purchasing department can get you into the jug as fast if it puts the screws on vendors too tightly? My lawyers tell me that beating down prices too far can be construed as demanding an unfair advantage over competitors. Had you thought of that?"

Harvey: "No, I hadn't. I know our purchasing personnel are paid to get the best buys they can, and I know they've been crowing about how much they contribute to profits. But I suppose if they get too rough—especially if one of our competitors starts screaming about 'chiseling'—we may have some fast explaining to do. I think I'll look into this pronto."

Pretty Clean Detergent, Inc., is a diversified laundry products firm with annual sales of around $230 million. Each of its three plants has its own purchasing setup, staffed by thirty buyers in all. They do business with 2,000 vendors, contracting for $110 million worth of chemicals, equipment, and supplies per year. The plant purchasing agents report to the local plant managers and are responsible for the cost and size of purchases.

Jack Rumquist is the director of purchasing at headquarters. He has two assistants to help on policy and research. He reports to the president, Mr. Goldberg. After battening down the hatch, Goldberg called in Rumquist. "Jack, all the talk you hear these days about selling and buying at unfair prices has me on edge. Take our case. We're buying for three locations, and I know every one of our purchasing people is under the gun from the plant manager to reduce materials cost and inventories. As a matter of fact, I know our fellows saved $540,000 for us last year alone. That's great, but do our buyers really have any clear idea of the law? Do you have any general policies on proper prices? What I'm really driving at is this: If a fellow from the Justice Department walked in here tomorrow morning and said 'You're violating this or that law,' could we defend ourselves? I want to be absolutely sure we know what we're doing."

1 How does the Robinson-Patman Act constrain buyers?
2 What are some of the potential problem areas for buyers?
3 What action should Jack have taken (or what action should he now take) in this area?

THE PRIVILEGED FLY

You are a privileged fly: You are allowed to be on the wall of a corporate boardroom during a high-powered discussion. The corporation is an engineering firm whose sales total approximately $140 million a year. Up to now, things appear to have been going well. Production does an efficient job and inventories have been reduced. But danger signs are cropping up. Although no orders have been lost as yet, several shipments have missed their deadlines. Customers are beginning to complain. In addition, transportation costs on incoming and outbound freight shipments are mushrooming. It is 9 A.M., and several people are nervously sitting at the conference table. A stern-looking individual enters.

THE CAST

- *Production manager:* Heinrich Holtz, former blue-collar worker. Loves his machines and hates to see them idle. But beneath his "good of the corporation" exterior lies the soul of a power maniac who seeks control over traffic and purchasing.
- *Marketing manager:* Harold Levi, a stereotype. Is afraid of losing sales because of late deliveries. Generally, echoes presidential statements. Appears ready to support Heinrich Holtz's power play.
- *President:* Joe Gish, old-line type. Extremely successful. Has just attended a National Industrial Conference Board (NICB) seminar and is throwing a lot of new buzz words and thoughts around. From his subordinates' point of view, he is dangerous.
- *Traffic manager:* Harold Tracks, another old-liner, but much less successful. Not good at verbalizing, except to quote percentage increases. His freight bills are going up and he is being made to look bad by comparison.
- *Purchasing manager:* Joan Glass, much younger than her associates. Does her best. Understands president Gish's words and tries to put some of them into action. Extremely inventory conscious.
- *Director of finance:* Sol Stein, dedicated to cost reduction.

ACTION

(This is what the privileged fly observes and hears.)

President Gish brings the meeting to order. "Look at these air freight bills! Here's one for $955—more than the damn part is worth! I know, *I checked!* These things are murdering us. You must realize that in our business today, transportation has great cost-cutting potential!"

Traffic manager Tracks responds, "I know that freight bills have risen 30 percent in the last six months, but what can I do? Miss Glass here is cutting inventories so hard that she never has anything in stock. Her short lead times force me to use air freight. And the way she spreads small orders, I almost never find a way to consolidate them to get volume rates. And I'm having the same problems on outgoing shipments. I'm caught in a two-bladed buzzsaw!"

Purchasing manager Joan Glass interrupts to say, "Harold, we're operating on low inventories because we save money doing it. Many times air freight is the only way I can be sure of getting what I need on time."

Production manager Holtz comments, "And ven I need something, I need it. Take spares. This 'downtime' is an awfully expensive proposition, and ve all know it. Further, by the time Miss Glass here gets me needed production materials, ve are so late that the only way to meet delivery dates is mit overtime and the use of air freight."

Marketing manager Levi joins in, "Whatever the trouble, it seems there must be a way to get an efficient pipeline. If Heinrich is late, then I'm late. We're losing our image as a reliable supplier. Soon, we'll be losing sales!"

Traffic manager Tracks defends himself by saying, "I don't want to seem bitter, but it looks like I'm getting the short end of the stick."

President Gish interrupts to say, "No more excuses. I want action! Costs must come down."

Purchasing manager Glass defends herself by saying, "The lead time problem goes right back through production and eventually to Harold's sales forecasts. I need earlier information."

Marketing manager Levi says, "I have to promise prompt delivery. We all know that the problem is at the other end."

Production manager Holtz suggests, "Like I've been zaying for a long time, ve should combine purchasing and traffic and get them closer to production."

At this point, purchasing manager Glass sounds frustrated when she says, "Heinrich, we're right back where we started. We need lower freight costs, but at the same time we must keep inventory down."

Director of finance Stein says, "Inventory carrying cost is over 30 percent a year. I think that Joan has done a great job. But I do agree with Mr. Gish that transportation costs are way over budget."

President Gish concludes the meeting by saying, "Heinrich's idea is a possibility. We could create a materials management setup. I understand it's the coming thing. I'll give each of you one week to put all your ideas on paper. Be prepared to deliver your reports at our next meeting. I want us out of this fix...and soon!"

1 Discuss the basic inventory problem confronting this firm.
2 Air freight firms keep growing both in numbers and in total dollar value of freight transported. What are the factors that have contributed to the development of this situation? Do they reflect efficient or inefficient management of purchasing, inventories, and production in firms such as this one? Discuss.
3 What should Joan Glass do?
4 Should Glass suggest a materials manager?
5 Should Glass build up her inventories?

A PROBLEM OF PRICE

Sue Jones sat at her desk reflecting on a pricing problem. Sue was a graduate of State University, where she majored in materials management. Since joining the small manufacturing firm of Prestige Plastics in Des Moines, she has been promoted from assistant buyer to buyer. She was responsible for purchasing the chemicals used in producing the firm's plastic products.

Sue was really perplexed by a particular procurement involving the purchase of X-pane, a chemical that was formulated specifically for Prestige Plastics. Thirty-one days ago, she forwarded a request for bids to six vendors for Prestige's estimated annual requirement of 10,000 drums of X-pane. Yesterday morning, Sue opened the five bids that had been received. The bids, F.O.B. Des Moines, were as follows:

	Price per drum ($)	Total price ($) (for estimated requirement of 10,000 drums)
Greater Sandusky Chemical	312	3,120,000
Chicago Chemical Co.	297	2,970,000
Tri-Cities Chemical	323	3,230,000
St. Louis Industries	332	3,320,000
St. Paul Plastics	340	3,400,000

The Chicago Chemical Company was low bidder for the fifth straight year. On the face of it, a decision to award the annual requirements contract to Chicago Chemical looked obvious. The day after the bid opening, the sales engineer from Greater Sandusky Chemical threw Sue a ringer. He said that no one would ever be able to beat Chicago Chemical's price. His firm estimated that setup costs associated with producing X-pane would be approximately $750,000. He went on to say that due to the uncertainties of follow-on orders, his firm would have to amortize this cost over the one-year period of the contract to preclude a loss.

Sue checked with the other unsuccessful bidders. They said substantially the same thing: $700,000 to $850,000 in setup costs were included in their prices.

Next, Sue looked at the history of past purchases of X-pane. She saw that on the initial procurement five years ago, Chicago Chemical's bid was $202 per barrel, $3.00 lower than the second lowest price. Since that time, bid prices had increased, reflecting cost growth in the materials required to produce X-pane. Each year, Chicago Chemical's prices were $3 to $15 lower than those of the unsuccessful competitors.

Sue knew from her purchasing course at State University that when five prerequisites were satisfied, under most conditions, competitive bidding normally resulted in the lowest price. She also knew that it was important to maintain the integrity of the competitive bidding process. But Sue felt a strong sense of uneasiness. Something did not seem right.

1 Under what conditions does competitive bidding normally assure the buyer of obtaining the lowest possible price?

2 Under what conditions may a buyer fall into the "competitive bidding trap"?

3 Which situation existed at Prestige Plastics for the *first* contract? Why?

4 Which situation existed at Prestige Plastics for the *current* buy? Why?

5 Describe three approaches to overcoming Sue's pricing problem.

RANDALL CORPORATION

Bill Huff was a subcontract buyer for Randall Corporation, located in Houston, Texas. His major supplier for mechanical subassemblies was Qualco Corporation of Los Angeles, California. In late 1989, Bill found out that Qualco was experiencing some financial difficulties. By May of 1990, these financial problems had worsened, and Bill wondered what, if anything, he should do.

RANDALL CORPORATION

Randall Corporation was a large supplier to the military, with total sales in 1989 in excess of $3 billion. Depending on the nature of the contract and Randall's capabilities, some military work would be subcontracted. Bill Huff was responsible for a variety of subcontracts, including mechanical subassemblies to machine shops.

Because of the critical nature of the subcontracted subassemblies, Bill thought that quality was the most important criterion for selecting suppliers. The next most important criterion was on-time delivery. Delivery times were important to ensure that the prime contract was completed on time and to avoid penalties for late completion that were usually part of the prime military contract.

Randall's policy was to maintain a minimum of three suppliers, and this was frequently a requirement that was included in the prime military contract as well. Furthermore, Randall's policy was to add suppliers as the volume of purchases increased. The volume of purchases of mechanical subassemblies required five suppliers under this policy. A supplier could not be added without eliminating another; if a supplier were dropped, another had to be added.

SUPPLY MARKET

In Bill's opinion, there were many machine shops in the United States that could produce good-quality mechanical subassemblies of the type required by Randall. These companies were typically small businesses owned by inde-

Copyrighted by the National Association of Purchasing Management. Reprinted by permission. This case was written by Alan Brokaw during one of the NAPM-sponsored case writing workshops.

pendent entrepreneurs. The profit margins for these companies were typically 10 to 12 percent of sales. For the mechanical subassemblies that Bill bought, location was not an important consideration because the freight costs were very low in comparison to the price of the products.

When a military contract required mechanical subassemblies, Bill would award the business among his five suppliers. In 1989, Bill had placed 40 percent, or $2.5 million, of his total mechanical subassembly volume with Qualco; the remaining 60 percent was evenly divided among the other four suppliers. In 1985, just before Qualco became a supplier for Randall, Qualco's sales were $900,000.

Qualco had become Randall's major supplier for mechanical subassemblies because of its superior performance. The company always met its delivery schedule, and the quality of its products was unsurpassed. In addition, its prices were about 12 percent below competitive machine shops. When Bill originally started to contract with Qualco, he was concerned about these low prices. He wanted his suppliers to make reasonable profits and therefore become good, long-term sources of supply. He found that Qualco's labor rates, machinery, and capabilities were similar to other machine shops he was using. However, Qualco was able to obtain much lower scrap rates than the rest of the industry. As a result, Qualco could charge lower prices and still maintain healthy profit margins.

Over the last three years, Qualco had been an excellent supplier. Qualco had also helped Randall by producing prototypes of subassemblies, which were useful in evaluating military systems before production.

FINANCIAL PROBLEMS AT QUALCO

In December 1989, Bill was told by the sales representative for Qualco that Qualco was having difficulty paying its representatives. At the same time, Bill observed that Qualco had remodeled its offices in a luxurious style. The owner of the company had recently taken his family on two cruises, and he had purchased a new luxury automobile.

In April 1990, the sales representative for Qualco told Bill that Qualco owed him $18,000 for back salary and bonuses. At about the same time, the owner called Randall's accounts payable department. He complained that a $40,000 invoice was two days overdue. He said to them, "I need the money. I may have to shut down if you don't pay me now." In May 1990, Bill learned that Qualco had "factored" its accounts receivable at 3 percent with National Acceptance Corporation.

Based on these events, Bill was concerned about the financial management and stability of Qualco. He was worried that he would suddenly be faced with the loss of his major supplier of mechanical subassemblies. Bill also knew that he would have to award subcontracts for a new $320,000 mechanical subassembly within two weeks. This requirement could grow to $2 million worth of subassembly business.

1 What is the relationship between financial soundness and supplier performance?
2 What action should Bill take?

RIPLEY ENGINE COMPANY

In early 1989, Tom Kemp, procurement specialist for R&D at Ripley Engine Company, Birmingham, Alabama, and a three-man team were responsible for recommending which potential suppliers should receive a request for proposal (RFP) for an important new component for small turbine aircraft engines. One of the four potential suppliers in the market, Aerolog, Inc., had been disqualified as a supplier to Ripley in early 1987. Tom wondered whether to include Aerolog, Inc., on the RFP list.

RIPLEY ENGINE COMPANY

In its nearly four decades of operation, Ripley had built more than 45,000 turbine engines for a wide variety of commercial, industrial, and military applications. Annual sales in 1988 were about $1 billion. Major product lines included aircraft propulsion systems, compact and powerful gas turbines for power generation systems, and larger, more rugged turbine systems for high-precision industrial applications. Noted for its research and development and innovation, Ripley led the very profitable market for small gas turbines. The company had a reputation for high quality and had always leaned on its suppliers for both quality products and on-time deliveries. The product lines all had worldwide applications in existing markets. Major customers looked to Ripley for research and development activities to improve overall operations.

In the mid-1980s, Ripley initiated actions to miniaturize the fabricated metallic components of certain engines to reduce both their weight and size. Several of these special efforts had progressed to the design and procurement phase.

PROCUREMENT AT RIPLEY

Procurement operations for turbo machinery projects were divided into four major activities under the management of David Nelson. (See Exhibit 1.)

Procurement to support research and development projects was accomplished by eight procurement specialists under the supervision of Joseph Moncreif. Typically, this work to support R&D was completed in very close

EXHIBIT 1
Organizational chart.

coordination with the engineers and quality control personnel responsible for the research project. Indeed, for major projects, a two-step supplier selection process was used. Step 1 involved selecting potential suppliers to receive the RFP, while Step 2 involved evaluating the supplier proposals actually received.

The two-step process was completed by a team of specialists representing engineering, procurement, and quality assurance. The procurement specialist was usually the team leader.

In early 1989, a supplier-selection team was appointed to select suppliers for an RFP for a highly complex fabricated metal component for small turbine engines for the aircraft market. The team was headed by Tom Kemp of R&D Procurement. The other members of the team were two engineers and a representative from quality control. The members of the team brought the following expertise to the task:

- *Tom Kemp*, team leader, had been with the company about two years. He graduated from Whittier College in 1975 with a major in physics. After college, he worked two years with the committee to re-elect President Ford and then was a lobbyist in Washington, D.C. A contact with business led to a major job in purchasing with a California firm. In 1987, he moved to the Ripley Company in Birmingham, Alabama.

- *George Smith*, the senior engineer on the team, had been with the company for fifteen years. He was a highly respected R&D engineer. He held an undergraduate degree from MIT and had done graduate work at Cal Tech.
- *Fred Brown*, the other engineer, had been with the company about ten years. He held an engineering degree from Purdue University and had worked as an R&D engineer at Ripley since graduating from college.
- *Paul Logan*, quality control, had been with the company about four years. He was a quality control engineer by training with an M.B.A. from Case Western University. Paul had a reputation for being a very tough man when quality was in question.

PROCEDURES FOR SELECTING POTENTIAL SUPPLIERS TO RECEIVE THE RFP

Typically, the RFP team responsibilities included:

1 Identifying all potential suppliers.
2 Developing a detailed analysis of each potential supplier.
3 Recommending the potential list of suppliers to a corporate-level review board, consisting of the vice president of engineering, the director of purchasing, and the program manager. The board decided which firms were to be on the RFP list.
4 Conducting the analysis of the proposals actually received from the firms on the RFP list.
5 Recommending a firm for contract negotiations.

COMPLEX METAL FABRICATION INDUSTRY

The team members discovered rather quickly and somewhat to their surprise that the industry capable of supplying the needed fabricated metal components consisted of only four firms. Their initial research uncovered the fact that one of these four firms, Aerolog, Inc., had been disqualified two years earlier as a supplier to Ripley for both quality and delivery problems. The Aerolog incident had required extensive litigation in 1986–87. Aerolog had a bad reputation with the old timers at Ripley.

The team listed these facts about the firms:

1 Aerolog appeared to be fully qualified as a bidder based on the criteria developed for technology, plant capacity, utilization rates, managerial team, and finances.
2 Two other firms, Reck Aerospace and Crum Aerospace, also appeared to be fully qualified.
3 The fourth firm, Northeast Machine Works, was questionable in the context of plant capacity and utilization rates. The firm appeared to have a superior managerial team.

EXHIBIT 2
COMPARATIVE DATA ON POTENTIAL SUPPLIERS

	Aerolog, Inc.	Reck Aerospace	Crum Aerospace	Northeast Machine Works
Technology (scale 1 to 50)[a]	48	47	49	46
Capacity				
sufficient	Yes	Yes	Yes	Yes
utilization rate	80%	82%	79%	90%
Financial status				
current ratio	2.36	2.22	2.02	2.56
quick ratio	1.35	1.10	.93	1.50
debt to equity	.75	.73	.76	.76
Sales (millions)—1988	$41,759.9	$18,653.0	$9,653.4	$7,543.8
Sales growth over past year	10%	9.8%	11%	3%
Cost of goods sold	89.6%	88.7%	90.3%	89.3%
Change from last year	−3%	−.5%	+2%	+ 3.5%
Managerial team (scale 1 to 10)	9.4	9.2	9.1	9.6
Quality reputation[b] long term (scale 1 to 10)	5	9	8.5	9.3
Last two years	9.5	9	8.7	9.4

[a]All scales 1 to 50, etc., are based on big being best.
[b]Based on information collected from other customers.

4 Many senior managers, engineers, and others were strongly opposed to considering Aerolog for anything at Ripley.

5 Word that Aerolog might get its foot back in the door spread throughout R&D, engineering, marketing, and quality control like a prairie fire.

6 Phone calls and comments to the team all seemed to say "not again," or more specifically, "You will be sorry you did that!" and "It's been nice knowing you."

7 See Exhibit 2 for comparative data on the suppliers developed by the team.

As Tom and the team met early on July 21, 1989, they knew they had to bite the bullet on this issue. Should Aerolog be included on the list for the RFP? Their list and analysis was to be presented to the Corporate Review Board at 9 A.M. on July 23, 1989.

1 What are the arguments favoring Aerolog's inclusion on the list?
2 What are the arguments against Aerolog's inclusion?
3 What would you recommend?

ROBOTICS, INC.

Robotics, Inc., of Chicago placed an order for four automatic welders with the Michigan Manufacturing Company. The order was on a fixed price basis of $200,000 per unit, F.O.B. Detroit (shipping point). The Robotics traffic manager designated a carrier and routes, and Michigan Manufacturing acknowledged the order without change.

Within six months the welders were completed, and they were shipped by Michigan Manufacturing. However, instead of shipping via Conrail, Robotics' designated carrier, Michigan shipped by truck. As was customary, Michigan invoiced Robotics immediately. Robotics paid immediately to take advantage of the cash discount.

En route to Chicago, the truck, a common carrier, collided with a tractor-trailer. The truck rolled over an embankment causing total loss of the four automatic welders.

When the buyer contacted the Michigan Manufacturing Company concerning the loss-in-transit, he was told that Michigan Manufacturing disclaimed all responsibility. "The units were sold F.O.B. Detroit, and title passed to Robotics at that time." When the buyer pointed out that Michigan Manufacturing Company did not ship via Robotics' designated routes or carrier, he was told, "We saved Robotics transportation costs by shipping via a less expensive carrier. You approved of our method of shipment by paying our invoice. The responsibility of filing a claim with the trucker clearly must be yours."

1 What is the significance of the F.O.B. point? What are the advantages and disadvantages of F.O.B. point of delivery? F.O.B. shipping point?
2 Whose responsibility is it to file claim with the carrier? Discuss.

RUHLING MANUFACTURING COMPANY

The Ruhling Manufacturing Company was founded in 1901 by Cyrus Ruhling. Until 1915, the firm made electric motors. In 1915, Mr. Ruhling was persuaded by the War Department to take on several defense contracts. Ruhling expanded rapidly. After World War I, Ruhling found itself the possessor of much excess capacity. Cyrus decided to cater to the small but growing home appliance industry. Today, Ruhling is one of the nation's largest appliance manufacturers.

Although appliances account for all the firm's sales, a small electric motor capacity has been retained, partly for historic purposes and partly to protect against unforeseen contingencies. Whenever feasible, Ruhling follows a dual sourcing policy. In some cases, three sources may be under contract.

Last month, purchasing issued an invitation for bids for $11/32$-horsepower motors for a six-month period. Ruhling's estimated price for the motors was $29.00. The quantity estimated was 48,000 motors over the six-month period. Orders were to be placed daily through the firm's automated material requirements planning system, with deliveries to be within one week of release of an order.

Three days ago, the bids were opened. They were as follows:

Able Electric	$30.00
Beta Products	28.00
Gamma Manufacturing	32.00
Delta Electric	29.25
Epsilon Products	30.00

Today, prior to the award of a purchase order, Epsilon Products contacted the buyer and submitted an alternative proposal. Under the proposal, Epsilon would reduce its bid to $23.75 if Ruhling would agree to purchase all its requirements for this size motor from Epsilon for a period of one year. Ruhling would be free to release delivery quantities at its own convenience and Epsilon would guarantee to meet them within three days. Epsilon would carry three months of normal inventory (24,000 motors) and would increase its capacity if demand warranted.

1 Should Epsilon's alternative proposal be considered?
2 Comment on the practice of dual sourcing, when part of the requirement is produced internally. Relate this practice to the advantages and disadvantages of a 100 percent requirements contract.

SAMPSON PRODUCTS

Sampson Products Corporation was a major manufacturer of electrical equipment used extensively by consumer goods manufacturers. The company sold most of its products to manufacturers of refrigerators, automatic washers, and electric stoves to be installed as original equipment that usually retained the Sampson brand name. In addition to the original equipment market, Sampson had obtained a significant portion of the replacement market for the products it manufactured. Sales of Sampson replacement parts were normally made through channels such as small hardware stores and other home repair retail outlets. Another substantial part of Sampson's revenue was derived from manufacturing electrical equipment for large electrical supply houses under the brand names of those outlets.

Sampson's annual sales averaged approximately $400 million. Of this total, the production and sale of small electric motors accounted for over $100 million. Although Sampson was one of the largest producers of small motors in the United States, there were four other competing companies of comparable size, as well as several smaller manufacturers. Approximately one-fourth of the company's production of motors was used to fill contracts with manufacturers of air conditioners, vacuum cleaners, and other power equipment for the home. These motors carried the brand name of the retailer; hence, Sampson referred to these contracts as "special brand business."

In 1986 Sampson Products obtained a special brand contract with General Company to manufacture $20 million of "General" motors. General was a major U.S. electrical products manufacturer with annual sales of approximately $750 million. Sampson had been awarded the contract after bidding competitively against one of the other large motor manufacturers and five of the smaller firms. Sampson's sales manager believed his bid had been accepted because of the excellent quality and reputation of the firm's motors, not because it offered the lowest price. Although the contract terminated annually, new contracts had been negotiated each year to the satisfaction of both parties, and Sampson had obtained the contract to manufacture motors for General again during 1991. Sampson succeeded in making an average before-tax profit of 9 percent on this contract, which management considered very satisfactory for this type of business.

While General Company had become an important customer for Sampson Products, General also *sold* to Sampson small rotor shafts used in some of Sampson's small high-speed motors. General manufactured these shafts in its machine shop division, which had been acquired in a merger seven years ago. Mr. George Smithe, director of purchases for Sampson, estimated that his department had purchased approximately $200,000 of shafts a year since 1987. In February 1989, Mr. Smithe negotiated a five-year contract with General, which obligated General to sell $200,000 of shafts each year at a fixed price of $3.10 per shaft (with escalation for labor and materials provided these costs rose by more than 10 percent). When the contract was developed, it contained a clause that provided General with an option to cancel the agreement at any time, with a three-month notice to Sampson. However, Mr. Jones, sales manager for the machine shop division of General, assured Mr. Smithe that his company would exercise the option only in the case of highly unusual, unforeseen circumstances.

The shafts were made of a special alloy that was in very short supply. Moreover, there were strong indications that the U.S. government might restrict all nonmilitary applications of the material to conserve supplies for military use. Accordingly, Sampson decided to purchase several years' supply of shafts before any government regulations could materialize. Consequently, Mr. Smithe was working on the procurement of approximately $1 million of motor shafts during 1990. Although Sampson was impressed by the performance of General shafts, Mr. Smithe decided to solicit competitive bids from several prospective suppliers. After investigation, he selected four major motor shaft manufacturers that had outstanding reputations for quality, service, and efficient operations. General Company was one of the producers from whom a quotation was requested.

The day following the receipt of General's quotation, Mr. Smithe was visited by Mr. Jones and the president of the machine shop division of General. Mr. Smithe understood that the president had a widely recognized reputation as an extremely aggressive, hard-hitting, sales-minded executive. Smithe's impression was quickly confirmed. From the beginning of the conversation he was the target of the president's well-known pressure tactics. The president informed Smithe in no uncertain terms that he felt the "friendship" of the two companies was at stake and reciprocal considerations were in order. Smithe informed the president that his bid was the highest received, and he suggested that the president knew by approximately how much he was high. Smithe stated that normally second bids were not accepted, but because of previous friendship he would in this case accept a revised bid from General. The president's reaction was to leave the meeting in anger with the parting comment that Smithe had better think again about awarding the contract to General—and fast.

Mr. Smithe set aside the shaft contract during the ensuing two weeks, partly as a result of his offer to the General representatives and also because he wanted to devote time to other problems. At that point, the president of Sampson Products asked Mr. Smithe to come to his office. The president stated that he had "just had a lengthy conversation with the chairman of the board of directors of the General Company. The chairman appeared to be exceedingly interested in getting that motor shaft contract you are presently considering. It seems the president of the machine shop division needs the work and is eager to get the order. He told the chairman that General's case might be strengthened if he brought the situation to my personal attention."

Mr. Smithe proceeded to outline the events surrounding the contract to the president. He also stated that he had not decided what action should be taken, but thus far had been against awarding General any portion of the shaft contract for four reasons:

1 There was no economic basis for General to insist on a premium price. In his opinion, General was attempting to take advantage of its substantial motor purchases to obtain a higher shaft price than was economically justified.

2 Doing business on a reciprocal basis, in his opinion, was a dangerous precedent and presented difficult administrative and control problems. "People are buying our products because they feel we provide the best value at the best price. If we start paying premiums for purchased materials, regardless of the reason, we risk losing that reputation as well as sales to those who are not our suppliers."

3 Mr. Smithe also believed General was bluffing. In his opinion, General was well satisfied with the quality and price of the motors, which was or should be the primary consideration of its purchasing them.

4 Finally, Mr. Smithe stated that he felt the only repercussion would be a possible cancellation of the long-term shaft contract. However, he believed that even the possibility of General exercising this option was remote since it would practically shut the door on any future shaft business from Sampson.

The president concluded the conversation by saying, "I see you have a good grasp of all the facts involved, George. In my opinion, this is a purchasing problem. You are our director of purchases, so it's your decision to make—and I wish you luck."

During the next week, Mr. Smithe received a second visit from Mr. Jones and the president of the machine shop division of General. During this visit, the conversation became very heated. The president of the machine shop division of General stated, "You get $20 million of business from us and we get $1 million of business from you; you can't find a better deal than that!" The president also reminded Smithe that the long-term contract could be canceled. After making this statement, the machine shop division president abruptly stormed out of the room in a very angry mood. Mr. Jones was a few steps behind the president. Before they reached the door, Mr. Smithe reminded them that he was going to complete the motor shaft contract the next day. He added that he hoped General would submit a new price by 10 A.M. the following morning. Mr. Jones replied that they would see what could be done, but the president left the office without another word or an acknowledging glance.

By 3:00 P.M. the following day, Mr. Smithe had not received any communication from the representative of General Company.

1 What are the basic policy issues in this situation? Analyze and discuss each of them.
2 What action should Mr. Smithe take? Why?

SDC CORPORATION

SDC Corporation is a large, high-technology manufacturer of sophisticated electromechanical devices. Its current manufacturing operations are diversified between several major product lines. Recently, SDC developed a new product line centered around the production of an electronic tracking device. The tracking device is placed in fleet vehicles such as taxi cabs, delivery trucks, and courier vans. During operation, it emits an electronic signal that is monitored at a central tracking console located near the dispatcher.

To facilitate a rapid entry into the market, SDC decided to rely on Hangsu Manufacturing Company in Japan to provide four critical electromechanical switching devices. Hangsu has a proven track record in supplying these components for Japanese applications. Hangsu had produced 40,000 of these components used in a similar tracking device in Japan. At the time of the decision, the exchange rate was acceptable.

SDC had experience *selling* finished goods on the international market; however, this was the firm's first attempt to use foreign subcontractors. SDC decided to use MTC, a Japanese trading company, to negotiate the initial

This case was developed by Christine Grambling, Robert Balderas, David Guebert, and Loven Lasche under the direction of Professor David N. Burt.

agreement with Hangsu. The agreement was negotiated, and Hangsu supplied the components in accordance with the SDC performance specification.

SDC has only one major competitor in the tracking device market. The total domestic market is estimated to be 100,000 units. SDC had already won one contract with Fleetway Trucking for 2,700 units, contingent on a successful pilot test of 100 units. Unfortunately, Fleetway subsequently terminated the contract due to nonperformance of the test units. The operating problem was attributed to failure of the Japanese components to perform according to specification.

Another contract for 1,000 units was awarded to SDC by Nationwide Cab Service. Having heard about Fleetway's problem, however, Nationwide placed the contract "on hold" pending the outcome of a more stringent pilot test to be performed by SDC.

SDC deals directly with Hangsu on technical and production problems. MTC operates as Hangsu's representative for all financial and contractual decisions. SDC feels that the device's operating problems are confined to the four components produced by Hangsu. To resolve the problem, SDC has requested that Hangsu rework the components contained in the original 2,700 units, and ensure that the next 1,000 units fully meet the performance specification.

Relations with MTC/Hangsu have deteriorated somewhat at this point in time. Hangsu feels that the SDC specification has been extensively modified and does not reflect the original design agreed on for the components. With over 40,000 similar tracking devices operating successfully in Japan—all using the Hangsu components—Hangsu is confident that it has met all specification requirements.

Frustrated by the inability to reach an agreement, Tom Decker, purchasing manager for SDC, has decided to withhold $1 million from MTC/Hangsu to establish a better negotiating position. In addition, deterioration of the yen/dollar exchange rate has made future dealings with Hangsu uncertain, at best. Tom Decker realizes that the Japanese will negotiate with a long-term perspective (four to five years) in mind, while he is being pressured to address SDC's current bottom-line difficulties.

1 How could Tom Decker have avoided the problems encountered with Hangsu? Discuss in detail.
2 What negotiation skills should Decker rely on to achieve SDC's objectives?
3 How can Decker get the 3,700 units reworked to meet specification?

SELECTION OF A PRESSURE VESSEL MANUFACTURER

On August 1, the engineering department hand-carried a purchase requisition to Jack Toole, buyer, purchasing department, Oceanics, Inc. The requisition covered the purchase of one pressure vessel to Oceanics' specifications as outlined in the requisition. Immediately, Jack went to work. He prepared a request for quotations asking twenty major pressure vessel manufacturers to have their proposals in his hands no later than Wednesday, August 31st. The response to Jack's request for quotations was amazing.

During the month of August, eighteen of the twenty companies hurriedly prepared their proposals and submitted them to Jack within the allotted bidding time. As each proposal was received on Jack's desk, copies were forwarded to the engineer and manufacturing engineer for preliminary evaluation. By September 5, Jack called a meeting in his office with the engineer, Mr. Holpine, and the manufacturing engineer, Mr. Grinn.

During the course of the meeting, proposals were carefully screened and bidders were eliminated one by one until two companies remained. It was a difficult decision for the group to decide which of the two companies submitted the better proposal. The advantages and disadvantages of each supplier appeared to be about equal. Jack pointed out that Atomic Products Company submitted a lower estimated price, guaranteed the equipment, was more suitably located, and would meet the required delivery date. Jack also pointed out to Grinn and Holpine that Nuclear Vessels, Inc., offered Oceanics lower hourly and overhead rates, a minimum amount of subcontracting, and excellent past experience in making similar vessels. Jack stated that a field trip would be necessary to talk with both suppliers to determine which one was best qualified. At this point the meeting was adjourned and plans were made to visit both companies the following week. (See Exhibits 1 and 2, pages 806 and 807.)

In following through with purchasing policy, Jack called the vice president of Oceanics' New York sales office and advised him of the potential trip. Jack learned that Atomic Products was a potential customer for Oceanics' products, but Oceanics' sales representatives were unable to get into the plant to meet key people responsible for procurement of major equipment. The vice president of sales stated that a sales rep would be at the airport to meet Oceanics' representatives and take them to the Atomic Products Company first thing Monday morning. Jack phoned the president, Mr. Wilcox, and advised him that representatives from Oceanics would like to be at his plant Monday morning to review his plant facilities and meet the responsible people. The president did not appear to be enthusiastic, but said that he would be pleased to see them when they arrived.

Another call was also made to Nuclear Vessels' president, Mr. Winninghoff, who was quite enthusiastic about the potential visit and asked if he could meet the group at the airport, make hotel reservations, or perform other courtesies. Jack advised Mr. Winninghoff that these matters were taken care of and that an Oceanics' sales representative for the Houston, Texas, area would accompany the group during the visit.

Monday morning, Messrs. Toole, Grinn, and Holpine took off from Pittsburgh and arrived at Kennedy Airport in New York. Mr. Morgan, the

---

EXHIBIT 1

ATOMIC PRODUCTS COMPANY, NEW YORK, N.Y.

We are pleased to submit a proposal in accordance with your request for the manufacture of one pressure vessel in accordance with your sketch #835 and all referenced specifications pointed out in your letter of August 2.

Price. Because of the potential changes pointed out in your invitation to bid, and in line with your request, the work will be performed on a cost-plus-a-fixed-fee contract detailed as follows:

a. Total price:	Estimated cost	$1,120,000
	Fixed fee	112,000
	Total	$1,232,000
b. Costing rate:	Estimated shop rate	$24/hour
	Shop overhead	180%
	Material	Cost+10% handling charge

Shop facilities. There are adequate facilities at our New York Plant to manufacture the vessel and meet the specification to the fullest extent possible. We invite you and your associates to visit our facilities.

Past experience. Our company has not made vessels of this size but does have the equipment and know-how necessary to perform the work. Our experience has been in working with vessels up to 60″ in length, I.D. 30″ and 3″ wall.

Subcontracting. We will be able to fabricate the entire vessel without exception in our shop.

Organization. A total of 2000 employees is directly associated with our division.

Delivery. The pressure vessel will be shipped f.o.b. shipping point via rail in 6 months providing there are no engineering changes.

Guarantee. We guarantee workmanship and materials to be in accordance with the specifications which were supplied to us at the time of this proposal.

---

sales manager of Oceanics' New York office, met the group and drove them to the main office of the Atomic Products Company. The group registered, obtained passes, and went to the conference room. Shortly thereafter, the manager of production, Mr. Strickland, entered, introduced himself, and stated that the president was tied up but would see them later in the day. Jack Toole opened the meeting by stating that Atomic Products' proposal was among the top contenders for supplying the pressure vessel and it was Oceanics' desire to look over Atomic Products' facilities and meet the people responsible for the job. Jack Toole asked Holpine to explain in greater detail the use of the vessel in the reactor system and to give Mr. Strickland some background on the engineering work relating to the vessel. Mr. Grinn reviewed the manufacturing aspects of the vessel as required by the basic specifications. Near the end of this discussion, Jack Toole asked Mr. Strickland if Holpine's and Grinn's comments had the same meaning as Atomic Products' interpretation of the specifications. Mr. Strickland agreed, but was somewhat concerned over the rigid cleaning specification. As he told the group, "It is difficult for a shop our size to construct a temporary building

EXHIBIT 2
NUCLEAR VESSELS, INC., HOUSTON, TEXAS

Reference is made to your invitation to bid dated August 2 to manufacture the pressure vessel in accordance with your negative #835, and referenced specifications and any future changes necessary.

Price. The work will be performed on a cost-plus-a-fixed-fee basis, broken down as follows:

a. Total price:	Estimated cost	$1,560,000
	Fixed fee	1
	Total	$1,560,001

b. Costing rates:	Estimated shop rate	$16/hour
	Shop overhead	160%
	Material	At cost

Shop facilities. We have adequate shop facilities to manufacture and deliver the vessel and would be pleased to have representatives from your company visit our facilities at any time.

Past experience. The company has had extensive experience in manufacturing pressure vessels of heavy plate. Vessels 80" I.D., 49' long, 5" thick and many others have been handled by this company.

Subcontracting. It will not be necessary for the company to subcontract any of the forming, welding, machining, or testing for this work. However, forgings will be purchased from a competent vendor after he has satisfied the company's metallurgist that his forgings will meet the specifications.

Organization. The Purchasing, Expediting, Quality Control, Production and other departments will each have one man assigned to follow this project from start to finish. Forms and records are available for your review. Our organization is familiar with Oceanics' requirements from knowledge gained as a result of previous work accomplished for your division.

Delivery. The pressure vessel will be shipped f.o.b. shipping point, Houston, Texas, to your Pittsburgh location within your required delivery time of six months or shortly thereafter.

Guarantee. This company will guarantee only workmanship. The rigid material specifications make it difficult for our supplier to furnish plate without any inclusion of slag deposits. Oceanics will have to stand the costs of any plate rejected or repaired after being tested by ultrasonic methods. Such costs can be negotiated after such defects are found.

around the pressure vessel, make such a building airtight, and compel our workmen to wear white coveralls, gloves, and to adhere to surgical cleanliness requirements. I doubt if we can erect such a building in our present shop area. Instead, we may add a lean-to to the outside of our existing buildings."

The meeting with the production manager lasted one hour; then the group commenced to tour the shop. Grinn noted that most of the machines, such as the vertical boring mill, horizontal mill planer, radial drills, and beam press, were comparatively new and well maintained.

Jack Toole wondered why Atomic Products' estimated cost was lower than Nuclear Vessels', yet Atomic Products' costing rates were somewhat higher. With this thought in mind, he asked Mr. Strickland, "Do you consider your shop to be better equipped than your competitors'?" Mr. Strickland replied that it was their management's feeling that this shop was the best equipped in the United States to handle such vessels, and that even though the shop rates were higher than other shops, they would turn out more work in less time than any competitor. Holpine asked Mr. Strickland why their past experience was limited to smaller-sized vessels, to which Mr. Strickland replied that they could handle any size vessel up to and beyond the one required by Oceanics, but had never received a contract for such vessels.

Atomic Products Company was a union shop that had several major strikes during the past few years. There were a total of 2,000 people employed, and the plant covered approximately 470,000 square feet of floor area.

The general appearance of the shop was excellent. The group noticed that the aisles were clean, that there was ample lighting, adequate ventilation, up-to-date laboratories, good inspection facilities, and that the overall appearance of the building was extremely neat and well ordered.

The group pointed out several items in production and asked Mr. Strickland the ultimate use of these products. They received a vague reply, such as, "These are a number of special jobs we have in the shop that we can handle without any trouble."

Mr. Strickland interrupted a group of employees standing in a corner and asked one of them to show the group the inspection and quality control departments. Both departments were well staffed and had up-to-date equipment.

The group asked Mr. Strickland to show them control of incoming materials vital to potential Oceanics' work. Wrong material that might possibly get into such a pressure vessel would contaminate the entire nuclear system. Mr. Strickland did not offer the group any evidence of materials control, but stated that they had produced hundreds of smaller vessels and had no trouble in the segregation of materials.

The metallurgical and chemical laboratories were well staffed and could provide Oceanics with adequate test specimens required by the specifications.

At the end of the tour, the group met with the president, who asked, "Do you think that our facilities are adequate to do the job?" Jack Toole replied that the facilities were impressive, but that the final selection of the supplier would be determined by many factors and that facilities were only part of the total evaluation. The president then replied, "If you want us to do the work, let us know and we will commence contract negotiations."

Several days later, Messrs. Toole, Grinn, and Holpine left New York and flew to Houston, Texas, for a visit to Nuclear Vessels, Inc. When the group registered in the hotel at 5 P.M., they found a call waiting for them from Mr. Winninghoff, president of Nuclear Vessels. Mr. Winninghoff asked the group to meet that evening at the Houston Country Club for dinner and business discussions. At 1:30 A.M., the group returned to the hotel.

The following morning, the Nuclear Vessels' chauffeur met Oceanics' team and the representative from Oceanics' sales office at the hotel and took them to Mr. Winninghoff's office. In the office, Mr. Winninghoff was waiting with the vice president of engineering, vice president of marketing, vice president of manufacturing, and other key figures in the organization. Jack Toole opened the meeting in much the same manner as was done at Atomic Products Company. After the Oceanics' people had gone into detail on the vessel, Jack Toole asked Mr. Winninghoff if they had any questions concerning the specifications. There were no comments, so the entire group commenced to tour the shop.

Mr. Grinn immediately noticed that the company's machines were of considerable age and not of large capacity, but adequate for the job. Some outside subcontracting work for the close machining tolerances would be required. Mr. Winninghoff stated: "True, we may not have all the necessary machines here, but there are ample machines available at other divisions, such as the large vertical boring mill at our El Paso, Texas, subsidiary plant. The schedule is such that we can move work into other divisions without delay." It was noted that general working conditions such as heating, lighting, ventilation, and cleanliness were not as adequate as Atomic Products'. Jack Toole noted that the higher estimated cost resulted from more man-hours required to make the vessel because of less adequate machines.

Mr. Winninghoff stopped by one of the shop foremen and asked, "Say, Sam, how about giving these gentlemen from Oceanics an idea of what your group will be doing in the forming and rolling of the pressure vessel?" Sam had several of his men stop work to show the equipment available and its intended use. Mr. Winninghoff mentioned to the group that their plant had been on a profit-sharing plan since it was organized. The employees never organized a union.

There appeared to be effective control between management and the shop. For instance, to carry out the work fully, one member each from purchasing, expediting, quality control, and scheduling was assigned to a task force headed by a project engineer. It was the responsibility of this task force to follow the entire project through the shop and keep the project engineer informed on a day-to-day basis.

Nuclear Vessels had constructed one vessel considerably larger than the vessel required by Oceanics. Mr. Winninghoff claimed that they ran into numerous problems at the beginning of manufacturing and that the experience gained in the production of such a large vessel made them change their organization for closer follow-up. They also changed the type of paperwork and records for better control of material. The group noticed that each piece of material in the shop was marked for the project of its intended use. The metallurgical and chemical laboratories were very large, but much of their equipment was old. They appeared to have adequate room for the location of a cleaning room.

On Friday of the same week, Toole called a meeting of Holpine and Grinn to evaluate the two companies being considered. Holpine argued strongly that Nuclear Vessels should be given a contract because of their extreme enthusiasm to carry out the job, their past experience in manufacturing pressure vessels of equal size, and their previous Oceanics experience. Said Holpine, "Atomic Products has not had experience with our rigid specifications and the price and delivery will probably slip." Grinn argued that Atomic Products should be the company selected because of their adequate shop and laboratory facilities, location, ability to meet delivery date, and ability to guarantee the vessel.

Neither Holpine nor Grinn took into consideration the cost, the company's organization, guarantees, and other business considerations. It was Jack Toole's responsibility to evaluate both of these companies and show which company should be given the contract.

1 What specific areas and activities should the Oceanics group have investigated on its two visits?
2 Evaluate each supplier on each of the above items using information obtained on the field visits.
3 Based on the face value of the written proposals, which company appeared to submit the better offer?
4 Based on the proposal plus information obtained from the case history, which company is likely to be the better supplier?
5 What do you recommend?

SENATOR FOGHORN

Senator Foghorn was a powerful political figure from the South who secretly enjoyed Yankee land far more than he could ever let anybody know. During his stay in Washington, he made some important business and political connections. As a result, when he was not reelected, he was able to secure several positions as a director for large companies and banks. This served as a sufficient excuse to keep him from going back to the South.

It was not too long a time until he was able to acquire a majority interest in a plating plant in New Jersey. The plant had good facilities and some excellent customers. The former senator naturally wished to expand its operation and started to use some of his political influence in business contacts to that end.

He was also able to get himself enmeshed in a very large housing project in Washington. Through his business affiliations and political contacts at local, county, state, and national levels, Mr. Foghorn maintained that he could exert powerful pressures on the architect and contractors for the housing project to buy from manufacturers of his selection. He said they were very receptive to pressure of this type. His recommendations carried much weight, said Senator Foghorn, and would be the deciding factor in the selection of suppliers on the housing project. With this in mind he approached selected manufacturers to obtain business for his plating plant and offered them in return his help in obtaining orders for the housing project.

One of the companies he approached was Maryland Electric, a firm in a position to supply all the electrical equipment and all the electrical appliances that would be required for the housing project. Foghorn went to see several vice presidents of Maryland, as well as Mr. Selby (in charge of trade relations), and explained that he was in a position to influence greatly the placement of the electrical work. While he did not say so, he intimated that he could almost guarantee it. Knowing that such influence did not come gratuitously, Mr. Selby tried to probe the former senator for the amount and the form of the return favor. His answer was a detailed explanation of the fine plating plant Foghorn controlled and the excellent quality of the plating it produced.

Mr. Selby knew that the amount of business that Maryland would have to place with the plating plant would be considerable in view of the fact that the order for the electrical equipment and appliances would run into several million dollars. The completely decentralized operation of Maryland Electric posed a problem in such cases, because many division managers and purchasing managers would have to be sold on the advantages of such a move.

In addition, Maryland owned its own plating facility, which was currently producing more than 75 percent of the company's requirements. The plating facility was operating at 60 percent of capacity at best, and it was trying to secure more work. In spite of these problems, Mr. Selby decided to investigate the possibilities of using Senator Foghorn's plant. This investigation showed that the 25 percent of the company plating requirements that were bought "outside" were purchased from basic raw material producers or from highly specialized platers who did nothing but intricate work. All of them were good Maryland customers.

Several days passed and Mr. Selby was still unable to resolve the problem. Naturally, he wanted to participate in the housing development, but there was no easy way of giving Senator Foghorn's plating plant any of Maryland's business. During this period Senator Foghorn had produced a very good contract for Maryland in molded plastic parts. He had done this, he said, to prove his value and show his good intentions toward Maryland. In addition, he spoke of other contracts, including one for an extremely large hydroelectric project in Asia. About this time Mr. Selby learned that Mr. Johnson, a recently retired president of one of the largest mail-order companies in the world, had joined forces with Senator Foghorn. The mail-order company handled Maryland equipment exclusively, and the retired president had been singly responsible for this purchasing agreement. Mr. Johnson visited Mr. Selby and reiterated the great influence that Senator Foghorn had with the housing project contracts, as well as his many other areas of influence.

1 Should Maryland Electric become involved with Senator Foghorn? If so, to what degree?

2 Should business be taken from Maryland's own plating plant or regularly good sources of supply to satisfy Senator Foghorn?

SIGNAL-TEK CORPORATION

BACKGROUND

Signal-Tek Corporation was founded in 1963. Following a series of new product developments, mergers, and acquisitions, the company evolved into an $82.5 million corporation with wholly owned subsidiaries operating in Colorado, Indiana, England, and Germany. The Denver division generates approximately $30 million in revenues, primarily from function generators. These general-purpose test and measurement instrumentation products are used in a variety of industrial, laboratory, and defense applications.

The Denver division had enjoyed several years of market leadership in these products based on innovative design, low cost, and high product quality. However, in recent years, Signal-Tek's product brand recognition has begun to slip due to its inability to meet competition. Based on more timely introduction of newer, low-cost products, two larger instrument manufacturers have been taking some of the division's market share. Signal-Tek has been unable to respond quickly enough to these competitive pressures and, as a result, has had to reduce its work force by almost 15 percent recently. It has become clear that the division must regain its market position by refocusing on its goals of timely introduction of low-cost, solid-performance, high-reliability instruments.

THE OPPORTUNITY

In late July 1990, the U.S. Army released a request for sealed bid quotes on a new low-cost signal generator that would eventually replace several thousand pieces of test equipment that the Army had in the field. The company with the lowest unit cost for the instrument would get the award.

The division estimated that the design and testing requirements alone would cost between $1 and $1.2 million and, based on the Army's request, had to be completed within one year after the release of the contract. The initial award included a first-year commitment of 900 units with a second and third year requirement of an additional 900 units each year. These additional requirements were to be awarded at a future date. Since the request also included an option to double the requirements in each of years two and three, the contract could be worth 4,500 units over the next three years with the potential of even more as the Army eventually replaced its entire field stock.

This case was developed by Dana Collins and Christine Childers under the direction of Professor David N. Burt.

In reviewing this request, the Denver division saw its opportunity to develop the most utility/cost efficient signal generator that has been built to date. However, given the potential volume of product that was at stake, Signal-Tek also recognized that competition for the contract could be very heavy. Marketing inquiries confirmed that the two competitors that had recently been taking market share, plus one foreign competitor, were planning to bid the contract. The division felt that the price of the unit would have to be under $1,900 in order to have a real chance at winning the award.

The bids were to be opened by the Army on August 25, 1990. Thus, the division had only enough time to make cost estimates based on current materials and labor standards used in similar products, rather than on a detailed analysis of the new product design. Typically, the cost of the division's products were 50 percent materials and 50 percent labor and overhead. Costs, when compared to the estimated required selling price, left a very low margin on the product. However, the decision was made to proceed with the bid with the expectation that somehow it would be possible to reduce the unit cost during the design and development stages. The price for the first 3,600 units was established at $1,799 each, with a reduction in price made available for units in excess of 3,600.

THE PROCUREMENT ENVIRONMENT

The purchasing department at the Denver division consisted of a purchasing manager named Barry Etcher and a staff of five buyers—two senior buyers and three junior buyers. Although this staff had experience in buying electronic components, neither Barry nor any of his buyers had any formal engineering background. Therefore, the engineering staff rarely worked with the purchasing group during the design and prototype stages of new products. Typically, the purchasing group would become involved at the point just prior to the new product being turned over to manufacturing for preproduction runs. By this time the design had been fairly well completed, frequently requiring parts that were not currently used by the division. In addition, the engineers had already spent a considerable amount of time talking with suppliers about new products that were being developed by these potential suppliers and how these items might enhance the new design.

After the Army reviewed the bids, Signal-Tek was awarded the contract. The division's management now had to focus on the issues of limited design time and the necessary cost reduction programs.

1 How can early purchasing involvement assist in low-cost and timely new product development?
2 How does purchasing's involvement enhance an early supplier involvement program? What are the potential benefits?
3 How can the division increase cooperation/communication between the engineering and purchasing departments?

4 How will standardization improve the new product development process?
5 How does more effective purchasing involvement change engineering's role?
6 What can the division do to help expand purchasing's contribution?

SMITH-JONES ELECTRONICS CORPORATION

Mr. George Brown was promoted in January to the position of senior procurement specialist, a procurement staff position at Smith-Jones Electronics Corporation, a Fortune 100 company in the northeastern United States. Within the first few months on the job, he found it difficult to do his work well and wondered what action to take.

COMPANY BACKGROUND

The Smith-Jones Electronics Corporation was a forty-year-old electronics manufacturing company selling in three primary markets: defense electronics, commercial aviation, and consumer appliances. The company was a financially sound multiplant organization. Current sales were $6 billion, and the company was enjoying a rapid growth rate, according to Mr. Brown. It was a multinational company with 77,000 employees worldwide.

PROCUREMENT PRACTICES

Procurement at Smith-Jones was conducted primarily in a decentralized mode. Staff functions such as large contract procurement, training, policy and procedure administration, and consulting on an as-needed basis were centralized in a corporate procurement department. Purchasing research was conducted using resources outside the company, mainly supplier surveys. Plants had a dotted line responsibility to the corporate procurement manager.

MR. GEORGE BROWN

Mr. George Brown was a purchasing professional with more than thirty years of procurement experience. Prior to joining Smith-Jones over fifteen years ago, he was employed by two large companies in the same industry. When his predecessor left Smith-Jones to work for another firm, Mr. Brown was promoted from purchasing manager in the data systems group to his current position as senior procurement specialist.

CHALLENGES TO IMPROVING PURCHASING'S OPERATIONS

A short time after Mr. Brown began his new assignment as senior procurement specialist he became disturbed about the difficulties he encountered in attempting to do his job well. Drawing on his substantial procurement experience to evaluate job performance, he was able to identify those areas that he felt needed improvement. He concluded that they could be classified as a lack of effective procurement methods. For example, he found that production was not being supported in a timely fashion. In general, production management perceived purchasing as conducting price auctions and not as professionals making a contribution. A lack of effective criteria for an in-depth evaluation of responses to requests for quotation resulted in bids being awarded to low bidders without considering other factors, such as quality, that impact on cost. This perception was further reinforced by an unusually large incidence of late deliveries. Cost comparisons with the then-current market activity revealed that prices being paid were too high. Buyers were reacting to requisitions as they were generated. Due to lack of communication among plant buyers, they were not making effective use of the company's buying power since they were operating independently of each other. They were consequently left to buy at the mercy of the marketplace. He found that a major contributing factor was that there were too few internal resources available to procurement specialists and buyers. The company did not have a strategic purchasing plan to provide direction for the procurement group. Attempts to collect meaningful data were not successful because the collection of data was inconsistent and usually incomplete throughout the procurement community.

Requests for forecasts could not be complied with since there was no internal base for developing purchasing forecasts. The only forecast data available in the procurement group was that supplied in response to requests to potential suppliers. Markets were not monitored by buyers. The absence of current market status, prediction of future market conditions, and an accurate forecast prevented buyers from reacting to market conditions to assure consistent sources of supply at competitive prices. Difficulties in assessing department productivity were encountered because the lack of credible data did not allow measurement of performance. However, even if such data were generated, their usefulness would be restricted by lack of historical data on performance. Without historical data for use as a base or an index, any attempt to measure productivity would yield flawed results. Proper use of suppliers as resources could not be realized since no vehicle existed to obtain, verify, and use data obtained from them. There was no formal supplier recognition program to encourage and reward supplier participation in performance, achievements, product development, cost containment, market awareness, and, when appropriate, brainstorming.

Some internal resistance to change existed due to a lack of understanding of how to react to market conditions. The one encouraging area Mr. Brown discovered was quality. There were few complaints about quality and it was not considered an issue.

He realized that any initiative for change would have to come from himself and wondered where to start.

1 Identify and discuss the basic issues in this case.

SPRINGER-BRIGHTON ELECTRONICS

Springer-Brighton Electronics is a small firm located in Chicago. Its major product is a line of automobile electrical system analyzers. These analyzers are used by auto repair shops in tune-up work to identify and diagnose problems in a car's electrical system. Although the market is highly competitive, Springer-Brighton's products compete well, and the firm is reasonably profitable.

The firm's production operation is ideally suited for management with an MRP-type planning and control system. Consequently, three years ago such a system was installed. Initially it did not work well, because it was not properly coordinated with the purchasing operation, and the planning data used in the system were not reliable. In time, however, the bugs were worked out, the system was refined, and it is now working well.

One of the organizational changes Springer-Brighton implemented was the creation of a materials management department that includes purchasing, production control, traffic, inventory management, and the warehouse operations. This arrangement seemed to facilitate effective operation of the MRP system.

More recently, the firm has adopted the use of the buyer-planner concept. That is, a buyer's job and a production planner's job have been combined into a single job. The number of materials handled by each buyer-planner has been reduced, but the scope of the task has become more extensive and more integrated in nature. For a given group of materials, a single individual prepares the production schedule and works directly with suppliers to make it function correctly.

Like most MRP systems, the one used by Springer-Brighton is computer operated. However, when a new buyer-planner is hired, he or she is "broken in" to the planning portion of the job by developing and managing the plan for one or two materials *manually*. The purpose of this approach is to teach the newcomer how the operating routine works, so he or she can understand clearly what the computer does when it runs the MRP planning and operating system.

Assume that you have just joined the firm's materials management department as a junior buyer-planner. One of the materials you have been assigned to handle is the metal housing for the Model 48A analyzer. The housing is formed by stamping and fabricating operations—and is single-sourced with a large metalworking shop in a north Chicago suburb.

As you begin to get organized during your second day on the job, your boss gives you the Model 48A housing requirements projection for the next ten weeks. The data are shown in the table below.

Model 48A Housing Requirements Projection

Order Quantity = 140 Lead time = 4 weeks Safety Stock = 80	Weeks → Firm Reqts.										Tentative	
	1	2	3	4	5	6	7	8	9	10	11	12
Requirements	40	40	50	40	40	50	40	40	60	50	50	50
Receipts		140										
OH-end of week 130												
Planned Order Releases												

1 Manually complete the ordering/operations plan for the Model 48A housing. Simultaneously, construct a table showing when you would expect order points to be reached during the first eight weeks.
2 List and discuss briefly the types of operating problems you might encounter that could require replanning and rescheduling work. What are the implications for supplier relations?

TEMPLETON ENGINE COMPANY

The Templeton Engine Company, located in eastern Wisconsin, was a major producer of aircraft jet engines. On December 15, 1989, Dave Giltner, sales manager for Precision Cutting Tools, called Neil Carlson, a purchasing supervisor for Templeton, to tell him that Precision planned to increase its prices 6 percent across the board on February 15. When he replaced the telephone, Neil wondered how to respond to this news in view of Templeton's plan to reemphasize its cost reduction program in January.

THE COMPANY

The Templeton Engine Company produced turbo-jet and turbo-prop engines for use on small- and medium-sized jet aircraft. It did not compete in the commercial jet engine market, although it did produce smaller engines used to power auxiliary equipment on commercial airliners. Templeton's sales totaled approximately $1 billion per year, divided roughly 80–20 among private and governmental purchasers. The firm employed 6,200 people, including approximately 50 professionals in the purchasing department. Because of the technical character of its products, over the years the company developed a strong engineering orientation which pervaded all aspects of its operations.

PURCHASING ACTIVITIES

Templeton spent approximately $600 million a year for materials, most of which were used in producing its finished products. All buying activities were based on material specifications generated in the firm's various design engineering departments. As a general rule, technical factors were the controlling considerations in specification development.

When considering potential new suppliers for major purchases, the purchasing department coordinated an extremely thorough investigation of the operations and capabilities of each firm reviewed. In addition to an investigation of the normal commercial and service considerations, personnel from Templeton's quality assurance and manufacturing engineering departments carefully analyzed each vendor's production and quality control operations. The objective was to evaluate both effectiveness and efficiency, as well as compatibility with Templeton's requirements. After selection, when a supplier proved its ability to meet the buyer's requirements consistently, Templeton frequently utilized a vendor certification program that allowed the supplier to perform a great deal of its own part inspection and acceptance.

Templeton's buyers used both competitive bidding and negotiation techniques in determining price, depending on the prevailing buying and market conditions. Since some of Templeton's products were sold to federal agencies, buyers had to follow government regulation, which stipulated the use of competitive bidding and negotiation, and set guidelines for the use of each. The Defense Contract Audit Agency periodically audited such purchases to ensure compliance. Once a supplier was selected, however, buyers frequently negotiated numerous contract details and service arrangements with the supplier.

An additional complication faced by some buyers stemmed from a Federal Aviation Agency (FAA) requirement. Each of Templeton's products and related components produced by specific suppliers had to be tested and certified initially by the FAA. Whenever a new supplier for such a part was used, Templeton was required to subject the new item to a rigorous and costly 150-hour operating test. Hence, buyers did not change suppliers without considerable analysis and effort to rectify problems with existing sources.

Like many major firms, over the years Templeton's purchasing philosophy evolved to view suppliers as partners that, in reality, functioned as extensions of Templeton's own production operations. Thus, while buyers evaluated a supplier's performance rigorously, they worked closely with the supplier to optimize the benefit of the relationship for both organizations. When it was advantageous, buyers liked to utilize long-term contracts—often up to three years in duration—to assure compliance with quality and pricing objectives. As a rule, Templeton's buyers had responsibility for the full range of activities involved in their respective transactions—everything from market research to expediting.

COST AND QUALITY

For obvious reasons, quality requirements in the jet engine industry were stringent and extremely important. No producer of shoddy work survived for long. At the same time, however, competition among major producers had become increasingly intense. Consequently, the incentives to keep costs down were substantial. For this reason, buyers at Templeton diligently sought out potential opportunities to reduce materials costs without jeopardizing quality. The company, in fact, was currently in the process of reemphasizing its corporatewide cost reduction program.

THE PURCHASE OF TOOLING

The Templeton manufacturing organization used approximately $1 million worth of tooling each year. Because of the tight tolerances required in the manufacturing process, tooling that performed with precision and reliability was essential.

The special tooling supplied by Precision Cutting Tools was a major dollar item for Templeton. In addition, after extensive testing Templeton's design engineers specified the Precision organization as a single-source supplier.

As Neil Carlson pondered the pending 6 percent price increase on Precision's special tooling, he was acutely aware that he had less than sixty days to resolve the problem.

1 What alternatives does Neil have?
2 What are the advantages and disadvantages of each?
3 What should Neil do?

WORLD-WIDE INDUSTRIES

Alice Baxter recently joined the purchasing department of World-Wide Industries (WWI). Alice had been a buyer in a machine shop in the nearby town of Clarence. While at the machine shop, she completed her A.A. degree with a major in materials management. Her new job with WWI resulted in a handsome increase in salary and a great potential for promotion. Alice's first assignment at WWI was buyer for all purchased components for WWI's line of power mowers. Alice's new boss and the individual responsibility for hiring her was Gayton Hackman, the purchasing manager.

Alice received as her first major buying assignment the purchase of a metal housing for a 19-inch power mower. Her previous experience had given her a familiarity with drawings and specifications, particularly as they were related to sheet metal work. She was not disturbed at all by the magnitude of the assignment. It involved not only a high-priced assembly, but a major investment in tools. Alice requested advice from Mr. Hackman as to those sources that could fabricate the housing at low cost. Mr. Hackman gave her the names, addresses, and contacts for four companies currently in the business of manufacturing this type of product, and recommended that they be sent drawings and specifications.

On receipt of the drawings, all the potential suppliers visited Miss Baxter to make sure that all the details were understood and to offer helpful suggestions as to ways in which the housing could be made at a lower cost. In the meetings that ensued, both Miss Baxter and Mr. Hackman discussed the details with the suppliers and the design engineer. At that time it was pointed out very clearly by Miss Baxter that this housing purchase was highly competitive, that other sources were also quoting on the same drawings and specifications, and that the power mower was a low-profit-margin item. Accordingly, the company was forced to make every conceivable effort by negotiation of design and price to purchase the housing at the rock-bottom price. She also pointed out that there would be substantial volume over a period of twelve to eighteen months, which should make the business very attractive. In a few days following these separate meetings, quotations were received from the suppliers. They were carefully reviewed by Miss Baxter, with the resultant determination on her part to place the business with the lowest bidder who apparently would meet all the drawing and specification requirements. The low bidder, the Troy Iron Works, quoted $19.56. The next lowest bidder, the Tipton Machine Company, quoted $19.80. The other two companies were over $21.00 and were not given any consideration by Miss Baxter.

In the course of a discussion about the placement of this business, Miss Baxter was quite surprised to find that Mr. Hackman did not consider that the business was ready for placement. He contended that the price of $19.56 was too high, and that the business should really be placed with the Tipton Machine Company. Miss Baxter argued with Mr. Hackman that, inasmuch as the suppliers had been told that they must bid at the lowest possible price, they had negotiated out all of the design features possible. The price must be right. She saw no reason for procrastination or further discussion. Mr. Hackman, on the other hand, calmly stated that they were now in a position for the first time really to negotiate the purchase and that Miss Baxter should go back to the low bidders and tell them that their prices were too high and that they should submit new quotations. Miss Baxter stated that she was of the opinion that this was unfair to the Troy Iron Works. She felt the quotations were already based on the suppliers making a fair profit and that such a quotation might injure their opportunity to negotiate further business with these suppliers. Mr. Hackman agreed that any company that does not receive the business is apt to be unhappy regardless of the circumstances, but he would not agree that the question of profit should concern the buyer. After all, no consideration was being given to the profitability of the power mower, which had already been clearly defined as marginal.

Mr. Hackman further explained to Miss Baxter that it was highly desirable for the business to be placed with the Tipton Machine Company, as the Troy Iron Works was already making all the other mower housings. Unless the company provided some split of the business, it would lose its negotiating effectiveness for future business (it being accepted by the suppliers that no one but the Troy Iron Works could get business from World-Wide Industries). Mr. Hackman further explained that the company was not in a position to pay Tipton more than Troy and that the negotiations should be conducted to ensure that Tipton Machine Company not only received the business but that it was the low bidder. The degree of determination on the part of Mr. Hackman that this must be true, and the lack of acceptance by Miss Baxter of the fact that it either could or should be done, resulted in Mr. Hackman taking over the completion of the negotiations with both the Troy and Tipton companies.

The net result of this second-look negotiation was that the business *was placed* with the Tipton Machine Company at a price of $18.60. The initial and revised bids are as follows:

	Initial bid	Second bid	Change
Troy Iron Works	$19.56	$18.75	−$0.81
Tipton Machine Co.	$19.80	$18.60	−$1.20

Miss Baxter was very upset on two counts: Her supervisor had proved that additional costs could be taken out of the part, and supplier relations had in no way been disturbed.

1 Why was Mr. Hackman able to reduce the price? How did he know that a reduction was possible?
2 Did Mr. Hackman treat Miss Baxter fairly?
3 Can this type of buying approach be broadly applied to all commodities and industries?
4 Do you believe that either Miss Baxter or Mr. Hackman was right in disregarding the high initial bids submitted by the third and fourth companies?

WVC INDUSTRIAL CHEMICALS COMPANY

WVC Industrial Chemicals Company was a large producer of several industrial chemicals that were widely used in the manufacture of steel, glass, and rubber, and in various types of food processing operations. The WVC operation itself was a continuous, twenty-four-hour-a-day processing operation in which the ingredients for a finished chemical underwent a series of a dozen or more purifying, mixing, and concentrating operations. After each operation was completed, the chemical was put in liquid form and pumped to the next processing operation, in some cases at high temperatures and in others at low temperatures. In total, the plant had over 400 pumps and 50 major processing machines in operation.

WVC's purchasing department was organized into four sections: (1) operating materials, (2) capital equipment, (3) maintenance parts for capital equipment, and (4) MRO supplies. In terms of purchase order activity, the maintenance parts section was the largest of the four.

WVC had developed an extensive and carefully planned two-phase preventive maintenance program. In the first phase, each pump and each major piece of equipment was taken out of service for a short period of time each month and given preplanned, routine maintenance, such as replacement of bearings, seals, and other parts subject to predictable wear. The second phase involved a production shutdown and complete overhaul of each piece of equipment every eighteen months. Bills of material and engineering drawings for all machines were on file, and a list of specific parts required for the overhaul of each machine were available approximately four months before the work was to be done.

For the upcoming phase-two shutdown, maintenance parts buyer Jan Allen was handling the requirement for three large cast pump housings. The large housings were first cast using special alloy steel, and then machined to very close tolerances to meet WVC's precise operating requirements. Because of the high cost involved, Jan solicited bids from four area foundries. All of the foundries responded; their quoted prices and lead times varied considerably. Because of the tight timing requirements, Jan elected to go with Western Foundry, which quoted a twelve-week delivery, even though Western's price was approximately 10 percent higher than the low bidder. Jan had done business with Western before and knew that it was a reliable, high-quality firm. In addition, the Western sales representative assured Jan that his firm could easily meet her twelve-week delivery requirement.

Four weeks before the scheduled delivery for the castings, Jan received a call from the inside sales department at Western. The young man on the other end of the line told her that two of the three castings had to be scrapped because of problems that developed during the machining operations. This unexpected turn of events left Jan speechless—she did not know what to say next.

1 What should Jan do now?
2 If you had been Jan, how would you have handled the follow-up function?

SELECTED
BIBLIOGRAPHY

GENERAL PURCHASING AND MATERIALS REFERENCES

Ammer, Dean S.: *Materials Management and Purchasing*, 4th ed., Richard D. Irwin, Inc., Homewood, Ill., 1980.

Bierman, Edward J. (ed.): *The CPM Study Guide*, rev. ed., National Association of Purchasing Management, Tempe, Ariz. 1988.

———(ed.): *Guide to Purchasing*, Vol. 1–4, National Association of Purchasing Management, Tempe, Ariz., 1990.

Burt, David N.: *Proactive Procurement: The Key to Increased Profits, Productivity, and Quality*, Prentice-Hall, Inc., Englewood Cliffs, N.J., 1984.

———, Warren E. Norquist, and Jimmy Anklesaria: *Zero-Base Pricing: Achieving World Class Competitiveness through Reduced All-in-Cost*, Probus Publishing, Chicago, Ill., 1990.

Cavinato, Joseph L.: *Purchasing and Materials Management: Integrative Strategies*, West Publishing Company, New York, 1984.

Dowst, Somerby R.: *Basics for Buyers: A Practical Guide to Better Purchasing*, Cahners Books, Boston, 1971.

———: *More Basics for Buyers: Purchasing Principles and Procedures*, CBI Publishing Company, Inc., Boston, 1979.

Farrell, P. V., and G. W. Aljian (eds.): *Aljian's Purchasing Handbook*, 4th ed., McGraw-Hill Book Company, New York, 1982.

Harris, George: *Purchasing Policies*, Business Laws Inc., Chesterland, Ohio, 1988.

Heinritz, Stuart F., P. V. Farrell, and C. L. Smith: *Purchasing Principles and Applications*, 7th ed., Prentice-Hall, Inc., Englewood Cliffs, N.J., 1986.

Karrass, C. L.: *Give and Take: The Complete Guide to Negotiating Strategies and Tactics*, Thomas Y. Crowell Company, New York, 1974.

Leenders, Michiel R., and D. L. Blenkhorn: *Reverse Marketing*, Free Press, New York, 1988.

————, Harold E. Fearon, and Wilbur B. England: *Purchasing and Materials Management,* 9th ed., Richard D. Irwin, Inc., Homewood, Ill., 1989.

Magad, Eugene L., and John M. Amos: *Total Materials Management,* Van Nostrand Reinhold Inc., New York, 1989.

Monczka, R. M., P. L. Carter, and J. H. Hoagland: *Purchasing Performance Measurement and Control,* Division of Research, Graduate School of Business Administration, Michigan State University, East Lansing, Mich., 1979.

Murray, John E., Jr.: *Purchasing and the Law,* Purchasing Management Association, Pittsburgh, 1980.

Nierenberg, Gerald I.: *The Complete Negotiator,* Nierenberg and Zeif Publishers, New York, 1986.

Reck, Ross P., and Brian Long: *The Win-Win Negotiator,* Blanchard Training and Development Inc., Escondido, Calif., 1985.

Ritterskamp, James J.: *Purchasing Manager's Desk Book of Purchasing Law,* Prentice-Hall, Inc., Englewood Cliffs, N.J., 1987.

Scheuing, Eberhard E.: *Purchasing Management,* Prentice-Hall, Inc., Englewood Cliffs, N.J., 1989.

Schorr, John E., and T. F. Wallace: *High Performance Purchasing,* Oliver Wight Publications, Essex Junction, Vt., 1986.

Sherman, Stanley M.: *Contract Management: Post Award,* Woodcrafters Publications, Gaithersburg, Md., 1987.

Woodside, Arch G., and Nyren Vyas: *Industrial Purchasing Strategies,* Lexington Books, Lexington, Mass., 1987.

Zenz, Gary J.: *Purchasing and the Management of Materials,* 6th ed., John Wiley & Sons, New York, 1987.

SELECTED TOPICAL REFERENCES

Specialized Purchasing

Ammer, Dean S.: *Purchasing and Materials Management for Health Care Institutions,* D. C. Heath and Company, Lexington, Mass., 1983.

Elderkin, Kenton W., and Warren Norquist: *Creative Counter Trade,* Ballinger Publishing Company, 1987.

McDonald, Paul R.: *Government Prime Contracts and Subcontracts,* Procurement Associates, Glendora, Calif., revised annually.

Page, Harry R.: *Public Purchasing and Materials Management,* Lexington Books, Lexington, Mass., 1981.

Sherman, Stanley M.: *Government Procurement Management,* Woodcrafters Publications, Gaithersburg, Md., 1985.

Federal Acquisition Regulation (FAR): Superintendent of Documents, Washington, D.C., published annually.

Try Us 1989, National Minority Business Directories, Minneapolis, 1989.

Accounting, Finance, and Economics

Horngrun, C. T.: *Accounting for Management Contol,* 5th ed., Prentice-Hall, Inc., Englewood Cliffs, N.J., 1980.

————: *Cost Accounting: A Managerial Emphasis,* Prentice-Hall, Inc., Englewood Cliffs, N.J., 1982.

Samuelson, P. S.: *Economics*, 11th ed., McGraw-Hill Book Company, New York, 1980.
Weston, J., and E. F. Brigham: *Essentials of Managerial Finance*, Dryden Press, Hinsdale, Ill., 1974.

Forecasting and Commodities Markets

Arthur, Henry B.: *Commodity Futures as a Business Management Tool*, Division of Research, Harvard Business School, Boston, 1971.
Dauten, C. A., and L. M. Valentine: *Business Cycles and Forecasting*, South Western Publishing Company, Cincinnati, 1978.
Spurr, W. A., and C. P. Bonini: *Statistical Analysis for Business Decisions*, 2d ed., Richard D. Irwin, Inc., Homewood, Ill., 1973, chaps. 18–24.

Inventory and Production Planning

Buffa, E. S., and Jeffrey Miller: *Production—Inventory Systems: Planning and Control*, 3d ed., Richard D. Irwin, Inc., Homewood, Ill., 1979.
Janson, Robert: *Handbook of Inventory Management*, Prentice-Hall, Inc., Englewood Cliffs, N.J., 1987.
Orlicky, Joseph: *Material Requirements Planning*, McGraw-Hill Book Company, New York, 1975.
Wight, Oliver W.: *The Executive's Guide to Successful MRP II*, Prentice-Hall, Inc., Englewood Cliffs, N.J., 1983.

Management

Cohen, Stephen, and John Zysman: *Manufacturing Matters*, Basic Books, Inc., New York, 1987.
Drucker, Peter F.: *Managing for Results*, Harper & Row, Inc., New York, 1964.
McGregor, D.: *The Human Side of Enterprise*, McGraw-Hill Book Company, New York, 1960.
Monks, Joseph G.: *Operations Management*, McGraw-Hill Book Company, 1988.
Morris, Michael H.: *Industrial and Organizational Marketing*, Merrill Publishing Company, Columbus, Ohio, 1988.
Newman, W. H., C. E. Summer, and W. E. Kirby: *The Process of Management: Concepts, Behavior, and Practice*, Prentice-Hall, Inc., Englewood Cliffs, N.J., 1971.
Ouchi, William G.: *Theory Z*, Addison-Wesley Publishing Co., The Phillippines, 1981.

Quality

Crosby, Philip B.: *Quality Is Free*, McGraw-Hill Book Company, New York, 1979.
Grant, Eugene L., and R. S. Leavenworth: *Statistical Quality Control*, McGraw-Hill Book Company, New York, 1971.
Imai, Masaaki: *Kaizen*, Random House Business Division, New York, 1986.

Traffic and Transportation

Lochlin, D. P.: *Economics of Transportation*, Richard D. Irwin, Inc., Homewood, Ill., 1977.

National Motor Freight Classification, American Trucking Association, Washington, D.C., published annually.

Taff, Charles A.: *Management of Physical Distribution and Transportation,* 6th ed., Richard D. Irwin, Inc., Homewood, Ill., 1978.

Uniform Freight Classification, Tariff Publishing Office, Chicago, published periodically.

Value Analysis

Miles, Lawrence D.: *Techniques of Value Analysis and Engineering,* 2d ed., McGraw-Hill Book Company, New York, 1972.

Mudge, A. E.: *Value Engineering, A Systematic Approach,* McGraw-Hill Book Company, New York, 1971.

Purchasing, annual value analysis issue, published each spring.

Purchasing World, annual value analysis issue, published each summer.

Name Index

Pinkerton, Jeff, 87n.
Pinkerton, Richard L., 23n.
Pinto, Peter A., 436n.
Placido Engine Company, 785–788
Polaroid, 315
Pretty Clean Detergent, Inc., 788–789

Qualco Corporation, 793–795

Randall Corporation, 793–795
Rathjen, J. A., 521n.
Raytheon, 679
RCA, 9
Reagan, Ronald, 533
Reck, Ross P., 824
Reddy, Jack, 125, 204n.
Reese, S. A., 513n.
Reich, Caroline, 470n.
Reichard, R. S., 337n., 512n.
Remington Rand Corporation, 365
Ridgeway, James, 663
Ripley Engine Company, 795–798
Robertson, T. S., 502n.
Robotics, Inc., 798–799
Rockwell International, 46, 679
Rogers, Amy J., 654n.
Ruhling Manufacturing Company, 799–800

Sampson Products Corporation, 800–803
Samuelson, Paul, 244n.
Schlesinger, James, 704, 705n.
Schorr, J. E., 416n., 431n.
SDC Corporation, 803–804
Sears, Roebuck and Company, 184
Selden, Doyle, 654, 654n.
Sherman, Stanley M., 824
Shewhart, Walter, 395
Signal-Tek Corporation, 812–814

Smith, A. W., 436n.
Smith, Clifton L., 76n., 639, 639n.
Smith, Larry L., 677n.
Smith, Robert M., 385n.
Smith-Jones Electronics Corporation, 814–816
Sony, 220
Spekman, Robert E., 555, 556n.
Springer, Steve, 84n., 87n.
Springer-Brighton Electronics, 816–817
Stanford University, 62, 136n., 525
Stigler, George, 244n.
Stock, James R., 348n.
Storage Technology Corporation, 56, 59
Sudweeks, Brian, 718
Sunstrand Corporation, 702n.

Templeton Engine Company 817–819
Tennant Company, 220, 371, 407–408
Texas Instruments, Inc., 220, 371
Thies, J. B., 340n.
Thomas, Michael H., 652n.
Timex, Inc., 20
Tonkin, Lea, 567n.
Transportation Data Coordinating Committee, 90
Trevisan, Richard E., 644n., 646n.
Tunnel Machinery Exchange, 532
Twin Cities Purchasing Management Association, 644

Unisys Corporation, 654
United Parcel Service (UPS), 496
United States Navy, 365, 561
United States Steel Corporation, 573–574
United Technologies, 679

Subject Index